Monday's child is fair of face,
Tuesday's child is full of grace,
Wednesday's child is full of woe,
Thursday's child has far to go,
Friday's child is loving and giving,
Saturday's child has to work for its living,
But a child that's born on the Sabbath day
Is fair and wise and good and gay.

Anonymous Nursery Rhyme

Literature for Thursday's Child

SAM LEATON SEBESTA
University of Washington

WILLIAM J. IVERSON
Stanford University

SCIENCE RESEARCH ASSOCIATES, INC.
Chicago, Palo Alto, Toronto
Henley-on-Thames, Sydney, Paris, Stuttgart

A Subsidiary of IBM

To the memory of my beloved grandmother, Sadie Klepper Leaton; also to Diane Monson and Ron Watters, dear friends; to Dorothy Giles and Cliff Foster for their support and patience. And to Judy Garland. (If I hadn't had her to inspire me since 1939, I'd never have dared get up in public and make a fool of myself, which is what college teaching is so far as I'm concerned).—S.L.S.

For my wife, my family, and my students.—W.J.I.

Printed in the United States of America

Library of Congress Cataloging in Publication Data

Sebesta, Sam Leaton.
    Literature for Thursday's child.

    Includes bibliographies and index.
    1.   Children's literature—Study and teaching.
I.   Iverson, William J., joint author.   II.   Title.
LB1575.S42   372.6′4   74–32421
ISBN 0–574–18615–8

Contents

Preface

We began this book as countless others have begun their books: with confidence, a neat list of chapters and other features, and a deadline. Gradually, our confidence began to fall away. We discovered that two lifetimes of reading, teaching, and loving children's literature didn't raise us above the watchful criticism of teachers who work day by day to bring the joy of literature to children. Our writing sessions became reading and re-reading sessions. Literary theories that seemed too safe a distance from classroom practice became suspect. Our outline began to totter. Why, we were advised, should activities for teaching literature be separate from the content of literature and its purposes? Why not present literary teaching techniques while identifying literary types and examples? The gulf between theory and practice would then disappear. We took the advice and came up with a new plan: we agreed never to present a theory without also presenting its tested outcome in practice.

Our deadline came and went. Only the unfailing aid and patience of our two talented editors, Karl Schmidt and Barbara Carpenter, sustained us. In addition, we owe a debt of gratitude to the many people who helped us along the way. These include Elaine Aoki, Caroline Allen, and Sally Chadbourne, who gave help with book listings; Toni Marshall and Ted Overman, who reviewed materials for special sections; Ellen Buckley and Emily Sisson, the devoted children's librarians who checked the bibliographies, and Mark Hammarlund, Joan and Andrea Klyn, Carol and Rob Wilkinson, and John Spiers, who assisted in preparing the index. Special contributors who deserve our thanks include Mary Jett Simpson, John Smith, William A. Brochtrup, and Hans J. Schmidt. For their reviews and suggestions at various stages of the manuscript, we are also indebted to Theodore A. Mork, Andre Favat, Allan Jacobs, Nancy Johansen, Alleen Nilsen, Norma Livo, Geneva T. Van Horne, Alan C. Purves, M. Jean Greenlaw, and Donald J. Bissett.

All of these people and many more have aided in preparing this book. The mistakes are our own, but many of the good things could not have been accomplished without the help of our friends.

Because of them—and you—we'd do it all again.

S.L.S.
W.J.I.

November, 1974

Introduction

The rabbits in *Watership Down* are about to be invaded; the survival of their world is at stake. What can they do? They listen as one of their members tells a story, the myth of how a legendary rabbit hero defeated the bad Rowsby Woof. The rabbits go to sleep with the confidence that they, too, will survive. Thursday's children they are, having far to go. So are we all Thursday's children with far to go—but with the promise of a safe, fruitful journey aided by literary tradition.

That literary tradition is the backbone of this book. It is fleshed out with examples from modern works—some that emulate tradition and some that flaunt it. For literature is dynamic, its tradition changing with time while maintaining a core of stability.

Our aim has not been to dissect literature or to separate it from its purpose and the reader's response. You'll find discussion of literary types and examples alongside suggestions for teaching literature to enhance response. The *why, what,* and *how* of literature are intermingled. We believe that you will be able to use them best in this way.

This book doesn't stand alone. You'll need access to a collection of children's books—a good library with a substantial sampling of the growing wealth of paperback and hardcover titles. Of course you'll want to encourage children to share the experience with you, noting their reactions. This book is intended as the liaison between books and children as you develop your own program of children's literature. The wide margins on the page are not accidental. They are intended as space for you to add titles, ideas, and reactions.

The teaching suggestions we've presented have been tried by us with good results. For instance, the "Taking Stock" quiz in chapter 1 has stimulated teachers and children to read some of the books mentioned. Several people have responded by giving us some quiz items of their own, based on their favorite works. We didn't design this quiz to elevate us and intimidate you; rather, it's intended as a quick way to dramatize how many good things there are for children to read. The question types and sequence described in chapter 9 come from several years of courses and workshops followed by reports of their effects and suggestions for their improvement. We hope the suggested pattern will stimulate you to develop your own techniques.

Whenever possible, we've cited exemplary titles that we've read, studied, and valued. We don't assert that every work cited is a "classic." Some of the literature we mention is of temporary value, its presence justified because it catches the tone of the moment. Nor do we pretend that all the works we've highlighted will have instant appeal for a wide audience. Some works need you to introduce them and motivate their acceptance. Others are better left to a small, appreciative audience. Deciding what approach best suits the children you work with is always a unique, creative task. All we can do is try to help you.

People who help children choose literature sometimes want to know exactly what age level is appropriate for reading a selection. Certainly selection would be easier if a book could be labeled "for age eight" or "for a child with sixth-grade reading ability." But such exact labeling is impossible. Interests and other factors peculiar to individuals preclude assigning precise age levels to books. Readability formulas are estimates only. The way you present a book and guide the literary experience always affects how well the work matches the children who experience it. So, after careful consideration, we've chosen to indicate age groupings very approximately:

E indicates Early Childhood level, up to about age eight;

I indicates Intermediate Childhood level, ages eight to eleven;

U indicates Upper Childhood level, ages eleven to young adult.

To assist you further, we've prepared information on the match in chapter 3.

No book is the last word on anything. This book, like any other, reflects the authors' states of mind at the time it was completed. Of course you will not accept everything we say; of course you will question and explore. Looking back now that the manuscript is in final form, we still have some second thoughts and afterthoughts. Let us share three of them with you:

1. *Tone* as a literary concept is very important, though difficult to define. Perhaps it's more important than our discussion indicates. The objective, distant tone of a folk tale permits readers to observe gross actions and amplified character traits that are less likely to appear in other works. The tone embodied in works by writers such as Lucy Boston, E. Nesbit, or Lloyd Alexander is what emerges through style, plotting, and theme. It's the "feel" of a work—the reason that one author's apparent skill in plot and style leaves readers cold while another author's no greater skill strikes the imagination and emotions. Tone is a useful concept to be kept in mind as you read literature.

2. *Suspense* as an ingredient of fiction receives higher marks from many child readers than from well-meaning adults who read children's literature. Some adults most admire a gentle book with fine characterization and substantial theme. But some children read primarily to find out that happens next—and for them, that happening must renew hope through overcoming danger. There may be an adult-approved, gentle tradition in children's literature that does not offer suspense for child readers who want it badly. There may be a double standard: some avid child readers go their suspense-prone, tightrope-walking way while some adult specialists continue to prize other qualities in literature. To be sure, not every fiction work must depend on suspense—but we hope you won't neglect this element as you consider selections that will interest children in reading literature.

3. Finally comes the concept of *values.* We've attempted to show how elements

in literature contribute to theme, communicating an author's sense of values. Most literary criticism centers on how well an author has presented those values. The author's opinion—the values contained in a work—are those of one individual. A skillfully presented work may still fall short of enduring wisdom. Age-old value questions are not necessarily answered wisely through only one author's opinion. Is violence an acceptable means of accomplishing nonviolent ends? Is social acceptability always the criterion for solving personal problems? Is the conflict between generations as common and inevitable as some modern authors would have us believe? A literary work tells how an author perceives something about the world. But wise adults will constantly check the wisdom of an author's value system against the values expressed in other works, as well as comparing them with their own experiences. No work stands alone as the only way of knowing.

We offer these afterthoughts to encourage you to inquire into your own ideas about literature as you read this book. We hope your journey through its pages will be a pleasant and profitable one.

part I

Choosing Literature

I *chapter*

Literary Purposes, Literary Sources

Literature brings high joy to children. It spreads warmth in much the same way as does music, painting, or sculpture. Like music, literature brings the stimulation of sound and rhythm. Like painting, it brings the illumination of imagery and design. Like sculpture, literature brings the awareness of texture and space. When it is well conveyed, literature, like all art, leaves a lasting radiance.

But did it ever strike you as odd that there is a planned curriculum of literature in the high school and college but usually none before or during elementary school? There is, instead, a curriculum in basic reading instruction. But, you may say, since the basic reader is mostly stories, isn't that teaching literature? No, for while the teaching is done through stories, the principal objective is not to develop enjoyment of the stories as literature but to teach "basic reading skills," the *language* skills on which all reading depends. These include the ability to identify words, to group words within sentences syntactically, to grasp the meaning of the kernel sentence patterns, to respond to the sentences in connected discourse. The stories are selected and used as a vehicle for teaching those skills.

Think for a moment about your experience in literature classes in high school and college. In those classes you were taught to appreciate literature for its own sake, not to develop basic reading skills. Put aside, if you can, whether the teaching was good or bad and just think about what the objective was. Was it not to help you experience what made a fine story, a stirring poem, a provocative play, a stimulating biography? We're not arguing that one objective is good (the literary teaching) and the other is bad (the basic reading instruction). The only point we want to make is that the objectives are quite different.

You can see this difference most vividly in the first years of instruction in the elementary school. Generally speaking, teaching in the primary grades focuses sharply on basic reading skills. The stories in basic readers are chosen and taught with that focus in mind. Indeed, some are written directly to that focus and others are selected and rewritten to the same end.

Let's look, for example, at word identification. To make the teaching task manageable only a certain number of new words are permitted within a sentence. More than that, only a certain kind of new word is allowed: the kind of word that exemplifies the particular linguistic approach being used, whether it is what has been traditionally called *phonics* (letter-sound relationships) or *structure* (prefixes, roots, suffixes, syllables). So if in a story the writer has chosen a word on literary grounds (to achieve imagery, rhythm, emotional impact, or another aesthetic effect), that choice can no longer enjoy first priority if the word is to satisfy the skill objective. For example, is it the right word to teach the way a given letter or combination of letters represents a certain sound? If the literary word does not fit the skill objective, it is removed and a more suitable word substituted. Obviously, a story can't meet both objectives—it can't be an equally effective vehicle for literary enjoyment and for basic skill teaching.

We have illustrated the point with only one basic reading skill, word identification. We could discuss comprehension skills with sentences and connected discourse. The more skills the piece is required to exemplify, the less emphasis can be put on literary quality.

By the intermediate grades the basic readers are no longer held to the same tight restrictions about number and kinds of words introduced or length of sentences. But the skill objective still holds. Indeed it is reinforced because the demands on reading skills rise sharply during these years, especially those made by disciplines such as social studies, science, and mathematics. The information in these fields is communicated primarily through expository rather than literary means, through explanations rather than through stories. We say *primarily* because the difference between expository language and literary language is not absolute but a matter of degree. The field of social studies, for example, consists of history, political science, geography, economics, sociology, and anthropology. History is more a humanities subject, more a literary subject, than a science; geography and economics are almost straight science. The others fall somewhere in between. The closer the field is to science and mathematics, the more likely that its language will be expository.

Exposition is governed by logic. The language of expository writers must be precise and detailed, with a minimum of ambiguity and redundancy. In exposition the ideal word has *a* meaning, not diverse meanings (mathematical symbols come closest to this ideal), and the ideal sentence conveys a message that is identical as issued by the writer and received by the reader. To achieve this end, sentences must be logically patterned, employing the format of logic common to all expository fields: deduction, induction, and analogy.

On the other hand, the literary emphases in language rarely heed logical order. Indeed, as a witness to human conduct, literature may portray deliberate violations of reasoning. Emotional responses, the primary aim in literature or any fine art, escape the tidy rubrics of logic. Many literary effects are not stated but merely suggested. In experiencing a poem, for example, each reader must supply in his imagination a response to what the poem only implies.

Exposition restricts this kind of freedom. The reader is not allowed to supply his own data if the logic is less than comprehensive, but rather must be sensitive to such gaps in logic as inadequacies occur.

Clearly these two emphases in language, the literary and the expository, cannot prosper in the instructional program unless differentiated.

In the elementary school an emphasis on children's literature is needed equal to the emphasis on basic reading instruction. In all too many schools the distinction between expository and literary emphasis in language has been ignored. In basic reading instruction in the elementary school, literary materials (stories) are used almost exclusively but are taught largely as if they were expository pieces. If skill-practice materials are used, whether commercially prepared or teacher prepared, they may force an emphasis on expository answers. "Who did it?", "What happened?", and "Where did it happen?" are important questions in exposition, but they fall far short of producing imaginative, individual responses to literature. Even in exposition such questions do not probe the organization or application of ideas.

Stories do not lend themselves well to logical analysis for organization or application of ideas. For example, one skill in basic reading instruction is reading for main ideas. If the materials used were expository, such an objective would be attainable. A reader could read for main ideas within paragraphs or in longer pieces of connected discourse. But stories are not developed that way. The paragraphs in a typical story are usually very short and are not devoted primarily to explaining. Most of them, indeed, use dialogue to carry on the movement of the story. When teaching is directed toward reading for main ideas in story materials, it is almost always aimed at simply reading for main events. A main event is a happening arranged primarily under considerations of aesthetic impact. A main idea, on the other hand, is a theory or a process arranged primarily under considerations of logical development. Reading for main ideas cannot be taught by reading for main events. Certainly a reader of stories can read for theme or infer the idea behind the events, but that is a very different task from reading for main ideas in exposition.

So what do we propose? We propose that basic reading instruction and the teaching of literature be treated as distinctive enterprises; that the skills on which literary reading depends continue to be developed, but that it be recognized that literary reading serves distinctive purposes beyond those basic skills. We propose that a curriculum be planned to meet those purposes and that teaching explicitly help children achieve them.

PURPOSES

Literature brings to children a world of healthy entertainment. It heightens sensitivity to people, places, and things and synthesizes experience in imaginative relationships. Literature presents human options for action and belief. It offers measures for caring for others, for developing the trait of empathy so necessary to all people, young or old, if they are not to feel isolated. Literature offers language rich in the aesthetic, in the sense of beauty all around us. We

From MA nDA LA by Arnold Adoff, illustrated by Emily Arnold McCully. Text copyright © by Arnold Adoff. Illustrations copyright © by Emily Arnold McCully. By permission of Harper & Row, Publishers, Inc.

will examine some of the many purposes of literature, not to separate them artificially but simply to freshen our awareness of them.

Literature as Entertainment

To say that literature is an amusement, a diversion from perplexing problems or a relief from boredom, is to suggest only a part of its value. Its effect is, after all, different from the pleasure of eating an ice cream sundae or enjoying a warm bath. Literature is true recreation, in the root sense of that word: it re-creates the reader as it actively engages thought and feeling.

Adults sometimes associate reading for entertainment with escapism and mere time-killing. But those who guide children in their literary experience and who observe their responses see the entertainment motive in a more positive light.

For example, literature may be thought of in part as play. Play is voluntary. Children can be commanded to "go and play" but genuine entry into play remains their own decision. In play, a balance is established between relaxation and tension, conditioned by order rather than by chaos. Play results in a renewal

Wanda Gág's modern folk tale presents a simple plot with a recurrent rhyme that invites children to join in the telling of the story. Her illustrations further enhance the folk-tale quality of the book. Reprinted by permission of

of vigor for living and a new perspective on reality, though it is not undertaken specifically for these effects. It is self-contained, finding its own reward in its own performance.[1]

Play, with all its enlivening power, needs especially to be preserved in a society subject to social, economic, and technological pressures. "When the play spirit dies, the freshness, joy, and spontaneity of life are quenched, and routine, compulsion, and mechanization supervene," warns Philip Phenix.[2] Huizinga notes sadly that "Civilization today is no longer played, and even when it seems to play, it is false play. . . ."[3]

---

[1]See J. Huizinga, *Homo Ludens: A Study of the Play-Element in Culture* (Roy, 1950), p. 197.
[2]Philip H. Phenix, "The Play Element in Education," *The Educational Forum,* 29 (March 1965), p. 298.
[3]J. Huizinga, *Homo Ludens,* p. 197.

Cats here, cats there,
Cats and kittens everywhere,
Hundreds of cats,
Thousands of cats,
Millions and billions and trillions of cats.

Coward, McCann & Geoghegan, Inc. from MILLIONS OF CATS by Wanda Gág. Copyright 1928 by Coward-McCann, Inc.; renewed ©1956 by Robert Janssen.

So let us consider the purpose literature serves when it stimulates play in children. Historically, the play motive in literature for children has been admitted only with reluctance. Today, when literature is valued for its part in giving insight, in developing social consciousness, in influencing behavior, we ought to consider as well its importance in developing children through the restorative power of play.

From the beginning, you can bring children literature that appeals to their sense of play. By reading well, by eliciting active response, you can augment the entertainment purpose of literature. You can help provide literature that invites relaxation and at the same time brings the pleasant tension of expectation.

For the early childhood years there is the great tradition of nursery rhymes, the language play paralleling the child's spontaneous attempts to develop lan-

past the mill

Bright, warm colors dominate the illustrations for this story, contributing an important plot element as they show the hungry fox trying unsuccessfully to pounce on the unsuspecting Rosie as she goes for a pleasant walk. Used

guage. The rhythm and rhyme of "hickory dickory dock" and "higglety pigglety" and all the rest are natural invitations to play. The repetition and simple dramatization of "Jack and Jill" and "Sing a Song of Sixpence" promote early appreciation of literature as entertainment.

Modern works presenting simple play with language can also be used. Many of these are in picture book form, adding the visual dimension to literary entertainment. *MA nDA LA* (1)[1] by Arnold Adoff uses only a few rhyming syllables to sing the song of planting and harvesting in an African setting: MA and DA to identify the parents, LA for singing, HA for laughing, NA for "no," RA for victorious shouting, and AH for a sigh of happiness. Richly colored pictures make the meaning of the rhymes explicit.

Following the connected events of a plot is an age-old pleasure recognized by all storytellers and their listeners. The miniature plots of nursery rhymes introduce children to this pleasure. The rise and fall of Jack and Jill or of Humpty Dumpty is a perfect place to begin this facet of literary entertainment. The simplest of folk tales somehow become more exciting with repeated readings and tellings. The invitation to join in the tale becomes irresistible. In a few moments children hum the recurrent rhyme in *Millions of Cats* (2) by Wanda Gág, and are ready to supply it whenever the story calls for it.

Some of the more recent picture books also highlight the pleasure of following a simple story line. *Mr. Gumpy's Outing* (3) by John Burningham accumulates, one by one, a large cast of characters in Mr. Gumpy's boat—children, a rabbit, a cat, a dog, a pig, a sheep, chickens, a calf, a goat—until the overloaded boat capsizes

---

[1]Figures in parentheses refer to the list of references at the end of each chapter.

with permission of Macmillan Publishing Co., Inc. and The Bodley Head from ROSIE'S WALK by Pat Hutchins. Copyright ©1968 by Patricia Hutchins.

and they all swim to shore and go home to tea. With just one sentence and some exciting action pictures Pat Hutchins's *Rosie's Walk* (4) shows a hen on a pleasant journey, unaware that a hungry fox has tried unsuccessfully many times to pounce upon her.

Plot with a single incident but with insight into how characters feel about each other and deal with each other's problems is within the reach of young listeners. In James Marshall's books, such as *George and Martha* (5) and *George and Martha Encore* (6) it is a high form of entertainment. George and Martha are hippopotamuses. In one story George peeks through the window at Martha while she's taking a bath. Martha doesn't like that. "We are friends," she tells George, "but there is such a thing as privacy!"[1]

Literature for intermediate- and upper-grade children meets the entertainment purpose, too. Fanciful works alter some aspect of reality to permit play in a world somewhat different from the familiar one. Humor and suspense surround the adventures of young Ralph in *The Mouse and the Motorcycle* (7) by Beverly Cleary. The mouse hero in this story learns to power a toy motorcycle by making a noise *pb-pb-b-b-b*. George, the title character in Evelyn Sibley Lampman's *The Shy Stegosaurus of Cricket Creek* (8), is many a child's dream come true: a gigantic friendly creature who loves children and does his bumbling best to help them. And there is sanctuary as well as a rousing good time in breathing the world of a rabbit civilization in Richard Adams's *Watership Down* (9).

Realistic fiction and nonfiction, light-hearted or serious, can also invite play, for play needn't be the opposite of seriousness. Readers may worry tremen-

---

[1]*George and Martha*, p. 28.

From GEORGE AND MARTHA written and illustrated by James Marshall. Copyright ©1972 by James Marshall. Reprinted by permission of the publisher, Houghton Mifflin Company.

dously about the future of *Harriet the Spy* (10), for Harriet's imagination runs on candor rather than kindness. Yet few would say that Harriet's barbed efforts to become Harriet M. Welsch, the famous writer, aren't entertaining. Tony in Judy Blume's *Then Again, Maybe I Won't* (11) is entertaining not just because of his funny moments but because the story provides an orderly look at this newly rich boy's highly specific, very personal problems. Readers voluntaily enter his

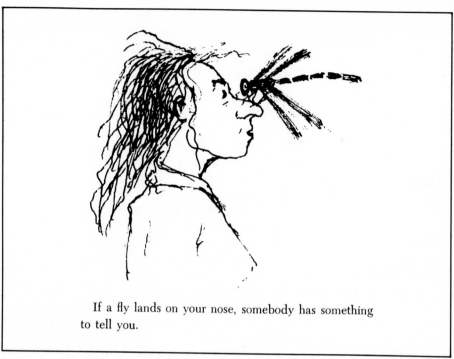

If a fly lands on your nose, somebody has something to tell you.

world, just as they enter the zany world of Peter Hatcher and his turtle-swallowing little brother Fudge in the same author's *Tales of a Fourth Grade Nothing* (12). Barbara Corcoran's *The Winds of Time* (13), in which Gail Abrams really does have to run away from home and place herself at the mercy of strangers, offers readers suspense and a slowly-developing mood of warmth and kindness. In reading *I'm Nobody! Who Are You?* (14) one may be shocked by the evil attempt of one girl to control the mind of another, but this strange tale that explores the limits of psychic power does not skimp entertainment.

Enthusiastic readers and tellers of *Witcracks—Jokes and Jests from American Folklore* (15) will attest to this collection's entertainment value and to the hilarity of the same collector's *Cross Your Fingers, Spit in Your Hat* (16). Entertainment may also be the chief purpose of the child who enters the special domain of *Yoga for Young People* (17) by Michaeline Kiss, the chatty suggestions of *How to Play Baseball Better Than You Did Last Season* (18) by Jonah Kalb, or the precise painstaking diagrams of *Ships through History* (19) by Ralph T. Ward.

As entertainment, then, literature invites voluntary entry for a limited time into experiences that might otherwise be unknown. The experience is orderly and invites active participation but frees the reader from the long-range commitment and effects which first-hand experience often requires.

Literature Provides Insight through Information

Literature, both fiction and nonfiction, provides insight. It synthesizes; it provides an imaginative and valid framework for relating and organizing various bits of information.

Superficial definitions of fiction may indicate that it is "made up" and doesn't deal with factual details or events. But fiction has its basis, its claim to credibility, in fact. Even fantasy has a realistic system from which the fantastic elements clearly depart. Furthermore, fiction is especially rich in the type of insight that can be described as *soft knowledge,* a term defined by Weinberg as "a set of facts about human behavior which we cannot observe or record."[1]

What soft knowledge, for example, is implicit in the fiction cited in the preceding section? In *MA nDA LA* the shifting moods of the African farm family are determined by the cycle of planting, waiting in the rain for the crop to grow, and harvesting. Illustrations show a family working and playing together. Even the chickens and the pet goat are a part of the family's unity. This perception of family comfort in each other's presence is communicated more effectively than it could be by any explicit statement.

At first glance *Millions of Cats* might seem to have little relation to the real world. It's unlikely that a man would encounter trillions of cats or that they'd follow him home! Yet the repetition of action and language in *Millions of Cats,* the pattern of setting out on a search and coming home again, does provide insight into human behavior in an effective way.

Fiction contains *hard knowledge,* too: human behavior that can be observed and recorded directly. This hard knowledge is put to immediate use within the framework of the story. When you read authentic historical fiction about any period or place, you gain hard knowledge about an assortment of human activities—production, protection, transportation, communication, education, recreation—each performed in a manner unique to the time. These activities are placed within the fabric of living, not as disconnected bits of knowledge. Thus in works of fiction about the Middle Ages you can hear the clear ring of a bell on quiet air and note the significance of that sound; you perceive the crash of armor and the flash of the sun; you become aware of the heavy, dusty, musty clothing. The upper-age novels of Rosemary Sutcliff, Howard Pyle's *Otto of the Silver Hand* (20) and *Men of Iron* (21), and Elizabeth Janet Gray's *Adam of the Road* (22) synthesize soft knowledge and hard knowledge to bring fiction's special touch to communicating human behavior in the Middle Ages.

A central purpose of nonfiction is to provide information. Nearly all subjects

---

[1]Carl Weinberg, "Education and Literature," *Humanistic Foundations of Education,* ed. Carl Weinberg (Prentice-Hall, 1972), p. 138.

of interest to children are available for nearly all levels of comprehension: from abacus to aerodynamics, to anarchism, to archeology, to astronomy, to Aztecs —and on down the alphabet of topics the world over. An author's purpose to inform and a reader's purpose to receive information are clearly served by nonfiction.

The manner of presenting these subjects is as varied as the subjects themselves. Information in *Books for You to Make* (23) by Susan Purdy is unadorned hard knowledge of the how-to-do-it type. David Macaulay's beautiful book *Cathedral* (24) seems almost as straightforward, but the purpose and effect is wondrous respect for the masterwork of architecture. The crystal clear style and dignified format of *Women Themselves* (25) by Johanna Johnston is appropriate to the subjects it treats, including succinct, but unhurried biographies of Abigail Adams, Elizabeth Blackwell, Carrie Chapman Catt, and others.

Hendrik Willem Van Loon's world history for children, *The Story of Mankind* (26), was the first winner of the celebrated Newbery Medal—and the only nonfiction book other than biographies to receive this distinction. The hard knowledge imparted through its pages is breathtaking, a factual history spanning a half-million years. Yet there is soft knowledge as well, including Van Loon's poetic account of the rise of Greek theater and the playful, childlike, all-encompassing animated chronology at the end of the book. Edward Osmond's *A Valley Grows Up* (27) synthesizes history through poetry and fact by presenting the changes occurring in one small setting over the years 5000 B.C. to 1900 A.D., ending with a sentence that brings the information home to British readers:

"The prehistoric hunters may have camped where your house stands, or the remains of a Roman farmhouse may lie beneath your local cricket ground; and it may even be you who will bring these things to light."[1]

Biography as a special class of nonfiction combines the appeal of narrative, or storytelling, with the imparting of authentic information. At least, that's the *intent* of biography. The Crowell Biographies series edited by Susan Bartlett Weber shows how well this can be done for young children's entertainment and information-getting purposes.[2] Cornelia Meigs's early Newbery Medal biography *Invincible Louisa* (28) helped set standards for children's biography. If you have had long, loving acquaintance with *Little Women,* you may wish to compare the Meigs biography with one written for adults. It is generally faster in pace, more concerned with incident than with speculation about motives; yet it has depth and, above all, integrity. You will feel that almost nothing has been added beyond the known facts, but the reporting and pervading spirit of the work give it unity and excitement quite in keeping with its subject's best work. When at last you hear publisher Thomas Niles say, "I think, Miss Alcott, that you could

---

[1] p. 82.

[2] The series includes *Maria Tallchief* (29) by Tobi Tobias, *Wilt Chamberlain* (30) by Kenneth Rudeen, *Cesar Chavez* (31) by Ruth Franchere, *Malcolm X* (32) by Arnold Adoff, *Leonard Bernstein* (33) by Molly Cone, and others.

In the Osage Indian language, *Ki He Kah Stah* means "the tall chiefs." America's greatest ballerina comes from the family with this name. Maria Tallchief was born on January 24, 1925, in Fairfax, Oklahoma. Fairfax is a sleepy, small town on the Osage reservation in the southwest of the United States.

Her father, Alexander Tallchief, was a full-blooded Osage, and her grandfather, Peter Big Heart, had been chief of the tribe. Her mother, Ruth Porter Tallchief, came from Scottish and Irish people. She was given the name Elizabeth Marie Tallchief. Her family and friends called her Betty Marie.

As a child, Betty Marie liked to watch the dancing of the Osage tribe. But she saw these

From MARIA TALLCHIEF by Tobi Tobias, illustrated by Michael Hampshire. Copyright ©1970 by Tobi Tobias. Illustrations copyright ©1970 by Michael Hampshire; with permission of Thomas Y. Crowell, Co., Inc., publisher.

write a book for girls," you will have a sense of drama and human emotion quite beyond a purely factual account.[1]

In another Newbery Medal book, published a few years later, the ingredients of biography are changed. Kate Seredy's *The White Stag* (34) places "legendary truth" over fact, presenting the exploits of Attila the Hun as descendants of the hero might wish to recall them, complete with Moonmaidens and strange visions. "It is a fragile thread; it cannot bear the weight of facts and dates," says the author to her readers.[2] Instead the biography reveals the spirit of a people and their reverence for a legendary leader.

Recent biographies for children combine entertainment and insight. They attempt to present lives authentically in spirit and incident but, when appropriate, to bring the material to life through the creation of imagined conversation and detail. Jean Lee Latham's Newbery Medal biography of a mathematical genius in American colonial times, *Carry On, Mr. Bowditch* (35), and her heartbreaking account of the Jamestown colony, *This Dear-Bought Land* (36), are striking examples.

All types of literature can provide insight in the form of either soft knowledge

---

[1] p. 200.
[2] p. 8.

From THE WHITE STAG by Kate Seredy. Copyright 1937, copyright © renewed 1965 by Kate Seredy. Reprinted by permission of The Viking Press, Inc.

or hard knowledge. The authenticity and appropriateness of the insight, whatever its type and form of presentation, must be considered when selecting books to meet the insight-developing purpose of literature.

Literature Illuminates Human Options

A useful education involves more than merely learning to recall facts. Developing the ability to recognize and define problems, to speculate about possible solutions, to make decisions regarding problem solving, to carry out solutions and assess the consequences—these are also recognized goals of education. Literature can aid in achieving them, not only through providing hard and soft knowledge as data for the problem-solving process but through practice in the process itself.

Most narrative literature centers in human options. A principal character finds himself or herself faced with a conflict. To resolve that conflict, the character must make a choice in thought and action; or, when no choice is possible, the character must find a way to live with the inevitable consequence. Thus he or she chooses among options for solution or acceptance, and some evidence is usually given as to the suitability of that outcome.

The result should be recognition of the relation between the character's problems and one's own problems in living, the options that are available, and a manner of choosing among the options. For example, in *Millions of Cats* the main character is faced with a specific problem: what is he to do when he arrives home with trillions of cats? You can stop the story at this point, decide how you would solve the problem, and then return to the story to see how the old man solved it. Mr. Gumpy in *Mr. Gumpy's Outing* faced the problem of what to do when his boat tipped over. His solution was to take everyone home to tea, but he might have chosen some other course of action. Both characters faced a problem and both characters made choices from available options.

In more complex stories the range of options and the process of making choices are often more explicit. Near the end of *The Mouse and the Motorcycle* Ralph the mouse finds that his human friend Keith badly needs an aspirin. Ralph decides to help him, but the solution isn't simple for a mouse. After one attempt, two ladies discover Ralph and daintily put him out the window, where a predatory owl lurks. Escaping from that plight, Ralph decides again whether the problem is worth solving, and tries a new solution. If you follow Ralph into the book's sequel, *Runaway Ralph* (37), you'll find him in more extended peril as a result of his initial decision to run away from home.

Tony's problems in *Then Again, Maybe I Won't* will strike most readers as far more serious than Ralph's. Tony must cope with some embarrassing problems having to do with physical maturation in reaching adolescence. He's involved with an acquaintance who shoplifts and must decide what to do in this circumstance. Most serious of all, Tony slowly realizes that his parents have sacrificed family solidarity in their pursuit of social success in a snobbish society. With this realization comes the knowledge that solutions aren't always immediately possible. For the time being, to cope rather than to solve may be Tony's only recourse.

A wide range of options is presented in literature for children. The problem-solving process is laid out before them, with implications for decision-making in their own lives.

Literature and Empathy

Literature develops empathy by helping the reader relate more fully to the human condition. At the motor level empathy means that you react with your body as the character reacts. Viewers of a live performance may raise an arm when the pitcher throws a ball or breathe deeply as they watch a character on the run. Readers of literature also react with their bodies when deeply moved, tensing at a moment of crisis, laughing openly at a time of humor.

Empathic identification with a character may exist without any outward signs. You feel a character's emotions as your own or think through a character's problems with concern as great as if those problems faced you. Empathy, then, is caught up with emotional and thinking responses.

Empathy permits you to feel *into* a character, to assume his or her point of view. So great is your identification with the character that you seem temporarily to forget yourself and view the world as the character views it. Related terms such as sympathy (feeling *with* a character) or antipathy (feeling *against* a character) are less intense, for in these instances you cling to your own identity and view the character from your own perspective.

Stories with strong heroes and heroines are powerful invitations to empathy for many readers. Because the reader knows that the character actually lived, biographies often encourage empathic relationship. For the understanding reader or listener or viewer, empathy may reach across centuries and cultures to include legendary heroes or characters who exist in the world's mythology.

But the literary sources of empathy needn't always be characters who embody all the heroic virtues. Empathy can be generated from understanding even when admiration is limited. Benji, nicknamed Mouse, in Betsy Byars's *The 18th Emergency* (38), has none of the fearlessness generally attributed to a hero. He's scared stiff of his tormentor, a big bully named Marv Hammerman, and he spends most of the book avoiding an encounter with Marv. Even when he dares to stand up to the bully, you may be left with the feeling that Mouse fell short of being the active sort of hero you might have liked him to be. But you understand him. With the understanding and the sympathy, most readers will go a step further and empathize with Mouse. Similarly, Dozie Western in Betty K. Erwin's *Behind the Magic Line* (39) may not seem to be strong enough to meet the problems of poverty and indifferent family members at the beginning of the book, but her situation and her quiet way of accepting it will probably arouse a reader's empathy.

Does empathy derived from literary experience transfer to other life experience? Will you, in a first-hand experience, have greater empathy for a child threatened by a bully as a result of reading *The 18th Emergency*? Will you have greater empathy for poverty-stricken people from having read about Dozie? David Russell and others who have studied the effects of literary response say they can't be certain.[1] But case studies and self-reports indicate that this purpose

---

[1]David H. Russell, "The Effects of Reading," in *The Dynamics of Reading,* ed. Robert B. Ruddell (Ginn, 1970), pp. 178–203.

of literature does serve a wider goal: to permit an individual to reach out from himself to understand others.

In the literature of here and now—modern realistic fiction—there is an increasing opportunity to develop empathy. We want to insure that a significant proportion of that literature really does liberate children from narrow enclaves. Children can read realistic fiction without confining themselves to the kind of experience they already know. We all know that fulfilling laughter is needed in our classrooms, but we need enlarging sadness too. If life is sometimes ugly, it is not damaging for the more fortunate to learn of such ugliness. If there is bitterness and sorrow, children should know of that anguish.

None of us is so naive as to believe that books alone shape children. We all know that many forces play upon their malleable spirits. But literature can lift children's eyes above their immediate circumstance, and the added vision can make long-term differences.

We are not advocating evangelistic tracts. What children need to experience is writing that employs all the wonderful resources of the English language to open life wider, so that they see sights never seen in suburbia and hear sounds never heard on well-manicured streets and taste tastes never imagined in ranch-style homes and smell smells never smelled in two-car families and touch textures never felt in all of middle class life.

More importantly, when literature opens life wider, children will come to know, as John Donne knew long ago:

> No man is an Island, entire of it selfe; every man is a piece of the Continent, a part of the maine; if a clod bee washed away by the Sea, Europe is the lesse, as well as if a Promontorie were, as well as if a Mannor of thy friends or if thine owne were; any mans death diminishes mee, because I am involved in Mankinde; And therefore never send to know for whom the bell tolls; It tolls for thee.

For children, it is not too soon to hear the bell toll.

Aesthetic Purposes in Literature

We have reserved to the last the most important purpose that literature serves. Literature is an art form. It heightens an awareness of the beauty all around us. Readers are encouraged to make individual creative responses out of the suggestions of the writer. They make out of their own beings, their own thinking, their own feelings, responses that are uniquely theirs. They join imaginatively with the writer to make new artistry.

One facet of the power of literature to stimulate individual creative response derives from the distinctive ways in which the sounds of language are employed. Examples are quickly found in the "sound effects" of nursery rhymes and in other poetry—from the "splishes and sploshes" of Susie's galoshes[1] to the gentle insistent rhythm of A. A. Milne's "Disobedience":

James James
Morrison Morrison
Weatherby George Dupree[2]

Additional examples can be found in almost any good literary prose for children. The repeated initial sounds describing Mole's emergence into the above-ground world in *The Wind in the Willows* (40) are richly descriptive: "So he scraped and scratched and scrabbled and scrooged and then he scrooged again and scrabbled and scratched and scraped. . . ." The expansion to describe the river a page later—"this sleek, sinuous, full-bodied animal, chasing and chuckling, gripping things with a gurgle and leaving them with a laugh"—is another form of sound to stimulate the imagination.[3]

The aesthetic purpose of literature contributes to the well-being of the individual in terms of his or her humanities education. Aesthetic unity—the synthesis of literary elements such as those to be examined in chapter 2—provides a basis for the appreciation of beauty just as a painting or a musical composition gives aesthetic enjoyment and a sense of well-being. This is a part of the entertainment value of literature, but with an outcome beyond the "play" purpose.

Whose Purposes?

We have now examined five main categories of literary purpose: providing entertainment, developing insight through information, presenting human options, encouraging empathy, and heightening awareness of beauty. We've tried to suggest the interplay of purposes that underlies literary experience. But, belatedly, we need to ask whose purposes we're discussing. Are these the purposes of authors when they write, of film-makers when they produce a literary film? Are they the purposes of adults—the teachers, librarians, parents, and others involved in presenting literature to children? Or are they the purposes of the children themselves as they approach literature?

Quite clearly, purposes may differ. You, as an adult, may have different purposes from a child, even though you both read the same piece of literature. Typically, the adult, nostalgic over a childhood experience with *The Secret Garden* (41) or *Charlotte's Web* (42), may, from an adult perspective, assign purposes to the experience that he or she did not discern when first encountering these books. Perhaps the interplay of purposes differs in most literary undertakings—that is, purposes differ from author to adult reader to child reader.

---

[1]Rhoda W. Bacmeister, "Galoshes," in *Bridled with Rainbows,* sel. Sara and John E. Brewton (Macmillan, 1949), p. 24.
[2]A. A. Milne, "Disobedience," in *When We Were Very Young,* illus. Ernest H. Shepard (Dutton, 1924), pp. 32–35.
[3]chapter 1.

Inviting Jason

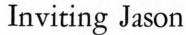

illustrated by Mercer Mayer

THE FIRST BIRTHDAY PARTY I ever had in my life was when I was ten years old. One whole decade old. And I had to invite Jason.

The big thing in birthday parties where we live is slumber parties, only it isn't called a slumber party because that's what girls call it. On the invitation where it says FROM . . . , I wrote "Supper at 7:00 P.M., May 15." May 15 being my birthday. Where

2

it says UNTIL . . . , I wrote "After breakfast on May 16." That and the fact that I wrote at the bottom to please bring a sleeping bag lets everyone know that it is a slumber party. I had been to two slumber parties since we moved here; one of them had been Jason's.

My mother checked the invitations for spelling. When she noticed the FROM and UNTIL, she said that she had no idea that a slumber party meant a life sentence cooking and washing dishes. My mother gets sarcastic at the slightest thing. She knew that I wouldn't care if she used paper plates. Mother also noticed that Jason's name wasn't on any of the envelopes. That was besides disapproving of the way that I abbreviated Ohio. *Cleveland, Oh.* I had put. Mother said that if that was the way I abbreviated Ohio that I should use exclamation points instead of periods. Sarcastic.

"Well, where is Jason's invitation?" she asked.

"You limited me to six kids, and Jay was number seven on my list," I explained.

"Take someone off," she suggested, the way an umpire *suggests* to a batter that he's out.

I took off John Beecham; he was the only one I had invited who I didn't really like. I had added him even though he hadn't invited me to his party. Dick

3

liked him. Dick was the fastest runner in the fourth grade and the second fastest in the whole school. As a matter of fact, if Dick couldn't make it on May 15, I would have to change the date. I thought about it again and decided that I ought to have John Beecham to give Dick something extra to come for.

"I don't think Jason can come," I told Mother. "He has dyslexia."

"It's not contagious," Mother said. "Invite him," she added.

I forgot that Mother would know what dyslexia was. She had explained it to me in the first place. Mother is big on education. Dyslexia has to do with education, or at least reading. If you have dyslexia it's like your brain is a faulty TV set; the picture comes through the wires all right, but some of the tubes are missing or are in the wrong places. So that when you tune in to one channel you may get the sound from another. Or spots of the picture may be missing or be backwards or upside down. Kids with dyslexia read funny.

Jason used to read funny in class until they discovered that he had it. Then they quit making him read out loud and sent him down to special reading during our regular reading. They also sent him down during our P.E., P.E. being physical educa-

4

tion. And it was too bad about that; Jason could handle a ball like there was nothing wrong with him. But his reading was like the Comedy Hour; that's about how long it took. Except that Mrs. Carpenter wouldn't let us laugh. And when Jay was called to the board to write something, it was like he was writing sideways, and that took three hundred hours.

Jason's mother, Mrs. Rabner, told Mother that he had improved a lot since he had been tutored in dyslexia. The nicest thing about Jason was his mother. She did everything she could to make my mother and me feel welcome when we moved here in September. But we had moved around enough for me to know that your first friends aren't always your best friends.

I ripped up the envelope that had John Beecham's address and addressed the last one to Jason Rabner. The invitations came eight in a package, but I had ruined one envelope spelling *boulevard* wrong. I had thought that spelling everything out and writing in ink made it look more important. After two bad mistakes of which I could fix only one, I wrote the rest in pencil instead of ink and abbreviated everything I could, including *Ohio*.

Inviting Jason was a mistake from before the time the party began because that's when he arrived.

Fifteen minutes before. I didn't like the idea of everyone else arriving and Jay looking buddy-buddy with me like some cousin or brother-in-law.

Mother served fried chicken, and the only person with a real appetite was Jason. He ate thirds. Everyone else was anxious to get on with the party and stopped at seconds. Jason cleared his plate and carried it to the sink where Mother was standing. She said, "Thank you, Jay; you're a real gentleman." No one else took the hint. I looked at Dick and rolled my eyes to the top of my head long enough for him to get the message but not long enough for Mother to get it, too.

When it was time to blow out the candles, Jason sang Happy Birthday with such concentration that when he got to Happy Birthday, dear Stanley—Stanley being my name—his *St* wet the icing and everyone kind of picked at the cake. Except, of

course, Jason who ate his all gone. I caught Dick's eye again.

The first thing we did after eating was to get on with the party. I had opened each present as it arrived so that there didn't have to be any grand opening; I don't think that that is bad manners. Just girls (mothers) think so.

Our first game was a drawing contest to see who could draw the best. We drew girls. With their clothes off. Grown-up girls. We passed the pictures all around. Since it was my party, I got to be judge.

Dick held on to Jason's picture for a long time before passing it back to me for judging. There was something sort of spooky about it. I awarded Dick first prize; his drawing was neat, and I decided that neatness counts. We crunched the pictures up and put them in the garbage can right after.

Next we sat around on the floor and played cards. Jason made a real fool of himself. He wanted to lose. He kept throwing down his cards and saying things like "Gol dang it, I thought I had him." A measly pair of fours. Then old Jason would throw in his M & M's. That's what we were playing for—the M & M candies that Mother had put in our party cups. Jay had only about ten brown ones left, and they were worth the least. Dick had cashed in a red for five brown and had bid three brown plus one yellow when Mother broke up the game. I told her that it wasn't for money. True, but it *was* gambling.

8

Also true. It was also messy. Someone had stepped on my winnings.

"Bed time," she said.

We pushed back all the furniture in the den and laid out the sleeping bags. Now was the time for ghost stories, but the truth is that no one could tell a ghost story and tell it right. They were all full of *uh's* and *and's* and they never told them in order. We told jokes full of swear words; I told one that I had heard my father tell the man from the office who he had brought to the house for supper. Everyone laughed. I was relieved because if someone had asked me to explain it, I would have had to fake it. But they either understood or else no one wanted to be the one to ask.

Mom and Dad took turns coming in to tell us to quiet down and go to sleep. Jason was the first to konk out; at least he didn't snore. It wasn't long before it was morning and everyone was ready for breakfast.

Everyone was more ready than Mother was. She put on a bright dress and make-up, but I knew what was going on underneath both.

Mother made bacon and eggs and put out two different kinds of cold cereal and orange juice and told everyone to pick up a plate and serve himself.

9

We almost ran out of bacon after Jason filled his plate. Almost. Mother told everyone to roll his sleeping bag and gather up his belongings and then play outside until he got picked up.

One by one they left. Two called their mothers to remind them. Jason sure didn't call his mother. Dick's mother had called us to tell us that she would be late picking up Dick since she had a beauty parlor appointment every Saturday; she said she would stop by for him on her way home, if that would be all right with us. I took that call, and I said that that would be fine with us.

By that time, it would have been nice if Jason's mother would come for him so that I could have some time alone with Dick. I guess she wasn't anxious to get him back, either. I had to help Mother push the den furniture back in place, and Dick and Jay were looking through LIFE magazines while I did that.

When I finished, I asked Jay if he would like to call his mother. "I'll dial it for you," I suggested. Jason did not look enthusiastic. After I finished that call, Jay and Dick were still sitting together. Jason had one of the pads we had drawn our girl pictures on last night. He was writing something when his mother arrived. I carried his sleeping bag out for him, meeting Mrs. Rabner halfway up the walk. I figured there was no point in having her come in. All she'd do would be to have coffee with Mother, and Jay would hang around for that.

Dick said goodbye to Jason and said, "I enjoyed talking with you." Dick also said "See ya" to him.

Jason said goodbye and thanked both me and my mother for the party. At last he was gone. I said to Dick, "Too bad about Jay." Saying that allowed room for Dick to say the first bad thing.

Dick said, "You know, dyslexia makes things come out different. Like I read him the story about the astronauts and here is how he wrote it." I looked at what Jay had written:

They nogged down and stepped onto the glans. Nothing looked farc wol, so Allen lo men . . .

"He sure can't spell," I said.

Dick glanced over the paragraph again. "The way he writes seems better for the moon than what the magazine said."

"That's one way of looking at it."

"Yeah," Dick added. "And here's a picture I asked him to draw. Doesn't it look kind of the way that moon pictures should."

"Maybe," I said, "but it sure don't rate hanging in any museum."

"No *earth* museum," Dick explained. And then Dick said three more nice things about Jason.

When Dick's mother came for him, I had had enough of the party. Mother made me help her load the empty Coke bottles into the car. "Aren't you glad that you asked Jason, after all?" she asked.

I answered, "No!"

Which was the same answer I would have given before the party, and I would have meant it just as much. Only my reasons would have been different.

special activities

Read the preceding selection and consider the following:

1. What might have been the author's dominant purpose in presenting this story? It is a modern story that you may find atypical and disturbing. Nevertheless some author purposes are strongly at work. What might these be?

2. If you were to present this story to children, what might be your dominant purposes in doing so? These purposes might help determine the manner and emphasis of your presentation. How would you present it?

3. What purposes might a child have in reading this story?

4. Using this selection as an example, what can you say about the importance of determining literary purposes as aids to facilitating literary experience? What purposes might be worth adding to those discussed in this chapter?

TAKING STOCK

If literature is to achieve the purposes we've explored, you'll want to know a wide variety of selections. You will recall some of these from your own childhood. Your reading in adulthood has, of course, added to your knowledge of literature. Even now you are expanding your knowledge of children's literature by exploring new and old works.

In this section you are invited to take stock of your knowledge of children's literature. Seventy-five books have been selected from the great wealth available today. Recently another version of this Taking Stock Quiz was given to more than a hundred teachers who distributed it to their pupils and requested help. The scores were surprisingly high, for children pooled their knowledge and reportedly enjoyed the challenge. In fact, sixteen percent of the teachers returned after a week with perfect scores. See how well you can do—alone, working with a partner, or inviting children to help you. (Answers to the Taking Stock Quiz will be found on pages 44–45.)

"How is Your Folklore Quotient?"

That's the question asked by Sister Margaret Mary Nugent in *Newsletter for Professors of Children's Literature.*[1] She comments: "The clues in the test which follows are intentionally slightly obscure, but accurate." Here are five of the original twenty items. The directions are: "Identify the story by writing the title in the space at the right." (Percentages at the end of each item tell how well 134 students did, sampled over a three-year period in Sister Nugent's classes.)

---

[1] *Elementary English,* 45 (May 1968): 667, 668, 671.

1. "Open Sesame" was the password._____(50.7%)
2. A man and his wife discover who brings them good fortune each night. _____ (14.9%)
3. Trouble brews in a gingerbread house in the forest. _____ (91.0%)
4. A story that involves the actions of a donkey, a dog, a cat, and a rooster. _____ (14.1%)
5. A troll is outwitted by those he planned to kill. _____ (65.6%)

CLASSICS

Having literary distinction or recognized lasting value, forming standards of excellence—such definitions of the elusive term *classic* apply to the five books for older children described below. Match them to their titles.

6. ____Four friends with very different ideas about the proper way to live join together to rid Toad Hall of the Weasels and Stoats, ending the adventure with a civilized banquet.
7. ____Where a robin led Mary Lennox—and generations of readers have followed.
8. ____Of Ummanodda in particular, and also of Oomgar. And of Tishnar.
9. ____Henry James said that the quarrel scene between David Balfour and Alan Breck in this book is the best episode in all adventure fiction.
10. ____"Man is the weakest and most defenceless of all living things, and it is unsportsmanlike to touch him." Besides, "man-eaters become mangy, and lose their teeth."

   a. *Kidnapped* by Robert Louis Stevenson, 1880.
   b. *The Wind in the Willows* by Kenneth Grahame, 1908.
   c. *The Jungle Books* by Rudyard Kipling, 1895.
   d. *The Secret Garden* by Frances Hodgson Burnett, 1911.
   e. *The Three Royal Monkeys* by Walter de la Mare, 1919.
   (Original title: *The Three Mulla-Mulgars*)

PICTURE BOOKS

Usually composed with an eye to pleasing younger children, but by no means limited to early childhood level, picture books present avenues to happy literary experience. For example:

A seagull with an intense, caring look follows the hero in (11) _____, causing him much embarrassment. African animals in vivid woodcuts practice their grunts and groans for saying hello, watch out, help, who are you, and CROCODILE! in (12) _____. Balance these with a grim realistic narrative about (13) _____, who is intent on survival in the big city. Or relax by watching a goose with a book under her arm in (14) _____. And laugh some more as you find out how (15) _____ gets into trouble and lands in the zoo.

a. *Petunia* by Roger Duvoisin, Knopf, 1950.
b. *How, Hippo!* by Marcia Brown, Scribner's, 1969.
c. *Nobody's Cat* by Miska Miles, illus. John Schoenherr, Atlantic, 1969.
d. *Thy Friend, Obadiah* by Brinton Turkle, Viking, 1969.
e. *Curious George* by H. A. Rey, Houghton, 1941.

With a picture book you can discover how a rainy day becomes not so boring after all if you are visited by (16) _____. Even if you don't read words, you can read pictures, and that's all you need to enjoy wordless books: for instance, the one about the marvelous man and woman who build their own world out of blocks and manage to escape flood and fire in (17) _____. Or the wordless book about a lady who's accosted by a robber, aided by a kindly gentleman, and is spunky enough to throw a party that very evening: (18) _____. Or a hip, modern, wand-waving fairy named Mabel Mae Jones, who has delighted ages four through a hundred and four, in (19) _____.

Or the Terrible Turner Twins, who show (20) _____ that she can't boss their town, even on one special night of the year. Or a boy and his dog named Laird Angus McAngus, who terrify the cows but capture a tiger in (21) _____. Admirable heroes all! And so is an elephant who insists that "A person's a person, no matter how small" and practices that doctrine in the midst of trouble in (22) _____. Pay tribute, too, to Grandmother and Grandfather for a tidy extraction in (23) _____.

Finally, for a chill, you must admit that, although the knitting turned to ashes, that was better than losing the maid altogether in (24) _____ (a recent Caldecott Medal book). And stop with the danger of being roasted and eaten, the naughty "just a joke" in (25) _____. Want some hints?

a. *Horton Hears a Who!* by Dr. Seuss, Random, 1954.
b. *Henry Explores the Jungle* by Mark Taylor, illus. Graham Booth, Atheneum, 1968.
c. *The Pumpkin Smasher* by Anita Benarde, Walker, 1972.
d. *Shrewbettina's Birthday* by John S. Goodall, Harcourt, 1971.
e. *The Cat in the Hat* by Dr. Seuss, Random, 1957.
f. *Duffy and the Devil* retold by Harve Zemach, illus. Margot Zemach, Farrar, 1973.
g. *The Turnip* by Janina Domanska, Macmillan, 1969.
h. *Changes, Changes* by Pat Hutchins, Macmillan, 1971.
i. *Roland the Minstrel Pig* by William Steig, Harper, 1968.
j. *The Dragon Takes a Wife* by Walter Dean Myers, illus. Ann Grifalconi, Bobbs-Merrill, 1972.

Caldecott Medal Books

Each year since 1938 the Caldecott Medal has been presented to "the artist of

Ananse spun a web round Osebo,
Mmboro, and Mmoatia.
Then he spun a web to the sky.
He pulled up his captives
behind him, and set them down
at the feet of the Sky God.

26. Caldecott Medal Book

the most distinguished American picture book for children." A complete list of recipients of this award appears on pages 543–45. Here are five illustrations, each taken from a Caldecott Medal book. Can you identify the books and the artists?

27. **Caldecott Medal Book**

28. Caldecott Medal Book

29. Caldecott Medal Book

30. Caldecott Medal Book

Made-up Dust Jacket Blurbs

Children like to create dust jacket blurbs to identify favorite books. Here are some samples, arranged by topics. See if you can match titles to blurbs.

MAINLY HISTORICAL

31. _____ Once a Forest Girl loved a prince of the Sun. Based on a real archaeological find, this story might have happened in ancient Denmark.
32. _____ Shut out of her own house, Maddy Franklin ran away to picket the White House. Her reason: Women's Rights. The time: 1917.
33. _____ A slave boy, a hermit saint, and a strange friend search for a kidnapped heiress in early medieval times.
34. _____ The murder of an old prospector was solved by a flapjack-eating burro and Uncle Jimmy.
35. _____A collage-of-the-city book: a birthday party and the main gift was a parrot. Maybe, a first-love story. The leading character appeared in a Caldecott Medal book, and now he's growing up a bit.
36. _____ First I got in trouble at the water spout, then I made like a rock and got rained on, then I missed the bell because of my snake, and—oh, well, they finally let me do it anyway.
37. _____ I am Mary Call Luther. When Roy Luther, our father, died, I and Romey served as his undertaker, preacher, and grave-digger.

MODERN VIEWPOINTS

38. _____ I'm a compulsive scribbler who learned that maybe too honest is dumb. Will I ever grow up to become H. M. Welsch, the noted writer? You can't say I'm not trying. Very trying.
39. _____ My mother left, and then my father. I thought I found them in the tavern. I thought they came home. I thought—but maybe I dreamed it all.
40. _____ DDT, automobile exhaust, sewage pollution, PCB, and mercury are the "realities" that I, Tony Isidoro, got into focus.
41. _____ A very serious matter this. Mark and me were friends like brothers, until I learned he was selling drugs, even to innocent people like M&M.
42. _____ My mother and I had a little altercation and next morning—well—"You are not going to believe me. . . . When I woke up this morning, I found I'd turned into my mother."

    a. *Never Jam Today* by Carole Bolton, Atheneum, 1971. (I-U)
    b. *Did You Carry the Flag Today, Charley?* by Rebecca Caudill, illus. Nancy Grossman, Holt, 1966. (E-I)
    c. *The Dancing Bear* by Peter Dickinson, Little, 1973. (U)
    d. *The Faraway Lurs* by Harry Behn, World, 1963. (U)
    e. *A Letter to Amy* by Ezra Jack Keats, Harper, 1968. (E)
    f. *Where the Lilies Bloom* by Vera and Bill Cleaver, Lippincott, 1969. (I-U)

g. *Brighty of the Grand Canyon* by Marguerite Henry, illus. Wesley Dennis, Rand, 1953. (I)

h. *Who Really Killed Cock Robin?* by Jean Craighead George, Dutton, 1971. (I-U)

i. *Freaky Friday* by Mary Rodgers, Harper, 1972. (U)

j. *Harriet the Spy* by Louise Fitzhugh, Harper, 1964. (I-U)

k. *The Jazz Man* by Mary Hays Weik, illus. Ann Grifalconi, Atheneum, 1966. (I)

l. *That Was Then, This Is Now* by S. E. Hinton, Viking, 1971. (U)

THINGS THAT GO BUMP IN THE NIGHT

43. _____ Noises and flashing lights frightened a modern guy like me: Thomas Small, who lives in a place where the Underground Railroad went through, long ago, and where it's rumored two slave ghosts still walk.

44. _____ Orphaned Sylvia and Bonnie, at the mercy of the terrible Miss Slighcarp, in this chilling tale that might have been written a hundred years ago.

45. _____ In this earthquake year, 1750, I traveled in strange company: a giant lately come from the gallows, a mad girl, and a quack medicine caravan.

46. _____ The "mice" who knocked back, precisely matching knock for knock. A bewitched girl tracing the design of a dinner plate.

47. _____ A dastardly scheme to control Europe by causing earthquakes is foiled by a clever family named Bird.

48. _____ Keith, Julio, or Fallen Arches—which one sent the false bracelet to Ellen?

49. _____ I spent so much time trying to get rid of something by any means possible—chasing it, feeding it, putting it in a sack, boiling it away—that when I got through not succeeding, I was too tired to enjoy what I liked.

50. _____ Although we're not human, we'll show you human foibles, such as list-making and dreaming of glory.

51. _____ The saga of Jennie, who had everything, even a master who loved her, but who went away. Today she's the star of The World Mother Goose Theatre. How she got that way is the story.

52. _____ Found at a certain London train station, arrived from Darkest Peru, he soon dampened the Brown household but brightened spirits everywhere.

53. _____ A modern adventure about the Brontë family's wooden soldiers, who belonged in the museum but couldn't get there because of the robbers and other things.

54. _____ Commences with a slip of the Fourth Fiddler's bow: ends with a dance of death and the winning of a princess.

55. _____ Leaving my Porcelain Pagoda once again, I, the President of the Mouse Prisoners' Aid Society, with the aid of my ever-faithful Bernard, rescued Patience from the horrible Grand Duchess.

56. _____ I have a monkey named Mr. Nilsson and a horse on my perch here at Villa Villekula, while daddy is off being a cannibal king.

a. *The Ice Ghosts Mystery* by Jane Louise Curry, Atheneum, 1972. (U)
b. *Black Jack* by Leon Garfield, Pantheon, 1968. (U)
c. *The Wolves of Willoughby Chase* by Joan Aiken, Doubleday, 1962. (I-U)
d. *Mystery of the Museum* by Betty Cavanna, Morrow, 1972. (I-U)
e. *The House of Dies Drear* by Virginia Hamilton, Macmillan, 1968. (I-U)
f. *The Owl Service* by Alan Garner, Walck, 1967. (U)
g. *Hildilid's Night* by Cheli Durăn Ryan, illus. Arnold Lobel, Macmillan, 1971. (E)
h. *The Return of the Twelves* by Pauline Clarke, Coward, 1963. (U)
i. *A Bear Called Paddington* by Michael Bond, Houghton, 1958. (I-U)
j. *The Marvelous Misadventures of Sebastian* by Lloyd Alexander, Dutton, 1970. (I-U)
k. *Pippi Longstocking* by Astrid Lindgren, Viking, 1951. (I)
l. *Frog and Toad Together* by Arnold Lobel, Harper, 1971. (E)
m. *Higglety Pigglety Pop! or There Must Be More to Life* by Maurice Sendak, Harper, 1967. (I-U)
n. *Miss Bianca* by Margery Sharp, illus. Garth Williams, Little, Brown, 1962. (I-U)

THE FUTURE, THE UNKNOWN

57. _____ Who on Moon would ever go there? Everyone knows it's a dead planet.
58. _____ After a long journey by helicopter, a strange group of scientists finds a young man whose life is saved by taking a bath!
59. _____ Four brothers on a quest to kill a dragon become entangled with a set of "missionaries" from planet Andrecia.
60. _____ Many years ago the Demons left the earth to the People, the Barkers, and the Tusked Ones. Now they have come back.
61. _____ I never even won a prize in a Cracker Jack, but I won this one—the most important prize of all. Look where it got me!

a. *The Day of the Drones* by A. M. Lightner, Norton, 1969. (I-U)
b. *Breed to Come* by Andre Norton, Viking, 1972. (U)
c. *Have Space Suit—Will Travel* by Robert A. Heinlein, Scribner, 1958. (I-U)
d. *Enchantress from the Stars* by Sylvia Louise Engdahl, Atheneum, 1970. (U)
e. *Matthew Looney's Voyage to the Earth* by Jerome Beatty, Jr., illus. Gahan Wilson, Addison-Wesley, 1961. (E-I)

BY POPULAR REQUEST

Some books and their characters are popular with children and adults alike. Here are four pictures denoting such characters. Identify them and the book from which they derive.

62. Popular Characters

63. Popular Characters

64. Popular Characters

65. Popular Characters

66. Two hounds named Old Dan and Little Ann bring momentary happiness to Billy Colman on the banks of the Illinois River in _____.

67. _____ blew down from the sky, brought by the East Wind, and stayed as governess until the West Wind came.

68. _____ was a toy until, through his love for the Boy and the kindness of the nursery magic fairy, he became the real thing, with real hind legs.

69. Spiders are not necessarily illiterate, not if you believe the writing in _____.

Newbery Medal Books

Each year, since 1922, the John Newbery Medal is presented to "the author of the most distinguished contribution to American literature for children." A complete list of recipients of this award appears on pages 540–43. Can you match the five brief descriptions below to the appropriate titles, all Newbery Medal books?

70. _____ The ship is called the Moonlight, the adventure begins with a kidnapping, the story that follows is of unrelieved brutality.

71. _____In Boston, on the brink of the Revolution, a young man's pride is weakened by a cruel accident.

72. _____ With one quick decision she altered the entire course of her life to help her brother Ramo. Later, she befriended the wild dog who killed Ramo.

73. _____ After her mother died, Julie went to live with spinster Aunt Cordelia and tipsy Uncle Haskell. In their different ways, both adults were kind to Julie. Through their love she found her way across the perplexities of adolescence.

74. _____ An oracular pig, an assistant pig-keeper—and how the threads of the fates completed a puzzle in Prydain.

75. _____ A famous seventeenth-century painted portrait is suffused with life in this narrative about the painter and his subject, a slave.
    a. *Up A Road Slowly* by Irene Hunt, Follett, 1966. (I-U)
    b. *I, Juan de Pareja* by Elizabeth Borton de Treviño, Farrar, 1965. (U)
    c. *The Slave Dancer* by Paula Fox, Bradbury, 1973. (U)
    d. *Island of the Blue Dolphins* by Scott O'Dell, Houghton, 1960. (I-U)
    e. *Johnny Tremain* by Esther Forbes, Houghton, 1943. (U)
    f. *The High King* by Lloyd Alexander, Holt, 1968. (U)

ANSWERS

1. *"Ali Baba and the Forty Thieves"* from *The Arabian Nights*
2. *The Elves and the Shoemaker*
3. *Hansel and Gretel*
4. *The Bremen Town Musicians*
5. *Three Billy Goats Gruff*

6. b	10. c	14. a	18. d	22. a
7. d	11. d	15. e	19. j	23. g
8. e	12. b	16. e	20. c	24. f
9. a	13. c	17. h	21. b	25. i

26. *A Story—A Story* by Gail E. Haley
27. *May I Bring a Friend?* by Beatrice Schenk de Regniers, illus. Beni Montresor
28. *Drummer Hoff* by Barbara Emberley, illus. Ed Emberley
29. *The Funny Little Woman* by Arlene Mosel, illus. Blair Lent
30. *Sam, Bangs & Moonshine* by Evaline Ness, Holt, 1966

31. d	38. j	44. c	50. l	56. k
32. a	39. k	45. b	51. m	57. e
33. c	40. h	46. f	52. i	58. a
34. g	41. l	47. a	53. h	59. d
35. e	42. i	48. d	54. j	60. b
36. b	43. e	49. g	55. n	61. c
37. f				

62. Babar from *The Story of Babar* by Jean de Brunhoff
63. Homer Price from *Homer Price* by Robert McClosky
64. Ribsy from *Ribsy* by Beverly Cleary, illus. Louis Darling
65. Raggedy Ann from *Raggedy Ann Stories* by Johnny Gruelle
66. *Where the Red Fern Grows* by Wilson Rawls
67. *Mary Poppins* by P. L. Travers, illus. Mary Shepard
68. *The Velveteen Rabbit* by Margery Williams Bianca, illus. William Nicholson
69. *Charlotte's Web* by E. B. White, illus. Garth Williams

70. c	71. e	72. d	73. a	74. f	75. b

SELECTED SOURCES

About two thousand new children's book titles are published each year, besides numerous films, tapes, and other products in the field. These, combined with older works still in print, comprise a book offering of about 40,000 titles. Fortunately, since no one can read them all, a variety of sources is available to help you locate and select good literature for children. In this section we shall acquaint you with some of the most useful sources.

General Sources

Children's Books in Print and *Subject Guide to Children's Books in Print* are annual publications of R. R. Bowker Company.[1] The 1973 editions list over 40,000 titles, attempting to provide the necessary information for obtaining all the children's books, hard and soft cover, currently in print.

Children's Books in Print is divided into three main sections: Author, Title, and Illustrator Index, with a handy Publisher Index that includes publishers' addresses. Here is a column from the Author Index of this source:

---

[1]R. R. Bowker Co., a subsidiary of Xerox Corp., 1180 Avenue of the Americas, New York, N.Y. 10036.

Fenner, Phyllis & Hughes, Avah. Entrances & Exits. (gr. 4-6). 1960. 4.00 (ISBN 0-396-04431-X). Dodd.

Fenner, Phyllis & McCrea, Mary. More Stories for Fun & Adventure. (gr. 4-9). 1964. 4.50 (ISBN 0-381-99834-7, A50600). John Day.

— —Stories for Fun & Adventure. (gr. 4-9). 1961. 4.50 (ISBN 0-381-99833-9, A75000). John Day.

— —Strange but True: Stories of Many Things. Etheredges, illus. (gr. 4-9). 1970. 4.95 (ISBN 0-381-99832-0, A74050). John Day.

Fenner, Phyllis, ed. Desperate Moments: Stories of Escapes & Hurried Journeys. Geer, Charles, illus. Fenner, Phyllis, compiled by. (Illus.). (gr. 7 up). 1971. 4.75; PLB 4.32. Morrow.

— —Where Speed Is King: Stories of Racing. Geer, Charles, illus. Fenner, Phyllis R., compiled by. LC 78-39618. (Illus.). (gr. 7-9). 1972. 4.95; PLB 4.59. Morrow.

Fenner, Phyllis R. Feasts & Frolics: Special Stories for Special Days. Durney, Helen R., illus. (gr. 3-7). 1949. 3.00 (ISBN 0-394-81152-6); PLB 4.59 (ISBN 0-394-91152-0). Knopf.

Fenner, Phyllis R., ed. Adventure: Rare & Magical. Pitz, Henry C., illus. (gr. 3-7). 1945. 3.00 (ISBN 0-394-80894-0); PLB 4.39 (ISBN 0-394-90894-5). Knopf.

— —Behind the Wheel: Stories of Cars on Road & Track. Geer, Charles, illus. (gr. 7 up). 1964. 4.50. Morrow.

— —Brother Against Brother: Stories of the War Between the States. Lohse, William R., illus. (gr. 7-11). 1957. 4.25. Morrow.

— —Circus Parade: Stories of the Big Top. Ames, Lee, illus. (gr. 3-7). 1954. 3.00 (ISBN 0-394-81030-9); PLB 4.82 (ISBN 0-394-91030-3). Knopf.

Fenner, Phyllis R., compiled by. Consider the Evidence, Stories of Mystery & Suspense. Geer, Charles, illus. LC 73-792. (gr. 7-9). 1973. 4.95; PLB 4.59. Morrow.

Fenner, Phyllis R., ed. Contraband: Stories of Smuggling the World Over. Geer, Charles, illus. (gr. 7 up). 1967. 4.50; PLB 4.14. Morrow.

— —Crack of the Bat: Stories of Baseball. (gr. 3-7). 1952. 3.00 (ISBN 0-394-81058-9); PLB 4.99 (ISBN 0-394-91058-3). Knopf.

— —Danger Is the Password: Stories of Wartime Spies. Geer, Charles, illus. (gr. 7 up). 1965. 4.50. Morrow.

— —Dark & Bloody Ground: Stories of the American Frontier. Geer, Charles, illus. (gr. 7 up). 1963. 4.25. Morrow.

— —Finders Keepers: Stories of Treasure Seekers. Geer, Charles, illus. (gr. 7 up). 1969. 4.50; PLB 4.14. Morrow.

— —Fools & Funny Fellows: More Time to Laugh Tales. Pitz, Henry C., illus. (gr. 3-7). 1947. 3.00 (ISBN 0-394-81160-7); PLB 4.59 (ISBN 0-394-91160-1). Knopf.

— —Ghosts, Ghosts, Ghosts. Lee, Manning, illus. (gr. 4-6). 1952. PLB 4.95 (ISBN 0-531-01676-5). Watts.

— —Giants & Witches & a Dragon or Two. Pitz, Henry C., illus. (gr. 3-7). 1943. 3.00 (ISBN 0-394-81183-6); PLB 4.79 (ISBN 0-394-91183-0). Knopf.

— —Giggle Box: Funny Stories for Boys & Girls. Steig, William, illus. (gr. 3-7). 1950. 3.00 (ISBN 0-394-81185-2); PLB 4.59 (ISBN 0-394-91185-7). Knopf.

— —Horses, Horses, Horses. Crowell, Pers, illus. (gr. 4-6). 1949. PLB 4.95 (ISBN 0-531-01690-0). Watts.

— —Hunter & the Hunted: Stories of Field & Forest. Geer, Charles, illus. LC 68-21003. (gr. 7 up). 1968. 4.25. Morrow.

— —Kick-off. Ames, Lee, illus. (gr. 3-7). 1960. 3.00 (ISBN 0-394-81301-4); PLB 4.89 (ISBN 0-394-91301-9). Knopf.

— —No Time for Glory: Stories of World War Two. Lohse, William R., illus. (gr. 7 up). 1962. 4.50; PLB 3.94. Morrow.

— —Open Throttle: Stories of Railroads & Railroad Men. Geer, Charles, illus. (gr. 7 up). 1966. 4.50. Morrow.

— —Over There: Stories of World War One. Lohse, William R., illus. (gr. 7 up). 1961. 4.25. Morrow.

— —Perilous Ascent, Stories of Mountain Climbing. Geer, Charles, illus. (gr. 7 up). 1970. 4.50; PLB 4.14. Morrow.

— —Pirates, Pirates, Pirates. Lee, Manning, illus. (gr. 4-6). 1951. PLB 5.95 (ISBN 0-531-01767-2). Watts.

— —Price of Liberty: Stories of the American Revolution. Lohse, William R., illus. (gr. 7 up). 1960. 4.25. Morrow.

— —Princesses & Peasant Boys: Tales of Enchantment. Pitz, Henry C., illus. (gr. 3-7). 1944. 3.00 (ISBN 0-394-81521-1); PLB 4.39 (ISBN 0-394-91521-6). Knopf.

— —Quick Pivot: Stories of Basketball. (Illus.). (gr. 5 up). 1965. 3.50 (ISBN 0-394-81530-0); PLB 4.99 (ISBN 0-394-91530-5). Knopf.

— —Stories of the Sea. Werth, Kurt, illus. (gr. 5-9). 1953. 3.00 (ISBN 0-394-81678-1); PLB 4.99 (ISBN 0-394-91678-6). Knopf.

— —Time to Laugh: Funny Tales from Here & There. Pitz, Henry C., illus. (gr. 3-7). 1942. 3.00 (ISBN 0-394-81752-4); PLB 4.39 (ISBN 0-394-91752-9). Knopf.

— —Yankee Doodle: Stories of the Brave & the Free. (Illus.). (gr. 3-7). 1951. 3.00 (ISBN 0-394-91841-X); PLB 4.79. Knopf.

Reprinted from CHILDREN'S BOOKS IN PRINT 1973 by permission of R. R. Bowker Company (A Xerox Education Company). Copyright ©1973 by Xerox Corp.

ACTIVITIES

1. Phyllis R. Fenner has edited a number of short story collections. List five topics indicated by the titles of these books. Write *I* by those suitable for intermediate levels and *U* beside those suitable for upper level.

2. Who publishes *Horses, Horses, Horses* by Phyllis R. Fenner? How much does this edition cost?

Subject Guide to Children's Books in Print arranges children's books according to 7000 subject categories.[1] In the Foreword to this source Lillian N. Gerhardt helps pinpoint its utility:

---

[1] The subject categories themselves are of interest. They are taken from a guide called *Sears List of Subject Headings*, 10th ed., edited by Barbara M. Westby (H. W. Wilson, 1972).

JAPAN—HISTORY

Dilts, Marion M. Pageant of Japanese History. 3rd ed. Onishi, Toyojiro, illus. (gr. 7 up). 1961. 6.50 (ISBN 0-679-20143-2). McKay.

Fitzgerald, Charles P. Concise History of East Asia. LC 66-17361. (Illus., Orig.). (gr. 9 up). 1966. 8.50x. Praeger.

Leonard, Jonathan N. Early Japan. (Illus.). (gr. 7 up). 1968. PLB 7.60 (Pub. by Time-Life). Silver.

——Early Japan. (Illus.). (gr. 7 up). 1968. 6.95. Time-Life.

Powell, Brian. Modern Japan. (Illus.). (gr. 8-10). 1969. PLB 3.96 (ISBN 0-381-99735-9, A49600). John Day.

Seth, Ronald. Milestones in Japanese History. LC 76-99601. (Illus.). (gr. 9 up). 1969. 4.95 (ISBN 0-8019-5389-8); PLB 4.73 (ISBN 0-8019-5393-6). Chilton.

Tamarin, Alfred. Japan & the United States: The Early Encounters, 1791-1860. LC 78-99126. (Illus.). (gr. 9 up). 1970. 6.95 (78881). Macmillan.

Williams, Barry. Emerging Japan. (Illus.). (gr. 10 up). 1969. 4.95 (ISBN 0-07-070542-9); PLB 4.72 (ISBN 0-07-070543-7). McGraw.

JAPAN—SOCIAL LIFE AND CUSTOMS

Appel, Benjamin. Why the Japanese Are the Way They Are. (Illus.). (gr. 7 up). 1973. 5.95 (ISBN 0-316-04866-6, 048666). Little.

Buell, Hal. Young Japan. (Illus.). (gr. 4-7). 1961. PLB 4.50 (ISBN 0-396-04766-1). Dodd.

Dunn, C. J. Everyday Life in Traditional Japan. (gr. 7 up). 1969. 5.00x (ISBN 0-399-20072-X). Putnam.

Hearn, Lafcadio. In Ghostly Japan. (Illus.). (gr. 9 up). 1971. pap. 2.20 (ISBN 0-8048-0965-8). C E Tuttle.

Peterson, Lorraine D. How People Live in Japan. (gr. 4-7). 1963. 3.20 (055095). Benefic.

Sternberg, Martha. Japan: A Week in Daisuke's World. Aoki, Minoru, photos by. (Illus.). (gr. k-2). 1973. 4.50g (70556, CCPr). Macmillan.

Sugimoto, Etsu I. Daughter of the Samurai. (gr. 9 up). 1966. 5.45 (ISBN 0-8048-0136-3). C E Tuttle.

Vining, Elizabeth G. Windows for the Crown Prince: An American Woman's Four Years As Private Tutor to the Crown Prince of Japan. (Illus.). (gr. 7-9). 1952. 8.95 (ISBN 0-397-00037-5). Lippincott.

Yashima, Taro. The Village Tree. (Illus.). (ps-3). 1972. pap. 1.25 (ISBN 0-670-05072-5, VS72, Seafarer). Viking Pr.

JAPANESE IN THE U. S.

Dowdell, Dorothy & Dowdell, Joseph. Japanese Helped Build America. Ebert, Len, illus. (gr. 3-6). 1970. PLB 3.64 (32257). Messner.

Leathers, Noel L. Japanese in America. (Illus.). (gr. 5-11). 1967. PLB 3.95 (ISBN 0-8225-0211-9). Lerner Pubns.

JAPANESE IN THE U. S.—FICTION

Blackburn, Joyce. Suki & the Invisible Peacock. (Illus.). (ps-3). 1968. 2.95 (ISBN 0-87680-078-9); record 1.98. Word Bks.

——Suki & the Magic Sand Dollar. (Illus.). (ps-3). 1969. 2.95 (ISBN 0-87680-096-7). Word Bks.

——Suki & the Old Umbrella. (Illus.). (ps-3). 1968. 2.95 (ISBN 0-87680-077-0). Word Bks.

Bonham, Frank. Burma Rifles: A Story of Merrill's Marauders. (gr. 7 up). 1960. 4.95 (ISBN 0-690-16147-6). T Y Crowell.

——Mystery in Little Tokyo. Mizumura, Kazue, illus. (gr. 3-7). 1966. PLB 3.95 (ISBN 0-525-35560-X). Dutton.

Breck, Vivian. Two Worlds of Noriko. LC 66-17447. (gr. 7-11). PLB 1.69 (ISBN 0-385-06305-9). Doubleday.

Christopher, Matt. Shortstop from Tokyo. Kidder, Harvey, illus. LC 72-97141. (gr. 4-6). 1970. 4.50g (ISBN 0-316-13951-3). Little.

Haugaard, Kay. Myeko's Gift. Ternei, D., illus. (gr. 3-7). 1966. 3.95 (ISBN 0-200-71454-6, B58590). Abelard.

Hawkinson, Lucy. Dance, Dance, Amy-Chan. (Illus.). (gr. k-2). 1964. 3.75, s.p. 2.81 (ISBN 0-8075-1451-9). A Whitman.

Lancaster, Clay. Michiko: Or Mrs. Belmont's Brownstone on Brooklyn Heights. Lancaster, Clay, illus. (gr. k-4). 1966. 3.50 (ISBN 0-8048-0402-8). C E Tuttle.

Means, Florence C. The Moved-Outers. (gr. 7-9). 1945. 4.95 (ISBN 0-395-06933-5). HM.

Politi, Leo. Mieko. Politi, Leo, illus. (ps-3). 1969. 6.39 (ISBN 0-516-08728-2, Golden Gate). Childrens.

Taylor, Mark. Time for Flowers. Booth, Graham, illus. (gr. k-3). 1967. 5.70 (ISBN 0-516-08704-5, Golden Gate). Childrens.

Uchida, Yoshiko. Journey to Topaz. Carrick, Donald, illus. (gr. 4-6). 1971. PLB 4.95 (ISBN 0-684-12497-1). Scribner.

——Promised Year. Hutchinson, W. M., illus. (gr. 4-6). 1959. 4.95 (ISBN 0-15-263866-0). HarBraceJ.

——Samurai of Gold Hill. Forberg, Ati, illus. (gr. 4-7). 1972. PLB 4.95 (ISBN 0-684-12955-8). Scribner.

Yashima, Taro. Umbrella. Yashima, T., illus. (ps-1). 1958. PLB 3.37 (ISBN 0-670-73859-X). Viking Pr.

Reprinted from SUBJECT GUIDE TO CHILDREN'S BOOKS IN PRINT 1973 by permission of R. R. Bowker Company (A Xerox Education Company). Copyright ©1973 by Xerox Corp.

Subject Guide to Children's Books in Print is now the starting point for answers to such stumping requests as, "How many books are there on bionics for kids?" or "Can I get a children's book on the care and training of elephants?" . . . *Subject Guide to Children's Books in Print* is designed as an aid, not a replacement, for the children's book specialists who can read any number of thematic overtones into the fiction and picture books published for children. It is intended to be the bibliography from which to start, but only knowledgeable, well-read personnel can follow through on the sensitive, always challenging task of finding the right books at the right time for the children who want them.[1]

ACTIVITIES

1. Is there a book on Japanese history written at the Early Childhood level?
2. Which books about Japanese-Americans were written since 1960?

---

[1]Lillian N. Gerhardt, "Foreword," *Subject Guide to Children's Books in Print* (Bowker, 1973).

811   BP731
FISHER, AILEEN. Up, up the mountain; illus. by Gilbert Riswold. Crowell c1968.
unp col illus.
Another of the poet's works in which she narrates a universal family
experience. Father suggests that they "drive through summer and walk to
spring" by climbing a western mountain. Excellent for reading aloud; the
illustrations of the "weathery mountain" add to its value as a picture-story
book.
SUBJ: Seasons--Poetry./ Nature in poetry.
                                                   Ph-3 I $3.83

811   BP732
FOSTER, DORIS VAN LIEW. Feather in the wind, the story of a hurricane; illus.
by Ati Forberg. Lothrop, Lee & Shepard c1972. unp col illus.
A prose/poetry description of the formation and destruction of a hurricane,
and of a boy in it who finds a half-dead creature that he nurses to health.
SUBJ: Hurricanes--Poetry.
                                                   Ph-3 P-4 $3.95

811   BP733
FRASER, KATHLEEN. Stilts, somersaults, and headstands; game poems based on a
painting by Peter Breughel. Atheneum c1968. 37p col illus.
One of Breughel's panoramic paintings is illustrated by a series of poems
about games--an unusual combination of poetry and the work of a master
artist stimulated by the author's discovery that the children in the painting are
playing many of the games she herself played as a child. You too may make
the same discovery.
SUBJ: Play--Poetry./ Games--Poetry.
                                                   Ph-3 I $3.87

Selected Lists

The most comprehensive selected lists attempt to recommend best items in all
subject categories. *The Elementary School Library Collection: A Guide to Books and Other
Media* is published by Bro-Dart Foundation[1] each year. Note that this source
includes films, filmstrips, and other nonbook media items. Section I is a Classified Catalog arranged by Dewey Decimal subject categories. In addition to
bibliographic information (author, title, publisher, date, price), entries include
a brief description of the item; the notations "Ph-1," "Ph-2," or "Ph-3" to
indicate whether purchase of the item should have top priority (phase one),
second priority (phase two), or third priority (phase three); and an estimate of
the item's readability according to the Fry Reading Estimate (e.g., P for Primary,
see page 120). For example, here are entries taken from the poetry segment
of the catalog. This collection includes author, title, and subject indexes in
addition to the Classified Catalog. An asterisk (*) indicates a newly included
title.

Since 1909 a leading source for selection has been the *Children's Catalog.* The
twelfth edition, edited by Estelle A. Fidell and published by H. W. Wilson
Company, includes over 5000 selected book titles. Annual supplements keep

---

[1]Bro-Dart Foundation, New Brunswick, New Jersey 08901.

Volcanoes
    Irving, R. Volcanoes and earthquakes
    (4-7)   551.2
    Lauber, P. Junior science book of vol-
    canoes (2-4)   551.2
    Marcus, R. B. The first book of vol-
    canoes and earthquakes (4-7)   551.2
    Matthews, W. H. The story of volcanoes
    and earthquakes (4-6)   551.2
    May, J. Why the earth quakes (2-4) 551.2
    Poole, L. Volcanoes in action (5-7) 551.2
        See also pages in the following books:
    Lauber, P. This restless earth p45-67
    (5-7)   551
    Matthews, W. H. The story of the earth
    p49-62 (5-7)   551
Volcanoes and earthquakes. Irving, R.
                                    551.2
Volcanoes and glaciers. Cary, S. F. 914.91
Volcanoes in action. Poole, L.   551.2

551.2 Volcanoes. Earthquakes

Irving, Robert
    Volcanoes and earthquakes; illus. by Ruth
Adler and with photographs. Knopf 1962
123p illus maps lib. bdg. $4.29 (4-7)   551.2
    1 Volcanoes 2 Earthquakes
    A "study describing the various kinds of
volcanoes and earthquakes and giving examples and historical accounts of the most deva-
stating ones. Examines the scientific basis for
understanding their activity and points out
need for continued research." Library J
    "With diagrams, cross-sections, and photo-
graphs of famous volcanoes and earthquake
areas." Chicago Sch J
    "The book is useful; the writing is authori-
tative. . . . The bibliography gives good source
material, but the titles are really adult." Chicago. Children's Book Center

Reprinted from CHILDREN'S CATALOG by permission. Copyright ©1971 by the H. W. Wilson Company.

this source up to date, and a complete revision cumulation is done every five years. You may want to begin with Part II, the Author, Title, Subject, and Analytical Index. The above is a sample entry for a topic that might be requested by a child, such as "volcanoes." The boldface numbers at the end of each entry (e.g., 551.2) refer to the modified Dewey Decimal classification system so that you can find out more about a book by turning back to Part I, or so that you can locate the book in the library. In Part I, called the Classified Catalog, books are arranged under a modified Dewey Decimal system corresponding to the numbers in Part II. Note that information in Part I includes selections from book reviews.

Similar to *Children's Catalog* in arrangement and scope but on the upper levels are the *Junior High School Library Catalog* and *Senior High School Library Catalog.*

Briefer selective lists include *Books for Children* published annually by American Library Association, a paperback aid consisting of brief reviews drawn from the Association's semi-monthly periodical, *The Booklist.* Criteria used for selecting titles are "literary quality, accuracy, appropriateness of format to content, suitability of content and format to age level, appeal to children, and usefulness in libraries."[1]

Adventuring with Books: 2,400 Titles for Pre-K-Grade 8[2] arranges titles according to fourteen subject categories, with selection based on "the qualities of entertaining reading with literary merit."

---

[1]"Preface," *Books for Children: Preschool Through Junior High School 1970–1971* (American Library Association, 1972), p. v.
[2]Second edition, Citation Press, 1973, compiled by representatives for National Council of Teachers of English.

JUNIOR-HIGH AND HIGH-SCHOOL LEVELS

Arnold Adoff, editor. *Black on Black.* **ages 14 and up**
New York: Macmillan, 1968.

An outstanding collection of the writings of black Americans. Every high-school student should be required to read at least some of the selections. Teachers will find this book extremely helpful as supplementary reading in English and social-studies classes. Black Studies programs should include it. Hopefully, many readers will be motivated to read the books from which the excerpts are taken. Selections that interested me especially were those by Frederick Douglass, Walter White, Gordon Parks, Dick Gregory, Malcolm X, and Kenneth B. Clark. Many points of view are represented, sometimes humorous, often caustic, but always candid. Biographical notes help readers understand and appreciate the attitudes and opinions of the individual writers.

Elizabeth Baker. *Stronger Than Hate.* **ages 12 and up**
Illustrated by John Gretzer.
Boston: Houghton Mifflin, 1969.

This very current, relevant junior novel has a solid punch. It isn't always comfortable to read, but it is timely and realistic. It deserves the attention of parents and teachers seeking provocative, stimulating fiction for youth. The New England community described seemed familiar and the plot action seemed quite within the realm of possibility.

When the families of black industrial engineers try to move into a white community, aided by a local minister, life in a quiet town explodes into hatred and violence. Courageous teenagers, supported by adults, lead the way to changing social patterns and reconciliation through their expressions of compassion and love. The plot gripped me from the start.

Reprinted from BUILDING BRIDGES OF UNDERSTANDING BETWEEN CULTURES by permission of the author, Charlotte M. Keating, and the publisher, Palo Verde Publishing Co.

SPECIALIZED LISTS.   Various interest groups and individuals have devised book-lists to acquaint children with their concerns through reading. The best of these lists also take into consideration literary quality.

Reading Ladders for Human Relations, published by the American Council on Education,[1] contains a wealth of fine titles and preceptive comment. Four *ladders,* or human relations topics, are used to organize the book, with subdivisions for smaller, related categories and maturity-level designations: primary, intermediate, junior, senior, mature. The main topics are these: Creating a Positive Self-Image, Living with Others, Appreciating Different Cultures, and Coping with Change. The overall stated purpose of this volume is "to list books that may increase the social sensitivity of young people and to extend their experience, appreciation, and understanding of their own life styles and the life styles of others."[2] Criteria for selection include choice of books that are "most relevant" and the selection committee does not assume that all such materials must possess "superior literary merit."

Building Bridges of Understanding between Cultures by Charlotte Matthews Keating[3] provides useful discussion including children's reactions to about 500 titles listed under such topics as these: Black Americans, Indians and Eskimos, Spanish-Speaking Americans, Asian Americans, Nationality Groups, and Religious Minorities. The selection and the commentary make this a valuable guide, exciting to read in itself. On the next page is a segment of the "Black Americans" section for "Junior-High and High-School Levels."

ACTIVITIES

1. How useful would the above source be to the junior high or high school student? Could it serve as a reference for the reader as well as the teacher to use?

2. Each section in *Building Bridges of Understanding between Cultures* ends with blank pages for the use of readers who wish to update the material. What other sources discussed in this chapter would help you to add titles under appropriate categories?

A Multimedia Approach to Children's Literature, compiled and edited by Allen Greene and Madalynne Schoenfeld,[4] lists books, films, filmstrips, and recordings according to popular book titles. A Directory of Distributors in this source facilitates its use, and there are plans for frequent updating of materials.

For the traveler abroad, Alec Ellis's *How to Find Out About Children's Literature*[5] can be a godsend. The book tells you where one-in-the-world book collections

---

[1]Located at One Dupont Circle, Washington, D.C. 20036.
[2]*Reading Ladders for Human Relations,* ed. Virginia M. Reid, 5th ed. (American Council on Education, 1972), p. 1.
[3]Palo Verde Publishing Company, Inc., Tucson, Arizona, 1971.
[4]American Library Association, 1972.
[5]Third edition, Pergamon Press, 1973, Maxwell House, Fairview Park, Elmsford, New York 10523.

can be found in England and also lists children's book centers throughout Europe.

Books about Children's Authors

There was a time when favorite authors for children were hard to get to know. Today, you can hear and see them during speaking engagements around the country. You'll find articles by them and about them in periodicals, and there's a growing list of books devoted to word-portraits of authors.

At the time of this writing, there are five volumes in the series *Something About the Author,* compiled by Anne Commire.[1]

Authors and Illustrators of Children's Books: Writings on Their Lives and Works,[2] compiled by Miriam Hoffman and Eva Samuels, presents critical and biographical articles about approximately fifty individuals, drawing from articles first published in various periodicals, useful in any intensive study of their subjects. In addition, biographical sketches are included in the *Who's Who in Children's Literature* by Brian Doyle,[3] and the *Third Book of Junior Authors,* edited by Doris de Montreville.[4]

In a pair of books of unusual interest Lee Bennett Hopkins has recorded lengthy interviews with popular authors, giving us fresh material about them in their own words. These are most readable and are enjoyed by children of almost any age: *Books Are by People: Interviews with 104 Authors and Illustrators of Books for Young Children* and *More Books by More People: Interviews with Sixty-Five Authors of Books for Children.*[5]

Finally, there's a growing number of publications devoted to intensive critical analysis of works by important authors. Of these, John Rowe Townsend's *A Sense of Story*[6] is outstanding. To read the discussion of Joan Aiken's life and work will send you to the Aiken collection immediately.

Awards and Prizes

An annual compilation called *Children's Books: Awards and Prizes* is published in paperback by The Children's Book Council, Inc.[7] Included are international and foreign award-winning titles as well as the many award lists from various groups in America. In addition to the lists of well-known awards such as the John Newbery Medal, the Randolph Caldecott Medal, and the Greenaway and Carnegie Medals of England, you'll find a listing of awards based on children's choices.

---

[1]Gale Research Book Tower, Detroit, Michigan 48226. The fifth volume was published in 1973, bringing a total of 30,000 author sketches to its pages.
[2]Bowker, 1972.
[3]Revised edition, Schocken, 1971.
[4]H. W. Wilson, 1972.
[5]Citation Press, 1969, 1974.
[6]Longmans, London, 1971.
[7]175 Fifth Avenue, New York, N.Y. 10010.

Periodicals That Contain Current Book Reviews

The Horn Book Magazine[1] is published every other month. It has a long tradition of fine articles of interest to adults involved with children's literature and a center booklist of reviews of recently published works, selected carefully by a committee of reviewers.

Bulletin of the Center for Children's Books,[2] a most valuable guide to current selection, contains reviews and critiques by Zena Sutherland and an advisory committee. Each title is designated Recommended, Marginal, or Not Recommended. (This bulletin's recommended books from 1966–1972 are discussed in the reprinted reviews in *The Best in Children's Books.*[3])

School Library Journal, published monthly, and *Booklist,* published semi-monthly, provide advice to the book buyer together with carefully considered evaluative reviews of current children's books. (*School Library Journal* is published by Bowker and *Booklist* by the American Library Association.)

Elementary English, published eight times a year by the National Council of Teachers of English,[4] contains a Literature in the Classroom section which is of great interest to teachers and librarians. The reviews are done by specialists who embrace both the fields of education and literature.

A Final Word on Sources

We haven't attempted to list all the good sources for finding out about children's literature, but those we've included should help as you embark on an inquiry voyage through the children's literature world. We've discussed them here rather than in an appendix because we believe they're basic to your study, a necessary part of the beginning, most appropriate for the opening chapter. Some of these may already be familiar guides, and some may bring fresh enthusiasm and information. Now is a good time, in fact, to locate and examine the sources available to you.

special activities

1. Which of the sources listed are primarily of interest to the adult, providing help in presenting children's literature to its audience? Which sources, once made available, can be used by children?

2. What other sources will you add immediately to the list?

3. Which source first comes to mind as a help in each of the following situations?

---

[1]The Horn Book, Inc., 585 Boyleston Street, Boston, Massachusetts 02116.
[2]The University of Chicago Press, 5801 Ellis Avenue, Chicago, Illinois 60637.
[3]Zena Sutherland, ed., University of Chicago Press, 1973.
[4]1111 Kenyon Rd., Urbana, Illinois 61801.

- A four-year-old wants a book about snakes.
- An intermediate-age child wonders how in this world (and others) Lloyd Alexander happened to decide to write about Prydain.
- A junior-high girl, who has never before cared for reading, suddenly wants to obtain every paperback written by Zilpha Keatley Snyder.
- You want to know whether to order and buy the next volume in Susan Cooper's new series, having recently acquired her *Greenwitch* and having found it bewitching.
- You're given the mission of starting a small new library of "can't put it down" titles for a classroom or children's organization.
- Your're getting ready to teach a unit on South America and find the textbook dull and your own knowledge of South America pretty limited.
- A parent asks you to recommend some *real* alphabet books and other picture-book fare that will appeal to two preschoolers, explaining, "We don't want all fuzzy kittens and tricycles."
- You want to know what children all over the nation seem to enjoy reading: what books do they select?

4. To finish this chapter, here's a paragraph of literary allusions for you. How many can you identify from your reading? From your film-viewing? Which ones will cause you to seek the sources we've just mentioned?

You may already feel at home among the Borrowers. You may be a familiar visitor of Mother Goose. Your world may include Mrs. Tiggy-winkle clear-starching the pinny and pocket-handkins, the crisp style of her doings sharpening your language tools. Agba the mute boy may ride Sham the magnificent stallion through your dreams. A hopeful girl dances her unknown way up the Yellow Brick Road, her story having reached you through book or film. Pooh, Charlotte, Pippi, the crazy Huckabucks, Pierre with his "I don't care," and Jingo Django may already be close friends of yours. Do you know Toad's list of things to do, and what he did when he lost it? Do you know the end of Zeke's puzzling adventure or dream in Harlem? And do you know the beetle's command on a quest not so different from ours: "We must leave. We have a journey to try, and a work to attempt"?

CHAPTER REFERENCES

1. Adoff, Arnold. *MA nDA LA.* Illus. Emily McCully. Harper, 1971. (E)
2. Gág, Wanda. *Millions of Cats.* Coward-McCann, 1928. (E)
3. Burningham, John. *Mr. Gumpy's Outing.* Jonathan Cape, 1970; Holt, 1970. (E)
4. Hutchins, Pat. *Rosie's Walk.* Macmillan, 1969. (E)
5. Marshall, James. *George and Martha.* Houghton, Mifflin, 1972. (E)
6. _____. *George and Martha Encore.* Houghton, Mifflin, 1973. (E)
7. Cleary, Beverly. *The Mouse and the Motorcycle.* Illus. Louis Darling. Wm. Morrow, 1965. (I)
8. Lampman, Evelyn Sibley. *The Shy Stegosaurus of Cricket Creek.* Doubleday, 1955. (I)

9. Adams, Richard. *Watership Down.* Collings, 1972; Macmillan, 1974. (U)
10. Fitzhugh, Louise. *Harriet the Spy.* Harper, 1964. (I)
11. Blume, Judy. *Then Again, Maybe I Won't.* Bradbury, 1971. (U)
12. _____. *Tales of a Fourth Grade Nothing.* Dutton, 1972. (I)
13. Corcoran, Barbara. *The Winds of Time.* Atheneum, 1974. (U)
14. Anderson, Mary. *I'm Nobody! Who Are You?* Atheneum, 1974. (I-U)
15. Schwartz, Alvin, coll. *Witcracks—Jokes and Jests from American Folklore.* Illus. Glen Rounds. Lippincott, 1973. All ages.
16. _____. *Cross Your Fingers, Spit in Your Hat.* Lippincott, 1974. All ages.
17. Kiss, Michaeline. *Yoga for Young People.* Bobbs-Merrill, 1971. (I-U)
18. Kalb, Jonah. *How to Play Baseball Better Than You Did Last Season.* Illus. Kevin Callahan. Macmillan, 1974. (I)
19. Ward, Ralph T. *Ships through History.* Illus. Samuel F. Manning. Bobbs-Merrill, 1973. (I-U)
20. Pyle, Howard. *Otto of the Silver Hand.* Charles Scribner, 1888. (I-U)
21. _____. *Men of Iron.* Harper, 1891. (U)
22. Gray, Elizabeth Janet. *Adam of the Road.* Illus. Robert Lawson. Viking, 1942. (I)
23. Purdy, Susan. *Books for You to Make.* Lippincott, 1973. (I)
24. Macaulay, David. *Cathedral.* Houghton Mifflin, 1973. (I-U)
25. Johnston, Johanna. *Women Themselves.* Illus. Deanne Hollinger. Dodd, Mead, 1973. (I-U)
26. Van Loon, Hendrik Willem. *The Story of Mankind.* Liveright, 1921, 1972. (I-U)
27. Osmond, Edward. *A Valley Grows Up.* Oxford, 1953 (out of print). (I-U)
28. Meigs, Cornelia. *Invincible Louisa.* Little, Brown, 1933, 1968. (I-U)
29. Tobias, Tobi. *Maria Tallchief.* Crowell Collier, 1970. (E-I)
30. Rudeen, Kenneth. *Wilt Chamberlain.* Crowell Collier, 1970. (E-I)
31. Franchere, Ruth. *Cesar Chavez.* Crowell Collier, 1970. (E-I)
32. Adoff, Arnold. *Malcolm X.* Crowell Collier, 1970. (E-I)
33. Cone, Molly. *Leonard Bernstein.* Crowell Collier, 1970. (E-I)
34. Seredy, Kate. *The White Stag.* Viking, 1937. (I-U)
35. Latham, Jean Lee. *Carry On, Mr. Bowditch.* Houghton Mifflin, 1955. (I-U)
36. _____ *This Dear-Bought Land.* Harper, 1957. (I-U)
37. Cleary, Beverly, *Runaway Ralph.* Illus. Louis Darling. Wm. Morrow, 1970. (I)
38. Byars, Betsy. *The 18th Emergency.* Illus. Robert Grossman. Viking, 1973. (I)
39. Erwin, Betty K. *Behind the Magic Line.* Illus. Julia Iltis. Little, Brown, 1969. (I)
40. Grahame, Kenneth. *The Wind in the Willows.* Scribner's, 1908, 1933, 1960.
41. Burnett, Frances Hodgson. *The Secret Garden.* Lippincott, 1911, 1962. (I-U)
42. White, E. B. *Charlotte's Web.* Harper, 1952. (All ages)

BIBLIOGRAPHY

Bernstein, Joanne. "Changing Roles of Females in Books for Young Children." *Reading Teacher,* 27 March 1974, pp. 545–49. Encourages teachers to examine children's books that portray girls in a positive light: includes good annotated bibliography.

Bissett, Donald J. "Literature in the Classroom." *Elementary English,* 50 May 1973, pp. 729–38. An excellent monthly column; this issue presents Mr. Bissett's critical comments on the quality of paperbacks and includes publishers' addresses.

Cohen, Dorothy H. "The Effect of Literature on Vocabulary and Reading Achievement." *Elementary English,* 45 February 1968, pp. 209–13+. Experimental evidence that second-graders' word knowledge and reading comprehension are significantly increased through planned experience with literature.

Dennis, Lawrence. "Play in Dewey's Theory of Education." *Young Children,* 25 March 1970, pp. 230–35. Implications of the play theory for use of literature in the modern school curriculum.

Englebright, Curtis L. "61 Ways to Tell About Books." *Instructor,* 79 November 1969, pp. 70–71. Quick run-down on ways to share books.

Huus, Helen. "Teaching Literature at the Elementary School Level." *Reading Teacher,* 26 May 1973, pp. 795–801. Presents general objectives of a literature program.

Johnston, A. Montgomery. "The Classics of Children's Literature." *Elementary English,* 39 May 1962, pp. 412–14. Expresses concern that few pupils have read classics; recommends a short list to challenge readers.

Lehman, Lola D., and Osborn, Jeanne. "Fiction Recommendations in Two Popular Book Selection Tools." *School Libraries,* 20 Winter 1971, pp. 21–24. Careful comparison of *Children's Catalog* and *Elementary School Library Collection.*

Miller, Bernard S. "The Humanities—What You Don't Know Will Hurt You." *Reading Teacher,* 18 April 1965, pp. 557–62. A magnificent defense of the humanities, including literature, amid the pressures of today's education.

Odland, Norine. "Discovering What Children Have Learned About Literature." *Elementary English,* 47 December 1970, pp. 1072–76. Includes lists of books receiving awards from children's voting; questions to ask in order to evaluate children's reactions to books.

Pellowski, Anne. "Sources of Children's Books from Other Countries." *Top of the News,* 28 January 1972, pp. 133–37. Information, including addresses, about distributors of foreign-language books for children.

Porter, E. Jane. "Reflections of Life Through Books." *Elementary English,* 50 February 1973, pp. 189–95. How to share books and create interest in reading; includes bibliography of helpful "starters."

Purves, Alan. "Indoctrination in Literature." *English Journal,* 63 May 1974, pp. 66–70. Report of an international survey to determine the effects of culture and teaching upon high school students' responses to literature.

Root, Shelton R. "Children, Books, and Diagnostic Teaching." *Viewpoints,* 48 January 1972, pp. 75–87. How children's literature fulfills students' needs.

Sebesta, Sam Leaton. "How to Wash an Elephant." *Instructor,* 78 December 1968, pp. 56–62. How reading skills focus on literature.

Simpson, Elizabeth Léonie. "The Humanities and the Arts: A Practical View." *The Record,* 71 September 1969, pp. 11–16. The poets, says the author, cannot lie; literature contributes to many aspects of human endeavor.

Smith, Dora V. "Children's Literature Today." *Elementary English,* 47 October 1970, pp. 777–80. A wise attempt to place pressures for structuring literature study in proper perspective.

Sutherland, Zena. "Not *Another* Article on the Newbery-Caldecott Awards?" *Top of the News,* 30 April 1974, pp. 249–253. There have been many criticisms of these two awards. This author reviews the situation, offering some defense and some ideas for change.

Viguers, Ruth Hill. "Not Recommended." *Horn Book,* 39 February 1963, pp. 76–78. A famous article attacking controlled vocabulary in primary children's literature.

Ward, Pearl L. "College Classes Choose Favorite Children's Books." *Elementary English,* 39 November 1962, pp. 680–84. Good taste and good variety were exhibited by college students in this writer's children's literature class; you might try a similar survey.

Whisler, Nancy G. "Book Reporting Comes Alive." *Journal of Reading,* 16 February 1973, pp. 383–87. Extensive discussion of alternatives to stand-up-and-tell-the-book.

Wilner, Isabel. "What Is a Book?" *Top of the News,* 28 June 1972, pp. 423–26. A long rhymed-couplet poem with many titles, authors, and perceptive comments worked into it.

2 chapter

Literary Elements

We began our inquiry with the *why* of literature, exploring in chapter 1 its major purposes. These were age-old: to offer entertainment, provide insight through information, present options, develop empathy, and heighten a sense of the aesthetic.

Then we explored some of the *what* of literature, with examples and sources, because our inquiry needs to be operational, based on real items. It needs the focus afforded by a corpus of works to be explored as we go along. Otherwise, discussion would be impractical and inapplicable—a literary theory without a place to apply it.

Now let's examine some of the elements that help explain the *how* of literature. We do this, first, because understanding these elements will help us guide children in selecting literature. Second, appreciation of these elements will help children enjoy literature.

Our concern here is not so much with literary analysis as with literary *synthesis;* with how literature unifies its elements to create its special pleasure. In this chapter you will not see literature treated as the Duke in James Thurber's *The Thirteen Clocks* treated time—he slew it with his sword, "and wiped his bloody blade upon its beard and left it lying there, bleeding hours and minutes, its springs uncoiled and sprawling, its pendulum disintegrating."[1] We will leave literature's parts in good working order. We want you to take great joy in the way they work together.

Let's begin our discussion with narrative fiction, examining first elements of theme, character, setting, and plot.

THEME

There's no doubt that theme is a high-level concept, gradually evolving during a literary experience. You don't sit down to read *Charlotte's Web* with the theme

[1]James Thurber, *The Thirteen Clocks,* illus. Marc Simont (Simon and Schuster, 1950), p. 20.

fully in mind at the outset. You don't say to yourself as you begin to read, "Now I'm going to explore the interdependence of barnyard animals who must deal with the problem of impending death."

Theme is an ultimate outcome of literary experience. It has been described as the "significance of the action: a theme tells the reader what an experience means."[1] Brooks and Warren define theme as "the 'point' or 'meaning' of a story or novel," with a warning against an over-simple definition that threatens to turn literature into a "collection of moralizations on life."[2]

Using these definitions as our base, we'll begin with a general statement or question about "the underlying idea" and then examine the way in which that idea is given concrete expression by an author. We will distinguish between didactic works in which a theme-statement is explicit and works in which a "message" is posed in the manner of an implied question. Now we'll illustrate the process.

Finding Themes

Remember "Inviting Jason," which you read in chapter 1? Let's try to phrase its significance in a general statement.

We begin by citing Stanley's problem as he perceives it. Stanley wants friends, he wants to keep his friends, he want friends of his own choosing—and he doesn't want others competing for these friends.

But then we begin to see that Stanley's problem *as he sees it* is not his real problem. Stanley is really against inviting Jason. Once invited, Jason is perceived as a growing threat. Stanley's problem is the opposite of what he thinks it is. By ruling out Jason and trying to rule Jason out of the friendship circle of others, Stanley seems to be failing in his quest for friendship.

What, then, is the story about? Removing its particulars (its specific actions and characters) for just a moment, we might suggest some hunches about the underlying ideas it attempts to convey:

- People who get selfish about their friendships end up losing their friends.
- Some children get to be bigots; they want to throw out anything that's different. They can't stand the threat of difference.
- Some children are gifted, which makes them appear different, and you have to watch that they don't get picked on.

You may have an entirely different view of what the story is about. How would you write an abstract statement about the story's significance?

Perhaps the story doesn't exactly tell us which of these potential theme-statements is at its center. Perhaps it isn't didactic enough for this sort of thing. If such is the case, we may be better off with theme-questions. These, at least, won't close off our inquiry too soon:

---

[1]Bernice E. Cullinan, *Literature for Children: Its Discipline and Content* (William C. Brown, 1971), p. 36.
[2]Cleanth Brooks, Jr., and Robert Penn Warren, *Understanding Fiction* (Appleton-Century-Crofts, 1943), p. 608.

- Is modern life too other-directed, too dependent on the opinions of others?
- Are some suburban children forced (or forcing themselves) into a kind of bigotry through the urge to conform?
- Are the "Jasons" in our midst really the misunderstood gifted?

Again, you may want to make your own theme-questions. The story certainly permits a variety of ways in which the theme may be viewed. The theme may be a moral one, involving acceptance of others. It may be psychological, an observation about a personality that forbids traits unlike its own. It may be sociological, an observation about peer group behavior in a suburban neighborhood. The theme may unify all these fields of inquiry, as well as some others.

Now you see how theme helps increase literary pleasure. It provides a focal point for dealing with a story's important components: its characters, settings, and the series of episodes making up the plot. "Inviting Jason" seems to be a story with a rather serious central problem, even though its detail and episodes are often humorous. Other stories, just as significant, may deal with less serious matters, and the theme-statements or theme-questions can deal with them accordingly. In fact, some enjoyable books celebrate the happiness of everything-going-well.

One note of warning is needed at this point: we are inquiring into elements of literature here in order to increase our understanding of how literature carries out its purposes, of how the literary experience operates. We are definitely not prescribing a sequence for presenting literature. We began with theme because it is a central concept, but that doesn't mean you should begin so abstractly in your work with children. In fact, to ask a child "What is the theme?" is to begin too abstractly and too generally. Many a potentially productive exploration of literary experience has been throttled by such a beginning. After examining literary purposes, elements, and types, you can use this information in considering approaches and sequences for teaching.

Theme, then, is the significance of the work—what the work is really about and how it says whatever it wishes to say. We may focus on theme through a question or a statement, either explicit or derived by inference. The literary purpose of the theme, broadly stated, is to help the reader confront a problem or problems, or appreciate life as it is or could be.

special activities

1. Select a book from the list of Caldecott Medal winners (pp. 543–45). Examine it carefully for a few minutes, with special attention to the illustrations. How does the artist impart theme? How do the content and style of the illustrations represent a central idea identifiable by a theme-question or theme-statement? Compare your conclusions with the findings of others.

2. Select one literary example from the quiz answers (pp. 45–6) and develop a theme-question or theme-statement. Most of these books have been considered successful in achieving literary purposes; can you judge why, in terms of their themes? Again, compare your results with the observations of others.

CHARACTER

How Character Is Portrayed

Fiction (as well as some nonfiction and poetry) tells a story. A theme emerges as the story is told, usually involving the reader with characters—those who experience the happenings. As you read a story or biography, you get to know its characters, but the getting-to-know experience has varying qualities and degrees of development.

Characters may be *flat,* that is, not developed in depth; or they may be *round,* that is, developed with some dimension. Folklore usually employs flat characters. Folk tales celebrate the ingenuity of action using familiar character types quickly discernible and needing little development. The simpleton son, for instance, is thought to be stupid and useless but saves the day through cleverness or kindness. Clever animals and animal tricksters, fleet-of-foot warriors, and persevering young ladies in folklore the world over are recognized by their readers and listeners as stock characters, quite sufficient for their stories' purposes. The villains, including older favored sons and assorted wicked people, serve their dark purposes and that is all; we're seldom told anything more about them. In the same way, flawless princesses, handsome princes, and devoted suitors are all mere representatives of types that exist in order to get on with the plot. We accept them as flat characters.

Modern versions of traditional tales sometimes attempt to retain the flat character treatment. A fine example is Louis Untermeyer's adaptation of *Aesop's Fables* (1) with amusing, appropriate, flat illustrations by A. and M. Provensen. Or look at *Jack Kent's Fables of Aesop* (2) and its sequel to see how easily and delightfully these flat characters are depicted in the cartoonist's style.

On the other hand, modern authors sometimes do attempt to round out the traditional flat characters. Eleanor Farjeon did so in *The Glass Slipper* (3), a retelling of "Cinderella." The result may be quite disturbing; you may feel that you're being told too much, for instance, when confronted with "Inside the kitchen, in her narrow bed, Ella pulled the thin blanket over her ears and tried not to hear. . . ."[1] After all, you've been accustomed to imagining your own Cinderella from the flat character customarily presented. The famous Arthur Rackham illustrated version (4) also requires an adjustment of expectations from flat to round characterization.

---

[1] p. 11.

In modern stories expectation plays a similar role, only now you usually expect round characters. If a modern author tries flat characterization, he may have difficulty with his readers. He may leave the impression that too much is left out, or that he really hasn't visualized the story or felt its meaning and so is failing to communicate his characters' significance. This can be overcome when a modern author writes a story in the manner of a folk tale, such as Wanda Gág's *Millions of Cats* (5) and more recently *The Squirrel Wife* (6) by Phillippa Pearce. Brief picture-book stories with their visual emphasis on broad aspects of character may also present flat characterization. You wouldn't want it any other way in a jolly cartoon book such as *Father Christmas* (7) by Raymond Briggs or a one-idea-with-variations picture story as *Benjamin's 365 Birthdays* (8) by Judi Barrett. Flat characterization is also successful in the long, rather complex novel, *The Wolves of Willoughby Chase* (9) by Joan Aiken and in its sequels. But flat characterization isn't often so effective in modern works because of the complexity of their themes.

It is generally true that more complex themes require fuller development of characters. True, the characters may still represent familiar types, but authors attempt to show these types as individuals, with important variations from the types. To do this successfully isn't just a matter of describing a character's appearance and actions fully. No description can really be complete. The author must select his detail, based upon the character's significance in the theme being developed.

Characters' appearances can be described in a straightforward manner, for many readers seem to want to know these details. Picture book artists often aim at a realistic or slightly exaggerated reproduction of a character's appearance. See, for example, the works of Evaline Ness, Maurice Sendak, and John Schoenherr. More often, description of physical appearance is accompanied by some detailing of the character's unique traits. The first paragraph of T. H. White's *Mistress Masham's Repose* (10) tells us how the heroine looks and describes some of her traits:

> Maria was ten years old. She had dark hair in two pigtails, and brown eyes the color of marmite, but more shiny. She wore spectacles for the time being, though she would not have to wear them always, and her nature was a loving one. She was one of those tough and friendly people who do things first and think about them afterward. When she met cows, however, she did not like to be alone with them, and there were other dangers, such as her governess, from which she would have liked to have had a protector. Her main accomplishment was that she enjoyed music, and played the piano well. Perhaps it was because her ear was good that she detested loud noises, and dreaded the fifth of November. This, however, with the cows, was her only weakness, and she was said to be good at games.

More frequently in modern works, leading characters are introduced and portrayed through their speech and actions, with only fleeting references to appearance. The opening of John Lawson's fantasy *You Better Come Home with Me* (11) lets you "see" the Boy without an actual description:

Illustration from FATHER CHRISTMAS by Raymond Briggs, reproduced by permission of Coward, McCann & Geoghegan, Inc. and Hamish Hamilton Children's Books Ltd., London. Copyright ©1973 by Raymond Briggs.

Now the story begins with the Boy coming down the road—down the mountain from the west—into town. The curious thing was that no one actually saw him on the road. He simply appeared on Main Street walking from the west and so you know he must have come that way. . . .

A recent trend uses first-person narration, leaving the reader to infer character partially through the character's direct statements and partially through the way others react to him. You come to know him as you might come to know an acquaintance—from the way he talks. The opening of *Freaky Friday* (12) by Mary Rodgers uses this now common technique in a somewhat unusual situation:

"You are not going to believe me, nobody in their right mind could *possibly* believe me, but it's true, really it is!

"When I woke up this morning, I found I'd turned into my mother. There I was, in my mother's bed, with my feet reaching all the way to the bottom, and my father sleeping in the other bed. I had on my mother's nightgown, and a ring on my left hand, I mean her left hand, and lumps and pins all over my head."

Sylvia Louise Engdahl in *Enchantress From the Stars* (13) develops an unusual mixture of characterization techniques. The story begins like a folk tale, third person, with characters who are appropriately flat: "At the edge of the Enchanted Forest there lived a poor woodcutter who had four sons, the youngest of whom was named Georyn." But after a few pages there is a sudden change, and the next portion of the story is in first person, giving us the heroine, Elana, through her own description of the affair: "I was not supposed to be in the landing party at all—I was supposed to be studying. . . ."[1] As Elana and Georyn meet and become fond of each other, we come to know each of them through the other's impressions. Few books attempt so wide a range of characterization techniques.

Whatever the techniques, the most difficult task for the author in developing character is to convince the reader of the psychological "rightness" of the portrayal. The author's choice of presenting flat or round characters, of extensive description of physical traits or of relating his description only through action, and his selection of which facets of a character to reveal—all of these depend on the effect he wishes to achieve in terms of the story and its theme. Once this psychological intent is felt, we can accept a great range of appropriate techniques of character portrayal. We can even surrender ourselves to believing the unbelievable, as in *The Wind in the Willows,* where Toad changes his appearance and size whenever the plot calls upon him to do so.

special activities

1. Read the following selection from *A Bargain for Frances* (14) by Russell Hoban. In an introductory scene Frances prepares to visit her friend Thelma and is warned by her mother to be careful because she has been tricked by Thelma

---

[1]pp. 7, 10.

"How much does the tea set cost?"

said Thelma.

"I don't know," said Frances.

"I am sure they cost a lot,"

said Thelma.

"It will take you a long time

to save up all that money."

"I know," said Frances, "and I wish

I had a tea set now."

"Maybe I will sell you mine,"

said Thelma.

22

"I don't want yours," said Frances.

"I want a real china one

with pictures on it in blue."

23

From A BARGAIN FOR FRANCES by Russell Hoban, illustrated by Lillian Hoban. Text copyright ©1970 by Russell Hoban. Illustrations copyright ©1970 by Lillian Hoban. By permission of Harper & Row, Publishers, Inc. and World's Work Ltd., London. **A good selection for focusing on characterization. (Story continued on p. 66)**

in the past. Now, Frances tells Thelma that she is saving to buy a tea set. What technique of characterization predominates? Does the characterization enable you to predict what may happen next? From this excerpt, can you infer any potential themes for the story? The accompanying illustrations tell something of the characters' appearances. What do these illustrations add to the characterizations? Now read the selection aloud. What contrasts can you make based on each character's traits?

2. For some readers, certain literary characters are like trademarks to apply to people they know. Do you know a "Cinderella"; a "Little Miss Muffet"; a "Mad Hatter"; an "Eeyore"? Which of the following characters from children's literature do you know in this way? What qualities do they represent?
    Jo in *Little Women;* Max in *Where the Wild Things Are;* Sylvester in *Sylvester and the Magic Pebble;* Harriet in *Harriet the Spy;* Claudia in *From the Mixed-up Files of Mrs. Basil E. Frankweiler;* Hazel in *Watership Down.*

"I don't think
they make them anymore,"·
said Thelma. "I know another girl
who saved up for that tea set.
Her mother went to every store
and could not find one.

Then that girl lost
some of her money
and spent the rest on candy.
She never got the tea set.
That is what happens.
A lot of girls
never do get tea sets.
So maybe you won't get one."

25

SETTING

Setting and Purpose

At first glance, setting is a simple concept: the time and place of a story. But, beyond the simple idea of physical description, it includes imparting a *sense* of time and place. The same time and place will require different handling in two stories that differ in theme and mood. Setting, then, has its psychological dimension.

Setting may be conveyed through straightforward description, as if the author were showing the reader a map or photograph. Early in her Newbery Medal book, *Julie of the Wolves* (15), Jean Craighead George quickly sketches the North Slope of Alaska where the story is taking place:

> The barren slope stretches for three hundred miles from the Brooks Range to the Arctic Ocean, and for more than eight hundred miles from the Chukchi to the Beaufort Sea. No roads cross it; ponds and lakes freckle its immensity. Winds scream across it, and the view in every direction is exactly the same. . . .[1]

---

[1] p. 6.

In another Newbery Medal winner, *The Bronze Bow* (16), Elizabeth George Speare uses a similar descriptive technique, but this time the scene is described as it might be viewed through the eyes of a group of teen-agers hiding from the Romans in this Biblical story of Palestine:

> Just below them the village clung to the rocky slope, the dark blocks of the synagogue showing clearly among the clustering flat-roofed houses. Around it circled the gray-green olive orchards and the fresh, clear green fields of grain, banded by purple iris and shining yellow daffodils. To the south lay the lake, intensely blue. To the north, beyond the line of hills, through the shimmering, misty green of the valley, the silver thread of the Jordan wound up to the shining little jewel that was the Lake of Merom. . . .[1]

Both descriptions present settings that are likely to be somewhat unfamiliar to most readers. Both appear early in the narratives, setting the stage for what is to happen. Both are fairly objective, although the second attempts to visualize setting from the characters' point of view. Even in these descriptions of setting, however, the authors have selected their details: there is no such thing as a complete description in narrative. Authors must consider what is most important for their stories in terms of setting, what information readers are most likely to need and use, and what facets of setting will aid theme and characterization. Hence *Julie of The Wolves* highlights the barren, isolated qualities of the setting, while *The Bronze Bow* presents the panorama where various episodes of the story are to take place.

Authors use figurative language to aid readers' imaginations. *Freckle* and *scream* in the first description aren't literal terms but figurative expressions. In *The Bronze Bow* a sense of motion is conveyed by words such as *circled* and *banded* as if the orchards, fields, and flowers were swept past the eyes of the watchers.

When settings are likely to be more familiar to readers, their descriptions may be briefer and intertwined with the action. The Ross home, the scene of much of the action in Jean Little's *Take Wing* (17), is described gradually as the action progresses, and you are able to imagine it simply because you've probably known other homes like it. A character is "asleep in the bedroom at the far end of the hall"—and you need nothing more.

In most works setting supports the literary purposes we have assigned to theme and character. But setting may play a more pivotal role. Anita Lobel crowds every nook and cranny of a castle with figures and clothing and furniture to convey the sad, smothered tone that dominates *A Birthday for the Princess* (18). *The Fool of the World and the Flying Ship* (19) may be a simple foolish tale, but the Shulevitz pictures give it a setting at once noble and kingly, lending the peasant tale a sense of pleasing importance. The Caribbean island in Theodore Taylor's *The Cay* (20) isolates the two main characters physically and psychologically from the rest of the world.

Setting, then, serves several purposes within the framework of a narrative: to suggest literally the place and time of the story, to give the author's or artist's

---

[1]p. 10.

interpretation of the significance of the place and time, and to reflect the tone and theme of the story. Perhaps the unity of these purposes is most easily observed in illustrations. For instance, the illustrations done by Alice and Martin Provensen for the Golden Press edition of *The Iliad and the Odyssey* (21) give only a fleeting impression of how the scenes might really have looked or have been imagined by the Greeks who first heard the tales. The perspective in the drawings of walled cities and other architecture seems modern impressionistic, while the figures are styled after Greek drawings such as those once found on the bas-reliefs of the Parthenon and elsewhere. This interpretation suggests timelessness, a blending of modern and ancient memory. The sweeping lines may symbolize the physical strength, the heroic determination in keeping with the narrative. A similar unity is achieved by the quite different stone engraving medium of Ingri and Edgar Parin d'Aulaire for *Abraham Lincoln* (22).

special activities

1. First, examine a sample of Caldecott Medal books (pp. 543–45) to note the great variety in illustration available to the artist. Contrast two good selections. What details have the artists chosen to represent literal setting? What have they done to interpret? Are their representations symbolic of the theme or tone of the stories? Compare the style of Nonny Hogrogian in *One Fine Day* (23) with that of *The Funny Little Woman* (24). The first is a simple tale, modeled after folk tales. The second is a retelling of an actual folk tale. What is the difference in complexity between the two stories and how is this shown in the illustrations? Could the two styles be interchanged? What would be the effect if they were?

2. Now see if you can find two books that present similar settings, one a picture book or highly illustrated story, and the other a pictureless book in which setting is carried entirely through words. For instance, Ann Grifalconi showed us Rio de Janeiro and its surrounding hills in woodcuts for *The Ballad of the Burglar of Babylon* (25). A somewhat similar setting in Bogotà, Columbia, is conveyed in words by S. R. Van Iterson in *Pulga* (26). The wood-grain texture in Grifalconi's pictures combines with minimal detail to give us a feeling of bleakness, of psychological as well as visual squalor. In *Pulga* the poverty of the hero and his family is memorably shown through a few word pictures: the family sitting together in a single room while flood waters pour in, tourists staring through the back window of their automobile, remarking "Just one of those street urchins. . . . Don't bother about him." Illustration and writing are two quite different media available in creating children's books. How does each medium convey setting? In both cases, the illustration and the word picture, the effect is likely to be different from a literal photograph. How? What is the effect of this difference?

An Army helicopter
Came nosing around and in.
He could see two men inside it,
But they never spotted him.

Reprinted with the permission of Farrar, Straus & Giroux, Inc. from THE BALLAD OF THE BURGLAR OF BABYLON by Elizabeth Bishop, illustrated by Ann Grifalconi. Copyright ©1964, 1968 in text by Elizabeth Bishop. Pictures copyright ©1968 by Ann Grifalconi.

PLOT

Defining Plot

In literature, plot is more than just any sequence of events. Scholes and Kellogg define it as "the dynamic, sequential element in narrative,"[1] and others have pointed out that plot must have structure: that is, the description of actions must be *plotted* to show interaction of events and something more at work than mere random choice of events. To put it another way, the plot of a story consists of the selected actions of characters in a particular setting to reveal a theme.

---

[1]Robert Scholes and Robert Kellogg, *The Nature of Narrative* (Oxford University Press, 1966), p. 207.

Often a plot contains events that show a problem or conflict leading to a climax and some sort of solution, followed by a *denouement:* the final unwinding of the complications that make up the story. But some themes don't lend themselves to this structure. It's doubtful, for instance, that "Inviting Jason" (the story you read in chapter 1) would be improved if its real conflict were built to an outward climax or followed by a satisfying denouement. The up-in-the-air endings of some social problem novels, such as *The Peter Pan Bag* (27) by Lee Kingman or the Paula Fox story *Portrait of Ivan* (28), may leave the feeling that we are experiencing only part of a plot, that the rest is yet to come even when the books end. Again, it's doubtful that a more complete plot would be preferable.

Children's fiction, more often than adult fiction, suffers from "bad plot" epidemics, often arising from a constricted idea of what plot is. New, fresh themes don't always lend themselves to the plot structure that the past has deemed most suitable. Even experienced, dependable authors trying such themes sometimes round out their plots neatly when a variation on the age-old formula might be more effective. Look how freshly exciting books can be when theme directs plot out of old ruts. *William's Doll* (29) by Charlotte Zolotow has a restrained plot. The author doesn't invent excessive incidents to tell what is really a simple but neglected situation: a boy wants a doll more than he wants a basketball or an electric train:

> But he didn't stop wanting
> a doll
> to hug
> and cradle
> and take to the park.[1]

And examine, too, the grim, unforgettable experience that results from reading *The Slave Dancer* (30) by Paula Fox, a book that refuses to lighten its mood through comic incident or hopeful ending.

There are a number of stock plots in children's literature, frequently appearing, grasped by inexperienced writers as if they were new gold, and almost always deadly dull. Commenting on one such group of plots—those that appear in picture books—editor Jean Karl writes:

> They are bad because they have no depth, because they are dull, because they are like hundreds of others that have been received. The number of stories about pine trees that want to be Christmas trees, donkeys that carry Mary to Bethlehem, and items that become the Christmas star is almost legion. The stories about Santa Claus are almost equally repetitive. So are the varieties of animals who long to be something else.[2]

---

[1] p. 22.
[2] Jean Karl, *From Childhood to Childhood* (John Day, 1970), p. 82.

not often—I would pretend it was a British cruiser not afraid to displease the United States Government by boarding us. I imagined the slaves set free, the rest of us taken to England where Stout would be hanged, and Purvis and I sent by fast ship to Boston. From there, I would make my way home, and one day, in the freshness of a morning, I would open the door and step inside, and my mother would look up from her work, and—

But we were not pursued. And if we had been, it is unlikely *The Moonlight,* with all her sails stretched, could have been captured. Only pirates might take us, French pirates undeterred by any flag, eager to pounce on a tattered dirty little ship with a cargo of half-dead blacks, and a bunch of ailing seamen as hard and dry and moldy as the ship's biscuits they gnawed on.

When, one morning, I could not find my fife, I thought Cooley or Wick, longing for distraction, had hidden it from me. They swore they had not touched it. And no one else had either, said Purvis, because he would have heard anyone sneaking about and reaching into my hammock where I always kept it. But Purvis had been on watch the night before.

I searched frantically throughout the ship. Porter came looking for me and told me I was wanted on deck. I found Stout waiting aft, the Captain standing a few feet away looking through his spyglass at the horizon. There had not been a word between Stout and me since the night I'd run away from him.

"We're going to bring up the niggers, Jessie," he said. "Where's your music maker?"

The instant he spoke, I knew Stout had made off with the fife.

Adults who recommend books for children must keep themselves open and responsive to experimentation with plot, not always insisting that books fit the standard plot requirements. If a book's plot strikes you as dull and trite but "surely suitable for a child reader because it seems to be a typical plot," chances are your first judgment is right and your second is wrong. In short, don't define plot so narrowly that you rule out innovation.

Surprisingly, some of the most strongly held beliefs about what plot ought to be are shaken when you examine some children's books that have lived through the years. Some say, for instance, that "lots of action" is a necessity in a children's book. Try that criterion on *The Secret Garden* (31) by Frances Hodgson Burnett, a book that one large group of teachers recently named as their favorite from all childhood reading. Note that it takes Mary Lennox, the book's heroine, seventy-some pages to make that first step into the garden. Even after that you could hardly say there's lots of action. Yet people have cared more about Mary's entrance into that garden and its effect upon her than about practically anything else that happened in 1911!

A modern counterpart is E. L. Konigsburg's *Jennifer, Hecate, Macbeth, William McKinley, and Me, Elizabeth* (32) which, by the lots-of-action criterion, gets off to a slow start. Yet that slow opening scene with Elizabeth in her Halloween garb walking alone and spying Jennifer up in a tree is the scene in the book that no one ever seems to forget. (See pages 73–75.)

Other beliefs, including those held by many children, ought often to be reexamined as a "stretching exercise" in considering plot. Not all children's books must have happy endings. The action doesn't always have to revolve around one strong central character who dominates the book's events from beginning to end. A few years ago it was not usual to find flashbacks in books for young children because it was presumed that the mixup in sequence might be confusing. But that technique of plotting is more acceptable today; in fact, long flashbacks are used in the middle portion of two recent Newbery Medal winners *(Mrs. Frisby and the Rats of NIMH* and *Julie of the Wolves).*

The concept of plot must be quite broad. It must permit latitude in the selection and presentation of events so long as these serve the other elements of narrative, particularly the characterizations and themes. Without this attitude, you'll miss the pleasure of watching a skilled writer experiment with plot.

special activities

1. What are the plot qualities you remember responding to in your childhood reading? To find these, first think of two or three favorite stories, and list the incidents that held your interest. Then try to determine what these incidents had in common, either in the way they were told or assembled in a whole plot, or in the nature of the incidents themselves. What qualities

1 I FIRST MET JENNIFER ON MY WAY TO school. It was Halloween, and she was sitting in a tree. I was going back to school from lunch. This particular lunch hour was only a little different from usual because of Halloween. We were told to dress in costume for the school Halloween parade. I was dressed as a Pilgrim.

I always walked the back road to school, and I always walked alone. We had moved to the apartment house in town in September just before school started, and I walked alone because I didn't have anyone to walk with. I walked the back way because it passed through a little woods that I liked. Jennifer was sitting in one of the trees in this woods.

Our apartment house had grown on a farm about ten years before. There was still a small farm across the street; it included a big white house, a greenhouse, a caretaker's house, and a pump painted green without a handle. The greenhouse had clean

3

windows; they shone in the sun. I could see only the roof windows from our second floor apartment. The rest were hidden by trees and shrubs. My mother never called the place a farm; she always called it THE ESTATE. It was old; the lady who owned it was old. She had given part of her land to the town for a park, and the town named the park after her: Samellson Park. THE ESTATE gave us a beautiful view from our apartment. My mother liked trees.

Our new town was not full of apartments. Almost everyone else lived in houses. There were only three apartment buildings as big as ours. All three sat on the top of the hill from the train station. Hundreds of men rode the train to New York City every morning and rode it home every night. My father did. In the mornings the elevators would be full of kids going to school and fathers going to the train. The kids left the building by the back door and ran down one side of the hill to the school. The fathers left the building by the front door and ran down the other side of the hill to the station.

Other kids from the apartment chose to walk to school through the little woods. The footsteps of all of them for ten years had worn away the soil so that the roots of the trees were bare and made steps for walking up and down the steep slope. The little woods made better company than the sidewalks. I liked the smells of the trees and the colors of the trees. I liked to walk with my head way up, practically hanging over my back. Then I could see the patterns the leaves formed against the blue sky.

I had my head way back and was watching the leaves when I first saw Jennifer up in the tree. She was dressed as a Pilgrim, too. I saw her feet first. She was sitting on one of the lower branches of the tree swinging her feet. That's how I happened to see her feet first. They were just about the boniest feet I had ever seen. Swinging right in front of my eyes as if I were sitting in the first row at Cinerama. They wore real Pilgrim shoes made of buckles and cracked old leather. The heel part flapped up and down because the shoes were so big that only the toe part could stay attached. Those shoes looked as if they were going to fall off any minute.

did they have? Interview one or two children to find out what plots arouse their interest. Explore their reactions and compare them with your own. These qualities will help you predict one element in children's preferences and interests in books.

2. How interdependent are the elements of character and plot in the books you like? It was the opinion of Henry James in "The Art of Fiction" that the two elements were inseparable: "What is character but the determination of incident? What is incident but the illustration of character? What is either a picture or a novel that is *not* of character? What else do we seek in it and find in it?" Are there books for children in which this statement holds true? What evidence can you give? Can you cite good examples in which the statement is not supported?

3. To explore the ranges of plot and its purpose and effect upon readers, try to locate, read, and compare the following two selections:

   a. *Rosie's Walk* (33) by Pat Hutchins. Rosie the hen seems to be unaware that a fox is about to plunge upon her at each segment of her journey. One early childhood authority explained to a group of teachers that the repetition of the problem builds knowledge of the repetition element in all experience; and, further, that the outcome of each of the fox's attempts to capture Rosie becomes predictable so that young children gain experience in cause-effect relationship. Do you agree? Is that the whole purpose of the plot? Is that a feasible description of the effect of the book?

   b. *Annie and the Old One* (34) by Miska Miles. A Navajo grandmother, the Old One in the story, tells the family that she will die when the new rug is finished. The child Annie tries to prevent completion of the rug. To discover what setting (through text and drawings), characterization, and theme have to do with fleshing out bare bones of plot, try summarizing this plot. Then compare your summary with the effect of the book itself. Now compare *Rosie's Walk* with *Annie and the Old One.* What literary elements make these works different?

UNITY: SYNTHESIZING THE ELEMENTS OF NARRATIVE

Terms used to discuss unity of elements in a story are varied and sometimes confusing. We will use the term *unity* to designate the ways in which plot, character, setting, and theme are synthesized. A story may have a lively, attention-getting plot but its characters may only be sketched in; they don't seem to "live" the plot. Or settings may be haphazardly described so that the reader develops little sense of place. The final effect may be puzzling and weak, lacking in unity. *Ox: The Story of a Kid at the Top* (35) by John Ney is full of incident: a rich, fat boy accompanies his hard-drinking father on an extended weekend party-trip from Palm Beach to California to Mexico to Houston and back home again. It could be a good story, this plight of the neglected wealthy. But all we learn about Ox is that he cries easily and watches too much television, and the settings are no more real than dots on a map. In our opinion, unity is lacking, though many people express approval of this book and its sequel.

Erik Christian Haugaard's *Orphans of the Wind* (36) has similar difficulties. Jim is real enough for identification. The style contains sailor talk and action, the movement of the ship, the changing weather. But episodes are selected and arranged in such a manner that the focus shifts from concern about Jim to concern about the whole matter of slavery; the two ideas in this case don't mesh. Again, this is a structural fault. A unified story has not been achieved.

Unity is a very broad concept. To explore the unifying mechanisms more closely, let's examine four more components that contribute to unity. These are the *point of view* from which a story is told, the *pace* of the story, and the twin components of author's *distance* and *tone*.

Point of View

Brooks and Warren define *point of view* as "the mind through which the material of the story is presented."[1] As we'll see in chapter 9, the concept of point of view is a most useful one in designing inference activities for enjoying literature. Right now we'll focus on the unifying effect of point of view.

A story may be told in the first person, either from the point of view of the leading character or, less frequently, a supporting character. This device works best when the story is or seems to be autobiographical. *The Endless Steppe* (37) by Esther Hautzig is Esther's true account of a five-year confinement in Siberia when the Communist Russian government displaced the author and her family from Poland to the northern land. No one intervenes to prevent Esther from revealing what is important to her. She can confess that "Our garden was the center of my world, the place above all others where I wished to remain forever."[2] And later, amid hunger and cold, she can convince us that her viewing of the film *Charlie's Aunt* transcends all the hardship: "It was Jack Benny, cavorting around in his ridiculous wig, who was most present, the scenes of Oxford that were most real."[3] When the family is freed to go home to Poland, we can believe Esther's desire to stay in Siberia long enough to enter the declamation contest, for she tells us directly of her eagerness to do so. And, when the family reaches Poland, the reader, who has been addressed directly by Esther all through the book, can empathize with her as she describes an incident in the homeland: "At this village, there were some Polish people who had learned nothing from the blood bath. . . . 'Who needs you?' they screamed. 'Go back to Siberia, you dirty Jews.' "[4]

---

[1]Brooks and Warren, *Understanding Fiction*, p. 607.
[2]p. 1.
[3]p. 124.
[4]p. 421.

Other semi- or pseudo-autobiographical accounts—for instance, . . . *and now Miguel* (38) by Joseph Krumgold and Scott O'Dell's *Island of the Blue Dolphins* (39)—could hardly be imagined except through the first-person narration of their leading characters. In such instances, the story's style seems dependent on the diction and rhythm of speech of these character-narrators.

When a minor character tells the story, the purpose is to give the reader a unique perspective on a main character or event. Amos, the mouse in Robert Lawson's *Ben and Me* (40), describes Ben Franklin; and the same author's *Mr. Revere and I* (41) presents the whole colonial panorama from the first-person viewpoint of the horse Scheherazade.

First-person narration has some distinct advantages. A character's direct address can enable us to know him. Plot, setting, and character are likely to be unified by the approach which says, "this is what happened to me, this is where it happened, this is how I felt." Insofar as the character's perceptions serve those of the theme, we are given a direct line to the theme—or, as in the case of "Inviting Jason," we may be addressed by a character whose consistent perceptions we react against.

But first-person point of view also has some strong limitations. It can't work effectively in presenting episodes in which the storytelling character does not appear. Nor does it enable the author to step outside the point of view to comment on important matters that lie beyond the perception of the storytelling character. Nowhere is this shortcoming more apparent than in some of the social-issues books of the late 1960s and early 1970s.[1]

Because, for example, twelve-year-old Michael tells the story of *Edgar Allan* (42), we are barred from the wider social context that Michael couldn't be expected to know but that is needed for understanding the story's significance, or theme. S. E. Hinton's *That Was Then, This Is Now* (43) can't explore the basic conflict in motives between loyalty and honesty because the storytelling character lacks the perception to do so.

Some stories, then, are better told in third person. In that case the author may choose to see the story through the eyes of a central character, still retaining his distance by using the third-person technique. Mab, the middle child in *The Ice Ghosts Mystery* (44) by Jane Louise Curry, observes the people in her family as they search for her missing father in the mountains of Austria. Since Mab plays the most prominent part in unraveling the mystery, and since she is fully capable of discerning the motives of everyone else in the story, this point of view is entirely acceptable. Even when Mab isn't present in a scene, as in the episode about her sister Oriole's search for help, we can accept the incident as one that Mab might learn about later. Mab, then, is the "entrance character" into the story, yet we are allowed to keep the third-person distance.

Some stories, however, seem to require the author's point of view. Those with a shifting cast of characters, those requiring considerable background for setting

---

[1]See Eleanor Cameron, "McLuhan, Youth, and Literature," *Horn Book,* 49 (February 1973): 79–85.

or theme, those that delve into crucial or puzzling issues—such stories seem to demand that the reader, particularly the child reader, have the guiding, sustaining mind of the analytic, sometimes omniscient author.

The author may then take the position of knowing all about his story. After all, it is his to tell! He is thus freed from the constraints imposed by revealing setting and plot through the senses of a character. He can keep his distance, telling only what he chooses to tell, or he can speak to the reader directly—over the heads of the characters, you might say. He can, if he's so disposed and skilled, make a clean approach to the description of setting and action without any concern about features that might not be noticed by characters in the story. Most important, he can build rapport with his audience, giving us the feeling that we are safely in the hands of a storyteller who has the widest grasp of the story.

If he so chooses, the omniscient author can step aside for a time to describe an incident through a character's eyes. He may, for example, permit a character to tell part of the story to another character, as Nicodemus the rat does in the long central section (pp. 98–177) of *Mrs. Frisby and the Rats of NIMH* (45) by Robert C. O'Brien. But the author can return to fill in more complete detail, to inform us about matters that help us understand the story's significance.

We've examined three rather distinct points of view used by authors of narrative for children: first person from a character's viewpoint, third person from a character's viewpoint, and third person from the author's viewpoint (though on rare occasions an author may decide to address his reader in first person as himself). The three points of view may be mixed in a single book, but the mixture must be handled deftly to avoid confusion.

special activities

1. Contrast point of view in these two books about inanimate objects: *Paddle-to-the-Sea* (46) by Holling Clancy Holling and *Hitty, Her First Hundred Years* (47) by Rachel Field. How would the latter be changed in effect if written from the author's third-person viewpoint? Could the carved "Paddle Person" in the little boat going from Lake Superior to France tell his own story? What would be the difference in effect?

2. The first-person point of view is effectively used in *Where the Lilies Bloom* (48) by Vera and Bill Cleaver. Here is a passage in which the heroine, Mary Call Luther, describes her older sister: "Like I say, Devola is cloudy-headed and this is one thing I cannot understand because none of the rest of us Luthers is that way, but Devola is for sure, so each day I have to explain the whole of our existence to her. Her confidence in my ability to do this is supreme though there are four whole years difference between her age of eighteen

and mine of fourteen."[1] How would a third-person, omniscient author style have dealt with this message?

3. We've mentioned two books by Robert Lawson *(Ben and Me* and *Mr. Revere and I)* which use the first-person point of view. But Lawson's best-loved work is probably *Rabbit Hill* (49). The story is about Little Georgie, the young rabbit, and his acquaintances. After reading the book, can you tell why Georgie wasn't allowed to tell the story himself?

A more sophisticated rabbit saga is Richard Adams's famed *Watership Down* (50). Readers attest to the closeness they feel to Hazel, Bigwig, and the rest of the valiant group in this book. One reader insists that this closeness derives from the author's writing "just as if he were a rabbit." Do you agree? Whose point of view is used to tell the adventures in *Watership Down?*

Pace

The *pace* of a narrative and its episodes contributes to a sense of unity. Hence, an incident of little central importance can be dealt with quickly, while in another work the same incident may require more detail because it figures more strongly in the concept of the whole story. The historical battle of Thermopylae in Greek history is only parenthetically related to Anne Rockwell's account of the building of the Parthenon in *Temple on a Hill* (51). Pace dictates that the battle be described in only two paragraphs:

> When morning came, one of the Spartans reported to Leonidas on the size of the Persian army he had seen approaching at the rear of the pass. He described it as so vast that its flying arrows would hide even the sun. But to this terrible news, a Spartan soldier named Dienekes only answered: "Good. Then we shall fight in the shade." For it was a hot day in July.
>
> They fought in the shade; all were killed. And most of the Greeks who had departed were overtaken by the Persians and also killed. Four thousand Greek soldiers fell that day to Xerxes, and his army marched on.[2]

But a very different pace holds for Mary Renault's *The Lion in the Gateway* (52) and Caroline Dale Snedeker's *The Spartan* (53). In all three cases, the sense of a unified structure—the place and importance of the Thermopylae battle in relation to the entire work—has determined the pace of its telling.

The pace problem is apparent in narratives that transfer a central character from a realistic world to a fantasy world. The everyday events must be dealt with quickly but solidly to establish credibility. The transition to an imaginary world full of imaginary events shouldn't be delayed too long. Note the transition that occurs in the third paragraph of *Alice's Adventures in Wonderland:* ". . . nor did Alice think it so *very* much out of the way to hear the Rabbit say to itself

---

[1] p.9.
[2] p. 21.

New Folks co-ming, Oh my! New Folks co-ming, Oh my! New Folks co-ming, Oh my! Oh my! Oh my!

From RABBIT HILL by Robert Lawson. Copyright 1944 by Robert Lawson, copyright © renewed 1972 by John W. Boyd. Reprinted by permission of The Viking Press, Inc.

'Oh dear! Oh dear! I shall be late!' " We learn by the fourth page of *Bed-Knob and Broomstick* (54) that Miss Price rides a broom, and shortly after this she confesses: "I am studying to be a witch." In Sheila Moon's fantasies, *Knee-Deep in Thunder* (55) and *Hunt Down The Prize* (56) characters jump almost at once into the unknown. Pace in these works doesn't slow our progress in reaching the place of importance.

In contrast, *Mindy's Mysterious Miniature* (57) by Jane Louise Curry begins with a realistic and sustained scene at a farm auction, the discovery of a strange dollhouse, a visit from a mysterious man who seems to want the dollhouse, and a collection of family incidents. We are nearly a third of the way through the book before it springs into fantasy: Mindy and her companion become miniature occupants of the dollhouse. The fantastic idea is appealing, but pace has by this time dampened our enthusiasm.

THEN she combed their tails and whiskers (this is Tom Kitten).

Tom was very naughty, and he scratched.

16

17

Extract from THE TALE OF TOM KITTEN by Beatrix Potter. Copyright © Frederick Warne & Co. Ltd., London and New York.

Picture books and highly illustrated stories must have a sense of pace that takes visual experience into account. Beatrix Potter achieves pace not only in her clear, succinct style but in her manner of ending each page with an implicit invitation to stop and examine the picture. As we learn, for instance, that "Tom was very naughty, and he scratched,"[1] we see Tom, claws extended, while Mrs. Tabitha Twitchit stands back in disturbed surprise, holding the comb. Ezra Jack Keats's illustrations for Lloyd Alexander's *The King's Fountain* (59) engulf the text, providing a leisurely look at the elaborate settings and the characters' moods.

Some picture books go at break-neck pace, piling one incident on another in rhythmic fashion, an incident per page. See, for example, H. A. Rey's *Curious George* (60) and other books in this series. Other writers effectively slow the pace to sustain high moments in the narrative. In *Where the Wild Things Are* (61) Maurice Sendak presents three wordless, double-page panoramas of the "wild rumpus" of Max and the Wild Things. Similarly, Sendak's *In the Night Kitchen* (62) contains five frames showing Mickey falling out of bed and into the batter,

---

[1]Beatrix Potter, *The Tale of Tom Kitten* (58), p. 17.

ten frames for the transformation of the batter into an airplane, and seven frames of Mickey performing in the milk bottle! (See pp. 84–85.)

Pace, then, is determined psychologically. It can be slowed to emphasize and explore an incident, a character, or a setting that is important in the unified structure; or it can be rapid to speed us onward to the climax.

Distance and Tone

Point of view is rather easily discerned. It's an objective quality that can be identified and agreed upon by knowledgeable readers. To a large extent, pace can also be discerned and discussed with some agreement. But the concepts of *distance* and *tone* aren't so readily identified. They are metaphoric terms, used to point out qualities that somehow make a difference in telling a story.

Distance refers to the relationship between the author and his story. He may seem to watch the story unfold as if he were viewing a film—from some vantage point outside it. Or he may seem to be almost a part of the story, his feelings and attitudes clearly involved in each incident.

Some very popular, lasting works radiate warmth from the author's closeness to the story. For example, *The Secret Garden* begins: "When Mary Lennox was sent to Misselthwaite Manor to live with her uncle everybody said she was the most disagreeable-looking child ever seen. It was true, too." Nothing in those two sentences tells us directly about the author's distance from Mary Lennox and her story, but somehow from the start we sense that the author is there, ever sympathetic, to Mary's thrust into an alien world, burdened with her disagreeable look. The reader, together with the author, seems to stand very close to Mary. Note that the third-person point of view may help you view Mary empathically with the author's suggestion.

But other popular, lasting works may achieve their unified effect with greater distance. Despite the fact that *My Side of the Mountain* (63) by Jean Craighead George is a first-person narration by its hero Sam Gribley, we seem to be experiencing the story from some distance away: "I left New York in May. I had a penknife, a ball of cord, an ax, and $40, which I had saved from selling magazine subscriptions," says Sam,[1] and we eagerly follow his progress as he ingeniously learns to live alone in the Catskill Mountains. Yet our interest is in *how* Sam manages, not particularly in *why*. We don't know, for instance, the motives that sent him to live in the wilderness, and we probably don't care. To make him too particularized, to delve too far into what makes him tick would spoil the structure. Most of us at one time or another would like to have the experience Sam has had, and that is enough. Our enjoyment needs some distance, a distance that author Jean George achieves. When we do come close to Sam, it is only for a moment. The warm feelings shared with him are objectified through response to a specific incident—for instance, when Sam describes his falcon pet in such a way that his feelings are implied:

[1] p. 19.

From IN THE NIGHT KITCHEN by Maurice Sendak. Copyright ©1970 by Maurice Sendak. Reprinted

The food put the bird to sleep. I watched her eyelids close from the bottom up, and her tail quiver. The fuzzy body rocked, the tail spread to steady it, and the little duck hawk almost sighed as it sank into the leaves, sleeping.[1]

---

[1]p. 56.

by permission of Harper & Row, Publishers, Inc. and The Bodley Head.

Tone is related to distance in describing a story's overall effect, the mood of the telling and the mood expected of the reader. The term also refers to style—the choice and arrangement of words. Noting the tone of the above passage, we might cite the repeated *s* sounds in the final sentence, the soft, quiet sounds conveyed by *sighed* and *sleeping.*

Such terms as distance and tone help describe overall reaction and response to a work. They direct our attention to the importance of a narrative's unity of effect. They remind us that we can't usefully consider elements separately without returning at last to the work as a whole.

PUTTING IT ALL TOGETHER

We've examined some elements of narrative literature, and some techniques that give a story unified structure. These elements and their structure are meant to serve the purposes of literature implicit in the literary experience. We believe knowing about them enhances the appreciation. We've explored them here because we believe they can help you guide children in selecting and enjoying good literature. They can give you knowledge of what you are doing and why you are doing it.

Unifying Elements in Literature

Let us see how one skilled writer unifies the elements of his story, *Charlotte's Web* (64). In a way, the author of a story creates something out of nothing. He weaves a web to be held up against the light to show its miracle of structure, the unifying relationship among elements that transform experience into a meaningful pattern. Perhaps E. B. White, whose years of craftsmanship are climaxed in *Charlotte's Web,* had this metaphor in mind when he ended his book about the famous spider: "She was in a class by herself. It is not often that someone comes along who is a true friend and a good writer. Charlotte was both."[1]

The book is considered a modern classic, and rightly so, for its freshness and impact are undimmed by countless readings, television adaptation, and a full-length cartoon film. Third- and fourth-grade teachers read it aloud to their classes, children reread it later to experience in solitude the bright sunlight of the Zuckerman farm and Charlotte's lonely death at the fairground, and college students discover it all over again—a renewal of the surrender to a book that, like its heroine, seems to give more than it requires in return.

For, as Margery Fisher said about another book, *Charlotte's Web* never *pesters* its readers. It is clearly about important things—living life gently, loving life, growing up, and facing death. It is concerned with survival but, beyond that, with the quality of happiness even when survival is not assured. Its optimism pervades, gathering strength while gazing into the eyes of destruction. Even so, the book never preaches, never presses down upon a theme-statement.

Like *The Wind in the Willows* (65), it is partially idyllic, a Golden Age book celebrating the best of all possible worlds. "The early summer days on a farm

---

[1]p. 184.

are the happiest and fairest days of the year. Lilacs bloom and make the air sweet, and then fade. Apple blossoms come with the lilacs, and the bees visit around among the apple trees." So begins chapter 6, and soon we are reveling in the white-throated sparrow's song "Oh, Peabody, Peabody, Peabody!", in "things for a child to eat and drink and suck and chew", and the hatching of seven goslings: " 'Fine!' said Charlotte. 'Seven is a lucky number.' 'Luck had nothing to do with this,' said the goose. 'It was good management and hard work.' "[1]

Good management and hard work are implicit in *Charlotte's Web,* but neither is allowed to strain the reader. The two opening chapters present human conversation and the human point of view. Then, almost without warning, Wilbur the pig begins to speak: "I'm less than two months old and I'm tired of living. . . ." But the transition seems natural. We realize that, after all, it's Wilbur's life we are interested in. Later, when credibility might begin to slip, there is a visit to Dr. Dorian to inquire whether it's unusual for a child to overhear animals talking—and the good doctor assures us that there's no need to worry. That clears up the matter.

The tranquil summer days, when the web of detail about the farm seems most idyllic, are pierced by an old sheep's bad news for Wilbur:

> "Kill you. Turn you into smoked bacon and ham," continued the old sheep. "Almost all young pigs get murdered by the farmer as soon as the cold weather sets in. There's a regular conspiracy around here to kill you at Christmastime. Everybody is in the plot—Lurvy, Zuckerman, even John Arable."
> "Mr. Arable?" sobbed Wilbur. "Fern's father?"
> "Certainly. When a pig is to be butchered, everybody helps. I'm an old sheep and I see the same thing, same old business, year after year. Arable arrives with his .22, shoots the . . ."
> "Stop!" screamed Wilbur. "I don't want to die! Save me, somebody! Save me!"[2]

Pierced but not shattered. The summer is more beautiful than ever: "I want to breathe the beautiful air and lie in the beautiful sun," moans Wilbur,[3] and the idyllic tone continues, now with a sense of urgency, with a problem to be faced and the threat of darkness.

For Wilbur, the darkness never descends. He is saved by Charlotte's "miraculous" web-writing and the gullibility of the humans. He lives in the spring sunlight, innocently blissful among Charlotte's descendants. And Charlotte herself, her final egg-sac miracle completed, has died a natural death. The child Fern has grown beyond the age of hearing animals talk, her maturation forming a part of the tranquil process of nature's inevitable change.

Even Templeton the rat, the potential villain of the piece, has been manipulated to help save Wilbur. Everything has been brought into line—to serve

---

[1]p. 45.
[2]pp. 49–50.
[3]p. 51.

nature's way. Comments the *New York Times Book Review:* "The book is not about the charmed life of Wilbur, but about real life and all that implies."[1]

Perhaps, then, this is the book's theme: that the best life moves with nature, taking its cues from nature's cycles. The breadth of theme encompasses death— the threat of death and the fact of natural death—and perhaps this reality fulfills a need to examine early the inevitability of the ultimate mystery.[2]

Plot and setting support such a theme. Episodes balance the joy of living with a conspiracy to stay alive. The rural scene, filled with specific multi-sensory images, seems most suitable for examining the theme simply, avoiding the confused problems and values of a more complex civilization. The pace and tone are right.

Best of all, E. B. White is able to present characters unhampered by the small rules of consistency that sometimes prevent lesser writers from joining with their readers in meaningful make-believe. He is the lovable storyteller, never actually intruding but always there to invite our trust and direct our attention. In a way, the author is the main character of the book. As such, he can alter point of view from Fern to Wilbur to Charlotte, wherever needed to provide the best vantage point.

Given this author and reader distance, we can accept the contradictions within Wilbur. He is easily duped, he sometimes talks like a fussy child, and yet he can deliver a line of careful semantic reasoning:

> "What do you mean, *less* than nothing? . . . I don't think there is any such thing as *less* than nothing. Nothing is absolutely the limit of nothingness. It's the lowest you can go. It's the end of the line. How can something be less than nothing? If there were something that was less than nothing, then nothing would not be nothing, it would be something—even though it's just a very little bit of something. But if nothing is *nothing,* then nothing has nothing that is less than it is."[3]

He can embroider a salutation with the best of toastmasters:

> Welcome to the barn cellar. You have chosen a hallowed doorway from which to string your webs. I think it is only fair to tell you that I was devoted to your mother. I owe my life to her. She was brilliant, beautiful, and loyal to the end. I shall always treasure her memory. To you, her daughters, I pledge my friendship, forever and ever.[4]

In short, Wilbur is capable of almost anything needed to serve the situation— not a real-life pig to be validated by real-life experience but a projection of the author's own warm acceptance of all life.

---

[1]Gerald Weales, "The Design of E. B. White," *The New York Times Book Review,* (May 24, 1970): 40.
[2]See Robert Kastenbaum, "The Kingdom Where Nobody Dies," *Saturday Review,* 55 (January 1973): 33–38.
[3]p. 28.
[4]p. 182.

Perhaps the pace can be described as leisurely. Seasons are examined without a sense of having to get on with the action. There are side trips, such as the funny explosion of a rotten egg, that bear no weight of the main problem and theme.

All these elements and their structural unity form the author's web and serve to balance his purposes: to inform and persuade us of the feasibility of a gentle, peaceful existence—above all, to give us the pleasure of sharing the author's mature wisdom. It is this latter quality that Eleanor Cameron expertly describes:

> It is the burden of feeling and meaning in *Charlotte's Web* which makes it memorable, which will speak to all times and not just to our own time. It is that burden which gives all the great children's books their greatness, a burden which is the natural result of their author's ability to invest a tale for children with wisdom and truth. It is this burden of feeling and meaning which speaks not only of the goodness of the raw material and the author's handling of it, but of the essence of the writer himself: his point of view, the roots from which he has sprung, roots which in White's case go deep into the natural world and are responsible for the tone and import of his book.[1]

teaching ideas

Book-sharing activities may be used as a basis for demonstrating literary response. If the suggestions are good ones, they can aid response in the following ways: (1) they help relate the book to the visual and performing arts, (2) they encourage related reading, (3) by instigating overt response, they may help pinpoint implicit response. But such lists of suggested activities need to be matched to books. To select from them at random fails to highlight the special qualities that each book possesses.

Here then is a list of sixteen suggestions for book-sharing activities. For each activity, decide which literary elements or unifying structural techniques are likely to be highlighted. If you can, suggest titles that might be used in conjunction with each activity:

1. Make a poster about the book, using at least four different textures. Can you include something to give third-dimension? Can you include something that makes a sound?

2. Imagine you are one of the characters in the book. Tell what role you play. Use first person; in other words, *be* that person. Tell what you think of the author for putting you into the book, and what you think of the other characters.

---

[1]Eleanor Cameron, "McLuhan, Youth, and Literature: Part II," *Horn Book,* 48 (December 1972): 576–77.

3. Imagine you are an author. Do some biographical research and explain what in your life caused you to write the book. Invite questions from your audience about your writing.

4. Use a camera, even a movie camera, to do a scene from the book. Or plan a scenario, showing main scenes and some good camera angles.

5. Write a different ending for the story. Try it out on the class. Try using a suitable musical accompaniment or other sound effects.

6. Use information from the book to make a scrapbook about a subject or a collection of things written about in the book.

7. Do a monolog or dialog from the story. Or do a pantomime and challenge the class to guess the title of the book.

8. Do a miniature stage set for the story, using a cardboard box as the frame. Choose a crucial scene and pose the characters to illustrate the scene. Can you get characters and background into the right perspective? Do you need to show what the characters are saying? How can you solve these problems?

9. Make a map of an imaginary country found in a book of fantasy. Show on your map what incidents occurred where. Show the incidents through small pictures on the map (a picto-map). Connect the incidents with tracks. Tell the story of the traveler(s) in this imaginary country. How might you convert your picto-map into a game for children?

10. Take two or more highly familiar folk tales. Mix the characters. Write the story that results. Goldilocks, taking a basket of food to the Three Bears, encounters a wolf who. . . .

11. Take a familiar story and, midpoint, ask what would have happened if a character had made a different decision from the one he or she made. What if the hero in *The Matchlock Gun* (66) had not fired the gun?

12. Debate unpopular positions in familiar stories: "Rumpelstiltskin should have been given the Queen's son to raise because of his magical powers. . . . Stoats should be allowed to live in Toad Hall in *The Wind in the Willows.*"

13. Bring a book into your home: What would your home be like if it belonged to a "Borrower"? To Charlotte in *Charlotte's Web?* To Pippi Longstocking?

14. Bring a book character from past to present: How would Huckleberry Finn or Johnny Tremain react to the world of today, to problems you face today? Show the reaction through discussion, through role-playing (see pages 446–51), or through creative writing.

15. Have a book character masquerade. Each class member should dress as a book character. Each should attempt to write down whom the other class member is impersonating and the name of the book or story in which the character appears.

16. Find passages in favorite books that can appropriately be recopied into lines of blank verse. Display it on a chalkboard or chart and try varying the size and shape of the letters to fit the meaning. For instance, this passage from the beginning of A. A. Milne's *Winnie-the-Pooh* (67):

Here is Edward Bear

Coming

down

the

stairs

now

bump

bump

bump

On the back of his head

Behind Christopher Robin.[1]

17. Collect cartoons whose meaning depends on a knowledge of literary allusions. Delete each caption and have class members make up new captions after they have identified the story source behind each cartoon.

CHAPTER REFERENCES

1. Aesop. *Aesop's Fables.* Louis Untermeyer, sel. Illus. Alice and Martin Provensen. Golden Press, 1965. (P-I)
2. Aesop. *Jack Kent's Fables of Aesop.* Illus. Jack Kent. Parents, 1972. (I)
3. Farjeon, Eleanor. *The Glass Slipper.* Illus. Ernest Shepard. Viking, 1955. (E-I)
4. Evans, C. S. *Cinderella.* Illus. Arthur Rackham. Viking, 1919. New "Studio Book" Edition, 1972. (I-U)
5. Gág, Wanda. *Millions of Cats.* Coward-McCann, 1928. (E)
6. Pearce, Phillippa. *The Squirrel Wife.* Illus. Derek Collard. Crowell, 1972. (E-I)
7. Briggs, Raymond. *Father Christmas.* Coward-McCann, 1973. (E-I)
8. Barrett, Judi. *Benjamin's 365 Birthdays.* Illus. Ron Barrett. Atheneum, 1974.
9. Aiken, Joan. *The Wolves of Willoughby Chase.* Doubleday, 1962. (U)
10. White, T. H. *Mistress Masham's Repose.* Putnam, 1946. (I-U)
11. Lawson, John. *You Better Come Home with Me.* Crowell Collier, 1966. (I)
12. Rodgers, Mary. *Freaky Friday.* Harper, 1972. (U)
13. Engdahl, Sylvia Louise. *Enchantress from the Stars.* Atheneum, 1970. (U)
14. Hoban, Russell. *A Bargain for Frances.* Illus. Lilian Hoban. Harper, 1970. (E-I)
15. George, Jean Craighead. *Julie of the Wolves.* Harper, 1972. (U)
16. Speare, Elizabeth George. *The Bronze Bow.* Houghton Mifflin, 1961. (U)
17. Little, Jean. *Take Wing.* Little, Brown, 1968. (I)
18. Lobel, Anita. *A Birthday for the Princess.* Harper, 1973. (E)
19. Ransome, Arthur. *The Fool of the World and the Flying Ship.* Illus. Uri Shulevitz. Farrar, Straus, 1968.

---

[1]This idea is from Myra Weiger, explained in her article "Found Poetry," *Elementary English,* 48 (December 1971): 1002–4.

20. Taylor, Theodore. *The Cay.* Doubleday, 1969. (I-U)
21. Homer. *The Iliad and the Odyssey.* Jane Werner Watson, sel. Illus. Alice and Martin Provensen. Golden Press, 1956. (I-U)
22. d'Aulaire, Ingri and Edgar Parin. *Abraham Lincoln.* Doubleday, 1939. (E-I)
23. Hogrogian, Nonny. *One Fine Day.* Macmillan, 1971. (E)
24. Mosel, Arlene. *The Funny Little Woman.* Illus. Blair Lent. Dutton, 1972. (E-I)
25. Bishop, Elizabeth. *The Ballad of the Burglar of Babylon.* Illus. Ann Grifalconi. Farrar, Straus, 1968. (U)
26. Van Iterson, S. R. *Pulga.* Tr. Alexander and Alison Gode. William Morrow, 1971. (I-U)
27. Kingman, Lee. *The Peter Pan Bag.* Houghton Mifflin, 1970. (U)
28. Fox, Paula, *Portrait of Ivan.* Bradbury, 1969. (U)
29. Zolotow, Charlotte. *William's Doll.* Illus. William Pene DuBois. Harper, 1972. (E-I)
30. Fox, Paula, *The Slave Dancer.* Bradbury, 1973. (U)
31. Burnett, Frances Hodgson. *The Secret Garden.* Lippincott, 1911, 1962. (I-U)
32. Konigsburg, E. L. *Jennifer, Hecate, Macbeth, William McKinley, and Me, Elizabeth.* Atheneum, 1967. (I)
33. Hutchins, Pat. *Rosie's Walk.* Macmillan, 1968. (E)
34. Miles, Miska. *Annie and the Old One.* Illus. Peter Parnall. Little, Brown, 1971. (E-I)
35. Ney, John. *Ox: The Story of a Kid at the Top.* Little, Brown, 1970. (I)
36. Haugaard, Erik Christian. *Orphans of the Wind.* Illus. Milton Johnson. Houghton Mifflin, 1966. (I-U)
37. Hautzig, Esther. *The Endless Steppe.* Crowell Collier, 1968. (U)
38. Krumgold, Joseph. *. . . and now Miguel.* Crowell Collier, 1953. (I-U)
39. O'Dell, Scott. *Island of the Blue Dolphins.* Houghton Mifflin, 1960. (I-U)
40. Lawson, Robert. *Ben and Me.* Little, Brown, 1939. (E)
41. ———. *Mr. Revere and I.* Little, Brown, 1953. (I)
42. Neufeld, John. *Edgar Allan.* Phillips, 1968. (I-U)
43. Hinton. S. E. *That Was Then, This Is Now.* Viking, 1971. (U)
44. Curry, Jane Louise. *The Ice Ghosts Mystery.* Atheneum, 1972. (I-U)
45. O'Brien, Robert C. *Mrs. Frisby and the Rats of NIMH.* Atheneum, 1971. (I-U)
46. Holling, Holling Clancey. *Paddle-to-the-Sea.* Houghton Mifflin, 1941. (E-I)
47. Field, Rachel. *Hitty, Her First Hundred Years.* Macmillan, 1929. (I)
48. Cleaver, Vera and Bill. *Where the Lilies Bloom.* Lippincott, 1969. (I-U)
49. Lawson, Robert. *Rabbit Hill.* Viking, 1944. (I)
50. Adams, Richard. *Watership Down.* Macmillan, 1974. (I-U)
51. Rockwell, Anne. *Temple on a Hill.* Atheneum, 1969. (I-U)
52. Renault, Mary. *The Lion in the Gateway.* Harper, 1964. (I-U)
53. Snedeker, Caroline Dale. *The Spartan.* Doubleday, 1912. (I-U)
54. Norton, Mary. *Bed-Knob and Broomstick.* Illus. Erik Blegvad. Harcourt, 1943, 1957. (I)
55. Moon, Sheila. *Knee-Deep in Thunder.* Atheneum, 1967. (I-U)
56. ———. *Hunt Down the Prize.* Atheneum, 1971. (I-U)
57. Curry, Jane Louise. *Mindy's Mysterious Miniature.* Harcourt, 1970. (I)
58. Potter, Beatrix. *The Tale of Tom Kitten.* Frederick Warne, 1907. (E)
59. Alexander, Lloyd. *The King's Fountain.* Illus. Ezra Jack Keats. Dutton, 1971. (E)
60. Rey, H. A. *Curious George.* Houghton Mifflin, 1941. (E)
61. Sendak, Maurice. *Where the Wild Things Are.* Harper, 1963. (E)
62. ———. *In the Night Kitchen.* Harper, 1970. (E)
63. George, Jean Craighead. *My Side of the Mountain.* Dutton, 1959. (I-U)
64. White, E. B. *Charlotte's Web.* Harper, 1952. (I)
65. Grahame, Kenneth. *The Wind in the Willows.* Scribner's, 1908, 1933.
66. Edmonds, Walter D. *The Matchlock Gun.* Dodd, 1941. (I)
67. Milne, A. A. *Winnie-the-Pooh.* Harper, 1926. (P-I)

BIBLIOGRAPHY

Baker, Augusta. "What Makes a Book a Good Book?" *Instructor,* 72 November 1963, pp. 47–48. The deep values of classics forbid rewriting; a good book has values implicit in the writing. Excellent criteria suggestions.

Carr, Robin L. "Death As Presented in Children's Books." *Elementary English,* 50 May 1973, pp. 701–5. How authors present themes dealing with death in fanciful and realistic fiction; excellent annotated book list.

Drury, Roger W. "Realism Plus Fantasy Equals Magic." *Horn Book,* 48 April 1972, pp. 113–19. Fresh ingredients are needed if children's literature is to move forward; ingredients here are discussed in terms of literary components—characterization, style, and theme.

Eisenberg, William D. "Morals, Morals Everywhere: Values in Children's Literature." *Elementary School Journal,* 72 November 1971, pp. 76–80. Suggests that no amount of clever loading of the text with "intrinsic" values will satisfy young readers; characters must be true to their own nature, and settings must be those where children can imagine themselves taking part in the events.

Greaves, Delia D. "Manhattan Children Through the Pavements." *School Library Journal,* 94 December 1, 1969, pp. 24–25. Long lovely poem about the importance of reading for inner-city children's development.

Kuhn, Doris Young. "Needed: Critical Evaluation of Trade Books." *The National Elementary Principal,* 47 February 1968, pp. 44–48. Excellent questions to be asked in selecting literature.

Lewis, C. S. "On Three Ways of Writing for Children." *Horn Book,* 39 October 1963, pp. 459–69. Fascinating analysis of the components that make up great literature for children—and for adults.

Livingston, Myra Cohn. "Literature, Creativity and Imagination." *Childhood Education,* 48 April 1972, pp. 346–61. Literature as private discovery rather than objective analysis is the premise of this fine article.

Lowry, Heath W. "Evaluative Criteria To Be Used as Guides by Writers of Children's Literature." *Elementary English,* 48 December 1971, pp. 922–25. Criteria cited by children's book editors as important in judging the worth of books. Highest rank is given to "message" or theme.

Reimer, Bennett. "Teaching Aesthetic Perception." *The Educational Forum,* 30 March 1966, pp. 349–56. Insisting that every individual possesses aesthetic sensitivity, this writer discusses the interaction between artist and receiver.

Shachter, Jaqueline, and Blake, Howard E. "Promoting Composition and Literature: A School-Wide Thematic Program." *Elementary English,* 51 May 1974, pp. 625–30. Twenty explicit suggestions for a school literature program. Books for each level are cited according to such theme topics as Courage, Loneliness, Growing Up, Humor.

Squire, James R. "Form Consciousness, an Important Variable in Teaching Language, Literature, and Composition." *Elementary English,* 42 April 1965, pp. 379–88. An unusual, interesting theory of the contribution of literature.

Stott, Jon C. "The Artistry of *Blue Willow.*" *Elementary English,* 50 May 1973, pp. 761–65+. Intensive, brilliant analysis of the components that make Doris Gates's *Blue Willow* a lasting achievement to be read for years to come.

Tway, Eileen. "Children's Literature Tomorrow." *Elementary English,* 49 March 1972, pp. 387–89. Argues for literary criticism to guide book selection in the future; cites critical works to help guide the selection.

3 chapter

Matching Children and Books

A young father recently announced that his four-year-old loved to hear a chapter of *The Hobbit* (1) every night at bedtime. A teacher described the excitement of "story time" in her class during which, over a six-month period, she had read nine volumes of the Nancy Drew series to her fourth-graders. A twelve-year-old came to the librarian with a request for six *short* books: "I'm trying to fill up my reading card so I can have a new bike."

What do these incidents have in common? Each gives evidence that children don't always have the ultimate power in choosing their literary fare. The choices are often made for them: by a parent or teacher, or by circumstances extrinsic to the content of literary materials.

Of course, this isn't always true. Today, more often than in the past, the values of free reading and free choice of reading material are recognized—to say nothing of the freedom given many children to select movies, records, and television programs. But here, too, there seem to be some limitations imposed not only by adults but by other children. Studies show, for instance, that children's reading choices are most often influenced by advice from their peers. Their choices are also heavily conditioned by culturally generated interests, such as horses, sports, science, family, and the occult.

All these influences on children's reading may lead to a rich, varied life of literature. If they do, then a chapter designed to provide help in matching children and literature is unnecessary.

But it doesn't always work out that way. You can argue that literature, any literature, is a "good" experience. *The Hobbit* for a four-year-old may be just the right book—and besides that child is fortunate to have a father who reads to him. Six months of Nancy Drew seems excessive, but still, nothing forbids more varied reading later; in fact, this teacher's enthusiasm may encourage it. But sooner or later you must decide whether such incidents build to maximum satisfaction in literary experience. Even the apparent desirability of selecting literary fare according to research-established interest patterns may be in doubt.

When we speak of matching literature and children, we are seeking a firmer basis for selection. The aim of the match isn't to produce an assigned reading list or to establish a precise diagnosis of a child's needs and abilities, resulting in a computer-like prescription of "appropriate" literature. Nor is it intended as a means by which an adult makes the choices. It is the boy or the girl who must choose. Ultimately, each child makes or fails to make his or her own match with literature. But you can assist this process by helping children discover their own options for literary experience. The best base for selection is a wide knowledge of the options available.

In other chapters we'll examine some of those options. Literary purposes, components, and types are all ways of looking at the options. Similarly, we'll show in later chapters how the ways of sharing literature and of responding to literature can open more options to children. But the choices themselves require a closer look at factors in human development, in interests, and in reading abilities than would appear in an inquiry otherwise devoted to literature and its potential effects. Those factors are our concern in this chapter.

FACTORS IN HUMAN DEVELOPMENT

Return for a moment to the four-year-old listening to chapters from *The Hobbit*. Are there facts about four-year-old abilities that tell you *The Hobbit* is too difficult, too fantastic, or too something else? Is present knowledge of human development such that you can safely assign *The Hobbit* to age twelve or age twenty-two or a certain mental age or some emotional quotient? More broadly, when a booklist assigns a book to "ages four-to-seven," are there factors in human development known to the reviewer to justify that classification?

Or take the Nancy Drew example again. For literary reasons some people consider this series inferior to some other mystery-and-adventure titles. Stereotypes in characterization, plot, and style seem to abound in Nancy Drew books, as they do in many a popular TV show. If demand were the only consideration, Nancy Drew's popularity would be evidence enough that the books meet some basic need, perhaps required in human development.

What do we really know about this matter? Can this information help us expand children's options for literary experience?

Theories of Human Development

SOME EARLY THEORIES. Freudian psychology cites a biological base to denote stages of development that affect the individual's entire being. Children seek security in a safe, known world, while at the same time meeting inevitable conflicts in attempting to grow into the roles of their parents. They struggle to control this security-conflict dilemma while progressing through biologically-ordained stages. The struggle is complicated by the "unconscious" self which demands that needs be satisfied, sometimes without consideration of outside reality.

The influence of Freudian theory on literature and literary interpretation is vast. Freud and his followers explain folklore, especially Greek myth and epic, in terms of the security-conflict struggle. Modern authors, too, have been strongly influenced by this theory.

The acting out of conflict, especially child-parent conflict, appears widely in literature for children. Sometimes the use of battle as a theme in modern works is defended on Freudian grounds. The child in Tomi Ungerer's picture book *No Kiss For Mother* (2) gets a nod of approval from some children because he so bitterly rejects any show of affection from his mother. In recent works such as John Donovan's *Remove Protective Coating a Little at a Time* (3) there may be an implicit Freudian theme: that parents are sometimes mixed-up people and children may have to transfer their affection to substitute parent-figures.

Another psychologist of the nineteenth century, G. Stanley Hall, attempted to explain child development as "cultural recapitulation," meaning that each child must re-experience the evolution of humanity. This led some specialists to recommend that a full range of classical literature be presented very early in a child's life to assist his living through the history of civilization. The myths, the folk tales, the epics of various cultures were considered a part of the process of catching up with modern times. Hall's theory and others of its type, including Jung's "collective unconscious," partly support this position.

During the first half of the twentieth century, Arnold Gesell and his co-workers attempted scientific observation of children at specified ages, collecting data to show commonalities, or *norms,* of development in motor activity, language, self-activity, and sociability.[1] When these norms were published and distributed, they were widely interpreted as standards for development. Many a parent and specialist used them as a sort of yardstick for determining whether a child was "living up to the standards," although Gesell himself specifically warned against such use.[2] The idea of matching literature to observed common behavior patterns should, however, be a part of the matching process.

In children's literature this concept appeared in the theories of Lucy Sprague Mitchell and in the books for two- to seven-year-olds of "the City and Country School" devised by Mitchell and her followers. These are stories or sketches attempting to enrich the child's here-and-now experience. Such a theory of child development did not tolerate the folk tale in early years. Here is what Mitchell had to say about the matter:

> Does not Cinderella interject a social and economic situation which is both confusing and vicious? Does not Red Riding-Hood in its real ending plunge the child into

[1]Arnold Gesell, *The Mental Growth of the Pre-School Child* (Macmillan, 1925) and *Infancy and Human Growth* (Macmillan, 1928); Arnold Gesell and others, *The First Five Years* (Harper, 1940); Arnold Gesell and Frances L. Ilg, *The Child From Five to Ten* (Harper, 1946) and *Infant and Child in the Culture of Today* (Harper, 1954), and other volumes.
[2]*Infant and Child in the Culture of Today,* p. 70.

an inappropriate relationship of death and brutality or in its "happy ending" violate all the laws that can be violated in regard to animal life? Does not "Jack and the Beanstalk" delay a child's rationalizing of the world and leave him longer than is desirable without the beginnings of scientific standards?[1]

It's probably fortunate that no single theory of child development has dominated the field of children's literature for very long. Mitchell's influence and similar influences have given us a great wealth of gentle here-and-now literature, including the works of Margaret Wise Brown, Virginia Lee Burton, and Marjorie Flack. These books meet a need for simple reality far from the shores of conflict outlined by Freud and folklore. Fortunately, Mitchell's attack on folklore didn't lead to its abandonment for young children.

In 1953 Robert J. Havighurst published *Human Development and Education,* which presented a kind of compendium of cradle-to-grave, culturally-demanded developmental tasks. These were defined as "those things that constitute healthy and satisfactory growth in our society."[2] As such, they defined developmental levels to be attained by each individual—his or her physical skills, attitudes toward self and others and institutions, cooperation, sex role, conscience and morality, and personal independence—at various stages of growth. Included were ways of assessing a person's success or failure in achieving each task and suggestions for furthering development.

The basic premise of this theory has an almost ominous tone today. It seems to view society as a dominating and constricting force in the life of the individual and warns that "failure [in meeting the developmental tasks] leads to unhappiness in the individual, disapproval by society, and difficulty with later tasks." That view of a child's development now appears narrow; in the words of one critic, childhood appeared to be "a defect to be overcome." Thus the younger child, as perceived by Havighurst, should, at the age of about five years, "show a marked decrease in fantasy." Then: "The special mental activity of middle childhood is the exploration and cataloguing of facts."[3]

The tasks are filled with stereotypes. A boy of middle years was termed successful if he spent most of his free time with a "loose-knit play-group," while a girl should have a "reputation of being ladylike, clean, friendly." Failure for either the boy or the girl was specified as "usually spends spare time alone."[4]

How much these developmental tasks influenced the production or the selection of literature is difficult to judge. At one point Havighurst suggested what he considered to be appropriate literary works for helping older children succeed in the developmental tasks. Viewed today, the list consists mostly of nearly forgotten works with an obvious didactic bent.

Not surprisingly, other theorists of the decade objected to the movement to view human development exclusively in terms of cultural conformity. Studies of creativity seemed to show that being different, or balancing conforming and nonconforming behavior through autonomy, is a desirable factor in human

[1]Lucy Sprague Mitchell, "Introduction," *Here and Now Story Book* (Dutton, 1921), p. 21.
[2]Robert J. Havighurst, *Human Development and Education* (McKay, 1953), p.2.
[3]pp. 2, 79, 80.
[4]p. 291.

development. Although we find themes of conformity in children's literature in every period, we also find themes pointing to the dangers of mass conformity. For instance, nine years after Havighurst's theory was developed, a Newbery Medal book, Madeleine L'Engle's *A Wrinkle in Time* (4), presented a hellish planet with a perfectly conforming community:

> As the skipping rope hit the pavement, so did the ball. As the rope curved over the head of the jumping child, the child with the ball caught the ball. Down came the ropes. Down came the balls. Over and over again. Up. Down. All in rhythm. All identical. Like the houses. Like the paths. Like the flowers.
>
> Then the doors of all the houses opened simultaneously, and out came women like a row of paper dolls. The print of their dresses was different, but they all gave the appearance of being the same. Each woman stood on the steps to her house. Each clapped. Each child with the ball caught the ball. Each child with the skipping rope folded the rope. Each child turned and walked into the house. The doors clicked shut behind them.[1]

MASLOW'S THEORY OF BASIC HUMAN NEEDS.   A quite different view of society was that of the late Abraham Maslow, whose theory of basic needs is drawn from a knowledge of psychology, anthropology, and the humanities. "Culture," he wrote, "can be basic need-gratifying rather than need-inhibiting."[2] As one aspect of culture, literature and the other humanities can help the individual fulfill his needs in ways that energize the culture.

Maslow identified the following basic needs:

(1) Physiological needs. These are the most basic because they mean physical survival. "For the man who is extremely and dangerously hungry, no other interests exist but food." But Maslow believed that once physiological needs are fulfilled, they do not remain powerful influences on behavior.

(2) Safety needs. For a child, this may mean a predictable world up to a point: a world that permits excitement and exploration but within the necessary level of safety.

(3) Belongingness and love needs. These needs involve both giving and receiving love. The love relationship need not be sexually based, as Freud would have it, but it must include mutual trust.

(4) Esteem needs. These include self-respect as well as the respect of others.

(5) Self-actualization needs. Maslow explored these at great length in *Toward a Psychology of Being*.[3] It is the need to become "everything that one is capable of becoming." By learning the process whereby this need is fulfilled, the individual is not unduly hampered by fear or by the temporary absence of other need fulfillment. Energy originates from and is directed toward the process of self-actualization.

(6) The need to know and understand. Interestingly, Maslow postulates a human curiosity drive quite independent of other needs.

---

[1]Madeleine L'Engle, *A Wrinkle in Time* (Farrar, Straus, 1962), pp. 103–4.
[2]Abraham H. Maslow, *Motivation and Personality*, 2nd ed. (Harper, 1954, 1970), p. 102.
[3]Published by Van Nostrand, 1962.

(7) Aesthetic needs. A commentator on Maslow's work makes this observation: "Behavioral science has generally ignored the possibility that people have an instinctual, or instinctoid, need for beauty. Maslow found that, at least in some individuals, the need for beauty was very deep, and ugliness was actually sickening to them."[1]

Maslow believed that these needs, operating concurrently, motivate human behavior. Further, they form something of a hierarchy of lower and higher needs, requiring that individuals satisfy needs for physical well-being, safety, and love before they can attain respect and self-actualization. Although Maslow did not perceive higher needs in infants, he nevertheless theorized that child development entails attempts to fulfill the entire range of needs.

Maslow's theory has many implications for the place of literature in child development. If the needs do form a hierarchy, then certain fundamental needs must be satisfied before any literary experience is likely to take place. A hungry child, a frightened child, or an unloved child is not likely to become engaged in a challenging bout with literature. Literary sessions aimed at developing aesthetic appreciation or satisfying the curiosity drive are destined for failure unless you have earlier presented literature in the light of fulfilling some needs lower on the hierarchy, such as meeting the needs for belonging and achieving esteem. Perhaps this is the appeal of Nancy Drew, even to the teacher we cited at the opening of this chapter. The series may fulfill some safety needs, since Nancy seems always successful in solving mysteries and defeating the "bad guys." Or the story may help satisfy the need for esteem through experiencing vicariously the esteem Nancy wins from her friends and father. But at this point on the hierarchy the power of the Nancy Drew books begins to wane, since higher needs are ignored.

Maslow's theory may help you become more sensitive to needs that growing boys and girls have and, therefore, may help you match them to literature. Above all, Maslow suggests a challenge to people who work with children's literature: Can you somehow help children impart richness to their lives through literature that satisfies the higher needs—the need for self-actualization, the need to know and understand, and the need for aesthetic satisfaction?

special activities

1. Is it possible to identify Maslow's levels in relation to specific books? Try it. Select three books discussed in the picture book section of chapter four (pp. 127–48) and attempt to list the hierarchy needs they treat according to emphasis. Then compare your list with that of a classmate to see if your judgments agree.

---

[1]Frank G. Goble, *The Third Force*, (Grossman, 1970), p. 42.

2. Is it feasible to construct a reading hierarchy, a list of books that appeal to sequential need levels on the Maslow hierarchy? Try it.

3. Consider for a moment the "safety" level on the hierarchy. Would you infer that a safety-level book must present a safe, sane world? How about a book whose humorous tone conveys the slapstick idea that shocking happenings might be funny or even safe? Consider, for example, Steven Kellogg's zany edition of *There Was an Old Woman* (5). Could this book appeal to safety needs? Discuss. List other favorites that might fit Maslow's levels. Where, for example, would you place John Donovan's *Remove Protective Coating a Little at a Time*, with its talk of masturbation and circumcision? Where would you place *Fair Day, and Another Step Begun* (6) by Katie Letcher Lyle, with its pregnant heroine pursuing her one-time lover into a hippie commune? How viable is the Maslow hierarchy in book selection? in book presentation? in determining the type of literary experience a book might promote?

KOHLBERG'S STUDIES OF MORAL DEVELOPMENT.   Lawrence Kohlberg of Harvard University studied the development of seventy-five boys, beginning when they were ten years old or older and ending fifteen years later. At three-year intervals the boys were asked to respond to problem-type stories or situations in which a leading character made a moral decision. One situation, for instance, described the plight of a husband who stole food in order to save his sick wife from dying. The boys were asked: "Should the husband have done that? Why?"

From the results of this study Kohlberg devised a hierarchy of six stages of moral development. The boys in his study displayed moral reasoning that advanced from one stage to another up the scale. The movement, says Kohlberg, "is always upward and occurs in an invariant sequence." When Kohlberg extended his study to other cultures (Great Britain, Canada, Taiwan, Mexico, and Turkey), he found that the stages, their sequence, and generally the rate of development were common to all these cultures, revealing, in his own words, "culturally universal elements to morality at every stage. . . ."[1]

Kohlberg's table of "Definitions of Moral Stages" is reproduced on pages 101–2 for use in the discussion that follows. (An interesting and highly readable discussion of his findings appears in *Psychology Today*.[2]

Further studies of Kohlberg and his co-workers indicated that when children are confronted with the explanation of a stage of moral reasoning above their current level, they tend to move upward on the scale. From this, we might conjecture that literary experience involving moral reasoning could produce similar effects. A character's stated reasoning for an act involving morality may serve as a model or clarification of a moral stage. This alone would appear to

[1]Lawrence Kohlberg, "From Is to Ought," in *Cognitive Development and Epistemology*, ed. Theodore Mischel (Academic Press, 1971), p. 180.
[2]Lawrence Kohlberg, "The Child as a Moral Philosopher," *Psychology Today* 2 (September 1968): 25-30.

TABLE I

DEFINITION OF MORAL STAGES

I. Preconventional level

At this level the child is responsive to cultural rules and labels of good and bad, right or wrong, but interprets these labels in terms of either the physical or the hedonistic consequences of action (punishment, reward, exchange of favors), or in terms of the physical power of those who enunciate the rules and labels. The level is divided into the following two stages:

Stage 1: *The punishment and obedience orientation.* The physical consequences of action determine its goodness or badness regardless of the human meaning or value of these consequences. Avoidance of punishment and unquestioning deference to power are valued in their own right, not in terms of respect for an underlying moral order supported by punishment and authority (the latter being stage 4).

Stage 2: *The instrumental relativist orientation.* Right action consists of that which instrumentally satisfies one's own needs and occasionally the needs of others. Human relations are viewed in terms like those of the market place. Elements of fairness, of reciprocity, and of equal sharing are present, but they are always interpreted in a physical pragmatic way. Reciprocity is a matter of "you scratch my back and I'll scratch yours," not of loyalty, gratitude, or justice.

II. Conventional level

At this level, maintaining the expectations of the individual's family, group, or nation is perceived as valuable in its own right, regardless of immediate and obvious consequences. The attitude is not only one of *conformity* to personal expectations and social order, but of loyalty to it, of actively *maintaining,* supporting, and justifying the order, and of identifying with the persons or group involved in it. At this level, there are the following two stages:

Stage 3: *The interpersonal concordance or "good boy—nice girl" orientation.* Good behavior is that which pleases or helps others and is approved by them. There is much conformity to stereotypical images of what is majority or "natural" behavior. Behavior is frequently judged by intention—"he means well" becomes important for the first time. One earns approval by being "nice."

Stage 4: *The "law and order" orientation.* There is orientation toward authority, fixed rules, and the maintenance of the social order. Right behavior consists of doing one's duty, showing respect for authority, and maintaining the given social order for it's own sake.

III. Postconventional, autonomous, or principled level

At this level, there is a clear effort to define moral values and principles which have validity and application apart from the authority of the groups or persons holding these principles, and apart from the individual's own identification with these groups. This level again has two stages:

TABLE I (*continued*)

Stage 5: *The social-contract legalistic orientation,* generally with utilitarian overtones. Right action tends to be defined in terms of general individual rights, and standards which have been critically examined and agreed upon by the whole society. There is a clear awareness of the relativism of personal values and opinions and a corresponding emphasis upon procedural rules for reaching consensus. Aside from what is constitutionally and democratically agreed upon, the right is a matter of personal "values" and "opinion." The result is an emphasis upon the "legal point of view," but with an emphasis upon the possibility of changing law in terms of rational considerations of social utility (rather than freezing it in terms of stage 4 "law and order"). Outside the legal realm, free agreement and contract is the binding element of obligation. This is the "official" morality of the American government and constitution.

Stage 6: *The universal ethical principle orientation.* Right is defined by the decision of conscience in accord with self-chosen *ethical principles* appealing to logical comprehensiveness, universality, and consistency. These principles are abstract and ethical (the Golden Rule, the categorical imperative); they are not concrete moral rules like the Ten Commandments. At heart, these are universal principles of *justice,* of the *reciprocity* and *equality* of human *rights,* and of respect for the dignity of human beings as *individual persons.*

justify unabashed didacticism: the presentation of high-stage models who clearly state their moral purpose. But blatant didacticism is a poor handmaiden to literary quality. Such preachments, too accurately and readily discerned as crass persuaders, may cause the story to lose its credibility. Ultimately, the theme and the author's good will in presenting it are likely to be discredited.

This doesn't mean, however, that good literature shuns moral concerns, or even that these moral concerns might not be relevantly examined through Kohlberg's hierarchy. The external consequences or the internal effect of a character's decisions can be observed through the workings of the story. Furthermore, the author's theme—the author's own moral judgment as he structures his work—may be discussed with children.

Return for a moment to "Inviting Jason," the modern story in chapter 1. Stanley's attitude and behavior toward Jason seem to be motivated by the attempt to satisfy his own needs. There is little loyalty, gratitude, or justice in Stanley's reasoning about his behavior. He seems drawn to conformity and attempts to please others of his own choosing. Perhaps he'd be placed at Stage 2 or Stage 3 on the Kohlberg Scale.

This is not to say that "Inviting Jason" represents to the reader a doctrine of rather low moral reasoning. The author makes sure that Stanley is not presented as a model suitable for emulation. Instead, there is an implicit case against his moral reasoning, revealed through a theme that seems to say that Stanley's reasoning isn't working out very well.

Literature, then, need not be blatantly didactic to be relevant to moral reasoning.

special activities

1. Choose one traditional and one modern story that involve moral reasoning on the part of a character. Discuss the reasoning and place it on Kohlberg's scale.

2. Read George and Fannie Shaftel's *Role Playing for Social Values* (Prentice-Hall, 1967), or see our discussion of role-playing, pp. 446–51. Select one problem story to be used as a basis for sociodrama. Either conduct the session or describe how you think a group of children might play out the story. Analyze the enactment in the light of Kohlberg's scale.

Matching Human Development Factors and Literature

It seems that the more you know about child development, the better you can guide literature selection and experience. Our brief survey of theories has yielded at least one important point: that the theories vary greatly in their emphases and conclusions. To be guided by any single theory to the exclusion of others is unwarranted and unwise.

You can feel free to present a great wealth of literature, the whole array, as it were: stories including conflict-security dilemmas; traditional literature reaching clear back to the dawning of civilization; narratives relating here-and-now realism; works satisfying basic needs and aspirations; and stories dramatizing problems of moral reasoning.

Most of these theories deal with generalizations. Their findings apply to norms for groups of children. The discerning adult, however, in observing individual children and listening to their talk, can make tentative inferences about human development factors. Tools for organizing information about individuals can be used if care is exercised. See, for example, the informal assessment instruments in *Studying the Child in the School* by Ira J. Gordon[1] and in *Child Development: The Emerging Self* by Don C. Dinkmeyer.[2] These may supplement your more general observations. Almy warns, however, that we must guard against bias:

---

[1]Ira J. Gordon, *Studying the Child in the School* (Wiley, 1966). Chapter Three, pp. 52–88, includes a self-report, "How I See Myself" (pp. 56 ff.), a self-concept inventory profile (pp. 75–80), and similar items.

[2]Don C. Dinkmeyer, *Child Development: The Emerging Self* (Prentice-Hall, 1965). Pp. 410–13 provide an interest record and a sentence completion instrument.

What is infuriating Terrible Turtle?

Why is he fussing so?

Why is he throwing a temper tantrum?

Where does he want to go?

From The Temper Tantrum Book by Edna Mitchell Preston, Illustrated by Rainey Bennett. Text Copyright ©1969 by Edna Mitchell Preston; Illustrations Copyright ©1969 by Rainey Bennett. Reprinted by permission of The Viking Press, Inc. and Curtis Brown, Ltd.

No matter how much experience in observation teachers have, they are bound to feel more sympathetic toward some children than others, to find certain kinds of behavior more disturbing or more satisfying, to be more involved with some youngsters and less with others. Such biases grow out of their own personal experiences and have to do in part with the kinds of children they once were or would have liked to be.[1]

Any conclusions about children's needs and any decisions to match a specific type or content of literature with needs must be tentative. And, as we've stated before, the child himself must have the last say about the choice.

---

[1]Millie Almy, Ruth Cunningham, and Associates, *Ways of Studying Children: A Manual for Teachers* (Bureau of Publications, Teachers College, Columbia University, 1959), p. 47. Chapter Two, "Observation: the Basic Way to Study Children" (pp. 25–61), contains useful information for the purposes discussed above.

Every day Leo's father watched him for signs of blooming.

Reprinted from LEO THE LATE BLOOMER by Robert Kraus, Illustrated by Jose Aruego. Copyright © 1971 by Robert Kraus and Jose Aruego, with permission of Thomas Y. Crowell, Inc.

BIBLIOTHERAPY.   Sometimes literature is selected by or for an individual because it may help him or her define or solve a specific problem. For instance, a child struggling with fear or with apparently unreasonable expectations of adults may read *Shadow of a Bull* by Maia Wojciechowska (7) and discover a kindred spirit in the struggle of Manolo, who is terrified of becoming a bullfighter. Or children may read *Pippi Longstocking* by Astrid Lindgren (8) and find that their lively misbehavior is not so bad after all when it's seen to parallel Pippi's wild antics. Or, reading Ezra Jack Keats's *A Letter to Amy* (9), the child discovers a parallel between his own social misbehavior and that of Peter, who knocks Amy onto a wet sidewalk.

When a personal problem is matched in this way with a problem in literature, the result is sometimes termed bibliotherapy. Hoagland defines this term rather broadly as "the attempt of an individual to promote his mental and emotional health by using reading materials to fulfill needs, relieve pressures, or help his development as a person."[1]

Conceivably, any of the human needs cited in our preceding discussion might be dealt with through literature. Bibliotherapy simply means that literary selection is related to those needs and that discussion and activity using the literature

[1]Joan Hoagland, "Bibliotherapy: Aiding Children in Personality Development," *Elementary English* 49 (March 1972): 390.

I'd give her my last piece of chalk.
I'd give him my last Chicklet.
Michael is my
Rosie is my
Friend.

emphasizes the parallel between the selection and the reader's own problems.

According to Shrodes, bibliotherapy produces its effect through identification, catharsis, and insight. The reader first identifies with a character or situation in literature. Living through the situation vicariously, the reader experiences catharsis—an emotional release. The overall result is insight into the problem, with the hope that such insight will transfer to the individual's own confrontation and solution of the problem as it appears in his or her life.[1]

Does it work? Some evidence, usually in the form of case studies, does seem to support the idea; but there are dangers. Serious problems, such as mental illness, physical abuse, or drug misuse, require help beyond the experience of the layman and beyond the identification and insight afforded by a literary work. Also, some proponents of bibliotherapy seem to be so enthusiastic about its possibilities that they would discard literary quality: they would seize any work that seems to pinpoint a problem. The result would make literature a stepchild to clinical case study. Finally, there is a question of the individual's dignity and self-respect. For example, it may be less than kind—and perhaps harmful—to match a neglected, poverty-stricken child with Marilyn Sachs's *The Bears' House* (10), even though this book's spunky little heroine shares these

booklist

Sources of Bibliotherapy Books

Edmonds, Edith. "Matching Books to a Child's Need." *Instructor* 82 (October 1972): 160–64.

Edwards, Beverly Sigler. "The Therapeutic Value of Reading." *Elementary English* (February 1972): 213-18. Specifies the role of bibliotherapy in self-concept development.

Moody, Mildred T., and Limper, Hilda K., eds. *Bibliotherapy: Methods and Materials.* Association of Hospital and Institution Libraries, American Literary Association, 1971. The books matched to problem areas here are carefully annotated, with specified reading levels and interest levels.

Smith, Henry P., and Dechant, Emerald V. *Psychology in Teaching Reading.* Prentice-Hall, 1961, pp. 316-20. Two hundred books for children, assembled under "Responsibility and Cooperation," "Emotional Conflicts," "Physical Handicaps," "Intergroup Relations," and "Achievement through Hardship."

Zaccaria, Joseph S., and Moses, Harold A. *Facilitating Human Development through Reading.* Stipes Pub. Co., 1968. Part II of this book (pp. 104-227) arranges titles according to "General Problems of Life and Adjustment," including "Poverty and cultural deprivation," "Self acceptance," "Blindness and impaired vision," "Speech and hearing difficulties."

---

[1]Caroline Shrodes, "Bibliotherapy," *Reading Teacher* 9 (October 1955): 24–29.

problems. Sometimes it's better to treat a child's personal problems as you would his secret treasure chest: open it only on invitation, and gently.

With this precaution in mind, the series of questions devised by Lundsteen for use in bibliotherapy are helpful. They emphasize the problem-solving aspects of the process and may aid in avoiding what might be interpreted as a too-direct attack:

What Are Types of Questions Useful in Bibliotherapy?[1]

What happened to the character?
What else was there?
How do you think he feels? (Facts and conditions)
What would *you* call it?
What do you mean? (Clarification)
But why?
Why did he do that? (Cause-effect)
What else might have caused it? (Multiple causes)
Would you do it?
Has anything like this happened to anyone you know or to you?
What if you put yourself in Mama's place? (Empathy and transfer)

booklist

Selected Books for Use in Bibliotherapy: Overcoming Handicaps[2]

Butler, Beverly. *Light a Single Candle.* Dodd, Mead, 1962. (U) A fictional account (based on the author's own experiences as a blind person) of a girl who has glaucoma at age 14.

Davidson, Margaret. *Helen Keller.* Hastings House, 1969. (I)

Herman, William. *Hearts Courageous.* Dutton, 1949. (U) Men and women who have overcome such handicaps as crippling, deafness, blindness, stuttering.

Orgel, Doris. *Next Door to Xanadu.* Harper, 1969. (E-I) The overweight heroine has no close friends.

Robinson, Veronica. *David in Silence.* Lippincott, 1966. (I-U) Thoroughly researched story of boy born deaf who moves to new town, faces derision, finds friends.

Southall, Ivan. *Let the Balloon Go.* St. Martin's Press, 1968. (I-U) An act of assertion by a twelve-year-old spastic boy that lets him decide for himself what his limitations are instead of having others decide for him.

Wrightson, Patricia. *A Racecourse for Andy.* Harcourt, 1968. (I-U) The importance of a supportive environment provided by peer and adult groups for a boy who has become increasingly detached from reality.

---

[1]Sara W. Lundsteen, "A Thinking Improvement Program through Literature," *Elementary English* **49** (April 1972): 510.
[2]This and other special booklists in this section were compiled by Toni Marshall, Palo Alto, California.

What could be done to change the situation?
How would you have handled it?
What difference would that make? (Alternatives)
What do you think the story is trying to show?
How would you summarize?
How could you use this idea some place else? (Principles, values, attitudes and their transfer)

INTERESTS

Is an individual driven or self-propelled? Older theories about need-fulfillment may make you wonder. Even the highest needs may connote an organism trying to keep its balance. And the concept of literature as bibliotherapy may begin to sound like repairing a dam at floodtime.

But humans do reach out. They are seekers, explorers, risk-takers. They have

booklist

Selected Books for Use in Bibliotherapy: Family Situations

Barnwell, Robinson. *Shadow on the Water.* McKay, 1967. (I-U) This story is about marital conflict that does not end in divorce since there is a last-minute resolution.

Blume, Judy. *It's Not the End of the World.* Bradbury, 1972. (I-U) The trials and tribulations of a twelve-year-old suffering the agonies of her parents' divorce.

Garfield, James B. *They Like You Better.* Viking, 1959. (I) A love of animals and the aid of an understanding adult help a neglected boy to a useful, satisfying life.

Goff, Beth. *Where Is Daddy?* Beacon Press, 1969. (E) A compassionate book for the troubled preschool child.

Hobson, Laura Z. *I'm Going to Have a Baby!* John Day, 1967. (E) Intended to help a child adjust to the realization that a new younger sibling is on the way.

Keats, Ezra Jack. *Peter's Chair.* Harper, 1967. (E) Learning to accept a new baby in the family.

Little, Jean. *Spring Begins in March.* Little, Brown, 1966. (I-U) Deals with problems of adjusting to sharing a room with a handicapped sister, school failure, and adjusting to a grandparent.

Marshall, James. *Willis.* Houghton Mifflin, 1974. (E) Problems and difficulties in connection with money.

Reyher, Becky. *My Mother Is the Most Beautiful Woman in the World.* Illus. Ruth Gannett. Lothrop, 1945. (E) Discovering that one's parents don't have to look like those in the commercials.

Sharmat, Majorie Weinman. *I Want Mama.* Illus. Emily Arnold McCully. Harper, 1974. (E) Accepting the situation when parent is sick in the hospital.

not only passive needs but active interests as well.[1] Interest may be an important factor in achieving the match between a child and his literature.

Some people believe interest is the only important factor: match a child's present interests with the right books and your job is done. Other theorists agree that interest is an important initial factor, but they point to the function of literature in broadening interests, even in creating new ones. They urge guidance in developing tastes that change and deepen interests.

At any rate, this tendency to seek and explore should be a part of your inquiry into the match. If you know enough about books and other materials and are aware of the main interests of children, you may be able to help them make a good start.

booklist

Selected Books for Use in Bibliotherapy: Understanding Emotions

Burnett, Frances Hodgson. *The Secret Garden.* Lippincott, 1962. (I-U) This book is not too far removed from the present day to speak to contemporary children who experience prolonged loneliness.

Fujikawa, Gyo. *Gyo Fujikawa's A to Z Picture Book.* Grosset, 1974. (E) Alphabet book showing that strong, sometimes negative feelings are natural and universal.

Lee, Virginia. *The Magic Moth.* Seabury Press, 1972. (I-U) A family of seven learns to accept the death of one of the children from a heart condition.

Lopshire, Robert. *I Am Better Than You.* Harper, 1968. (E) Boasting doesn't aid friendship.

Rey, Margaret Elizabeth, (Waldstein). *Curious George Goes to the Hospital.* Houghton Mifflin, 1966. (E) A read-aloud book written in collaboration with the Children's Center of Boston.

Viorst, Judith. *Rosie and Michael.* Atheneum, 1974. (E) Tolerating differences for friendship's sake.

———— *The Tenth Good Thing about Barney.* Illus. Eric Blegvad. Atheneum, 1971. (E) Acceptance of death.

Welber, Robert. *The Train.* Pantheon, 1972. (E) Many everyday things, such as trains, noises, or being alone, are sources of fear for children. This book shows that such fears can be overcome with a little understanding.

Zolotow, Charlotte. *A Tiger Called Thomas.* Illus. Kurt Werth. Lothrop, Lee, 1963. (E) The need to belong is the focus of this book.

---

[1]See J. W. Getzels, "The Problem of Interests: A Reconsideration," in *Reading: Seventy-Five Years of Progress,* ed. H. Alan Robinson (University of Chicago Press, 1966), pp. 97–106.

Interest Studies and Their Findings

In 1967 Ethel M. King found that more than 300 studies of children's interests had been published.[1] The intervening years have brought a great many more. It would be helpful if from these we could give you a clear, definitive guide—if we could say, for instance, that the seven-year-old now sitting before you is most likely to be captivated by literature about snakes.

But we can't. For many reasons, the studies themselves don't have that kind of precise agreement. The most obvious reason is that they reflect different populations at different times. Less obvious is that a great many studies differ in their results because they differ in the way they achieved those results. The most important reason is that interest studies report information about groups, whereas you must necessarily approach the subject of interests by meeting them head-on in the searching and seeking of an individual.

Let's not forget that last point. If sixth-grader Jeff is interested in butterflies, then that's that—all the interest studies of the century won't change that fact. If studies show, as many do, that girls like mystery, home, and school stories,

booklist

Selected Books for Use in Bibliotherapy: Social Concerns

Boles, Carol Ann. *Kevin Cloud, Chippewa Boy.* Reilly & Lee, 1972. (E) Documentary style text of an Indian boy's life in a big city and the numerous problems he encounters.

Caudill, Rebecca. *Did You Carry the Flag Today, Charley?* Holt, 1966. (E) A realistic and sympathetic account of an obstreperous five-year-old's problems in adjusting to classroom routine.

Clifton, Lucille. *Good, Says Jerome.* Illus. Stephanie Dougles. Dutton, 1973. (E) The story of a black boy making friends after the family moves.

Ets, Marie Hall. *Bad Boy, Good Boy.* T. Y. Crowell, 1967. (E) Emphasis on the language problem of a small boy who speaks only Spanish.

Harris, Janet, and Hobson, Julius U. *Black Pride,* McGraw-Hill, 1969. (U) The pride of tradition and the beginnings of the black power movement are detailed.

Konigsburg, E. L. *The Dragon in the Ghetto Caper.* Atheneum, 1974. (I) Facing crime realistically.

Newlon, Clark. *Famous Mexican-Americans.* Dodd, Mead, 1972. (I-U) A message of pride in being Chicano.

---

[1] Ethel M. King, "Critical Appraisal of Research on Children's Reading Interests, Preferences, and Habits," *Canadian Education and Research Digest* 7 (December 1967): 321–26.

you still shouldn't be surprised to find that the girls in your present group are interested in drug abuse, flying saucers, and football. Interest studies are of little interest to children.

Interest studies, however, do more than list winners in the contest. Some of them try out intriguing ways of finding interest. Some ask questions which often provide embarrassing answers: for instance, whether children really prefer the story topics found in their basal readers and whether adults are good at predicting which book topics children will choose. These are the matters we'll emphasize in our discussion here.

A series of studies done in the 1920s by Miriam Blanton Huber and Arthur I. Gates[1] generally used paired literary examples: a group of children who chose selection *A* over selection *B* were assumed to have interests that coincided with selection *A*. As has since been pointed out, such a technique indicates a preference, not necessarily an interest. If you ask a child whether she chooses to read about the Amazon or agriculture, she'll indicate whether she prefers one or the other, but she may not be *interested* in either. The Huber and Gates studies, however, seemed to show some consistent preferences such as fiction over nonfiction, and the fanciful and humorous over the familiar family-experience story.

Carrying the study further, Gates identified six fiction elements that children seemed to prefer: surprise, liveliness, animals, conversation, humor, and plot.[2] There's little doubt that even today such studies have influenced the content of reading instruction materials.

A problem in interest studies is knowing the range of books from which children have made their choices. If you ask children which books are their favorites, you can't know about the variety from which they have chosen. If you do a preference study, as Gates and Huber did, you limit children to the selections you present to them. In 1941 Robert L. Thorndike tried to surmount this problem in a unique way: he created eighty-eight fictitious annotated titles and asked children to indicate whether or not they would like to read each of these hypothetical books. For example:

Yes   No   ?   *Bowser the Hound*
                Bowser went hunting rabbits with his master. What happened when
                they met Jimmy Skunk instead.[3]

Thorndike's study indicated that the greatest difference in interests during that period were those attributed to sex differences. It is important to emphasize that attitudes toward sex differences in the 1970s are clearly different from those of the 1940s.

---

[1]See Arthur I. Gates, *Interest and Ability in Reading* (Macmillan, 1930), Chapters II and III, pp. 42–93.
[2]p. 89.
[3]Robert L. Thorndike, *A Comparative Study of Children's Reading Interests* (Bureau of Publications, Teachers College, Columbia University, 1941), p. 41.

A landmark in interest studies is George W. Norvell's *What Boys and Girls Like to Read*. A large number of third- to sixth-graders were asked to specify whether a selection, indicated by title only, was "very interesting," "fairly interesting," or "uninteresting." The results, reported in extensive tables in Norvell's book, yield fascinating information on specific titles. For instance, Edward Lear's "The Owl and the Pussy Cat" received an 87.4 percent approval from third-graders (83.6 percent from boys, 91.2 percent from girls) and 87.1 percent from the combined fourth- through-sixth-grade sample. Robert Frost's "The Pasture" received 67.2 percent from third-graders, while the fourth- through-sixth-graders gave it 37.8 percent.[1]

Norvell's general conclusions are really more important than the ratings achieved by specific selections. He concluded, for example, that content rather than "form or high literary quality" is the dominant influence in choices.[2] While the fairy tale and fable dominated interests in traditional folklore at grades three through five, older children preferred myths and legends. The influence of age on interests was greatest in early years; sex, in this study, was a less important factor than in most previous studies; the preference of highly intelligent children for works of superior literary quality was also less pronounced than in earlier research.

Norvell emphasized in his findings that children's choices didn't always coincide with those selections that adult experts considered most suitable and most popular. He concluded that experts "are usually wrong in their designation of poets children enjoy." Stories such as *Alice's Adventures in Wonderland* placed low in the ratings despite their high critical success with adults. There is one reservation we must have about Norvell's conclusions in these matters: his study failed to include many current prose selections of that time, a factor that might have changed his findings.[3]

Norvell's study does, however, suggest a way of gaining information about children's choices in literature. You could ask, for example, whether percentages indicating interest in certain selections might change as a result of your work. If, as some studies suggest, Newbery Medal books are generally rated somewhat low, would their popularity increase as a result of careful presentation?

Over the years, Paul A. Witty and his associates have made extensive investigations of children's interests in reading, play, vocations, and television. Witty's findings are summarized in chapter three of *The Teaching of Reading*. There's a wealth of information in these studies, many of them based on extensive, carefully devised questionnaires. Witty, more than any other investigator, has attempted to define the influence of non-reading media on the reading of literature. His earlier studies seemed to show that television, for example, had a stimulating influence on reading. This effect apparently didn't hold, for in 1966

---

[1]George W. Norvell, *What Boys and Girls Like to Read* (Silver Burdett, 1958).
[2]p. 27.
[3]p. 123.

he wrote: "Certainly, a disproportionate amount of time seems to be given to the mass media as compared with that accorded worthwhile reading."[1]

More recent studies of children's interests and preferences have focused on more specific groups and questions. One such study compared the content of stories in twelve series of first-grade basal readers with the content of books selected from the library by first-grade pupils.[2] The results showed wide discrepancies. Boys preferred information books, although the basal readers contained little such material. Both sexes chose a predominance of material about animals, make-believe, and inanimate objects; but their basal readers contained a predominance of child-character stories. Children's choices in library materials emphasized urban and rural settings as well as make-believe lands; their basal readers, however, were dominated by suburban settings. Children chose folk tales, nature selections, and real-life stories with negative affect; their readers presented imaginative play, pets, and real-life stories with positive affect. This study was published in 1970. You might wish to compare its findings with basal reader selections published since that time.

The interests of children living in urban areas have been studied with different results. Ford and Koplyay asked inner-city primary children to indicate picture and sentence preferences in relation to their reading interests. Highest preference was given to black heritage (79 percent), second was children in ghetto (65 percent), then history and science (59 percent), with fantasy (35 percent) and animals (22 percent) at the foot of the list. Rather surprisingly, children in suburban areas gave approximately the same preferences.[3]

On the other hand, Robert Emans's study of inner-city children showed a preference for "family-friends-pets" themes over "city" themes.[4] (This was in response to hearing paired stories dealing with the contrasting themes.) Using brief passages from books and slides of the illustrations, Jerry L. Johns sought intermediate-grade preferences and found that inner-city children at this level preferred "pleasant" settings, characters with a positive self-concept, and positive rather than negative group interaction.[5]

We have cited these discrepant results for a purpose. Interest studies reveal information about groups that is often useful, but the findings can be generalized only with caution. They necessarily reflect the past literary experience of children and probably the type and depth of literary study being provided in schools at the time of the study. A study of the books children like now may

---

[1] Paul A. Witty, Alma Moore Freeland, and Edith H. Grotberg, *The Teaching of Reading* (Heath, 1966), p. 52.

[2] John L. Wiberg and Marion Trost, "A Comparison Between the Content of First Grade Primers and the Free Choice Library Selections Made by First Grade Students," *Elementary English* 48 (October 1970): 792–98.

[3] Robin C. Ford and J. Koplyay, *Reading Teacher* 22 (December 1968): 233–37. See also Sam Sebesta, Dianne L. Monson, and Frank Love, "Research Critiques," ed. Patrick Groff, *Elementary English* 48 (May 1970): 651–54.

[4] Robert Emans, "What Do Children in the Inner-City Like to Read?" *Elementary School Journal* 69 (December 1968): 118–22.

[5] Jerry L. Johns, "What Do Inner-City Children Prefer to Read?" *Reading Teacher* 26 (February 1973): 462–67.

or may not tell us what books they will like next. The interest inventories, questionnaires, interviews, and even the more recent attempts to gain information through taped free discussion are limited by time and place; it seems unwise to generalize beyond those contexts.

What the studies do show is that temporary, specific interests can be assessed through a variety of techniques. These interests are likely to play a part in children's initial reading preferences. Knowing these interests can help you guide children in their selection and may enable you to help them extend and deepen their interests.

In addition, there have been some observable trends in interests over the years that may become apparent as you compare interest studies from various decades. There appears, for example, to be a trend toward more non-fiction reading. Interest areas such as adventure, action, mystery, and humor seem consistently to rank high. Sex differences appear strong in early studies and tend to persist in later studies; but recent examination of sex roles in and out of children's literature makes this finding tentative indeed. We may no longer conclude that girls will read what appeals to boys but not the opposite. A broadening definition of sex roles will surely result in less differentiation of interests by sex. There are some indications, too, that television and other mass media are supplying an escapist type of experience with the result that reading interests may assume a different quality.[1]

Studying a Child's Interests

As we've said, matching a child's interests to his reading is a matter of individual study. It can be highly informal: perhaps the most productive information is derived simply from talking with children and observing them. If you watch children choosing books, you may find that they don't really know how. They look here and there—at a pretty cover, at a first paragraph, or at whatever is handy. Your knowledge of books, of the child, and of the importance of the match can help here. You need not be either a dictator or a passive observer.

You may borrow some of the techniques of the interest researchers, perhaps reading or telling sample passages from an assortment of books and giving children an opportunity to use this knowledge of options in making their selections. Some adults working with younger children have devised their own preference tests including sets of pictures and interesting book covers for comparison purposes. Their aim is to discover general preferences leading to selection.

Open-ended inquiry into interests has some advantages. Suppose, for example, that you provide a child with a wide assortment of picture magazines and ask him to make a collage showing his "favorite things." Suppose that you initiate a "let's make up a story" session and let the child take the story wherever he or she wishes. Or suppose you just sit back and let the child tell about his

---

[1]See Bernice E. Cullinan, "Teaching Literature to Children," *Elementary English* (November 1972): 1028–37.

favorite programs, activities, and books. You can make a few notes about what you learn through these open-ended activities, and then see if your unforced guidance in matching such information to the child's reading options gives encouraging results.

Various interest inventories are available for use with individuals. They should be used orally, not handed to the child like an income tax form. Paul A. Witty's "Inventory for Primary Grades" and "Inventory for Intermediate and Upper Grades" (in collaboration with Robert A. Sizemore, Ann Coomer, and Paul Kinsella) are included in the aforementioned *The Teaching of Reading*. These include general questions ("When you have an hour or two to spend as you please, what do you like best to do?") as well as specific questions about television, radio, and movie preferences and items eliciting attitudes toward books. Use these questions selectively, choosing those that seem most suitable for each child. They can be valuable in pursuing the important goal of matching children's interests with their selections for literary experience.

special activities

1. Locate an interest inventory such as the one mentioned above and administer it orally to two children of approximately the same age. Summarize your findings and then locate two good choices in literature for each child. Share the results. How helpful did you find the inventory?

2. List other means of discovering interests. Try beginning with open, general questions: "What would you like to read about? What sort of books interest you?" Then consider nonverbal methods of assessing interests: a drawing, a collage, a mobile. What others can you think of?

3. Discuss the limitations of interests in assessing literature "needs." What other information might be helpful in matching children and literature?

READING LEVELS AND READABILITY

Of all areas dealing with the match between children and their reading, the matter of reading level and readability is the most controversial. Some critics say that children's literature is in a kind of squeeze: the hypothetical "average" American child has earlier maturity in development and interests than in former times, while his reading ability seems to have decreased. The first half of this allegation seems warranted: one critic has said that if the teen-age novel *Seventeen* were written today, it would have to be called *Twelve!* But studies of children's reading ability do not support the charge of lower teaching standards. Children today do as well as, or slightly better than, comparable groups of two or three generations ago.

There is also an opinion that children can read anything they're interested in, no matter how difficult it may be. That's a romantic notion. Observe the first-grade girl fascinated by astronomy who bears home a book on the topic, drawn from the adult section of the library. She may enjoy the illustrations and may tease out part of the text, but enthusiasm and interest aren't sufficient to surmount the reading barrier for very long.

Some of this controversy has roots in the over-attention paid to reading levels, as if third-grade or fourth-grade level were an absolute, precise designation. Similarly, there has been overconfidence in readability formulas. There's nothing in the whole of readability research which makes possible matching precisely a child with 3.6 reading level to a book with 3.6 readability. As with other factors, these are estimates only, but they can, if used wisely, help in your pursuit of the match between children and books.

Reading Levels

A child's reading level pertains to his reading ability on the basis of comparison with others. If you sample the reading performance and find it resembles that of an average fourth-grader, then you have some basis for saying that he reads on a fourth-grade level. At best, this is only an estimate. The child's performance may have been atypical on the day of your sample, or something may be wrong with the estimate of fourth-grade standards. But the estimate is more accurate than a wild guess. If you are using it to help find suitable reading material for a particular child, it's likely to lead to a better match than mere guesswork would provide.

Children's reading levels are often estimated through standardized reading tests which may help determine the methods or materials of instruction that will bring better results. But standardized group reading tests do not precisely measure an individual child's independent reading. Moreover, if he's shy at test-taking or disinclined to perform well on the fragments of content that usually make up such tests, the margin of error is increased. The test may underestimate his reading level. If he's a sophisticated test-taker, his level may be overestimated.

You may want to estimate a child's reading level by asking her or him to read, both silently and orally, from a whole selection. If you want to know, for example, whether he can manage a social studies or science textbook, ask him to read from it; you can estimate his ability from that. If you want to know if she or he can independently manage a free-choice story selection, ask him to read a sample from it. Better yet, help him discover this information for himself.

Such a practice requires some standards for estimating. If, say, a child stumbles on seventeen words on a page or finds himself miring down in the syntax or the sentence rhythm several times in a chapter, does this mean the book is too hard? Or will the difficulty "make him grow?" If he appears to read silently with ease but can only give you a partial report of what he's read, does this mean he's unlikely to get the message of the book? How do you decide?

One aid to making such decisions is the informal reading inventory, which really isn't difficult to adapt to your purpose.[1]

In its most basic form, this inventory yields the following information:

- If a child can read about 99 percent of the running words and can answer 90 percent of your questions about what he's read, the material is designated at his *Independent Level.* He should be able to read it without difficulty, without help. This assumes that his oral reading is smooth and that silent reading is fairly rapid.
- If a child can read about 95 percent of the running words and can answer 75 percent of your questions about what he's read, the material is designated at his *Instructional Level.* He can manage it with help in figuring out new words or managing difficult sentences. This assumes that he reads it orally with a conversational tone or silently with a fairly rapid rate (as fast as or faster than oral reading).
- If a child can read less than 90 percent of the words—if he misses more than one out of ten words—and can't answer at least half of your questions about what he's read, the material is designated at his *Frustration Level.* This is a warning sign. It means that he isn't likely to get much out of it nor is he likely to find the reading task a pleasant one, no matter how high his ambition or how inviting the cover. Above all, it means that his experience will be that of learning frustration, not reading, not enjoyment of the reading act. Accompanying signs at the Frustration Level may be a strained voice and lack of expression in oral reading and, eventually, inability to go on in oral or silent reading.

These criterion percentages are arbitrary. They are informal estimates only and must be employed in that light.

Questions for the informal reading inventory will, of course, vary in difficulty. You must judge what it is that you hope children will understand from their reading. Generally, one of your questions should be a *vocabulary* item; one should be a *factual* item, a literal question dealing with some fact the child must discover from the reading; one should be an *inference* item showing whether the child can use logic in dealing with the material; one may be a highly *interpretive* item to see whether he or she can give a reaction to what he's read. Judging the answers to your questions is somewhat subjective too, but you'll have to proceed on good faith that your judgment is better than a wild guess.

There are problems, of course, in deciding whether a word is "missed" or not. Some reading errors aren't errors at all but *miscues.* If a miscue is the wrong word

---

[1]A simple and very useful book is *Informal Reading Inventories* by Marjorie Seddon Johnson and Roy A. Kress (Newark, Delaware: International Reading Association, 1965). A more technical explanation of the informal reading inventory is that of Emmett A. Betts in *Foundations of Reading Instruction* (American Book Company, 1957).

but it makes the right sense, you should give the child the benefit of the doubt. After all, it's the meaning of the passage that is important.

Of course, it isn't practical or desirable to use the informal reading inventory with every child on every prospective reading selection. There isn't time—and you don't want to hound them. Some reading authorities, including proponents of individualized reading such as Jeanette Veatch, recommend that you instruct children in giving their own informal reading inventory. Help them learn to estimate a hundred words somewhere in the book, to read them and count the number of difficult words. Tell them to put a finger down each time they come to a "hard" word they can't manage in the selected passage. Five fingers mean that a child may have some difficulty with the book and will require help. Fewer than five indicates the book is one he can manage, providing he can summarize the passage.

This is, as we've said, only an estimate. But it presents some security, some means of ascertaining whether or not a book's readability is suitable for the reading level of a child.

Readability

Publishers often indicate the readability of a book, giving a range of reading levels that it should accommodate. Usually these are estimates, sometimes mere guesses. A few publishers use readability formulas which again are estimates. In fact, one critic alleges that the formulas generally used to estimate readability are only about 50 percent accurate.[1] For various reasons, they measure only a few of the factors that underlie a selection's difficulty, usually sentence length and vocabulary.

This should be enough to warn against depending too heavily on readability estimates. A better way to decide whether a book is readable for an individual child is to use the informal reading inventory or similar device to see if she or he can manage it. But, lacking this, you can avoid random guessing by the quick application of a readability formula. The simplest of these is Edward Fry's "Graph for Estimating Readability," reproduced on p. 120.[2] To use the graph, select a passage of a hundred words from the book under consideration. Count the number of sentences in the passage, to the nearest tenth and the number of syllables in the hundred words. Find the number of sentences on the vertical scale of the graph and the number of syllables on the horizontal scale of the graph. Follow the vertical and horizontal lines from the two scales until they meet. If the area indicated is in the "5" range, that means the passage is some-where around the fifth-grade level. Do at least three passages from the book

---

[1]George R. Klare, *The Measurement of Readability* (Iowa State University Press, 1963), p. 5.
[2]Edward Fry, "A Readability Formula That Saves Time," *Journal of Reading* 11 (April 1968): 513–16+. Graph is on p. 577.

Graph for Estimating Readability

by Edward Fry, Rutgers University Reading Center

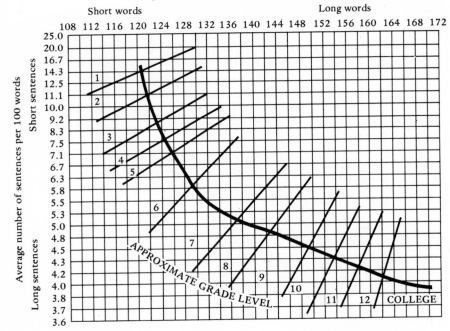

Average number of syllables per 100 words

Short words   Long words

DIRECTIONS: Randomly select 3 one hundred word passages from a book or an article. Plot average number of syllables and average number of words per sentence on graph to determine area of readability level. Choose more passages per book if great variability is observed.

From Edward Fry, "A Reading Formula That Saves Time," published in *Journal of Reading* (April 1968): 513–16+.

in this way, so that you have three or more estimates. When you average them, you have an estimate of the book's readability.

Now, for one aspect of the match, you can estimate a child's reading level and then estimate the readability of a prospective selection. Bring the two together, or bring them into approximate alignment. It isn't a scientifically precise decision, but it will help.

Recently, a new device for determining whether reading material is suitable for a child's reading ability has been offered. Its main proponent, John R. Bormuth, offers some evidence that it has greater accuracy than readability formulas. This is the *cloze* procedure, requiring construction of a "cloze test" from a selected passage in a book you're considering. Here are Bormuth's instructions for making a cloze test:

> (a) passages are selected from the material whose difficulty is being evaluated, (b) every fifth word in the passages is deleted and replaced by underlined blanks of a standard length, (c) the tests are duplicated and given, without time limits, to students who have *not* read the passages from which the tests were made, (d) the students are instructed to write in each blank the word they think was deleted, (e) responses are scored correct when they exactly match (disregarding minor misspellings) the words deleted.[1]

Scores of approximately 57 percent or better on the cloze test indicate that the passage is on the reader's independent level, while scores between 40 percent and 56 percent indicate the instructional level.[2] Note that to succeed in this test, the reader must be able to infer the context of the material, hence the test is said to be a measure of comprehension as well as word recognition.

The point of all this discussion about needs and interests and readability is the necessity of using every possible cue to help children find the proper panorama of literature for themselves. As we've emphasized, these are only aids to help with the match between children and books. They are estimates based on the study of children, on the study of the culture in which children are maturing, and on the study of the literature itself. The guidance, based on these estimates, may not be as definitive as you might wish. But it is better than simply hoping that the encounters between children and books will just naturally bring increasing satisfaction.

special activities

1. Conduct an informal reading inventory with a child. Discuss your findings and how you might use them to guide further selection of books.

2. Analyze a passage from a book using Fry's "Graph for Estimating Readability." Then check the book's readability rating in one of the source references mentioned in chapter 1. Compare how closely they agree, and comment on your findings.

3. Here is a random assortment of books to challenge you to use the various tools of the match. For instance, which of these books has an aesthetic dimension which you might use in conjunction with Maslow's hierarchy? Which book could you use in relation to a Kohlberg level? Which titles might

---

[1] John R. Bormuth, "The Cloze Readability Procedure," *Elementary English* 45: 429–36. See also John R. Bormuth, *Readability in 1968* (National Council of Teachers of English, 1968), in which the aforementioned article is reprinted, pp. 40–47.
[2] Earl F. Rankin and Joseph Culhune, "Comparable Cloze and Multiple-Choice Comprehension Scores," *Journal of Reading* 13 (Dec. 1969): 193-98.

lend themselves well to bibliotherapy and with what problems? Which might present problems in readability in relation to the age level at which they appeal?

Cain, Arthur. *Young People and Crime.* John Day, 1968. (U) A realistic view of crime and why people turn to crime and drugs. List of suggested readings is included.

Cleaver, Vera. *I Would Rather Be a Turnip.* Lippincott, 1971. (I-U) The eight-year-old illegitimate child of her older sister is difficult for a young girl to accept, but she learns tolerance through experience.

Dobrin, Arnold. *The New Life—La Vida Nueva.* Dodd, Mead, 1971. (I-U) An historical overview of the Chicanos with coverage of a variety of current problems.

Friis, Baastad Babbis. *Don't Take Teddy.* Scribner's, 1967. (I-U) A story about a retarded fifteen-year-old as told by his younger brother.

Grollman, Earl A. *Talking About Death.* Beacon, 1970. (All ages) A dialog between parent and child on the subject of death.

Harris, Janet. *A Single Standard.* McGraw-Hill, 1971. (U) A good basic handbook of the feminist movement; it gives some background, but the major concern is what's happening now.

Kerr, M. E. *Dinky Hocker Shoots Smack.* Harper, 1972. (U) Not about dope but overweight. Parents too busy running encounter groups for drug addicts to recognize their child's need for attention which leads to overeating.

Konigsburg, E. L. *(George).* Atheneum, 1970. (I-U) The title represents the hero's alter ego. Psychiatric help is effective in working out personal and family problems.

Little, Jean. *Take Wing.* Little, Brown, 1968. (I-U) Sibling retardation and the problem of shyness are dealt with in this story.

McBain, W. N., and Johnson, R. C. *The Science of Ourselves.* Harper, 1962. (I-U) Concerned chiefly with experimental psychology at a level that can be understood and taken part in by junior high students.

Orgel, Doris. *The Mulberry Music.* Harper, 1971. (I) Deals with a child's love for her grandmother and the acceptance of the death of a loved one.

Platt, Kin. *The Boy Who Could Make Himself Disappear.* Chilton, 1968. (U) Rejection, hostility, and a speech problem face a boy who is the butt of his newly divorced mother's cruel behavior. His difficult adjustment to a new city and a new school contribute to his deep unhappiness.

Ross, Pat, comp. *Young and Female.* Random House, 1972. (U) Personal accounts of American women who have been successful in politics, photojournalism, sports, writing, and other fields.

Sommerfelt, Aimee. *My Name Is Pablo.* Criterion Books, 1966. (I-U) Set in Mexico City, about the problems that beset a pair of shoeshine boys (one Mexican, the other Norwegian): poverty, social pressures, drugs, reform school.

Snyder, Zilpha Keatley. *The Witches of Worm.* Atheneum, 1972. (I-U) Rejection, hostility, and deceitfulness are dealt with in this story of a teen-age girl who has problems with her divorced mother.

CHAPTER REFERENCES

1. Tolkien, J. R. R. *The Hobbit.* Houghton Mifflin, 1938. (I-U)
2. Ungerer, Tomi. *No Kiss for Mother.* Harper, 1973. (E)
3. Donovan, John. *Remove Protective Coating a Little at a Time.* Harper, 1973. (U)
4. L'Engle, Madeleine. *A Wrinkle in Time.* Farrar, Straus, 1962. (U)
5. Kellogg, Steven. *There Was an Old Woman.* Parents, 1974. All ages.
6. Lyle, Katie Letcher. *Fair Day, and Another Step Begun.* Lippincott, 1974. (U)
7. Wojciechowska, Maia. *Shadow of a Bull.* Harper, 1964. (U)
8. Lindgren, Astrid. *Pippi Longstocking.* Viking, 1950. (I)
9. Keats, Ezra Jack. *A Letter to Amy.* Harper, 1968. (E)
10. Sachs, Marilyn. *The Bears' House.* Doubleday, 1971. (I)

BIBLIOGRAPHY

Bernstein, Edna. "Reaching Children Who Withdraw." *Instructor,* 82 April 1973, pp. 98–100. Techniques and materials to accompany literature so that the withdrawn child may find an outlet through reading.

Blatt, Gloria T. "The Mexican-American in Children's Literature." *Elementary English,* 45 April 1968, pp. 446–51. Content analysis of 32 books concerning Mexican-Americans, with encouraging conclusions.

Cianciolo, Patricia Jean. "A Recommended Reading Diet for Children and Youth of Different Cultures." *Elementary English,* 48 November 1971, pp. 779–87. Cites evidence of a commonality in reading interests across cultures; presents sample titles and reactions.

Gans, Roma. "19 All-Time Favorites Children's Stories." *Grade Teacher,* 82 March 1965, pp. 75–78. A list of titles for all levels, guaranteed to enhance literary experience.

Goodman, Kenneth. "Up-Tight Ain't Right." *Library Journal,* 97 October 15, 1972, pp. 3424–25. Language in early literature should reflect speech familiar to the child, argues this writer.

Hamilton, Aileen. "Books for the Retarded Child." *School Library Journal,* 93 February 15, 1968, pp. 48–49. Bibliography includes recordings and filmstrips.

Jacobson, Judith Grover. " 'Teach a Book' for Spring Reading." *Instructor,* 82 February 1973, pp. 176–77. How a primary teacher instigated shared reading in her classroom.

Johns, Jerry L. "What Do Innercity Children Prefer to Read?" *Reading Teacher,* 26 February 1973, pp. 462–67. Although the findings may be limited, the method of discovering interests is of value.

L'Engle, Madeleine. "The Danger of Wearing Glass Slippers." *Elementary English,* 41 February 1964, pp. 105–11. Stories that produce an upsetting reaction are needed in the process of growing up.

Mitchell, Edna. "The Learning of Sex Roles through Toys and Books: A Woman's View." *Young Children,* 28 April 1973, pp. 226–31. Warns against stereotypes but also notes that books presenting a "liberated" view of women must have a story worth reading.

Oakley, Madeleine Cohen. "Juvenile Fiction about the Orthopedically Handicapped." *Top of the News,* 30 November 1973, pp. 57–68. Perceptive analysis of such books as *The*

Door in the Wall, The Little Lame Prince, and *Johnny Tremain* in terms of what they may contribute to the "forgotten children."

Sebesta, Sam Leaton. "Developmental, Interest, and Reading Levels." pp. 16–26 in *Evaluating Books for Children and Young People,* ed. Helen Huss, International Reading Association, 1968. Defines aspects of the match, with plea for subjective analysis as well.

Strang, Ruth. "Motivation: As Adolescents See It." *Education,* 86 April 1966, pp. 473–78. The motives of teen-agers with implications for selection of literature.

Vanecek, Erich. "Measuring Readability—A Fundamental Part of Reading Research." *Bookbird,* 11 1973, pp. 16–22. Germany's use of cloze procedure to determine readability of its recent books for children. Example of application.

Worley, Stinson E. "Developmental Task Situations in Stories." *Reading Teacher,* 21 November 1967, pp. 145–48. This study of whether a basal reader series presents materials conjunctive with developmental tasks could be applied to a modern analysis of literary works.

part II

Surveying Literature

4 chapter

Picture Books and Folk Literature

In chapter 2 we looked at elements of literature and how these are unified to form a literary work. Our attention was focused mainly on modern stories, although we might have extended our search for elements to other literature as well. We emphasized what goes into a good work of literature and what pleasure comes out of it for the reader.

Now we'll examine types of literature for children. A literary type, as we'll define it, is a category of works with similar elements and often with a similar way of synthesizing these elements. It's a broad and somewhat arbitrary term.

We use the term *types* instead of the more scholarly *form, genre,* or *motif* because we want to be more flexible than these terms allow. Form emphasizes technical details of literary design, considerations of the critic that can be only of partial concern to us here—and of even less concern to children. Genre combines the concept of form with that of thematic idea or subject, a suitable arrangement until you start to apply it to the wide range of modern works. Motif denotes a recurrent element in a literary selection. For instance, what stories do you know about a hero or heroine who goes off on a dark journey and encounters monsters? The journey, the mysterious environment, the meeting with a monster—these could all be called motifs.

But these technical terms are not flexible enough for our purposes. Children, for example, may want "funny" books or books about ghosts or witches, or "books that really make you feel like you're part of the family." A topic category may range across a wide variety of categories of form: a collection such as Helen Hoke's *Witches Witches Witches* (1) contains folk tales, modern fantasy, Oscar Wilde's allegory, "The Fisherman and His Soul," a small segment from *Macbeth,* and three poems. A single work such as Maurice Sendak's *Higglety Pigglety Pop!* (2) is fantasy, allegory, myth, and picture book. Ivan Southall's *Josh* (3) follows the motif of *Captains Courageous* only so far and no further, and then turns on it, deliberately making a shambles of it. It seems that if we did succeed in getting the categories right, next year's authors would overturn them.

We will instead discuss the following types of literature in this and succeeding chapters: Picture Books and Folk Literature (chapter 4), Fanciful Fiction (chapter 5), Realistic Fiction (chapter 6), Poetry (chapter 7), and Nonfiction (chapter 8).

The literary elements in these six types may vary. You'll find plot, setting, character, and theme in most picture books, nearly all stories, in biography and some other subtypes of nonfiction, and in many poems. But there are some differences in elements between types and within types. In the picture book these differences are visual rather than verbal. In poetry the patterning of rhythm and sound, more pronounced than in prose, is likely to be the unique synthesizer of elements. While biography and history do contain characters, themes, settings, and sometimes plot in the story sense, there are generally some essential differences between these nonfiction types and the stories that spring from imagination.

Why examine literature by types? Given a topic or other entry to children's interests, the types present a variety from which to choose. Each has a special contribution to make, each is necessary to provide a balanced life of literature. To know about the types, to know fine examples within each type or across the variety of them is to help fulfill the wish of Eleanor Cameron when she writes, "I should like to travel up and down the country going to elementary schools and saying to all the teachers: Find out about the good children's books. . . . We must not *let* stories written with truth and wisdom die out."[1]

PICTURE BOOKS

What do you know about picture books? Can you remember them from your childhood? Can you recall specific pictures that impressed you then? Watch children in a bookstore or library as they look through picture books. What's their rate of picture-looking? What kinds of pictures cause them to stop?

Beni Montresor, who was awarded a Caldecott Medal for *May I Bring a Friend?* (4) says, "For me a picture book is a book whose content is expressed through its images."[2] The good picture book is more than a portfolio of pictures. It is designed to give a unified effect, its visual style reflecting the tone, mood, and theme of its verbal content. In other words, its merit stands or falls not just on the quality of its pictures but on the suitability of the artist's conception of the whole project. Ezra Jack Keats's paintings for Lloyd Alexander's *The King's Fountain* (5) have been criticized for having a style that may be too elaborate for the simple parable of a poor man's simple persuasion of a king.[3] On the other hand, Blair Lent's equally elaborate painting and line drawing art for *The Angry Moon*

---

[1]Eleanor Cameron, "McLuhan, Youth, and Literature," *Horn Book* 48 (October 1972): 433-40.
[2]Beni Montresor, "Caldecott Award Acceptance," *Horn Book* (August 1965): 371.
[3]See Paul Hein's review of *The King's Fountain*, "Summer Booklist" in *Horn Book* 48 (August 1971): 373.

From THE ADVENTURES OF PADDY PORK, Copyright ©1970 by John S. Goodall. Reproduced by permission of Harcourt Brace Jovanovich, Inc. and Macmillan London and Basingstoke.

(6) has been praised for providing an imagination stirring, authentic Tlingit Indian quality for this story of a boy who tricks the moon. Marcia Brown's woodcuts for *Once a Mouse* (7) seem to recapture the rough essence of a first telling of the fable. All three artists—Keats, Lent, and Brown—are among the most distinguished contributors to the picture-book type. You might begin your inquiry by examining the wide variety of style and content of their work. Note the versatility with which they meet the challenge of each new project.

Literary Elements in the Picture Book

The literary elements discussed earlier are generally present in picture books. Most, though not all, contain plot. If there is a plot, pictures may tell the entire sequence of events by showing each event or a sampling of events, allowing the reader to infer what happened between pictures, with or without the help of written text. Pictures tell the whole story in John Goodall's wordless books (see list pp. 136–37). In *Rosie's Walk* (8) by Pat Hutchins, the pictures provide the crucial plot element. In John Schoenherr's superbly drawn, realistic pictures for *Nobody's Cat* (9) by Miska Miles, the plot is elaborated, while the main events are rather completely told through the text.

Setting is an element naturally suited to pictures. In the books cited above the artist's prime concern has been in revealing setting visually, beyond the scope of words. But here, as in writing, it is the psychological aspect of setting that counts. Only in rare cases, such as the work of Sandra Weiner or Tana Hoban, do photographs succeed in conveying the psychological dimension of a picture book. The ever popular *The Story about Ping* (10) by Marjorie Flack, illustrated in painted sketches by Kurt Wiese, shows just enough detail about China to give viewers a realistic idea of setting, yet avoids the clutter of too much detail. The four-volume *R. Caldecott's Picture Books* (11), on the other hand, takes for granted that a child knows the basic settings and therefore introduces

He planted himself in the center of the road, raised one
hand to stop the traffic, and then beckoned with the other,
the way policemen do, for Mrs. Mallard to cross over.

From MAKE WAY FOR DUCKLINGS by Robert McCloskey. Copyright 1941, Copyright © renewed 1969 by Robert McCloskey. Reprinted by permission of The Viking Press, Inc.

many imaginative elements into the setting—spoons with legs, plates with smiling faces—all keeping with the nursery rhymes that form the text. Robert McCloskey's *Make Way for Ducklings* (12) with its sensible ducks requires a believable, matter-of-fact setting. The pictures are therefore as realistic as one could wish. But the wildly improbable "whopper" story of *Milton the Early Riser* (13) by Robert Kraus uses poster-like pictures to convey a tall-tale jungle setting that never was and never could be.

Character in picture books emerges through a great variety of styles. Sometimes the artists use caricature, especially in tales requiring flat characters who represent one simple trait. A master of this form of character presentation is Dr. Seuss (Theodor Seuss Geisel) whose *And to Think That I Saw It on Mulberry Street* (14) and *The 500 Hats of Bartholomew Cubbins* (15), among many others, haven't been surpassed in the art of adapting the cartoon-caricature style to the picture book.[1]

Sometimes the picture treatment reveals more about a book's characters than the text. For an example of this effect, see Evaline Ness's *Sam, Bangs & Moonshine* (16). Sam (Samantha) is presented in the text as something of a liar, and one of her lies is a dangerous one; but the line drawings with watercolor wash give

---

[1]See John P. Bailey, Jr., "Three Decades of Dr. Seuss," *Elementary English* 42 (January 1965): 7–11.

From SAM, BANGS & MOONSHINE written and illustrated by Evaline Ness. Copyright ©1966 by Evaline Ness. Reproduced by permission of Holt, Rinehart and Winston, Inc.

a deeper view of Samantha—that of a splendidly dreaming child preoccupied with the textures, sights, and smells all about her. The first picture of her friend Thomas tells all that you need to know about him: that he is intent, gentle, and

However, the last day of the eleventh month he takes her to a room she'd never set eyes on before. There was nothing in it but a spinning wheel and a stool. And says he, "Now, my dear, here you'll be shut in tomorrow with some victuals and some flax, and if you haven't spun five skeins by the night, your head'll go off." And away he went about his business.

Well, she was that frightened, she'd always been such a gatless girl, that she didn't so much as know how to spin, and what was she to do tomorrow with no one to come nigh her to help her? She sat down on the stool and

LAW, HOW SHE DID CRY!

Illustrations reprinted by permission of Charles Scribner's Sons from Tom Tit Tot illustrated by Evaline Ness. Illustrations copyright ©1965 Evaline Ness. Text reprinted by permission of G. P. Putnam's Sons from English Folk and Fairy Tales selected and edited by Joseph Jacobs.

gullible! (No wonder imitations of Thomas are found in illustrations by lesser picture book artists.) Now contrast the character pictures of *Sam, Bangs & Moonshine* with the same artist's *Tom Tit Tot* (17), a retelling of an English folk tale which exemplifies caricature appropriately at work.

Just as pictures can present a crucial element of plot omitted from the text, they can also present a crucial element of character. Jan Wahl's text for *Push Kitty* (18), illustrated by Garth Williams, presents a straightforward story, told in first person, about a child who dresses her pet cat in doll clothes. It's rather dull until you study the pictures. There you find the cat's point of view so thoroughly presented, so spread from whisker to whisker with self-contained feline agitation, that the impact of the book changes sharply. The whimsical, jocular nature of young Melkon, who defeats three awkward bandits in *Rooster Brother* (19), an Armenian folk tale retold and illustrated by Nonny Hogrogian, is apparent in every line and shade of the distinguished art work.

Books such as these, and picture books listed elsewhere in our discussion, use pictures not as mere illustrative accompaniment to text but rather to convey the tone, mood, and theme of the work. This is really the essence of the picture book. If you study the Caldecott Medal books and the world-wide survey of

Even the milkman's horse likes Mama's child—

From PUSH KITTY by Jan Wahl, illustrated by Garth Williams. Illustrations copyright ©1968 by Garth Williams. Reprinted by permission of Harper & Row Publishers, Inc.

fine picture books presented in *Picture-Book World* by Bettina Hurlimann,[1] you will discover the important contribution this type of literature has made.

Picture Books for Various Ages

The earliest picture books, those designated for pre-kindergarteners, should logically be the simplest. Many specialists, basing their judgment on observa-

[1]Bettina Hurlimann, *Picture-Book World* (Oxford, 1968).

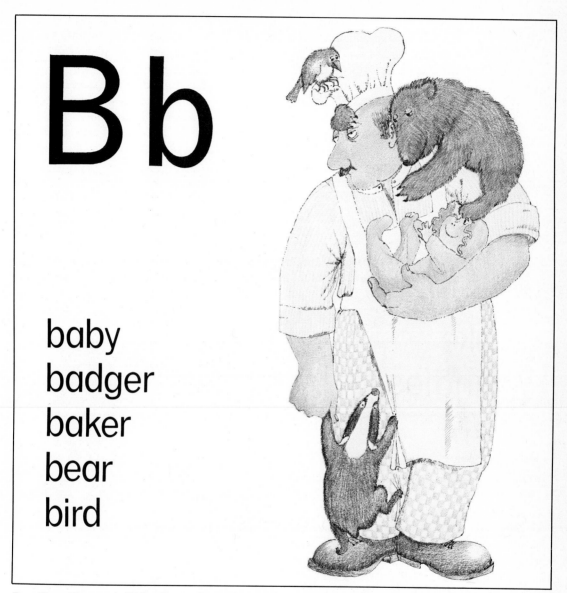

Bb

baby
badger
baker
bear
bird

From HELEN OXENBURY'S ABC OF THINGS. Copyright ©1971 by Helen Oxenbury. Used by permission of Franklin Watts, Inc., New York, and William Heinemann Ltd., London.

tion, subscribe to a here-and-now theory in choosing books for early childhood. An "awareness" school of writing and illustrating, fostered by Lucy Sprague Mitchell[1] and transformed into some pleasant-sounding picture book texts by Margaret Wise Brown, has shown us that everyday sights and sounds, even without crucial incident, can convey a memorable literary experience well

---

[1]See Lucy Sprague Mitchell, *Here and Now Story Book,* illus. Hendrik Willem Van Loon (Dutton, 1921, 1948).

within the grasp of very young children. In Richard Scarry's simplest books—those that group well-known items with labels—the cartoon style adds its own dimension to the here-and-now. [See, for example, *What Do People Do All Day?* (20) and *Richard Scarry's Great Big Schoolhouse* (21).]

You can discover for yourself the range of picture books that very young children respond to. Dorothy M. White's charming account of sharing books with her daughter Carol in *Books Before Five* presents many instances in which first-hand experience appeared necessary before the child could appreciate and comprehend the pictures. Only after such realism does the author observe that "Carol, I imagine, has sufficient grip on reality now to depart from it cheerfully."[1]

The artful but plain and simple picture books of objects to name are good beginnings: Françoise's *The Things I Like* (22), the series of pictures that comprise *Teddy* (23) by Grete Janus, perhaps the uncomplicated images of L. Leslie Brooke for the nursery rhymes in *Ring O' Roses* (24), or Tasha Tudor's paler and kindlier paintings for her *Mother Goose* (25). Add to them the counting books and alphabet books that take few liberties with reality but enhance photographic literalism with art. (See list, pp. 138–39.)

If you miss this stage with children, something is lost that can never be regained. The idea that pictures can convey reality, that books are windows to the world, must be introduced early and with care. No less important is the

booklist

Alphabet Books

Barton, Byron. *Applebet Story.* Viking, 1973.

Chardict, Bernice. *C is for Circus.* Illus. Brinton Turkle. Walker, 1971. Illustrations are like old circus posters.

Cooney, Barbara. *A Garland of Games and Other Diversions: An Alphabet Book.* Holt, 1969.

Feelings, Muriel. *Jambo Means Hello: Swahili Alphabet Book.* Illus. Tom Feelings. Dial, 1974.

Fife, Dale. *Adam's A B C.* Illus. Don Robertson. Coward, McCann, 1971. An easy to read book for letter identification and alphabet sequence; illustrations depict one day in the life of a black child.

Fujikawa, Gyo. *Gyo Fujikawa's A to Z Picture Book.* Grosset and Dunlap, 1974.

Fuller, Catherine L. *Beasts An Alphabet of Fine Prints.* Little, Brown, 1968.

Gág, Wanda. *The ABC Bunny.* (Woodcuts by author). Coward-McCann, 1933. An old favorite still popular with children and adults alike.

Garten, Jan. *The Alphabet Tale.* Illus. Muriel Batherman. Random, 1964.

---

[1]Dorothy White, *Books Before Five* (Oxford, 1954), p. 160.

rhythmic sound that emerges from the text of these books. Margery Fisher observes, "What goes in one ear does *not* come out the other. It stays embedded in the memory."[1]

Later, introduce more imaginative fare. Try the unusual, challenging alphabet and nursery rhyme books. Leonard Baskin designed *Hosie's Alphabet* (26), aided by his children Hosea, Tobias, and Lisa, with dramatic varieties of typography and illustration for such items as the "carrion crow" and the "rhinoceros express." Beni Montresor's *A for Angel* (27) has an ocean, oranges, oars, owls, and an octagon-bearing octopus for the "O" double-page. His wildly colored *I Saw a Ship A-Sailing* (28), a collection of sixteen nursery rhymes, is one of our favorites. "Hickory, dickory, dock" shows, instead of the traditional grandfather clock, an immense orange cat with a mouse leaping off his nose onto a stretcher held by two strange cat-beasts. These are "joke" books, perhaps enjoyed only by the special child. A more representative collection, departing from the here-and-now but still within range of experience might include such old favorites as the Little Tim books, the Babar books, the Curious George books, *Madeline* (29) by Ludwig Bemelmans, *The Little House* (30) by Virginia Lee Burton, and *The Little Island* (31) by Golden MacDonald.

This is also a time when wordless books and near-wordless books can be profitably used, for children can tell the story as they study the pictures. (See accompanying list.) Our happiest experience with this subtype was in using

booklist

Alphabet Books (cont.)

Grant, Sandy. *Hey Look At Me: A City ABC.* Photos Larry Mulvehill. Bradbury, 1973. Stresses verbs.

Greenaway, Kate. *A Apple Pie.* Warne, n.d.

Grossbart, Francine. *A Big City.* Harper, 1966.

Lear, Edward. *A Nonsense Alphabet.* Illus. Richard Scarry. Doubleday, 1962.

————. *The First ABC.* Ed. Frank Waters. Illus. Charles Mozley. Watts, 1971.

Munari, Bruno. *Bruno Munari's ABC's.* World, 1960.

Oxenbury, Helen. *Helen Oxenbury's ABC of Things.* Watts, 1971. Droll drawings delicately painted: an otter riding an ostrich, a hare and a hippopotamus in a hospital.

Rasmussen, Halfdan. *Halfdan's ABC's.* Illus. Spang Olsen. H. Rasmussen, 1967.

Sendak, Maurice. *Alligators All Around,* in Nutshell Library. Harper, 1962. Alphabet in rhyme.

Wildsmith, Brian. *Brian Wildsmith's ABC.* Watts, 1963.

---

[1]Margery Fisher, *Intent upon Reading* (Watts, 1961), p. 20.

Fernando Krahn's *How Santa Had a Long and Difficult Journey Delivering His Presents* (32). Each page in this book presents a problem that invites the child to create a solution: for example, Santa's reindeer get loose from the sleigh and fly away

booklist

Wordless Books[1]

Alexander, Martha. *Bobo's Dream.* Dial, 1970.
———. *Out, Out, Out.* Dial, 1970.
Amoss, Bertha. *By the Sea.* Parents, 1969.
Anderson, Laurie. *The Package.* Bobbs-Merrill, 1971.
Anno, Mitsumasa. *Dr. Anno's Magical Midnight Circus.* Weatherhill, 1972.
———. *Topsey Turvies.* Weatherhill, 1970.
Ardizzone, Edward. *The Wrong Side of the Bed.* Doubleday, 1970.
Aruego, Jose. *Look What I Can Do.* Scribner's, 1971.
Asch, Frank. *The Blue Balloon.* McGraw-Hill, 1972.
———. *In the Eye of the Teddy.* Harper, 1973.
Barton, Byron. *Elephant.* Seabury, 1971
Baum, Will. *Birds of a Feather.* Addison-Wesley, 1969.
Billout, Guy. *The Number 24.* Dial, 1973.
Bolliger-Savelli, Antinella. *The Knitted Cat.* MacMillan, 1972.
Carle, Eric. *Do You Want to Be my Friend.* Crowell, 1971.
———. *I See a Song.* Crowell, 1973.
———. *The Very Long Tail.* Crowell, 1972.
———. *The Very Long Train.* Crowell, 1972.
Carrick, Donald. *Drip Drop.* MacMillan, 1973.
Carroll, Ruth. *The Chimp and the Clown.* Walck, 1968.
———. *Rolling Downhill.* Walck, 1973.
———. *What Whiskers Did.* Walck, 1965.
———. *The Witch Kitten.* Walck, 1973.

Chamberlin, Bob, and Bergman, Donna. *I'm Not Little, I'm Big.* Puppet Press, 1973.
Espenscheid, Gertrude. *The Oh Ball.* Harper, 1966.
Fromm, Lilo. *Muffel and Plums.* MacMillan, 1973.
Fuchs, Erich. *Journey to the Moon.* Delacorte, 1969.
Goodall, John S. *The Adventures of Paddy Pork.* Harcourt, 1968.
———. *The Ballooning Adventures of Paddy Pork.* Harcourt, 1969.
———. *Jacko.* Harcourt, 1971.
———. *The Midnight Adventures of Kelly, Dot, and Esmeralda.* Atheneum, 1972.
———. *Paddy's Evening Out.* Atheneum, 1973.
———. *Shrewbettina's Birthday.* Harcourt, 1970.
Hamburger, John. *A Sleepless Day.* Four Winds (Scholastic), 1973.
Hoban, Tana. *Look Again.* MacMillan, 1971.
———. *Shapes and Things.* MacMillan, 1970.
Hogrogian, Nonny. *Apples,* MacMillan, 1972.
Hutchins, Pat. *Changes Changes.* MacMillan, 1971.
Krahn, Fernando. *A Flying Saucer Full of Spaghetti.* Dutton, 1970.
———. *How Santa Claus Had a Long and Difficult Journey Delivering His Presents.* Delacorte, 1970.
———. *Journeys of Sebastian.* Delacorte, 1968.

---

[1] Compiled by William A. Brochtrup, University of Washington. Reprinted by permission of the author.

and Santa's airplane toys upset the sleigh. We found that the early pages drew great excitement and a stream of speculative language from even the shyest child. A simpler wordless book, *What Whiskers Did* (33) by Ruth Carroll is in

booklist

Wordless Books (cont.)

Lisker, Sonia. *The Attic Witch.* Four Winds, 1973.

Mari, Iela. *The Apple and the Moth.* Pantheon, 1970.

————. *The Chicken and the Egg.* Pantheon, 1970.

————. *The Magic Balloon.* S. G. Phillips, 1969.

Mayer, Mercer. *Bubble Bubble.* Parents Magazine Press, 1973.

————. *A Boy, A Dog, and A Frog.* Dial, 1967.

————. *A Boy, A Dog, A Frog and A Friend.* Dial, 1971.

————. *Frog on His Own.* Dial, 1973.

————. *Frog Where Are You.* Dial, 1969.

Meyer, Remate. *Hide and Seek.* Bradbury, 1972.

————. *Vicki.* Atheneum, 1969.

Miller, Barry. *Alphabet World.* MacMillan, 1971.

Mitgutsch, Ali. *In the Busy Town.* Golden, 1973.

Mordillo, Guillermo. *Damp and Daffy Doings of a Daring Pirate Ship.* Harlin Quist, 1971.

Olschewski, Alfred. *Winterbird.* Houghton Mifflin, 1969.

Reich, Hanns. *Animals of Many Lands.* Hill and Wang, 1966.

————. *Dogs.* Hill and Wang, 1973.

————. *Laughing Camera.* Hill and Wang, 1967.

————. *Laughing Camera II.* Hill and Wang, 1969.

————. *Laughing Camera for Children.* Hill and Wang, 1970.

————. *Lovers.* Hill and Wang, 1968.

Rice, Brian and Evans, Tony. *English Surprise.* Flash, 1973.

Ringi, Kjeli. *The Magic Stick.* Harper, 1968.

————. *The Winner.* Harper, 1969.

Schick, Eleanor. *Making Friends.* MacMillan, 1969.

Simmons, Ellie. *Cat.* McKay, 1968.

————. *Dog.* McKay, 1967.

————. *Family.* McKay, 1970.

————. *Wheels.* McKay, 1969.

Steiner, Charlotte. *I Am Andy.* Knopf, 1961.

Sugano, Yoshikatsu. *The Kittens Adventure.* McGraw-Hill, 1971.

Sugita, Yutaka. *Goodnight 1,2,3.* Scroll Press, 1971.

————. *My Friend Little John and Me.* McGraw-Hill, 1973.

Ueno, Noriko. *Elephant Buttons.* Harper, 1973.

Ungerer, Tomi. *One, Two, Three.* Harper, 1964.

————. *One, Two, Where's My Shoe.* Harper, 1964.

————. *Snail, Where Are You.* Harper, 1962.

Ward, Lynd. *The Silver Pony.* Houghton Mifflin, 1973.

Wezel, Peter. *Good Bird.* Harper, 1966.

Wondriska, William. *A Long Piece of String.* Holt, 1963.

inexpensive paperback. Buy two copies, cut them apart, mount the pictures on cardboard, and you have a puzzle in sequence so that a child can arrange the pictures in order and tell the story. A difficult wordless book, *Changes, Changes* (34) by Pat Hutchins, tells an epic-like story by arrangement of play blocks.

The language development stimulated by wordless books seems evident, but their possibilities for promoting a child's interest in reading and his readiness for the task have only begun to be explored. Certainly the child struggling with his first reading lessons is entitled to a rich accompanying diet of picture books, including those whose vocabulary is unlimited (and therefore to be read to him) as well as the better examples of picture books with easy words and syntax. The Beginner Books published by Random House and the I Can Read Books published by Harper & Row may not always be high in literary quality, yet many a child has found Dr. Seuss's fifty-word vocabulary and absurd drawings a good cut above his primer fare when he opens *Green Eggs and Ham* (35). The prepositions in easy phrases in *Bears in the Night* (36) by Stan and Jan Berenstain

booklist

Mother Goose and Other Nursery Rhymes

Alexander, Frances. *Mother Goose on the Rio Grande.* National Textbook Corp., 1960. Traditional Mexican nursery rhymes, riddles, and singing games, printed with facing English and Spanish texts.

Aliki, illus. *Hush Little Baby.* Prentice-Hall, 1968.

Baring-Gould, William S. and Cecil. *The Annotated Mother Goose Nursery Rhymes Old and New.* Illus. Water Crane, Randolph Caldecott, Kate Greenaway, Arthur Rackham, Maxfield Parrish. Potter, 1962.

Briggs, Raymond. *The Mother Goose Treasury.* Coward-McCann, 1966. Greenaway Medal winner.

Burroughs, Margaret Taylor, comp. *Did You Feed My Cow? Street Games, Chants, and Rhymes,* rev., ed. Illus. Joe E. DeValasco. Follett, 1969.

Caldecott, Randolph, illus. *Hey Diddle Diddle Picture Book.* Warne, n.d.

DeForest, Charlotte B. *The Prancing Pony; Nursery Rhymes from Japan adapted into English verse for Children, with "Kusa-e,"* Illus. Keiko Hida. Walker, 1968.

DeKay, Ormonde, Jr. *Rimes de La Mére Oie.* Illus. Seymour Chwast. Little, Brown, 1971. Mother Goose rhymes in French.

Greenaway, Kate, illus. *Mother Goose.* Warne, 1882.

_____. *Under the Window: Pictures and Rhymes for Children.* Warne, 1879.

_____. *Marigold Garden.* Warne, n.d.

Grover, Eulalie Osgood, ed. *Mother Goose: The Classic Volland Edition.* Illus. Frederick Richardson. Hubbard, 1971. (First published in 1915).

are effortlessly alive for the beginning reader. The Frog and Toad books by Arnold Lobel and the Little Bear books by Else Holmelund Minarik, illustrated by Maurice Sendak, all published in the I Can Read series, are also useful members of the picture book type. See, too, Lillian Hoban's Arthur books in the same series. These books, such as *Arthur's Honey Bear* (37), are a bit longer, increasing the attention span of the beginning reader.

teaching ideas

1. Try using wordless books these two ways: First, "read" it yourself to a child. Include references beyond what is shown in the illustrations. Include conversation; name the characters. Second, using a different book, ask the child to "read" to you. Note inference-making and direct conversation. After you

booklist

Mother Goose (cont.)

Hogrogian, Nonny., illus. *One I Love, Two I Love; and Other Loving Mother Goose Rhymes.* Dutton, 1972.

Latham, Hugh, tr. *Mother Goose in French: Poésies de la vraie mére Oie.* Illus. Barbara Cooney. Crowell, 1964.

Reed, Phillip, illus. *Mother Goose and Nursery Rhymes.* Atheneum, 1963.

Reid, Alastair and Kerrigan, Anthony, tr. *Mother Goose in Spanish: Poesias de la Madre.* Illus. Barbara Cooney. Crowell, 1968.

Sendak, Maurice, illus. *Hector Protector, and As I Went Over the Water.* Harper, 1965.

Tenggren, Gustaf, illus. *The Tenggren Mother Goose.* Little, Brown, 1956.

Tucker, Nicholas, comp. *Mother Goose Lost.* Illus. Trevor Stubley. Crowell, 1971.

Wildsmith, Brian. *Brian Wildsmith's Mother Goose.* Watts, 1964.

Winsor, Frederick. *The Space Child's Mother Goose.* Illus. Marian Parry. Simon and Schuster, 1958.

Wood, Ray, comp. *The American Mother Goose.* Illus. Ed Hargis. F. A. Stokes, 1940.

Wyndham, Robert. *Chinese Mother Goose Rhymes.* Illus. Ed Young. World, 1968.

Montgomerie, Norah and William, coll. and ed. *A Book of Scottish Nursery Rhymes.* Illus. N. Montgomerie and T. Ritchie. Oxford Press, 1965.

The Only True Mother Goose Melodies. Lothrop, Lee, 1905. (Originally published by Munroe and Francis, 1833).

Potter, Beatrix. *Appley Dapply's Nursery Rhymes.* Warne, 1917.

——. *Cecily Parsley's Nursery Rhymes.* Warne, n.d.

Here come the elephants, ten feet high,
elephants, elephants, heads in the sky.
Eleven great elephants intertwined,
one little elephant close behind.

Elephants over and elephants under,
elephants bellow with elephant thunder.
Up on pedestals elephants hop,
elephants go and elephants stop.

Elephants quick and elephants slow,
elephants dancing to and fro.
Elephants, elephants twice times six,
elephants doing elephant tricks.

Elephants strutting, elephants strolling,
rollicking elephants frolicking, rolling.
Elephants forming an elephant arch,
elephants marching an elephant march.

Elephants there and elephants here,
elephants cheering an elephant cheer.
Elephants, elephants, trunks unfurled,
in a wonderful, elegant elephant world.

study chapter 8, return to this section. Which of the procedures described in chapter 8 might best be practiced using wordless books?

2. Dramatize *Bears in the Night* using a story theater approach. This means you read the book a phrase at a time; let children study the drawings and then act out the story. Dramatize it twice; then see whether, without any urging, the child "reads" the book.

It has been customary to confine picture books to early years and distinguish them from the illustrated stories with longer texts that children "grow into."

Neither assertion is accurate. As we examine other literary types in the ensuing sections, we shall see that there are many illustrated books suitable for early years and that many picture books are quite appropriate for later years. A fascinating account of the use of picture books with inner-city fifth-graders reveals the motive power and sophisticated response stimulated by such stories as *Stevie* (38) by John Steptoe, *The Ballad of the Burglar of Babylon* (39) by Elizabeth Bishop, *Charles Addams Mother Goose* (40) and *Harriet and the Promised Land* (41) by Jacob Lawrence. In each instance, a carefully planned sequence of questions and activities resulted in increased visual awareness.[1]

Recent picture books with appeal to intermediate-level children cover a wide range of art styles and language. *A New Day* (42) by Don Bolognese contains complex color mixes and great detail as it tells a modern version of the Nativity story with a cast of migrant workers in the Southwest. A Spanish fable, *The Elephant and His Secret* (43) by Gabriela Mistral (written in Spanish with English text by Doris Dana) presents striking solid-block designs in orange, purple, and black. Humor in geometric cartoon style fills the pages of Ellen Raskin's *Franklin Stein* (44). Jack Prelutsky's *Circus* (45) is a picture book in verse with enough detail and word play to last many an hour.

Teaching Picture Books

Using picture books in the classroom can be difficult. When you're working with a group of children, you may wish that the book were six times larger.

Seat children on the floor or on a closely arranged circle of chairs. Avoid waving the book over their heads; put it down to eye level. Can you read upside down? If so, hold the open book in front of you at lap-level. If not, try holding it firmly at your side, the open page turned toward your class, not aslant. Hold the book still. If you need to face it in the usual reading position, then do so: show a few pictures, invite comments, then turn the book away from your group and read the story. Afterwards, you can turn it around again for picture study.[2]

The following sample questions, applicable to most picture books, will help you direct attention to the *how* of the picture process. Such questions can be interspersed with interpretation items such as those suggested in chapter 9. You will, of course, need to change the wording to suit your group's maturity level.

• How did the artist decide what mood or theme to follow in making his pictures? How did the artist achieve his effects and what are they?

---

[1]M. Jean Greenlaw. "Picture Books: No Age Limit for Enjoyment," *Top of the News* (January 1972): 189–97.

[2]See Joanna Foster, *How to Conduct Effective Picture Book Programs: A Handbook* (Westchester Library System, 1967). An accompanying film is called "The Pleasure is Mutual: How to Conduct Effective Picture Book Programs," available through The Children's Book Council, Inc., 175 Fifth Avenue, New York, N.Y. 10010.

Every time Benjamin passed Tulip's house, she said, "I'm gonna beat you up."

In a departure from traditional roles, this story features a female character, Tulip, as the bully and a male character, Benjamin, as the victim. Excerpted from BENJAMIN & TULIP by Rosemary Wells. Copyright © 1973 by Rosemary Wells.

- How did the artist decide what scenes to present? Did he attempt an item-by-item presentation to show everything described in the text? What did he omit? What did he add, and why? When appropriate, try blocking out an important part of a picture, using heavy paper or cardboard. Ask what should be included in the masked portion.
- What items are repeated in the pictures? Where do you find repetition of shapes, of lines, of colors? Where do you find repetition with variation?
- How else, other than through repetition, does an artist draw attention to something important? Note contrast through color, size, and interruption of repeated design.

Don't use all the questions in the same session. Use only a few that are especially right for the book you're presenting.

As you work with picture books, you'll discover that every worthy one is unique in some special way. You and your children will return again and again to those intrinsically unique books, teasing out the quality that makes them special, the quality that inspires you to present the books. We'll point out our own discoveries about a handful of excellent picture books.

Marjorie Flack's Angus books, about a pet Scottie, have timeless appeal. First of all, these books are well plotted. Events happen *to* Angus and his reactions are expertly shown in the drawings. The first book, *Angus and the Ducks* (46), is a reversal story. Angus chases the ducks until they turn about and chase him.

And she did.

Used with permission of The Dial Press.

What stays in the memory are the final four pages, a sort of slow-motion sequence of Angus crawling under a sofa, his eyes turning from white alarm to blue puzzlement. *Angus Lost* (47) has a final page worth studying: its picture synthesizes the basic elements of all three books. *Angus and the Cat* (48) is a good example of economy in prose style, neither too terse nor too wordy. Note, too, the "body English" revealed in its drawings. In each picture of the two animals, one is reacting to the other. When the cat is asleep, Angus is skulking and curious. When she jumps in alarm to the sofa back, Angus's head and tail invite instant open communication. Angus's movements exactly complement the cat's aggression or withdrawal. (See pp. 144–45.)

Where the Wild Things Are (49) by Maurice Sendak begins realistically and then sets off into fantasy without the conventional bridge between the two worlds. You're not told that it was all a dream. Sometimes teachers attempt to build the bridge for the book, asking, "Which is real and which is make-believe?" or "Didn't Max have a frightening dream?" But such questions spoil the spirit and unity of the book. Within the framework of the story, all events are real.

Sendak has varied the size of his drawings in an interesting way. The early scenes are small, but the scenes showing the dance of the Wild Things several pages later are so large they seem to carom off the pages. Interlaced lines unify the texture of realistic and fanciful depictions alike. Claws on Max's wolf suit are amplified into the terrible claws and teeth of the Wild Things. Faint color gives the pictures an air of not-quite-reality, of half-remembered dreams, but that's the only hint of fantasy. Sendak loves motion; he has described his book

Up jumped the CAT onto the arm
of the sofa. Angus came closer and—

The author/artist uses alternating pages of black and white and then color to depict the encounter between Angus and the cat. From ANGUS AND THE CAT by Marjorie Flack. Copyright 1931 by

in choreographic terms. Noting that a picture shows an arrested action, ask your pupils to go on with the dance. Ask them to imitate the pose of one of the creatures and then show his next movement.

A picture book worth owning for the joy of many lookings is *Rain Makes Applesauce* (50) by Julian Scheer, illustrated by Marvin Bileck. "The stars are made of lemon juice," shouts the first line, and three very busy children in outlandish dress, stabilized by parachutes, are squeezing a lemon to create swirling stars, while Appleseed Mary, beneath a cloud, greets two young visitors. In a later scene "the wind blows backwards all night long"—and there's the wind, his great face bulging with effort, and in his dark wake a host of people, teapots, and UFOs flying through the air.

The book revels in floating, sliding, lounging, and eating. It's a celebration of verbs, a radiation of imagery. Its words have melody: "Monkeys mumble in a jellybean jungle." Its pictures are so delicately detailed that you need much time to sort them out. This book seems to flaunt the very idea that every book must have a point, must "say something." The theme, if there is one, is that the joy of drawing and coloring is sufficient in itself. It may inspire imaginative drawing and painting and wild word experiments. Above all, it shows how happily a picture book can abandon the literary components of other types— plot, theme, and the rest—to gain a visual unity all its own.

Drummer Hoff (51), adapted by Barbara Emberley and illustrated with gaily inked woodcut outlines by Ed Emberley, has a sturdy cumulative text based on

SISS-S-S-S-S-S!!!
That little CAT boxed
Angus's ears!

Marjorie Flack Larsson. Reprinted by permission of Doubleday & Company, Inc.

an English folk rhyme. Beginning with the lowest rank, the men in an army build a cannon. A cannon part is brought by each man. When the cannon is finished, it is fired: KAHBAHBLOOM. But the man who accomplishes this climactic task is of the lowest rank: the drummer, the title character, who gets exclusive mention in the book's refrain. An unusual feature for such a simple story is the second ending. We see the cannon on the last page, now fallen apart with birds and spiders and grasshoppers in command. No men, no words.

The text is like a series of headlines—no adjectives, no commentary. The pictures provide the description beyond the basic actions and open the way for interpretation. The theme might be that cannon firing is triumphant and it's the "little" man who really does the job; or, considering the irony of the final page, the theme might be that cannon firing is a short-lived triumph.

teaching ideas

1. One way to introduce Drummer Hoff is to re-create the artist's picture-making process. Since woodblock printing is difficult and dangerous, you might substitute print-making with soap, potato, or linoleum. Talk about the effect. Try coloring in the spaces. Even try photographing the result. Read or tell about the artist's explanation of his technique, described in his own

words.[1] Show the book jacket or a page near the middle of the book. Talk about the art process, then gradually shift to the content.

2. You may decide to highlight the book's structure. With the text at hand, note the two progressions: the ranks of the men and pieces of the cannon, related like this:

KAHBAHBLOOM

GENERAL --Order
MAJOR --Shot
CAPTAIN --Rammer
SERGEANT --------------------------------------Powder
CORPORAL --------------------------------------Barrel
PRIVATE--Carriage

DRUMMER

To "read" the book requires filling in the names. Children can anticipate some of these names because they rhyme with the progression of cannon parts:

Private_____brought the carriage.
Corporal_____brought the barrel.

3. Teach the book's cumulative style: each new rank and part is followed by a repetition of the whole rhyme up to that point. As you present the cumulative rhyme, use the above chart to aid the memory. It won't be long before all children can read the book with you. When pictures and text have been thoroughly absorbed, invite children to dramatize the narrative, using pantomime and choral speech. Props aren't really necessary, but characters may wear tagboard signs bearing names. This might also be the time to view the Weston Woods film based on the book.[2] It's likely to gain a hearty reception.

4. Taking care not to dampen enthusiasm for the book, you might use such questions as these, aimed at understanding and appreciating art composition:
   How is yellow used in each picture? Why does red increase as the pictures go along? In what picture do you find the most red? What are the main colors in the final picture, when the cannon is broken? Why did the artist use this contrast?
   In which direction do the characters look and walk? Why isn't Drummer Hoff looking in that direction, too? The artist added grass, birds, insects, and flowers to the pictures even though the story as told doesn't mention them. Would you have expected these in a story about firing a cannon? What else might be added?

---

[1]Ed Emberley, "Caldecott Award Acceptance Speech," *Horn Book* 44 (August 1968): 399–404.
[2]"Drummer Hoff" film and filmstrip (#108) are available from Weston Woods, Weston, Connecticut 06880.

The intent of using a few selected questions is to direct children toward appreciation by discerning how effects are achieved by the artist. Visual literacy is one goal in picture book presentation. The direct question approach can sometimes be a means to achieving it.[1]

Toward the end of your sessions with *Drummer Hoff,* you may examine the book's possible themes: is it, for instance, a celebration or a denunciation of military status and endeavor? What have the author and artist intended through the two endings?

Oh, No, Go (A Play) (52) by David McPhail is one of the most lively and complex of near-wordless books for children. Using only the three words of the title, spoken by various members of the large cast of animal and human characters, the author-artist plays upon a motif of transformations. An airborne balloon is transformed into a tent containing a theater in which a strange play is enacted while a hen member of the audience hatches chicks. The proceedings of the play bring about a flood that engulfs the audience, which presently finds itself underwater with a mermaid and swordfish, all threatened by a monstrous fish and a personified wind. There's a daring rescue, and the tent (or is it an octopus?) is transformed back into a balloon bearing the chief characters away, presumably to a new adventure.

As children examine the forty-four pictures that comprise this book, they discover several plots operating simultaneously, offering an opportunity for describing sequences from the viewpoints of various characters. Ask children, for instance, to "be the hen and tell what happened in the story," and to do the same from the point of view of the white rabbit, the bespectacled dog, or the mermaid. The drawings show a collection of incidents often without a single focal point. As such, they provide a real challenge for answering the most basic question in picture-book discussion: "What is happening in this picture?"

special activities

1. Choose a work by any of the artists listed earlier in this section. Describe or demonstrate how you can incorporate recognition of unique visual elements into your presentation of the picture book.

2. Study the pictures and texts of the most recent Caldecott Medal book and the Honor Books designated by the Caldecott List. How do texts and pictures in these works combine to produce their effects? How do the differences in purpose of text and pictures affect the manner in which you present selected picture books?

3. Sometimes commentaries on picture books emphasize color. Which of your

---

[1]See Catharine M. Williams, *Learning from Pictures,* 2nd ed. (Department of Audiovisual Instruction, National Education Association, Washington, D.C., 1968), p. 25.

favorite picture books use color as an important element? Which do not? What color processes and, more widely, what art processes are most frequently used in the picture books children prefer?

4. Sometimes it's better to plan several brief related discussions dealing with a fine picture book than to attempt to present it in one lengthy session. Using a good selection, such as those mentioned in our discussion, plan a sequence of short discussions. Which elements should you highlight for their unique contribution to the book's effect? If possible, try out your plan.

FOLK LITERATURE: TALES, MYTHS, LEGENDS, AND EPICS

Folk literature includes "all forms of prose narrative, written or oral, which have come to be handed down through the years." This is the definition used by Stith Thompson, who adds:

> The important fact is the traditional nature of the material. In contrast to the modern story writer's striving after originality of plot and treatment, the teller of a folk tale is proud of his ability to hand on that which he has received. He usually desires to impress his readers or hearers with the fact that he is bringing them something that has the stamp of good authority, that the tale was heard from some great story-teller or from some aged person who remembered it from old days.[1]

booklist

African Folk Tales[2]

Aardema, Verna, reteller. *Behind the Back of the Mountain: Black Folktales from Southern Africa.* Illus. Leo and Diane Dillon. Dial, 1973. Ten short South African folk legends from the Hottentot, Zula, Bantu, Bushman, Thongu, and Tshindao languages. Stories deal with trickery, outwitting acts, foolishness and impossible tasks among talking animals, flying maidens, beasts, princesses, and witches.

Bryan, Ashley, reteller/illus. *The Ox of the Wonderful Horns and Other African Folktales.* Atheneum, 1971. Five fun trickery stories of familiar African folk characters such as Anansi the spider, Frog Kumbota, and Hare the born trickster. Included is the title story of Mungalo, the mistreated chief's son who is aided by a pair of magic ox horns.

Berger, Terry. *Black Fairy Tales.* Illus. David Omar White. Aladdin, 1969.

Heady, Eleanor. *When the Stones Were Soft: East African Fireside Tales.* Illus. Tom Feelings. Funk, 1968.

Savoy, Phyllis. *Lion Outwitted by Hare and Other African Tales.* Whitman, 1971.

---

[1]Stith Thompson, *The Folktale* (Dryden, 1946), p. 4.
[2]Folk tale booklists were compiled by Elaine Aoki, University of Washington.

We have followed the Stith Thompson definition and included in our discussion of folk literature the folk tale, fable, myth, legend, and epic.

Folk Tales

Folk tales are as old as people. All around the world from the earliest times people have told tales to carry a sense of what has been, what is, and what might be. Long before people learned to write they told stories to one another and to their children. The telling helped them to preserve what they cared about. Even after more and more people learned to write, the old tales drew the plain people together.

Today folk tales still have that communal power, especially for children who retain many of the qualities of the plain people. The power of folk tales to make people feel their common humanity is heightened by the way they are told—a way that is characteristic of folk tales regardless of the culture of their origin.

Folk tales are good stories. Their action begins at once; the conflicting forces

booklist

Asian Folk Tales

Carpenter, Frances. *People From the Sky: Ainu Tales from Northern Japan.* Illus. Betty Fraser. Doubleday, 1972. Ekashi, an Ainu chief of a Hokkaido village, relates tales of origin and creation to his grandchildren Toki and Haruko.

Picard, Barbara Leonie. *Tales of Ancient Persia.* Walck, 1973. Dignified tales taken from the epic poem, Shah-Nana, the King's Book by Iranian poet Firdausi. Stories tell of Persian history from creation to conquest by Arabs in seventh century.

Sharma, Partap. *The Surangini Tales.* Harcourt, 1973. Illus. by Demi Hitz. A woven carpet, Kalu, a poor weaver, and the disappearance of Surangini, daughter of India's wealthiest man set the stage for suitors to tell their stories of rescue. A collection of 17 short series-like tales recounting the rescue attempts of suitors to gain Surangini's love.

Wyndham, Robert. *Tales the People Tell in China.* Illus. Jay Yang. Julian Messner, 1971. A beautiful collection of ancient Chinese myths, legends, folktales, anecdotes, and sayings. Both writing and illustrations reflect the tradition and accuracy of these Chinese tales.

Bany, Garrett, tr./illus. *Men From the Village Deep In the Mountains and Other Japanese Folk Tales.* Macmillan, 1973.

Durham, Mae. *Tobei.* Illus. Mitsu Yashima. Bradbury, 1974.

Ginsburg, Mirra, tr. *The Kaha Bird; Tales from the Steppes of Central Asia.* Illus. Richard Cuffari. Crown, 1971.

Spicer, Dorothy Gladys. *The Kneeling Tree and Other Folktales from the Middle East.* Illus. Barbara Morrow. Coward-McCann, 1971.

are quickly identified. Characters are graphically sketched with clear motives and uncomplicated actions. The settings, too, are projected economically. Once these essentials are established the tales move with dispatch to final resolutions. And the resolutions are of the same quality as the rest of the tales: clear, unambiguous, and supremely just.

The style of folk tales is tempered to the tongue. The better versions of the tales show that they are meant to be told; ornate, complicated syntax is generally avoided, for it cannot be handled orally. So the telling flows along in ways which the voice can manage and the listener can remember. Flavored words and patterned phrases abound, sometimes in a mixture of prose and verse.

Behind the clear plot lines of the stories, ideas and attitudes are expressed with clarity. The good do triumph and the evil suffer. The persisting virtues survive: bravery, compassion, perseverance, love, honesty. What the plain people care most about is dramatized in a thousand different ways: a good home, a good feeling in the family, enough food and drink. True, in the tales they dream about kings, princes, and princesses, but the dreams are tempered by reality. The privileged aren't always noble. Sometimes they are seen as vain and foolish. They dream about the giants, ogres, and dragons who *might* exist, and they find relief from their fears by defeating with gusto these protagonists of the vast unknown. They dream about enchanted people—fairies, elves, and other wee folk—and find them as various as the ordinary people they know: generous and selfish, wise and foolish, honest and deceitful. In short, wherever the plain people pitch their tales, the basic values they cherish come through quite unmistakably.

These tales are not, however, full of the dull moralizing that was to characterize the stories of later eras. Folk tales all around the world underline the point of the story with delightful inventiveness. We have seen that they extend the theater of action beyond ordinary people and places to enchanted creatures and mystic lands. Magic is everywhere; beasts are transformed into people; people are transformed into beasts. Magical rings, lamps, mirrors, and a thousand other objects have wondrous powers to solve the most difficult problems. The granting of wishes may be a special magic that surmounts obstacles or, if used unwisely, compounds the dilemmas. Magic and shrewd, untutored wit conquer difficulties as often as not. Sometimes the solutions are really tricks, in which the simple bests the sophisticated, or the slow and weak defeat the quick and powerful. Broad humor is often an added ingredient in these conflicts, especially in the stories of fools and simpletons who become enmeshed in ridiculous situations. The opponents in the tales are not always men and women; animals often replace human beings as principal figures. Actually, they are more human than animal, but the animal guise lends a new perspective through which human strength and frailty can be viewed. All these story devices—motifs as they are called by folklorists—exist in almost unending variety. They are surely one of the best testaments to the creative power of the plain people.

How will you select and use folk tales with children to help them feel all the linguistic, ethical, and creative power that is found in these old, old stories?

Wisely chosen tales will cast their own spell. Watch the children as you tell or read the tale. Does its power bring the rapt look, the faraway gleam into the eyes? Draw your audience close and seize a good time for the telling. If necessary, clarify terms or settings before you begin, but once you've started, stick to the pace inherent in the tale. (See pp. 463–77, chapter 10 for additional help in storytelling and reading aloud.)

Don't assume that folk tales are limited to any certain grade level or age, nor that older children are too old to hear a story or to sit on the floor to listen as a community. Purists may discourage you from telling a tale unless you're an expert, or disparage attempts to have children tell folk tales. It's true that through the ages there have been skilled storytellers whose fame and livelihood rested on their ability to tell certain stories better than anybody else. (At one time, Russian mill-owners hired gifted storytellers to attract customers, just as breakfast food and soap companies hire TV personalities today.) There are still a few professional storytellers around, but, lacking these, you can do as the plain folk have always done: tell the stories yourself and inspire your children to tell them.

And read aloud. A folk tale need not be told in order to preserve the oral tradition. Some of that tradition is safely alive in the best editions of folk tales, and you may well begin by reading them aloud.

The oldest English-language versions include Robert Samber's translation (1730) of the French tales collected by Perrault and John Edward Taylor's translation of an Italian collection, *The Pentamerone* (50 stories) published in 1848. The German tales assembled by the Brothers Grimm, *Kinder- und Hausmarchen* (1812–1815), appeared in English in 1824, and with terrifying illustrations by George Cruikshank in 1826. Margaret Hunt's translation, *Grimm's Household Tales*, published in 1884, was republished by Follett in 1968 under the title *Grimm's Fairy Tales*, with an introduction by Frances Clarke Sayers. *The Household Stories From the Collection of the Brothers Grimm*, which first appeared in 1886, is still of interest for two reasons: the engravings by Walter Crane are beautifully composed, and the translation by Lucy Crane weaves a melancholy spell when read aloud. The most famous historical version of the Grimm folk tales is probably *Grimm's Fairy Tales*, first published in 1909, with the distinguished illustrations of Arthur Rackham.

Two turn-of-the-century Englishmen are famed for their multi-volume collections of folk tales from many parts of the world, and their versions are still read today. Joseph Jacobs's five volumes began with *English Fairy Tales* (1890) and include *Celtic Fairy Tales* (1892) and *Indian Fairy Tales* (1892). The author attempted to translate the tales authentically, yet with an eye and voice to aid the reader. The other English collector of about the same time was Andrew Lang, whose twelve "color" volumes of folk tales began with *The Blue Fairy Book* (1889) and continued through a number of color titles through 1910. These, too, are worldwide collections, each source briefly identified as a footnote to each story.

In terms of translation, the Wanda Gág versions are no less authentic. The author writes charmingly of her intent in the introduction to this collection, and critic Eleanor Cameron has added detail about the painstaking research and literary endeavor that underlie *Tales From Grimm* (53) and Gág's subsequent *More Tales From Grimm* (54).[1]

You must choose carefully, thinking how you mean to use the collection or single work and for what audience you intend it. Later, you should involve children in the problems of selection. In *A Comparative Anthology of Children's Literature* (55) Mary Ann Nelson has provided nine widely different versions of "Cinderella," including one from ancient Egypt, one from Africa, and a Chinese Cinderella. Seeking to condemn or defend the actions of "Rumpelstiltskin," one group of sixth-graders dug out twelve versions of this tale to document their case!

Modern collections of folk tales invite you to scan for good fare to begin with. Stith Thompson's *One Hundred Favorite Folktales* (56) is limited mainly to European tales, but they are well selected, as you might expect of a scholar whose life work has been the study of folklore. A much wider assortment is found in *A Harvest of World Folk Tales* (57), edited by Milton Rugoff. The typography and sometimes the principles for selection in these collections make them more suitable for the adult, but this may be a good way to start your own collection of folk tales to use with children.

For intermediate-age children, the *Favorite Fairy Tales* series of Virginia Haviland are most readable.[2] The prose is clear and there is a steady pace to the narrative, although you aren't likely to find great variety in style from one volume to another. For the most part, these are tales adapted and abridged from various other published versions.

The collections of Ruth Manning-Sanders can be placed with confidence into the hands of intermediate-age children with interest in a specific topic. Drawn from almost everywhere, the tales are assembled under such interest-catching titles as *A Book of Dwarfs* (1964), *A Book of Wizards* (1966), *A Book of Witches* (1965), *A Book of Dragons* (1964), *A Book of Ghosts and Goblins* (1968), *A Book of Charms and Changelings* (1971), *A Book of Princes and Princesses* (1969), and *A Book of Sorcerers and Spells* (1974). There are many more. (All, with the exception of *A Book of Magical Beasts,* published by Thomas Nelson in 1965, are published by Dutton.)

Collections drawn from one continent, country, or locale are numerous. Sometimes you must be guided by availability rather than a booklist of recommended titles. We will mention a few with brief annotations to give you a beginning. The study of a country's folklore gives you a sense of the spirit and guiding themes of its people. A Near East spirit, for instance, emerges from *Turkish Fairy Tales* (58) by Selma Ekrem, illustrated by Liba Bayrak. Their unvary-

---

[1] Eleanor Cameron, *The Green and Burning Tree* (Little, Brown, 1962, 1969), pp. 311–15.
[2] *Favorite Fairy Tales Told in England* (1959), *Favorite Fairy Tales Told in France* (1959), *Favorite Fairy Tales Told in Germany* (1959), *Favorite Fairy Tales Told in Norway* (1961), and parallel titles for Ireland (1961), Russia (1961), Scotland (1963), Italy (1965), Sweden (1966), Spain (1963), Czechoslovakia (1966), Denmark (1971), and India (1973), all published by Little, Brown. *Favorite Fairy Tales Told in Japan* (1969) is illustrated by George Suyeoka, and a sampling of the series appears in *The Fairy Tale Treasury* (Coward-McCann, 1972).

Illustration from THE FIRE PLUME, edited by John Bierhorst. Illustrated by Alan E. Cober. Copyright ©1969 by Alan E. Cober. Used with permission of The Dial Press.

ing opening—"Once there was and once there was not, in the time before—" is like the unwinding of a spool of priceless stuff. The author comments, "I have tried to write these tales the way my old nurse used to tell them." The *Australian*

Legendary Tales (59), collected by K. Langloh Parker in the nineteenth century, are of the *pourquoi* genre: stories explaining the origin of animals, natural phenomena, and customs. *Men from the Village Deep in the Mountains and Other Japanese Folk Tales* (60), translated and illustrated by Garrett Bang, has exceptional variety in its dozen stories—variety of length, motif, and tone.

Terry Berger's *Black Fairy Tales* (61) are excellent to read or tell. "The Serpent's Bride" has an elaborate underwater setting that deserves the author's own

booklist

European Folk Tales

Brown, Michael, ed. *A Cavalcade of Sea Legends.* Illus. Drystyna Turska. Walck, 1972. Selected stories and ballads from classical, Teutonic and Celtic sources interpreting the mysterious, powerful sea, in poetry, fiction and nonfiction.

D'Aulaire, Ingri and Edgar Parin, tr./illus. *D'Aulaires' Trolls.* Knopf, 1970. Imaginative art and stories tell of Norwegian beliefs and superstitions.

Ginsburg, Mirra, tr. *The Lazies: Tales of the Peoples of Russia.* Adapt. M. Ginsburg. Illus. Marian Parry. Macmillan, 1973. Lazy people and animals are the center of this collection of humorous Russian tales.

Mehdevi, Alexander, reteller. *Bungling Pedro and Other Majorcan Tales.* Illus. Isabel Bodor. Knopf, 1970. Unique to these stories are onomatopoetic sounds as "ki-ki-ketty-ki" and "tup-tup-nyak", used for missing words.

Pugh, Ellen. *More Tales from the Welsh Hills.* Illus. Joan Sandin. Dodd, Mead, 1971. Humorous, adventurous, and ghastly tales set in a Welsh country village. Stylish Welsh speech make these excellent for storytelling and reading aloud.

Quinn, Zdenka and Paul, John. *The Water Sprite of the Golden Town: Folk Tales of Bohemia.* Illus. Deborah Ray. Macrae Smith, 1971. These magic tales of Bohemian princes and princesses, beasts, hunters, and honest men reflect dreamy, mysterious moods of quiet fishing streams, hazy village scenes, and high castles. Excellent for storytelling

Tashjian, Virginia A. *Three Apples Fell From Heaven, Armenian Tales Retold.* Illus. Nonny Hogrogian. Little, Brown, 1971. Armenian tales poking fun at the common people and their weaknesses of laziness, foolishness, greed, and trickery.

Whitney, Thomas P., tr. *In a Certain Kingdom: Twelve Russian Fairy Tales.* Illus. Dieter Lange. Macmillan, 1972. Adventures of golden feathered firebirds, princes disguished as falcons, and others are translated from the tales and legends of the classic Afanasyev collection.

Green, Roger L., ed. *A Cavalcade of Dragons.* Illus. Krystyna Turska. Walck, 1971.

Lundbergh, Holger, tr. *Great Swedish Fairy Tales.* Illus. John Bauer. Delacorte, 1973.

Danaher, Kevin. *Folktales of the Irish Countryside.* Illus. Harold Berson. White, 1970.

Sorche, Nic Leodhas. *Twelve Great Black Cats and Other Eerie Scottish Tales.* Dutton, 1971.

Durham, Mae, ed. *Tit for Tat and Other Latvian Folktales.* Illus. Harriet Pincus. Harcourt, 1967.

Wojciechowska, Maia. *Winter Tales From Poland.* Illus. by Laszlo Kubinyi. Doubleday, 1973.

words. Children with whom we've worked, however, like best the first story in the collection, "The Moss-Green Princess." This tale of a Cinderella-like princess named Kitila, cruelly clothed in the monster skin of the Nya-Nya Bulembu, ought to be told rather than read.[1] The informal, storyteller style of Julius Lester's *Black Folktales* (62) should probably be read aloud. Very readable, brief, and delightful are the ten tales in *Behind the Back of the Mountain: Black Folktales from Southern Africa* (63) retold by Verna Aardema.

A good introduction to some familiar folk figures of the United States is *American Tall Tales* (64) collected by Adrien Stoutenburg. Here we find Paul Bunyan, Pecos Bill, Old Stormalong, and John Henry—not to mention assorted rattlesnakes, "squonks," and feathered floppers. French Canadian stories with

booklist

Folk Tales of North America

Baker, Betty. *At the Center of the World.* Illus. Murray Tinkelman. Macmillan, 1973. A continuous narrative incorporating ancient myths and legends of the Pima and Papago Indian tribes of Southern Arizona and Northern Mexico.

Field, Edward, sel./tr. *Eskimo Songs and Stories.* Illus. Kiakshuk and Pudlo. Delacorte, 1973. Eskimo customs and folklore are intertwined in these tales about creators and elements of sickness, death, and afterlife.

Jones, Hettie, ed. *Longhouse Winter: Iroquois Transformation Tales.* Illus. Nicholas Gaetano. Holt, 1972. The foreword sets the stage for these magical transformation tales. By will or for punishment, Indian characters are given back their lives and transformed into many forms: a robin who welcomes spring, a bride of the ruler of all fish, a despised, hated rattlesnake.

Lester, Julius. *The Knee-High Man and Other Tales.* Illus. Ralph Pinto. Dial, 1972. These six animal tales from American slave lore include the prankster tales of cunning Mr. Rabbit and Mr. Bear, and a pourquoi tale, "Why the Waves Have Whitecaps." Told in colloquial style, good for storytelling.

Carter, Dorothy Sharp, ed. *The Enchanted Orchard and Other Folktales of Central America.* Illus. W. T. Mars. Harcourt, 1973.

Courlander, Harold. *People of the Short Blue Corn: Tales and Legends of the Hopi Indians.* Illus. by Enrico Arno. Harcourt, 1970.

Gillham, Charles Edward. *Medicine Men of Hooper Bay: More Tales from the Clapping Mountains of Alaska.* Illus. Chanimun. Macmillan, 1966.

Harris, Christie. *Once More Upon a Totem.* Illus. Douglas Tait. Atheneum, 1973.

Lyons, Grant. *Tales the People Tell in Mexico.* Illus. Andrew Antal. Messner, 1972.

Reid, Dorothy M. *Tales of Nanobozho.* Illus. Donald Grant. Walck, 1963.

---

[1]Compare it with another African Cinderella-motif tale, *Nomi and the Magic Fish,* retold by fifteen-year-old author Phumla, illus. Carole Byard (Doubleday, 1972).

broad humor are deftly told by Natalie S. Carlson in *The Talking Cat and Other Tales of French Canada* (65). The famed *Jack Tales* (66) and *Grandfather Tales* (67) reveal the wit and wisdom of North Carolina mountaineers.

Recently picture-book artists have turned more and more often to the folk tale as a source of inspiration, using older versions or creating their own but always breathing the life of visual art into the telling. We think that a gem in this group is neglected: Charles Mikolaycak's *Grimm's Golden Goose* (68). Done in browns, ochers, and lavenders in a Renaissance style, the pictures are sweepingly composed. The first shows Simpleton gazing at butterflies while the rest of the family stands away from him making fun of his behavior. A recent picture-book version of *Snow White and the Seven Dwarfs* (69) is unsurpassed for its rich, authentic detail and is likely to be enjoyed for many years to come. Though not basically a picture book, *The Juniper Tree and Other Tales from Grimm* (70) selected by Lori Segal and Maurice Sendak contains illustrations that, in one reviewer's words, "are monuments to intense moments of the author's imagination."[1]

Some folklore begs for humorous illustration, a quality sometimes lacking in over-respectful older versions. Anita Lobel's stupid-looking people, bunched together as if in a dance, are the very essence of Elizabeth Shub's adaptation of *Clever Kate* (71). A Rumpelstiltskin plot as it might be envisioned by Carol Burnett is the subject of Margot Zemach's pen-and-wash Caldecott Medal pictures for *Duffy and the Devil* (72).

Among the most versatile artists in this picture-book-of-folklore field are Marcia Brown and Blair Lent. Marcia Brown's *The Three Billy Goats Gruff* (73) has long-necked, bleary-eyed goats who look like comedians, contrasted with a

booklist

Folk Tales of Australia and the Pacific

Bates, Daisy (Gatson), comp. *Tales told to Kabbarli: Aboriginal Legends.* Ret. Barbara Ker Wilson. Illus. Harold Thomas. Crown, 1972. Barbara Ker Wilson retells these aboriginal Australian tales recorded by Daisy Bates, the white grandmother Kabbarli. Tales display beliefs, culture, and values of the aboriginal tribes.

Thompson, Vivian I., ret. *Hawaiian Tales of Heroes and Champions.*Illus. Herbert Kawainui Kane. Holiday House, 1971. Twelve Polynesian tales recounting the feats of Kapua, the supernatural heroes of old Hawaii, who roamed the islands taking various forms of "shape shifters" who could change from man to shark to rat to bunch of bananas. Writing maintains Hawaiian vocabulary.

Robertson, Dorothy Lewis, ed. *Fairy Tales From the Philippines.* Illus. Howard M. Burns. Dodd, Mead, 1971.

---

[1]Paul Heins, "Review of *The Juniper Tree and Other Tales from Grimm,*" *Horn Book* 50 (April 1974): 136–38.

knotty-legged troll guaranteed to scare the wits out of wiser folk. Her contribution to the Arabian Nights folklore is *The Flying Carpet* (74), so rich in purples, coarse black outlines, and daubs of orange, yellow, and green that it resembles an Oriental rug. Her *Cinderella* (75) and *Once a Mouse* (76) are examples of contrasting art styles to suit contrasting tales, the first an elaborate treatment of a fairy tale, the second a sparse design for a fable.

Blair Lent doesn't attempt to imitate Oriental art in his pictures for *Tikki Tikki Tembo* (77) but brings instead an originality of design and movement to explain the near-drowning of Tikki tikki-tembo-no-sack rembo-chari bar-ruchi-pipperi pembo, who fell down a well and almost didn't get out because no one could pronounce his name fast enough. Lent's Newbery Medal book *The Funny Little Woman* (78) is really a double story told through the pictures. We see the underground adventures of the little woman and at the same time the search for her above ground.

"Tell us a story . . . Read us a story!" say the children. Don't always try to meet that request with a modern short story, for there aren't that many good ones for children of all ages. Nor should you always turn to the long continued book, the novel for children. Instead dip into the folk heritage, share the magic, the tasks and matching inventiveness, the meetings of the wise and foolish, the visions and journeys into other worlds, the trickery and greed offset by wisdom and kindness, the supernatural, and the improbable but intoxicating events of folklore. Even today, they give balance to the literary feast. Eric Quayle observes as he sets out to describe folk tale collections of the past:

> Children have never ceased to enjoy reading fairy tales since the first collection of them appeared in print early in the seventeenth century. They were the first literature for children to escape from the stifling toils of didacticism and were attacked and condemned by the puritanical writers precisely for this reason.[1]

Today when most of that condemnation is past, these stories deserve even more of our time and our love.

Fables

Fables are brief tales, with an acknowledged moral purpose, often peopled by animals, and sometimes including inanimate objects brought to life. Sometimes human beings are in the cast. Whatever the characters, fables concern the everlasting verities—good and evil, wisdom and folly, justice and chicanery.

Although fables do have a moral, either stated or implied, they still thrive, even in an age that disclaims didacticism in its literature. To help you understand why, let's examine the Indian fable, now several thousand years old, about a rabbit and a monkey who decide to trick a man coming along the road with a load of bananas and sugar. The rabbit causes the man to set down his bundle to give chase, and the monkey steals it. But when the rabbit returns, there sits the monkey in a tree, eating the food. The rabbit climbs the tree to see if the

---

[1]Eric Quayle, *The Collector's Book of Children's Books* (Clarkson N. Potter, 1971), p. 36.

food is really gone and he can't get down again. So he flatters an old rhinoceros into standing underneath the tree, then jumps so hard on the rhino's neck that the poor gullible animal dies, whereupon the rabbit, now badly frightened, runs all the way to the king and hides beneath the silken robes—only to be discovered when he sneezes.

"Who dares sneeze in the presence of the king?" demands the king. The rabbit is condemned to death. But trickery is still at work: the rabbit escapes his punishment by telling the king that there's a dead rhinoceros out there whose horn can be ground into fine medicine. The king is so pleased he awards the rabbit a fine robe and a horse.

"Where did you get that fine robe and horse?" asks the monkey, returning to the scene.

"From the king," replies the rabbit, "because I sneezed."

You can guess the rest. The monkey rushes to the king and sneezes in the regal presence and the circle of trickery is completed.[1]

What the definitions can't disclose is the ingenuity of the fable. Each is a little tragedy or comedy with an unswerving theme from which a moral emerges like an egg out of a magician's hat. It's the most painless way of teaching a lesson ever devised.

Nearly all countries claim a fable collection, though the similarities suggest that a great deal of borrowing has taken place. India has some of the oldest and liveliest. Those from the *Panchatantra* (five books) of 200 B.C. and other sources, form the basis of Gaer's *Fables of India* and a nicely told, appropriately illustrated edition, *Tales from India* (79).

The Western world is most familiar with the fables attributed to Aesop, who may or may not have existed. If he did, he lived in Greece about the seventh century B.C. His name means, however, "the man from Ethiopia," and he was probably a slave. If you go to Delphi, your tour guide is sure to show you the steep cliff from which Delphic priests are said to have flung Aesop for doubting the prophecies of the oracle. Most of the fables of Aesop seem to have been borrowed from the folklore of Egypt, Persia, and the Far East.

One difficulty with several otherwise attractive editions of Aesop's fables is that old versions are used for the text, making them abstract and difficult for children. This may be the case with Boris Artzybasheff's collection (80), although the wood engravings are splendid. Through the years these animated tales have inspired many artists, some of whom are represented in *Aesop: Five Centuries of Illustrated Fables* (81), selected by John J. McKendry.

An unusual recent edition, quite readable and illustrated with highly stylized art work, is Jacob Lawrence's *Aesop's Fables* (82). Bright, cartoon-style illustrations intermix with text in *Aesop's Fables* (83), selected and adapted by Louis Untermeyer, with pictures by A. and M. Provensen. This, too, is a very readable

---

[1]Joseph Gaer, "Greedy and Speedy," *The Fables of India* (Little, Brown, 1955), pp. 14–18. This fable is from the *Panchatantra*.

From AESOP'S FABLES, retold by Anne Terry White, illustrated by Helen Siegl. Copyright ©1964 by Anne Terry White. Reprinted by permission of Random House, Inc.

edition. Much of it is recorded with voice and music by Marshall Izen.[1] Poet James Reeves's version, *Fables from Aesop* (84), expands the stories, filling out

[1]Columbia Records, No. CC24501. Write to Columbia Book and Record Library, CBS, Inc., 51 W. 52nd St. New York, N.Y.

characterization with witty conversation. Funniest of all are the very simple tellings and droll drawings of *Fables of Aesop* (85) and *More Fables of Aesop* (86) by Jack Kent.

A French collection of fables—by Jean de la Fontaine in the seventeenth century—draws heavily from Aesop although the author cited the fables of India as his main sources. Richard Scarry's simple version of these, *The Fables of La Fontaine* (87), is humorously illustrated. An important version in poetry form for older children is Marianne Moore's *The Fables of La Fontaine* (88).

Like folk tales, fables have become a source for picture-book artists. Katherine Evans, Paul Galdone, Brian Wildsmith, Marcia Brown, and others have brought their skill to this subtype.

teaching ideas

1. Fables can be introduced early in a child's literary experience. Their brevity and action appeal even when their abstract morals do not. Tell fables as "quick" stories, or as material for dramatization. They also provide an impetus for art work such as cut-outs or paintings. The Untermeyer-Provensen edition, cited above, is especially suitable for this purpose.

2. Older children will recognize that the stated morals are often in the form of proverbs. Since proverbs apply to all times and places, try giving older children a set of proverbs from which to choose, to create their own modern fables. In *Proverbs of Many Nations* (89), compiled and illustrated by Emery Kelen, each page presents several examples based on a common theme:

How Rumors Spread

One dog barks because it sees something; a hundred dogs bark because they heard the first dog bark. (Chinese)
If you pull one pig by the tail, all the rest squeal. (Dutch)
One rooster wakens all the roosters in the village. (German)
If you kick one walnut in the sack, all the rest chatter. (Hungarian)[1]

Now, if you present a page such as this and ask children to create a fable to fit the theme, they will be led to transcend the imagery and look instead at the theme behind the imagery. They will discover the meaning behind the metaphor.

Myths, Legends, and Epics

These stories were intended to bring a unifying spirit to a culture or nation, to bind together past, present, and future. In their oral creation, and in some of their earliest written forms as well, they were meant to be believed.

---

[1]p. 19.

The myth, Stith Thompson tells us, is "a tale laid in a world supposed to have preceded the present order. It tells of sacred beings and of semi-divine heroes and of the origins of all things."[1] The legend is less concerned with origins than with human heroism. It tells, in circumstances based on history but not historically verifiable, how heroes surmounted fear and selfishness to achieve, or be defeated by, a larger purpose. The epic, a sustained narrative often in poetic style, combines elements of myth and legend into a unified story of the workings of gods and heroes to achieve something of value as a symbol of what man might be or become.

In the Chinese myths of the origin of the world, P'an Ku holds the sky above his head as he grows, until earth and sky are far apart. When he dies, his body enriches the earth, his breath becomes the wind and clouds, his eyes become the sun and moon, and his blood flows to become the rivers. In the mythology

booklist

Other Modern Editions of Fables

Three Aesop Fox Fables. Illus. Paul Galdone. Seabury Press, 1971. Bright colors; blank verse helps the reading.

Androcles and the Lion. Illus. Paul Galdone. McGraw-Hill, 1970.

Aesop's Fables. Sel. and illus. Gaynor Chapman. Atheneum, 1971. Brief, but difficult vocabulary. Since the morals are not stated, children might state them, using a set of proverbs and matching them to the stories.

Aesop's Fables. Thomas James and George Tyler Townsend, cols. Illus. Glen Rounds. Lippincott, 1949. (I) Very readable with many examples.

Aesop. *Lions and Lobsters and Foxes and Frogs.* Edward Gorey, col. Illus. Ennis Rees. Young Scott Books, 1971. A verse version with sophisticated cartoons.

Aesop's Fables. Anne Terry White, ed. Illus. Helen Siegl. Random House, 1964. (E) Quite simple, with much narrative.

Montgomerie, Norah, col. and illus. *Twenty-Five Fables.* Abelard-Schuman, 1961. (E) Wide assortment, including fables from Tibet. Much conversation, much expansion on the fable as a literary type.

Cooper, Lee. *Five Fables From France.* Illus. Charles Keeping. Abelard-Schuman, 1970. Combines folk tales and fables, drawn from originals by lesser known authors—Pezard, Lannion, and Levron.

Upadhyay, Asha. *Tales From India.* Random House, 1971. Difficult but inclusive.

The Blue Jackal. Col. and illus. Mehlli Gobhai. Prentice-Hall, 1968. Well-formed tale with bright color and skillful artistry.

---

[1] Stith Thompson, *The Folktale*, p. 9.

of Native Americans the earth is supported on the back of a giant turtle, or by a post in danger of being dislodged by a gnawing beaver, or by the shoulders of a man. The Nigerian goddess Yemonja, mother of rivers, binds the earth together and withstands the abuse of lesser divinities. The Greek gods, grandchildren of heaven and earth, divide and rule the world of the living, the sea, and the underworld of the "piteous" dead.

This is not to say that all myths are of such primal stuff. They also tell of the origins of traits, beliefs, and customs, both animal and human: how the bear learned to hibernate or the squirrel to find buried nuts (Chippewa), or even how a statue came to life at the behest of Aphrodite in order to please a sculptor named Pygmalion (Greek).

In legend, the Frankish hero Roland sounds his horn at the start of hopeless battle, and this call echoes down the centuries. The differing quests of Sir Gawain, Sir Percival, Sir Galahad, and all the others of King Arthur's Round Table weave a net of legend to hold the ideal of knighthood. Chicovaneg, legendary hero of the Indians of Mexico, dons eagle's wings to capture stars to make a new sun. In *Kiviok's Magic Journey: An Eskimo Legend* (90) Kiviok and his snow-goose wife Kungo brave giants and gods in order to be together. The three epic-size tales in Christie Harris's *Once More upon a Totem* (91) show native America of the Pacific Northwest linked to nature through its heroes. Hawaiian heroes—the "shape-shifters" endowed with gifts of magical transformations —overcome evil to save their people.

These fragmentary glimpses of gods and heroes are brought together in the epic, synthesized by a poet genius into a story whose existence invites its own kind of belief. Here the characters magnify a thousand times those traits and emotions that we find in ourselves: the grief and final resolve of Achilles and the desperation of Hector in the *Iliad* of the Greeks, or the determination to make the best of it that seems to characterize the wily Odysseus. The epic plots teem with action, each episode so intricately jigsawed into the others that the most improbable happenings are believable. Theme, in the sense of an author's intent or moral message, seems for the most part nonexistent, except in Virgil's *Aeneid,* which was devised specifically to enhance the stature of the Romans. Instead, the sweep of the epic usually seems to say, "This is the way it was or should have been, and you can make what you will of it!"

To the Western world, the Homeric epics—the *Iliad* and the *Odyssey*—are probably best known. The *Iliad* describes the long seige of Troy, or Ilium, though the specific action of the story tells only the final days of the battle. The *Odyssey* describes its hero's ten-year journey from Troy back to his homeland, the island of Ithaca west of the Greek mainland. But it is also the story of Odysseus's son Telemachus, who must set out to find his father, and of the homecoming itself, when Odysseus must defeat his wife's suitors. Both epics are set within a context of the workings of the gods and of huge frameworks of incidents presumed to be known to the audience and only partially told within the stories themselves. Reading them or hearing them, you feel yourself a part of an ancient Greek community, where countless myths and legends are considered familiar.

The Hindu epic *Ramayana* of India has recently become more available to children. It begins like a fairy tale, with its hero Rama (whose name means Great Delight) winning the hand of Princess Sita. But Rama and Sita are soon banished from the kingdom to live (more happily than you might expect) in the deep forests. This idyll is interrupted by battles and Sita's abduction in a flying chariot driven by Ravana, the King of Giants. How Rama is aided by a kingdom of monkeys in slaying the giants and rescuing his princess forms the rest of the story. There is magic in it, as well as religious teaching, but the dominant spirit is that of simple human kindness embodied in the love of Rama and Sita and the faithfulness of their companion, Rama's brother Lakshman.

The oldest epic known to the world may be that of *Gilgamesh,* the story of a king of the Sumerians in the land that became Babylonia. The hero's search for immortality and his subsequent visit to the land of the dead are, in our experience, the finest, clearest episodes for introducing epics to intermediate-age and older children.

The Norse *Volsung Saga* and the German *Nibelungenlied* are epics of Sigurd, or Siegfried. But he is only the human hero whose bravery and final defeat through trickery are the will of the gods. The adventures of the gods make up the major part of the stories in most versions for children. The oldest epic in English is *Beowulf.* This gory tale, describing the hero's fights with the monster Grendel and Grendel's mother, has a clarity of plot that is sometimes less apparent in larger epics. There are some good versions for children.

For the child who falls in love with epic—or the adult who discovers that epic serves him or her well in continued storytelling to children—there are many lesser known but powerful works at hand. The Persian epic of Rustam (original version *Shah Namah* by Firdausi), the Japanese epic of Yoshitsune, recently made available in a children's edition, and various others can be located in the sources mentioned in chapter 1. The Bible can be viewed as epic, and its inclusion as an epic type enhances its beauty and historical significance.

MODERN ADAPTATIONS OF MYTHS, LEGENDS, AND EPICS.   The modern author's task in adapting myths, legends, or epics for children is difficult. He must be a good storyteller, able to capture and hold the interest of children in what may be an unfamiliar setting and form. He must decide whether to tell the story in a familiar style, as if it were a sort of everyday adventure, or whether to risk stylized language in keeping with the often elaborate style of poets and early storytellers.

Selecting the right version for the children you teach is also difficult. If there are several to choose from, you may wish to dip into each and compare specific passages before selecting. Children who love the story may devour several versions anyway.

We will suggest a few outstanding selections here and comment on them and simply list a few others. Almost every year brings the publication of several new versions of these tales. Each new issue of *Hornbook* provides you with careful reviews in the "Booklist" section.

Older versions of the Greek and Roman myths include Thomas Bulfinch's *Mythology,* first published as three books: *The Age of the Fable* (1855), *The Age of Chivalry* (1858), and *Legends of Charlemagne* (1863). A recent edition, *Bulfinch's Mythology* (92), is difficult reading but a good source book. Charles Kingsley's *The Heroes* and Nathaniel Hawthorne's *The Wonder Book* are both highly praised, the first for its music and rhythm of style, the second for the author's inventions to enliven the stories. Various editions of these two classics are available in most libraries.

A frequently read version of the Greek myths, *Stories of the Gods and Heroes* (93) by Sally Benson, is based on the Bulfinch work, but simplified and shortened. Tom Galt's *The Rise of the Thunderer* (94) is even simpler, perhaps cutting the gods down too closely to human size, but it is a highly readable version. Two popular picture-book versions which give clarity to setting are *D'Aulaire's Book of Greek Myths* (95) by Ingri and Edgar Parin D'Aulaire and *The Golden Treasury of Myths and Legends* (96) by Anne Terry White, illustrated by Alice and Martin Provensen. The latter includes Celtic, Persian, French, and Norse tales as well.

Greek Myths (97) by Olivia Coolidge retains the complexity of the stories but is told in a clear style. More recently, Doris Gates, an experienced children's author, has begun a series of graphic retellings of Greek tales: *Lord of the Sky: Zeus* (98), *The Warrior Goddess: Athena* (99), and others.

One new version of the Greek myths is different from all the others. It reads like a scenario with thoughts and motives filled in. Its style is often elaborate —you can almost see the storyteller beating his fist on the table and hear him raise his voice—but it is never long-winded, as some of the older versions are. The language is fairly easy, but it holds nothing back:

> Wild of aspect and terrible in her anguish, the great goddess stood before her greater brother on the rocky steeps of high Olympus. The clouds trembled and the stars crept frightened into their holes as Demeter cursed the sky that had looked down on the rape of her child by Hades, hateful god of the dead.[1]

This version, though not difficult, is not for the faint-hearted. *The God Beneath the Sea* (100) by Leon Garfield and Edward Blishen was originally published in England, where it won the Carnegie Medal (the English equivalent of the Newbery Medal). It was followed by an even more dramatic sequel, *The Golden Shadow* (101), with the original Keeping illustrations. These are monumental works, ranking with the best modern versions of myths, legends, and epics.

Many artists have singled out myths for picture-book treatment. *Persephone and the Springtime* (102), retold by Margaret Hodges and featuring Arvis Stewart's tantalizing line drawings washed with pale color, is an exciting addition to the myth-into-picture-book type. (It is part of the author's Myths of the World series.) The style is well suited to reading aloud.

Artist Barbara Cooney went to Greece to get the right background for *Hermes, Lord of Robbers* (103) and *Demeter and Persephone* (104). Cooney's painting is best in

---

[1]Longmans edition, p. 122.

Everyone, everywhere, loves the springtime. The ancient Greeks said that spring was a beautiful young girl. Her name was Persephone and she always followed in the footsteps of her mother, Demeter, the earth goddess.

Demeter loved the singing birds, and the poppies blowing in the fields of wheat. She took care of the crops in summer, and in the autumn she gathered in the golden harvest. She watched over her child with tender care. Demeter was happy all year long and in those first days of the world there was no winter. But one terrible year the springtime was lost.

From PERSEPHONE AND THE SPRINGTIME by Margaret Hodges, illustrated by Arvis Stewart, by permission of Little, Brown and Co. and the author's agent, Caroline S. Lehman. Text copyright ©1973 by Margaret Hodges. Illustrations copyright ©1973 by Arvis Stewart. This illustration originally appeared in color.

showing textures—countrysides, buildings, garments—and carefully selected details. These qualities make her *Hermes and Apollo* work the better of the two books, for it makes greater use of the contrasting light and shadow of the landscape. How Greek myth personifies the constellations is told in *Stars—Their Facts and Legends* (105) by Florence Armstrong Grondal. Issac Asimov's *Words from the Myths* (106) presents mythology's contributions to the English language.

Some of the books cited above go beyond the myths to tell parts of the Greek epic. Olivia Coolidge's *Greek Myths* was followed by *Trojan War* (107). If you and your children delve long into the epics, you will soon want many versions, taking delight in your own discoveries.

The Norse myths and epics are less frequently adapted for children. Dorothy Hosford's *Sons of the Volsungs* (108) tells the youthful and tragic tale of Sigurd, and her *Thunder of the Gods* (109) is wonderful for reading aloud. Both Olivia Coolidge and, earlier, Padraic Colum, have treated the Norse gods and heroes in their narratives. Barbara Leonie Picard's *Norse Gods and Heroes* (110) is a no-nonsense, difficult version, and for these reasons it may have special appeal for certain children. A very popular picture-book edition is *Norse Gods and Giants* (111) by Ingri and Edgar Parin D'Aulaire.

Books of King Arthur, the Once and Future King, are numerous enough to give you a fair variety of selection, though we wonder as we read them whether the classic version of this story is yet to be written for children. Most experts seem to prefer Sidney Lanier's treatment of the Malory epic, accompanied by the great paintings of N. C. Wyeth in *The Boy's King Arthur* (112). The language, though, is often archaic: "full woe am I of thy departing" and "I am right heavy of your hurts." Also well known is Howard Pyle's *The Story of King Arthur and His Knights* (113). *Stories of King Arthur and His Knights* (114) by Barbara Leonie Picard is more readable for children today. The briefer adventures of the knights are told in a somewhat light-hearted manner by Constance Hicatt in *Sir Gawain and the Green Knight* (115), *The Sword and the Grail* (116), and *The Castle of Ladies* (117). A nonfiction book called *The Search for King Arthur* (118) by Christopher Hibbert makes an interesting companion volume to any of the narratives of Arthurian legends or epic.

The Ramayana is told in simple style by Joseph Gaer in *The Adventures of Rama* (119). Elizabeth Seeger's *The Ramayana* (120) has a slow beginning which you may want to tell briefly, but once the narrative starts rolling, you should read it aloud, all of it. Its prose has the ring of epic—of monumental, well-remembered events clothed in the best of language. Another Indian epic, the Mahabharata, is retold by the same author under the title *The Five Sons of King Pandu* (121).

The story of Beowulf appears in various editions that invite comparison. Ian Serraillier's *Beowulf the Warrior* (122) retains some of the alliteration of the original and adds iambic meter. The following passage recounts the height of the struggle between the hero and the monster Grendel in the mead-hall:

Spilling the benches,
They tugged and heaved, from wall to wall they hurtled.
And the roof rang to their shouting, the huge hall
Rocked, the strong foundations groaned and trembled.[1]

booklist

Other Versions of Greek Epics

Cox, Miriam. *The Magic and the Sword.* Illus. Harold Price. Row, Peterson, 1956. (I) Semi-textbook form with a running commentary about vocabulary and the significance of events. Proper names are given a pronunciation key in parentheses within the text.

Green, Roger Lancelyn. *Heroes of Greece and Troy.* Walck, 1961. (I-U) Fairly difficult but highly skilled retelling.

McLean, Mollie and Wiseman, Anne. *Adventures of the Greek Heroes.* Illus. W. T. Mars. Houghton Mifflin, 1961. (E-I) Notable for its simplicity, this book can be read by low intermediates, yet it is very inclusive.

[1] p.13.

Rosemary Sutcliff's *Beowulf* (123) treats the same incident in prose in this way: "Trestles and sleeping benches went over with crash on crash as they strained this way and that, trampling even through the last red embers of the dying fire; and the very walls seemed to groan and shudder as though the stout timbers would burst apart."[1] In a third version by Robert Nye, *Beowulf: A New Telling* (124), illustrated by Alan E. Cober, the emphasis is on Grendel's towering rage: "Hall Heorot rocked down to its stone roots with the rage of the demon's struggling."[2] Comparisons such as these show how much of the effect of epic is controlled by the teller, and how greatly adaptations can vary.

Briefer heroic tales referred to in the preceding discussion include *Warlord of the Genji* (125), the story of Yoshitsune of Japan, B. Traven's distinguished retelling of the Mexican legend of Chicovaneg, *The Creation of the Sun and the Moon* (126), and *Chinese Myths and Fantasies* (127), retold by Cyril Birch.

Bible selections in the King James language are presented in free verse form in *God and His People* (128), edited by Harold Bassage, and in the Revised Standard Version language, beautifully illustrated by Lynd Ward in *Bible Readings for Boys and Girls* (129). Another recent edition retold by Philip Turner and accompanied by distinguished art work is *Brian Wildsmith's Illustrated Bible Stories* (130).

Teaching Folk Literature

You may ask whether these stories, some of them arising from primitive cultures, have been outgrown by modern civilization. They are often violent, and their ways of explaining the world are notably unscientific. Their heroes often prevail through brute force and downright dishonesty. Are they, then, still suitable? Do they have something worthwhile to offer? We think they do.

booklist

Short Tales of Biblical Heroes

Petersham, Maud and Miska. *David* and *Joseph and His Brothers*. Macmillan, 1958. (E-I)
Bulla, Clyde Robert. *Jonah and the Great Fish*. Illus. Helga Aichinger. Crowell, 1970. (E-I)
———. *Joseph the Dreamer*. Illus. Gordon Laite. Crowell, 1971. (E-I)
Shadrach, Meshach and Abednego. Illus. Paul Galdone. McGraw-Hill, 1965. (E-I) From the King James version of the Book of Daniel, illustrated in magnificent yellow and gold.
Graham, Lorenz. *Every Man Heart Lay Down*. Illus. Colleen Browning. Crowell, 1946, 1970. (E-I) A black version of the story of Jesus.
———. *David He No Fear*. Illus. Ann Grifalconi. Crowell, 1946, 1971. (E-I) A companion volume, also with black characters.

---

[1] p. 37.
[2] p. 49.

From Beowulf: A New Telling by Robert Nye, illustrated by Alan E. Cober, by permission of Farrar, Straus & Giroux, Inc. Copyright ©1968 by Robert Nye.

First of all, it isn't likely that children will emulate the heroes of folk literature, except in their play. The worlds of folk heroes are set apart from our own world, but there is reassurance in these other worlds. The heroes (especially epic heroes) are sorely tried. They may make grave mistakes and sometimes falter, but they struggle on, rising above human failings, and remaining to the end "bloody but unbowed."

The trickery and violence often found in folklore are balanced by ageless, desirable human qualities: kindness and devotion to friends, loyalty to causes, and, above all, a zest for life. The hero, whatever his shortcomings, embraces life in an effort to work out his own identity, to become whatever he is capable of becoming. Within this framework, the means by which he makes his quest are sometimes seen to be the only means at his disposal, or they are culturally determined behavior, sometimes dictated by the gods or other supernatural powers.

In the end, these stories reach the level of allegory. The good survive or accept a mission, performing it against great odds, or they attempt to transcend human frailty. The bad are personified in the monsters, the unfriendly elements, and sometimes in man himself. But the allegorical level is never presented in an abstract manner. Folk literature doesn't stop to sermonize. The action moves on in brilliant display, and readers can interpret at whatever level they wish.

No child in modern cultures is likely to believe a folk tale, a fable, a myth, or an epic—not literally. Yet, in an aesthetic realm, these stories are to be believed. They exist, and therefore someone has invented them. To believe in the human power to invent the forms and their content is to believe in humanity's great capability to create.

At the outset, these may not appear to be persuasive reasons for presenting folk literature. But when you read these stories to your children, you are likely to find the reasons real enough. Folklore does fire the imagination. Children do ask for more. Those are finally the persuasive reasons.

Many of the examples and editions we've mentioned need little more than good reading aloud. This applies especially to shorter stories, such as folk tales and fables. If you can tell them, all the better. Longer stories, especially the epic, often require summarizing. You might, for instance, mark a copy of the story of King Arthur and his knights to indicate stretches of narrative that are better told, reserving crucial scenes for the more leisurely or dramatic pace of reading aloud. Sometimes, as with the Odyssey, you may need to give narrative background before beginning the story. (Here you can rely on adult versions presenting summaries, such as Edith Hamilton's *Mythology,* published by Little, Brown in 1940 and 1942.)

Informational materials accompanying your reading or telling of folk literature will help lend a sense of place and time. The look of Odysseus's ships and the weapons used in the contest with the suitors help children visualize the story. The walls built by Gilgamesh and even the clay tablets on which his story was written fuel the imagination. Information about Stonehenge, conjecture about this monument's origin and ancient use, enlivens the legend of Merlin's

part in building it. There is every reason to use one literary type—in this case, nonfiction—to aid another.

Virtually all art forms have been used to explore and interpret folk literature: opera, orchestral composition, songs, paintings, sculpture, drama, film, dance, poetry, the novel with a modern setting, and even the lowly comic book. Children in literature—including Booth Tarkington's Penrod, Tom Sawyer, and the modern children of the Green Knowe series—read and act out folk literature. You can encourage such response, not with a peremptory "Go draw a picture of the story" but with a lively discussion of the possibilities for transforming a story into another art form. Pantomime is a good way to begin and will gradually develop into spoken as well as acted drama. Striking visual imagery, such as that of the episodes in the African tales of *Zomo the Rabbit* (131), may legitimately lead to cartoon-drawing or colorful painting. A song or poem composed to celebrate or sustain the attention—Demeter's search for her daughter Persephone, the triumph of the musicians of Bremen[1]—is sometimes surprisingly within the capabilities of children who would balk at trying to create music or verse about more familiar topics.

special activities

1. Folk literature has arisen from cultures of the past. What sort of folk literature do we have today? What can you cite from television, from cartoon strips, and other sources that might fit the folk literature category in years to come?

2. Many longer items in folk literature are episodic. After reading such works, think of additional incidents that could be created, retaining the tone and intent of the works. Brainstorm ideas through which additional incidents might be created.

3. Certain universals have been found in folk tales of many cultures. A recurring theme or motif often appears, for example, wish-fulfillment, *pourquoi* or origins, and compensation. First, think of well-known tales that illustrate these motifs. Then, examine folk literature of other cultures less familiar to you. Can you spot such motifs in these tales? Finally, can you find the same motifs in today's literature? Cite examples. Why do such motifs recur? What do they tell us about literature and its purposes?

4. The list of distinguished picture-book artists is long. We can't begin to cite them all here. The following is a partial list of artists whose works will give pleasure to reading and examining picture books. Select several and explore their works; then share your findings with classmates.

---

[1]See Wanda Gág, "The Musicians of Bremen," in *Tales from Grimm* (Coward-McCann, 1936), pp. 87–97.

Picture-Book Artists

Adrienne Adams
L. Leslie Brooke
Virginia Lee Burton
Walter Crane
Jean de Brunhoff
Ed Emberley
Don Freeman
Edward Gorey
Berta and Elmer Hader
Nonny Hogrogian
Robert Lawson
Arnold Lobel
Gerald McDermott
Charles Mikolaycak
Evaline Ness
Celestino Piatti
Beatrix Potter
John Schoenherr
Uri Shulevitz
William Steig
N. C. Wyeth

Edward Ardizzone
Marcia Brown
Randolph Caldecott
Ingri and Edgar d'Aulaire
Laurent de Brunhoff
Marie Hall Ets
Wanda Gág
Hardie Gramatky
Gail E. Haley
Pat Hutchins
Lois Lenski
Mercer Mayer
Beni Montresor
Blair Lent
Harriet Pincus
Arthur Rackham
Maurice Sendak
Louis Slobodkin
Sir John Tenniel
Leonard Weisgard
Taro Yashima

Ludwig Bemelmans
John Burningham
Barbara Cooney
Marguerite de Angeli
Roger Duvoisin
Françoise
Paul Galdone
Kate Greenaway
Syd Hoff
Ezra Jack Keats
Leo Lionni
Robert McCloskey
Bruno Munari
Helen Oxenbury
Leo Politi
Feodor Rojankovsky
Ernest Shephard
Marc Simont
Tomi Ungerer
Brian Wildsmith
Harve and Margot Zemach

teaching ideas

1. Folk tales are filled with clear plots and lively action. Select one to use in a a story theater presentation. For story theater you need a reader and several actors. As the reader reads the story, the actors play what they hear. They mime the action and the meaning of the speeches. They even mime the scenery—for instance, a ship can be simulated by several actors joining hands. Critique the result and play it again, adding new mimes to make it come alive. When the session is completed, discuss the outcome in terms of oral reading, listening, and psycho-motor activity.

2. Collect from picture books illustrations that show the variety used by artists to depict certain items: a tree, a specific animal, a mood. Ask children to pose as the artists, explaining why they created pictures for their effects.

3. Tell a folk tale. First, read it carefully. Second, outline the scenes necessary for imparting the story. Use your own words, but try to recapture the tone of the tale. Practice a few times and then tell the tale to an audience, noting their reactions.

4. Longer folk literature, including legends and epics, can be introduced by taping a single incident, with a brief introduction to characters and setting. Outline your presentation, then tape it on a cassette and make it available to children who might be interested in reading the entire work.

CHAPTER REFERENCES

1. Hoke, Helen. *Witches Witches Witches.* Watts, 1958.
2. Sendak, Maurice. *Higglety Pigglety Pop!* Harper, 1967.
3. Southall, Ivan. *Josh.* Macmillan, 1971.
4. Montresor, Beni. *May I Bring a Friend?* Atheneum, 1964. (E-I)
5. Alexander, Lloyd. *The King's Fountain.* Illus. Ezra Jack Keats. Dutton, 1971. (I)
6. Sleator, William. *The Angry Moon.* Illus. Blair Lent. Little, Brown, 1970. (E-I)
7. Brown, Marcia. *Once a Mouse.* Scribner's, 1961. (E-I)
8. Hutchins, Pat. *Rosie's Walk.* Macmillan, 1968. (E)
9. Miles, Miska. *Nobody's Cat.* Illus. John Schoenherr. Little, Brown, 1969. (E-I)
10. Flack, Marjorie. *The Story about Ping.* Illus. Kurt Wiese. Viking, 1933. (E)
11. Caldecott, Randolph, comp. *R. Caldecott's Picture Books.* Warne, 1878–1885. (E)
12. McCloskey, Robert. *Make Way for Ducklings.* Viking, 1941. (E-I)
13. Kraus, Robert. *Milton the Early Riser.* Illus. Jose and Ariane Aruego. Windmill, 1972. (E)
14. Geisel, Theodor Seuss [Dr. Seuss]. *And to Think That I Saw It on Mulberry Street.* Vanguard, 1937. (E-I)
15. _____. *The 500 Hats of Bartholomew Cubbins.* Vanguard, 1938. (E-I)
16. Ness, Evaline. *Sam, Bangs & Moonshine.* Holt, 1966. (E-I)
17. _____. *Tom Tit Tot.* Scribner's, 1965. (E-I)
18. Wahl, Jan. *Push Kitty.* Illus. Garth Williams. Harper, 1968. (E-I)
19. Hogrogian, Nonny. *Rooster Brother.* Macmillan, 1974. (E-I)
20. Scarry, Richard. *What Do People Do All Day?* Random, 1968. (E)
21. _____. *Richard Scarry's Great Big Schoolhouse.* Random, 1969. (E)
22. Françoise. *The Things I Like.* Scribner's, 1960. (E)
23. Janus, Grete. *Teddy.* Illus. Roger Duvoisin. Lothrop, Lee, 1964. (E)
24. Brooke, L. Leslie. *Ring O'Roses.* Warne, 1923.
25. Tudor, Tasha. *Mother Goose.* Walck, 1944. (E)
26. Baskin, Leonard. *Hosie's Alphabet.* Viking, 1972. (E)
27. Montresor, Beni. *A for Angel.* Knopf, 1969. (E)
28. _____. *I Saw a Ship A-Sailing.* Knopf, 1967. (E)
29. Bemelmans, Ludwig. *Madeline.* Viking, 1939.
30. Burton, Virginia Lee. *The Little House.* Houghton, 1942.
31. Brown, Margaret Wise [Golden MacDonald]. *The Little Island.* Illus. Leonard Weisgard. Doubleday, 1946.
32. Krahn, Fernando. *How Santa Had a Long and Difficult Journey Delivering His Presents.* Delacorte, 1970. (E)
33. Carroll, Ruth. *What Whiskers Did.* Walck, 1932, 1965. (E)

34. Hutchins, Pat. *Changes, Changes.* Macmillan, 1971. (E)
35. Geisel, Theodor Seuss [Dr. Seuss]. *Green Eggs and Ham.* Random, 1956. (E)
36. Berenstain, Stan and Jan. *Bears in the Night.* Random, 1971. (E)
37. Hoban, Lillian. *Arthur's Honey Bear.* Harper, 1974. (E)
38. Steptoe, John. *Stevie.* Harper, 1969. (I-U)
39. Bishop, Elizabeth. *The Ballad of the Burglar of Babylon.* Illus. Ann Grifalconi. Farrar, 1968. (U)
40. Addams, Charles. *Charles Addams Mother Goose.* Harper, 1967. (I-U)
41. Lawrence, Jacob. *Harriet and the Promised Land.* Windmill, 1968; Simon and Shuster, 1969. (E-I)
42. Bolognese, Don. *A New Day.* Delacorte, 1970. (I)
43. Mistral, Gabriela. *The Elephant and His Secret.* English text, Doris Dana. Illus. Antonio Franconi. Atheneum, 1974. (I)
44. Raskin, Ellen, *Franklin Stein.* Atheneum, 1972. (I)
45. Prelutsky, Jack. *Circus.* Illus. Arnold Lobel. Macmillan, 1974. (I)
46. Flack, Marjorie. *Angus and the Ducks.* Doubleday, 1930. (E)
47. _____. *Angus Lost.* Doubleday, 1932. (E)
48. _____. *Angus and the Cat.* Doubleday, 1931. (E)
49. Sendak, Maurice. *Where the Wild Things Are.* Harper, 1963. (E)
50. Scheer, Julian. *Rain Makes Applesauce.* Illus. Marvin Bileck. Holiday, 1964. (E-I)
51. Emberley, Barbara, adapt. *Drummer Hoff.* Illus. Ed Emberley. Prentice-Hall, 1967. (E)
52. McPhail, David. *On, No, Go (A Play).* Little, Brown, 1973. (E-I)
53. Gág, Wanda. *Tales from Grimm.* Coward-McCann, 1936.
54. _____. *More Tales from Grimm.* Coward-McCann, 1947.
55. Nelson, Mary Ann, ed. *A Comparative Anthology of Children's Literature.* Holt, 1972.
56. Thompson, Stith, sel. *One Hundred Favorite Folktales.* Indiana Univ. Press, 1968.
57. Rugoff, Milton, ed. *A Harvest of World Folk Tales.* Viking, 1949.
58. Ekrem, Selma. *Turkish Fairy Tales.* Illus. Liba Bayrak. Van Nostrand, 1964. (I)
59. Parker, K. Langloh, coll. *Australian Legendary Tales.* Ed. H. Drake-Brockman. Viking, 1966.
60. Bang, Garrett, trans. and illus. *Men from the Village Deep in the Mountains and Other Japanese Folk Tales.* Macmillan, 1973.
61. Berger, Terry. *Black Fairy Tales.* Atheneum, 1969.
62. Lester, Julius. *Black Folktales.* Illus. Tom Feelings. Richard W. Baron, 1969.
63. Aardema, Verna. *Behind the Back of the Mountain: Black Folktales from Southern Africa.* Illus. Leo and Diane Dillon. Dial, 1973.
64. Stoutenburg, Adrien, coll. *American Tall Tales.* Viking, 1966.
65. Carlson, Natalie S. *The Talking Cat and Other Tales of French Canada.* Illus. Roger Duvoisin. Harper, 1952.
66. Chase, Richard. *Jack Tales.* Houghton Mifflin, 1942.
67. _____. *Grandfather Tales.* Houghton Mifflin, 1948.
68. Mikolaycak, Charles. *Grimm's Golden Goose.* Random, 1969.
69. Jarrell, Randall, trans. *Snow White and the Seven Dwarfs.* Illus. Nancy Ekholm Burkert. Farrar, Straus, 1972.
70. Segal, Lori, and Sendak, Maurice, sel. *The Juniper Tree and other Tales from Grimm.* Illus. Maurice Sendak. Farrar, Straus, 1973. (U)
71. Shub, Elizabeth, adapt. *Clever Kate.* Macmillan, 1973.
72. Zemach, Harve. *Duffy and the Devil.* Illus. Margot Zemach. Farrar, Straus, 1973.
73. *The Three Billy Goats Gruff.* Illus. Marcia Brown. Harcourt, 1957.
74. *The Flying Carpet.* Illus. Marcia Brown. Scribner's, 1956.
75. *Cinderella.* Illus. Marcia Brown. Scribner's, 1954.
76. *Once a Mouse.* Illus. Marcia Brown. Scribner's, 1961.
77. Mosel, Arlene. *Tikki Tikki Tembo.* Illus. Blair Lent. Dutton, 1968.

78. _____. *The Funny Little Woman.* Illus. Blair Lent. Dutton, 1972.

79. Upadhyay, Asha. *Tales from India.* Illus. Nickzad Nodjoumi. Random, 1971.

80. Artzybasheff, Boris, coll. *Aesop's Fables.* Viking, 1933.

81. McKendry, John J., sel. *Aesop: Five Centuries of Illustrated Fables.* Metropolitan Museum of Art, 1964.

82. Lawrence, Jacob. *Aesop's Fables.* Windmill, 1970.

83. Untermeyer, Louis, sel. and adapt. *Aesop's Fables.* Illus. A. and M. Provensen. Golden, 1965.

84. Reeves, James. *Fables from Aesop.* Illus. Maurice Wilson. Walck, 1962.

85. *Fables of Aesop.* Illus. Jack Kent. Pantheon, 1973.

86. *More Fables of Aesop.* Illus. Jack Kent. Pantheon, 1974.

87. Scarry, Richard. *The Fables of La Fontaine.* Doubleday, 1963.

88. Moore, Marianne. *The Fables of La Fontaine.* Viking, 1954.

89. Kelen, Emery, comp. and illus. *Proverbs of Many Nations.* Lothrop, Lee, 1966.

90. Houston, James. *Kiviok's Magic Journey: An Eskimo Legend.* Atheneum, 1973.

91. Harris, Christie. *Once More Upon a Totem.* Illus. Douglas Tait. Atheneum, 1973.

92. Bulfinch, Thomas. *Bulfinch's Mythology.* Thomas Y. Crowell, 1970.

93. Benson, Sally. *Stories of the Gods and Heroes.* Illus. Steele Savage. Dial, 1940.

94. Galt, Tom. *The Rise of the Thunderer.* Illus. John Mackey. Crowell, 1954. (I)

95. D'Aulaire, Ingri and Edgar Parin. *D'Aulaires' Book of Greek Myths.* Doubleday, 1962. (E-I)

96. White, Anne Terry. *The Golden Treasury of Myths and Legends.* Illus. Alice and Martin Provensen. Golden, 1959. (E-I)

97. Coolidge, Olivia. *Greek Myths.* Illus. Eduoard Sandoz. Houghton Mifflin, 1949. (I-U)

98. Gates, Doris. *Lord of the Sky: Zeus.* Illus. Robert Handville. Viking, 1972. (I)

99. _____. *The Warrior Goddess: Athena.* Illus. Don Bolognese. Viking, 1972. (I)

100. Garfield, Leon, and Blishen, Edward. *The God beneath the Sea.* Illus. Charles Keeping. Pantheon, 1971.

101. _____. *The Golden Shadow.* Illus. Charles Keeping. Pantheon, 1973.

102. Hodges, Margaret. *Persephone and the Springtime.* Illus. Arvis Stewart. Little, Brown, 1973. (E-I)

103. Proddow, Penelope. *Hermes, Lord of Robbers.* Illus. Barbara Cooney. Doubleday, 1971.

104. _____. *Demeter and Persephone.* Illus. Barbara Cooney. Doubleday, 1972.

105. Grondal, Florence Armstrong. *Stars—Their Facts and Legends.* Illus. Ralston Crawford. Garden City, 1940. (I-U)

106. Asimov, Isaac. *Words from the Myths.* Illus. William Barss. Houghton Mifflin, 1961. (I-U)

107. Coolidge, Olivia. *Trojan War.* Illus. Eduoard Sandoz. Houghton Mifflin, 1952. (I)

108. Hosford, Dorothy. *Songs of the Volsungs.* Illus. Frank Dobias. Holt, 1949. (I-U)

109. _____. *Thunder of the Gods.* Illus. Louden. Holt, 1952. (I-U)

110. Picard, Barbara Leonie. *Norse Gods and Heroes.* Illus. Joan Kiddell-Monroe. Oxford, 1953. (U)

111. D'Aulaire, Ingri and Edgar Parin. *Norse Gods and Giants.* Doubleday, 1967.

112. Lanier, Sidney, *The Boy's King Arthur.* Illus. N. C. Wyeth. Scribner's, 1952. (U)

113. Pyle, Howard. *The Story of King Arthur and His Knights.* Scribner's, 1903.

114. Picard, Barbara Leonie. *Stories of King Arthur and His Knights.* Illus. Roy Morgan. Oxford, 1955. (U)

115. Hicatt, Constance. *Sir Gawain and the Green Knight.* Illus. Walter Lorraine. Crowell, 1967. (I)

116. _____. *The Sword and the Grail.* Illus. David Palladini. Crowell, 1972. (I)

117. _____. *The Castle of Ladies.* Illus. Norman Laliberte. Crowell, 1973. (I)

118. Hibbert, Christopher. *The Search for King Arthur.* Horizon Caravel Book series, Harper, 1969. (I-U)

119. Gaer, Joseph. *The Adventures of Rama.* Illus. Randy Monk. Little, Brown, 1954. (I)
120. Seeger, Elizabeth. *The Ramayana.* Illus. Gordon Laite. William R. Scott, 1969. (I-U)
121. ————. *The Five Sons of King Pandu.* Illus. Gordon Laite. Scott, 1967.
122. Serraillier, Ian. *Beowulf the Warrior.* Illus. Severin. Walck, 1961. (I-U)
123. Sutcliff, Rosemary. *Beowulf.* Illus. Charles Keeping. Dutton, 1961. (I-U)
124. Nye, Robert. *Beowulf: A New Telling.* Illus. Alan E. Cober. Hill and Wang, 1968. (I-U)
125. Carlson, Dale. *Warlord of the Genji.* Illus. John Gretzer. Atheneum, 1970. (I-U)
126. Traven, B. *The Creation of the Sun and the Moon.* Illus. Alberto Beltran. Hill and Wang, 1968. (I)
127. Birch, Cyril. *Chinese Myths and Fantasies.* Illlus. Joan Kiddell-Monroe. Walck, 1961. (I-U)
128. Bassage, Harold, ed. *God and His People.* Illus. Clark B. Fitzgerald. Seabury, 1966.
129. *Bible Readings for Boys and Girls.* Illus. Lynd Ward. Thomas Nelson, 1959.
130. Turner, Philip. *Brian Wildsmith's Illustrated Bible Stories.* Watts, 1968, 1969.
131. Surton, High, coll. *Zomo the Rabbit.* Illus. Peter Warner. Atheneum, 1966. (E-I)

BIBLIOGRAPHY

Cianciolo, Patricia Jean. "Use Wordless Picture Books to Teach Reading, Visual Literacy and to Study Literature." *Top of the News,* 29 April 1973, pp. 226–35. Interesting analysis, with many examples, of the contribution of this picture book type.

Colwell, Eileen. "Folk Literature—An Oral Tradition and an Oral Art." *Top of the News,* 24 January 1968, pp. 175–80. The oral basis of this literary tradition, with implications for the best way to present folk tales.

Dill, Barbara. "Picture Books for Children." *Wilson Library Bulletin,* 48 January 1974, pp. 380+. The first in a series of columns evaluating picture books and including tips on how to use these books with children.

Groff, Patrick. "Children's Literature Versus Wordless 'Books.'" *Top of the News,* 30 April 1974, pp. 294–303. The author believes that alleged "visual literacy" gains through wordless books are damaging to a child's concept of reading.

Hopkins, Lee Bennett, and Arenstein, Misha. "From Apple Pie to Zooplankton: A Selected List of Alphabet Books for Use in the Elementary Grades." *Elementary English,* 48 November 1971, pp. 788–92. Cleverly assembled review of twenty-six alphabet books.

Kamenetsky, Christa. "The Brothers Grimm: Folktale Style and Romantic Theories." *Elementary English,* 51 March 1974, pp. 379–83. Why and how the Brothers Grimm worked; their answer to parents who worried about the violence in the tales.

Livo, Norma J. "Dragons I Have Known and Loved." *Reading Teacher,* 26 March 1973, pp. 566–71. A whole cavern of dragons and dragon stories and a long bibliography for dragon-lovers.

Pillar, Arlene M. "Selected Greek Myths: A Critical Appreciation." *Elementary English,* 51 March 1974, pp. 427–31. A unit for teaching myths: objectives, development, activities. Bibliography includes films and filmstrips.

Shulevitz, Uri. "Within the Margins of a Picture Book." *Horn Book,* 47 June 1971, pp. 309–12. The author, a Caldecott Medal winner, discusses the "coded language" of picture books penetrable only by those sensitive enough to "listen" to their content.

Toothaker, Roy E. "Folktales in Picture-Book Format, A Bibliography." *Library Journal,* 99 April 15, 1974, pp. 1188–94. Evaluation according to story, literary text, and picture book format.

Werner, Judy. "Black Pearls and Ebony." *Library Journal,* 93 May 15, 1968, pp. 2091+. Suitable and unsuitable presentations of black characters and "black" symbols in old and new picture books.

chapter 5

Fanciful Fiction

Folk literature, discussed in the previous chapter, takes for granted a community of understanding: its characters are immediately recognizable types; its settings are familiar; its plots are locked into a culturally determined sense of justice. The modern fanciful story, on the other hand, takes less for granted. Characters must make difficult decisions about the options available to them. Plots are more complex and less dependent on undeviating cause-and-effect. Settings are unique, requiring more elaboration of an author's special vision.

All these characteristics are apparent, for example, in Hans Christian Andersen's "The Little Mermaid." Here the initial setting is the underwater mermaid kingdom with its palace and special set of rules for rising to the surface of the sea to view the ships sailing by. Each of the six mermaid princesses meets adventure in a different way. The youngest falls in love with a handsome human prince and sacrifices her power of speech in order to become human so that she may follow him. Justice might decree that such sacrifice be rewarded by love and a fairy-tale marriage. But it is not. The prince marries a different princess, and the little mermaid must choose between killing him to escape the spell or joining the ocean foam in everlasting forgetfulness. When she chooses oblivion, the outcome is softened, but not completely reversed: "Unseen she kissed the bridegroom's forehead, smiled upon him, and then, with the rest of the children of the air, soared high above the rosy cloud which was sailing so peacefully over the ship."[1]

When the authors of modern fanciful stories base their work directly on folk literature, the difference is still notable. Compare the Grimm Brothers' unadorned version of "The Twelve Brothers" with Andersen's "The Wild Swans." The folk tale is, by comparison, terse and economical in its beginning: "Once upon a time there lived a king and a queen very peacefully together. They had twelve children, all boys. . . ."[2] But at the outset Andersen touches the tale

---

[1]*Hans Christian Andersen's Fairy Tales* (1), p. 124.
[2]"The Twelve Brothers," in *Tales of Grimm and Andersen*, p.8.

with magic, rounding the characters and adorning the setting like an elaborate painting rather than a simple sketch:

> Far, far away, in a land to which the swallows fly while we have winter, there once lived a King who had eleven sons and one daughter, Elise. The eleven brothers— Princes they were, of course—went to school with stars on their breasts and swords at their sides. They wrote upon golden slates with diamond pencils, and knew their lessons just as well by heart as if they were reading them from the book; one could tell at once that they were Princes. Their sister, Elise, sat on a little glass footstool, and looked at a picture book which had cost half the kingdom. These children had such a happy time, but it did not last long. . . .[1]

Much less ornate, but still with the characteristic expansion of the modern fanciful type, is Vsevolod Garshin's treatment of a fable in "The Frog Went A-Traveling." As folklore fable, the story is a brief tale about the downfall of pride: a frog bites onto a tree branch held between two flying ducks, soars with them happily for a time but falls to earth when she opens her mouth to brag. The Russian fanciful tale fashioned from this fable tells considerably more. The frog is given a set of manners and reflections; we learn her thoughts, including the interesting information that she doesn't think it dignified to croak in the wrong season! After her fall, we are told where she went—and that the ducks felt very sorry for her. Here the characters are given life outside the plot structure; details are presented to round out the incident.[2]

Many modern fanciful stories, in fact, are derived from folklore. The celebrated tales of Isaac Bashevis Singer in *Zlateh the Goat* (3) are amplifications of folklore. But there is also, as we shall see, a widening assortment of truly original tales in this type. Derivative or not, they possess the features we've examined, each uniquely conveying the author's perspective.

These differences between folk literature and modern fanciful stories suggest differences in the way we treat the two types. Folk literature is oral, meant to be told. Often we find the telling difficult and turn instead to good written versions, but always with the intent of capturing the storyteller's style. Modern fanciful stories, on the other hand, are written literature. They are meant to be read. The written style is intrinsic to the success of the story.

That is why it's seldom a good idea to *tell* a modern fanciful story except in rare instances in which these stories are written for telling. True, they can be memorized and recited (one form of storytelling), but not everyone has the time to master a tale word for word. What is needed is the ability to read well, to sense and convey the author's intent. To do the job poorly or to turn to simplified hurry-up versions (such as simpler versions of *Mary Poppins* or *Winnie-the-Pooh*) is to miss the spirit, the intimacy between author and reader, that such stories offer.

---

[1]Hans Christian Andersen, "The Wild Swans," in *It's Perfectly True and Other Stories,* tr. Paul Leyssac (Harcourt, 1938), p. 286.
[2]Vsevolod Garshin, "The Frog Went A-Traveling," in *A Harvest of Russian Children's Literature* (2), pp. 75–79.

The qualities that make these stories pleasurable can also make them difficult for children to read. Elaborate description slows plot. It may bore impatient readers. Sometimes you'll need to help them. But once stories such as those of Walter de la Mare and L. M. Boston are understood and felt, fantasy takes on the credence and immediacy of reality.

The plots in fanciful literature are often initially puzzling and sometimes exasperatingly slow in getting down to business. But there's a reason for this barrier: the author has to establish a solid, believable basis for the fantastic events to come. The folkteller launches into improbable events with no more than a "once upon a time"; but the fanciful writer attempts less author distance, taking readers by the hand and convincing them that anything is possible within the fantasy framework. It's a formidable goal which many authors fail to achieve.

Look how C. S. Lewis achieves it in the first of his Narnia series, *The Lion, the Witch, and the Wardrobe* (4). He introduces his human characters in a realistic setting and then leads them abruptly into a realistic wardrobe through which they enter at once into a fantastic world. Some critics contend that the abruptness of the device is too simple for the purpose, but it does move the plot along. This device may be preferable to a long drawn-out beginning, drifting between the real and fantastic worlds. As a middle way between abrupt and elaborate introductions, the first chapter of Mary Norton's *The Borrowers* (5) is a model of how to tease a reader into fantasy.

Whatever the style of introduction in the modern fanciful story, logic is not suspended. If the experience with this literature is to be pleasant, persuasive, or informative, it must begin with a sense of logic. Fantasy must travel logically, perhaps with a logic of its own, but still with logical consistency. As critic Eleanor Cameron says, "In good fantasy, anything does *not* go." She explains:

> Now, if the artist is to achieve this sense of reality, without which fantasy becomes embarrassing and unreadable, it is required of him that in the very beginning he establish a premise. It is required of him that he create an inner logic for his story and that he draw boundary lines outside of which his fantasy may not wander. The author . . . is working consistently within a frame of reference.[1]

teaching ideas

Children may need your help in exploring modern fanciful stories if they are to appreciate the literary effects. For instance, you can suggest the following activities to them:

1. Suppose you're sending an envoy to the Wonderland of *Alice's Adventures in Wonderland* (6). What five or ten or twenty rules of Wonderland behavior can you give in order to save her or his neck?

---

[1] Eleanor Cameron, *The Green and Burning Tree* (Little, Brown, 1962, 1969), p. 17.

2. The members of the amazingly versatile Finnfamily Moomintroll,[1] Tove Jansson's curious creation, have tails and big snouts. Otherwise, they seem to be like ordinary, normal people. Or are they? What consistent differences from people as you know them do the Moomintroll exhibit? If you sent a Moomintroll to Alice's Wonderland, would he be just as puzzled as Alice? How are the two fantastic worlds—Wonderland and Moominland—different from each other and from the world you know?

3. Beverly Cleary's *The Mouse and the Motorcycle* (7) and its sequel *Runaway Ralph* (8) are almost realistic. You sense right away that this is not a world that will contain a witch, a magic ring, a pill for growing larger or smaller, a new kind of animal, or even a spaceship to transport Ralph or the boy Keith to another planet. Now, what could you logically add as fantastic elements to these stories?

EARLY FANCIFUL WRITERS

Hans Christian Andersen (1805–1875) was one of the first writers to be identified with modern fantasy. His various biographers seem to agree on the facts of his life, but the spirit of the man—his motives and real feelings—may elude them. He wasn't handsome, he was awkward, and he might have placed higher value on social esteem than on artistic success. Hugh Walpole says quite bluntly that Andersen was not a charming person, that he was conceited, quick-tempered, and elusive.[2] Toward the end of his life he deplored his image as a writer solely for children: "My goal was to be a poet for all ages, and children could not represent me."[3]

Yet the facts of Andersen's life seem to contradict some of these views. Andersen had many friends—among them Dickens, the Grimm Brothers, Lewis Carroll, various artists, singers, and royalty. He was a welcome guest, and his acting ability brought him fame throughout Europe as a reader of his own stories. He could be kind, and he could sometimes be humble.

"The Ugly Duckling" is often cited as his symbolic autobiography—a rise from poverty to renown and moderate wealth, a triumph of beauty over ugliness. But the facts aren't quite so orderly. Andersen, the child of loving parents, grew up in the small, friendly community of Odense, Denmark. His childhood home was small, but abject poverty and squalor such as characterized Dickens' childhood don't appear to have existed in Andersen's life. True, his father's death changed the world of his childhood. After his move to Copenhagen at

---

[1]This series begins with *Tales from Moominvalley* tr. by Thomas Warburton, (Walck, 1964). There are many more, including *Moominsummer Madness* (1961), *Moominland Midwinter* (1962), *Finnfamily Moomintroll* (1965), and *Exploits of Moominpappa* (1966). The author received the Hans Christian Andersen International Award in 1966.
[2]Hugh Walpole, "Foreword" to *It's Perfectly True and Other Stories*, p. vi.
[3]Monica Stirling, *The Wild Swan: The Life and Times of Hans Christian Andersen* (Harcourt, 1965), p. 358.

the age of fourteen he became a disappointed youth unable to achieve immediate fame in the theater, but his misfortunes were alleviated by the kindness of those who gathered to help him.

No, biography doesn't explain genius. Even Andersen's two literal autobiographies can't reveal the inner intensity of the talent that produced satire ("It's Perfectly True!", "The Emperor's New Clothes," "The Darning Needle") as well as strange, sad personifications ("The Steadfast Tin Soldier" and "The Fir Tree") and even moralism saved by lyric beauty ("The Snow Queen", "The Nightingale," and so many others).

The tone of some of these stories is very close to the "pathetic fallacy": we are made to feel grief over objects incapable of feeling the tragedy bestowed upon them. But at the last moment, the balance is righted. Although the hopeful fir tree is burned to ashes and a thoughtless child wears its star, we are jarred at the end into remembering that this is just a story, a play of imagination: "Now that was done with, and the tree was done with, and the story is done with! done with! done with! And that's what happens to all stories."[1] The proud, silly darning needle is run over by a cart and left lying in a gutter, but the author smiles at the end: "Let's leave her there." Even "The Little Mermaid" ends with a not-quite-serious nod to moralists: naughty children, we are told, add years

booklist

Versions of Andersen

The Complete Fairy Tales and Stories: Hans Christian Andersen. Tr. Erik Christian Haugaard. Doubleday, 1974. (All ages) This is likely to be the authoritative edition for years to come. Translated directly from the Danish by an author skilled in both Danish and English.

The Complete Andersen. Tr. Jean Hersholt. Heritage, 1952. (All ages) Presents 168 tales. Pleasant rhythm, good for reading aloud to intermediates.

It's Perfectly True and Other Stories. Tr. Paul Leyssac. Harcourt, 1938. (All ages) Exciting storytelling material, translated by a storyteller-actor.

Fairy Tales. Tr. R. P. Keigwin. Ed. Svend Larsen. Scribner's, 1951. (All ages) Attempts to stick to the originals: a good edition to compare with others.

Seven Tales. Tr. Eva Le Gallienne. Illus. Maurice Sendak. Harper, 1959. (All ages) Especially suitable for primary-age children. Attractively done, reads well aloud.

Jacobi, Frederick, Jr., sel. *Tales of Grimm and Andersen.* Modern Library, Random, 1952. Contains a famous and helpful introduction to the Andersen tales (as well as those of the Brothers Grimm) written by W. H. Auden.

Look for picture-book editions of single Andersen tales, too numerous to mention here. See, for example, illustrations by Marcia Brown, Blair Lent, Adrienne.

[1]"The Fir Tree," in *It's Perfectly True and Other Stories*, pp. 246–58.

to the mermaid's probation. Only occasionally—such as in "The Little Match-Girl" or "The Red Shoes"—are we left without reassurance.

There is humor in Andersen, even in the tales that seem predominantly serious, and it evades some translators. Compare, for instance, various translations of the incident in "The Nightingale" in which the learned courtiers mistake a cow mooing and frogs croaking for the nightingale's song. Or examine in the same tale the subtle snobbery of the prime minister as he addresses the nightingale. The humor is often delicate, but it is quickly clear to child listeners when they are presented with a lively translation.

Charles Dodgson (Lewis Carroll), an Oxford mathematics professor, published *Alice's Adventures in Wonderland* in 1865, then withdrew the edition because he didn't like the reproduction of Tenniel's pictures and permitted a new printing to appear a year later. The Alice fantasies have the consistency of mathematics, once you grant the original assumptions. Some of us return to these works every year, always with a sense of renewing a joyous bond.

One of Dodgson's literary friends was George MacDonald, whose influence on later writers is probably equal to that of Lewis Carroll himself. C. S. Lewis wrote of MacDonald: "I have never concealed the fact that I regarded him as my master."[1] Such diverse figures as G. K. Chesterton and Maurice Sendak have paid high tribute to MacDonald. His major works for children—such as *At the Back of the North Wind* (1871), *The Princess and the Goblin* (1872), and *The Light Princess* (1893)—are available in numerous modern editions, the latter in a beautiful book illustrated by Maurice Sendak (9).

MacDonald was a Scottish Congregational minister dismissed by his congregation when he was twenty-nine years old, probably because he preached that the heathen would be saved. He never quite recovered from that dismissal. Although he never preached in a pulpit again, he preached in his many writings over the next fifty years. As one biographer says of him: "Scarcely any other writer of fiction in any literature so consciously regarded his function to be that of a teacher and preacher, rather than to be that of an entertainer, artist, or money-earner."[2]

Many modern readers find that MacDonald's preaching encumbers his otherwise enjoyable stories. The lovely lady who personifies his North Wind in *At the Back of the North Wind* (10) is a wonderful fanciful character who assumes whatever size suits her purpose and carries a little boy named Diamond upon adventures over land and sea. But she talks incessantly about her missions, even mystically justifying the sinking of a ship; and Diamond is tiresomely acquiescent and untempted: "He never touched any of the flowers or blossoms, for he was not like some boys who cannot enjoy a thing without pulling it to pieces, and so preventing everyone from enjoying it after them."[3]

Happily for the modern reader, *The Light Princess* is comic and direct. The princess and her parents are joyful characters. The princess's difficulty (she floats

[1] C. S. Lewis, *Surprised by Joy* (Harcourt Brace, 1955), p. 130.
[2] Richard H. Reis, *George MacDonald* (Twayne, 1972), p. 47.
[3] p. 47.

it makes rather a handsome pig, I think." And she began thinking over other children she knew, who might do very well as pigs, and was just saying to herself, "if one only knew the right way to change them—" when she was a little startled by seeing the Cheshire Cat sitting on a bough of a tree a few yards off.

The Cat only grinned when it saw Alice. It looked goodnatured, she thought: still it had *very* long claws and a great many teeth,

84

through the air without the gift of gravity until finally a prince marries her and brings her down to earth) is treated amusingly. This is the MacDonald story you should begin with.

Howard Pyle, an American writer and artist who struggled to fame in New York, ably imitated the form and structure of the folk tale in the eight stories of *Pepper and Salt, or Seasoning for Young Folk* (11) (1885) and the twenty-four stories (one for each hour of the day) in *The Wonder Clock* (12) (1887). In "The Skillful Huntsman" the hero succeeds in three quests to win a princess, makes a deal with the devil, and wins.[1] In "How Dame Margery Twist Saw More Than Was Good for Her," a crafty lady rubs ointment on her eyes and is enabled to see the fairy folk in her garden and at the market.[2] These charming stories are suitable for reading especially to primary-age or older children. Pyle's highly detailed, well-composed drawings, verse, and original fables add spice to the books. The style is more direct and the rhythm more abrupt than in other fanciful stories of the time. Pyle avoids the temptation to interrupt his tales to deliver asides to his readers, hence preserving the folk tale distance.

Another American, L. Frank Baum, ushered in the twentieth century with *The Wonderful Wizard of Oz,* first published in 1900. Today there are more than ten editions in print, and in Russia the book is used to teach English.[3] Rather unwillingly, Baum added thirteen more volumes to his Oz series, and other authors have stretched the series into forty volumes. The continuing popularity of the 1939 movie based on *The Wonderful Wizard of Oz* and a new generation of fantasy readers assure that the trip to the Emerald City with Dorothy, the Scarecrow, the Tin Woodman, and the Cowardly Lion will be repeated for years to come.

Each of the authors discussed here is of more than historical importance. Each contributes to literary experience today. Modern fanciful fiction has evolved from them, and they remain interesting to the modern reader.

Each author found his own way to impart a vision and to achieve a lasting literary transaction with readers. Hans Christian Andersen did it with convincing sincerity. He believed in his stories, and his balance and tone impart that belief to his audience. Lewis Carroll created in Alice a character to embody his own perplexities and even his nightmares. Above all, he found her adventures a way to express his well-integrated verbal humor. George MacDonald, despite all his conscious preaching, had the gift of suspending the laws of realism to ask, "What if . . .?" When his symbolism and moralizing are forgotten, the floating, changing characters remain in the memory. Howard Pyle internalized the structure and content of folklore and somehow succeeded in what almost no one else has done: he created folklore of his own. Baum, distinctly American, was resourceful. Like the well-seasoned television novelty performer, he drew upon a store of tricks and bits of action to keep his readers tuned in.

---

[1]In *Pepper and Salt,* pp. 1–13.
[2]pp. 28–42.
[3]See Ann E. Prentice, "Have You Been to See the Wizard?" *Top of the News* 27 (November 1970): 32–44.

When we compare these works to the general run of fantasy today, we have a good argument for keeping these older books alive. The television cartoon show, the forced gimmickry of the misguided author who tries to write coyly about funny little animals or objects aspiring to be something else—the existence of these works indicates the continuing need for food for the imagination, but the works themselves don't satisfy that need. Because time builds some barriers, many modern children won't voluntarily enter into a private transaction with MacDonald's strange lady or Andersen's storytelling storks in "The Marsh King's Daughter," but they will respond to being read to, to lively discussion, and to a myriad of activities built around these stories. The old fantasies are worth our time, for they impart a richness to life that can be gained in no other way. As L. Frank Baum noted in his preface to *Lost Princess of Oz:* "The imaginative child will become the imaginative man or woman most apt to create, to invent, and therefore to foster civilization."

With all this in mind, we'll examine four major fanciful fiction writers of the early twentieth century. Each writer raised this literary type to new heights.

E. Nesbit

The *E* is for Edith. There is no one like her in all of children's literature. She was born in London in 1858 to a wealthy family and was educated in England and France. At twenty-two, she married Hubert Bland and suddenly found herself the breadwinner for herself, her husband, and her child. She became an activist and "free-thinker." She was a leading member of the Socialist Fabian Society, a benefactor (when she could ill afford it) of countless down-and-outers, an organizer of literary clubs, a close friend of almost every literary figure of the time. She raised a sizable family, including two of her husband's illegitimate children. She managed several homes, tried to control her willful husband, survived the agony of the deaths of two babies and her fifteen-year-old son, saw her fortunes rise and fall, took lovers, acted in the theater, danced, rode, and swam. And all the time she wrote. She wrote to keep alive. She dashed off serials for magazines, sometimes a chapter in an hour or two. She wrote of anything and everything—whatever a publisher would pay her for. The list of her book-length publications is nearly a hundred strong. Between books, she wrote little verses and greeting cards to please herself and her friends. She was indomitable. As her biographer puts it, "Indeed, she had a child's flexibility almost all her life in recovering from every possible distress."[1]

When she was forty years old, Nesbit wrote *The Story of the Treasure Seekers* (13) (1899) and continued through two sequels to tell of the attempts of the Bastable children to make money. Told in first-person by the eldest brother, Oswald Bastable, these stories are models of humorous child interaction in realistic literature.

In *Five Children and It* (14) (1902), realism was combined with fancy. The four

---

[1]Doris Langley Moore, *E. Nesbit: A Biography* (Chilton, 1966), p.99.

children and their baby brother discover a Psammead, a Sand-fairy, in their diggings in the sandpit:

> It was worth looking at. Its eyes were on long horns like a snail's eyes, and it could move them in and out like telescopes; it had ears like a bat's ears, and its tubby body was shaped like a spider's and covered with thick soft fur; its legs and arms were furry too, and its hands and feet like a monkey's.[1]

The Psammead isn't at all an agreeable creature, but he is somehow compelled to grant the children's wishes. There are, however, two conditions: each wish is cancelled at sundown, and the fulfillment of each wish is evident only to the children and can't be discerned by others. The children are delighted with the arrangement. Each day brings a new adventure based on a wish: to be as beautiful as the day, to turn the sandpit into gold, to get rid of the baby, to fly, to be big, to grow up at once, and to make mother the finder of stolen jewels. But each wish is a disaster. Beautiful as day, the children aren't recognized as themselves; they become temporarily homeless. Gold coins from a sandpit aren't acceptable in any shop and lead to the police station. The wings are indeed wonderful—until they disappear at sundown, leaving the children trapped atop a far-off tower. "Reconsideration is the keynote of the book," comments Margery Fisher.[2] The children are finally glad to "promise faithfully never to ask for another wish after today."

The Phoenix and the Carpet (15) (1904) explores further the shortcomings of magic. The magic Phoenix visits the children trapped in a tower. Despite their pleas, he tells them he hasn't any power just then to help them escape: " 'Then how are we going to get home?' said Cyril, at last. 'I haven't any idea,' replied the Phoenix kindly. 'Can I fly out and get you any little thing?' "[3]

Subsequent adventures take the children to a tropical beach. At one point their living room is filled with 199 cats, a cow, and a burglar. After all these adventures, the carpet begins to wear thin so that if you stand on a thin part during a wish, you're in danger of being only half transported to somewhere. The Phoenix, stubbornly refusing to keep up with the time, sets a theater on fire, under the impression that it is his temple. All in all, it is a wonderful series of adventures, but the children are more than a little relieved to find a way to get rid of the overzealous carpet and the Phoenix, who goes back to sleep for another two thousand years.

The Psammead is off-stage during *The Phoenix and the Carpet*, but he reappears in a pet shop in *The Story of the Amulet* (16) (1906), no friendlier for having been rescued from captivity. This third (and last) book in the series has the children (four of them—the baby is conveniently away on a visit) and sometimes an adult stepping back and forth through an arch into the distant past or the just as distant future. "Time is only a mode of thought, you know," the characters are

---

[1]p. 22.
[2]Margery Fisher, *Intent upon Reading* (Watts, 1961), p. 147.
[3]p. 30.

fond of saying, as Nesbit alludes to *Through the Looking-Glass* and to H. G. Wells, perhaps her sources of inspiration on the matter.

As always, the characters and settings in distant places and times are carefully within range of what the children's imaginations might be expected to produce, hence they seem credible. The Babylonian Queen, for instance, is like a modern Englishwoman with an unusual mission. She says,

> Just make yourselves comfortable. . . . I'm simply dying to talk to you, and to hear all about your wonderful country and how you got here, and everything, but I have to do justice every morning. Such a bore, isn't it? Do you do justice in your own country?[1]

If you read the three fantasies in sequence, you detect a darker tone in the third. The children are more quarrelsome, and there's a growing social awareness. Modern London, viewed from the past or the future, is clearly not the best of all possible worlds. The hunger, unhappiness, and hurried lives of its people seem to affect the children and the author alike. There is more than one reference to the polluted condition of the Thames and the rising mechanical noise.

Nevertheless, Nesbit is never an angry writer, nor a bitter one, nor a social reformer. What is more rare, she is not, in the midst of her fantasy, a melancholy writer. Fantasy writers, including the three great ones we'll discuss next, are inclined in that direction: they create a special world and then wonder if it wouldn't be nice if we could all be children in it. Not Nesbit. At the end of *The Story of the Amulet* she lets the children cheerfully toss away their magic and trip down the steps to greet their parents and get on with their lives.

Nesbit's characters are normal, nonexceptional children who have unusual adventures. This quality is something of a relief from stories that take pains to portray characters who are exceptionally intelligent or sensitive or misunderstood. To write excitingly of everyday people, even when they experience unusual incidents, is a demanding art. Nesbit's influence in this sphere of fantasy is great: neither Mary Norton, nor Pamela Travers, nor Edward Eager could have done without her.

Her biography shows that the years in which she wrote these stories were full of personal troubles, but the voice that speaks so distinctly through these books is that of a confident adult who knows that life on almost any terms is wonderful. "The story is indeed a little difficult to believe," she remarks at one point, and adds, "Still, you might try."[2]

Kenneth Grahame

E. Nesbit and Kenneth Grahame were contemporaries, both living in and about London, but we have no evidence that they knew each other. They weren't at

---

[1] *The Story of the Amulet,* p. 110.
[2] *The Phoenix and the Carpet,* p. 86.

all alike, although some people point to similarities between Grahame's *The Golden Age* and Nesbit's *The Treasure Seekers*.

Kenneth Grahame was born in Scotland in 1859 and spent much of his childhood in and around Oxford. It was a dream-filled, somewhat solitary childhood whose main focus was the River—

> . . . this sleek, sinuous, full-bodied animal, chasing and chuckling, gripping things with a gurgle and leaving them with a laugh, to fling itself on fresh playmates that shook themselves free, and were caught and held again. All was a-shake and a-shiver—glints and gleams and sparkles, rustle and swirl, chatter and bubble.[1]

Grahame never left that river spiritually, nor did he wander very far from it physically. He returned to it and to his childhood in his many writings and was esteemed as a sensitive, skilled stylist even before the publication of *The Wind in the Willows* (17) in 1908.

At the same time, Grahame had a business career. For thirty years he was a very successful banker in London. Socially, he ranked high in both business and literary groups, a combination that is not frequently found today. He also had a wife named Elspeth and a son named Alastair, whom he affectionately called "Mouse."

It was to Mouse at bedtime that he began to tell the adventures of Mole, Rat, Badger, and Toad; and these were continued in a series of letters sent to Mouse and carefully preserved by a governess. The book itself was formed through much labor, and quieter chapters such as "The Piper at the Gates of Dawn" and "Wayfarers All" seem to have been inserted after the original manuscript was completed.

At the time of its publication, no one appeared to make much out of *The Wind in the Willows,* although it has been a steady favorite ever since. It defies the so-called laws of consistency. Good slapstick humor and great sadness, fascination with the machine age and pantheism, active life and the life of contemplation—all of these trot along side by side, bound together in a prose and poetry style that, more than in any other modern fantasy, derives from an author's lifetime of attitudes and unconscious symbols perfectly served by his craft.

Grahame himself commented on *The Wind in the Willows* as an animal fantasy: "Every animal, by instinct, lives according to his nature. Thereby he lives wisely, and betters the tradition of mankind. No animal is ever tempted to belie his own nature. Every animal is honest, every animal is straightforward. Every animal is true."[2] Grahame's biographer, Peter Green, takes great pains to show that the book reveals the author's terror that "the structure of society might be destroyed through social revolution."[3] Others see it as a parody of various classical works, especially The *Odyssey,* or, more simply, as the author's attempt to examine several life styles—the wanderer, the stay-at-home, the darer, the contemplator—that somehow couldn't find resolution in his own life.

---

[1] Kenneth Grahame, *The Wind in the Willows,* p. 30.
[2] Cited in Clayton Hamilton, "Frater Ave Atque Vale," *The Booksman* 76 (January 1933): 71-72.
[3] Peter Green, *Kenneth Grahame: A Biography* (World, 1959), p. 247.

There really isn't any way to explain *The Wind in the Willows.* You have to read it. Its style reflects the easy flow of speech and is best when read aloud. But don't mistake this liquid language for spontaneous, everyday speech. The language is more mature than that; it's wonderfully susceptible to the modulations of emotion and meaning that good reading can provide.

The edition illustrated by Ernest H. Shepard has a useful map in the frontispiece. We've used this in presenting the book to a class of sixth-graders, along with a bulletin board display of wise and wild one-line quotes from the book: "Toad is busy arraying himself in those singularly hideous habiliments"; "Then the brutal minions of the law fell upon the hapless Toad"; "There was panic in the parlour and howling in the hall . . ." We've used the "Dulce Domum" chapter (chapter 5) as a special December holiday reading, with a Robert Shaw Chorale musical background. For most children, *The Wind in the Willows* isn't a you-can't-lay-it-down book, but keep it around and you'll find that children and adults go back to it.

teaching ideas

1. Can you find a river setting for reading *The Wind in the Willows?* Perhaps a change of setting—getting back to Grahame's inspiration—will aid literary experience with this book.

2. Fantasy logic in *The Wind in the Willows* includes the idea that any character can at any time change size to suit the plot. Toad at one moment impersonates a woman, and a few pages later is so small that a woman throws him halfway across a river. Discuss with children what might be a suitable way to illustrate this book, possibly combining realism (in the settings) and the abstract. Try combining art forms into illustrations for *The Wind in the Willows.*

Walter de la Mare

In one of his fanciful short stories for children Walter de la Mare comments: "But there is a music in the voice that tells more to those who understand it than can any words in a dictionary."[1] Such word music is the triumph of his work, especially in his long book, *The Three Royal Monkeys* (18). From its beginning, it is filled with strange lulling language that must be read rhythmically aloud:

> On the borders of the Forest of Munza-Mulgar lived once an old grey Fruit Monkey of the name of Mutta-matutta. She had three sons, the eldest Thumma, the next Thimbulla, and the youngest, who was a Nizzaneela, Ummanodda. And they called each other for short, Thumb, Thimble, and Nod.[2]

---

[1] Walter de la Mare, "The Lord Fish," in *A Penny a Day* (Knopf, 1925), p. 183.
[2] p. 3.

The three sons set out for the Valley of Tishnar to find their father. Nod is separated from his brothers and captured by the Oomgar Mulga, a man. This relationship (chapters 9 through 12 in the book) forms one of the strangest, most captivating passages in all imaginative literature. Not until L. M. Boston's *A Stranger at Green Knowe* (19), wherein a Chinese boy and an escaped gorilla befriend each other in the woods of an English estate, do we find anything that tells so movingly of an animal and a human attempting to understand each other. Nod and the Oomgar, whose name is Andy Battle, find part of this understanding through the music of a bell and a lute and dancing. There's an unforgettable glimpse of the other forest animals longing to join this harmony:

> But the leopards and other prowling beasts, when they heard the sound of their strings and music, went mewing and fretting; and many a great python and ash-scaled poison-snake would rear its head out of its long sleep and sway with flickering tongue in time to the noisy echoes from the rocky and firelit shelf above. Even the Jack-Alls and Jaccatrays squatted whimpering into their bands to listen and would break when all was silent into such a doleful and dismal chorus that it seemed to shake the stars.[1]

Andy and Nod try to communicate, too, through speech, and it's difficult not to believe in their small successes. Eventually, though, they must part, and Nod bids good-bye in his own language: "Oomgar, Oomgar . . . ah-mi, ah-mi; sulani ghar magleer."[2] This farewell is a surprising moment, for the reader who has gone this far in the relationship finds that he understands and believes the Munza-Mulgar language.

If you develop a love for the sounds and rhythms of language through a book such as *The Three Royal Monkeys,* you have gained a great gift of aesthetic and communicative value. This facet of language has sometimes been neglected in modern teaching, although its power ought to be apparent as you witness the often fumbling attempts of modern rock lyricists to tap it. At any rate, the language of Walter de la Mare, borne by his animal kingdom, ought to be sampled. The book may have retreated in popularity, but we predict that it will return.

teaching ideas

1. The *Three Royal Monkeys* needs a map. Have children help you make one as you read the story.

2. One way to foster interest in language sounds and rhythms is through the creation of a special, made-up language. Use *The Three Royal Monkeys* to encourage children to think up new, appropriate names for things, finding suitable-sounding verbs and an original syntax for a language of their own.

---

[1] pp. 112–13.
[2] pp. 147.

A. A. Milne

It is a long way to the Valley of Tishnar and a great distance back to the social structure of *The Wind in the Willows;* but the Hundred Acre Wood in *Winnie-the-Pooh* (20) and *The House at Pooh Corner* (21) is a stuffed-animal, child-dominated, familiar world.

The animals are introduced one at a time, each with simple, consistent characteristics: Pooh, the gentle bear of Very Little Brain who on occasion acts with bumbling heroism; Rabbit, busy and scheming; Piglet, small and uncertain; melancholy, complaining Eeyore; sour, pretentious Owl; and Kanga with her bothersome child Roo are there to make up the balanced community. Tigger, introduced in the second book, is bouncy and unmanageable—he offers just the right touch of variety.

The stories are told to Christopher Robin, who insists that he already knows them but who likes to be reminded of them again. Christopher lives peacefully in the knowledge that he is the most important character of all, and, at the end, goes away with Pooh to the gentle music of his father's words: "So they went off together. But wherever they go, and whatever happens to them on the way, in the enchanted place on the top of the Forest, a little boy and his Bear will always be playing."[1]

The ingredients of these books are deceptively simple. The characters lose something (a tail, a house) or search for something (a strange animal, the North Pole) or misunderstand each other or try simple strategies that never quite work. *Winnie-the-Pooh* is climaxed by a flood and *The House at Pooh Corner* by a windstorm, but even these potential disasters have the gentle feel of the nursery. Milne knew (before psychologists noted it) that early childhood thrives on small dangers quickly defeated by the reassertion of security. He knew (before language development specialists noted it) that "big" words and word play are more intriguing to the child than controlled vocabulary. He never paused to explain what Hostile Animals with Hostile Intent might be up to, nor did he straighten out Pooh's confusion between an Ambush and a gorse-bush. He left Pooh wondering if Woozle is the plural of Wizzle or the other way around. He knew that small children can relish the type of humor in which the reader knows something the characters don't know, even when the understanding can only be derived by inference.

Above all, Milne presented childhood respectfully but without sentimentality. His autobiography makes clear his belief that the child is grossly egotistical.[2] It is something of a surprise to discover again, after this observation, that he presented childhood with such tenderness.

Critics aren't all at ease with the Pooh books. Fisher says that Milne "does

---

[1] *The House at Pooh Corner,* pp. 179-80.
[2] A. A. Milne, *Autobiography* (Dutton, 1939), pp. 282–85.

not seem to me entirely at home in the child's world."[1] Humorist Dorothy Parker wrote a famous scathing review of *The House at Pooh Corner* (which Milne answers with spirit in his Autobiography). We place him here beside Nesbit, Grahame, and de la Mare without the slightest hesitation or apology. Surely most readers will know why.

In these pages we've looked happily at some of the early modern fanciful stories that continue to enchant many modern readers and to influence more recent writers. It is difficult to leave them, for they are among our favorite things.

We should have mentioned Rudyard Kipling's *The Jungle Books* (1894) and *Just So Stories* (1902); James Barrie's *Peter Pan* (1904); Lucretia Hale, *Pinocchio,* and perhaps *The Water-Babies.*

And now we have done so.

MODERN FANCIFUL STORIES

In a fanciful story one or more of the literary elements is altered from what the reader expects based on his own experience. Think of the flexibility this permits.

Characters can be given attributes they don't possess in real life. Animals talk, inanimate objects move about and have emotions, a person can be three inches high or a mile high, or a new type of being can be created.

Settings unknown in the real world can be invented as the author wishes. There can be places without gravity or where gravity doesn't harm you when you topple. There can be regions of strange encounters, as if the setting consciously took part in the struggles of characters who work through the maze of their fates.

Plots can present bizarre problems and consequences, consistent with the author's logic but not necessarily consistent with cause and effect in the real world.

Authors sometimes experiment with other elements of their craft in telling fanciful stories. For instance, when Meg and Mr. Jenkins, a school principal, are in the microcosmic world of Charles Wallace's blood cells in *A Wind in the Door* (22), author Madeleine L'Engle describes their struggle in page after page of free verse—disjointed sentence fragments attempting to reflect their state of half-consciousness. This stylistic variation seems warranted, since she has transported her readers to a world where neatly formed sentences might seem out of place.

Form may be altered from expectation. Maurice Sendak in *Where the Wild Things Are* (23) used a series of double-page, textless pictures to show the dance of Max and the wild creatures. In Mercer Mayer's *Mrs. Beggs and the Wizard* (24) the text stops short of the horrifying end of the story, allowing visual effects to take over the form.

---

[1] *Intent upon Reading,* p. 38.

A key criterion in fantasy is credibility. Can an author vary one or more of these elements and still make you want to believe, make you suspend your disbelief sufficiently to enter into the story? If the tale is paced too quickly, you grow suspicious of the author's invention; too slow a pace makes you lose the motivation to go on. If the writer seems to stand too far away to care, you also become indifferent; but if he nudges and cautions and delivers asides to you to coax belief, you may grow impatient.

Likewise, when tone varies without a valid reason, you're likely to abandon belief. One such story starts with a pig who worries, quite believably, about the fate of his kind: he's destined to become ham and bacon on the farmer's table. A few pages later the story takes off on a light-hearted journey—the pig has joined the circus, to chat with the customers and make his way in the world as a young man might do. The tone has shifted abruptly and the reader may not shift with it.

Of all literary elements theme is the most crucial in fanciful fiction. Theme—the significance of the story—is most convincing when it comes from the story's context, not when it is tacked on as a moral lesson or an abstract observation by the author. How can you judge whether a theme is intrinsic to the tale?

In fanciful literature, as in any literary type, theme must somehow convey a sense of truth. Even though the story has an unfamiliar setting or characters whose actions are different from the reader's experience, theme should still tell us something about ourselves and our world. The fantasy gives it focus, but theme must not be distorted by the unreality contained in other literary elements. Some authors of fanciful stories cannot manage this matter of truth in theme. In one story a country pigeon flies to the city to live. Everything goes wrong. The city is smoke-filled and ugly, other pigeons drive the hero away from food handouts in the park, the pigeon's wing is injured, and he's almost eaten by an alley cat. He returns to the country, and the author concludes that the country is the best place to live. A closed case, but a questionable truth, even in terms of the story. Aren't there any cats in the country? Is ugliness really confined to cities? You shouldn't be hypersensitive about one-sided thematic arguments, but in that case a story should have compensating features.

A theme in fanciful literature ought to be in balance with the tone and substance of the story's other elements. If the plot and characters are presented as serious and complex, and the author imparts a sense of urgency, then the story should have a theme of some significance. If the story is light and playful, it needn't be overwhelmed by a weighty theme. To examine this point, let's look at an example. In one collection of fanciful stories there's a cow happily browsing in her pasture until she happens to read a billboard advertising orange juice. Thereupon she's dissatisfied: why can't she produce orange juice instead of milk? Toward this end, she undergoes a series of adventures all ending in apparent failure: orange juice production just isn't her profession. The story ends with the cow's pronouncement that we must all be content to be ourselves. This sort of plot is slender and unlikely for such a theme.

Theme in fine fantasy can be simple if the story itself is simple in tone and mood. John Burningham's *Mr. Gumpy's Outing* (25) is a simple story adorned with light, free drawings and bright colors. The theme is that a simple accident (a boat overturning in shallow water) need not ruin a life or even a day: you just go home and have tea. A heavier theme would have upset the book as well as the boat. The brilliant, light-hearted story of *The Cat Who Wished to Be a Man* (26) by Lloyd Alexander says that people can be corrupt and mean but that it's wonderful to be a person after all. Alexander has the good grace to leave it at that. He doesn't break the mood to try to explain that this theme is profound. But *Tom's Midnight Garden* (27) by Philippa Pearce is serious, almost tragic, in all its elements. The theme that evolves—that time inexorably moves on unaltered by one's sorrows—is consistent with the content and the style.

Modern Fanciful Stories for Early Childhood

Picture books as a literary type overlap with the category of modern fanciful stories for early childhood. The young child's literary medium is visual as well as auditory; therefore, many of the works discussed in the picture book section are relevant here.

If a child is especially sensitive to the "language" of pictures, he may respond best to books that emphasize picture quality and detail, whether they convey a strong fanciful narrative or not. Other children are fascinated by language—for instance, by repeated magic phrases and unusual combinations of images. Still other young readers prefer an explicit, full narrative—a fanciful story that uses pictures and language to move the narrative along, rather than a story in which fanciful elements are to be relished in themselves.

Crockett Johnson's very popular *Harold and the Purple Crayon* (28) and its sequels depend on a visual joke: Harold draws his environment as he wants it to be, then steps into it and lives there. The fanciful content depends on the pictures, although the author ends with a verbal-pun flourish: at the end of the day Harold draws a bed, climbs into it, and, the author tells us, "he drew up the covers."

Milton the Early Riser (29) by Robert Kraus gives only a hint of its simple fanciful narrative through language, but the pictures make all the difference. Milton the panda wakes before the other animals have finished sleeping and tries to entertain himself. He creates an earthquake and a great windstorm with his singing. The animals are scattered all over the place, but Milton puts them all back in their original positions before they wake up. No child would listen twice to such a story, if it were just told or read. But the pictures create a world of fancy and make Milton the panda a winning, enchanting character.

Margaret Wise Brown, a prolific writer of tone poems about realistic topics, could also weave gentle fanciful stories. Her *Little Fur Family* (30) doesn't have much plot, but the pleasant lines are memorable. They convey the bliss of a group of creatures unknown to zoologists:

There was a little fur family
warm as toast
smaller than most
in little fur coats
and they lived in a warm
wooden tree.

This is word magic to capture any child's fancy, even those who aren't interested in fanciful narrative. The same is true of Charlotte Zolotow's *Mr. Rabbit and the Lovely Present* (31). The entire text is a conversation between the little girl and Mr. Rabbit, and the plot is the search for a present for her mother's birthday. Sendak's kindly rabbit contributes to the fancy; the author's soft crooning lines give the story a mood and tone that lodge it securely in one's memory.

To weave a spell of fancy through words, not really depending on suspense to keep the reader on his toes, is difficult. One self-conscious word and the spell fades. If rhythm is overstressed, the resulting sing-song effect spoils the tone; but if rhythm is ignored, the spell doesn't work. Jan Wahl's *A Wolf of My Own* (32) catches the thought patterns of a little girl who receives a puppy and imagines what she could do with him if he were a wolf named Fred. There are other good books of this kind, but they're still a precious and scarce commodity.

Fanciful stories that depend upon suspenseful events are more numerous. Such stories for young children often include enticing illustrations and pleasant or lively language, but they can stand on their own as stories to be remembered and loved simply because of a fanciful character involved in fanciful events. *The Sailor Dog* (33) by Margaret Wise Brown is a fine choice (available in various Golden Book editions). "Born at sea in the teeth of a gale, the sailor was a dog. Scuppers was his name."[1] The book follows Scuppers through his adventures, including shipwreck and repairs, a visit to the East, and the choice of a lone life at sea. It ends with Scupper's salty sea song, a tribute to independence that children appreciate.

We must also mention Richard Scarry's *Busy, Busy World* (34) as a special favorite. Thirty-three countries (shown on a map at the back of the book) are represented by thirty-three fast, wildly illustrated tales, some admittedly filled with stereotypes but all rollicking in the plot devices of best-loved farce. There are mistaken identities (Professor Dig's Egyptian mummy is mistaken by his near-sighted friend for his mommy), naughty but harmless villains (such as Klondike Kid, who steals lollipops), and a host of cartoon animals with serious intent. *The Great Pie Robbery* (35), featuring Sam Cat and Dudley Pig as detectives, and other books in Scarry's collection are also popular. Their themes aren't any more substantial than those of television cartoons, but the drawing is much better and the plots more original. These aren't great books beloved by critics, but they're very readable and provide a fine introduction to fanciful plot.

---

[1] Margaret Wise Brown, *The Sailor Dog* (Simon and Schuster, 1953), p. 1.

A number of early childhood fanciful stories that have remained popular through the years aren't exactly critical favorites. The sixteen volumes about Raggedy Ann and Raggedy Andy, beginning with *Raggedy Ann Stories* (36) by Johnny Gruelle, are cloying to most adults, but some children still like them. Each chapter has just enough gentle incident—a bit of danger followed by a return to security—to entice a child. Raggedy Ann herself is indestructible and dependably cheerful, even when she loses her stuffing.

Many books in series, carrying fanciful characters through several episodes and beloved by children and critics alike, present an author-artist's unique vision. The first book of the Babar series, *The Story of Babar* (37) by Jean de Brunhoff, appeared in 1933. In it Babar, the little elephant, left the jungle to visit Paris, returned home, became king, and married happily. Through the years Babar has continued his adventures throughout the world and finally to the outer world in *Babar Visits Another Planet* (38) by the original author's son, Laurent de Brunhoff. The illustrations look as if a gifted child had drawn them. The English translations from the French are rhythmical and are scrawled in cursive writing, as if each book were produced by hand. The authors seem aware of a young child's fondness for lively plots. Problem incidents are quickly solved and the plot moves on.

Ludwig Bemelmans's *Madeline* books are more sophisticated. They begin with *Madeline* (39) and continue through five books, ending the series with *Madeline in London* (40). Each book begins with slight variations on a setting in verse:

In an old house in Paris
that was covered with vines
lived twelve little girls in two straight lines.
In two straight lines they broke their bread
and brushed their teeth
and went to bed.[1]

The first book in the series, dealing with Madeline's appendectomy, is soothing to children concerned about illness and hospitals.

Many very young children seek stories about witches and other things that go bump in the night, so a number of fanciful stories have been written to meet such requests. Patricia Coombs has a successful series about a witch girl named Dorrie, her mother Bit Witch, and Gink the cat. In one of the more recent books, *Dorrie and the Goblin* (41), a baby goblin is found in a basket on Dorrie's doorstep, and poor Dorrie discovers that goblin-sitting is an impossible job. The Old Witch stories by Wende and Harry Devlin, such as *Old Witch Rescues Halloween* (42), have predictable plots. In one story, for example, a boy and his mother are troubled by the witch who lives in their attic, but the witch always helps them solve their problems. These books are especially popular around Halloween.

---

[1]*Madeline,* p. 1.

But I was saying—suppose you met a witch,
up in that murky waste of wood
where you play your hide-and-seek. Suppose
she pounced from out a bush,
she touched you, she clutched you,
what would you do? No use
in struggling, in vain to pinch and pull.
She's pinned you down, pitched you into her sack,
drawn tight the noose.

There's one way
of escape, one word you need to know—
W–A–N–D. Well,
what does that spell?...

From SUPPOSE YOU MET A WITCH by Ian Serraillier, illustrated by Ed Emberley, by permission of Little, Brown and Co. and Ian Serraillier. Text copyright ©1952 by Ian Serraillier. Illustrations copyright ©1973 by Edward R. Emberley. This illustration originally appeared in color.

A promising new series about Arthur the mouse and Sampson the cat is loaded with incident and crowded with lively pictures. (See *The Church Mouse* (43) and *The Church Mice and the Moon* (44) by Graham Oakley.) In the first book, the mouse and cat are abandoned on an island. They paint themselves in strange colors to pass as new species for the benefit of visiting zoologists. Old problems with new solutions form the delightful themes in these books.

Many picture books and some illustrated stories are short. If they're intrinsically good, they don't strain children's attention. Yet you may wonder sometimes if a whole book devoted to one brief story is worth the price. One solution is to make ample use of the library. You can check out a stack of books about Babar, read one to a child at each sitting, and perhaps select a favorite to buy so that the child can return to it often. Then you have the advantages of both a wide selection and ownership.

But, you may ask, aren't there books for young chilren that contain many good, short selections that don't depend on each other to gain their effect? There are, of course, numerous collections of "bedtime stories" that provide 365 stories, one for each night in the year. But after examining such collections, you may decide that 365 good stories (fanciful or otherwise) aren't within the capabilities of most books.

There are, however, a growing number of books that contain in a single volume several fanciful tales, each complete in itself. Most of these are well worth your attention. We hope their number will continue to grow as publishers become aware of the need. Let's examine a few promising ones.

Perhaps the most exciting recent volumes of this type are James Marshall's *George and Martha* (45) and *George and Martha Encore* (46), which we discussed in chapter 1. Several books in Harper's I Can Read collection also present a number of fanciful tales suitable for young children. Else Holmelund Minarik's *Little Bear* (47) and others in this series, illustrated by Maurice Sendak, are fine examples. Arnold Lobel's *Frog and Toad Are Friends* (48) and *Frog and Toad Together* (49) are pleasant friendship stories with somewhat sustained, occasionally subtle plots. The same author's *Mouse Tales* (50) are simpler in structure and perhaps more suited to this category: the seven short tales in this book use cumulative incidents, repetition of incidents and phrases, and even a rebus to bring delight in small helpings.

A few short story collections featuring modern fanciful works from various sources have been well received. *Told under the Magic Umbrella* (51), illustrated by Elizabeth Orton Jones, contains thirty-three stories of varying length. (It was selected by the Literature Committee of the Association for Childhood Education.) Anthologies edited through the Child Study Association of America contain carefully selected fanciful stories. Maybe your best anthology would be a suitcase filled with the fanciful literature you discover to be most exciting as you work with young children. Let it grow as your life with literature and children grows.

Modern Fanciful Stories for Middle Childhood

You might begin at this level with fanciful humor—fantasy whose chief concern is laughter rather than credibility. Well-written, modern tall tales are a good start, especially the Josh McBroom stories by Sid Fleischman, illustrated by Kurt Werth. In the first of these, *McBroom Tells the Truth* (52), McBroom and his large family farm a swamp. Their watermelon crop will never again be equaled, as their cruel landlord Heck Jones will attest. *McBroom's Zoo* (53) introduces fascinating beasts such as Teakettler, a Descot Vamposer, a Galoopus bird who lays square eggs, a Sidehill Gouger, and the Great Prairie Hidebehind, who can't be seen because you can't turn around fast enough to more than glimpse him. McBroom himself tells the stories, assuring us "Why, I'd rather sit on a porcupine than tell a fib." The author says that he was once a magician—and, in a way, he still is.

All tall tales have wish-fulfillment at their centers. The McBroom stories appear to be based on the sort of wishes you might expect of rural people in an unsophisticated time. The wishes implicit in Roald Dahl's *Charlie and the Chocolate Factory* (54) are more modern and perhaps more cynical. Charlie and four unsavory children, together with assorted parents, are awarded a tour of Willy Wonka's fantastic production plant, a world made of candy and gum. Satisfaction of the taste buds dominates the whole value system in this story, although toward the end a new satisfaction is added: flying through the air in a glass elevator, a motif that Dahl develops in a sequel *Charlie and the Great Glass Elevator* (55).

A multitude of readers and movie-goers profess to love Charlie and all that happens to him though it's hard to see that Charlie amounts to anything more than a passive appetite. Eleanor Cameron has attacked the first book at considerable length; the heated exchange between this critic and author Dahl ought to be read before you decide whether to include Charlie Bucket in your selection of good fanciful fare for intermediate-age children.[1]

You and your children might compare Charlie with Pippilotta Delicatessa Windowshade Mackrelmint Afraim's Daughter Longstocking, better known as Pippi Longstocking in Astrid Lindgren's book of that name (56). Pippi is very much alone in the world, and no Willy Wonka comes along to save her. She's very strong and lives resourcefully in her Villa Villekulla with her monkey Mr. Nilsson and her horse. In the first volume of this series she finds it necessary to pick up her horse, a cow, a brazen bull, two uncooperative policemen, and a couple of robbers. She can't fly, although she tries to, but she can dive from the roof into a tree without getting hurt and run all the way around the kitchen without touching the floor!

In addition to strength and agility, Pippi possesses several qualities that endear her to many less fortunate children. She can create a great whopper of a story in an instant, and social convention doesn't prevent her from sharing it. Pippi departs from convention rather often, usually with a reason that sounds quite sensible. Why *not* use the floor instead of a breadboard to roll out the dough if you're making an extra large batch of cookies? Why *not* use your big cartwheel hat for carrying in the wood?

It's always difficult for an author and readers to say good-bye to a beloved fanciful character such as Pippi. She has just returned to her home, celebrating Christmas with her friends. We see her sitting alone at the kitchen table, staring at the flame of a candle. Then she blows out the candle, and that is all.

We are inclined to compare author Lindgren with E. Nesbit because both writers are so joyous and readable. The voice of both is that of a wise, happy adult who loves to amuse children without sentimentalizing over their innocence. In *The Nesbit Tradition* a British critic asserts: "Astrid Lindgren's books are the outstanding masterpieces of much-larger-than-life portraiture."[2]

Let's briefly mention one other modern tall tale before you explore this sub-type on your own. Robert McCloskey's *Homer Price* (57) and its sequel *Centerburg Tales* (58) derive from the author-artist's childhood in a small Ohio town. Homer, an engaging character, is usually in the midst of an overwhelming problem and is doing his straightforward best to solve it. The townspeople are recognizable types and generally pleasant. The episodic adventures, each complete in itself, contain splendid exaggeration (a doughnut machine that won't stop production), literary allusion (a pied piper named Mr. Murphy who demonstrates a musical mousetrap), and local lore (ragweed plants that burst out of the green-

---

[1]See Eleanor Cameron, "McLuhan, Youth, and Literature," *Horn Book* 48 (October 1972): 433–40; *Horn Book* 48 (December 1972): 572–79; *Horn Book* 49 (February 1973): 79–85. Then see Roald Dahl, "Charlie and the Chocolate Factory: a Reply," *Horn Book* 49 (February 1973): 77–78, and Eleanor Cameron, "A Reply to Roald Dahl," *Horn Book* 49 (April 1973): 127–29.
[2]Marcus Crouch, *The Nesbit Tradition* (Rowman and Littlefield. 1972), p. 103.

house to threaten all hay fever victims). In at least two instances (the skunk-and-robbers chapter and the knitting chapter) the illustrations provide the clue to the story's secret and McCloskey leaves you to work it out. The writing style is precise, providing an excellent context for a rather difficult vocabulary; many chapters, including the famous doughnut incident, invite exciting dramatizations.

ANIMALS IN FANCIFUL FICTION.   Animals abound in fanciful fiction for intermediate-age children. Walter R. Brooks's many books about Freddy the pig have worn well and are still favorites of many children with average and below-average reading ability. Freddy and his animal pals (including a black cat named Jinx, Charles the rooster, and a delightful cow named Mrs. Wiggins, who becomes president of the First Animal Republic) talk easily with their human owners, Mr. and Mrs. Bean. Their adventures on and away from the farm are fraught with funny, sometimes suspenseful happenings, usually involving animal and human villains. Freddy deals skillfully with both the animal and human worlds. Unlike some series, this one has variety: each book draws upon a new setting and unique plot ideas.[1]

The events at number thirty-two Windsor Gardens in London are more sophisticated than those on the Bean farm. That's the home of *A Bear Called Paddington* (62) a sixteen-pound stowaway from Darkest Peru who was adopted by Mr. and Mrs. Brown, their children, and their housekeeper, Mrs. Bird. You might expect the addition of a bear to the household to cause a terrible upheaval, but not in the Brown household. When, for example, Mrs. Bird learns that a bear has joined the family, she exclaims: "Mercy me . . . I wish you'd told me. I haven't put clean sheets in the spare room or anything."[2]

Paddington always means well, and Londoners are kind and accepting in their dealings with him. As a result, his hectic adventures always turn out well. As an unexpected participant in a large department store display window, he draws a fine group of customers. When he tries to restore a painting, he wins first prize. Readers know that Paddington will survive whatever difficulties he encounters and be received at home with love and understanding. It's a reassuring theme, since we so easily identify with Paddington and can hope for such acceptance for ourselves.

All of the Paddington books are well written.[3] Although the character was inspired by a toy bear, there's nothing of the stuffed animal in Paddington. He's flesh and blood, a remarkable creation to help us feel at one with the animal world. Peggy Fortnum's free sketches add to credibility and humor, never telling too much of the story ahead of the text.

[1]See *Freddy and the Bean Home News* (59), *Freddy and the Space Ship* (60), *Freddy and the Dragon* (61), and others, illus. Kurt Wiese (Knopf 1943, 1953, 1958).
[2]Michael Bond, *A Bear Called Paddington*, p. 23.
[3]See Michael Bond, *A Bear Called Paddington*, illus. Peggy Fortnum, and others in this series. The most recent is *Paddington Takes to TV* (Houghton Mifflin, 1974).

Illustrations from A Bear Called Paddington by Michael Bond, illustrated by Peggy Fortnum (cont. on p. 202). Copyright ©1958 by Michael Bond. Reprinted by permission of Houghton Mifflin

These books read well aloud. A few British terms—*underground* for subway, *marrow* as a vegetable—may need explaining for children to understand the plot. Some of the humor is verbal, requiring a good reading to be appreciated. For example, when asked if he's resting on his laurels, Paddington replies that he isn't—he's sitting on his begonias!

In the words of a well-known poem, *mice are nice*—at least, writers of fanciful stories appear to think so. They are tidy, well-spoken, tolerant of the unkindness of humans, and sometimes as brave and daring as Odysseus. As junior members of the animal kingdom, mice may seem to parallel the place of human children. In modern fanciful stories mice are the underlings destined to overcome obstacles through courage and ingenuity.

Nathaniel Benchley's *Feldman Fieldmouse* (63) and his nephew Fendall are such mice. The book, subtitled "A fable," offers a rather explicit pair of themes. First, we see Fendall learning a lesson of freedom: that it's better to risk life in the open rather than remain a safe prisoner in a cage. Second, there's the tragic knowledge that one wild dance of joy may be worth dying for. The adventures

Company and William Collins Sons & Co., Ltd., London.

in which a human boy named Lonny assists the two mice as they survive encounters with a fox and an owl have a good storyteller's balance of humor and suspense, although we keep wondering how these otherwise naive characters can know so much about vitamin C and various ecological matters.

The central character in George Selden's *The Cricket in Times Square* (64) is probably Tucker Mouse, despite Chester Cricket's billing in the title. Tucker, Chester, and Harry Cat occupy the newsstand operated by the Bellini family in a Times Square subway station. Under Tucker's sponsorship, Chester astonishes the human world with his performance of operatic arias. As a result, the newsstand business flourishes, and the Bellinis are saved from financial disaster; but Chester tires of the city and goes home to Connecticut. In a sequel, *Tucker's Countryside* (65), the three friends help to preserve Chester's homeland against the onslaught of human housing. These attempts to up-date animal fantasy are pleasant, though ironically their plots often resemble the comic drama of old movies. Selden's recent book, *The Genie of Sutton Place* (66), places its modern hero, Tim Farr, in the company of a well-meaning genie. A fake occultist with many aliases—an Auntie Mame type of character—joins in the harmless fun.

Of all mouse characters, Margery Sharp's Miss Bianca is the most distinguished. Beginning with *The Rescuers* (67), this white-furred, brown-eyed pet of the ambassador's son earns immortality as Perpetual Madam President of the Mouse Prisoners' Aid Society. Accompanied by the gallant but very ordinary mouse Bernard, she saves human prisoners—a poet, a little girl, Teddy-Age-Eight—from horribly dangerous villains and captivities. Her remarkable physical courage is matched by her refinement, her ability to speak with conviction to mouse and human worlds alike, and her talent as a poet. The writing style in these books is complex. The sentences include many subordinate clauses and parenthetical statements. Some good readers are able to manage them, but others will enjoy the stories only if they are read aloud.[1]

Occasionally you'll find a reader who prefers E. B. White's *Stuart Little* (68) to the same author's *Charlotte's Web* (69). *Stuart Little* is a remarkable fantasy, worth many readings. Its theme is somber: the individual who doesn't fit into the world must wander through it finding some transitory happiness in the quest. But the tone is light, often humorous. Stuart is a brave, trusting little fellow and, in the author's eyes, the alien world is as gentle as one could hope.

As you may have already noticed, the English seem to dominate the field of fantasy, although Americans such as E. B. White and Lloyd Alexander have made unique contributions. The British have another American counterpart in Carol Kendall, whose small-peopled land sets the theme of nonconformity in *The Gammage Cup* (70) and its sequel *The Whisper of Glocken* (71). But fanciful literature seems to belong primarily to the British, although, fortunately, it can be understood and enjoyed by American children as well.

The British draw upon a longer, more consistent tradition, and this is observable in their fanciful stories. Their love of theater (including children's theater) seems to feed directly into their literary works for children. It's no accident that several leading British writers of fantasy have also had careers on the stage. The English writers also have a unique perception of a child's interest in *things* —umbrellas, pins, spools, opera glasses—not necessarily the toys purchased especially for play and regarded as special possessions, but the items that keep cropping up in one's life, sometimes taken for granted and nearly forgotten. English writers are often adept at conveying a sense of setting, an especially important element in fanciful literature. The setting may become almost a living being with its own active role in determining the plot.

Several British fanciful stories are gaining wide acceptance in America, especially the works of the four authors we will discuss next.

MARY NORTON.   Mary Norton's five books about the Borrowers almost convince you that the tiny people who live in the small spaces under the floor and behind

---

[1]See also Margery Sharp, *Miss Bianca,* illus. Garth Williams, *Miss Bianca and the Bridesmaid,* illus. Erik Blegvad (Little, Brown, 1962, 1972) and others in this series.

the wall really do exist. They're "as like to humans as makes no matter," says one adult as he describes them to a curious child in *The Borrowers Afield*. (72).[1]

Borrowers view normal-size humans as their unknowing benefactors. Examine the wonderful drawings in the first book to see how cleverly the Clock family of Borrowers (Pod, Homily, and their daughter Arrietty) have adapted items from the full-size human world to their own needs—a handwritten letter as wallpaper, a thimble for a water container, a child's building block as a work table, a safety pin to secure the front door, a cigar box for a bedroom, a kitchen funnel for a chimney, a glove for a rug, a chess piece as sculpture, a postage stamp as a portrait hung on the wall. (Since such things do get lost in every home, it is easy to believe that the Borrowers have borrowed them.)

But Borrowers also view normal-size humans as potentially dangerous. To be seen by them is to risk such danger that the best solution is to move away at once. In *The Borrowers* this doctrine is reluctantly ignored by the Clock family. Arrietty is not only seen by the boy in the house but strikes up a friendship with him and lets him bring gifts to the Clock home. For a time the family lives in riches, rivaling the snobbish Overmantel family of Borrowers in the drawing room. And then one night come the dogs, the ferret, and the poison gas.

In subsequent adventures the Clocks are victims of famine, flood, and thievery. Relatives aren't very kind to them, nor are they very well adapted to total outdoor life. They don't find life easy when humans aren't around to provide for them. In the words of Margery Fisher, they "remind us of all the dispossessed, the small and valiant and under-privileged people of this world and of all worlds."[2] Yet the Clocks are never completely overcome—they are too resourceful for that. Nor are they ever shaken from their family solidarity. They seldom stop to bewail their fallen estate, but, instead, they make do.

Paralleling the travail of the Borrowers is an emerging theme of human belief and disbelief in their existence. At first, we learn of them through the handed-down tales of a young boy, long since grown to manhood and killed in a war. Later, the story is continued through the account of old Tom Goodenough, who is thought to be senile. Gradually, the author takes over and in the fourth book tells the saga directly. Human characters who believe in the Borrowers are presented as empathic to all nonhuman, fanciful creatures, while the nonbelievers are the practical, pragmatic skeptics in our midst. Mrs. Driver, the mean housekeeper who actually sees the Borrowers, denies their existence. Her orderly world, designed to be controlled for her own purposes, simply won't permit that belief. The fantasy has a serious core within its literary device for credibility: empathy includes reaching out to the unknown and caring about its existence.

In these stories there is a touching alliance between the young and the elderly.

---

[1]See also Mary Norton, *The Borrowers, The Borrowers Afloat, The Borrowers Aloft,* and *Poor Stainless,* illus. Beth and Joe Krush (Harcourt, 1953, 1959, 1961, 1971).
[2]Margery Fisher, *Intent Upon Reading* (Watts, 1961), p. 106.

Children learn of the Clock family's existence through the tipsy, bedridden Great-Aunt Sophy, a "some kind of relation" oldster named Mrs. May, senile Old Tom, one-legged Mr. Pott, and others like them. Perhaps the implication is that only the old and the young have the time and the will to "see."

The first four books in the Borrowers series form a continuous chronology, telling how the Clock family was driven from its home and finally found another suitable place to live.

P. L. TRAVERS.   No such overall plot line is to be found in P. L. Travers's famed Mary Poppins books.[1] Instead, there are thirty-six chapter-long adventures, apparently in no particular order, bound together by the arrivals and departures of the world's most astonishing governess. Almost every episode explores a new facet of magic brought (but not acknowledged) by Mary Poppins. Because each episode has its own unity, there can be a variety of tone—from the faintly sad and nostalgic "John and Barbara's Story" (chapter 9 in *Mary Poppins*) and the wistful "Marble Boy" (chapter 4 in *Mary Poppins Opens the Door*) to the delightful revenge of "Miss Andrew's Lark" (chapter 2 in *Mary Poppins Comes Back*) and the hilarious gravity-free effects of "Laughing Gas" (chapter 3 in *Mary Poppins*).

The basic ingredient of the plots in this series is magic—not the dangerous, threatening magic that so often haunts folklore but magic that brings pleasure to the Banks children. Such a variety of magic would lose its novelty and appeal within a few pages if it were not so stringently controlled by Mary Poppins. You want to read on, not only to find out what happens next but to be assured repeatedly that a strict, no-nonsense adult can bring limitless fun. That's a theme to give hope to us all, adult and child alike!

NICHOLAS STUART GRAY.   Gray is one of the most light-hearted modern fanciful writers, yet he never loses respect for the literary art or turns it into parody. In one of his earlier books, *Grimbold's Other World* (73), a boy hero receives a ring from the finger of a witch, who tells him: "Take this with my love and thanks. . . . A small reward. But, if ever you are bored—rub the stone. Nothing will happen, but it whiles away the time."[2] When even a witch can talk like that, you know you are on safe ground.

The agreeable balance of humor and suspense is even stronger in Gray's more recent *Over the Hills to Fabylon* (74). In this story a pesky door follows the Lord Chamberlain's son about and can't be gotten rid of; a lovely white hound is discovered to be the bewitched mother of the young man; and a friendly bear takes the princess's crown and won't give it back. The author, a Scot with a lilt in his style, is a stage actor with a fine eye for visual effects and an ear for amusing conversation.

---

[1] See P. L. Travers, *Mary Poppins, Mary Poppins Comes Back,* and *Mary Poppins in the Park,* illus. Mary Shepard (Harcourt, 1934, 1935, 1952) as well as *Mary Poppins Opens the Door,* illus. Mary Shepard and Agnes Sims (Harcourt, 1943).
[2] p. 36.

LUCY M. BOSTON.   Finally, let us present Lucy M. Boston, the enigmatic stylist who didn't begin to write for children until she reached the age of sixty. It is said of the American painter, Grandma Moses, that she began at the top of a picture, painted the sky and the rest of the landscape, then the buildings, and finally the animals, the people, and the action. That is also the impression created by Boston—a predominance of setting and atmosphere from which the actions of the rather flat characters evolve. Because of this tableau quality, her work doesn't appeal to all tastes. You and certain children may still find yourselves among the many Boston enthusiasts.

Her first book, *The Children of Green Knowe* (75), takes a little boy, nicknamed Tolly, through a vast flood to the castle called Green Noah, sometimes known as Green Knowe. The entrance room is full of mirrors so that "he almost wondered which was really himself."[1] His grandmother, Mrs. Oldknow, who lives alone in the castle, watches the boy kindly and tells him many stories of his ancestors, including three children who perished long ago in the plague of 1665. Gradually, Tolly begins to see the three children. They are ghosts who sometimes play with him and who at other times take no notice of him. The reader gradually begins to wonder what this strange story is all about. Is it about the ghosts or about Tolly? Who is "real" in this work? At the terrifying climax, Tolly's reality seems to win, but only because a supernatural statue of Saint Christopher steps in to save him.

The second book, *Treasure of Green Knowe* (76), also has a double plot. Tolly returns to Green Knowe for the holidays, finds his beloved grandmother in need of money, and searches for treasure to help her. But the ghost of a blind girl named Susan interrupts his search, as do Mrs. Oldknow's stories of how Susan was enabled to "see" through her other senses with the help of an African boy named Jacob. There's great cruelty in these episodes—especially in the way people of the past locked defective children away from society and in the racially-based abuse directed at Jacob.

The River at Green Knowe (77) has a lighter tone, and the scene shifts to the outer boundaries of the estate. Tolly is gone and so is Mrs. Oldknow; three children of different nationalities meet weird, fantastic creatures, such as winged horses and a giant. The effect is idyllic and splendid. Whereas the earlier books are weighted with a past that threatens to engulf the present, this book celebrates the unity between children and the earth.

Lucy Boston's next book in this series, *A Stranger at Green Knowe* (78) (considered by some critics to be her best), presents the underside of the theme: a child's unity with nature ends in tragedy. There's no fantasy in this book. Instead, there's an escaped gorilla and an Oriental boy named Ping, who understand each other perfectly without words. Never has an animal been more insightfully described than Hanno, the gorilla.[2]

---

[1] p. 15.

[2] *A Stranger at Green Knowe* really belongs in the discussion of realistic fiction in chapter 6, but we include it here because it is part of this otherwise fanciful series.

An Enemy at Green Knowe (79) features a modern witch named Melanie Powers, a student of witchcraft who is uncomfortably adept at applying the latest theories of behavior shaping. She's defeated, of course, by the cunning of Tolly (who returns for this adventure) and by Ping, the boy from the previous book.

Western literature seems to take conflict for granted as a component of plot. But Boston's *The Sea Egg* (80) is a plotted tone poem without conflict other than momentary impatience and a mother's brief anxiety that her sons seem to be growing up so quickly. The Green Knowe setting and the familiar characters are gone. But the theme of children's oneness with the universe remains and grows, as two naked boys join a Triton in the regions of the sea—". . . the sea, huge and wide and blue, and so full of light that it seemed hardly to be there at all, but it heaved gently, as if it breathed in its sleep, and whispered in an echoey way, both near and very far off."[1] So the sea setting dominates, and the characters and their actions are blended into it.

In these books, fancy serves theme more than plot. The mystical is made manifest and concrete through the fanciful. The symbolism is extended and complex—some say too complex for children's literature. The monstrous force that almost destroys Tolly in *The Children of Green Knowe* is a replication of Noah, who saved humanity from the flood to let it go on in sorrow. Tolly, through his ghosts, has absorbed that sorrow. But those same ghosts save Tolly by calling to the Saint Christopher statue, showing that the past brings strength along with its burden. The gorilla, the fanciful Triton, the African child (and to some extent the other children as well) stand in positive opposition to the human concept of evolution—that man's place in the world is to set himself above it and control it for his own purposes.

The Boston books are very difficult and sometimes considered tedious, but they support the conviction that fanciful literature can reveal reality with greater depth than almost any other medium.

Modern Fanciful Stories for Upper Childhood

HIGH FANTASY.   So-called *high fantasy* is of special interest to many upper-age children, though not limited to this age level. High fantasy enthusiasts cross all age boundaries and delight in each other's company, comparing notes and impressions about Narnia, Prydain, Earthsea, or whatever their specialty.

The works these enthusiasts most admire have certain similarities. A high fantasy is usually long, running to several volumes. Its setting is a world other than our own, with a different geography and history. By various references, the author lets readers know that this other world contains much more than the story presents, giving it a sense of reality akin to our perception of our own world. The plot in high fantasy likewise appears to be a sampling of adventures

---

[1]p. 14.

known to the author and presented in tip-of-the-iceberg fashion, so that we are left to fill in some of the incidents. The plot has an epic quality: a hero or heroine on a quest, a spell to be broken, a whole civilization to be saved. The plot is complex with episodic pieces, but it has a clearly definable overall structure.

Magic and supernatural forces appear in high fantasy but not just to fulfill wishes. They are double-edged devices, helping to solve problems but also creating them. Characters must learn to deal with the supernatural to avoid being overcome by it. The characters themselves, despite their otherworldly setting, are surprisingly like ordinary people and form our thematic bond to the story.

The three best-known high fantasy works present the worlds of Middle-earth, Narnia, and Prydain—created, respectively, by J. R. R. Tolkien, C. S. Lewis, and Lloyd Alexander. In the following excerpts, Mary Lou Colbath expertly summarizes these classic works.

WORLDS AS THEY SHOULD BE: MIDDLE-EARTH, NARNIA AND PRYDAIN

by Mary Lou Colbath[1]

Fantasy presents the world as it should be. . . . Sometimes heartbreaking, but never hopeless, the fantasy world as it "should be" is one in which good is ultimately stronger than evil, where courage, justice, love and mercy actually function. . . . [I]f we listen carefully, it may tell us what we someday may be capable of achieving.[2]

. . . Hobbits[3] make reluctant but dependable heroes, a kind of scaled-down man-size hero. They themselves are not men, of course, but creatures smaller than dwarves who like the "creature comforts" of good food, pleasant companions, a warm fire and not too much excitement.

In *The Hobbit,* a straight forward adventure story, Bilbo Baggins regrets leaving his home even as he sets out with Gandalf and thirteen dwarves on the quest of great treasure. All through the book he finds himself thinking, "not for the last time," of the comforts of home. Never does he consider himself capable of coping with the dangers and perils of the road. And yet he does. Bilbo is responsible, more than once, for saving the lives of his companions. He does the dangerous, courageous thing out of necessity—because there is no one else to do it. And he does it honestly—admitting his own fear and wishing that he were not the one on whom the others must rely.

But it is his nephew Frodo Baggins in *The Lord of the Rings* who gives the greatest demonstration of heroism, courage and sacrifice. Bilbo did not know what lay ahead when he set out on his quest. Frodo does. Knowing full well the awesome threat of the One Ring of Power, the terror and horror of Sauron and the armies of Mordor, recognizing his own weakness and fear, he assumes the responsibility of "ring-bearer" and the charge by the council of free peoples to carry the ring to the Mountain of Fire. With him goes his servant and companion Sam, no less brave to be sure, but less aware of the ultimate trials the two are to face. . . .

---

[1]Reprinted from *Elementary English 48* (December 1971): 937–45.
[2]Lloyd Alexander, "The Flat-Heeled Muse," *Horn Book* (April 1965): 141.
[3]From J. R. R. Tolkien, *The Hobbit* [and other books in this series.] (Houghton Mifflin, 1938).

It is without hope that Frodo sets out—he knows only that he must try to carry the ring to its destruction. That he is successful only through the help of Sam and the despised yet pitied Gollum does not diminish Frodo's heroism. And while not called upon to make the ultimate sacrifice of his life, Frodo does not accomplish his quest without sacrifice. Grievously wounded by the power of the Ring, he gives up that which he most loved and wanted to keep—the Shire, his home. . . .

The land of Narnia[1] also demands heroism and courage but on a different scale. . . . The adventures of Peter, Susan, Lucy, Edmund and later, Eustace and Jill, all the English children, are the adventures of school children called upon to do all the things they have always longed to do in their dreams.

They fight by the side of Aslan, the noble and mystical lion, are knighted on a field of battle, are crowned in a great palace to the cheers of their friends the talking animals. When Narnia is in danger, they come to her rescue.

But the children are never alone. Around them like a great cloak of warmth and light is the knowledge that, although he may not be with them physically, Aslan exists and will always be their guide and protector.

Uppermost in the values to be found in Narnia are those which the children learn from Aslan: loyalty; consideration for others; courage to do the right thing despite those who counsel otherwise; steadfast faith in the power of goodness. These values are attained not so much by sacrifice as by a painful learning process. Edmund in *The Lion, The Witch and The Wardrobe*, changes from an unpleasant, selfish, greedy little boy to a kind, brave young man. In the process, however, he suffers at the hand of the White Witch, plays the traitor to his brother and sisters and, worst of all, must acknowledge to himself that in the eyes of Aslan he had done grievous wrong. Given the chance to redeem himself, Edmund does so admirably and can ascend victoriously to one of the four thrones of Narnia. . . .

If one could venture a hope for the Land of Prydain[2] it would be this: that Prydain, Taran and Eilonwy would be available for all children to read about and dream about in these perilous years of the space age and for many years to come. Lloyd Alexander truly has created a story, a myth, that children can claim as their own—untouched by adult tampering or changing—unshared with adults unless the grown-up reader himself chooses to go adventuring. . . .

The Book of Three. . . . begins with a conflict that says much about Taran, about the stories that are to come, about young boys on their way to growing up:

> Taran wanted to make a sword; but Coll, charged with the practical side of his education, decided on horseshoes. And so it had been horseshoes all morning long. Taran's arms ached, soot blackened his face. At last he dropped the hammer and turned to Coll, who was watching him critically.
> "Why?" Taran cried. "Why must it be horseshoes?"[3]

More quickly than he had thought possible, Taran, assistant pigkeeper, finds himself involved with swords, battles, heroes and great danger. By the side of Prince Gwydion, fighting to save Prydain from King Arawn, the Death Lord, Taran begins to grow up—and to learn the importance of horseshoes.

But the growing up is not easily accomplished. His head full of dreams about battles and heroes, Taran comes face to face with the reality of death, danger and sacrifice.

It is in *The Black Cauldron* that Taran learns most painfully that honor is not lightly achieved; that much is demanded when one takes a man's place. Once again in the

---

[1]From C. S. Lewis, *The Lion, the Witch, and the Wardrobe* (Macmillan, 1950).
[2]From Lloyd Alexander, *The Book of Three* (Dell, 1969).
[3]p. 9.

battle field, Taran grows to admire and love the gentle bard Adaon who teaches him:

> I have marched in many a battle host. . . . but I have also planted seeds and reaped the harvest with my own hands. And I have learned there is greater honor in a field well plowed than in a field steeped in blood.[1]

It is with the greatest grief he has ever known that Taran sees Adaon die; he learns well the lesson of the Bard's life.

But the Chronicles of Prydain are not stories of unrelieved battle. Humor does exist by the side of gallantry and sheer exuberance of living is exhibited by Taran and his companions. The Princess Eilonwy, first met in *The Book of Three,* shares the adventures of growing-up. As Taran learns, so does she and readers will recognize and delight in Eilonwy's struggles with the problems of becoming a woman.

In a most un-didactic way, young readers (and for that matter, older readers as well) of the Chronicles of Prydain learn about the dreams of youth and the realities of growing up. They learn that dreams and dreamers can be honored and encouraged but that much is expected of those who would fulfill the dreams. In *Taran Wanderer,* the young man, Taran, sets out to fulfill a boyish dream—to discover who his parents were. Not through great adventure in battle (although there are adventures early in the book with a wicked enchanter and with three weird sisters), but through his own hard work, through his willingness and readiness to learn from others—a farmer, a smith, a weaver, a potter—Taran discovers himself. He leaves the Mountains and the Mirror of Llunet at peace with himself and ready to face his destiny.

It is in *The High King* that Taran completes the process of growing up. He is, at last, a full-fledged hero; through his efforts Prydain is saved and the Death-Lord slain. Given the chance to depart for the Summer Country with Dalben, Gwydion and his other companions, Taran is sorely tempted.

But during a sleepless night, Taran remembers the friends who died fighting with the forces of good—the peoples of Prydain who cast their lots with an Assistant Pig-Keeper. He chooses to stay—not to leave the realm with his companions and with the enchantment which no longer has a place in a country of free men. . . .

In three other books Lloyd Alexander has expanded his Prydain chronicles. *Coll and His White Pig* (81) is a picture book to accompany *The Book of Three. The Truthful Harp* (82) is for readers who have special fondness for the bard Fflewddur Flam. *The Foundling and Other Tales of Prydain* (83) has a special dedication: "For Friends of Prydain who promised to read more if I promised to write more." In this book the author is at the height of his powers. The first story, "The Foundling," revisits the three hags of fate and Dalben's discovery of their powers: "The thread you spin, and measure, and cut off . . . these are no threads, but the lives of men."[2] "The True Enchanter," with its motif of three suitors for a princess's hand, makes a fine dramatization. "The Sword" is Alexander's tale of treachery, without a grain of the author's characteristic humor. All six stories should be read aloud, for their prose rhythm and diction are matchless.

---

[1]Lloyd Alexander, *The Black Cauldron* (Holt, 1965), p. 43.
[2]p. 6.

Two American-based women have made recent important contributions to high fantasy. Susan Cooper (born in England, now living in America) began her series with *Over Sea, Under Stone* (84), a modern treasure hunt involving one of the "Old Ones"—ancient purveyors of magic. With the second book, *The Dark Is Rising* (85), the high fantasy element emerges: Will Stanton, a modern boy enjoying the Christmas holidays, is suddenly cast back into an ancient magic world where he must rescue the symbols of wood, bronze, iron, fire, water, and stone from the powers of Darkness. The mystical hold of ancient rites dominates the third volume, *Greenwitch* (86). (Cooper plans to add two more volumes to this series.)

Ursula K. LeGuin, well known to readers of adult science fiction, began with *A Wizard of Earthsea* (87) to tell how a goatherd became a wizard, an Archmage, and eventually a dragon-lord. This book has one particularly terrifying scene: the aspiring wizard misuses his power to summon up the dead and is severely punished. Its climax also contains one of the best surprises in high fantasy—one you should discover for yourself. In the second book, *The Tombs of Atuan* (88), the wizard, now called Sparrowhawk, has learned not to use his magic for self gain, a difficult denial when he's buried underground with apparently no other hope of escape. In *The Farthest Shore* (89), the third book in the series, a dark evil seems to be spreading all over Earthsea. The Archmage and his young apprentice set out to meet it. Here, as in the other two volumes, the theme deals with the time and appropriateness of using power over others. Unfortunately, *The Farthest Shore* is a confusing book. The lesson is driven home at the expense of clarity of plot.

LIGHT FANTASY.   Light fantasy is less demanding than high fantasy. Its other worlds aren't so far removed. They include an ant colony in Evelyn Sibley Lampman's *The City under the Back Steps* (90) and a number of brief, varied little worlds just beyond *The Swing in the Summerhouse* (91) by Jane Langton.

A very fine writer of light fantasy for upper-age children is Joan Aiken, whose somewhat tall tales bear a resemblance to Victorian novels. *The Wolves of Willoughby Chase, Black Hearts in Battersea, Nightbirds on Nantucket,* and *The Cuckoo Tree* (92) form a series in the sense of containing some of the same characters. *The Whispering Mountain* (93) has different characters and a more fanciful setting.

The plots of these books are fast-paced and near parody. A wolf is rumored to have eaten the train engineer. Another one leaps through the carriage window and is promptly dispatched by a good gentleman who throws his cloak over the creature and stabs it with a piece of broken glass. Little girls, presumed to be orphans, are locked in various ugly prisons. At one point in the third book a cannon, constructed to shoot clear across the Atlantic and hit King James, is instead safely towed away by a pink whale. Comic melodrama of the "Oh, my goodness—then you must be my long lost daughter" type abounds, almost straight out of Gilbert and Sullivan.

But, unlike most parodists, Aiken arouses empathy. When the plucky heroine Dido apparently dies at the end of *Black Hearts in Battersea* and is provided a "simple stone with a simple legend, 'Dido Twite, a Delicate Sprite,' " the reader is likely to be shamelessly saddened.

Quite different is the light fantasy of Mollie Hunter. Her *Thomas and the Warlock* (94) has a funny cast of adults ridding their land of witchcraft. In *The Haunted Mountain* (95) a foolish man is enslaved by the fairy "Good People" and then rescued by his son and dog. But Hunter attempts the rich, rhythmical style of the Scottish storyteller and a thematic depth not quite consistent with her playful plots. In *The Walking Stones* (96) a modern boy summons his own double, a mysterious Co-Walker, to foil three modern industrialists who would destroy ancient monuments. The past must give way, the new generation must supplant the old one, the unknown must be confronted—these are heavy themes caught in a light structure.

TIME FANTASY.   Time fantasy usually presents modern characters who are somehow transferred into the past, offering a unique perspective on history. H. G. Wells used it, as did Mark Twain in *A Connecticut Yankee in King Arthur's Court* (97). Alison Uttley in *A Traveler in Time* (98) wrote about the efforts of a time-traveler to avert the tragedy of Mary Queen of Scots. It is also the device that makes *Tom's Midnight Garden* by Philippa Pearce a gently moving love story across the ages. Penelope Farmer's *Charlotte Sometimes* (99) features Donald Jackson, a frustrated modern boy who learns to be brave by tackling a worm-monster outside a medieval village.

Recently, time fantasy seems to have borrowed some of the flashback and flash-forward techniques of the cinema. Half-described settings and floating shadows drift impressionistically across the plots, leaving readers confused about what is happening. Alan Garner's *Red Shift* (100) is a sort of association game. The modern boy and girl are so adrift in the past that their real actions never come to the surface.[1] Alison, the heroine of Garner's much praised *The Owl Service* (101), doesn't drift into the past, but she is bewitched by it, specifically by the characters in an old tragic legend who would force Alison to replay the past.

This vagueness about what is happening or what has happened may create an appropriate atmosphere for time fantasy. But often it puzzles and bores its readers. William Mayne has a wonderful beginning in *Earthfasts* (102): an eighteenth-century drummer boy, Nellie Jack John of Low Eskeleth, emerges into the modern world from an underground passage where he once went searching for the treasures of King Arthur. Two modern boys, David and Keith, try to befriend him, but he remains stubbornly uncomprehending. Then the past begins to envelop the present. Giants devastate the countryside, and one of the boys disappears. The theme has something to do with coming of age and with time being out of joint, but nothing is clarified by the jumble of scenes that complete the book. Similarly, Mayne's *The Hill Road* (103) begins well: a red-

---

[1]See Aidan Chambers, "Letter from England: Literary Crossword Puzzle . . . or Masterpiece?" *Horn Book* 49 (October 1973): 495–97.

haired girl of the past discovers she has powers of witchcraft and can help members of a Briton tribe just after the Romans have withdrawn. But the focus then shifts abruptly to three modern children (one of them red-haired) caught in the ancient turmoil. The two story fragments don't seem to come together.

In these stories events aren't so much told as commented upon. A collage of settings and situations asks the reader to project his feelings without very clear understanding of the fictional basis for doing so.

Limited ambiguity of a different sort helps make Mary Q. Steele's *Journey Outside* (104) a challenging and rewarding book. The clarity of her style and the purposeful pace add to the reader's enjoyment. Dilar, the hero, is a member of a diminishing tribe of Raft People, destined to travel round and round in their underground river till the end of their lives. But Dilar wants to know more than the colorless river and the adults of his tribe can tell him. In the first of a series of impulsive leave-takings, he jumps off the raft and climbs up a passageway to the world above. This world resembles our own. There is sun, grass, trees, hens, pumpkins—things that surprise and please Dilar and give readers a fresh look at familiar surroundings. Still, Dilar is looking for something more, perhaps a way of life or an answer to the question of what people should be. The people he meets are friendly enough and generous, but they take no thought of the morrow and harbor no curiosity. So Dilar moves on, into the winter mountains where tigers lurk and the freezing weather brings him to the door of death. For a time he lives with a jolly, storytelling caveman. Dilar should be happy: he has food and companionship, and he shares the man's mission—to bake cakes to feed the mountain animals. But this, too, begins to seem wrong, and one night Dilar discovers that he is a prisoner. Escaping down the mountain, he tries yet another life style—this time among solitary desert people.

Perhaps in the end Dilar finds what he seeks. He does learn the origin of the Raft People and determines to go and bring them up again into the sunlit world. But why? For themselves? For himself? The author doesn't permit an ambiguous theme to block clarity of setting, character, and plot. For this reason, her story remains worthwhile and interesting to the end.

ANIMAL FANTASY.   Richard Adams's *Watership Down* (105), a fantasy for upper ages and adults, may help to set things straight. This is a long work (nearly five hundred tightly crammed pages) in a real English setting, without the cosmic philosophies and overtones of high fantasy but also without the playful tone of light fantasy. It avoids any pretense of being anything other than an adventure story about rabbits. Eleven of them leave their warren just in time to escape the poison gas used by urban developers.

Hazel becomes their leader. Fiver is the "seer," his visions warning them against disaster and, in the end, saving them. Bigwig is their physical force, their weapon against enemies. They become as real as anyone you've ever known. And, without any author intrusion whatsoever, you learn from them—not just the less important though interesting things such as how to escape a cat or tease a dog, but matters of character that are both subtle and humanistic. Hazel is sincere but tactful even in the worst of circumstances, while Bigwig is far from the stereotype of brawn-without-brain.

The rabbits move on—to a false paradise where men bring food in plenty. Men, they decide, do not destroy rabbits as revenge for raiding of crops: "That wasn't why they destroyed the warren. It was just because we were in their way. They killed us to suit themselves."[1]

And, shortly, they find their new home at Watership Down—safety at last, and sufficient shelter and food. But now their attention turns to a different problem: the need for mates. So off go the hunting parties, this time to a totalitarian rabbit empire controlled by General Woundwort. The fight and flight, the counter-attack by the general, and a final chapter that leaves you reluctant to finish because then there won't be any more of it to enjoy—that's enduring fantasy. It's accomplished through superb craftsmanship, as well as through splendid, sustained inspiration. Here, for example, are some ways the inspiration is manifested:

- Rabbit language. Adams seems to have created a whole syntax and lexicon of rabbit language. Unlike some fantasy writers, he makes no attempt to teach it to the reader. It's there in fragments if you want it: *silflay* for grazing, *El-ahrairah* for the mythic hero, *elil* for enemies, *hrududu* for automobile.

- Rabbit mythology. The main narrative is frequently broken to permit the telling of a story, a myth usually known to the listeners but appreciated by them. On several occasions the myth provides the solution to a problem. At the conclusion, you discover how the adventures of the characters have begun to be converted to myth.

- Balance in plot and theme. There are many occasions when this book could have displayed great cruelty, preachy wisdom, or boundless terror. Or the book could have created episodes of character conflict to keep the reader temporarily alert (Bigwig and Hazel are potential contenders for leadership, for example). A sign of greatness in *Watership Down* is that the author keeps the balance. Nothing is used for momentary effect alone. Nothing is taken to an extreme just to give us a sharp jolt when interest might be flagging.

- Honest pathos. When Bigwig and General Woundwort have fought almost to the death and Bigwig is about to lose consciousness, he cries out: "The wire!" It is his earlier encounter with death half a lifetime ago, when he was caught in a snare, that Bigwig remembers. The effect is to show that he has lived with this terror almost from the beginning of the adventures. Likewise, Adams is able to show Woundwort, the arch-tyrant, in pathetic bravery, calling his soldiers back to face the monster: "Come back, you fools! Dogs aren't dangerous! Come back and fight!"[2]

---

[1] p. 165
[2] p. 457

Unlike most princesses in traditional folk tales who cringe in the background while the brave hero chases the dragon, this princess boldly encounters a modern dragon decorated with folk-art designs. From THE PRACTICAL PRINCESS by Jay Williams, illus. by Friso Henstra. Copyright © 1969. Used by permission of Parents' Magazine Press.

The Golden Goose

Then Simpleton set at once to hew down the tree. And when it fell he found among its roots a goose whose feathers were all of pure gold. He lifted it out, carried it off, and took it with him to an inn where he meant to spend the night.

Charles Mikolaycak uses soft ochres and orange and the rounded composition of Renaissance paintings to illustrate this favorite old tale. Copyright © 1969 by Charles Mikolaycak. Reprinted from GRIMM'S GOLDEN GOOSE by the Brothers Grimm, illustrated by Charles Mikolaycak, by permission of Random House, Inc.

John Burningham's charming pictures tell a simple tale from a child's point of view, using muted colors. This drawing assembles children, animals, and Mr. Gumpy with a child's quiet assurance, disposing of any thought that this is an unlikely group to gather

for tea. From Mr. Gumpy's Outing by John Burningham. Copyright © 1970 by John Burningham. Reproduced by permission of Holt, Rinehart and Winston, Inc. and Jonathan Cape Ltd.

Compare Charles Mikolaycak's interpretation of Red Riding-Hood's visit to Grandmother with his GOLDEN GOOSE (p. 215.) The elaborate quilt and drape designs heighten the drama as the puzzled heroine begins her immortal inquiry. From LITTLE RED RIDING-HOOD by the Brothers Grimm, illustrated by Charles Mikolaycak. By permission of the C. R. Gibson Company.

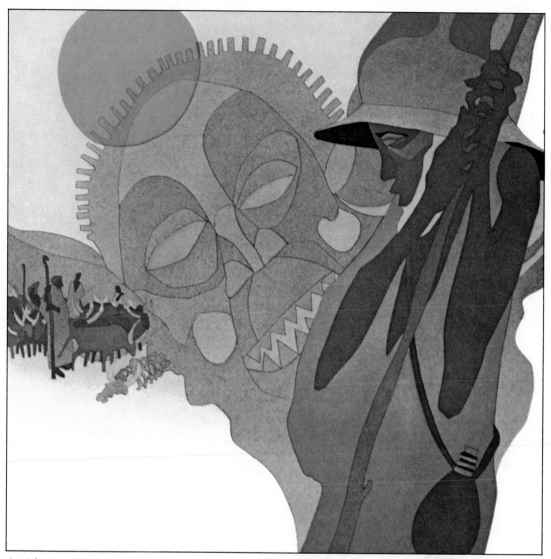

An African mask dominates the scene, a depiction of tone rather than actual incident. The artists, Leo and Diane Dillon, use design to comment upon the story, complementing the text of the storyteller. From THE THIRD GIFT by Jan Carew, by permission of Little, Brown and Co. Illustrations Copyright © 1974 by Leo and Diane Dillon.

The Dillons have treated this Shawnee legend as a stylized design. Out of the primal matrix the animals emerge. Excerpted from THE RING IN THE PRAIRIE by John Bierhorst; illustrated by Leo and Diane Dillon. Text copyright © 1970 by John Bierhorst; illustrations copyright © 1970 by Leo and Diane Dillon. Used with permission of the Dial Press.

←

Like a soap bubble reflecting the sun, the elaborately drawn figures and backgrounds in RAIN MAKES APPLESAUCE float and twinkle in their pastel beauty. Intricate, connecting lines and text direct the eye to a unity of design. From RAIN MAKES APPLESAUCE, words by Julian Scheer and pictures by Marvin Bileck. Used by permission of the publisher, Holiday House, Inc.

⟶

But his face you could not see,
On account of his Beaver Hat.
For his Hat was a hundred and two feet wide,
With ribbons and bibbons on every side,
And bells, and buttons, and loops, and lace,
So that nobody ever could see the face
Of the Quangle Wangle Quee.

Helen Oxenbury's opulent interpretation of Lear's mad tale adds to its hilarity. This artist's inventive style can also be seen in her Greenaway Medal book, THE HUNTING OF THE SNARK, another Lear tale. From THE QUANGLE WANGLE'S HAT by Edward Lear, illustrated by Helen Oxenbury. Copyright © 1970 by Helen Oxenbury. Used by permission of Franklin Watts, Inc., New York, and William Heineman Ltd., London.

Blair Lent's intricate, watercolored ink drawings for THE FUNNY LITTLE WOMAN show green-hued underground creatures contrasted with the orange-clad little woman. This artist varies his medium and style to attempt authenticity in depicting different cultures. Contrast this treatment of a Japanese tale with his mask-dance figures for an African myth, WHY THE SUN AND MOON LIVE IN THE SKY. From THE FUNNY LITTLE WOMAN by Arlene Mosel, illustrated by Blair Lent. Copyright © 1972 by Arlene Mosel; Illustrations copyright © 1972 by Blair Lent. Reprinted by permission of the publishers, E. P. Dutton & Co., Inc.

The rough, primitive quality of woodcuts seems especially appropriate to folk tales. Here Naoko Matsubara has fashioned a design keyed to the mood of this Japanese tale. Woodcut by Naoko Matsubara, reproduced from THE TALE OF THE SHINING PRINCESS by Hisako Matsubara by permission of Kodansha International Ltd., Tokyo, Japan. Copyright © 1966 by Kodansha International Ltd.

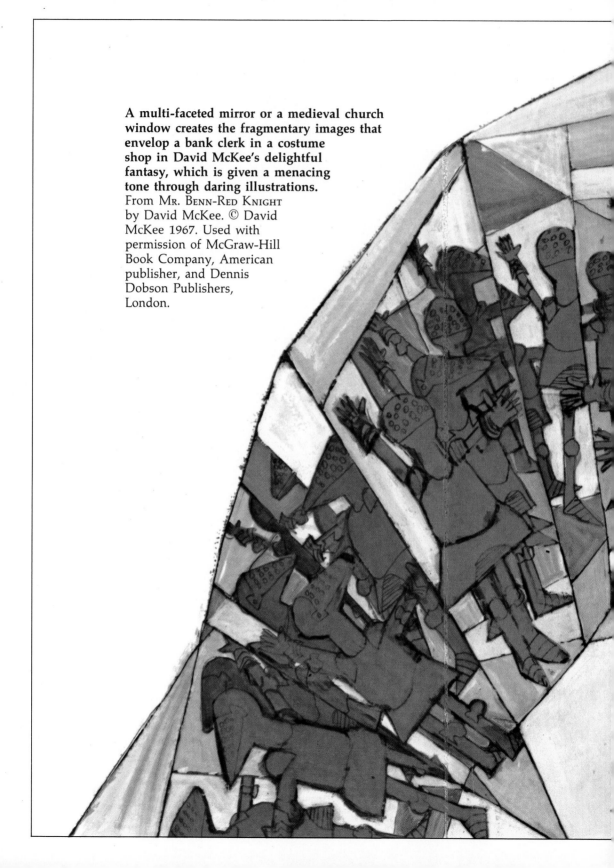

A multi-faceted mirror or a medieval church window creates the fragmentary images that envelop a bank clerk in a costume shop in David McKee's delightful fantasy, which is given a menacing tone through daring illustrations.

Maurice Sendak's illustrations picture creatures frozen in ballet-like motion, seeming about to leap off the page. This author/artist draws and paints to a musical background, a fact that is apparent in his work. From WHERE THE WILD THINGS ARE by Maurice Sendak. Copyright © 1963 by Maurice Sendak. By permission of Harper & Row, Publishers, Inc., and The Bodley Head.

Innumerable books testify to Mercer Mayer's fun-loving tone and his ability to balance a wealth of detail in a small space. In contrast with Sendak's ballet-like process. Mayer has projected a tangled melée. Reprinted by permission of Four Winds Press, a division of Scholastic Magazines, Inc., from WHAT DO YOU DO WITH A KANGAROO? by Mercer Mayer, © 1973 by Mercer Mayer.

The favorite of many children's book enthusiasts, Arthur Rackham gave his settings an eerie quality that suggests a magic world in which the earth, trees, and sky are all conscious of the significance of the story. From RIP VAN WINKLE by Washington Irving, illustrated by Arthur Rackham (1967 edition). Reproduced by permission of J. B. Lippincott Company.

Tootle-toot! **sang the flute
and up went her boot
and down again soon
to the tantivy tune.
Every thorn and twig
did dance to the jig
and the witch willy-nilly —
each prickle and pin
as it skewered her in
was driving her silly.**

A terrifying tale based on Grimm receives a fascinating, unpredictable treatment by Ed Emberley, the tone and style markedly different from his DRUMMER HOFF illustrations. The witch's boots are entangled by plants that are authentic herbs of witchcraft.

"Hi!
   Ho!"
      shrieked she,
and "Tickle-me-thistle!" and "Prickle-de-dee!"
And battered she was as she trotted and tripped,
and her clothes were torn and tattered and ripped
till at last,
all mingled and mangled,
   her right leg entangled,
      her left leg right-angled,
firm as a prisoner pinned to the mast,
she
      stuck
            fast.

There is surprisingly clear detail in Gerald McDermott's half-literal, half-symbolic illustrations for this and other tales and myths. Brilliant block color adds clarity and drama, giving a familiar tale immediacy and suspense. From ANANSI THE SPIDER, adapted and illustrated by Gerald McDermott. Copyright © 1972 by Landmark Production, Incorporated. Reproduced by permission of Holt, Rinehart and Winston, Inc. and Hamish Hamilton Children's Books Ltd.

SCIENCE FICTION

Proponents of science fiction in children's literature attest to its importance:

> The belief that children's science fiction is essentially escape literature associated with 'Bug-Eyed Monsters' and space opera plots is fallacious. The genre includes significant themes and values which are commentaries on society in general and the impact of technology on human values in particular. The literature can be used to help create in children an awareness of social problems and a more perceptive understanding of decisions one must make in the world.[1]

Notwithstanding, science fiction for children has a dual personality. It does contain bug-eyed creatures. In some of its stories there appears an ethnocentric attitude that anything not of this earth must be comic or of inferior intelligence or morality. Margery Fisher refers to the "brashly imperialistic flavour" of some science fiction that takes for granted the human right to conquer all worlds and make them as much like our own as possible.[2] The values behind such works are similar to those of the minister who asserted that if there are creatures on other planets, our task is to teach them to be Christians.

The other personality of science fiction, which is beginning to emerge in writing for upper levels, has a serious, thoughtful intent. It is best described in Sylvia Louise Engdahl's definition, which compares science fiction with fantasy: "(S)cience fiction differs from fantasy not in subject matter but in aim, and its unique aid is to suggest real hypotheses about mankind's future or about the nature of the universe."[3] Other definitions, however, indicate a difference in subject matter, specifically the use of technologically accurate data to establish credibility.

Adult science fiction began at least as early as ancient Roman times with Lucian's *True History,* purporting to be an account of a trip to the moon. More recently the Jules Verne and H. G. Wells scientifically-based fantasy stories appeared. They are still being read by adults and older children. A long-lived periodical, *Amazing Stories,* began in 1926 and established a tradition of escapist pseudo-science stories that, by World War II, had begun to sound more plausible than their writers at first intended. By 1952 the way was open for a science fiction work done expressly for children: Louis Slobodkin's *The Space Ship under the Apple Tree* (106).

By modern standards, this work and its two sequels[4] are a bit tame, though still entertaining. Eddie Blow, vacationing on his grandparents' farm, meets a three-foot-tall Martinean (whose planet is somewhere beyond our solar sys-

---

[1]M. Jean Greenlaw, "Science Fiction: Impossible! Improbable! or Prophetic?" *Elementary English* 48 (April 1971): 201.
[2]Margery Fisher, *Intent Upon Reading* (Watts, 1961), p. 203.
[3]Sylvia Louise Engdahl, "The Changing Role of Science Fiction in Children's Literature," *Horn Book* 47 (October 1971): p. 450.
[4]Louis Slobodkin, *The Space Ship Returns to the Apple Tree* and *The Three-Seated Space Ship* (Macmillan, 1958, 1962).

tem). Eddie takes his space guest to the Boy Scout Jamboree and helps him put his Astral Rocket Disk back into operation. By the third volume, Eddie and his grandmother are fellow flyers, traveling to London in the space ship and returning to the airport from which they began, the grandmother deciding that the whole adventure was "an educational dream."

Alongside these safe, merry, flying saucer escapades were still popular adventures of a live, far-from-young lady, Miss Pickerell, who first appeared in *Miss Pickerell Goes to Mars* (107) by Ellen MacGregor. The eight volumes in this series contain just enough technological information to avoid implausibility. Although Miss Pickerell doesn't emerge as one of fiction's most fascinating creations, she is amusing and admirable in her resourcefulness. She's the brains of any outfit; the scientists in these books are unimaginative and bumbling.[1]

Two well known authors in the science field made early contributions to science fiction for teen-agers. Robert A. Heinlein's early teen-age stories began with *Rocket Ship Galileo* (108). Isaac Asimov, using the pseudonym Paul French, wrote *David Starr: Space Ranger, Lucky Starr and the Pirates of the Asteroids,* and *Lucky Starr and the Oceans of Venus* (109). Heinlein's story tells of a rocket race to the moon, confounded by attacks from the Nazis. The Asimov series describes the struggles of an earth-based Council of Science to bring law and order to the galaxy, where crime and espionage are the greatest dangers. Unlike the stories for younger children, these do present technological information as accurately as possible. The settings, involving interplanetary travel to Mars and Venus, also aim at authenticity.

But the plots are concerned with interpersonal conflict, not with the struggle of science to conquer the unknown. Although the young heroes travel the universe, they remain cowboy types, definitely earth-centered and earth-bound in their problems and attempted solutions.

The writers of the 1950s never quite came to terms with space fiction for children, using it merely as a new setting for old plots. The results are often entertaining, however, and a later age may view them as a rather quaint security device for considering the unknown. *Space Cat* (110) and the other books in this series by Ruthven Todd make no pretense of authenticity. They are amusing fantasy, using space flights, the moon, and other planets as settings for comic-book creatures like talking cats who get into difficulty with their human masters. John M. Schealer's Zip-Zip books contain an over-abundance of sibling argument among four members of the Riddle family, who accompany a Martian all over the United States to bring back a steam shovel in *Zip-Zip and His Flying Saucer* (111). Later they help him locate his father in *Zip-Zip Goes to Venus* (112) and defeat primitive beings called Tubars in *Zip-Zip and the Red Planet* (113). Critic Eleanor Cameron uses an interesting hypothesis as the basis for her science fantasy series: that creatures from outer space might find earth children more adaptive

---

[1]See also Ellen MacGregor and Dora Pantell, *Miss Pickerell Goes on a Dig* (Whittlesay House, 1966), Dora Pantell, *Miss Pickerell and the Weather Satellite* (Whittlesay House, 1971), and others in this series.

and helpful than adults. *The Wonderful Flight to the Mushroom Planet* (114) presents two wholly engaging boys, David and Chuck, who help the wisemen of the Mushroom race save their endangered citizenry. There's a tribute to childhood's spirit of good will in this and the other books in the series.

Miss Pickerell, the space cat Flyball, young Sparky in the Zip-Zip series, and Tyco Bass of the spore people all invite laughter. You can laugh at them and with them without leaving the context of their stories. In the Matthew Looney books by Jerome Beatty, Jr. the humor goes further: readers share jokes about the story with the author. At the start of *Matthew Looney's Voyage to the Earth* (115) Matt, who was born on the moon, is reading a book called *Is There Life on Earth?* The stage is set for a science fiction satire. When Matt visits the planet Earth, he finds no life, for the space ship has landed in Antarctica, under the impression that the earth's white regions must be more inhabitable than its green and blue regions. Later stories about Matt are longer and a shade more serious, as the moon's Anti-Earth League and the earthlings themselves are determined to destroy each other.[1]

The best light science fiction is still Robert A. Heinlein's *Have Space Suit—Will Travel* (116). Kip, its hero, loses a moon flight contest but receives a second-hand space suit instead. (It smells like a locker room.) Like most boys with a newly acquired piece of complicated equipment, he reads the manual and then comments:

> You can die from oxygen shortage, be poisoned by too much oxygen, be crippled by nitrogen, drown in or be acid-poisoned by carbon dioxide, or dehydrate and run a killing fever. When I finished reading that manual I didn't see how anybody could stay alive anywhere, much less in a space suit.[2]

Soon the space suit is in working order and the serious adventure begins. As the captive of the worst space monster imaginable, Kip is reeled off to the moon and Pluto—helpless as a goldfish, as he puts it. He's aided but also hampered by a couple of fellow captives: a precocious little girl named Peewee and a mysterious Mother Thing, a sort of life force symbol.

Heinlein is a good plotter. He builds high plot barriers and makes his characters figure out how to overcome them. He seldom wheels in a convenient outer force to do the job for them. In some of his books a group of young men (associate heroes, you might call them) solve the problems together, with almost too much talk and cooperative effort. But Kip, though aided, is the only hero in this book. Although he's given no dramatic character flaw to overcome, he is required to develop ingenuity and understanding. He's even required to work out his adolescent relationship with women.

With Madeleine L'Engle's *A Wrinkle in Time* (117), a Newbery Medal book,

---

[1]The most recent book in this series is *Matthew Looney and the Space Pirates* (Young Scott, 1972).
[2]p. 32.

science fiction for children attained a new seriousness. The book is one long crescendo. It begins realistically with the Murry family—Mrs. Murry, daughter Meg, younger son Charles Wallace, and the twins—comforting each other during an especially bad storm. A tramp arrives—or, rather, a creature from outer space—named Mrs. Whatsit. There is such a thing as a tesseract, she tells them. And soon Meg, Charles Wallace, and their friend Calvin have tesseracted and are sweeping away to other planets without any passage of time. Their immediate problem is how to rescue Mr. Murry, but even more is at stake: a gigantic evil force, named simply IT, must be overcome before it conquers the universe. This is great drama so long as the settings are clear, especially in the terrifying scenes of forced conformity. Eventually, however, abstractions supplant the action. The evil force can be defeated only by strongly willed love. Some of the dramatic force is lost, although many readers will testify that the sometimes confusing events in the latter chapters of the book are exactly right. L'Engle revisited the Murry family in *A Wind in the Door,* a story with an even more mystical conclusion.

L'Engle's *The Arm of the Starfish* (118) tells of a marine biology student's involvement with the secrets of the regenerative process by which starfish grow new arms, a process which might be adapted to man. Someone is bent upon stealing the secret for evil purposes—but who? Is it Carolyn Cutter, who appears to be the heroine? Is it Canon Tallis, who appears to be the spiritual anchor for the story? The choice is more than an adventure story guessing game. It has to do with the theme: that good and evil aren't always easy to distinguish. The gang called the Alphabets in *The Young Unicorns* (119) is recognizably evil. Their headquarters is under Columbia University and their activities include the use of a laser beam to dispose of their enemies. In both of these stories L'Engle has woven her theme into the fabric of plot and character; no departure from the action is needed in order to explain the significance.

With increasing seriousness, recent science fiction for upper ages views the world of the present as an unfortunate condition. One vein of science fiction purports to show what will happen if the world continues on its present course. Another group picks up the strands of evolution and technology to explain how a new world might evolve or be created. As several critics have remarked, the characters in most of these books have the emotional and intellectual make-up of people today. The new beings envisioned by some of the writers are, ironically, stuck with familiar human strengths and frailties.

But this is not to discredit the very recent imaginative, hair-raising science fiction for upper ages. Here are several authors whose works you may want to investigate for older children:

- John Christopher. In his first trilogy, which began with *The White Mountains* (120), creatures from outer space have inhabited earth and are turning humans into robots. The stories would be a tribute to the bravery of men if it weren't for Christopher's pessimism. In the end, it is quite clear that once rid of alien monsters, men will quickly return to a condition of war among themselves. In the second trilogy, beginning with *A Prince in Waiting* (121), the pessimism is even deeper. Christopher doesn't seem to have a way out. His vision of man seems unalterably tragic, though he is certain that his heroes will rise—at least temporarily—above their will to destroy.

• Robert C. O'Brien. Best known for his science-fiction fantasy *Mrs. Frisby and the Rats of NIMH* (122), O'Brien also wrote *The Silver Crown* (123). The opening scenes in this book are very similar to the theater of the absurd. Ellen, who has just turned ten, finds a silver crown on her pillow, imagines herself a fairy tale princess, and goes for a little walk. When she returns, her home has burned to the ground, apparently with her parents in it. From nowhere, men in green masks appear on the streets and shoot down policemen. The man who offers Ellen a lift in his car is a brainwashed brainwasher, who pursues her through a Gothic-like forest. The latter half of the book, with its brainwashing colony and despotic government, is comparatively common stuff. But the first half is almost high fantasy, very daring and effective.

• Ben Bova. After writing many high action, science fiction adventures for upper grades, Ben Bova decides to rid the earth of scientists. In *Exiled from Earth* (124) the geneticists are tossed off earth in an elaborate twenty-first-century space ship. In the second volume, *Flight of Exiles* (125), the space vehicle is described in detail:

> Going outward, each ring was bigger and held more room for equipment and living space. The entire ship was turning, revolving slowly, to provide an artificial gravity. The outermost wheel, level one, was at one full Earth *g,* and everyone felt his normal Earth weight there. Going "upward," toward the hub, weight and gravity fell off consistently, until at the hub itself, there was effectively no gravity, weightlessness.[1]

The first generation of exiles decides to head off for another planet in another galaxy. Because such an undertaking will span more than a lifetime, the scientists place themselves in a deep sleep, remaining frozen in a cryonics area of the ship, in the hope that they will awake years later to help their children begin a new civilization. But something goes wrong: a fire, accidental or planned, destroys them, leaving only a younger generation, among whom there seems to be a murderer.

• Peter Dickinson. Editor of the English humor magazine *Punch,* Dickinson began writing for children with *The Weathermonger* (126). In this and two later science fiction works—*Heartsease* and *The Devil's Children* (127)—the basic situation is the same: England has been stricken by the Changes, a time when all machines are hated and outlawed, and the last remains of magic are pounced upon by

---

[1]p. 16.

an arrogant population. Only a handful of children and young people are left to break the spell of hatred and unleash progress again. The first book explains the reason for the Changes, a most surprising one but quite convincing within the book's context. The other two books are set in the same time as the first, with different sets of characters and equally surprising revelations at the end.

• Sylvia Louise Engdahl. Engdahl has an anthropology-based theory that life on various galaxies has advanced to differing levels of technology and human relations. *Enchantress from the Stars* (128) begins the series. The heroine Elana is an endangered observer in a situation involving nuclear destruction in *The Far Side of Evil* (129). There's no space travel here, no interaction of planetary civilizations. A young man named Noren lashes out at his advanced culture, is apparently punished by the ruling scholars, and reaches a new understanding of his world. Engdahl doesn't dwell on technology; her interest is in the evolution of social control with emphasis on the individual's relationship to society. Repeatedly, her best-intentioned characters use deception to educate or strengthen those who lack wisdom. It's a useful plot device but wears a bit thin thematically. The central characters' inner thoughts and motivations are explored at great length, with such author concern that the reader shares in their plights.

• A. M. Lightner. Although she has written other science fiction, Alice Lightner is best known for *The Day of the Drones* (130). The setting is Earth after nearly total destruction in which Africa (now called Afria) seems to be the only continent untouched by radioactivity. A group of scholars and a governmental informant depart in the only flying machine available—a not-too-trustworthy helicopter run by solar batteries. What this group finds in England is a mounting horror: a matriarchal survival society patterned after and controlled with gigantic mutant bees. A discarded male in this society is painted with scent and promptly brought to death by the bees. Inevitably, the Afria heroine of the story, Amhara, receives this death mark, too.

Lightner has more in mind than a horror story, however. She deals perceptively with racial prejudice: the black Afrians are as repelled by the racial features of their found society as by its customs. The Afrian society itself is almost bookless, its knowledge of history reduced to a dim memory of a Pre-Disaster Civilization where, it is argued, two great playwrights named Shakespeare and Bern Shaw were really one and the same. Their quest for knowledge has different purposes for those involved: the politician wants it to strengthen his power, while the scholars want it for more humane reasons. With the horror behind them, the travelers return to Afria, as the book's final page moves to a grim, truncated ending.

• Andre Norton. Norton is an under-rated writer of science fiction. She's so prolific—three books a year—that few can really claim to know her work. Her most original works are also her most complicated and slow-starting. The first chapter of *Dark Piper* (131) is so weighted down with names and generations that most readers have trouble following it, although the Pied Piper type of narrative that follows is worth the trouble.

Breed to Come (132), however, is a better one to begin with. "What monstrous folly, think you, ever led nature to create her one great enemy—man!" This quote from John Charles Van Dyke begins the book. As the story opens, man is gone—flown off into space to escape the earth he has ruined, leaving behind the mutant versions of animals who once shared the earth with him. Wisest of these are the People, the descendents of cats—their forepaws now divided into small fingers, bodies beginning to be devoid of fur, high domed skull to contain an enlarging brain. Norton tells of the People's struggle to climb upward on the ladder of evolution. No longer naturally gifted with claws, they carry metal ones in their belts and strap these onto their hands in time of battle. Etiquette forbids the typically feline vocalization: to growl or snarl in a moment of high emotion is an embarrassment.

These interesting creations are the gifts of an imaginative writer whose ideas differ greatly from the futurist's more usual conception of modern man dressed in a space suit but not altered within himself. The struggles between the People and the Barkers, dog mutants who haven't evolved as far, are a clear victory for feline cleverness. The People's encounter with the Tusked Ones is almost comic, because by now physical strength without equivalent intelligence simply doesn't stand a chance. But the Rattons, a totalitarian group operating with the unity of a fist, are a different matter. Norton lets this showdown between self-willed individuals and group-willed hordes run its course without comment. At the climax, she brings down a space ship filled with creatures whom the mutants fear most: man, the Demon.

Why Teach Science Fiction?

Some people believe that science fiction is a modern means of fulfilling the age-old purposes of folklore, explanation of the unknown, and wish-fulfillment. But serious science fiction is more than that. It attempts to define the future, to foresee change. True, the changes are limited to those influenced by technology. The possible alterations in nature are only dimly thought out. Most science fiction writers are also inclined to fall back on stock plot devices and rather predictable characterization. The intent, however, is to create a fanciful literature that is exciting, promising, and truly innovative.

In one of her adult science fiction novels, Ursula K. Le Guin presents a central character whose dreams come true. He can't will them—they arise from his subconscious—but they are outcomes of his experiences and his interpretation of those experiences. Serious science fiction attempts this major theme: to determine what will or might occur in a world in which technology makes dreams come true. Dream it and you can have it, the authors seem to say—but your potential for dreaming well requires greater wisdom than you now possess. It is a warning and a challenge. Most serious science fiction does not escape a tone of pessimism.

Just how valuable serious science fiction is for children is a matter you must judge for yourself. It is seldom if ever attempted for younger children; instead, you'll find the Bug-Eyed monsters and playful romps among planets. But for older children the range of selection is broadening and deepening, and well worth your study.

special activities

1. How can you use the material in chapter 3 for determining the place of fanciful fiction in your work with children? What literary purposes will you discuss explicitly with children as you present fanciful fiction?

2. Many of the fanciful fiction works we've discussed in this chapter originated in England. Compare and contrast these with American fanciful fiction. Can you account for the differences?

3. As you continue your study of this book, you will find activities suggested that include verbal responses (questions, retellings, dramatization), visual responses (drawing, collage-making, etc.), and psycho-motor responses (miming, other action items). Now is a good time to consider the type of activity best suited to a specific work. List ten works from this chapter that are familiar to you; then list types of activities that are appropriate to them. Attempt to balance your list among visual, verbal, and motor activities.

teaching ideas

1. Many modern fanciful stories focus on small objects and characters. Place such objects and models in a box: pins, small dolls, miniature items such as "Monopoly" houses and toy dishes. Ask children to draw from the box, selecting a small set of such objects; then ask them to create an oral story about the items, working alone or in brainstorming groups. Help them to critique the stories. Evaluate this activity in terms of creative output and the resulting interest in this literary type.

2. Some science fiction works stress inventions—things that might be used in the future. Ask children to discuss, draw, or diagram inventions for the future. Also, after a number of science fiction works have been read, make a list of science fiction writers' hypothetical inventions.

3. Ask pupils to pretend that they arrived from another planet to investigate earth. What items on earth might they be most surprised to see? How would they explain such items? List and discuss.

4. Some fantasy contains excellent examples of "found poetry." (See p. 91, chapter 2 for a description of found poetry.) Ask pupils to collect it from their fantasy reading.

5. Nearly all high fantasy requires careful visualization of an overall setting consisting of many scenes through which the action passes. As you read high fantasy with children, use a large surface to sketch a map of the territory. Make it a picto-map, containing some of the scenes of the action. Sometimes, as with the works of Tolkien and C. S. Lewis, commercial maps are available. If you can obtain these, use them as you read these works with children. Trace the action on the map as you go.

CHAPTER REFERENCES

1. *Hans Christian Andersen's Fairy Tales.* Illus. Jiri Trnka. Spring Books, n.d.
2. Morton, Miriam, ed. *A Harvest of Russian Children's Literature.* Univ. of California Press, 1970.
3. Singer, Isaac Bashevis. *Zlateh the Goat.* Illus. Maurice Sendak. Harper, 1966. (I-U)
4. Lewis, C. S. *The Lion, the Witch and the Wardrobe.* Macmillan, 1950. (I-U)
5. Norton, Mary. *The Borrowers.* Harcourt, 1952. (I)
6. Carroll, Lewis. *Alice's Adventures in Wonderland.* Illus. John Tenniel. Heritage Press, 1941.
7. Cleary, Beverly. *The Mouse and the Motorcycle.* Illus. Louis Darling. Morrow, 1965. (I)
8. _____. *Runaway Ralph.* Morrow, 1970. (I)
9. MacDonald, George. *The Light Princess.* Illus. Maurice Sendak. Farrar, Straus, 1969. (I-U)
10. _____. *At the Back of the North Wind.* Airmont, 1966.
11. Pyle, Howard. *Pepper and Salt, or Seasoning for Young Folk.* Harper, 1885.
12. _____. *The Wonder Clock.* Harper, 1887.
13. Nesbit, E. *The Story of the Treasure Seekers.* Coward-McCann, 1958. (I-U)
14. _____. *Five Children and It.* Illus. J. S. Goodall. Looking Glass Library, Random, 1948. (I-U)
15. _____. *The Phoenix and the Carpet.* Illus. J. S. Goodall. Looking Glass Library, Random, 1948. (I-U)
16. _____. *The Story of the Amulet.* Illus. H. R. Millar. Looking Glass Library, Random, 1960. (I-U)
17. Grahame, Kenneth. *The Wind in the Willows.* Illus. Ernest H. Shepard. Scribner's, 1960. (I-U)
18. de la Mare, Walter. *The Three Royal Monkeys.* Knopf, 1919. (I)
19. Boston, Lucy M. *A Stranger at Green Knowe.* Harcourt, 1961. (I)
20. Milne, A. A. *Winnie-the-Pooh.* Illus. Ernest H. Shepard. Dutton, 1926. (I)
21. _____. *The House at Pooh Corner.* Illus. Ernest H. Shepard. Dutton, 1928. (I)
22. L'Engle, Madeleine. *A Wind in the Door.* Farrar, Straus, 1973. (I)
23. Sendak, Maurice. *Where the Wild Things Are.* Harper, 1963. (E)
24. Mayer, Mercer. *Mrs. Beggs and the Wizard.* Parents, 1973. (E-I)

25. Burningham, John. *Mr. Gumpy's Outing.* Cape, 1970. (E)
26. Alexander, Lloyd. *The Cat Who Wished to Be a Man.* Dutton, 1973. (I-U)
27. Pearce, Philippa. *Tom's Midnight Garden.* Lippincott, 1959. (I-U)
28. Johnson, Crockett. *Harold and the Purple Crayon.* Harper, 1955. (E)
29. Kraus, Robert. *Milton the Early Riser.* Illus. Jose and Ariane Aruego. Windmill, Dutton, 1972. (E)
30. Brown, Margaret Wise. *Little Fur Family.* Illus. Garth Williams. Harper, 1946. (E)
31. Zolotow, Charlotte. *Mr. Rabbit and the Lovely Present.* Illus. Maurice Sendak. Harper, 1962.
32. Wahl, Jan. *A Wolf of My Own.* Illus. Lillian Hoban. Macmillan, 1969. (E)
33. Brown, Margaret Wise. *The Sailor Dog.* Illus. Garth Williams. Simon and Schuster, 1953.
34. Scarry, Richard. *Busy, Busy World.* Golden, 1965. (E)
35. _____. *The Great Pie Robbery.* Random, 1969. (E)
36. Gruelle, Johnny. *Raggedy Ann Stories.* Bobbs-Merrill, 1918. (E)
37. de Brunhoff, Jean. *The Story of Babar.* Random, 1933. (E)
38. de Brunhoff, Laurent. *Babar Visits Another Planet.* Random, 1973. (E)
39. Bemelmans, Ludwig. *Madeline.* Viking, 1939. (E)
40. _____. *Madeline in London.* Viking, 1961. (E)
41. Coombs, Patricia. *Dorrie and the Goblin.* Lothrop, Lee, 1972. (E)
42. Devlin, Wende and Harry. *Old Witch Rescues Halloween.* Parents, 1972. (E)
43. Oakley, Graham. *The Church Mouse.* Atheneum, 1972. (E)
44. _____. *The Church Mice and the Moon.* Atheneum, 1974. (E)
45. Marshall, James. *George and Martha.* Houghton Mifflin, 1972. (E)
46. _____. *George and Martha Encore.* Houghton Mifflin, 1973. (E)
47. Minarik, Else Holmelund. *Little Bear.* Illus. Maurice Sendak. Harper, 1957, 1960. (E)
48. Lobel, Arnold. *Frog and Toad Are Friends.* Harper, 1971. (E)
49. _____. *Frog and Toad Together.* Harper, 1972. (E)
50. _____. *Mouse Tales.* Harper, 1972. (E)
51. *Told under the Magic Umbrella.* Illus. Elizabeth Orton Jones. Macmillan, 1955. (E)
52. Fleischman, Sid. *McBroom Tells the Truth.* Illus. Kurt Werth. Norton, 1966. (I)
53. _____. *McBroom's Zoo.* Illus. Kurt Werth. Grosset & Dunlap, 1972. (I)
54. Dahl, Roald. *Charlie and the Chocolate Factory.* Knopf, 1964. (I)
55. _____. *Charlie and the Great Glass Elevator.* Knopf, 1972. (I)
56. Lindgren, Astrid. *Pippi Longstocking.* Tr. Florence Lamhorn. Viking, 1950. (I)
57. McCloskey, Robert. *Homer Price.* Viking, 1943. (I)
58. _____. *Centerburg Tales.* Viking, 1951. (I)
59. Brooks, Walter R. *Freddy and the Bean Home News.* Knopf, 1943. (I)
60. _____. *Freddy and the Space Ship.* Knopf, 1953. (I)
61. _____. *Freddy and the Dragon.* Knopf, 1958. (I)
62. Bond, Michael. *A Bear Called Paddington.* Illus. Peggy Fortnum. Houghton Mifflin, 1958. (I)
63. Benchley, Nathaniel. *Feldman Fieldmouse.* Illus. Hilary Knight. Harper, 1971. (I)
64. Selden, George. *The Cricket in Times Square.* Illus. Garth Williams. Farrar, Straus, 1960. (I-U)
65. _____. *Tucker's Countryside.* Farrar, Straus, 1969. (I-U)
66. _____. *The Genie of Sutton Place.* Farrar, Straus, 1973. (I-U)
67. Sharp, Margery. *The Rescuers.* Illus. Garth Williams. Little, Brown, 1959. (I)
68. White, E. B. *Stuart Little.* Illus. Garth Williams. Harper, 1934. (I)
69. _____. *Charlotte's Web.* Illus. Garth Williams. Harper, 1952. (I)
70. Kendall, Carol. *The Gammage Cup.* Harcourt, 1959. (I)
71. _____. *The Whisper of Glocken.* Harcourt, 1965. (I)
72. Norton, Mary. *The Borrowers Afield.* Harcourt, 1955. (I)

73. Gray, Nicholas Stuart. *Grimbold's Other World.* Illus. Charles Keeping. Meredith, 1963. (I)

74. _____. *Over the Hills to Fabylon.* Illus. Charles Keeping. Hawthorn, 1970. (I)

75. Boston, Lucy M. *The Children of Green Knowe.* Illus. Peter Boston. Harcourt, 1954. (I)

76. _____. *Treasure of Green Knowe.* Illus. Peter Boston. Harcourt, 1958. (I)

77. _____. *The River of Green Knowe.* Illus. Peter Boston. Harcourt, 1959. (I)

78. _____. *A Stranger at Green Knowe.* Illus. Peter Boston. Harcourt, 1961. (I)

79. _____. *An Enemy at Green Knowe.* Illus. Peter Boston. Harcourt, 1964. (I)

80. _____. *The Sea Egg.* Harcourt, 1967. (I)

81. Alexander, Lloyd. *Coll and His White Pig.* Illus. Evaline Ness. Holt, 1965. (I-U)

82. _____. *The Book of Three, the Truthful Harp.* Illus. Evaline Ness. Holt, 1967. (I-U)

83. _____. *The Foundling and Other Tales of Prydain.* Illus. Margot Zemach. Holt, 1973. (I-U)

84. Cooper, Susan. *Over Sea, under Stone.* Harcourt, 1965. (U)

85. _____. *The Dark Is Rising.* Illus. Alan E. Cober. Atheneum, 1973. (U)

86. _____. *Greenwitch.* Atheneum, 1974. (U)

87. LeGuin, Ursula K. *A Wizard of Earthsea.* Parnassus, 1968. (U)

88. _____. *The Tombs of Atuan.* Atheneum, 1971. (U)

89. _____. *The Farthest Shore.* Atheneum, 1972. (U)

90. Lampman, Evelyn Sibley. *The City under the Back Steps.* Doubleday, 1960. (I-U)

91. Langton, Jane. *The Swing in the Summerhouse.* Harper, 1967. (I-U)

92. Aiken, Joan. *The Wolves of Willoughby Chase, Black Hearts in Battersea, Nightbirds on Nantucket,* and *The Cuckoo Tree.* Doubleday, 1962, 1964, 1966, 1971. (U)

93. _____. *The Whispering Mountain.* Doubleday, 1968. (U)

94. Hunter, Mollie. *Thomas and the Warlock.* Illus. Joseph Cellini. Funk and Wagnalls, 1967. (U)

95. _____. *The Haunted Mountain.* Illus. Laszlo Kubinyi. Harper, 1972. (U)

96. _____. *The Walking Stones.* Illus. Trina Schart Hyman. Harper, 1970. (U)

97. Clemens, Samuel [Mark Twain]. *A Connecticut Yankee in King Arthur's Court.* Dodd, Mead, 1960. (U)

98. Uttley, Alison. *A Traveler in Time.* Illus. Christine Price. Viking, 1939, 1964. (U)

99. Mayne, William. *Game of Dark.* Dutton. (U)

100. Garner, Alan. *Red Shift.* Macmillan, 1973. (U)

101. _____. *The Owl Service.* Walck, 1967. (U)

102. Mayne, William. *Earthfasts.* Dutton, 1967. (U)

103. _____. *The Hill Road.* Dutton, 1969. (U)

104. Steele, Mary Q. *Journey Outside.* Illus. Rocco Negri. Viking, 1969. (U)

105. Adams, Richards. *Watership Down.* Macmillan, 1974. (U)

106. Slobodkin, Louis. *The Space Ship under the Apple Tree.* Macmillan, 1952. (I-U)

107. MacGregor, Ellen. *Miss Pickerell Goes to Mars.* McGraw-Hill, 1951. (I)

108. Heinlein, Robert A. *Rocket Ship Galileo.* Illus. Thomas W. Voter. Scribner's, 1947. (U)

109. French, Paul [Isaac Asimov]. *David Starr: Space Ranger, Lucky Starr and the Pirates of the Asteroids,* and *Lucky Starr and the Oceans of Venus.* Doubleday, 1952, 1953, 1954. (U)

110. Todd, Ruthven. *Space Cat.* Illus. Paul Galdone. Dutton, 1954. (I)

111. Schealer, John M. *Zip-Zip and His Flying Saucer.* Dutton, 1956. (I)

112. _____. *Zip-Zip Goes to Venus.* Dutton, 1958. (I)

113. _____. *Zip-Zip and the Red Planet.* Dutton, 1961. (I)

114. Cameron, Eleanor. *The Wonderful Flight to the Mushroom Planet.* Illus. Robert Henneberger. Little, Brown, 1954. (I)

115. Beatty, Jerome, Jr. *Matthew Looney's Voyage to the Earth.* Illus. Gahan Wilson. Scott, 1961. (I)

116. Heinlein, Robert A. *Have Space Suit—Will Travel.* Scribner's, 1958. (I-U)

117. L'Engle, Madeleine. *A Wrinkle in Time.* Farrar, Straus, 1962. (U)

118. _____. *The Arm of the Starfish.* Farrar, Straus, 1965. (U)
119. _____. *The Young Unicorns.* Farrar, Straus, 1968. (U)
120. Christopher, John. *The White Mountains.* Macmillan, 1967. (U)
121. _____. *A Prince in Waiting.* Macmillan, 1970. (U)
122. O'Brien, Robert C. *Mrs. Frisby and the Rats of NIMH.* Atheneum, 1962. (U)
123. _____. *The Silver Crown.* Atheneum, 1968. (I-U)
124. Bova, Ben. *Exiled from Earth.* Dutton, 1971. (U)
125. _____. *Flight of Exiles.* Dutton, 1972. (U)
126. Dickinson, Peter. *The Weathermonger.* Little, Brown, 1968. (I-U)
127. _____. *Heartsease* and *The Devil's Children.* Little, Brown, 1969, 1970. (U)
128. Engdahl, Sylvia Louise. *Enchantress from the Stars.* Atheneum, 1970. (U)
129. _____. *The Far Side of Evil.* Atheneum, 1972. (U)
130. Lightner, A. M. *The Day of the Drones.* Norton, 1969. (U)
131. Norton, Andre. *Dark Piper.* Harcourt, 1968. (U)
132. _____. *Breed to Come.* Viking, 1972. (U)

BIBLIOGRAPHY

Ellis, Alec. "E. Nesbit and the Poor." *The Junior Bookshelf,* 38 April 1974, pp. 73–78. English critic finds social commentary in Nesbit's fantasy and realistic fiction.

Fletcher, David. "The Book That Cannot Be Illustrated." *Horn Book,* 44 February 1968, pp. 87–90. The surrealistic nature of *The Wind in the Willows* suggests that illustrators can't cope with this fantasy form.

Haugaard, Erik Christian. "Random Thoughts by a Translator of Andersen." *Horn Book,* 48 December 1972, pp. 557–62. The author's testimonial to the effect of the Andersen tales on his childhood; comments on Andersen's relevance to modern times.

Lewis, Claudia. "Fairy Tales and Fantasy in the Classroom." *Childhood Education,* 49 November 1972, pp. 64–67. Six books used at each of four levels.

Livo, Norma J. "Lucy Boston at 80." *The Junior Bookshelf,* 36 December 1972, pp. 355–57. Photo and succinct description of the great author's works.

Nelson, Ravenna. "Fantasy and Self-Discovery." *Horn Book,* 46 April 1970, pp. 212-33. A psychologist's premise that fantasy yields wisdom about the ego.

Sicherman, Ruth. "Time to Tell an Andersen Tale." *Top of the News,* 30 January 1974, pp. 161–68. Discusses current appeal, current relevancy of such tales as "The Steadfast Tin Soldier" and "The Swineherd."

Tolkien, J. R. R. "On Fairy-Stories." *Horn Book,* 39 October 1963, p. 457. A great writer's tribute to the fairy tale, which taught him, he says, the "potency of words."

chapter 6

Realistic Fiction

Could it have happened? Is it likely to have happened? These questions point to one distinction between realistic fiction and fanciful fiction. The fanciful tale, as we've seen, alters one or more components from what we'd expect to find in our own world. Characters in fantasy may be larger or smaller than life, or they may possess magic powers. Settings may be clearly different from our world. Plot incidents may be believable only if we accept a system of cause and effect different from the one experience has taught us.

The credibility of realistic fiction, however, requires no such suspension of disbelief. Our willingness to believe rests in part on the accuracy of the report, the power with which the report is conveyed, the apparent honesty of the author in holding up a mirror to this world and its people.

Yet realistic fiction is more than an elaborate report, an expanded news story, or a detailed case study. It is an interpretation of reality intended to inform, to entertain, and usually to persuade. This is how experience brings reality to me, the author seems to say—hold it up to the light and decide if this confirms and deepens your own sense of reality.

The credibility of realistic fiction doesn't rest only on these simple questions: Could it have happened? Is it likely to have happened? Ultimately, it rests on the validity of the themes and the perspective these themes lend to reality.

Viewed in this way, realistic fiction may not differ so greatly from fanciful fiction as may first appear. Lloyd Alexander's Prydain series is fiction that explores the qualities of heroism, whether its noble Pig Keeper exists in Prydain or in modern reality. The Borrowers won't really be found scuttling beneath our floor, but their struggle for dignity and survival enlightens us about our own struggles. The circumstances of the two fictional types may be different, but their themes emerge from a common source. Both are intent upon discovering and defining truth.

Such commonality is bound to produce hybrids. Russell Hoban's Frances stories *(A Bargain for Frances, Bedtime for Frances)* deal with simple but sharp realities known to most readers through first-hand experience: trouble with a little sister, being tricked by a friend, dislike for certain foods. These are familiar realities, but the books contain one fanciful component: the characters are badgers, not people. Does this make them fanciful? Are they basically talking-animal stories? They wouldn't be very different if Frances were a little girl, though ironically Frances as a human being might cause some readers to identify less with her—to separate her reality from their own.

Martha Alexander in *And My Mean Old Mother Will Be Sorry, Blackboard Bear* (1) presents a plot that is definitely fanciful: in revolt against his angry mother, a boy draws a bear on the blackboard and has the satisfaction of seeing his drawing climb down and accompany him on a journey to freedom. But an almost identical theme in similar style of plot and illustration appears in the same author's realistic story, *We Never Get to Do Anything* (2).

Some of the best loved fiction for early childhood seems to straddle the wall between fancy and reality. Known for her tender portrayal of the here-and-now, Margaret Wise Brown nevertheless chose rabbit characters to convey the universal love of a mother for her playful, imaginative child in *The Runaway Bunny* (3). The lasting appeal of *The Fast Sooner Hound* (4) and *Slappy Hooper the Wonderful Sign Painter* (5), both by Arna Bontemps and Jack Conroy, rests on the fun of tall tale coupled with cracker-barrel realism. We know Lynd Ward's classic *The Biggest Bear* (6) can't quite be true, but Johnny Orchard's predicament with his unmanageable pet becomes all too painfully real through Ward's amazing drawings. Even James Daugherty's *Andy and the Lion* (7) begins to be plausible when you study the cartoon faces of these two characters in the modernized fable.

Many themes projected by authors and artists simply cannot be pigeon-holed. *Andrew Henry's Meadow* (8) by Doris Burn shows that an inventive child can upset the household—so he moves away into the meadow where he can invent to his heart's content. He's soon joined by other children who prize his inventions. The constructions are fantastic, as the illustrations show them, but the theme and the plot are intertwined with reality.

So the fanciful and the realistic may not be as sharply differentiated as one might suppose. Children are often asked "Did this really happen?" but in our opinion the distinction need not and cannot always be made.

special activities

1. Examine *Where the Wild Things Are* (9) by Maurice Sendak. The book is usually classified as fanciful. Some adults, however, ask a child to decide whether the story is real in the sense that Max merely dreamed his adventure. How does the book present the matter? How would you respond to the argument that *Where the Wild Things Are* confuses the fanciful and the realistic?

2. Some books present a thin narrative of the realistic fiction type when the intent seems to be to provide expository material. Examine, for example, Aileen Fisher's *We Went Looking* (10) and *My Mother and I* (11). When you share these books with children, will you emphasize story quality or nonfiction quality? How are the fictional and nonfictional aspects balanced in *A Pocketful of Cricket* (12) by Rebecca Caudill? Are there dangers in mixing literary types? If so, what are they? Are there advantages in combining types—presenting expository information through realistic or fanciful fiction? What other examples of mixed types can you think of or find?

We cannot attempt in a single chapter to acquaint you with all of realistic fiction. The sources you've encountered (see chapter 1) will enable you to locate many titles on a variety of subjects with an even greater variety of themes. Now we'll survey a few selections with you, turning our attention to examples and criteria that will help you discern the qualities of fine realistic fiction.

Our organization here will be somewhat arbitrary. While we might have chosen to discuss popular topics as they are treated in realistic fiction—sports, animals, mysteries, home life, adventure, humor—our examination of theme and other literary elements persuades us that topic alone may not yield the most useful information. Instead, we'll examine realistic fiction according to three broad, overlapping thematic characteristics:

- Works whose focus and audience appeal rest mainly on the exploration of *self.* In these, readers are likely to discover protagonists with whom they can readily identify, as well as settings and incidents that parallel their own experiences. Readers share in solving problems that are likely to be familiar. Examples will be drawn from stories intended for early-, middle-, and upper-age children.

- Works whose main concern with reality is the *self* in relation to the *outer world,* or reality outside the self. Here we'll include adventure away from familiar home settings, stories that attempt to portray animal characters realistically, stories in which the identity of characters and forces is likely to be unfamiliar to the reader. Again, examples will be drawn from books written for all ages.

- Works about *other times and other places.* All age levels need realistic fiction to take readers beyond themselves. Incidents, settings, and even characters in historical fiction may be strange; and yet this strangeness, when vividly and graphically presented, can be intriguing, adding to a sense of living in the midst of a vast world. Stories with a modern but far-removed setting also expand a reader's horizons. In a sense, this third category is an extension of the second, but it is more widely removed in time and place.

REALISTIC FICTION ABOUT SELF

These stories deal with commonly shared experiences, helping the readers to interpret their experiences, usually through a central character with whom they can identify. At the earliest level, these narratives may do little more than portray unremarkable events. At times, the illustrations accompanying the text are highly imaginative, augmenting the experience and sharpening the reader's perception.

Early Childhood Fiction about Self

Simple incidents based on first-hand experience are portrayed with stimulating pictures in *What Do the Animals Say?* (13) by Grace Skaar, with a simple pattern of questions and answers. In *What Do I Say?* (14) by Norma Simon, detailed, cross-hatched illustrations give individuality to the simplest of questions—"I get up in the morning. What do I say?"—without distracting from the experience.

Several authors and artists possess the skill to make ordinary experiences meaningful and significant through lyrical style and beautiful illustration. In *The Day We Saw the Sun Come Up* (15) by Alice E. Goudey, the celebration of early morning amounts to a high ritual, easily recognized and relished by young listeners. A series of "Quiet" and "Noisy" books from the lyrical pen of Margaret Wise Brown, including *The Seashore Noisy Book* (16) and *The Quiet Noisy Book* (17), have found their way into the loving hands of more than one generation. Many works by Marie Hall Ets and Charlotte Zolotow treat common, unremarkable experiences as if they were rich and significant. These books can help establish a beginning to the art of appreciating life in its simple, basic experiences. Similarly, there are several books that focus on one specific, comforting experience without resorting to conflict or cuteness. *On Mother's Lap* (18) by Ann Herbert Scott presents a happy Eskimo family to illustrate its single happy observation: "(T)here is always room on Mother's lap." And Tobi Tobias's *A Day Off* (19) pleasantly describes the times when a child can have his father all to himself.

Adults sometimes overlook the effects of such books—they seem to contain so little. They seem to lack conflict and resolution, elements we've come to expect in literature. They seem to present nothing new. They are idyllic. Such books must be read lovingly, their pictures examined with wonder at the artist's ability to pierce the ordinary to discover delight.

When authors and artists attempt to enhance the ordinary by clever interpretation, the result ought to be evaluated in terms of honesty as well as invention. *A Hole Is to Dig* (20) by Ruth Krauss consists of clever definitions ("The world is so you have something to stand on"). Although popular with adults, this book may not be appreciated by children, who often miss the whimsy. Yet the spirited drawings by Sendak probably transmit the book's real intent to young readers.

Seldom have children in motion been so lovingly portrayed. Betsy Byars's *Go and Hush the Baby* (21) is a very funny account of Will's attempts to placate his baby brother. The humor is honest and quite within the realm of a young child's appreciation. Charlotte Zolotow's *When I Have a Little Girl* (22), while amusing to adults, will strike young children as entirely sensible in its specific list of things a little girl intends to permit her future child to do: "She can have a friend stay overnight whenever she wants. . . . She can give milk to all the cats and if they don't go away afterward they can live with her."

More heavily plotted realistic books for young children include stories whose basic appeal lies not in the specific conflict but in the sense of a shared experience. For example, *Sleep Out* (23) by Carol and Donald Carrick describes the slightly scary adventures of young Christopher when he decides to stay out all night in his new sleeping bag. This type of book is a good introduction to realistic fiction if you match it with a child who has had a similar experience. In fact, there appears to be a need for constantly updated stories dealing with such experiences, not in terms of high conflict and ingenious twists of plot but in recognition that common experiences do exist in every era.

Stories involving real conflict and problem solving, such as those depicting the quest for identity or characters' learning to find their way in an often puzzling world, require a close bond between author and reader. The problem treated in the story may seem trivial to an adult, but the author's treatment of it must not show disrespect for the child's concern. For example, you can talk down to a smaller-than-average child by telling him to forget about height—or you can read him a book that takes his concern seriously, such as Jerrold Beim's *The Smallest Boy in the Class* (24). You can sympathize with a child's wish for privacy by sharing *Evan's Corner* (25) by Elizabeth Starr Hill. Note how every sentence in this book moves the narrative forward, how the pictures fill in the details of Evan's attempt to make his private corner a good place to be, how the suggestion of black dialect helps make the experience authentic and specific. Literary criteria shouldn't be neglected as you search for books on a specific topic or theme.

Books that treat simple problems in a way that will amuse adults may falsify the problem from the child reader's point of view. *I Do Not Like It When My Friend Comes to Visit* (26) by Ivan Sherman is funny to an adult, as the little girl visitor makes a shambles of the protagonist's possessions. But the humor may not be shared by a child who has experienced that problem. Only the ending—"Tomorrow I get to visit her"—may strike a chord of satisfaction. *Noise in the Night* (27) by Anne Alexander tells how Sherri tried to block out strange noises by playing her radio all night or wearing earmuffs, an unconvincing humorous attack on a problem that many children consider serious. In *Peggy's New Brother* (28) by Eleanor Schick, Peggy discovers her mother is pregnant and wishes she could have a dog or cat instead—a humorous idea, though not original, and perhaps not one that a child will find amusing. The audience for a problem story must be kept in mind: in this case, the young child, not the adult.

Illustration from STEVIE by John Steptoe. Copyright ©1969 by John Steptoe. Reprinted by permission of Harper & Row, Publishers, Inc.

Real problems dealt with honestly, with real regard for a young child's concerns, are welcome fare in realistic fiction. When the presentation also meets

And Grandmother's lap is best of all
when you don't want to do anything
but sit in the big chair,
and rock back and forth, and back and forth,
while Grandmother hums little tunes.
And her shoes make a soft sound on the floor.
        make
            soft
                sounds
                    on
                        the
                            floor.

Reprinted by permission of the publisher from GRANDMOTHER AND I by Helen Buckley; illustrated by Paul Galdone. Copyright ©1959 by Lothrop, Lee & Shepard Co., Inc.

high literary standards, the result is a book to be treasured for years. *Abby* (29) by Jeannette Caines convincingly shows us a little girl seeking answers to several pressing problems: Where did she come from? Why can't she be a boy? Is she adopted? *Stevie* (30) by John Steptoe, a remarkable creation by a teen-age black artist, catches the pathos of an older boy's dislike for the responsibility of caring for a younger child. In *Tom and the Two Handles* (31) Russell Hoban deals humorously but honestly with two boys who can't stop fighting. *Benjie* (32) and *Benjie on His Own* (33) by Joan M. Lexau deal with a black child struggling to help his aged grandmother. Chibi, the "forlorn little tag-along" in Taro Yashima's *Crow Boy* (34), and Momo in the same author-artist's *Umbrella* (35) are children whose problems touch empathically on the concerns of childhood. And Rebecca Caudill's story of an Appalachian child's small but serious attempts to succeed at school in *Did You Carry the Flag Today, Charley?* (36) sets a standard for honesty and literary excellence.

The light touch in illustration and style can still yield honest problem-confrontation in books for young children. In *Will I Have a Friend?* (37) by Miriam Cohen, Lillian Hoban's pleasant drawings show that a child who is lonesome on the first day of school can still have an enjoyable time. *Mommy, Buy Me a China Doll* (38), adapted by Harve Zemach from an Ozark folksong with illustrations by Margot Zemach, makes a realistic commentary on a child's unfulfilled wish for possessions. Books by Janice May Udry and Else Holmelund help lighten the load of serious problems without detracting from their significance for the young child.

Several problems clearly within the scope of young children tend to be ignored by the mass of realistic fiction or are confined to highly didactic lesson-filled books of dubious quality. One such problem has to do with the relationship between the young and the aged in a society that is sometimes accused of neglecting the elderly. In two wonderful books, *Grandfather and I* (39) and *Grandmother and I* (40) by Helen E. Buckley, the alliance of age and youth is unforgettably set forth. One searches for more books like these, books that have the wisdom and gentleness to meet problems that ail society. Slowly they begin to appear: books about children of divorced or unmarried parents, books about afflicted children and those living amid affliction, and books about other similar problems.

Rather surprisingly and reassuringly, the topic of death has been presented in a gentle, sensitive manner in several books for younger children. Margaret Wise Brown does it calmly and with just a touch of irony in *The Dead Bird* (41). The children hold a funeral for the bird and "Then they cried because their singing was so beautiful and the ferns smelled so sweetly and the bird was dead." In *The Tenth Good Thing about Barney* (42) by Judith Viorst, a deceased pet cat is regarded with a father's comforting words: "He'll help grow the flowers, and he'll help grow that tree and some grass. You know . . . that's a pretty nice job for a cat."[1] *My Grandpa Died Today* (43) by Joan Fassler, and *Growing Time* (44) by Sandol Warburg, are also recent books on this topic.

special activities

1. The sources mentioned in chapter 1 can guide you to selections on various realistic topics. Which of these sources are available and useful to you in finding books for early childhood in the realistic fiction category?

2. Author Mary Q. Steele writes: "The world has not spared children hunger, cold, sorrow, pain, fear, loneliness, disease, death, war, famine, or madness. Why should we hesitate to make use of this knowledge when writing for them?"[2] What are the dangers in presenting the "dark side" of reality early? What are the benefits of early presentation?

---

[1] p. 19.
[2] Mary Q. Steele, "Realism, Truth, and Honesty," *Horn Book* 47 (February 1971): p. 20.

Intermediate Childhood Fiction about Self

Children's literature of the past reveals a middle childhood full of excitement, joy, and important but nonthreatening incidents. Perhaps this was characteristic of middle childhood in several past generations of Western culture. Children of this age seem to have been free to operate happily and with safe independence, suffering neither the insecurities of early childhood nor the pangs of adolescence. Some of the best of this literature is almost idyllic; troubles and problems are transient and easily overcome. Some stories present deeper concerns, but the pervading tone is optimistic.

The family, viewed through the eyes and actions of an intermediate-level child, forms the basis of many of these stories. In other instances, the adults are moved farther offstage, leaving the child protagonist to deal with his peers, as if this age group existed in a world of its own.

The world of Tom Sawyer and Huckleberry Finn is such a world as this, and so is the world in Booth Tarkington's books about Penrod and Sam. In the late thirties and forties Carolyn Haywood produced two dozen lively books about the neighborhood adventures of Betsy, Eddie, and Penny. In *"B" Is for Betsy* (45) early, happy school days are recorded, a teacher, Miss Grey, demonstrates how lively early childhood education can be, and parents and peers ease Betsy along the way through her school experience. The hero of *Little Eddie* (46) is more enterprising. He brings home a whole telephone pole for firewood, manages to redistribute the neighborhood cats, and runs for election as dog catcher. There's never any doubt in these books that the audience is children. Haywood imparts genuine happiness, never resorting to contrived plots.

More difficult and thematically deeper are the Moffat books by Eleanor Estes, beginning with *The Moffats* (47) and including *Ginger Pye* (48), which won the Newbery Medal. A special favorite is *Rufus M.* (49), with its loving look at the smallest Moffat's perseverance in obtaining a library card, his earnest attempt to help the soldiers in World War II, and his solution to the mystery of who plays a player piano. The world of the Moffats is small, seen through the eyes of the children, but the family situation has the ring of truth about it. Honesty of presentation and affection for the time and characters make these books a happy reading experience today, just as Louisa May Alcott's books continue to appeal. It is not nostalgia alone that causes them to last but, rather, the embodiment of the universal in the specific.

The setting for Elizabeth Enright's *Gone-Away Lake* (50) and its sequel *Return to Gone-Away* (51) is rural and less familiar to most readers today, but readers can share in the children's discoveries. The lake, which has become a swamp, and the houses surrounding it are a mysterious, dangerous playground for the three children involved. Still the children's rapport, their joy in being together, predominates. Above all, in these and other books Enright captures children's conversation believably. One child describes another: "He has these big front teeth that look as if he could bite a tree down, like a beaver, and he wears glasses.

He's very, *very* nice." The other replies, "I guess he'd never be a success in the movies, though."[1] These books should be read aloud.

Today the dominant figure in happy-intermediate-childhood fiction is Beverly Cleary, whose fifteen or more books have made readers the next-door neighbors of Beezus, Ellen Tebbits, Otis Spofford, Ramona, and especially Henry Huggins. Until *Socks* (52), these books were illustrated by Louis Darling, and a more compatible author-illustrator collaboration is hard to find. Look, for example, at Henry and Ribsy as they stare into an aquarium in *Henry Huggins* (53). Parallel curiosity and wonder, shared by boy and dog, couldn't be captured better. Ribsy later gets a book of his own (54), and Darling's pictures form a portfolio of dogdom's moods.

Beverly Cleary's characters don't remain forever in a happy age of childhood. They grow older from book to book. They learn how to deal with each other, and successive episodes build on these changes and developments in character. Ramona in *Beezus and Ramona* (55) is something of a preschool-age tyrant. But in *Ramona the Pest* (56) we have hopes for this youngest member of the Quimby family. She may still be a nuisance to Henry, who is now on school patrol, and she does become a kindergarten dropout, but sympathy is on her side. She has moved from tyranny to trying to cope. At this writing, Beverly Cleary is reported working on the further adventures of Ramona. We await these eagerly.

Several authors present a happy exploration of self through adventures with pets. Molly Cone's *Mishmash* (57) and its sequels show how Pete Peters's alarmingly friendly big dog gives the boy a firm rein on the neighborhood. *Clarence the TV Dog* (58) by Patricia Lauber and its sequels are composed of family episodes centered on an unusual but believable rascal of a pet.

So far in these books, whose central characters are easily within the reader's ability to identify, the environment and its problems are within the hero or heroine's range of management. The dog can find his way home. The kindergarten dropout can get back in school. The small child struggling in the swamp quicksand can be rescued. The library card can be obtained even if Rufus has trouble writing his name on it.

Not all problems are so readily solved, and the quest for identity can take turns that are not so easily followed. Problems of minority people do not resolve themselves so readily, as in Molly Cone's story of an Indian boy's conflict in *Number Four* (59), Hila Colman's *Chicano Girl* (60), and the same author's *End of the Game* (61)—the latter about a black child's first encounter with adult prejudice. While the majority of these stories about minority group conflicts appear at upper levels, a growing number are written for younger children as well. You will find many of them listed by level at the end of each chapter in Ruth Kearney Carlson's most helpful source book, *Emerging Humanity.*[2]

Problems of minorities are present even if not central in some recent readable

---

[1] *Gone-Away Lake,* p. 15.
[2] Ruth Kearney Carlson, *Emerging Humanity,* illus. Louise Noack Gray (Little, Brown, 1972).

Easter, rabbits and baby chicks and ducks. Inside there was usually a parrot or monkey and once there had been a deodorized skunk. Henry thought it would be fun to have a skunk following him around, but when he found it cost forty dollars he gave up the idea.

But best of all Henry liked the fish. One side of the store was covered with rows of little tanks. Each aquarium contained green plants that grew under water, snails, and a different kind of tropi-

books for the middle level. Black characters are authentically portrayed in Kristin Hunter's *Boss Cat* (62), but the conflict is really over how to convince Mom that Pharaoh, the new cat, is an all-right member of the family. The central theme of Rebecca Caudill's *Somebody Go and Bang a Drum* (63) is the demonstration of how an eight-child family manages to live together, making joy out of squalor. The children are of various races, adopted from various parts of the world. Zilpha Keatley Snyder's memorable Newbery Honor book, *The Egypt Game* (64), includes a black child in the neighborhood group.

These books point to a welcome change in the variety of realistic fiction available for intermediate years. Writers are entering new areas of experience. For example, other recent middle-level novels by Zilpha Keatley Snyder are almost Gothic in that they hint at mysterious dark places and forces. They are not, for the most part, presented as real encounters with the occult, although three of them—*Season of Ponies* (65), *Black and Blue Magic* (66), and *Eyes in the Fishbowl* (67)—are outright fantasy. The rest are realistic, but realism in their characters' minds is clouded and darkened by the atmosphere of supernatural forces at work. All of this might be a simple basis for ghost-story thrills, but Snyder is more concerned with the effect of occultism on her growing characters—so much so that you remember the characters rather than the plots. You remember Martha Abbott in *The Changeling* (68) because Martha searches for her own uniqueness through her strange friend Ivy Carson. The troubled heroine of *The Witches of Worm* (69) gives us insight into the merging of occultism and aberration. The sources of influence of one child over another are examined painfully and dangerously in *The Truth about Stone Hollow* (70).

special activities

1. Other authors whose works belong in the intermediate-level category of realistic fiction are mentioned in various places in this book. Look, for example, at discussions of the books of Betsy C. Byars, Louise Fitzhugh, Betty Erwin, Virginia Hamilton, Robert McCloskey, Marilyn Sachs. What authors can you identify from your childhood or more recent reading of children's literature whose characters enter a quest for self? Which are the most memorable? How do they add to your knowledge of the variety of intermediate-level realistic fiction?

2. Animal stories, mysteries, sports stories, and other similar categories may or may not be included in the assortment of literature emphasizing the self. For example, a mystery story with characters whose sole purpose is to serve the plot might be realistic fiction but it does not attempt to examine the self. But other mystery works do have themes about self. One such story is Catherine Woolley's *Ginnie and the Mystery Light* (71) which deals with discovering the roots of superstition, ignorance, fear, and prejudice—all related to the mys-

tery and intrinsic to the plot of the story. What other mysteries can you name that fit into this category? Why is it worth noting this distinction?

Mary Calhoun's *The Horse Comes First* (72) begins with a startling episode that tells more about a boy's character than about harness racing: Randy, the main character, strikes a horse for stepping on his foot. The ensuing story shows Randy learning to examine situations from someone else's viewpoint—a discovery-of-self theme. What other animal stories from this category come to mind?

Upper Childhood and Adolescent Fiction about Self

Margaret Simon, the modern girl in Judy Blume's *Are You There, God? It's Me, Margaret* (73), is almost twelve. Her secret club rules that she must wear a brassiere although she's not ready for one. She talks secretly to God, begging him to help her be "normal." Margaret's male counterpart in Blume's *Then Again, Maybe I Won't* (74) is Tony Miglione, who is somewhat older. He worries about his erotic dreams and his compulsion to peek through binoculars into the bedroom window of the girl next door, about his friend who shoplifts, and about his mute grandmother who is ignored by the rest of the social-climbing family.

Davy Ross gets involved in what may be a socially unaccepted relationship with another boy in John Donovan's *I'll Get There. It Better Be Worth the Trip* (75). He fears that, by some illogical connection, this attachment has caused the killing of his dog. He resolves the situation to his own satisfaction in a brawl with his friend. In *The Man without a Face* (76) by Isabelle Holland, a brief taboo encounter between a boy and a man is resolved by the death of the adult.

As these examples illustrate, recent realistic fiction for upper childhood and adolescence includes topics once considered taboo, but now presented openly. A few appear to have been written to shock people, advertising that taboos are being broken. But in many the characters and plots are dealt with skillfully, not to shock but to expand the frontiers of realism in children's literature. These books are often welcomed by child and adult readers who seem glad to discover that previously undiscussed but real concerns are presented in fiction.

Many critics and authors approve the new realism in fiction for preadolescence and adolescence. Newbery Medal winner Maia Wojciechowska has called it "An End to Nostalgia,"[1] and Nancy Larrick notes with approval that in such literature "Baby Dolls Are Gone."[2] Other writers disagree. Some don't take issue with taboo-breaking but urge that literary quality be upheld: "(Y)ou can't turn a bad novel into a good one by filling it with pregnancy, pot and the pill,"[3] notes John Rowe Townsend.

---

[1]Maia Wojciechowska, "An End to Nostalgia," *School Library Journal* (December 1968): 13–15.
[2]Nancy Larrick, "Baby Dolls are Gone," *School Library Journal* (October 1969): 105–108.
[3]John Rowe Townsend, "It Takes More Than Pot and the Pill," *The New York Times Book Review* (November 9, 1969): 2.

Reading these taboo-breaking books, you become aware of other works that break with tradition, some reflecting the unique and personal views of their authors and some arising from readily observable changes in society, but all attempting to look more clearly into the face of reality. The characters in these books encounter sexual and social problems at a younger age than a generation ago. Childhood seems whittled away so that preadolescence is weighted with the concerns of adolescence and adulthood. An implicit theme in many of the stories is the longing for acceptance: young people in the new realistic fiction fear more than anything else that they won't be accepted by their peers.

These books approach their topics and themes with varying tones. Judy Blume writes just on the edge of humor. For her, there is a light at the end of the tunnel of adolescence and there's a good deal of pleasantness along the way. Quite understandably, a trace of bitterness underlies Marilyn Sachs's *The Bears' House* (77)—her heroine is somewhat at the mercy of poverty and her mother's insanity. But the same author's *The Truth about Mary Rose* (78) has a softer tone. This book combines suspense and surprise amid an array of social difficulties, including the conflict between generations, reversal of hitherto accepted sex roles, prejudice against Puerto Ricans, and big-city anonymity. In the works of John Donovan, Lee Kingman, John Neufeld, and Barbara Wersba the tone is equally serious—indeed, often tragic.

Only a few writers pierce the wall of heavy realism with unblunted humor. In M. E. Kerr's first novel, *Dinky Hocker Shoots Smack!* (79), there's a kind of bitter humor. Dinky's weight problem and the problem of her negligent, thoughtless mother can't extinguish Dinky's spirit. Brenda Belle Blossom in *The Son of Someone Famous* (80) is a bit less buoyant and the goings-on are more out of control, but this author's honest humor still dominates the tone of the writing. The buoyancy of youth amid pressing problems is also apparent in Vera and Bill Cleaver's *Grover* (81)—even when the hero must face his mother's suicide—and in the tough-conversation, fast-plot, black-character books of Frank Bonham, including *Mystery of the Fat Cat* (82) and *Hey, Big Spender!* (83).

Modern realistic fiction about self is distinguished from its forerunners by still another characteristic. The style is more intimate and draws on the vernacular, using the diction, phraseology, and sentence structures that the young characters themselves might use. Often it's a first-person style in which the author is trying to be unobtrusive, attempting to display not his own language but that of his central character. Sentence fragments, elliptical expressions, and at times an imprecise form of description loaded with repetitions of "you know" and "things like that" are intended to tell the reader that the account comes straight from the lips and thoughts of a character only partially skilled at writing.

It doesn't always work. Sometimes the principal character, from whom we must grasp the theme, is unable to communicate it. The author is stuck with him, and so are we. For example, near the end of Barbara Wersba's *Run Softly, Go Fast* (84), David Marks looks back over his account of the quarrel with his now-deceased father and admits that he has told only half the story, turning his father, he says, into a monster.[1] Perhaps the father-son conflict that forms the basis for this book is not well served by a vernacular, first-person style. On the other hand, *This Is a Recording* (85) by Barbara Corcoran makes an effort to tell in Marianne's own words how she slowly came to respect and love her unusual grandmother and her new surroundings. The theme develops from the heroine's growing awareness, and it seems natural to grasp this theme through the character's words.

Sometimes point of view presented through third-person narration can be just as constricting. The author, locked into the point of view of one principal character, can't show the variety of viewpoints needed to examine the theme adequately. Michael in John Neufeld's *Edgar Allan* (86) is furious with his minister father when the family capitulates to the town citizens by rejecting the black child whom they had adopted. The fury is understandable, but the family's position is not because we are given no means for examining it. Wendy in *The Peter Pan Bag* (87) by Lee Kingman demands her parents' sympathy after she has run away, but it is difficult for a reader to comprehend Wendy's situation because her own view—the only one we're permitted—often seems distorted.

Whether first person or third person, the intimate vernacular style of these self-searching, modern realistic books often provides new insight into the perplexing problems of youth. Used well, it is valuable and illuminating. Perhaps its beginnings can be traced to *The Adventures of Huckleberry Finn*, told in the first person, and to the warmth of youth in *Little Women*, told in the third person. Above all, it is indebted to *The Catcher in the Rye* (88), J. D. Salinger's first-person account of Holden Caulfield's adolescent odyssey into a world of phonies and false values. Modern authors of personal realistic fiction for upper childhood may have been more influenced by this novel than by any other.

At the time of its appearance, *The Catcher in the Rye* wasn't considered specifically written for adolescents, although it was widely read by them. Other authors of the 1950s, however, began to explore hitherto neglected situations in adolescent life. Mary Stolz and others examined teen-age romantic love and often found its sadder side, as Maureen Daley had in her unforgettable *Sixteen* (89). Henry Gregor Felsen, a sensitive writer who uses third-person narrative effectively, presented premarital sex and forced marriage in *Two and the Town* (90), a novel specifically for adolescent readers.

Madeleine L'Engle's *Meet the Austins* (91) is, for the most part, a pleasant family chronicle, but its opening pages vividly project the family's shock and sorrow when a beloved friend, "Uncle Hal," is killed in a jet crash. John Knowles's *A Separate Peace* (92), a popular selection in literature classes for adolescents, recounts the death of the romantic hero Phineas as a result of a foolish act committed by the book's narrator. While neither of these stories is in quite the naturalistic style and tone of *The Catcher in the Rye*, they seem to foreshadow the no-holds-barred realism of later works.

---

[1]p. 202.

In the Newbery Medal book *It's Like This, Cat* (93) by Emily Neville, the hero, Dave Mitchell, tells the story in first person, using present tense. "My father is always talking about how a dog can be very educational for a boy. This is one reason I got a cat," he begins; but what follows is more than a son-father conflict or a boy-and-his-pet idyll. Dave is real. He isn't a foil for a lecture about the struggle between generations or the difficulty of finding close personal contacts in New York.

Describing the way she began to write this book, the author explains: "At the end of the first page or so I stopped to reread, and a tingling thrill went up my spine. I thought: it's right, it's actually right! There is no excitement quite as great to an author—after the pages of nearly right, or all wrong—as feeling you have finally *hit* it."[1] There lies the secret of successful realistic fiction. The intimate portrayal of characters must feel right for the author and, therefore, for the reader. The characters' problems—the psychological and social issues presented through the characters—give substance to the characterizations.

Not all realistic stories of the self need be so intimate in tone, style, and author distance as those we've highlighted here. There's still room for the less personal story, told in the third-person language of an observant author who maintains some distance from the subject. In *A Trick of Light* (94) by Barbara Corcoran, Cassandra and her twin brother Paige are reunited in spirit as they search for their missing dog—a simple plot developed quietly in the author's own language. It is filled with detail about survival in the woods but makes no pretense that this theme of twin togetherness is an earth-shaking issue. The death of the beloved pet brings sadness, but this event is placed in proportion to the framework of the narrative; its significance is shown in the wider context. Mary Stolz also weaves her characters' problems into the wider fabric of living. In *Leap before You Look* (95), her heroine, Jimmie Gavin, gazes back over the year in which her parents were divorced, seeing her mother as a "fragile, furious, and fatigued" individual unable to cope with her husband's infatuation with another woman. Debates about Women's Liberation and the Peace Movement marches are balanced with Jimmie's growing love of nature and her wish to be attractive. We learn of her bitterness, her sense of living in very troubled times. Yet, beyond the issues, Jimmie learns how to find self-respect and autonomy.

Upper-level stories about minority characters have also gained balance and perspective. The issues of prejudice and inequality are still present. They are seen as an important part of reality, but only a part. Added to those issues is a firm, warm feeling for cultural diversity as an enrichment to living, as a positive force to discovery of self. Thus young Bradley Clarke, in *Bongo Bradley* (96) by Barbara Glasser and Ellen Blustein, energetically pursues the mystery of his family's musical past and present. Leaving his Harlem home to spend the summer with relatives on a North Carolina tobacco farm, Bradley finds cousin Ardetha singing gospels while learning her art from secret visits to a hermit teacher; he seeks out his late grandfather's trumpet and the jazz records the

---

[1] Emily Neville, "Newbery Award Acceptance: Out Where the Real People Are," in *Newbery and Caldecott Medal Books: 1956–1965,* ed. Lee Kingman *(Horn Book),* 1965, p. 132.

family has tried to hide. When he returns to Harlem, his knowledge of self has deepened. Throughout the adventure, Bradley is discernibly a black character, black in speech and behavior, black in dignity and pride. Such a book has permanence—an important step beyond works whose themes are merely topical.

Just One Indian Boy (97) by Elizabeth Witheridge is another satisfying achievement. This story of the growing up of an Ojibway named Andy Thunder isn't altogether a treatise about maladjustment resulting from prejudice. True, Andy is a victim: white students taunt him for eating baked rabbit heads for lunch, and Andy runs away from high school. Working in a lumber camp, he is again driven away by prejudice in the form of physical abuse and demeaning working conditions. We see him experiment with alcohol as a way out, but we also see him change and grow because of many kinds of love. Finally, we see that his self-discovery leads to his reaching out to help others, as Andy signs a teaching contract to work with high school students. This is not the story of an Indian who succeeds in becoming a white man, for Andy retains his identity as one of his people. The plot itself has some of the structure of Indian lore. Some episodes are only half-told, as if the reader might be already familiar with them. These add to the texture of the story and seem to be a successful experiment in creating an ethnic novel that reflects the structure and style of a people.

special activities

1. Authors write from their own experience and convictions. When you consider the themes and characterizations of recent realistic fiction for upper levels, what do you find about conformity? About conflict between generations? About discussion of topics once considered taboo in literature for young people? Would the views of these authors be considered representative of the views of society? Which of the books you've read seem to mirror recent societal changes in values or in beliefs? Which seem to place themselves in opposition to society? What is the role of such works in changing or establishing a culture's attitudes and values?

2. Some recent works of realistic fiction have been criticized for being too didactic—that is, for being too intent on driving home a lesson. Is this a valid criticism? Do some books in modern times attempt to specify a lesson to the reader? Is didacticism a valid and honest goal in literature? Discuss, citing examples.

3. Survey recent literature dealing with minority peoples. Which of these stories would you consider to be treatises aimed at identifying the problems of such groups? When do these stories also present characters in perspective so that their problems are universal as well as ethnic. When do such stories succeed best in bringing characters to life? What criteria can you devise for evaluating such literature?

4. What psychological and social issues are most important for authors to consider as they write realistic fiction for today's youth? Can you locate good examples for each of the issues you identify? Which issues are still ignored?

REALISTIC FICTION OF THE OUTER WORLD

The selections we've discussed in the previous section include a great variety of settings, plots, and characters. But they have a theme in common: an attempt to parallel their characters' search for self with that of their readers. Generally, their journey is inward rather than outward: events lead to self-enlightenment.

But there is another kind of journey—beyond the self and into the outer world. Realistic fiction helps expand horizons of experience to include characters and settings that readers can examine vicariously. These may be probable and convincing, though unfamiliar to many readers. Or they may be unusual and even improbable, clinging to realism for the sake of credibility while aiming at entertainment through novelty. Mystery, adventure, and suspense stories are included in this category—but so are tales of more probable, if unfamiliar, events, characters, and settings. The search for meaning in the outer environment rather than the search for self is the keynote.

Early Chilhood Fiction of the Outer World

Young children are sometimes viewed as egocentric and uninterested in the outer world. Nothing could be further from the truth. The young child is constantly exploring and, in fact, is eager to discover what lies beyond his immediate horizons. The books that aid such exploration are often subtle extensions of discovery-of-self books, but they do make the point that there's a world out there filled with exciting possibilities.

For instance, examine Harlow Rockwell's *My Doctor* (98). The emphasis is not upon the child visiting the doctor but upon the doctor herself—a woman with all sorts of specifically presented doctoring equipment including a "rubber mallet to tap my knees" and "a needle to give shots." To an adult, this may seem a small journey into the unfamiliar. To a child, it can be most absorbing.

The photographic presentations of Tana Hoban encourage a closer look at familiar, if unnoticed, phenomena. In *Look Again!* (99) cut-out pages direct the reader's attention to the textures and designs of parts of seashells and small animals, while *Where Is It?* (100) explores the posturing and movement of one delicate white rabbit. Admittedly, these books are not really fiction in that they contain little plot and characters are present only as subjects for photographs. Yet to the small child these are tantalizing ways of seeing into the outer world. They invite a closer look at outer reality, just as the thin story in Alice E. Goudey's lyrical *Houses from the Sea* (101) helps a child see the distinguishing characteristics of seashells.

These early explorations into outer reality are as important for what they do not attempt as for their inclusions. They do not attempt to personify objects or animals. They generally do not create a pseudo-story to make their information seem more palatable. They respect a child's native curiosity without false stimulation through cuteness. Such books should not go unnoticed or unrespected.

A certain amount of personification and a definite story line have helped make Virginia Lee Burton's *Mike Mulligan and His Steam Shovel* (102) a classic. The steam shovel named Mary Anne is given an expressive face; she's a willing coworker as Mike digs the foundation for the town hall. Yet this author/artist knows the limits of the device. She knows that her subject's major appeal is a realistic one, and her illustrations show how a real steam shovel works. The impact seems to derive from realistic presentation, even though the thin layer of fantasy may add to enjoyment. Such balance needs to be evaluated when you examine and present stories for early readers: is their realistic intent aided or hampered by fanciful overtones?

Fantastic overtones may come quite naturally in a realistic story for young readers or listeners. In *Humbug Witch* (103) by Lorna Balian, a little girl dressed as a witch tries all sorts of terrible spells to the amazement of Fred, her cat, but as she strips off her witch costume, there's no doubt that it's all in fun. The fire-breathing dragon who is really Great-Aunt Fanny and all the other mistaken identities in Ellen Raskin's *Spectacles* (104) are clearly the imaginings of the delightful heroine, Iris Fogel, who resists getting glasses to correct her strange visions. Once the glasses are obtained, Iris's friend Chester remarks that she looks different and her reply is, "You look pretty different yourself, Chester."

But there's no fantastic overtone and no personification in the wonderfully realistic narratives of Miska Miles, illustrated with magnificently composed drawings by John Schoenherr. In a warm, believable episode of *Mississippi Possum* (105), the animal makes friends with a flooded-out family. In *Fox and the Fire* (106) we enter the world of an animal dispossessed of his home and watch his reluctant entry into the human domain. In *Nobody's Cat* (107) there is the touch of poetry in word and picture as the cat crouches before a car speeding by: his grim, watchful eye stares into a headlight as if it were a matching eye. In these and other books tracing the believable encounters of solitary animals with often unfriendly environments, we enter unfamiliar worlds with amazingly sharp perception. More tenderly presented is the more familiar world of William as he talks to his aging dog in *Old Arthur* (108) by Liesel Moak Skorpen:

What a good, old dog you are. . . .
You're good for waiting
and walking
and sitting down
and for lying on your back and singing songs.
You're very good for playing hide-and-seek,
but what I like best
is the way you wag your tail.

So the variations in realistic fiction for young readers are many. Stories may contain realism with almost no plot but with careful attention to detail. They may include slight personification or a few fanciful elements merely as devices for sustaining their realistic intent. They may portray a realistic plot or tone unblinkingly, sometimes grimly, with confidence that style in writing and illustration will carry the reader into the outer world presented. These plots may be portrayed in a style alive with local color, bringing to life settings and characters of a particular, often unfamiliar, time and place. *Joey's Cat* (109) by Robert Burch tells of a black child's struggle to protect his pet in a semi-rural setting, where a possum with a snake-like tail plays the villain. Mark Taylor's *Old Blue* (110) brings realism to a folk song plot by telling quite believably how a hound climbed a tree to trap his quarry.

In all-out adventure stories for young children, the young protagonist is usually seen as remarkably superior to peers and adults, overcoming all obstacles to win the day. Such an adventure may be treated humorously, as in Crosby Bonsall's *The Case of the Dumb Bells* (111) in which four boys solve the mystery of a doorbell that rings by itself. But in the stories of Billy and his wonderful stallion, Blaze, by C. W. Anderson, the terse style and charcoal drawings depict a series of serious adventures in which the two heroes warn the countryside of an impending fire, defeat a band of gypsies, capture a wild horse, and survive to receive all sorts of honors. Although the cast of characters changes in Anderson's recent stories—for instance, in *The Rumble Seat Pony* (112)—the same heroic virtues are still present, and so is the escapist, wish-fulfilling action.

A distinguished contribution to escapist adventure for the very young is the series of "Tim" books by Edward Ardizzone. Tim and his friends, Charlotte and Ginger, go to sea, suffer much hardship, and come home again to receive the approval and heightened respect of parents. After ten books, this series of voyages grows a bit predictable, and even the staunchest readers may be relieved to learn of *Tim's Last Voyage* (113) in which he agrees never to go to sea again until he is grown.

The stories, all ten of them written over a period of thirty-five years, are told charmingly with a fine sea vocabulary. There's no attempt to write down to the small child. In *Tim in Danger* (114) the shipwreck plot includes terms such as *bollard, barquentine, port bow, grog,* and *lee shore.* Watercolor and cross-hatch pen drawings convey the storyteller's delight for invention with a sure air of knowing what a young viewer will want to know about. The plots contain a kind of Gilbert-and-Sullivan pattern of coincidence, but with serious respect for the characters' difficulties and their ability to overcome them. In *Tim and Ginger* (115) the character contrast between the two boys is underlined so that the most inexperienced listener can comprehend it. Ardizzone knows his art and his audience. Adventure lovers of all ages should relish his work.[1]

---

[1]See Nicholas Tucker, "Edward Ardizzone," in *Children's Literature in Education,* 3 (1970): 21–29.

'Hullo, my lad,'
said the captain.
'Come, stop crying
and be a brave
boy. We are
bound for Davey
Jones's locker and
tears won't help
us now.'

So Tim dried his eyes and tried not to be
too frightened.   He felt he would not mind

going anywhere
with the captain,
even to Davey
Jones's locker.
    They stood
hand in hand and
waited for the
end.

From Little Tim and the Brave Sea Captain by Edward Ardizzone. Used by permission of Henry Z.
Walck, Inc. and Oxford University Press, London.

Intermediate Childhood Fiction of the Outer World

For many children, social problem novels for the intermediate level provide experiences into unfamiliar territory. Some of these are mentioned in the previous section. Mary Stolz's *The Noonday Friends* (116) is at once an exploration of self and a study of contrasting ethnic backgrounds—Fanny's Anglo-Saxon home life and the Greenwich Village neighborhood of Simone, who is Puerto Rican. A black child's inquiry into his ancestry in Lucille Clifton's *All Us Come Cross the Water* (117) presents some unusual glimpses into an unfamiliar, removed setting. Successful efforts of neighborhood children to save the last vacant lot for a wildlife preserve form a kind of outer-world exploration story in *The Little Park* (118) by Dale Fife. And there are many others, with realistic, not-so-unusual charcters reaching outward, groping with social and environmental problems.

But a major characteristic of many outer-world books is that they are escapist in intent. Plot rather than character exploration is their hallmark. Mysteries, animal adventures, sports stories—their often superficial characterizations are only a means for moving the story along. Though the reader may identify strongly with the characters, he reads not primarily for character development or theme but for what happens next. Mary Adrian, for example, provides some background in ecology, in history, and in the study of nature, but these are incidental to her chief purpose—to grip her readers through suspense in such books as *The Skin Diving Mystery* (119) and *The Ghost Town Mystery* (120). Peggy Parish's *Key to the Treasure, Clues in the Woods, Haunted House* (121) and others form an interchangeable series in which the Roberts family sorts out clues and codes to solve puzzling but nonthreatening mysteries. Catherine Woolley's numerous stories of young girls' adventures move along through lively plots but without any major attempt at discovery-of-self themes. See, for example, *Ginnie and Her Juniors* (122) in which the young heroine forms a day school for three-year-olds, and *Ginnie and the Mystery Cat* (123) in which a trip through Europe brings an encounter with a dangerous villain. To entertain rather than to enlighten is the aim of such books.

In the Alden Family series by Gertrude Chandler Warner, escapist mystery plots are bolstered by warm family feeling and a cast of characters with real individuality. The first in the series, *The Boxcar Children* (124), embodies a genuinely original idea: that children, left to their own devices, might set up a household all their own. Their dependence on one another in their struggle to establish their own home makes a memorable story. Unusual settings and the relationship between the children and their grandfather lift subsequent adventures, such as *Houseboat Mystery* (125) and *Bicycle Mystery* (126), above the general run of adventure stories. Like most mystery and adventure books, these are filled with conversation. The action is related mostly through talk—but the Alden conversation is more alive, more specific and ingenious than that in most mystery fare. An additional feature of these books is their low readability, which makes them a substantial contribution to the high-interest low-readability category of realistic fiction.

Sports stories for intermediate level are predictably focused on winning the big game. The game may vary, as does the cast of characters, but the plots are all somewhat alike. A hero must overcome a problem: a physical limitation, difficulty in getting along with his teammates, an over-demanding or unfair adult, or a fellow player who is somehow different. But the problem is usually resolved rather easily as the big tournament rolls around and the team wins. The value of teamwork, of straining to overcome competition, and of fast, sports-laden talk seems to be taken for granted in these books. But sometimes this value system seems questionable. Here, for example, is how Jeff gets the good word about winning the tournament from his science teacher, Mr. Gregory, who has just managed to help Jeff squeeze through on his science test:

> Mr. Gregory put out his slender white hand. Jeff took it, felt Mr. Gregory's firm grip.
> "Destroy them," Mr. Gregory said. "Not savagely, of course. But by the rules."
> Jeff was astonished. But he felt overjoyed as he left the room. That Mr. Gregory! He's a real human being after all! And I thought he was a stupe![1]

Such an incident is faintly condescending toward the adult who isn't really involved in sports; it conveys the impression that people outside of sports are the "stupes." But this will probably go unnoticed by the sports enthusiast. In Matt Christopher's long list of popular titles, on nearly every team sport known to Americans, the case is made repeatedly that sports help resolve the more obvious personal and interpersonal problems. See, for example, *Wing T Fullback* (128) and *Mystery Coach* (129). Bill J. Carol in *Lefty's Long Throw* (130) and *Lefty Plays First* (131) presents a hero who faces a physical limitation: his pitching arm fails and he must retrain as a first-baseman. In the same author's *Fullback Fury* (132) a high school hero is haunted by the reputation of his deceased father, a theme that adds depth to the formula sports story. William Heuman, dealing with the world of professional sports and sports-writers, has a salty style that reads very well aloud. His humor is an antidote to other sports fare. *Horace Higby and the Gentle Fullback* (133) and *Home Run Henri* (134) are lively yarns to share with sports enthusiasts.

Nature stories, especially those with animals as central characters, have had wide, enduring popularity. Many of these were originally intended for upper levels but are increasingly sought out by intermediate readers whose enthusiasm overcomes some of the reading level difficulty. Certainly Jack O'Brien's *Silver Chief* (135) and its many sequels continue to be read. Without resorting to personification, O'Brien can describe animal behavior in long passages devoid of human intervention. The battle for survival and the motives underlying loyalty and cunning in animals are well related, though the author's asides attempting to set forth "laws of nature" seem somewhat dated. All the books in Walter Farley's Black Stallion series contain a bit of mystery to enhance the heroism of a mighty horse. Idyllic accounts of children's love for animals are to be found in Mary O'Hara's *My Friend Flicka* (136) and its sequels, Eric Knight's

---

[1]Matt Christopher, *Shadow over the Back Court* (127), p. 109.

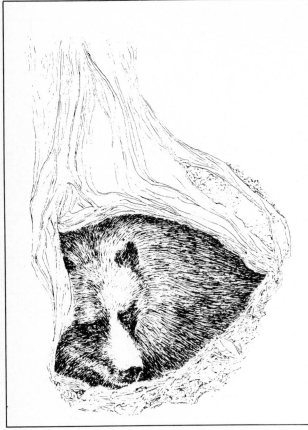

Part I

1

Deep in December the wheat-colored Grizzly stirred in her den. Outside on the eastern slope of the high ridge, snow piled up. She pawed listlessly at the mound of leaves and twigs she had packed into the den in October. It was a big den, close to the timber line. The entrance sloped down, following an underground ledge. The hollow where the bear lay was almost nine feet deep.

Although she had mated in June, the unborn cubs were still no more than three-quarters of an inch long. They would not be born until late January or early February, and when they were born, they would be the size of a chipmunk, blind, toothless, and hairless.

But the big bear was not concerned with unborn

3

Copyright ©1974 by Paige Dixon. Illustrated by Grambs Miller. From THE YOUNG GRIZZLY. Used by permission of Atheneum Publishers.

Lassie Come-Home (137), and Marjorie Kinnan Rawlings's distinguished *The Yearling* (138). When read aloud by an adult, these books are still within comprehension range of intermediate children.

Walt Morey's growing list of animal stories is deservedly popular. Each book creates a separate world of human and animal experiences in a style that is both dramatic and filled with realistic scenes of the north. The main character in *Gentle Ben* (139) is an Alaskan brown bear; he is at the mercy of ignorant adults but is saved by a boy's love. *Gloomy Gus* (140), a Kodiak bear, is forced temporarily to endure the indignities of the circus, but he is also saved by a boy hero. A more troubled hero is Dan in *Angry Waters* (141), who finds sanctuary in wildlife surroundings against the shadow of his own wrongdoings and the threat of prison. In *Canyon Winter* (142) a rather timid rich boy, Peter Grayson, is isolated for the winter with a hermit and learns to love wild animals and fight for their preservation. *Runaway Stallion* (143) begins with a long account of the escape of a fine horse, his efforts at survival, and the saving love of a farm boy who finds him. In these and other stories Morey argues for the civilizing influences of nature often contrasted with the destructive forces of society. But the tone is not romantic: animals and the natural environment are not idealized. Although the books are long, their plots are simple and clear. The style is simple enough for many intermediate readers, and the characters' motives are evident through the action.

Fiction that concentrates on the behavior of animals with little or no human intervention is a special challenge. It may personify the animals and do so effectively, as in *Bambi: A Life in the Woods* (144) by Felix Salton. By presenting the animal as different from others in his species, it may add a dimension of drama, as in Glen Rounds's *The Blind Colt* (145). In several recent works for the intermediate level, Paige Dixon argues for the preservation of animals and their domain. He describes animals as they might be observed by an objective by-stander, with little conjecture about motives and feelings. In *The Young Grizzly* (146) Dixon's ability to communicate his observation without intruding is most effective.

Upper Childhood and Adolescent Fiction of the Outer World

Formerly, the adolescent novel—sometimes called transitional because it seemed to pave the way to adult reading—dealt with high adventure, suspense, and careers. Today the focus has shifted to the highly subjective novels of the self, described earlier, and a fine array of historical fiction. This change is apparent in the works of new authors as well as in the style and subject matter of established authors. For example, John R. Tunis's early works dealt with big sports events and the struggles of young men to find their way in the world. In these books, such as *Iron Duke* (147), and *Go, Team, Go* (148), the hero's resolution centered upon having a steady girlfriend, winning the big game, and making the dean's honor list. Tunis's later stories are concerned with the grim topic of war and its aftermath. Likewise, Ivan Southall, after a decade of writing roman-tic adventure fiction, has more recently sought realism dealing with specific time and place.

There is, then, some evidence that mere escapism in upper-level realistic fiction is on the wane. It may occur in nostalgic accounts such as Sterling North's *Rascal* (149), in which the author recalls the capture and taming of a beloved raccoon pet. It may appear in perceptive stories of nature with an ecological theme, as in Paul Annixter's early book *Swiftwater* (150), the story of a sensitive boy named Bucky Galloway who attempts to save the wild geese from hunters, or in *The Great White* (151) by Jane and Paul Annixter, which brings the biography of a polar bear, Iskwao, to a bloody conclusion. But, increasingly, such tales turn inward to focus on a central character's discovery of self or outward to examine a unique geographical region or a specific historical period.

Undoubtedly, some older children still read adventure stories about easily identifiable characters and settings that require little realistic detail. Howard Pease's Ted Moran mysteries, written from 1926–1961, and Stephen W.

Meader's adventure stories of sports and machines may please the present generation almost as much as they entertained readers in the past. K. M. Peyton, in *Fly-by-Night* (152) and other horse stories, fulfills some children's continuing interest in horse stories. Romance in Florence Crannell Means's *Knock at the Door, Emmy* (153) and *Tolliver* (154) continues to draw readers. And perhaps most popular of all are stories containing the hint of dangerous doings, of young people threatened by evil surroundings. Joan Aiken's modern Gothic tale *Night Fall* (155), with Meg's discovery of a real murderer, is a good example, as is Mabel Esther Allan's *The Night Wind* (156), which tells of Robin Maybury's flight from an orphanage.

Perhaps the main route to escapism has now been directed to other media, such as movies and television. The more demanding experience of reading, particularly at the upper levels, seems concerned with realism of some depth. If this is true, we might rejoice in the growing amount of fiction that explores and attempts to resolve psychological and social problems and that presents historical and geographical settings, characters, and events in an engaging, en- lightening manner. Still, we might wonder at the apparent dearth of upper-level fiction that stimulates the mind and senses through modern plots well told, through characters representing our idealized selves, and settings that exist primarily for the sake of the adventure. At the moment, these are to be found in television offerings and science fiction—but less often in realistic fiction.

Surprisingly, career stories seem to have waned in popularity and availability. The range of career choices has certainly broadened over the years, and more than ever, young people need to know what careers are available. Perhaps authors need to re-examine the possibility of good realistic stories about people choosing and experiencing careers—not just glamorized professions, but the more available, sometimes neglected fields.

Unfortunately, most fiction in the past has not dealt realistically with careers. Noel Streatfeild's "Shoes" books—*Ballet Shoes, Circus Shoes* (157), and others—in- variably feature heroes and heroines who become stars of glamorous professions almost without effort. These are warm, escapist stories but can hardly be called realistic career stories. Betty Cavanna's *Fancy Free* (158) contains some informa- tion about archaeologists' work in Peru, but the sixteen-year-old heroine seems far more interested in protecting a baby llama than in pursuing a career. Series books about professionals have almost invariably been criticized for stock plots, tiresomely good characters, and overglamorized views of career pursuits. Exam- ples of this type are the Sue Barton series by Helen Dore Boylston and the Penny Marsh series by Dorothy Deming. W. E. Butterworth attempts to describe the world of auto racing realistically amid some incredible plots—but these, too, may give the career-seeker much misinformation.

In assessing realistic fiction for upper levels, you might ask what is the place of such fiction in the lives of modern young people? Is there still a need for escapist fiction that places exciting plot in the foreground, offering sanctuary from deeper concerns about character, time, and place? Is there a need for modern information about careers and other matters of the outer world that is best conveyed through the fictional mode?

special activities

1. In this section we have mentioned only a few of the available titles in adventure stories, animal stories, and suspense stories for each level. If *Subject Guide to Children's Books in Print* or similar sources are available to you, examine them to get a wider view. Look for titles listed under such topics as the following: Mystery and Detective Stories, Sports Fiction, Animals—Stories, Dogs—Stories, Horses—Stories, Adventure and Adventurers—Fiction. Note that fanciful as well as realistic titles are listed in most sources. Where would you find qualitative reviews of the selections you have located?

2. Select several career or occupation topics. Using available sources, determine which books are pertinent to these topics and when they were published. At what levels are they written? Read and evaluate at least two books related to each topic. If you were creating realistic fiction intended to describe a career or occupation, what information would you include? Would the information be better imparted through nonfiction? Discuss.

3. Interview children at several levels of age and development, asking them about their favorite reading experiences. If they mention realistic fiction, find out whether they select books for escapist purposes. Compare the information you obtain with adults' recollections of childhood reading. In what ways have attitudes toward realistic fiction of the outer world altered?

4. Many of the titles mentioned in this section are more than a decade old. This is partly because books such as those by Virginia Lee Burton, C. W. Anderson, Edward Ardizzone, Mary Stolz, Gertrude Chandler Warner, Jack O'Brien, Glen Rounds, Paul Annixter, and Howard Pease apparently have long-lasting appeal. Some of these works may have appealed to you as you read them in your childhood. How does your experience compare with the reports of modern children who have read these works? How much can you depend on your own childhood reading to guide you in helping modern children select realistic fiction?

HISTORICAL FICTION: REALISTIC FICTION OF OTHER TIMES AND PLACES

Historical fiction is an important complement to history textbooks and other nonfiction historical accounts. Fiction that clearly depicts geographical regions that contrast with the environment of most readers can be an accessible way to geographical information. An implicit purpose in both subtypes (historical and geographical fiction) is the presentation of factual information. Accuracy is required—both of fact and of perspective. But accuracy alone isn't sufficient. There must be, in addition, a good story with a theme appropriate to the time and place and authentic characters. The story must move along in a satisfying manner, synthesizing information without relinquishing its hold upon the reader.

This is a tall order, requiring a balance between storyteller and reporter. Happily, many modern writers can fill that order, often varying time and place from book to book so that their works provide an amazing historical and geographical array. One such writer is Patricia Beatty, who sometimes co-authors books with her husband John Beatty. In *Hail Columbia* (159), for example, information about ethnic struggles and the equally pertinent women's rights movement in 1893 is presented in a fresh, often light-hearted manner that becomes serious when appropriate. Readers see the happenings through the eyes and ears of Louisa Baines, whose astonishment and growing admiration for her suffragette Aunt Columbia are quickly shared and relished by the reader. In historical books about the Northwest region—such as *Bonanza Girl* and *O the Red Rose Tree* (160)—Patricia Beatty enlivens late-nineteenth-century history with never-failing invention. In *How Many Miles to Sundown* (161) the locale shifts to the Southwest. The spunky heroine's pursuit of her partners and her resistance to folks who would "curlize" her have a Mark Twain quality making this story a welcome addition to the Beatty shelf. In a parallel series of stories, Patricia and John Beatty have recreated Elizabethan England with all its rowdiness and brutality. In *Holdfast* (162), for example, a captive Irish orphan named Catriona vies with the aging, angry Queen to win back her freedom and her beloved dog. In this situation there's little room for the fun-filled English court comedy; instead, the supporting characters, noble and common alike, are selfish and brutal, their characteristic mood portrayed through the cruel sport of bear baiting. The plight of a sixteenth-century girl who must disguise her sex in order to join Shakespeare's acting company is the Beattys' topic in *Master Rosalind* (163).

Of course, fiction can lie—though historical lying is not limited to fiction alone. Readers can sharpen their critical reading skills by comparing and contrasting various accounts of particular historical incidents in fiction and nonfiction. The discovery that authors vary the tone to fit their purposes is a part of learning to evaluate all second-hand accounts. Readers of all ages can profit from considering when a one-sided report is permissible and when it is dangerously misleading. Many early works about little-known cultures, especially those designed to entertain younger readers through novelty, have fostered stereotypes—the wooden shoes and tulips of Holland and the endless tea ceremonies among cherry blossoms of Japan. Fortunately, accuracy is becoming more common and a wider choice of materials is being presented so that readers of almost any age can compare and evaluate. The somewhat pleasant, nostalgic episode of the slave ship in *Sophia Scrooby Preserved* (164) by Martha Bacon can be compared with the sordid account in *The Slave Dancer* (165) by Paula Fox. When various sources have been examined, a reader can determine from the evidence whether all these accounts contain psychological and objective truth. In this way, historical fiction aids development of the highest levels of reading skill.

You may approach the works in this category by selecting a specific period or place—for example, when you wish to enrich a unit of study, or when a child expresses interest in a particular subject and wants help in locating appropriate works. Subject listings and critical reviews of fiction in the historical and geographical categories are of great help. Look especially for the distinguished book about a period or era that may otherwise go unnoticed. The work itself may stimulate further exploration of that period. Peter Dickinson's *The Dancing Bear* (166), for example, is a thoroughly absorbing adventure set in early medieval times. You'll emerge from this reading experience with the conviction that this historical time and place have been neglected.

Early Childhood Fiction of Other Times and Places

Books from this category can open exciting new worlds hitherto unknown to the young child. The northern regions of the Old World, for example, are beautifully shown in the stone lithographs of Ingri and Edgar Parin d'Aulaire in the simple stories of *Ola* (167), *Children of the Northern Lights* (168), and *Nils* (169). Such books give evidence that well-executed picture books with substance retain their appeal over many decades. To some extent this is also true of the regional and ethnic picture books of Leo Politi, including his still popular *Song of the Swallows* (170) and *Emmet* (171). Although the narratives in Politi's books are rather unexciting and too obviously didactic, his highly elaborate color mixes and compositions give the books distinction.

Evaline Ness's woodcuts for *Josefina February* (172) have a solid rhythm with flowing orange, ochre, and lavender. The simple story of a little girl in Haiti searching for the owner of a burro she finds in a grove provides an attention-holding device for exploring the setting. *Do You Have the Time, Lydia?* (173), set "on a tropical island in the middle of a warm and noisy sea," has a theme in keeping with the culture and setting. More than most illustrators, Ness imparts a feeling for locale combined with themes and plot ideas.

Some books of this type are less successful, depending almost entirely on the novelty of setting to hold interest. Raymond Creekmore's *Little Fu* (174) is representative of quite a number of early childhood narratives whose all too apparent purpose is to impart information through a thin story. On his river boat Fu visits farmers and encounters bandits, but the action never quite emerges from the emphasis on description. However, in *Tia Maria's Garden* (175) by Ann Nolan Clark a lyric style helps to make such detail interesting in itself; the quiet desert comes alive in the eyes of its nameless hero. Theme is conveyed not through action, but instead in the magic of the language.

For many young readers, the most successful combination is a specific, exciting story intrinsic to the setting. The events of *The Cow Who Fell in the Canal* (176) by Phyllis Krasilovsky, illustrated by Peter Spier, could only happen in the Netherlands. Author and artist are careful to show us unique aspects of the setting to make the slightly outrageous story plausible: Hendrika the cow journeys on a barge from farm to village and is rescued only after she acquires a ridiculous hat. It's good fun, bordering on the fanciful but leaving no doubt that it all could happen in this very real, explicit setting. For even younger readers, using less connected plot but with similar merging of action and setting, Lois Lenski's "Little" and "Small" books are also a revelation: for example, *The Little Auto*, *The Little Farm*, *Cowboy Small*, and *Policeman Small* (177).

Brinton Turkle's Obadiah stories present exciting plots that could happen only in a Quaker community in the Nantucket region. The plots center on Quaker customs and values, and the themes are in keeping with the time and place. *Obadiah the Bold* (178) describes the young hero's happy imagination gently at work, while *Thy Friend, Obadiah* (179) shows him pursued by a too-friendly seagull. Liveliest of all is *The Adventures of Obadiah* (180), in which the boy's tall tales run afoul of his elders' strictures about lying.

Glimpses of history for the young child must not take for granted a knowledge of historical perspective. They are cameos of the past, presented for the purpose of introducing and arousing interest in specific periods. In *Jack Jouett's Ride* (181) by Gail E. Haley, a little known episode of post-Revolutionary times in America is given self-contained excitement and authenticity through linoleum-block prints. The argument that such accurately done historical settings are wasted on the young child, who hasn't the background for accurate interpretation of them, overlooks the value of such works in imparting a loving interest in the past. They are among the finest introductions to history that we possess. Beyond this, such books should be used with all age levels. The rewards of picture books are not confined to young children alone. Graphic historical presentations such as Peter Spier's panoramic paintings for *The Star-Spangled Banner* (182) serve a high informational and entertainment purpose.

History-based narratives for the young are usually intended to be read to the child, often with some accompanying explanation. In recent years these have been somewhat neglected; most authors seem to prefer writing historical narrative for older readers. Nathaniel Benchley in *Sam the Minuteman* (183) and other stories has been able to present historical episodes in a simple style. Betty Baker's *Little Runner of the Longhouse* (184) reflects the author's ability to portray Indians of the past, though the narrative may not hold interest. *The Fooling of King Alexander* (185) by Mervyn Skipper is an exciting achievement: an anecdote about Chinese persuading Alexander that their land is an impossible conquest is clearly and amusingly told for young readers.

In numerous fully developed, simple stories of America in the past, Alice Dalgliesh gives younger children a sense of what it might have been like to be a child in other times. *The Courage of Sarah Noble* (186) is based on a real incident, the encounter between a brave white girl and Indians in the early part of the eighteenth century. Sarah's counterpart in courage is Jonathan in *The Bears on Hemlock Mountain* (187), who ingeniously uses an iron kettle to make a celebrated escape. These are clever books, light-hearted without making light of the problems of survival. Very gently they invite the reader to reflect on the values of the pioneer. Sarah is indeed brave and quite able to adapt, yet almost any reader will notice her lack of understanding when she says to Indian children, "How foolish. . . . Why can't you speak English?"[1]

special activities

1. When do these historical and geographical stories for younger readers present stereotypes and when do they present accurate simplification? The Swedish characters in Maj Lindman's "Flicka, Ricka, Dicka" and "Snipp, Snapp, Snurr" series, all very popular a generation ago, are spanking clean and presented in rosy-faced laughter. The "Jeanne-Marie" stories of Françoise have the unvaried tone of continual bliss, as if the heroine were a doll. In Peggy Parish's *Granny and the Indians* (188) the serious matter of an elderly lady captured by the Indians becomes a joke: the Indians can't bear her meddling manner. Are these stereotyped presentations that result in misunderstanding, or will the young child understand them within the framework of their stories, without overgeneralizing about the values implied? Discuss.

2. Diction appropriate to time and place adds authenticity and spirit to some works in this category. To a large extent, young readers have been limited to diction in keeping with so-called standard English. But increasingly, authors attempt to incorporate suitable vernacular to help portray the tone of a place or time. In *Walk On!* (189) by Mel Williamson and George Ford, the entire text is a Black English commentary on the street life of young children: "You never played this game? It's fun. You have to watch out you don't step on the lines . . . you do—you out" and "If my daddy's home he gon' beat my butt good. . . ." What other example can you find to show this trend?

Intermediate Childhood Fiction of Other Times and Places

There is a need for new vibrant fiction of this type written for lower intermediate levels. The seven-to-nine-year-olds, emerging into independent reading, presumably possess some background for historical and geographical fiction based on their experience with picture books and stories read to them, on brief acquaintance with nonfiction materials featuring drawings and photographs, and on knowledge obtained from television and films. Some may be ready for longer works read to them, including the simpler books of Patricia Beatty, Nathaniel Benchley, Weyman Jones, Henry Winterfeld, and others. There are

---

[1] p. 28.

some titles in this category written at easy reading levels, but the supply of good ones is limited.

Certainly the regional stories by Lois Lenski continue to be good fare today. Lenski traveled to colorful regions of America, particularly the Southeast and North Central states. As evidenced by the ample conversation in her stories, she carefully recorded speech patterns typical of regional dialect and painstakingly attempted to transmit them through spelling and diction that dared to differ from standard English. In all her regional books the plots are heavily loaded with incidents highlighting ways of life peculiar to the regions. The title character in *Bayou Suzette* (190) discovers alligator eggs and is discovered by an alligator, learns of a ghost that supposedly inhabits the bayou, and encounters regional attitudes toward Indians. Tina, the *Coal Camp Girl* (191), faces near tragedy when her father is trapped in the flooded mine. The events in *Prairie School* (192) display the nobility and cheerfulness of children and their teacher during a bitter blizzard year in South Dakota.[1]

The Lenski books contain the author's own illustrations and maps, the latter often in the form of picto-maps to aid the reader in following the story. In fact, nearly every attempt is made to clarify the reader's concept of each region. Less successful, however, is the attempt to create memorable characters. Despite the local color, Lenski heroes and heroines seem somewhat abstract. They react in stereotyped ways, and incidents that should be crucial to character development are glossed over. For instance, in *Coal Camp Girl* Tina is so depressed about the injury of her uncle that she leaves school; a couple of pages later this depression is dismissed and Tina worries instead about a colt with the colic; shortly thereafter she is exploring an empty house, trying to solve its mystery. The pattern in all these books is one of quickly solved problems. The optimistic tone is preserved perhaps at the expense of heavier involvement and more deeply felt characterization. Nevertheless, on most grounds these are good books of the regional type, simply enough written for the lower intermediate level.

The regional and historical fiction of Clyde Robert Bulla is also easy to read. Bulla attempts less detail of setting and time than Lenski, yet there is a compensating depth of characterization. There is more sustained drama, resulting sometimes in genuine dramatic surprise. In one book, *Benito* (194), the Mexican hero is indebted to his uncle, who has rescued and reared him; but, in the end, Benito defies his uncle, announcing that from now on he will spend part of his time doing wood carvings rather than working on the farm. Kee Manygoats, the Navajo boy in *Indian Hill* (195), helps his parents decide to return to the city rather than live permanently on the reservation. The decision is difficult, and it is clear that neither place will bring an entirely satisfactory style of living.

In these and other books, including a wide range of biographies and several versions of epics and legends, Bulla places character and theme foremost, per-

---

[1]Other notable Lenski titles include *Cotton in My Sack, Corn Farm Boy, San Francisco Boy,* and *Houseboat Girl* (193).

mitting these to arise from details of time and place. He doesn't impose a simplicity that doesn't belong, trusting his reader's maturity even though writing at an easy level. His *Viking Adventure* (196) could be clarified by maps and more explicit detail, but the struggle and tragedy of Norse explorers are engaging and real. Simplicity need not mean that characterization and theme are written down to the reader.

Perhaps the most significant contribution to American historical writing for the intermediate ages is that of Laura Ingalls Wilder. These autobiographical books, cast in the form of fiction, achieve a good balance of style and content. They are nostalgic in their memory of family goodness in the midst of great difficulties encountered in pioneer life. Yet the nostalgia is not permitted to hide the darker side of reality. Because these books are so important for understanding the possibilities of historical fiction in children's literature, we present here a detailed examination of them done by a perceptive literature student.

A DESCRIPTION OF THE WORKS OF LAURA INGALLS WILDER
by T. R. Overman

No matter how complete your sense of what pioneer existence may have been like, a reading of the "Little House" series will enrich it immensely. When Laura Ingalls Wilder was in her sixties, she began the ten-year process of chronicling her childhood. With total recall and a gift for style, she presented an ethnography of American settlers of the late 1800s within the literary context of a family saga.

Readers watch young Laura abandon a corn cob wrapped in cloth when a genuine home-made rag doll takes its place. They see her grow from a watcher and mimic of the adult world, through a helping stage until, at fifteen, her courtship begins and she is no longer a child.

But more than Mrs. Wilder's own life is shown—the author re-creates the pioneer world as she knew it. Her description of Ma making cheese, for example, is so complete that any industrious reader could make his own. Watching Pa build a log cabin in Indian territory, the reader is overwhelmed by the effort involved. The result is an admiration for the pioneer attainable only through reading great fiction.

These books reveal a whole segment of society in transition from self-sufficiency to utilization of modern inventions—the coming of threshing machines, milled lumber, and the railroad. The world itself moves through time as the family's pioneer solitude changes to a town society.

Wilder's books have the excitement of adventurous existence—the bears, wolves, Indians, blizzards, and tornadoes; the sickness and accidents; the partings and painful memories of missions that failed and of deeds left undone. All of these are accompanied by the overpowering evidence that being alive is wonderful.

In *Little House in the Big Woods* (197) the Ingalls family lives in the paradise that was the Big Woods of Wisconsin in 1870. Beholden to no one, they live on the game Pa Ingalls shoots, the stock they raise, and the vegetables and grain they grow.

You watch with fascination as the Ingalls prepare for winter: Ma smokes the deer in the smokehouse, Pa butchers the pig, Ma stores vegetables in the attic. When winter comes, young Laura, who is five when the book opens, and sister Mary listen to Pa's stories and sing as he plays the violin. The image of this family, a happy, self-contained unit, is etched on the memory through beautiful prose.

But Pa grows restless. As more and more settlers come to the Big Woods, game becomes scarce. One day the Ingalls family sells the farm, loads their belongings into a covered wagon, and heads off into Indian territory where Pa will eventually build the *Little House on the Prairie* (198). After months of travel, with the little dog Jack trotting along underneath the wagon, the family arrives in what is now Oklahoma. Pa looks about the flat prairie until he finds the best spot. And slowly, over the next two months, he erects the log cabin that is to shelter the family through the next winter. Malaria, giant buffalo wolves, and a sweeping prairie fire are endured, until, just when better times seem in sight, the government tells the Ingalls to move on, for this is Indian land.

In *Farmer Boy* (199) we meet Laura's future husband, Almanzo. His upbringing provides something of a contrast to that of the Ingalls children, for he is an Easterner accustomed to better food on an average night than the Ingalls enjoy on their Christmas table. But Almanzo does change. Parental proddings help create a brave, self-reliant young man who will eventually save an entire town by defying blizzards to prevent starvation.

Back into the wagon go the Ingalls, driving north until *On the Banks of Plum Creek* (200) in Minnesota they find an unhappy Norwegian willing to swap his two oxen, his sod house, and his land. Now Laura is near town, near school and society, and encounters new problems: she now has friends and enemies to deal with. All this comes to an end as clouds of locusts descend, devouring every green thing in the territory. So the Ingalls must set off once more. *By the Shores of Silver Lake* (201) is set in the Dakota territory, where the family lives in a lineshack while Pa works for the railroad. Their move to town, their acquisition of a homestead, and the gradual emergence of the family from solitude to town society life are described in *The Long Winter* (202) and *Little Town on the Prairie* (203).

At fifteen, Laura obtains her first teaching job. Such early independence is difficult, but her earlier experiences have taught her to cope and survive. This experience, ending with her marriage to Almanzo, is described in *These Happy Golden Years* (204). The final book of the series, *The First Four Years* (205) published after the author's death, shows that Laura's struggles continue. But now Laura is at the helm. Her transition from childhood to adulthood is complete, and so, in a way, is the transition of the pioneer existence into a world of complex dependencies.

Other intermediate-level fiction pinpoints specific times and places in the American scene without attempting the total recall of Wilder or the breadth of regions in the Lenski stories. For example, in *A Spy in Williamsburg* (206) by Isabelle Lawrence, suspense is combined with a boy's eye view of one segment of Revolutionary War times. A slave in Georgia in Peter Burchard's *Bimby* (207) decides to attempt escape, thereby giving the reader a glimpse of the pre-Civil War period. In *The House of Dies Drear* (208) by Virginia Hamilton, the plot, involving a modern child named Thomas Small, enables readers to explore the workings of the Underground Railroad and its part in American history a century ago. In F. N. Monjo's *The Vicksburg Veteran* (209), a unique device—the fictional diary of Ulysses S. Grant's twelve-year-old son Fred—provides a very personal view of an American historical figure. These and other works enliven the past with the artistry of literature.

Numerous works of fiction highlight more recent history, often with a nostalgic tone reflecting the author's involvement. Robert Newton Peak's *Soup* (210) describes the life of a Vermont farm boy growing up in the 1930s. The author's voice relating the story seems geared to adults, though children may enjoy listening to the hero's escapades. After all, problems with teachers and parents are universal, no matter when or where they are faced. Robert Burch's nostalgic regional stories have much the same appeal. His *Skinny* (211), set in the Depression times in Florida, depicts a boy who longs to join the circus and find a permanent home. In the end, he must face the reality of life in an orphanage. The reader, who also has learned that many dreams cannot come true, empathizes with Skinny and hopes for his well-being. The title character of Burch's *Queenie Peavy* (212) is an embittered tomboy heroine who causes an accident and defies adults in her school and town. A memorable scene reveals that Queenie has good reasons for her bitterness—her jailbird father will have nothing to do with her. Such a story might happen anywhere, but Burch gives it credence and specificity through its Southern setting of a generation ago. More gently, Burch remembers a class of sixth-graders in rural Georgia during World War II. Their attempts to make their existence count within the framework of the distant war and their calm acceptance of tragedy make *Hut School and the Wartime Home-Front Heroes* (213) a quiet book, effective in its nostalgia.

Perhaps it should not be surprising to find that stories of adventures in America's past are predominantly rural and small-town in setting. Perhaps city life lends itself less well to regional and historical treatment. Sydney Taylor's *All-of-a-Kind Family* (214) and its sequels do present a nostalgic view of a big city—New York—in the opening years of the present century. More typical, however, is the Adenville, Utah, turn-of-the-century setting of John D. Fitzgerald's *The Great Brain* (215) about Tom Fitzgerald and his brothers, who meet the perplexities of their time—from water closets to small-town bank robbers—with an inventiveness that appeals to all children.

The modern city as a specific region with its niche in history is presented often, sometimes as mere background for characterization and universal plot but sometimes almost as a character itself. In *The Seventeenth Street Gang* (216) by Emily Cheney Neville, the waterfront and street traffic of New York are playmates as well as antagonists to the boys and girls of the playful gang. Sharon Bell Mathis uses the impersonal city as the foil in *Sidewalk Story* (217), showing how Lilly Etta, a staunch black heroine, asserts her presence against the bureaucracy. In the same author's *Teacup Full of Roses* (218) the poverty and drugs associated with the big city are not so easily defeated. As one student commented about the book, "The nice guy finishes dead." The big city as a strange region offering limited understanding to the newcomer is indelibly painted in Pura Belpre's *Santiago* (219), in which a Puerto Rican child seeks some association with the memory of his native land, and in *The Day Luis Was Lost* (220) by Edna Barth, which dramatizes the attitude of some city-dwellers toward a non-English-speaking child.

You may ask whether these and similar historical and regional books present a realistic perspective. Problems of the past are more clearly delineated than problems of the present. Villains are more easily identified as enemies who would do violence or as natural forces unfriendly to those who hope to inhabit the country. Viewed in modern perspective, values of the past appear simpler; there seems to be less ambiguity about "doing the right thing." Most modern books portray the modern city as unfriendly, at least in contrast to the nostalgic presentations of small-town and rural life. In fact, there are fewer stories that highlight modern regions than stories of modern characters seeking to clarify and follow their values in settings of incidental importance.

Adults may often, especially when writing for children, assume a nostalgic tone when attempting to convey the past. Conversely, in modern times, they may overemphasize the growing pains of the transition from rural to city life, from a "melting pot" concept of American character to that of plurality. The effects are most discernible in historical and regional fiction. The contrast drawn between past and present may not be a fair one. Whether or not this is true, you can seek out and benefit from realistic historical fiction that shines an honest light on the past, from regional fiction that presents an unbiased view of both past and present, and from works that attempt to show modern America with hope as well as candor.

Beyond the American scene, historical and regional fiction for the intermediate level is ample and admirable. Ancient times are well explored in stories with a great variety of tones and moods. The final section in Rosemary Sutcliff's *Heather, Oak, and Olive* (221) is a serious confrontation between two Greek boys, an Athenian and a Spartan, at the Olympic Games. The boys discover that, at least for the moment, friendship transcends civic pride. When it comes to light-hearted but historically accurate fiction of the ancients, *Detectives in Togas* (222) by Henry Winterfeld is a pace-setter. The phrase "Caius asinus est" ("Caius is a dumbbell") scribbled on a Pomeiian temple wall causes a group of Roman schoolboys to search for the scribbler. This is no trivial prank, for desecration of a temple means imprisonment and possible punishment by death. Winterfeld, despite his generous use of humor, makes clear the seriousness of Roman punishment: a suspect thrown into prison is fettered to other prisoners and forced to lie on the damp stone prison floor without food or water. Various intriguing examples of ancient beliefs are worked into the narrative without slowing it: "Right foot forward, please!" the boys are told as they enter a household, the reason being "to ward off the misfortune it would bring upon the household if anyone entered with his left foot foremost."[1]

In the midst of such information about an unfamiliar time and place, the narrative itself provides one of the best detective stories for intermediate readers. This is a fine book for reading aloud in the classroom and could be accompanied by reports and displays to amplify the ancient Roman setting.

Intermediate books of other times and places are cited in various other parts of this book. When you've read quite a number of books in this category, you will want to begin to formulate criteria for selection. Authenticity, as we've said, isn't sufficient. Theme, characterization, and other literary elements must also

---

[1]p. 65.

be evaluated. The balance between narrative (description of the action) and passages providing necessary information relevant to unfamiliar times and places is difficult to manage. So this balance, too, must be considered in your evaluation of realistic historical and geographical fiction.

Beyond these guidelines for criteria, consider an intangible quality: does the spirit of the time and place emerge from the pages? Some authors seem to provide all the parts, but the whole somehow lacks spirit. The situations in the story seem to have been rigged for the purpose of teaching a bit of history, or the explicitly described region seems to have no relevance to the events. Sometimes, too, the author's fine presentation of background is not matched by a story that shows awareness of children's interests and feelings.

Let us cite two examples, both by the renowned writer Meindert DeJong. *The Wheel on the School* (223) is highly acclaimed, a winner of the Newbery Medal. Six school children, inspired by their teacher, decide on a project: to bring storks to the roofs of their seaside village in Holland. Their efforts involve the entire community, hence providing the reader with much information about the locale. At the end storks do come to the village, the community rejoices, and the children feel heroic. Certainly DeJong is a master prose stylist, a skillful planner who examines the fishing community as thoroughly as if it lay in the palm of his hand. But one may admire the book without being wholly convinced that it's worth the effort: a rather contrived situation expanded to nearly three hundred pages may not really balance the regional background material or justify it in relation to the fictional purposes.

But *The House of Sixty Fathers* (224) is quite another matter. History and setting (China in World War II) form an intense, integral frame for a narrative that has seldom been equaled in children's fiction. In the beginning, Tien Pao and his family have been driven up the river by the Japanese invasion: "The family of Tien was now safe from the Japanese, but they were penniless in a strange, big city."[1] Presently, an accident sweeps Tien Pao and his pet pig, Beauty-of-the-Republic, back down the river into Japanese held territory. The ensuing journey homeward tells how Tien saves the life of an American pilot, how he himself is saved by Chinese guerillas, and how he is adopted by the "sixty fathers." Death by starvation and the violence of war surround Tien during his journey. The author doesn't soften the grim details but tells them through the deepening stoicism of the young hero. Tien becomes a touching symbol of all children in war, enduring horror as a part of living, somehow escaping bitterness, treasuring stolen moments of physical warmth and comfort with the bittersweet knowledge that they can't last. The conclusion of the book tells how Tien is reunited with his family. It seems an unlikely ending, though perhaps we oughtn't to take issue with a resolution so devoutly wished by readers.

The House of Sixty Fathers sets high standards with which to compare DeJong's other books, including his National Book Award winner, *Journey from Peppermint Street* (225). By contrast, this quiet story, back in the Netherlands setting, shows

---

[1]p. 7.

a sane, child-pleasing world. The revelation of incidents through the child's point of view remains effective, and cross-age relationships (between the boy Siebren and younger children, between Siebren and his grandfather) have a universality that contrasts with the regional background.

The light spirits in Natalie Savage Carlson's *The Happy Orpheline* (226) and its sequels seem to be authentically reflected by the French setting. Even the episodes about little Brigitte losing her way and trying to get back to Madame Flattet and the orphanage are acceptably jovial.

Some of these books are difficult for average children of lower-intermediate years to read by themselves. In those cases, the books may be read aloud. Historical and regional fiction should be experienced early, for it fulfills and enhances the purposes of literature examined in chapter 1.

special activities

1. What criteria for selecting realistic fiction have been suggested in the preceding discussion? What criteria will you add? Select an example of historical fiction for intermediate level; read it and discuss its merit in terms of the criteria you've listed.

2. Fiction authors can't be expected to provide complete background for historical and regional stories, although they should give information sufficient for following the plots. If you wish for more background, you have a fine opportunity for presenting fiction and nonfiction together. If, for example, you read *Detectives in Togas* or its sequel, *Mystery of the Roman Mansion* (227), to a group of children, what nonfiction about ancient Rome is available for them to read? What sources will help you locate it? When and how might you use such material?

3. Because our present category is a very broad one, it's impossible to include a complete array of authors and titles of historical and regional fiction. Although, as we've stated, historical fiction for children is more plentiful at upper levels, many of the authors listed below are within range of intermediates. Read one or two pieces of historical or regional fiction by one of the authors listed below and write a brief annotation and evaluation for each.

Betty Baker	Mehlli Gobhai	George Panetta
Mary Buff	Lorenz Graham	Louise Rankin
Betsy Byars	James Houston	Kate Seredy
Rebecca Caudill	Irene Hunt	Kerstin Thorvall
Ann Nolan Clark	Eleanor Lattimore	Yoshiko Uchida
Vera and Bill Cleaver	Robert McCloskey	Edith Unnerstad
Barbara Corcoran	Reba Mirsky	Jill Paton Walsh
Doris Gates		

Upper Childhood Fiction of Other Times and Places

The brilliant, complex historical romances for upper-age readers form an important segment of children's literature. Their authors make few concessions to immaturity in their audience, but instead, they speak directly to equals. They assume that the voluntary reader will find that his own world is enhanced by credible incidents and themes that connect the present to the past. This is a heavy demand. It is not surprising that many readers cannot meet it alone, preferring other types of fiction and nonfiction. But if you introduce these books carefully, using maps and brief factual material, the authors can soon take over. For example, reading the first Sutcliff novel may entail some effort for most adolescents, but it's unlikely that much urging will be needed for them to undertake a second or third Sutcliff work.

Older works in this category were often marred by an over-idyllic tone, ignoring real psychological and physical hardships of the past perhaps in an effort to portray the past as a Golden Age. In *Theras and His Town* (228) Caroline Dale Snedeker dismisses slavery in ancient Athens by remarking, "All people in the whole world bought slaves in those days. The only difference was that the Athenians were kinder to their slaves than were other people."[1] That, as scholars of ancient history will attest, is an observation of very doubtful validity. Slaves relegated to the silver mines owned by Athenian citizens were literally worked to death. In Snedeker's *The Spartan* (229) the historically verifiable heroism of Leonidas and his Four Hundred is magnificently described, but the book's earlier scenes make Spartan training and upbringing seem no more severe than schoolboy rivalry in many another day—certainly an understatement of the harsh realities of ancient Sparta. In Marchette Chute's *The Innocent Wayfaring* (230) the quiet Chaucerian English countryside forms the setting, almost trouble-free, for an idyllic journey and romance. In this instance, because the author so lovingly establishes the wish-fulfillment tone, the book seems right and rewarding. But it is not historical realism.

Most historical novels for upper ages written in the 1970s appear to draw their themes from modern concerns. There is no doubt that something is to be gained by revealing the past from a modern perspective. As such, the past is anything but idyllic. Instead, it is seen by some writers as the partial cause of present-day problems. Paula Fox's *The Slave Dancer* (231) is an unmitigated terror story focused on a sadistic slave dealer. Nathaniel Benchley's moving account of a Cheyenne named Dark Elk in *Only Earth and Sky Last Forever* (232) ends with the young man's rejection of "freedom": "It means whatever the winner wants it to mean, and nothing more."[2] Anguish instead of joy, the failure of human relationships— these are the dominant dark tones of much recent historical fiction.

Between those opposing tones—the idyllic optimism of early writers and the dark pessimism of many recent historical fiction works—lies a group of fine writers who have sought to make the past live again *as it was*. They people it

---

[1] p. 3.
[2] p. 189.

with characters of their own imaginations but their credibility derives from objective research, not from a superimposed tone. Sometimes the result is as powerful as anything in modern literature. As critic Eleanor Cameron observes in reading the account of a miracle credited to a misshapen boy named Drem in Bronze Age Britain:

> I would say that the power of imagination Rosemary Sutcliff needed in order to cast herself back into the minds and feelings of the Bronze Age peoples in *Warrior Scarlet* (233) is fully as vital and astounding as that required by Mary Norton or by C. S. Lewis or by Tolkien in order to conceive of their fantastical yet absorbingly real worlds of the Borrowers and Narnia and Hobbitry. Sutcliff's quality of imagination is different from theirs, no doubt, for there are many different kinds of imagination. But it is just as truly a wizard power to exist so completely in the past that the reader never stops once to question any action, any name, any practice or statement or habit of these ancient people. There is never once a false or hollow ring; on the other hand, every scene is packed with evocation and reality. We feel deeply what her boy Drem felt in that far-off time, not only because of his own nature but because of the nature and history of his culture. A sense of profound conviction is conjured out of this fusion of research and empathy and imagination.[1]

HISTORICAL FICTION SET IN EUROPE. While not all times and places are presented in such works, they do afford a fascinating, selective view of world history. The sources cited in chapter 1 can be consulted with a particular period in mind, and add to these *European Historical Fiction and Biography for Children and Young People* by Jeannette Hotchkiss.[2] Here we will cite a few of the best works and authors.

And the Waters Prevailed (234) by D. Moreau Barringer is an ambitious undertaking. The author attempts to support the theory that Stone Age people living in the Mediterranean basin were destroyed by waters that suddenly poured across the lowland of Gibraltar from the Atlantic Ocean. Whether or not the theory is correct is less important in this novel than the author's description of the hero Andor's attempt to convince his fellows of the impending disaster.

Harry Behn's *The Faraway Lurs* (235) was inspired by the discovery in 1921 in Denmark of a coffin containing the remains of a young girl apparently buried toward the end of the Stone Age and miraculously preserved through the centuries. From this finding Behn has fashioned a strange love story between a girl named Heather and Wolf Stone of the Sun People. From the start you know the romance is doomed, for over the story hangs the knowledge that the girl died young. Near the end, Behn's prose mounts to tragic beauty as Heather contemplates the end of her Age and the death of her lover:

> She had not forgotten the storm. But this sunny, golden morning was more real, as real as the dream she had just awakened from. In her dream, Wolf Stone came riding down into the glade. Bees were humming among the flowers as he sat there on his

---

[1]Eleanor Cameron, "The Dearest Freshness Deep Down Things," in *The Green and Burning Tree: On the Writing and Enjoyment of Children's Books* (Atlantic Monthly Press, 1969).
[2]Jeanette Hotchkiss, *European Historical Fiction and Biography for Children and Young People,* 2nd ed. (Scarecrow Press, 1972).

horse in his golden-bronze armor, waiting for her. She knew it was a dream. But it seemed as real as the morning world she ran down lightly to meet.[1]

Novels for this level about ancient Greece and Rome are fairly numerous but for one reason or another may not be entirely credible. Geoffrey Trease is justly praised for his story of the discovery of a Greek manuscript in medieval England in *The Hills of Varna* (236), but most critics agree that his attempt to provide the story of the Athenian origin of that manuscript in *The Crown of Violet* (237) is less successful. Trease's Greek characters act and talk like modern British people. The hero says to his younger brother, "Will you pipe down?" The slave nurse in the story tells her charges, "Ah've no time to bother wi' breakfast, love." Trease is much better on his own ground, as in his ninth-century story of two young people hurrying across England to warn of a Viking invasion in *Escape to King Alfred* (238).

A Danish writer, Erik Christian Haugaard, tells his historical stories through characters who sound as if they bridged two worlds—their own ancient one and our own. This is especially apparent in *A Slave's Tale* (239) in which the teller of the tale, a slave girl accompanying her master to Brittany and France and home to Denmark again to become his wife, seems to choose her words with such care that they might be written on stone. What Haugaard does best in this book, and in two other works, *Hakon of Rogen's Saga* (240) and *The Untold Tale* (241), is to portray violence from the point of view of simple men, women, and children who found themselves engulfed by it. Other writers seem to describe battles from a safe vantage point, with a storyteller's clear knowledge of what happened. In Haugaard's work, violence is the random sword slash and the sudden face of an unknown enemy that blots out the future. The stark illustrations in these books are done by Leo and Diane Dillon. Often their composition, like that of medieval pictures, is crowded and grotesque, driven by the urgency to explain the workings of fate before total darkness ensues.

The numerous works of Henry Treece and C. Walter Hodges form exciting accounts of early medieval Europe. Aboard a Viking ship called The Nameless in the eighth century, a Norse boy named Harald Sigurdson learns a strange code of bravery and faith among the raiders in *Viking's Dawn* (242) by Henry Treece. Two succeeding books carry Harald farther from home, to the Mediterranean and to the New World. The tragic story of the thirteenth-century attempt to cross from France to the Holy Land, and the capture and subjugation of the boys and girls who made the attempt, receives a happy-ending treatment in the same author's *The Children's Crusade* (243). A pair of first-person accounts of King Alfred, *The Namesake* (244) and *The Marsh King* (245) by C. Walter Hodges, are difficult to read but rewarding to those who persevere.

The acknowledged champion of early British history portrayed through fiction is Rosemary Sutcliff. Having begun as a painter, Sutcliff gazes back upon

---

[1] p. 187.

From THE UNTOLD TALE by Erik Christian Haugaard, illustrated by Leo and Diane Dillon. Copyright ©1971 by Erik Christian Haugaard. Reprinted by permission of the publisher Houghton Mifflin Company.

the murky periods of England's beginnings with the artist's genius for fashioning a world of events from a few scattered clues.[1] Her first book, *The Queen Elizabeth Story* (246), was a weak effort—an attempt to describe in folk language a little girl's desire to meet the queen, with a rather unexciting final scene of fulfillment. In terms of Sutcliff's later achievement, this is an interesting beginning, for it shows an author apparently trying to please her readers and, in doing so, attempting a lightness that was not natural to her. Sutcliff is not a humorist, and her best characters seem to experience few trivial moments. They move with heightening heroism through a dark-and-light world that has no stability. When they succeed—when they win the battle or return from the mission—the success is temporary. They must start out again or yield to a new generation. Response to change, to eventual defeat wrought by change, is the deep theme of Sutcliff's work, an epic theme that unifies her novels.

A good Sutcliff novel to begin with is *Outcast* (247). The hero Beric, of Roman parentage but reared by a tribe of Britons, is thrust out because he is different, sent back to Rome and slavery, and finally during a storm is cast out upon the shores of Britain to start life anew. Sutcliff penetrates to the heart of her scapegoat character, revealing his ultimate horror: while suffering the extremes of his ill fortune, Beric suspects that he is indeed a curse upon humanity. Only at the end does he find some measure of assurance: " 'This is my belonging-place,' he thinks. 'Whether I stay, or whether I go forth again, it will still be here. It will keep faith with me.' "[2]

The Eagle of the Ninth (248) and *The Silver Branch* (249) are stories of the aftermath of Roman rule in Britain, after the famed Ninth Legion has mysteriously disappeared in the north, and with it the Roman Eagle standard which symbolized Roman power. In the first of these books Marcus, badly injured in battle, frees his Briton slave Esca and the two men visit the Caledonian tribes to recover the standard. The second book, set some years later when Roman legions are leaving Britain, is a suspense plot of the underground with a new hero, a Roman surgeon named Justin. In a third book in this series, *The Lantern Bearers* (250), darkness descends over the land; the Romans have gone, but one of them remains behind to continue the struggle against anarchy. Sutcliff is fascinated with the question of Roman influence on England; she returns to this matter in the six stories that comprise *The Capricorn Bracelet* (251) to trace, as she puts it, "our link with Rome."

From this central focus on Roman Britain other novels by Sutcliff explore related times. *Dawn Wind* (252) and *Witch's Brat* (253) present an England emerging from the Dark Ages, with the promise of light ahead. Other stories add to the fabric of early English history with a vividness that only good fiction can provide. In Sutcliff's work the past does more than foreshadow the present; it becomes a metaphor for modern times. But Sutcliff does not underline the metaphor or even acknowledge that it is there. The comparison and contrast to the modern world is left to the reader, to make of it what she or he will.

---

[1]See Eileen H. Colwell, "Rosemary Sutcliff—Lantern Bearer," *Horn Book* 36 (June 1960): 200–205.
[2]p. 228.

The accomplishments of two other British novelists, Cynthia Harnett and Hester Burton, ought to be examined by potential readers of historical fiction. Of all historical writers, Harnett is most eager to narrow the distance between her material and her reader. Her books are filled with her own finely detailed drawings to explain exactly how things looked and how they were done. In an open, engaging letter to the reader at the end of each book she explains the process of her research, the factual and fanciful basis of her plotting, and her own quandaries in handling the material. *The Wool-Pack* (254) seems almost too inclusive, but that may not bother many readers. In this book Nicholas, son of a wealthy wool merchant in the Cotswolds, serves as the author's vehicle for describing British customs of church and state, the treachery of guilds and Lombardian money-lenders, and the news of the explorations of a sea captain:

> This Cristoforo Colombo was a fine seaman. Uncle John knew him well, and his brother Bartolomeo too. He'd once been on a voyage to Iceland with them. Since those days Colombo had been moving about Europe trying to get someone to pay for an expedition; three ships fitted out for a year was what he wanted. He'd even sent his brother to England to ask King Henry. It was a fine chance. But the King was so slow. By the time that he had made up his mind Colombo had got his ships from Spain. It was nearly a year since he had set sail. Perhaps he'd reached the Indies by now, but more likely he was at the bottom of the sea.[1]

Although Nicholas seems to believe that his is the best of all possible worlds, his creator shares no such idyllic view of the past. There is a certain bite in her observation that "He [Nicholas], and every other boy or girl, so far as he knew, was trained to complete and unquestioning obedience. Any trace of rebellion had been beaten out of him so early that he did not even remember it."[2]

The American edition of Harnett's *The Load of Unicorn* is titled *Caxton's Challenge* (255), a reasonable change since the book deals with the struggle between London scriveners, or copyists, and the printing press introduced by William Caxton of Westminster. Again, the author's drawings are an integral part of the book, showing the printing process and the London setting with a specificity that writing alone could not achieve. The note at the end, describing how the author wove into her book a thread of mystery about Caxton's printing of *Morte D'Arthur*, is as exciting as the story itself.

A fifteenth-century mystery, *The Writing on the Hearth* (256), shows once again Cynthia Harnett's remarkable gift for peopling history with understated characters and amazing events. While the author's contribution this time does not include drawings, the word pictures are completely captivating, such as when Meg the witch is swallowed up by the earth in a scene which the author attests to be possible.

Hester Burton's *Time of Trial* (257) has a convincing heroine in Margaret Pargeter, who learns something timeless about mob violence: that the mob, once

---

[1] pp. 41–2. The American edition of *The Wool-Pack* is retitled *Nicholas and the Wool-Pack* (Putnam, 1953).
[2] p. 52.

1. The Scrivener's Shop

THE RAIN was coming down in torrents when Bendy reached the back door. He could hear voices inside and he paused on the step to reckon his chances of getting upstairs unnoticed. Contrary to orders he had gone off to school without the cloak or galoches he was supposed to wear in bad weather. Cloaks and galoches were silly, considering that he had such a short way to go—just along Paternoster Row, under the arch into Paul's Alley, and then straight through the cathedral itself to St. Paul's Grammar School, less than a bowshot away.

Though the overhanging houses gave some shelter, the cobbled street was a swirling river of London muck, and he had to admit that he was soaked to the knees with filth. He would get a scolding from old Mother Collin and pos-

unleashed, can turn upon its sympathizers. Margaret's father in this story is a book-seller who wants to improve the lot of the poor. His Oxford counterpart, a radical newspaperman, appears in the same author's *The Rebel* (258). Burton seems to possess the accuracy and daring to break stereotypes. Perhaps this is best shown through a brief story, "Not the End of the World," in the collection of tales about a Victorian-Edwardian family in *The Henchmans at Home* (259). In this story a twelve-year-old girl, wealthy and slightly pampered, learns one summer day that her sixteen-year-old friend has given birth to an illegitimate child and has tried to abandon it on the beach.

In reviewing European historical fiction, we should mention two contrasting works by Americans: *I, Juan de Pareja* (260) by Elizabeth Borton de Treviño and *A Proud Taste for Scarlet and Miniver* (261) by E. L. Konigsburg. Pareja, the black slave who assisted the great painter Diego Velazquez in seventeenth-century Spain, tells his story almost too simply. The slave's love for his master and his hatred for bondage seem too balanced, achieving a mild tone not in keeping with that of Velazquez's famed painting of Pareja. In this instance, the fictionalized biography ought to be accompanied by a portfolio of other information, including portrait reproductions.

The Konigsburg work, purporting to be Eleanor of Aquitaine's memoirs written in Heaven, is something else again. You will have to read it yourself to decide whether it is a promising mix of fancy and history. At the very least, it's a lively experiment.

The most innovative historical writer for young people is an Englishman, Leon Garfield. His books begin with a full head of steam. In *The Sound of Coaches* (262) a baby is born at the inn, the unidentified mother dies during the event, and the inn's guests kindly, if short-sightedly, agree to take over the child's care. In *Black Jack* (263) a boy is locked in a room to guard the body of a hanged man; he stares at the body only to realize that the body is staring back at him with eyes that a moment ago had been shut. A few pages into *Smith* (264) finds the pickpocket hero an unwilling witness to murder, a deftly described scene that illustrates Garfield's compressed, emphatic style:

> They moved very neat—and with no commotion. They were proficient in their trade. The taller came at the old man from the front; the other took on his back. And slid a knife into it! The old gentleman's face was fatefully turned toward a certain dark doorway. He seemed to peer very anxiously round the heavy shoulder of the man who was holding him—as if for a better view. His eyes flickered with pain at the knife's quick prick. Then he looked surprised—amazed even—as he felt the cold blade slip into his heart. "Oh! Oh! my . . ." he murmured, gave a long sigh—and died.[1]

Such openings have won Garfield critical acclaim and popularity. His plots move along with what appears to be on-the-spot invention; it is difficult to detect a unified theme at work. *Black Jack,* filled with outlaws and a merry troupe

---

[1]p. 9.

DURING HER LIFETIME Eleanor of Aquitaine had not been a patient woman. While she had lived, she had learned to bide her time, but biding one's time is a very different thing from patience. After she had died, and before she had arrived in Heaven, it had been necessary for Eleanor to learn some patience. Heaven wouldn't allow her Up until she had. But there were times, like today, when she wasn't sure whether she had really learned any patience at all or whether she had simply become too tired to be quarrelsome.

Today she was restless. She paced back and forth so rapidly that the swish of her robes ruffled the treetops below. For today was the day when her husband, King Henry II of England, was to be judged. Today she would at last know whether or not—after centuries of waiting—he would join her in Heaven.

Henry had died even before she had. He had died in the year 1189, in July of that year, and Eleanor had spent fifteen years on Earth beyond that. But Eleanor's life had not been perfect; she had done things on Earth for which there had been some Hell to pay, so she had

of dishonest medicine sellers, turns for its climax to a London earthquake. *The Drummer Boy* (265) begins with a memorable scene of the aftermath of battle, but its climax is a high comedy scene of lovers at an inn far removed from any war.

History and the lives bound up in it, Garfield seems to say, are unplanned. The end is not predictable from the beginning. Come along and enjoy the ride. The ride is always a lively one, in a style closely packed with vivid, somewhat grotesque detail. Caricature abounds, and some of Garfield's characters remain in the memory like fugitives from a Dickens novel. But chaos seems to reign in most Garfield novels with all the pieces not quite meshing.

European historical fiction of the present century is generally more serious in tone; the close past is less romantic. James Foreman's novels of World War II are frightening studies of oppression. His *Ceremony of Innocence* (266) is based on the true story of the execution of two German youths for publication of anti-Nazi materials. A Danish novel, *North to Freedom* (267) by Anne Holm chronicles a twelve-year-old's escape from a prison camp and eventual reunion with his mother. Hester Burton's *In Spite of All Terror* (268) features Liz Hawtin, an orphan sent out of London during the bombings. The story tells of her sojourn with an aristocratic family in the country and her participation in the evacuation at Dunkirk. A fascinating story of guilt and revenge in the aftermath of World War II is John Tunis's *His Enemy, His Friend* (269). Judith Kerr's *When Hitler Stole Pink Rabbit* (270), despite its rather whimsical title and the child narrator's innocent point of view, is a chilling narrative of Jewish exile during the early years of Nazi Germany.

Somewhat in contrast to these stark accounts are the romantic adventures of the Russell family in England preceding and during World War I in K. M. Peyton's trilogy, *Flambards* (271), *The Edge of the Cloud* (272), and *Flambards in Summer* (273). A story of suffragettes during the same period combines humor and political purpose with a London setting: *Miss Rivers and Miss Bridges* (274) by Geraldine Symons. A pleasant Greek family with a lively outlook on life amid the turmoil of political upheaval during the 1930s is the subject of *Wildcat under Glass* (275) by Alki Zei.

AMERICAN HISTORICAL FICTION. Historical fiction of America is a vast matrix covering periods of discovery and exploration, settlement, the turmoil of development, facets of everyday life in various periods, and, recently, some re-evaluation of roles played by minority groups in the changing times. Two excellent sources, selecting from the entire breadth of historical writing for adolescents and emphasizing works having an American setting, ought to be consulted for a thorough listing of pertinent works. The first is *Historical Fiction* compiled by Hannah Logasa.[1] Categories in this volume include Ancient History, Medieval and Modern Europe, Canada, Latin America, and United States.

---

[1]Hannah Logasa, comp., *Historical Fiction*, 9th ed., McKinley Bibliographies, vol. 1 (McKinley Pub. Co., 1968).

Works for junior high level are designated, although some of these are actually written at lower levels. A one-line description follows each title, and works deemed "especially valuable" are so indicated. Within these categories books are listed according to historical period, pinpointing major dates covered by each.

History in Children's Books, compiled by Zena Sutherland, also includes a predominance of American history titles.[1] The majority are nonfiction, but biographies and fiction titles are designated. Slightly longer book descriptions are included, as are easy-to-read items. This volume also pinpoints the historical periods encompassed in each selection. Both references are of great value to the teacher or student intent upon either surveying or studying intensively the contributions relating to specific periods in American history. More recent titles can also be located in the general references cited in chapter 1.

There are many excellent selections in this category as well as quite a few "pot-boilers"—novels that exploit historical settings in a sensational manner with stock plots that distort historical perspective. The best writers, steeped in research, impart excitement enough through their accurate findings. They neither distort the facts nor over-assert the historical detail in a way that dampens the narratives. Considering the difficulty of the task, it's surprising that so many authors have produced many fine works of historical fiction about America.

Scott O'Dell's *The King's Fifth* (276) is, above all, a fully developed drama of a man's struggle to keep his values straight amid human greed for gold. At age 15, Estaban, the Spanish cartographer, accompanies a crew searching for Coronado. When mutiny brews, he must decide whether to be set ashore to continue the search, which by now has become a quest to find the Seven Golden Cities where it is rumored galleons of gold can be found.

A French novel translated into English—*The Wapiti* (277) by Monique Corriveau—begins in 1656 with fifteen-year-old Matthew Rousseau, a stowaway aboard the *Valiant* from France to Quebec. Matthew becomes a member of an Iroquois tribe and eventually plays his part in promoting peaceful relations between the Indians and the French in the New World. In contrast to O'Dell's Estaban, Matthew doesn't experience internal struggle; his goals appear to be set for him by external forces. But the action of the story is exciting, the pace unhampered by unnecessary detail.

Elizabeth George Speare's *The Witch of Blackbird Pond* (278) a Newbery Medal winner, presents Kit Tyler, who was brought to the Connecticut Colony in 1687. Rather gently, the author tells how Kit shocks the community with "unladylike" high spirits. She swims in the harbor, upsets her schoolroom's stolid atmosphere by having her pupils dramatize the Good Samaritan story, and finally faces trial accused of witchcraft: "guilty of actions and works which infer a court with the devil, which have caused illness and death to fall upon many

---

[1]Zena Sutherland, comp., *History in Children's Books,* McKinley Bibliographies, vol. 5 (McKinley Pub. Co., 1967).

innocent children in this town."[1] But the trial is short lived, and the ending is happy. The "witch hunt" in tragic perspective is described indelibly in Ann Petry's *Tituba of Salem Village* (279). In this story, a black slave girl from Barbados, a real character from history, is convicted of witchcraft. Details of the trial evidence a temper in the times quite different from the easily appeased accusers of Kit Tyler.

Calico Captive (280), also by Elizabeth George Speare, is based on a real incident: the kidnap of a Vermont family in 1754 by Indians who sold their captives to the French in Montreal. On the whole, *Calico Captive* is good reading. For the most part it maintains its lightness convincingly by presenting the story through the point of view of its heroine Miriam. She is inclined to overlook the larger horror, to concentrate instead on trivialities that affect her vanity. The meanness of the moment, not the threat of tragedy in the future, affects Miriam, as when the kidnappers steal her best dress: "There in the wilderness, surrounded by savage enemies, bound for a fate she dared not imagine, she wept her heart out for a flowered dress she would never wear again."[2] Epic-minded fiction writers who present their settlers gazing nobly into the future, as if only a bit of cement were needed to turn them into monuments for the park or the city hall, ought to examine Speare's theme: that concerns of the moment and persistent self-interest are also a part of the pioneer spirit.

The American Revolution is, quite naturally, the subject of many fictional and semi-fictional works. Of the latter type, Mary Kay Phelan's *Four Days in Philadelphia—1776* (281) and *Midnight Alarm: The Story of Paul Revere's Ride* (282) are good examples of important historical events presented in elaborate narration. Jean Fritz's *Early Thunder* (283) describes through fiction the fierce debate of colonists preceding the war—whether to remain loyal to the king or to join the "patriots." An unusual side-light on the War itself is given in a biographical fiction book, *The Incredible Deborah* (284) by Cora Cheney. This real-life heroine disguised her sex and joined patriot soldiers to fight in the Revolutionary War. A particularly strong first novel, *Rebel in the Night* (285) by Peter Jones, begins with some earthy details of the fight for Long Island and then describes the prison ship existence of the captured hero Evan Stoddard. Throughout, the book presents a candid look at common motives behind the Revolution.

In *Johnny Tremain* (286) Esther Forbes has created one of historical fiction's unforgettable characters. The opening scenes show Johnny as an apprentice silversmith, gifted but too proud, sharp-tongued, high-spirited, and thoroughly appealing. His visit to the Boston wharf is worth pages of description in a history book: "Already the day's bustle had begun up and down the wharf: A man was crying fish. Sailors were heave-hoing at their ropes. A woman was yelling that her son had fallen into the water. A parrot said distinctly, 'King Hancock.' "[3]

Johnny breaks the Sabbath and, in what appears to be true justice of the times,

---

[1] p. 210.
[2] p. 26.
[3] p. 7.

burns his hand, apparently beyond repair. His career is ended; he is "No more good than a horse with sprung knees." A child in his master's home screams at him: "Don't touch me! Don't touch me with that dreadful hand! . . . Go away, Johnny, go away! I hate your hand."[1] So Johnny goes away. The slow recovery of his pride, the acceptance of his handicap—this is a masterful story. But wider events engulf the narrative so that the troubled hero and his friend Rab, a "Son of Liberty," are the reader's entry to the Boston Tea Party, the opening of the Revolution, the confusion and doubts of rebels who were quickly driven to resolve by the British attempt to starve Boston into submission.

Paul Revere, John Hancock, Sam Adams, and a prophet James Otis walk through these pages not as hallowed historical figures but as men fashioning solutions to problems of the moment.

Without preaching, without explicit theme-stating, the book gives a view of history as a leavener of character. Johnny's handicap is his greatest problem in the first half of the story; by the end, the sudden hope that the hand can be healed is less important to him than the rush of wider events. The reader leaves the book wishing that there might have been another, to tell what became of this hero as he grew further to manhood.

A series of books by Leonard Wibberley explores three generations of the fictitious Treegate family, from 1769 to the War of 1812. The elder John Treegate in *John Treegate's Musket* (287) changes his sympathies from the British to the rebel cause, and the book ends at a high-pitched moment at the Battle of Bunker Hill in 1775. *Peter Treegate's War* (288) examines a father-son conflict, its roots in personalities more than in political beliefs. Two supporting characters—a Scot named Maclaren and a navigator with new-found religious convictions, Peace of God Manly—add zest and the feeling of life to this book. By the time of *Red Pawns* (289) the family is well known to the reader, and the author's style is comfortable and assured. The major tone is one of conflict; often as not, the conflict is among generations and factions rather than with an identified enemy. The fighting spirit of the early nationalists is thus seen to turn upon itself, though the progress of settlement continues.

The diverse settings of the new nation are exciting backgrounds for many skilled authors' stories of young men and women of those times. Stephen Meader's *Who Rides in the Dark?* (290) shows early New Hampshire through the eyes of Daniel Drew, an orphan stable boy at the Fox and Stars Inn. Dan barely escapes death at the hands of highway robbers and eventually gains status in his community. He's an appealing boy but lacks the internal struggle of Johnny Tremain and so is less well remembered when the book is ended. Meader's *Boy with a Pack* (291) follows a similar hero, Bill Crawford, on his dangerous lone journey from New Hampshire through Ohio. Rebecca Caudill tells of a family's move to Kentucky during Revolutionary War times in *Tree of Freedom* (292); Stephanie, the heroine, plants an apple seed, a symbol of growth in the frontier.

---

[1] pp. 35, 62.

Caudill's *The Far-off Land* (293) tells of a different journey, that of Ketty Petrie in 1780 from Salem to the Cumberland Mountains. The role played by resourceful young women in the settlement of America is well displayed in such fiction. *The Taken Girl* (294) by Elizabeth Gray Vining is especially noteworthy, for its heroine Veer Schuyler must surmount the obstacles of orphanhood and servanthood to become a leader in the Quaker community during Abolitionist times and a respected acquaintance of John Greenleaf Whittier. The latter is revealed as a supporter of women's rights, explaining to Veer that "Women's labor is placed on an equality with that of men. They are not paid as much, even though they stand beside the same machines, but that will come later."[1] The otherwise quiet novel is climaxed by the burning of an orphanage for black children in Philadelphia and by portents of the Civil War to come.

Irene Hunt's complex novel of the Creighton family in Illinois in *Across Five Aprils* (295) begins in a leisurely manner with its characters' concern about farm work, but soon their closed world is penetrated by the Civil War. Family closeness is dissolved when the two older brothers join the opposite sides in the war, and the younger brother Jethro writes a letter to the President pleading for clemency in regard to his brother's desertion. Jethro, in fact, is fashioned after the author's grandfather, as she explains in an end-note. The Civil War has seldom been so capably described in fiction, all from the perspective of one rural family.

Rifles for Watie (296) by Harold Keith, set in the Oklahoma-Kansas region, takes as its central situation the selling of munitions by northerners to the Confederacy. A Kansas boy spies on the Confederates, is captured, and manages to befriend his captors, which include Stand Watie, a Cherokee Indian. This is an exciting, believable narrative by an author who combines exhaustive research with break-neck pace in storytelling. The same author's *Komantcia* (297) provides a closer look at Indian ways in the 1860s, when a young Spaniard is forced to join the Comanches. William O. Steele's *The Perilous Road* (298) is set in Tennessee, where the Brabson family divides its alliances between the North and the South.

Older stories of the settling of America sometimes present stereotypes: the noble pioneer, the "savage," the brave but subservient female. Walter D. Edmonds's *The Matchlock Gun* (299) is a frightening story of an Indian raid upon pioneers, but some people have objected to it because the author seems to generalize about Indians in a negative manner. *Caddie Woodlawn* (300) by Carol Ryrie Brink is a light-hearted pioneer story set in Civil War times, with a heroine who refuses to act like a "lady." The book is intended to reflect the spirit of the times when it shows that in the end Caddie decides to conform.

It's refreshing to discover that balance is now beginning to be established in current fiction about pioneer America. In addition to his superb, tragic story of a nineteenth-century Cheyenne in *Only Earth and Sky Last Forever,* Nathaniel

---

[1] p. 133.

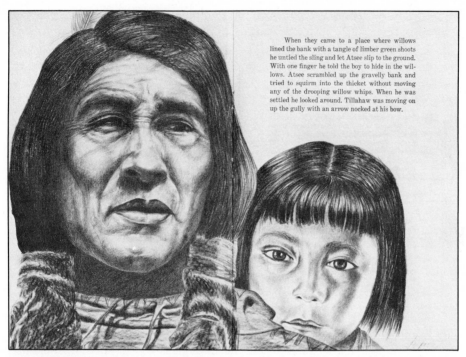

When they came to a place where willows lined the bank with a tangle of limber green shoots he untied the sling and let Atsee slip to the ground. With one finger he told the boy to hide in the willows. Atsee scrambled up the gravelly bank and tried to squirm into the thicket without moving any of the drooping willow whips. When he was settled he looked around. Tillahaw was moving on up the gully with an arrow nocked at his bow.

Excerpted from THE TALKING LEAF by Weyman Jones. Copyright ©1965 by Weyman Jones. Used with permission of The Dial Press.

Benchley shows the less-than-heroic underside of pioneer life in *Gone and Back* (301). Betty Baker examines America of a century ago through the puzzled eyes of an Apache, Hatilshay, in *And One Was a Wooden Indian* (302). In this and many other novels with varied historical settings, the author brings a rare tone of respectful humor to her work. Weyman Jones's two novels about Sequoyah, the Cherokee who brings written language to his people, are *The Talking Leaf* (303) and *Edge of Two Worlds* (304). The first is quiet, telling of a young boy's acceptance of the condition that his people must learn to live in harmony with the settlers. The second hurls its reader a painful contrast: a hunger-crazed white boy who has just witnessed his family's destruction by Indians finds that his only hope of survival is through alliance with the old, lone man Sequoyah. The kidnap of Navaho girls by white slavers in Scott O'Dell's *Sing Down the Moon* (305), their escape and return to the tribe, and the forced march of the Navahos in the 1860s are the authentic events of memorable historical fiction. Ann Nolan Clark, a gifted lyrical stylist, imparts respect and understanding for the Pueblo people clinging proudly to their culture in *Circle of Seasons* (306). And Frank Bonham in *Chief* (307) presents one of the best of several modern accounts of the struggle of the Indian to live with dignity in a "white" culture that is learning belatedly to alter its ethnocentrism.

Several purposes are at work in fiction that attempts to eliminate stereotypes. The author must present factual information; he may also attempt to persuade through an argument implicit in the theme; and he writes to entertain. At times, historical fiction may not permit a suitable balance among these purposes. Modern authors dealing with unfamiliar cultures often seek combinations that may result in new forms. Christie Harris's *Raven's Cry* (308) combines straight factual history about the exploitation of the Haidas in Canada by white traders with a fragmentary fictional narrative. In *Secret in the Stlalakum Wild* (309) she blends a modern fanciful narrative with accurate historical fact, an effective combination so clearly rendered that readers will not be confused. *At the Mouth of the Luckiest River* (310) by Arnold A. Griese is a story of intrigue: the crippled Indian boy named Tatlek must avert war with the Eskimos. The book also contains anthropological insights into the Athasbascan tribe of a hundred years ago. The combination of fictional conversation and occasional fictional incident with true biographical data may appear to be a questionable form, requiring a discerning reader and a writer who avoids the temptation to distort; but recent biographical fiction, inspired perhaps by Jean Latham's *Carry On, Mr. Bowditch* (311), proves that this form contributes to literary experience. New forms and new emphases develop our empathy and understanding for other cultures.

America's recent history as portrayed through fiction almost invariably includes current social concerns in its themes. Such works provide material for social studies curricula and are therefore discussed with nonfiction in chapter 8. Here we shall cite a few examples, each to some extent combining historical detail with an intent to persuade. *Never Jam Today* (312) by Carole Bolton presents the unpleasant facts of cruelty dealt to members of the women's suffrage movement during World War I. Its heroine, Maddy Franklin, goes to jail for her beliefs and, when she is released, spurns marriage and conformity in order to pursue her cause. Irene Hunt's excellent novel of the Depression of the 1930s, *No Promises in the Wind* (313), brings the painful realization that physical deprivation resulting from poverty often led to anger and real hatred among family members. The Polish immigrant father in this story vents his anger upon his older son Josh, and only at the end is there a hint that Josh may learn to cope with this injustice. The book's view of the effects of poverty contrasts to the theme of family solidarity in William H. Armstrong's masterful *Sounder* (314), a story of tragic injustice suffered by a black sharecropper family.

Amid these rather grim themes, you may seek nostalgic fiction for upper levels as reassurance that modern times do have a pleasant side. For example, two books purporting to be the month-by-month diary of Letitia Chambers Sterling (Tish) give a lively, warming account of a Bronx family in 1901: *The Keeping Days* (315) and *Glory in the Flower* (316) by Norma Johnston. Tish is a happy character. Her first romance and her helter-skelter production of *Romeo and Juliet* show that turn-of-the-century life was not unduly weighted down with manners and morals. Best of all is the stereotype-breaking character of Mama, who, pregnant and mad, berates her family: "Hell and damn! . . . Tarnation children can't take responsibility for anything without I tell you three times! All the thanks I get!

Pa not home again when I need him! Me in this condition!"[1] This book might inspire you to begin a list of modern historical fiction works that have an assortment of things to say about "reality."

Fiction about World War II includes an exciting group of short stories, *No Time for Glory* (317), one of the many fine upper-level collections of Phyllis R. Fenner. The war in action strikes school children in Alaska, resulting in the death of a patriotic teacher, in Theodore Taylor's *The Children's Way* (318). Karl Bruckner's story of Hiroshima in 1945, *The Day of the Bomb* (319), includes statistics of the devastation wrought by the first use of the atomic bomb in war, but the plight of one Japanese family following the event arouses greater empathy than the statistics. P. L. Travers's *I Go By Sea, I Go By Land* (320) is the America-based diary of a British girl displaced by the war. C. L. Rinaldo's impressive first novel, *Dark Dreams* (321), is set in a New England city during World War II. This story of Carlo's personal war against three hoodlums and his socially unacceptable friendship with a brain-damaged adult is a reminder that historical fiction set in war times may not always place national events at its center.

Racial struggles of the 1950s and 1960s are among those social themes treated in upper-level literature. Two early, comparatively quiet works about school integration have earned a lasting place in modern reading. *Mary Jane* (322) by Dorothy Sterling features a charming heroine with refreshing humor in the midst of anguish. "You'd think that when people were grown up they'd have more sense," she grumbles when prejudice threatens to turn her out of school. The book ends with a dignified joke and a saving touch of realistic hope. The tone of Natalie Savage Carlson's *The Empty School House* (323) seems mild in spite of the racially-based hatred at its core. Its heroine meets violence with believable calm and takes her place among memorable characters of historical fiction.

The recent past as a central subject for serious upper-level fiction seems somewhat neglected. Time will tell whether fiction can deal effectively with it, or whether nonfiction will predominate. *Cross-Fire: A Vietnam Novel* (324) by Gail Graham is a searing, soul-searching account of tragedy that follows an American soldier's adoption of children victimized by war. It stands alone, a reminder that the history of only yesterday needs the interpretive power of fictional literature, too.

We have not attempted here to survey all periods and places in historical fiction. You can utilize sources to locate others of your choice. What we have attempted to show is that fiction plays an important part in revealing the dynamics of history. Viewed as a whole, historical fiction and fiction dealing with unique, often unfamiliar settings reveals that the reality of the past is not to be grasped as a series of stable, unchanging plateaus. Nearly always, characters and plots move through transitional times. This is a concept that seems best developed through fiction, for the nonfiction historian often appears to view history as a sequence of unified periods, one following another. Historical fiction at its best gets at the gaps between the periods. It highlights the dynamics.

---

[1]*Glory in the Flower*, p. 4.

Our entire chapter has surveyed realistic fiction in three large categories: the fiction of "self," the fiction of "outer world," and the fiction of "other times and places." We would not pretend that these categories are mutually exclusive, but they help us observe some distinctions. To some extent, the first category emphasizes fiction whose depth derives from character study; the second from the unique romance of action or plot based upon possibilities afforded by unusual or unfamiliar settings; the third from the dynamics of time-settings and place-settings comprising our heritage. Hence character, plot, and setting emerge and merge in the exciting array of this literary type.

special activities

1. Select one period to explore through historical fiction. Using sources mentioned in this section and in chapter 1, list all works pertaining to that period, or confine your list to one level of childhood. Then locate as many as you can and survey them. How can you determine, through a brief overview, which of the works are likely to be of greatest value? What criteria are suggested in this chapter's discussion to help you? What sources of book evaluation will help? Read several of the works you've selected. From this study, make a selected list of fiction pertaining to the period, including a brief summary and opinion of any listed books you've read. If you are involved in a class studying this chapter, reproduce your selected list and exchange with other class members. Discuss ways in which this activity can be useful in your work with children and children's literature.

2. Suppose you were selecting a theme, setting, and group of characters to portray what is known to you of the present—to be read ten years from now as a portrayal of recent history. What events would you include as typical? What tone would your work attempt? Compare your notes with those of others. What problems common to authors of historical fiction present themselves as you attempt this activity?

3. Some critics assert that historical fiction has neglected various cultures and times. In particular, historical fiction often seems to focus on Western cultures and on times most focal to a Westernized audience of readers. What examples can you find to show that this view is not entirely correct? Can you locate, for example, fictional works portraying life in Russia at various points in its history? in modern China? in countries of Africa? One unusual novel, *Walk the World's Rim* (325) by Betty Baker, presents co-heroes—Indian and black—against a background of early Mexico. Contrasting cultures, unusual combination, can place themes in strong light. Can you find other examples?

CHAPTER REFERENCES

1. Alexander, Martha. *And My Mean Old Mother Will Be Sorry, Blackboard Bear.* Dial, 1972. (E)
2. _____. *We Never Get To Do Anything.* Dial, 1970. (E)
3. Brown, Margaret Wise. *The Runaway Bunny.* Illus. Clement Hurd. Harper, 1942. (E)
4. Bontemps, Arna, and Conroy, Jack. *The Fast Sooner Hound.* Houghton, 1942. (E-I)
5. _____. *Slappy Hooper the Wonderful Sign Painter.* Houghton, 1946. (E-I)
6. Ward, Lynd. *The Biggest Bear.* Houghton, 1952. (E-I)
7. Daugherty, James. *Andy and the Lion.* Viking, 1936, 1966. (E-I)
8. Burn, Doris. *Andrew Henry's Meadow.* Coward, 1965. (E-I)
9. Sendak, Maurice. *Where the Wild Things Are.* Harper, 1963. (E)
10. Fisher, Aileen. *We Went Looking.* Illus. Marie Angel. Crowell, 1968. (E)
11. _____. *My Mother and I.* Illus. Kazue Mizumura. Crowell, 1967. (E)
12. Caudill, Rebecca. *A Pocketful of Cricket.* Illus. Evaline Ness. Holt, 1964. (E-I)
13. Skaar, Grace. *What Do the Animals Say?* Scott, 1950, 1968. (E)
14. Simon, Norma. *What Do I Say?* Illus. Joe Laker. Whitman, 1967. (E)
15. Goudey, Alice E. *The Day We Saw the Sun Come Up.* Illus. Adrienne Adams. Scribner, 1961. (E)
16. Brown, Margaret Wise. *The Seashore Noisy Book.* Illus. Leonard Weisgard. Harper, 1941. (E)
17. _____. *The Quiet Noisy Book.* Illus. Leonard Weisgard. Harper, 1950. (E)
18. Scott, Ann Herbert. *On Mother's Lap.* Illus. Glo Coalson. McGraw, 1972. (E)
19. Tobias, Tobi. *A Day Off.* Illus. Ray Cruz. Putnam's, 1973. (E)
20. Krauss, Ruth. *A Hole Is to Dig.* Illus. Maurice Sendak. Harper, 1952. (E)
21. Byars, Betsy. *Go and Hush the Baby.* Illus. Emily A. McCully. Viking, 1971. (E)
22. Zolotow, Charlotte. *When I Have a Little Girl.* Illus. Hilary Knight. Harper, 1965. (E)
23. Carrick, Carol and Donald. *Sleep Out.* Seabury, 1973. (E)
24. Beim, Jerrold. *The Smallest Boy in the Class.* Illus. Meg Wohlberg. Morrow, 1949. (E)
25. Hill, Elizabeth Starr. *Evan's Corner.* Illus. Nancy Grossman. Holt, 1967. (E)
26. Sherman, Ivan. *I Do Not Like It When My Friend Comes to Visit.* Harcourt, 1973. (E)
27. Alexander, Anne. *Noise in the Night.* Illus. Abner Graboff. Rand, 1960. (E)
28. Schick, Eleanor. *Peggy's New Brother.* Macmillan, 1970. (E)
29. Caines, Jeannette. *Abby.* Illus. Steven Kellogg. Harper, 1973. (E)
30. Steptoe, John. *Stevie.* Harper, 1969. (E)
31. Hoban, Russell. *Tom and the Two Handles.* Illus. Lillian Hoban. Harper, 1965. (E)
32. Lexau, Joan M. *Benjie.* Illus. Don Bolognese. Dial, 1964. (E)
33. _____. *Benjie on His Own.* Illus. Don Bolognese. Dial, 1964. (E)
34. Yashima, Taro. *Crow Boy.* Viking, 1955. (E)
35. _____. *Umbrella.* Viking, 1958. (E)
36. Caudill, Rebecca. *Did You Carry the Flag Today, Charley?* Illus. Nancy Grossman. Holt, 1966. (E-I)
37. Cohen, Miriam. *Will I Have a Friend?* Illus. Lillian Hoban. Macmillan, 1967. (E)
38. Zemach, Harve. *Mommy, Buy Me a China Doll.* Illus. Margot Zemach. Follett, 1966. (E)
39. Buckley, Helen E. *Grandfather and I.* Illus. Paul Galdone. Lothrop, Lee, 1959. (E)
40. _____. *Grandmother and I.* Illus. Paul Galdone. Lothrop, Lee, 1961. (E)
41. Brown, Margaret Wise. *The Dead Bird.* Illus. Remy Charlip. Scott, 1938. (E)
42. Viorst, Judith. *The Tenth Good Thing about Barney.* Illus. Erik Blegvad. Atheneum, 1972. (E)
43. Fassler, Joan. *My Grandpa Died Today.* Behavioral Publications, 1971.
44. Warburg, Sandol. *Growing Time.* Illus. Leonard Weisgard. Houghton Mifflin, 1969. (E)

45. Haywood, Carolyn. *"B" Is for Betsy.* Harcourt, 1939. (I)
46. _____. *Little Eddie.* Morrow, 1947. (I)
47. Estes, Eleanor. *The Moffats.* Illus. Louis Slobodkin. Harcourt, 1941. (I)
48. _____. *Ginger Pye.* Harcourt, 1951. (I)
49. _____. *Rufus M.* Harcourt, 1943. (I)
50. Enright, Elizabeth. *Gone-Away Lake.* Illus. Beth and Joe Krush. Harcourt, 1957. (I)
51. _____. *Return to Gone-Away.* Illus. Beth and Joe Krush. Harcourt, 1961. (I)
52. Cleary, Beverly. *Socks.* Morrow, 1973. (I)
53. _____. *Henry Huggins.* Illus. Louis Darling. Morrow, 1950. (I)
54. _____. *Ribsy.* Morrow, 1964. (I)
55. _____. *Beezus and Ramona.* Morrow, 1955. (I)
56. _____. *Ramona the Pest.* Morrow, 1968. (I)
57. Cone, Molly. *Mishmash.* Houghton, 1962. (I)
58. Lauber, Patricia. *Clarence the TV Dog.* Illus. Leonard Shortall. Coward, 1955. (I)
59. Cone, Molly. *Number Four.* Houghton, 1972. (I)
60. Colman, Hila. *Chicano Girl.* Morrow, 1973. (I)
61. _____. *End of the Game.* World, 1971. (I)
62. Hunter, Kristin. *Boss Cat.* Illus. Harold Franklin. Scribner's, 1971. (I)
63. Caudill, Rebecca. *Somebody Go and Bang a Drum.* Dutton, 1974. (I)
64. Snyder, Zilpha Keatley. *The Egypt Game.* Illus. Alton Raible. Atheneum, 1967. (I)
65. _____. *Season of Ponies.* Atheneum, _____. (I)
66. _____. *Black and Blue Magic.* Atheneum, _____. (I)
67. _____. *Eyes in the Fishbowl.* Atheneum, _____. (I)
68. _____. *The Changeling.* Atheneum, 1970. (I)
69. _____. *The Witches of Worm.* Atheneum, 1972. (I)
70. _____. *The Truth about Stone Hollow.* Atheneum, 1974. (I)
71. Wooley, Catherine. *Ginnie and the Mystery Light.* Morrow, 1973. (I)
72. Calhoun, Mary. *The Horse Comes First.* Atheneum, 1974. (I)
73. Blume, Judy. *Are You There, God? It's Me, Margaret.* Bradbury, 1970. (I-U)
74. _____. *Then Again, Maybe I Won't.* Bradbury, 1971. (I-U)
75. Donovan, John. *I'll Get There. It Better Be Worth the Trip.* Harper, 1969. (I-U)
76. Holland, Isabelle. *The Man without a Face.* Lippincott, 1972. (U)
77. Sachs, Marilyn. *The Bears' House.* Doubleday, 1970. (I-U)
78. _____. *The Truth about Mary Rose.* Doubleday, 1973. (I-U)
79. Kerr, M. E. *Dinky Hocker Shoots Smack!* Harper, 1972. (U)
80. _____. *The Son of Someone Famous.* Harper, 1974. (U)
81. Cleaver, Vera and Bill. *Grover.* Lippincott, 1970. (I-U)
82. Bonham, Frank. *Mystery of the Fat Cat.* Dutton, 1968. (U)
83. _____. *Hey, Big Spender!* Dutton, 1972. (U)
84. Wersba, Barbara. *Run Softly, Go Fast.* Atheneum, 1970. (U)
85. Corcoran, Barbara. *This Is a Recording.* Atheneum, 1971. (U)
86. Neufield, John. *Edgar Allan.* Phillips, 1968. (U)
87. Kingman, Lee. *The Peter Pan Bag.* Houghton Mifflin, 1970. (U)
88. Salinger, J. D. *The Catcher in the Rye.* Little, Brown, 1951. (U)
89. Daley, Maureen. *Sixteen and Other Stories.* Dodd, Mead, 1961. (U)
90. Felsen, Henry Gregor. *Two and the Town.* Scribner's, 1952. (U)
91. L'Engle, Madeleine. *Meet the Austins.* Vanguard, 1960. (I-U)
92. Knowles, John. *A Separate Peace.* Macmillan, 1961. (U)
93. Neville, Emily. *It's Like This, Cat.* Illus. Emil Weiss. Harper, 1963. (U)
94. Corcoran, Barbara. *A Trick of Light.* Illus. Lydia Dabcovich. Atheneum, 1972. (I-U)
95. Stolz, Mary. *Leap Before You Look.* Harper, 1972. (U)
96. Glasser, Barbara, and Blustein, Ellen. *Bongo Bradley.* Hawthorn, 1973. (I-U)
97. Witheridge, Elizabeth. *Just One Indian Boy.* Atheneum, 1974. (U)

98. Rockwell, Harlow. *My Doctor.* Macmillan, 1973. (E)
99. Hoban, Tana. *Look Again!* Macmillan, 1971. (E-I)
100. _____. *Where Is It?* Macmillan, 1974. (E)
101. Goudey, Alice E. *Houses from the Sea.* Illus. Adrienne Adams. Scribner's, 1959. (E)
102. Burton, Virginia Lee. *Mike Mulligan and His Steam Shovel.* Houghton Mifflin, 1939. (E)
103. Balian, Lorna. *Humbug Witch.* Abingdon, 1964. (E-I)
104. Raskin, Ellen. *Spectacles.* Atheneum, 1968. (E)
105. Miles, Miska. *Mississippi Possum.* Illus. John Schoenherr. Little, Brown, 1965. (E-I)
106. _____. *Fox and the Fire.* Little, Brown, 1969. (E-I)
107. _____. *Nobody's Cat.* Little, Brown, 1969. (E-I)
108. Skorpen, Liesel Moak. *Old Arthur.* Illus. Wallace Tripp. Harper, 1972. (E-I)
109. Burch, Robert. *Joey's Cat.* Illus. Don Freeman. Viking, 1969. (E)
110. Taylor, Mark. *Old Blue.* Illus. Gene Holtan. Golden Gate, 1970. (E-I)
111. Bonsall, Crosby. *The Case of the Dumb Bells.* Harper, 1966. (E)
112. Anderson, C. W. *The Rumble Seat Pony.* Macmillan, 1971. (E)
113. Ardizzone, Edward. *Tim's Last Voyage.* Walck, 1973. (E)
114. _____. *Tim in Danger.* Walck, 1953. (E)
115. _____. *Tim and Ginger.* Walck, 1965. (E)
116. Stolz, Mary. *The Noonday Friends.* Harper, 1965. (I)
117. Clifton, Lucille. *All Us Come Cross the Water.* Illus. John Steptoe. Holt, 1973. (I)
118. Fife, Dale. *The Little Park.* Illus. Janet LaSalle. Whitman, 1973. (I)
119. Adrian, Mary. *The Skin Diving Mystery.* Hastings, 1964. (I)
120. _____. *The Ghost Town Mystery.* Hastings, 1971. (I)
121. Parish, Peggy. *Key to the Treasure, Clues in the Woods,* and *Haunted House.* Macmillan, 1966, 1968, 1971. (I)
122. Wooley, Catherine. *Ginnie and Her Juniors.* Morrow, 1963. (I)
123. _____. *Ginnie and the Mystery Cat.* Morrow, 1969. (I)
124. Warner, Gertrude Chandler. *The Boxcar Children.* Scott, Foresman, 1942, Whitman, 1950. (I)
125. _____. *Houseboat Mystery.* Whitman, 1967. (I)
126. _____. *Bicycle Mystery.* Whitman, 1970. (I)
127. Christopher, Matt. *Shadow over the Back Court.* Watts, 1959.
128. _____. *Wing T Fullback.* Watts, 1960. (I)
129. _____. *Mystery Coach.* Little, Brown, 1973. (I)
130. Carol, Bill J. *Lefty's Long Throw.* Steck-Vaughn, 1967. (I)
131. _____. *Lefty Plays First.* Steck-Vaughn, 1969. (I)
132. _____. *Fullback Fury.* Steck-Vaughn, 1972. (I)
133. Heuman, William. *Horace Higby and the Gentle Fullback.* Steck-Vaughn, 1968, 1970. (I)
134. _____. *Home Run Henri.* Steck-Vaughn, 1970. (I)
135. O'Brien, Jack. *Silver Chief.* Illus. Kurt Wiese. Winston, 1933. (I-U)
136. O'Hara, Mary. *My Friend Flicka.* Lippincott, 1941. (I-U)
137. Knight, Eric. *Lassie Come-Home.* Holt, 1940, 1971. (I-U)
138. Rawlings, Marjorie Kinnan. *The Yearling.* Scribner's, 1939, 1962. (I-U)
139. Morey, Walt. *Gentle Ben.* Dutton, 1965. (I-U)
140. _____. *Gloomy Gus.* Dutton, 1970. (I-U)
141. _____. *Angry Waters.* Dutton, 1969. (I-U)
142. _____. *Canyon Winter.* Dutton, 1972. (I-U)
143. _____. *Runaway Stallion.* Dutton, 1973. (I-U)
144. Salton, Felix. *Bambi: A Life in the Woods.* Grosset, 1929. (I)
145. Rounds, Glen. *The Blind Colt.* Holiday, 1941, 1960. (E-I)
146. Dixon, Paige. *The Young Grizzly.* Atheneum, 1974. (I)
147. Tunis, John R. *Iron Duke.* Harcourt, 1938. (U)
148. _____. *Go, Team, Go.* Morrow, 1954. (U)

149. North, Sterling. *Rascal.* Illus. John Schoenherr. Avon, 1969. (I-U)
150. Annixter, Paul. *Swiftwater.* Wyn, 1950. (U)
151. Annixter, Jane and Paul. *The Great White.* Holiday, 1966. (U)
152. Peyton, K. M. *Fly-By-Night.* World, 1968. (U)
153. Means, Florence Crannell. *Knock at the Door, Emmy.* Houghton, 1956. (U)
154. _____. *Tolliver.* Houghton, 1963. (U)
155. Aiken, Joan. *Night Fall.* Holt, 1969, 1971. (U)
156. Allan, Mabel Esther. *The Night Wind.* Atheneum, 1974. (U)
157. Streatfeild, Noel. *Ballet Shoes* and *Circus Shoes.* Illus. Richard Floethe. Random, 1937, 1939. (U)
158. Cavanna, Betty. *Fancy Free.* Morrow, 1961. (U)
159. Beatty, Patricia. *Hail Columbia.* Morrow, 1970. (I-U)
160. _____. *Bonanza Girl* and *O the Red Rose Tree.* Morrow, 1962, 1972. (I-U)
161. _____. *How Many Miles to Sundown.* Morrow, 1974. (I-U)
162. Beatty, Patricia and John. *Holdfast.* Morrow, 1972. (I-U)
163. _____. *Master Rosalind.* Morrow, 1974. (I-U)
164. Bacon, Martha. *Sophia Scrooby Preserved.* Little, 1968. (I-U)
165. Fox, Paula. *The Slave Dancer.* Bradbury, 1973. (U)
166. Dickinson, Peter. *The Dancing Bear.* Little, Brown, 1973. (U)
167. D'Aulaire, Ingri and Edgar Parin. *Ola.* Doubleday, 1932. (E)
168. _____. *Children of the Northern Lights.* Viking, 1935. (E)
169. _____. *Nils.* Doubleday, 1948. (E)
170. Politi, Leo. *Song of the Swallows.* Scribner's, 1948. (E)
171. _____. *Emmet.* Scribner's, 1971. (E)
172. Ness, Evaline. *Josefina February.* Scribner's, 1963. (E)
173. _____. *Do You Have the Time, Lydia?* Dutton, 1971. (E)
174. Creekmore, Raymond. *Little Fu.* Macmillan, 1947. (E)
175. Clark, Ann Nolan. *Tia Maria's Garden.* Illus. Ezra Jack Keats. Viking, 1963. (E)
176. Krasilovsky, Phyllis. *The Cow Who Fell in the Canal.* Illus. Peter Spier. Doubleday, 1953, 1957. (E)
177. Lenski, Lois. *The Little Auto, The Little Farm, Cowboy Small,* and *Policeman Small.* Walck, 1934, 1942, 1949, 1962. (E)
178. Turkle, Brinton. *Obadiah the Bold.* Viking, 1965. (E)
179. _____. *Thy Friend, Obadiah.* Viking, 1969. (E)
180. _____. *The Adventures of Obadiah.* Viking, 1972. (E)
181. Haley, Gail E. *Jack Jouett's Ride.* Viking, 1973. (E)
182. Spier, Peter. *The Star-Spangled Banner.* Doubleday, 1973. All ages.
183. Benchley, Nathaniel. *Sam the Minuteman.* Illus. Arnold Lobel. Harper, 1969. (E)
184. Baker, Betty. *Little Runner of the Longhouse.* Illus. Arnold Lobel. Harper, 1962. (E)
185. Skipper, Mervyn. *The Fooling of King Alexander.* Illus. Gaynor Chapman. Atheneum, 1967. (E-I)
186. Dalgliesh, Alice. *The Courage of Sarah Noble.* Scribner's, 1954. (E)
187. _____. *The Bears on Hemlock Mountain.* Scribner's, 1952. (E)
188. Parish, Peggy. *Granny and the Indians.* Illus. Brinton Turkle. Macmillan, 1969. (E)
189. Williamson, Mel, and Ford, George. *Walk On!* Odarkai Books, 1972. (E-I)
190. Lenski, Lois. *Bayou Suzette.* Stokes, 1943. (I)
191. _____. *Coal Camp Girl.* Lippincott, 1959. (I)
192. _____. *Prairie School.* Lippincott, 1951. (I)
193. _____. *Cotton in My Sack, Corn Farm Boy, San Francisco Boy,* and *Houseboat Girl.* Lippincott, 1949, 1954, 1955, 1957. (I)
194. Bulla, Clyde Robert. *Benito.* Crowell, 1961. (I)
195. _____. *Indian Hill.* Crowell, 1963. (I)
196. _____. *Viking Adventure.* Crowell, 1963. (I)

197. Wilder, Laura Ingalls. *Little House in the Big Woods.* Illus. Garth Williams. Harper, 1932. (I)
198. _____. *Little House on the Prairie.* Illus. Garth Williams. Harper, 1935. (I)
199. _____. *Farmer Boy.* Illus. Garth Williams. Harper, 1933. (I)
200. _____. *On the Banks of Plum Creek.* Illus. Garth Williams. Harper, 1937. (I)
201. _____. *By the Shores of Silver Lake.* Illus. Garth Williams. Harper, 1939. (I)
202. _____. *The Long Winter.* Illus. Garth Williams. Harper, 1940. (I)
203. _____. *Little Town on the Prairie.* Illus. Garth Williams. Harper, 1941. (I)
204. _____. *These Happy Golden Years.* Illus. Garth Williams. Harper, 1943. (I)
205. _____. *The First Four Years.* Illus. Garth Williams. Harper, 1971. (I)
206. Lawrence, Isabelle. *A Spy in Williamsburg.* Rand, 1955. (I-U)
207. Burchard, Peter. *Bimby.* Coward-McCann, 1968. (I)
208. Hamilton, Virginia. *The House of Dies Drear.* Macmillan, 1968. (I)
209. Monjo, F. N. *The Vicksburg Veteran.* Illus. Douglas Gorsline. Simon & Schuster, 1971. (I)
210. Peak, Robert Newton. *Soup.* Illus. Charles C. Gehm. Knopf, 1974. (I-U)
211. Burch, Robert. *Skinny.* Illus. Don Sibley. Viking, 1964.
212. _____. *Queenie Peavy.* Viking, 1966. (I)
213. _____. *Hut School and the Wartime Home-front Heroes.* Viking, 1974. (I)
214. Taylor, Sydney. *All-of-a-Kind Family.* Follett, 1941. (I)
215. Fitzgerald, John D. *The Great Brain.* Viking, 1967. (I)
216. Neville, Emily Cheney. *The Seventeenth Street Gang.* Illus. Emily McCully. Harper, 1966. (I)
217. Mathis, Sharon Bell. *Sidewalk Story.* Viking, 1971. (I)
218. _____. *Teacup Full of Roses.* Viking, 1972. (I)
219. Belpre, Pura. *Santiago.* Illus. Symeon Shimin. Warne, 1969. (I)
220. Barth, Edna. *The Day Luis Was Lost.* Illus. Lilian Obligado. Little, Brown, 1971. (I)
221. Sutcliff, Rosemary. *Heather, Oak, and Olive.* Illus. Victor Ambrus. Dutton, 1972. (I)
222. Winterfield, Henry. *Detectives in Togas.* Tr. Richard and Clara Winston. Harcourt, 1956. (I)
223. DeJong, Meindert. *The Wheel on the School.* Illus. Maurice Sendak. Harper, 1954. (I)
224. _____. *The House of Sixty Fathers.* Illus. Maurice Sendak. Harper, 1956. (I)
225. _____. *Journey from Peppermint Street.* Illus. Emily McCully. Harper, 1968. (I)
226. Carlson, Natalie Savage. *The Happy Orpheline.* Illus. Garth Williams. Harper, 1957. (I)
227. Winterfeld, Henry. *Mystery of the Roman Mansion.* Illus. Fritz Biermann. Harcourt, 1969, 1971. (I-U)
228. Snedeker, Caroline Dale. *Theras and His Town.* Doubleday, 1924. (U)
229. _____. *The Spartan.* Doubleday, 1912. (U)
230. Chute, Marchette. *The Innocent Wayfaring.* Schribner's, 1943. (U)
231. Fox, Paula. *The Slave Dancer.* Illus. Eros. Keith. Bradbury, 1973. (U)
232. Benchley, Nathaniel. *Only Earth and Sky Last Forever.* Harper, 1971. (U)
233. Sutcliff, Rosemary. *Warrior Scarlet.* Walck, 1958. (U)
234. Barringer, D. Moreau. *And the Waters Prevailed.* Illus. P. A. Hutchinson. Dutton, 1956. (U)
235. Behn, Harry. *The Faraway Lurs.* World, 1963. (U)
236. Trease, Geoffrey. *The Hills of Varna.* Vanguard, (U)
237. _____. *The Crown of Violet.* Vanguard, 1952. (U)
238. _____. *Escape to King Alfred.* Vanguard, 1958. (U)
239. Haugaard, Erik Christian. *A Slave's Tale.* Houghton Mifflin, 1965. (U)
240. _____. *Hakon of Rogen's Saga.* Houghton Mifflin, 1963. (U)
241. _____. *The Untold Tale.* Houghton Mifflin, 1971. (U)
242. Treece, Henry. *Viking's Dawn.* Criterion, 1956. (U)

243. _____. *Children's Crusade.* Criterion, 1958. (U)
244. Hodges, C. Walter. *The Namesake.* Coward, 1964. (U)
245. _____. *The Marsh King.* Coward, 1967. (U)
246. Sutcliff, Rosemary. *The Queen Elizabeth Story.* Oxford, 1950. (I-U)
247. _____. *Outcast.* Walck, 1955. (U)
248. _____. *The Eagle of the Ninth.* Walck, 1954. (U)
249. _____. *The Silver Branch.* Walck, 1957. (U)
250. _____. *The Lantern Bearers.* Walck, 1959. (U)
251. _____. *The Capricorn Bracelet.* Walck, 1973. (U)
252. _____. *Dawn Wind.* Walck, 1962. (U)
253. _____. *Witch's Brat.* Walck, 1970. (U)
254. Harnett, Cynthia. *The Wool-Pack.* Methuen, 1951. (U)
255. _____. *Caxton's Challenge.* World, 1960. (U)
256. _____. *The Writing on the Hearth.* Viking, 1973. (U)
257. Burton, Hester. *Time of Trial.* World, 1963. (U)
258. _____. *The Rebel.* Crowell, 1971. (U)
259. _____. *The Henchmans at Home.* Crowell, 1970. (U)
260. deTreviño, Elizabeth Borton. *I, Juan de Pareja.* Farrar, 1965. (I-U)
261. Konigsburg, E. L. *A Proud Taste for Scarlet and Miniver.* Atheneum, 1973. (I-U)
262. Garfield, Leon. *The Sound of Coaches.* Viking, 1974. (U)
263. _____. *Black Jack.* Pantheon, 1968. (U)
264. _____. *Smith.* Pantheon, 1976. (U)
265. _____. *The Drummer Boy.* Pantheon, 1969. (U)
266. Foreman, James. *Ceremony of Innocence.* Hawthorn, 1970. (U)
267. Holm, Ann. *North to Freedom.* Harcourt, 1963. (U)
268. Burton, Hester. *In Spite of All Terror.* World, 1968. (U)
269. Tunis, John. *His Enemy, His Friend.* Morrow, 1967. (U)
270. Kerr, Judith. *When Hitler Stole Pink Rabbit.* Coward, 1971. (U)
271. Peyton, K. M. *Flambards.* World, 1968. (U)
272. _____. *The Edge of the Cloud.* World, 1970. (U)
273. _____. *Flambards in Summer.* World, 1970. (U)
274. Symons, Geraldine. *Miss Rivers and Miss Bridges.* Macmillan, 1971. (U)
275. Zei, Alki. *Wildcat under Glass.* Holt, 1968. (I-U)
276. O'Dell, Scott. *The King's Fifth.* Houghton, 1966. (U)
277. Corriveau, Monique. *The Wapiti.* Trans. J. M. L'Heureux. Macmillan, 1968. (U)
278. Speare, Elizabeth George. *The Witch of Blackbird Pond.* Houghton Mifflin, 1958. (U)
279. Petry, Ann. *Tituba of Salem Village.* Crowell, 1964. (U)
280. Speare, Elizabeth George. *Calico Captive.* Houghton Mifflin, 1957. (U)
281. Phelan, Mary Kay. *Four Days in Philadelphia—1776.* Crowell, 1967. (I)
282. _____. *Midnight Alarm: The Story of Paul Revere's Ride.* Crowell, 1968. (U)
283. Fritz, Jean. *Early Thunder.* Coward, 1967. (U)
284. Cheney, Cora. *The Incredible Deborah.* Scribner's, 1967. (U)
285. Jones, Peter. *Rebel in the Night.* Dial, 1971. (U)
286. Forbes, Esther. *Johnny Tremain.* Houghton Mifflin, 1943. (U)
287. Wibberley, Leonard. *John Treegate's Musket.* Farrar, 1959. (U)
288. _____. *Peter Treegate's War.* Farrar, 1960. (U)
289. _____. *Red Pawns.* Farrar, 1973. (U)
290. Meader, Stephen. *Who Rides in the Dark?* Harcourt, 1937. (U)
291. _____. *Boy with a Pack.* Harcourt, 1939. (U)
292. Caudill, Rebecca. *Tree of Freedom.* Viking, 1949. (U)
293. _____. *The Far-Off Land.* Viking, 1964. (U)
294. Vining, Elizabeth Gray. *The Taken Girl.* Viking, 1972. (U)
295. Hunt, Irene. *Across Five Aprils.* Follett, 1964. (U)

296. Keith, Harold. *Rifles for Watie.* Crowell, 1957. (U)
297. _____. *Komantcia.* Crowell, 1965. (U)
298. Steele, William O. *The Perilous Road.* Harcourt, 1958. (U)
299. Edmonds, Walter D. *The Matchlock Gun.* Dodd, Mead, 1941. (U)
300. Brink, Carol Ryrie. *Caddie Woodlawn.* Macmillan, 1935. (I-U)
301. Benchley, Nathaniel. *Gone and Back.* Harper, 1971. (U)
302. Baker, Betty. *And One Was a Wooden Indian.* Macmillan, 1970. (U)
303. Jones, Weyman. *The Talking Leaf.* Dial, 1965. (U)
304. _____. *The Edge of Two Worlds.* Dial, 1968. (U)
305. O'Dell, Scott. *Sing Down the Moon.* Houghton Mifflin, 1970. (I-U)
306. Clark, Ann Nolan. *Circle of Seasons.* Ferrar, 1970. (I-U)
307. Bonham, Frank. *Chief.* Dutton, 1971. (U)
308. Harris, Christie. *Raven's Cry.* Atheneum, 1966. (U)
309. _____. *Secret in the Stlalakum Wild.* Atheneum, 1972. (U)
310. Griese, Arnold A. *At the Mouth of the Luckiest River.* Illus. Glo Coalson. Crowell, 1969, 1973. (I-U)
311. Latham, Jean. *Carry On, Mr. Bowditch.* Houghton Mifflin, 1955. (U)
312. Bolton, Carole. *Never Jam Today.* Atheneum, 1971. (U)
313. Hunt, Irene. *No Promises in the Wind.* Follett, 1970. (U)
314. Armstrong, William H. *Sounder.* Harper, 1969. (U)
315. Johnston, Norma. *The Keeping Days.* Atheneum, 1973. (U)
316. _____. *Glory in the Flower.* Atheneum, 1974. (U)
317. Fenner, Phyllis R. *No Time for Glory.* Morrow, 1962. (U)
318. Taylor, Theodore. *The Children's Way.* Doubleday, 1971. (U)
319. Bruckner, Karl. *The Day of the Bomb.* Van Nostrand, 1962. (U)
320. Travers, P. L. *I Go by Sea, I Go by Land.* Harper, 1941. (I-U)
321. Rinaldo, C. L. *Dark Dreams.* Harper, 1974. (U)
322. Sterling, Dorothy. *Mary Jane.* Doubleday, 1959. (I-U)
323. Carlson, Natalie Savage. *The Empty School House.* Harper, 1965. (I-U)
324. Graham, Gail. *Cross-Fire: A Vietnam Novel.* Pantheon, 1972. (U)
325. Baker, Betty. *Walk the World's Rim.* Harper, 1965. (U)

BIBLIOGRAPHY

Abel, Midge B. "American Indian Life as Portrayed in Children's Literature." *Elementary English,* 50 February 1973, pp. 202–8. Thoughtful analysis of many fictional and nonfictional works with Indian characters. Excellent bibliography.

Alm, Julie N. "Young Adult Favorites." *Top of the News,* 30 June 1974, pp. 403–9. What Hawaiian high schoolers like to read. Shows a definite preference for current realistic fiction of the self.

Arth, Alfred A., and Whittemore, Judith D. "Selecting Literature for Children that Relates to Life, the Way It Is." *Elementary English,* 50 May 1973, pp. 726–28+. Includes annotated bibliography of books dealing with contemporary issues.

Banks, James A. "Developing Racial Tolerance with Literature on the Black Inner-City." *Social Education,* 34 May 1970, pp. 549–52. Perceptive discussion of how fiction may generate discussion of social and psychological problems.

Bird, Kathy. "The Value of Individualism." *Elementary English,* 50 May 1973, pp. 707–14. How American historical fiction for children and young people reveals the changing idea of individualism.

Bontemps, Arna. "Old Myths, New Negroes." *Top of the News,* 26 January 1970, pp. 138–47. Discusses many welcome changes in realistic fiction about black characters.

Burch, Robert. "The New Realism." *Horn Book,* 47 June 1971, pp. 257–64. Contends that recent "slice-of-life" stories needn't neglect happy endings in favor of the harsher side of things.

Carlson, Julie. "Jean Lee Latham—'A Memorable Person'." *Elementary English,* 47 February 1970, pp. 281–84. One of the many author profiles in the *Elementary English* collection; includes personal glimpse of the author and annotated list of her fictional biographies.

Casmir, Fred L. "Children's Books: A Search for Reality." *Elementary English,* 39 December 1962, pp. 803–5. Still fresh is this writer's argument for "sanity" rather than "reality" in realistic fiction for children.

Cianciolo, Patricia Jean. "Meindert De Jong." *Elementary English,* 45 October 1968, pp. 725–30. Biographical data and survey of the works of a distinguished writer.

Cullinan, Bernice E. "Reality Reflected in Children's Literature." *Elementary English,* 51 March 1974, pp. 395–98. Argues that there's a need for quality as well as relevancy in current literature; recommends titles with a modicum of both characteristics.

Goodrich, Catherine. "The Many Faces of Aloneness." *Elementary English,* 40 February 1963, pp. 135–41. A classic article, citing titles arranged by categories of living in isolation.

Holland, Isabelle. "Tilting at Taboos." *Horn Book,* 49 June 1973, pp. 299–305. Interesting argument: that taboos often motivate a story and have contributed to the creation of some of our best literature.

Johnson, G. S. "Going Down Under?" *Elementary English,* 51 March 1974, pp. 432–34. Twenty-five fiction titles about Australia, carefully annotated.

Knudson, Rozanne. "My Mother, the Censor." *Teachers College Record,* 47 February 1966, pp. 363–66. Lively argument for more light and less heat in evaluating realistic fiction.

Neumeyer, Peter F. "What Is Relevant Literature?" *The Record,* 71 September 1969, pp. 1–10. The themes of great literature are "relevant" whether or not their subjects are specifically based on current happenings.

Nilsen, Alleen Pace. "Books about Drugs." *English Journal,* 63 May 1974, pp. 89–91. Critical review of *Go Ask Alice, We Were Hooked, Richie, Dinky Hocker Shoots Smack!* and others, all for upper levels.

Odland, Norine. "Marguerite Henry: Mistress of Mole Meadows." *Elementary English,* 45 January 1968, pp. 7–11. Photos, brief biography of the author, and summary of her books.

Parrott, Phyllis. "Cynthia Harnett: A Tribute on Her Eightieth Birthday." *The Junior Bookshelf,* 37 August 1973, pp. 233–34. Those who read Ms. Harnett's work will appreciate this information about her life style and manner of working.

Peterson, Barbara G. "Life Maladjustment through Children's Literature." *Elementary English,* 40 November 1963, pp. 716–18. Review of selected titles shows that empathy for personal difficulties is developed through books of realistic fiction.

Prida, Dolores, et al. "Feminists Look at the 100 Books: The Portrayal of Women in Children's Books in Puerto Rican Times." *Interracial Books for Children,* 4, 1973, pp. 7–10. The committee examines a selected list, having set criteria for their evaluation.

Stavn, Diane G., and Lanes, Selma. "On Feminist Criticism." *Library Journal,* 99 January 15, 1974, pp. 182–87. Discusses feminist promoted children's literature as a distinct form of propaganda, suggesting that it should be welcomed provided that literary quality is also considered.

Stavn, Diane G. "Reducing the Miss Muffet Syndrome: An Annotated Bibliography." *Library Journal,* 97 January 15, 1972, pp. 256–59. Books that, in the author's opinion, depict women and girls realistically and fairly.

Stevens, Carla. "Attitudes Toward Gypsies in Children's Literature." *Interracial Books for Children,* 5, 1974, p. 1+. Especially worthwhile study because the author obviously has read carefully the works she discusses.

chapter 7

Poetry

Poetry composed for children has had a predominantly gentle tradition, celebrating the pleasing moment, the nonthreatening view. The best-remembered poems of Robert Louis Stevenson, for example, describe simple acts—going up in a swing, building a ship upon the stairs—and his ingenious, smoothly flowing lines catch the happiness behind commonplace experiences:

> When I was down beside the sea
> A wooden spade they gave to me
> To dig the sandy shore.

And:

> I should like to rise and go
> Where the golden apples grow.[1]

Similarly, Christina Rossetti's short lyrics gaze upon a garden mouse, upon wrens and robins; her lines echo the ringing bells of the country and village. Rachel Field in America and Eleanor Farjeon in England present the city and the quiet landscape of another day, celebrating names and games, buses and buildings, rains, flowers, and fresh mornings. The master of pleasant dreams, Walter de la Mare, following Pope's dictum that "sound must seem an echo to the sense," gives us singing, lulling lines:

> Softly, drowsily,
> Out of sleep;
> Into the world again
> Ann's eyes peep.[2]

And:

---

[1] From "At the Seaside" and "Travel," respectively, in *A Child's Garden of Verses* (Scribner's, 1905), pp. 5, 13.
[2] From "A Child's Day," in *Rhymes and Verses* (Holt, 1947), p. 307.

> Slowly, silently, now the moon
> Walks the night in her silver shoon.[1]

Even now, Harry Behn among contemporary poets is fond of soft meditation:

> Dreaming of honeycombs to share
> With her small cubs, a mother bear
> Sleeps in a snug and snowy lair.[2]

True, a hint of frustration distinguishes Dorothy Aldis's verse:

> *No*
> He did not want to do it.
> He would not do it: No.
> She led him firmly to it
> But still he wouldn't do it—
> He never would, he knew it—
> NO!

> *Bad*
> I've been bad and I'm in bed
> For the naughty things I said.
>
> I'm in bed. I wish I had
> Not said those things that were so bad.
>
> I wish that I'd been good instead.
> But I was bad. And I'm in bed.[3]

But the mood is mild. We don't find trauma in these poems.

A number of poems in the gentle tradition rely on sound alone to capture an image, inviting bright "all-stops-out" reading. David McCord's "The Pickety Fence" is a good example:

> The pickety fence
> The pickety fence
> Give it a lick it's
> The pickety fence
> Give it a lick it's
> A clickety fence
> Give it a lick it's
> A lickety fence
> Give it a lick
> Give it a lick
> Give it a lick
> With a rickety stick
> Pickety
> Pickety
> Pickety
> Pick.[4]

---

[1]From "Silver," in *Peacock Pie* (Knopf, 1961), p. 103.
[2]From "Waiting," in *Time for Poetry*, ed. May Hill Arbuthnot (Harcourt, 1949), p. 374.
[3]From *All Together* (Putnam's, 1952), pp. 81, 109.
[4]David McCord, "The Pickety Fence," from *Far and Few* (Little, Brown, 1952).

Each of these verses and verse-makers in one way or another conforms to a gentle tradition, derived perhaps from Wordsworth and Blake. Each supports a world of childhood that is pleasant, curious, appreciative of the ridiculous, sometimes softly mystical, and dependably beautiful. Who's to say that this is unfortunate or even unduly limited? Poetry as an aria of cadence and sound ought to celebrate the quiet miracles of life, as the heart of the matter, especially for children.

In the past, poetry for children has served other purposes. Long passages of metered history were memorized, we are told, by the Greek schoolboy. The awful rhymes of old alphabet books were read not for enjoyment but for making information memorable. Exhortative, persuasive tales of woe were meant to frighten children into good behavior on earth and eternal reward in heaven; these were the verses that Lewis Carroll mocked in many a parody and that inspired Hillaire Belloc's *The Bad Child's Book of Beasts* (1) and *Cautionary Tales* (2).

Of course, the choices of children have never really been limited to what was written or selected for them. Mother Goose rhymes, though reportedly written as political satire, have long been the property of children, appropriated by them along with versified riddles, game-songs, and tongue twisters and passed from childhood to childhood down through the centuries. Older children have borrowed the ballads and lyrics from the adult level. There has always been, alongside the gentle fare, a parallel current of red-blooded sound and meaning.

Recently, however, poetry for and by children has been extended even further. Poems of social protest, of personal anguish, poems sometimes composed in rough blank or free verse, have thrust their way into anthologies and the classroom, a new, counter influence to the gentle tradition. If you contrast two important anthologies of poetry written *by* children—*Children's Voices* (3) compiled by Bertha E. Roberts and Aneta T. Beckman and *The Voice of the Children* (4) collected by June Jordan and Terri Bush—you will see that the intervening years have wrought a great change. The former consists of rhymed, metered verses about pretending, fishing, keeping a garden, looking at a mountain, enjoying pets, and observing the weather and the seasons. The latter, composed almost entirely in free verse, is concerned with war, change, and social injustice. Another recent collection, *Here I Am!* (5) compiled by Virginia Olsen Baron contains this poem by a child named Veronica Bryant:

> The world was meant to be peaceful
>   nice and quiet,
> Not like killing and crying the
> world was meant to be peaceful.
> If Adam and Eve didn't eat that
> fruit the world would be
> in the garden of Eden.
> I wish the world had a better chance.[1]

---

[1] p. 47.

Similar concerns of children are shown in Nancy Larrick's *I Heard a Scream in the Street: Poems by Young People in the City* (6).

The work of some adult poets writing for children also stands in contrast to the gentle tradition, a recognition that honest children's poetry does not always say that this is the best of all possible worlds. The poems in *Only the Moon and Me* (7) by Richard J. Margolis have an undertone of despair:

> Sometimes
> when I'm teased
> I don't cry,
> I go away.
> When I come back
> they're doing something else.
> I remember.
> They forget.[1]

> Very very
> quietly
> I
> got up
> and stood
> at the door
> and listened.

booklist

Poetry by Children[2]

Have You Seen a Comet? John Day, 1971. A collection of children's poetry, prose, and art from around the world, published in cooperation with UNICEF. The selections are in both the original language and in English. A good book to use for stressing the universality of poetry.

Joseph, Stephen M., ed. *The Me Nobody Knows: Children's Voices from the Ghetto.* World, 1969. The title speaks for itself. Shows that the language of poetry and the sensitivity of the poet are universal and reside in diverse places.

Larrick, Nancy, ed. *Somebody Turned on a Tap in These Kids: Poetry and Young People Today.* Delacorte, 1971. The material for this book grew out of a poetry festival in 1969 at the School of Education at Lehigh University.

Lewis, Richard. *Miracles.* Simon and Schuster, 1966. Poems written by children of the English-speaking world, ranging in age from five to thirteen. The poems are unedited, except for spelling corrections.

---

[1] p. 42.

[2] This and other poetry booklists were compiled by Toni Marshall, Palo Alto, Ca.

They were talking about someone else.
I
went back
to bed.[1]

Irony and penetrating sadness are not considered by writers such as Nikki Giovanni to be out of place in poetry for children. Note this example from her *Spin a Soft Black Song: Poems for Children* (8):

Mommies Do
in summer
mommy goes to work and locks
me in
and i peep outside through the iron
gate at the children playing
ball and rope and scaley and break
bottles and run and jump
and laugh
and i ask mommy why can't i
go out and mommy says because
she loves me[2]

We have painted a contrast between older poems in the gentle tradition and newer ones which are more robust. But we have also emphasized that poems chosen by the children themselves have always covered a wide range. Our aim has been to reveal the variety in form, in subject, in intent; to show that poetry chosen by children deals with matters both lovely and abhorrent. The long standing purpose of poetry to entertain is augmented to include a new kind of persuasion, a new mission to inform, with a greater understanding of the individual's right to consider his world in both its good and bad qualities—his right to try to make sense out of his reality.

With so broad an array, one can't treat poetry as a "yes-no" matter, making broad statements about selecting all types of poetry at all levels. There was a time in our culture when teachers might reject poetry in the mistaken notion that it did not conform to gentle, pretty appreciation. But poetry—as ad-writers and rope-jumpers, as activists and observers of early childhood language usage have long known—is broader than the gentle tradition, is firmer, more basic, tougher fibered.

Begin with the premise that poetry in whatever form is a feeling display of language, from a tripping "Good morning" or a "get outa my way" to the mumbled lyric of a popular ballad to the cheerleader's chant to the finely wrought verse. It is not confined to a tombstone, a tv commercial, or a greeting card. It is here now and is ready to elicit response. All poetry needs is a real place in the classroom and a genuine welcome in teaching. Begin by looking more closely at the domains of poetry, then at techniques for selecting and reading it, and finally at some activities for presentation.

---

[1] p. 10.
[2] p. 18.

As a sort of prelude, we'll offer these four general suggestions for you to consider about teaching poetry:

- It is better to present poetry than to teach about it, especially if children are just discovering that poetry is a basic part of their language.

- If you as an adult memorize a poem, you have found a way to own it. Each time you say it and think it, the poem will show a new facet of cadence and meaning. (It isn't inaccurate, by the way, to say that you learn a poem "by heart.") Other people will probably learn it from you with little conscious effort. This is far better than requiring that students memorize a poem.

- Although there are many good anthologies of poems for children (we'll point out a few later), the best is the one you carry around in your head and on cards you've carefully assembled. Let the children join you in making personal discoveries of good poems.

- To read a poem well, to select a poem wisely, and to broaden your own and children's tastes in poetry demand some knowledge of the techniques poets use. This doesn't mean that you must become a specialist in prosody, the study of metrical structure in verse. It does suggest, however, that you'll need to possess some knowledge of various techniques and types of poetry in order to present them well.

booklist

Aids for Teaching Poetry

Arnstein, Flora J. *Poetry and the Child.* Dover, 1962. Answers basic questions regarding the why and how of helping children to enjoy and create poetry. Even considers the fearsome question of what to tamper with and what to leave alone in children's writing. Offers specific teaching ideas for each age group from six-year-olds through junior high.

Hughes, Ted. *Poetry Is.* Doubleday, 1970. Based on BBC talks, this book is intended for young writers, grade six and up.

Koch, Kenneth. *Wishes, Lies, and Dreams: Teaching Children to Write Poetry.* Chelsea House, 1970. (Distributed by Random House.) The author reports results of his experiment in teaching children from grades one through six to write poetry. His techniques are explained and successful writing ideas are presented, discussed, and illustrated.

Livingston, Myra Cohn. *When You Are Alone/ It Keeps You Capone.* Atheneum, 1973. Don't let the title stand in your way. This is a helpful book that discusses such basics as: where to start when you teach writing, how to reach the nonwriter, when it's time for disciplined writing, form versus no-form, the collective poem.

Mearns, Hughes. *Creative Power: The Education of Youth in Creative Arts.* Dover, 1958. The work of Mearns has been around for a number of years and is well worth looking into.

Illustration for "Mommies Do" by Nikki Giovanni. Reprinted with the permission of Farrar, Straus & Giroux, Inc. from Spin a Soft Black Song by Nikki Giovanni, illustrated by Charles Bible. Illustrations copyright ©1971 by Charles Bible.

special activities

1. Examine anthologies of poetry for children, including one collection of traditional verse and one collection of modern verse. (A few examples of each type appear on p. 316.) What is the range of poetry presented in these two types of collections—traditional and modern? What are the principal contrasts in their contents? Which poems might you choose to represent poetry at its best?

2. Examine volumes of poetry for children by individual poets, seeking especially recent works by one or more of the following: Dorothy Aldis, Harry Behn, Gwendolyn Brooks, John Ciardi, Elizabeth Coatsworth, Aileen Fisher, Frances Frost, Karla Kuskin, Myra Cohn Livingston, David McCord, Eve Merriam, Mary O'Neill, May Swenson. Which poems would you choose as the most exciting, most skillfully composed, or in some other way most deserving of an audience? You may wish to check *Index to Children's Poetry,* compiled by John E. Brewton and Sara W. Brewton[1] or *Subject Index to Poetry for Children and Young People,* compiled by Violet Sell and others.[2]

THE DOMAINS OF POETRY

Every good poem is unique. Put six "spring" poems or six "sports" poems or six "angry" poems or six limericks, sonnets, or quatrains side by side and compare them—and you'll find that their differences stand out, making each poem alive and worth its own special effort. If they don't, then all the classifying, analyzing, and effort at appreciation aren't likely to improve the poetic experience they afford. We join Eve Merriam in her advice to readers of poetry:

> Don't be polite.
> Bite in.
> Pick it up with your fingers and lick the juice that may run down your chin. . . .[3]

Finding the unique poem and discovering what is unique and important about it require several ways of viewing poetry. We can examine poetry's domain by topic, by purpose and effect, and by certain techniques used by poets. We'll look at these domains briefly, then discover how each is involved in selecting, reading, and presenting a poem.

Poetry by Topic

Indexes and anthologies of poetry often arrange their fare by topic: poems about nature, about everyday life, about the city. And teachers often select poems by topic. They seek a Halloween poem, or a spring poem, or a poem to suit a group of baseball players.

There's nothing wrong with that, so far as it goes. You must realize, though, that topic alone cannot include all that a poem means. A special occasion or interest isn't always the key to discovering a poem that will have the effect

---

[1]John E. Brewton and Sara W. Brewton, *Index to Children's Poetry* (H. W. Wilson, 1942). Periodic supplements keep it up to date.
[2]Violet Sell, et al, *Subject Index to Poetry for Children and Young People* (American Library Association, 1957). Supplemented periodically.
[3]Eve Merriam, "How to Eat a Poem," *It Doesn't Always Have to Rhyme* (Atheneum, 1964).

you're looking for. It's an entry, a way of finding a number of poems that may have potential for your particular situation.

Don't treat topics too narrowly. The Halloween mood doesn't necessarily require that you search for a poem about witches, goblins, black cats, or even one containing the word *Halloween.* Put the tone above topic, and above that, put the quality of the poem: whether its unique way of presentation is likely to arouse positive response. Poets themselves state that topic alone isn't a sufficient guide to what the poem is really about. As James Reeves puts it:

> It cannot be too strongly stated that a poem, however much it may have been shaped or altered in the process of composition, emerges *as a poem,* not as a thought, a story, a description to which a verse form is applied, as it were, from the outside.[1]

In addition, grouping poetry by topic creates strange bedfellows. It isn't very helpful to place William Blake's little lamb beside E. V. Rieu's happy hedgehog—a mystical poem beside a comic one—even if both poems are grouped under the heading of Familiar Animals. Wind and Weather as a topic contains both Laura E. Richards's playful "The Umbrella Brigade" and Carl Sandburg's mood-piece, "Fog," but the mixing of highly metered, rhythmic verse with free verse isn't likely to provide much help in selection and presentation.

Many recent anthologies have discarded the topical arrangement and simply scatter the poems, grouping a few by interests, some by contrasts, and placing some by pure whim. The deservedly popular collection *Reflections on a Gift of Watermelon Pickle and Other Modern Verse* (9) is done that way. Other recent anthologies arrange poems under impressionistic, mood-building headings, sometimes using a line from one of the poems. "Bring the Day," "The Lamb White Days," and "Aye, My Dear and Tender" are sample headings used in the poetry section of *Anthology of Children's Literature* (10). A few recent anthologies devote themselves exclusively to one very broad topic, presenting highly varied fare.

If you're looking for poetry and how to present it, consider topic as sometimes necessary but never sufficient.

Poetry by Purpose and Effect

The poet's purpose in producing his poem and your purpose in presenting it are features you'll want to consider carefully. At this point, your poetry selection departs from concern with topic only and entails consideration of tone: the tone the poet attempts to convey, the mood that listeners are likely to achieve as a result of the experience.

Traditionally, poems have been classified as lyric, narrative, or dramatic. The term *lyric,* which literally refers to a song to be sung to the accompaniment of a lyre, may indicate that a poet wishes to impart a mood through showing a specific scene. Her or his concern is to convey mood by drawing attention to

---

[1] James Reeves, *How to Write Poems for Children* (Heinemann, 1971), p. 83.

the scene, a character, or directly to the mood itself. To poetry readers intent on "getting the story" the lyric may at first seem disappointing, since it appears that nothing happens. Of course, the scene in a lyric can contain some action, as in the first stanza of Harry Behn's "Near and Far":

> What do hens say
> With all their talking?
> *What luck! What luck!* they cluck,
> *Look, look!* they say
> As they settle
> In a sunny nook
> And scoop
> Dust under their feathers. . . .[1]

The poet's primary purpose, however, is to capture the scene and the feeling imparted by the scene. Listeners or readers must appreciate that scene, not expect that the action will develop into a story.

A lyric poem may also present a collage or other arrangement of details, all related in some way to achieve a purpose. Harry Behn's "Hallowe'en" consists of such details: leaves flying, elves and sprites flitting, pumpkins staring. It's not

booklist

Poetry Anthologies for Children

Traditional Collections

Arbuthnot, May Hill, and Root, Shelton L., Jr., eds. *Time for Poetry,* 3rd ed. Scott, Foresman, 1968.

Ferris, Helen, ed. *Favorite Poems Old and New.* Doubleday, 1957.

Johnson, Edna, Sickels, Evelyn R., and Sayers, Frances Clarke, eds. *Anthology of Children's Literature,* 4th ed. Houghton, Mifflin, 1970. (pp. 909–1000)

Modern Collections

Dunning, Stephen, Lueders, Edward, and Smith, Hugh, eds. *Reflections on a Gift of Watermelon Pickle and Other Modern Verse.* Scott, Foresman, 1966.

Adoff, Arnold, ed. *I Am the Darker Brother.* Macmillan, 1968.

Cole, William, ed. *Pick Me Up: A Book of Short Short Poems.* Macmillan, 1972.

Fleming, Alice, ed. *Hosannah the Home Run!* Little, Brown, 1972.

---

[1]Harry Behn, "Near and Far," *Windy Morning* (Harcourt, 1953), pp. 26–27.

one particular scene but a collection of related details intended to illustrate a Halloween mood:

> Tonight is the night
> When dead leaves fly
> Like witches on switches
> Across the sky,
> When elf and sprite
> Flit through the night
> On a moony sheen.
>
> Tonight is the night
> When leaves make a sound
> Like a gnome in his home
> Under the ground,
> When spooks and trolls
> Creep out of holes
> Mossy and green.
>
> Tonight is the night
> When pumpkins stare
> Through sheaves and leaves
> Everywhere,
> When ghoul and ghost
> And goblin host
> Dance round their queen.
> It's Hallowe'en![1]

This collection of details intended to convey a unified effect may be difficult for children to appreciate. It's a fairly common pattern in lyric for children, but it does require a great amount of visualization. As you consider the intended effects of your lyric selections, consider as well how you will achieve these effects.

Unlike lyric poems, narrative poems do relate an incident or sequence of incidents and, in doing so, take on some of the attributes of a story. But there must be a reason, integral with the poet's purpose, for casting the story into poetry form. If the reason is superficial—an attempt to make a thin story seem more important—the narrative poem is no better than its prose version would be. (Each year brings its small, undistinguished group of picture books for small children in the form of narrative verse. Many of these lapse into tired verse and forced rhyme and must be rejected outright.) There has to be something in the author's purpose—and therefore in the effect you wish to achieve in presenting the work—that justifies a story's presence in poetry.

There are a number of good examples of narratives in verse, such as A. A. Milne's "The King's Breakfast," "Disobedience," and others. Look at almost any story poem that has lasted over the years, from "Get Up and Bar the Door" and

---

[1]Harry Behn, "Hallowe'en," *The Little Hill* (Harcourt Brace Jovanovich, 1949), p. 41.

"Robin Hood and Little John" to "The Three Little Kittens" and "A Visit from St. Nicholas"; examine the varied story poems in *Story Poems New and Old* (11), edited by William Cole. If you do a prose treatment of a narrative poem that appeals to you, you'll discover just how much the poetry form contributes to the narrative. Let's use Countee Cullen's "Incident" as an example:

> Once riding in old Baltimore,
>   Heart filled, head-filled with glee,
> I saw a Baltimorean
>   Keep looking straight at me.
> Now I was eight and very small
>   And he was no whit bigger,
> And so I smiled, but he poked out
>   His tongue, and called me, 'Nigger.'
>
> I saw the whole of Baltimore
>   From May until December;
> Of all the things that happened there
>   That's all that I remember.[1]

Often the story line in a narrative poem consists of one central incident, sometimes leaving the reader to infer the intended mood. The above poem is just one piercing moment in the speaker's life and an understated reaction to that moment. But the brief narrative intends much more than the usual something-that-happened-to-me-in-my-childhood incident. In working with this poem, you'll need to consider how to build the context and a subsequent activity or time for reflection that will permit the effect to sink in.

Similarly, a simple-sounding conversation verse such as Rachel Field's "Elfin Berries" requires more consideration of poet's intent and potential effect than a mere prose meaning treatment would require:

> "Elf, will you sell me your berries bright
>   For to make me a pot of jam?"
> "No, for they grew in Fairyland,
>   I'm very sorry, ma'am."
>
> "Not if I let you lick the spoon
>   When the sweet juice bubbles red?"
> "My berries are not for pots and spoons
>   Or earthen crocks," he said,
>
> "They came from a bush that no man knows
>   Whose name is 'Never-Grow-Old,'
> And they shall be meat and drink to me,
>   And warmth when the nights are cold."
>
> "Here's a ring, Sweet Elf, and a purse of gold,
> And beads as blue as the sea—?"
> "Elfin berries are not for sale,
>   Good-day to you, ma'am!" said he.

---

[1]Countee Cullen, "Incident," *Color* (Harper & Row, 1925), p. 15.

With narrative as well as lyric poetry, there's something more at stake than painting a picture in the mind or relating a series of incidents. There's a theme, just as you find in prose, and a mood bound up with the author's purpose. And these are intrinsic to the poems, providing their real reason for being. To know that a poem has lyric or narrative intent, to comprehend its prose meaning in terms of the scene or incidents it depicts, is a step deeper than topic. It should lead to the deep structure, the poet's real concerns, which you want to communicate to your listeners.

booklist

Poems to Dramatize

Benet, Rosemary Carr and Stephen Vincent. "Abraham Lincoln," in *A Book of Americans.* Holt, 1933. (I-U) The scenes and characters depicted can be pantomimed as the passages are read. There might be a total of ten narrators in addition to the six characters involved.

Carroll, Lewis. "Father William," in *100 Poems about People.* Sel. Elinor Parker. Thomas Y. Crowell, 1955. (I-U) Presents challenging opportunities for acting. Instead of one son, the lines can be divided among four people.

Ciardi, John. "Little Bits," in *You Read to Me, I'll Read to You.* Lippincott, 1962. (E) The parts of the two characters can be read aloud or ad libbed, depending on the children's abilities. This poem could stimulate children to make up counting poems or perhaps do a collective poem.

Hopkins, Lee Bennett, sel. *Girls Can Too!* Illus. Emily McCully. Watts, 1972. (E) A good beginning book for miming.

Lear, Edward. "The Owl and the Pussy Cat," in *Nonsense Songs.* Orig. published Warner, 1871. Picture book edition, illus. William J. DuBois. Doubleday, 1961. (E-I) This classic can be memorized, read, or ad libbed. Characters are an owl, a pussy cat, a pig, and a turkey. One to three narrators can be used.

Mitchell, Lucy Sprague. "It Is Raining," in *Another Here and Now Story Book.* Ed. Lucy Sprague Mitchell. Dutton, 1937. (E) A background of storm music and an illustrated backdrop painted by the children can help establish mood. From one to three narrators can be used in addition to the three respondents.

Saxe, John G. "The Blind Men and the Elephant," in *The World's Best Loved Poems.* Ed. James Gilchrist Lawson. Harper, 1927. (I-U) This can be done in pantomime with a narrator or taped reading. There are six characters besides the narrator.

Smith, William Jay. "Raccoon," in *Boy Blue's Book of Beasts.* Little, Brown, 1957. (E-I) Can be read twice in succession, with the whole class joining the characters the second time. The cast includes a raccoon, an evening star, and a boy, who has no lines but who listens and reacts.

A special kind of narrative is dramatic poetry, which can be performed as a monologue, dialogue, or as full drama. "Incident," printed above, might be treated as a dramatic poem, but its effect would probably not be achieved by a reader pretending to be the character saying the poem. The recitation might seem authentic, but the poem's reader should probably convey more understanding of the poem's intent than character portrayal would permit.

"Elfin Berries" might be treated as a drama, but its intent doesn't really seem to be a play-acting one. On the other hand, some ballads are clarified and interaction with readers is made more intense through treatment as dramatic poetry, even with full dramatization. Older children may dramatize the ballad "Sir Patrick Spens," for example, using characters and a reader who describes the action.

PRIVATE-WORLD AND PUBLIC-WORLD POEMS.   Another way of examining a poet's intent is to note the distinction cited by Archibald MacLeish in *Poetry and Experience* (12). Some poems are intended to reveal a poet's "private world": his unique, personal way of responding to experience. "Public-world" poems, on the other hand, celebrate an occasion or display a sense of community. The effect of a private-world poem is to enable the reader to glimpse the world through another's eyes, with the connotations the poet attributes to an experience. Take, for example, a group of poems based on a common topic—dogs. Irene Rutherford McLeod in "Lone Dog" conveys her private-world image of a dog who shuns society, protecting his rough lonely freedom. It is the projection of a mood that the poet sometimes longs for: a private feeling revealed through the image. In contrast Marchette Chute in "My Dog" tells of warm feelings toward an entirely civilized dog, projecting a much different private world.

Lone Dog

I'm a lean dog, a keen dog, a wild dog, and live;
I'm a rough dog, a tough dog, hunting on my own;
I'm a bad dog, a mad dog, teasing silly sheep;
I love to sit and bay the moon, to keep fat souls from sleep.

I'll never be a lap dog, licking dirty feet,
A sleek dog, a meek dog, cringing for my meat,
Not for me the fireside, the well-filled plate,
But shut door, and sharp stone, and cuff, and kick, and hate.

Not for me the other dogs, running by my side,
Some have run a short while, but none of them would bide.
O mine is the lone trail, the hard trail, the best,
Wide wind, and wild stars, and hunger of the quest.[1]

My Dog

His nose is short and scrubby;
His ears hang rather low;
And he always brings the stick back,
No matter how far you throw.

---

[1]Irene Rutherford McLeod, from *Songs to Save a Soul* (B. W. Huebsch, 1916).

He gets spanked rather often
For things he shouldn't do,
Like lying-on-beds, and barking,
And eating up shoes when they're new.

He always wants to be going
Where he isn't supposed to go.
He tracks up the house when it's snowing—
Oh, puppy, I love you so.[1]

In Robert L. Tyler's "Puppy" (see page 340) the poet relishes a simple world consisting of a lawn and sprinkler hose, a private world of simplest freedom and joy of the moment. When you read a private-world poem, your concern is with responding to the poet's private feelings, almost becoming the poet for a time in order to share his private world.

A public-world poem is more objective, perhaps fulfilling a more conscious obligation to its audience. Harry Behn's "Hallowe'en," quoted earlier, may embody some of the poet's private feelings, but it is primarily a catalog of images to celebrate the event, images that most people would agree upon. Narrative poems, in which the poet's subjectivity is present only in his selection of events and his choice of words and rhythms to describe them, are likely to be public-world poems. Toad's elaborate recitations in Kenneth Grahame's *The Wind in the Willows* proclaim his bravery in a public way. The poems celebrating heroes and heroines, holidays and events, commonly shared and commonly experienced happenings—these have their public-world focus. Look for examples of such poems in *A Book of Americans* (13) by Rosemary and Stephen Benet, and in John Updike's *A Child's Calendar* (14).

Private-world poems ask that the reader or listener be able to enter the poet's mood, to grasp and value the poet's perception of the world. If a child reader doesn't share a poet's excitement over the bubbling spring or the daffodil, you must find another private world for him to enter or else do something to make the worlds of the bubbling spring or the daffodil accessible. In other words, you must anticipate effect as well as purpose in this private-world experience.

Public-world poems, on the other hand, run the risk of being mundane. If they do nothing to enhance the image, their effect is little different from a newspaper account. Seek poems which lend a special effect to a public experience, and be clear as to what that special effect is.

Poetry by Versification

Unless you pay some attention to the technical side of poetry, you are unlikely to know the full range of poetry's domains. In such instances, appreciation stops short of feeling the power of the poet's language, and you are likely to miss opportunities for bringing a poem to life.

We know that taking such a position is swimming upstream against a current of modern thinking that attributes all dislike of poetry to forced poetic analysis.

---

[1]Marchette Chute, from *Rhymes about Ourselves* (Macmillan, 1932).

Yes, it is true that young children are likely to love poetry given to them freely and naturally, as a living part of their language without sermons and without analyzing. And it is probably true that many children begin to dislike poetry because it is thrust at them with instructions to analyze. Many teen-agers and college students have rejected poetry because of the bitter experience of being required to strip it down to its springs and gears. We know these reactions and acknowledge their validity; yet we ask you for a moment to consider versification, the *how* of a poem's assemblage.

Why? Our first reason is quite pragmatic. Knowing little or nothing about the techniques of sound and rhythm available to poets and trusting instinct alone to tell you whether a poem "sounds right" narrows your appreciation. When you present poetry to children, you are in some sense a teacher or guide. To *listen* to a poem may require little knowledge of techniques, but to *read* a poem aloud and to guide children to appreciate the full power of a poem requires more know-how and know-what.

The second reason is pedagogic. Poetry analysis sessions have often really been exercises in learning to state banality, in learning stock responses couched in too-abstract dead language: "The poem makes me feel happy and nice. . . . I like the pretty way the words make my tongue feel. . . . I have a singing feeling in my head." Such reactions may indeed be honest, but they often conceal empty responses because the respondents lack a minimal knowledge of how poetry works, how it gains its effects.

What minimum knowledge do you need? First, be aware that all literature has rhythm. The flow of words may be conversational, as if the teller paid little attention to their rhythm. But the rhythm is there, pulling the reader along:

> Last night I got the idea to put the whole thing into song. I've been writing songs again lately, but this wasn't like the others. What I had in mind was a kind of ballad, a song story like the ancient troubadors used to make up about an important event so it would never be forgotten.[1]

That's the opening of Zilpha Keatley Snyder's *Eyes in the Fishbowl* told from a fourteen-year-old's point of view: two rather short sentences followed by a third longer one, beginning to unfold the story. No heavy interruptions—an easy-to-read beginning to capture the character and to lead into an important event.

A quite different rhythm occurs in a heavy action scene in the midst of John Rowe Townsend's *Hell's Edge:*

> Norman and Cliff ran. Jack Raynor and his gang ran after them. Footsteps echoed along the narrow side road. Somebody threw a stone, which missed Cliff by a yard. Norman stumbled, caught his foot in the kerb, and fell. Half a dozen lads closed in.[2]

---

[1]Zilpha Keatley Snyder, *Eyes in the Fishbowl* (Atheneum, 1968), p. 1.
[2]John Rowe Townsend, *Hell's Edge* (Hutchinson, 1963), p. 56f.

I eat my peas with honey,
I've done it all my life,
They do taste kind of funny,
But it keeps them on the knife.

Each brief sentence, like the pounding of footsteps, advances the action; and the reader rushes on.

Sometimes prose style exhibits a unity of meaning and sound that is close to poetry. Erik Christian Haugaard's *The Slave's Tale* is a kind of prose-poem wherein rhythm and imagery are intended to weave a spell of sound:

> Once upon a time . . . with those words do all tales start, even when the storyteller does not bother to say them. For once upon a time in everyone's life the world was created, the sun rose, and the stars were fixed in the sky.[1]

Each of these prose passages is rhythmical and unrhymed, though their words are chosen with regard to other features of sound. These literary prose passages are akin to *free verse*, the rhythmic, unrhymed form of poetry such as that used in Veronica Bryant's poem (p. 309) and "Mommies Do" (p. 311). Rhythmic literary prose and free verse really differ only in the way the lines are printed on the page. Free verse is printed in separate lines; the separation is designed to emphasize the rhythmic patterns.

Most poetry, however, goes a step further with rhythm. Its rhythm is *metered*, which means that it has a steadier beat. The steady beat (an accented syllable) and its surrounding unaccented syllables comprise a *foot*; the feet are combined to make a *line*; and the lines may be grouped to form *stanzas*.

One poet likens the feet, lines, and stanzas in poetry to the left-hand accompaniment in piano music: it sets the rhythm, makes it metrical, and provides the background for the melody. Note, however, that meter doesn't imply that all feet are equal, giving a sing-song stress to each foot. Some beats are heavier than others, and the variety in beat is determined by the sound and meaning.

Hence the sounds support the meter: repeated consonant sounds (alliteration) and repeated vowel sounds (assonance) may combine with rhyme to support the repetition. They highlight the meaning and enhance it.

Most poetry, using these elements, is metered, rhymed, and filled with an interplay of repeated sounds. Let's look at the first stanza of E. V. Rieu's "The Lost Cat":

> She took a last and simple meal when there were none to see her steal—
> A jug of cream upon the shelf, a fish prepared for dinner:
> And now she walks a distant street with delicately sandalled feet,
> And no one gives her much to eat or weeps to see her thinner.[2]

The meter is entirely regular: eight feet in the first and third lines, seven feet in the second and fourth lines, each foot consisting of an unaccented syllable followed by an accented syllable. An unaccented syllable occurs at the end of

---

[1]Erik Christian Haugaard, *The Slave's Tale* (Houghton Mifflin, 1965), p. 1.
[2]E. V. Rieu, "The Lost Cat," *The Flattered Flying Fish and Other Poems.* Illus. E. H. Shepard (Dutton, 1962), p. 27.

the second and fourth lines. Note the rhymes: internal rhyme (*meal* and *steal* in the first line, *street* and *feet* in the third line) and the two-syllable rhymes (*dinner, thinner*) at the end of the second and fourth lines. There is another rhyme within the fourth line, carried over from the third line—and there are repeated consonant and vowel sounds throughout the poem—for instance, the long *e* sounds in the fourth line.

Now, suppose that Rieu had made a different arrangement of poetic line:

> She took a last and simple meal,
>   When there were none to see her steal—

A poetic line ought to be read as a unit. If you read the poet's original version, you'll have a long flowing line, whereas the second version with a split in the middle begins to have a sing-song effect not at all appropriate to the serious effect attempted by the poem.

Now, see if this knowledge about the poem's versification can make a difference. First, force yourself to read the stanza as if it were prose, paying no attention whatsoever to meter and sound repetition. A prose meaning comes through, but something is lacking.

Second, read the poem in an exaggerated sing-song rhythm, emphasizing the meter only. This reading also lacks something: the meaning, the prose meaning, begins to disappear, leaving an unthinking rhythm, a *bass* accompaniment and little else.

Third, read the poem carefully—with a little emphasis on the meter but with variations to bring out feet that need emphasis to underline meanings, allowing just a hint of emphasis to pin down the rhymes and repeated consonant and vowel sounds. All this attention to sound and rhythm factors must still be subordinate to the meaning you're attempting to convey and the mood that accompanies it.

The result, if you've done it well, is an enhancement of meaning and mood through a balance of attention to features of rhythm and sound.

We've attempted to show how the essentials of versification can help you in reading a poem aloud. You may need to consider these elements in selecting poetry as well. Consider criteria such as the following:

- Does the meter support the sense of the poem? If the poem has a serious intent, is the meter flexible enough to avoid sing-song repetition?

- Do repetitions of sound support the mood and overall intent of the poem? Rather than opting for every possible alliterative opportunity, does the poet repeat sounds to add emphasis in the right places?

Admittedly, these criteria are applied more or less spontaneously. You'll need to try out a poem to see how it fits your tongue. But some knowledge of the ways in which meter and sound support the meaning and mood helps you in selecting and presenting a poem.

Alice and Martin Provensen's colorful, stylish illustrations bring this classic Tennyson poem into the realm of child readers. From "The Charge of the Light Brigade" by Alfred Lord Tennyson, illustrated by Alice and Martin Provensen. ©Copyright

special activities

1. Eleanor Farjeon's "The Night Will Never Stay," reprinted below, is a popular poem, selected by many readers for the manner in which meter and sound support the sense. Why? The meter is simple: the first four lines are consistent, with feet composed of an unaccented syllable followed by an accented syllable. Then there's a break in which unaccented syllables are increased. Why? What is the effect? Where do you find alliteration, repeated consonant sounds? Where is the rhyme scheme broken so that you are surprised at the change? Some sounds are sustained, defying interruption. How does the poem use sustained sound?

"Forward, the Light Brigade!"
Was there a man dismay'd?
Not tho' the soldier knew
Some one had blunder'd.

II

Theirs not to make reply,
Theirs not to reason why,
Theirs but to do and die.
Into the valley of Death
Rode the six hundred.

The night will never stay,
The night will still go by,
Though with a million stars
You pin it to the sky,
Though you bind it with the blowing wind
And buckle it with the moon,
The night will slip away
Like sorrow or a tune.[1]

In reading the poem aloud, give some emphasis to meter and sound repetition. Some lines have no punctuation at the end, tempting you to rush on to the following line. Instead present each line as a unit, with a slight length-

[1]Eleanor Farjeon, "The Night Will Never Stay," *Gypsy and Ginger* (Dutton, 1920).

ening of the final syllable in a run-on line. (Such an ending is called an *enjambment*.) Robert Hillyer advises you to "draw out the last syllable" in such a line and then, without pause or change of pitch, launch into the second line.[1]

What is the topic of this poem? Is it really about the night, or is it about comfort and finding peace in the midst of threat? And what is the meaning of *binding* and *buckling* the night, when everyone knows that this is not possible?

2. Pace is another important element in presenting poetry. If your seventh reading of "The Night Will Never Stay" succeeded in making meter and sound support the sense, if you managed to convey the figure of speech in the fifth and sixth lines, did your reading slow down so that the poem held a quiet mystery? If so, try a contrast. A steady rhythm through consistent meter, internal rhyme, and word-sound play comprise this traditional poem from *Tongue Tanglers* (15) edited by Charles F. Potter. Your reading pace, with practice, ought to emphasize the excitement of an impending word mix-up:

> A tree toad loved a she toad
> That lived up in a tree.
> He was a two-toed tree toad,
> While a three-toed toad was she.
> The he-toad tree toad tried to gain
> The she toad's friendly nod,
> For the two-toed tree toad loved the ground
> That the three-toed tree toad trod.
> The two-toed tree toad tried in vain
> But couldn't please her whim,
> For from her tree toad bower
> With her she-toad power
> The three-toad tree toad vetoed him.[2]

3. If you need practice in reading poems aloud, try nursery rhymes. An excellent group appears on pages 3 to 39 in *Anthology of Children's Literature,* mentioned previously. (We have also listed a few on pp. 332–3.) In some of these rhymes the intent and effect bear careful scrutiny; it isn't always the sense that predominates but, rather, the sound and the meter:

> Bobby Shaftoe's gone to sea,
> Silver buckles at his knee;
> He'll come back and marry me,
> Bonny Bobby Shaftoe.

Which feet are emphasized and sustained? Which rhyme words do you empha-

[1]Robert Hillyer, *In Pursuit of Poetry* (McGraw-Hill, 1960), p. 48.
[2]p. 32.

size and sustain? The concluding line of each stanza, the refrain, needs special attention: how does the alliteration help you do this?

Try "One misty, moisty morning" or the familiar "Simple Simon met a pie-man" to practice your skills of using purpose-intent-effect and versification features to enhance your reading of a poem.

Poetry through Imagery and Metaphor

In this chapter we're discussing features of poetry that make a difference in: (1) your knowledge of the part poetry plays in a whole literary enterprise for children, (2) your selection of poetry—no longer will you search for poetry just by topic or nice feeling, (3) the way you read poetry, for that is the heart of how you present poetry to children, (4) the activities you'll design for enhancing response to poetry.

To further these purposes, we need to explore *imagery* and *metaphor,* two of the components that add meaning to the poetic effect.

An *image* is defined by Perrine as "the representation through sound of sense experience."[1] It can be a visual image or may refer to smell, taste, touch, or movement.

An image can be conveyed by a word. What words refer to sense experience, for example, in Eve Merriam's "Kitty Cornered"? (P. 330)

An image may consist of a mixture of sense impressions. For instance, the opening line of Alfred Noyes's "The Highwayman" speaks of a "torrent of darkness." *Torrent* usually refers to a swift, turbulent stream and may affect the sense of touch and motion, while *darkness* is visual. The two image words, used together, result in a multi-sensory image.

Images can be more than single words or phrases: a whole poem may really consist of an image whose purpose is to convey a mood. Even the description of night in "The Night Will Never Stay" could be considered an image with the intent of conveying calm and comfort.

Images don't really have to be "poetic" or unusual. This poem from *Beyond the High Hills: A Book of Eskimo Poems* (16), collected and translated by Knud Rasmussen, presents a set of images on the idea of youth:

> . . . youth seems a time
> when all meat was juicy and tender,
> and no game too swift for the hunter.[2]

But more often, as used by professional poets, images take a turn toward the unexpected, though they are surprisingly appropriate, as in these lines by Elinor Wylie:

---

[1] Laurence Perrine, *Sound and Sense,* 2nd ed. (Harcourt, 1956, 1963), p. 45.
[2] p. 29.

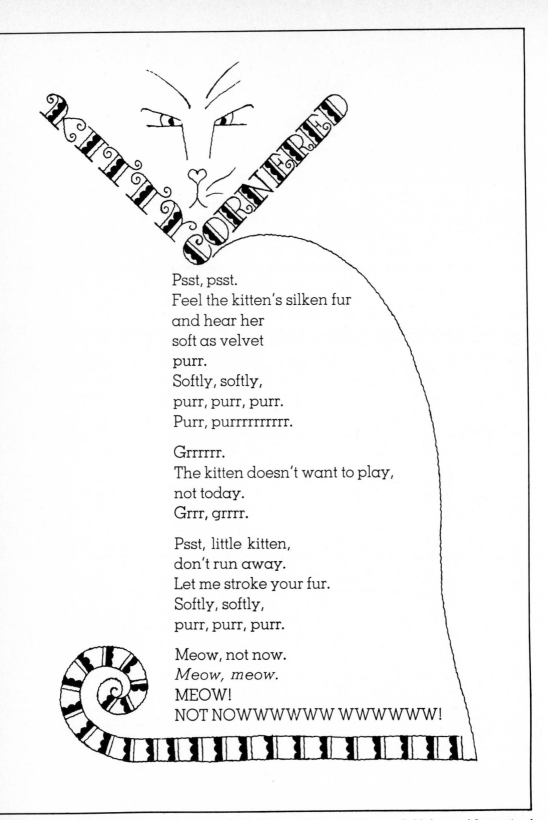

KITTY CORNERED

Psst, psst.
Feel the kitten's silken fur
and hear her
soft as velvet
purr.
Softly, softly,
purr, purr, purr.
Purr, purrrrrrrrrr.

Grrrrrr.
The kitten doesn't want to play,
not today.
Grrr, grrrr.

Psst, little kitten,
don't run away.
Let me stroke your fur.
Softly, softly,
purr, purr, purr.

Meow, not now.
Meow, meow.
MEOW!
NOT NOWWWWWW WWWWWW!

Parting Gift
I cannot give you the Metropolitan Tower;
I cannot give you heaven;
Nor the nine Visigoth crowns in the Cluny Museum;
Nor happiness, even.
But I can give you a very small purse
Made out of field-mouse skin,
With a painted picture of the universe
And seven blue tears therein.

I cannot give you the island of Capri;
I cannot give you beauty;
Nor bake you marvellous crusty cherry pies
With love and duty.
But I can give you a very little locket
Made out of wildcat hide:
Put it into your left-hand pocket
And never look inside.[1]

When and if you teach about imagery directly, you can attempt to excite children's awareness through it. Some ways for doing this are suggested in the last half of this chapter. Here we'll note two procedures to be avoided. Don't try to get at an image by using abstract language for describing it. In our judgment, to ask, "How does that word make you feel?" drives all the life out of an image. Such questions and discussions force vocabulary onto an abstract level that's meaningless or devoid of sensual ties. An image is presented to achieve just the opposite: specificity and sense awakening.

Also avoid insisting that every child understand at once all the allusions suggested by an image. Let children, once in a while, tolerate some ambiguity! If right then and there they don't have a firm picture or experience with all the allusions suggested, let them live with the poetry a while—the allusions will become clearer.

A *metaphor,* a specific form of imagery, is a comparison between two things that are essentially different. Some people consider metaphor to be the heart of poetry, even the heart of language itself. To construct a comparison that jars the listener into a new understanding of the two things compared, or provides a freshened perception of some familiar experience, is one of those seemingly impossible tasks that poets must face. Further, the ability to see unusual similarities is one of the basic abilities in all creative thinking, a part of problem-solving and synthesis.

A metaphor may be brief, a passing comparison in the body of a poem, or it may comprise the poem itself. The short ones are more easily identified. Carl Sandburg tells of the "splinter of singing" of the last cricket, a touch-and-sight image beside a sound image combined to show similarity between that kind of song and a splinter. "The hiss of tensing nozzle nose" in "Puppy," which

---

[1]From *Collected Poems of Elinor Wylie* (Knopf, 1938), p. 95.

appears later in this chapter, calls attention to a similarity between the hose and a snake. Even simpler are metaphors that directly state one thing to *be* another, as when snow on a fence post is said to be a marshmallow. In "Elegy for Jog" John Ciardi creates a daring, sustained metaphor by making death appear as a dog:

> Stiff-dog death, all froth on a bloody chin,
> sniffs at the curb. Skinny-man death, his master,
> opens the traffic's hedge to let him in.[1]

The quality of imagery and metaphor must be considered in selecting poetry. More important is one's comprehension of these figures of speech in reading the poem clearly. These and other techniques, including *onomatopoeia* (words that seem to sound like what they mean) and *personification* (attributing human qualities to nonhuman objects) are aids to meaning. They help us to experience poetry through all our senses. In fact, this experience is more than just arousal

booklist

Poems to Read Aloud: Early Childhood

Adoff, Arnold, ed. *My Black Me: A Beginning Book of Black Poetry.* Dutton, 1974. (E-I) Easy poems, old and new. A good book to begin on.

Ciardi, John. "I Wouldn't," in *You Read to Me, I'll Read to You.* Lippincott, 1962. (E) The internal and end-of-line rhymes call for careful enunciation of initial consonants. Catch the delightful rhythm that emphasizes the playful mood of the poem.

Hubbell, Patricia. "Breakfast Conversation," in *Catch Me a Wind.* Atheneum, 1968. (E-I) Lilting conversation with a wake-up quality. The kind of fantasy that is part of the delight of childhood.

Kuskin, Karla. "I'm swimming around in the sea, see," in *Any Me I Want to Be.* Harper, 1972. (E) Fast moving rhythm to match the movement of a whale. Imagination with a sprinkle of fun.

McCord, David. "Bananas and Cream," in *Take Sky.* Little, Brown, 1962. (E-I) The simple rhythm and repetition and the everyday words make it easily adaptable as accompaniment for marching, jump rope, or even singing.

Starbird, Kaye. "The Problem," in *A Snail's a Failure Socially.* Lippincott, 1966. (E-I) One of the many dilemmas of children is handled with humor and rhyme. Besides being entertaining, the poem makes visits to the doctor or dentist acceptable as part of living. It also makes a good jumping off place for a discussion of common problems.

---

[1]John Ciardi, "Elegy for Jog," reprinted in *Reflections on a Gift of Watermelon Pickle,* p. 87. [Originally printed in John Ciardi, *As If* (Rutgers Univ. Press, 1955).]

of the senses but rather it increases our sense of being alive. As William Saroyan puts it, "(The) vision is not the eye's, it is the spirit's. . . ."[1]

ACTIVITIES WITH POETRY

"Bite in. Pick it up with your fingers. . . ." Eve Merriam's words keep coming back to remind us that poetry has to be an *experience.* Your selection and your reading will lead children to make good selections, even though they may not know about the tools you use to bring poetry to life. Children will pick up good poetry reading habits from your model. And you'll find that your memory begins to be active: poems will begin to "stick like burs upon your mind."

booklist

Poems to Read Aloud: Intermediate and Upper Levels

Bierhorst, John, adapt. *Songs of the Chippewa.* Illus. Joe Servello. Farrar, 1974. All ages. Can be sung or recited. Chippewa language included.

Coatsworth, Elizabeth. "The House Plants," in *The Sparrow Bush.* Norton, 1966. All ages. Simplicity, imagination, empathy, make this a pleasant poem to read aloud. Could lead to deeper discussions about the feelings of plants and the oneness of all living things.

cummings, e.e. "little tree," in *100 selected poems.* Grove, 1959. All ages. This graceful poem is pure soul music guaranteed to soothe, to calm, to enrich the listener.

Giovanni, Nikki. *Ego-Tripping and Other Poems for Young People.* Illus. George Ford. Lawrence Hill, 1973. (U) Poems covering a wide range of moods from humor and fantasy to joy and anger.

Holman, Felice. "Voices," in *At the Top of my Voice.* Norton, 1970. (I) A lovely, relaxing poem laced with sibilant sounds that require special care in reading aloud. The persistent rhythm, like a small drum, can be emphasized.

Merriam, Eve. "Llude Sig Kachoo," in *Finding a Poem.* Atheneum, 1970. All ages. A rollicking laugh from a plugged head. Aside from the humor, the poem provides an irresistible opportunity to put in a strong word for enunciation.

Mezey, Robert, sel. *Poems from the Hebrew.* Illus. Moishe Smith. Crowell, 1973. (U) Excellent introduction sets the stage and mood for understanding.

Sandburg, Carl. "Old Deep-Sing Song," in *Wind Song.* Harcourt, 1960. (U) An uncommon lullaby whose sounds and rhythm imitate the sea in her moments of calm, in her swells of sadness overlaid with peace.

---

[1] William Saroyan, "How to See," *Theatre Arts* (March 1941): 25.

As we begin this discussion and illustration of activities for poetry, remember that no activity fits all poems. That would be gimmickry. An activity can be used when its intent fits and therefore can enhance the poem's intent. Your growing experience using the ideas in the first part of this chapter will lead you to use an activity only when it's appropriate.

A Poem as a Riddle

We dance round in a ring and suppose,
But the Secret sits in the middle and knows.[1]

Riddle poems, such as the above poem by Robert Frost, can help you introduce poetry to children. There are many traditional riddle poems:

Four fingers and a thumb,
Yet flesh and bone have I none.[2]

These poems by May Swenson are intriguing riddles for older children:

Was Worm
Was worm

swaddled in white
Now tiny queen
in sequin coat
peacockbright

booklist

Poems Strong in Imagery

Fisher, Aileen. "Like a Summer Bird," in *Feathered Ones and Furry.* Thomas Y. Crowell, 1971. (E)

Malam, Charles. "Steam Shovel," in *Upper Pasture.* Holt, 1931, 1958. (I-U)

Merriam, Eve. "Fingers," in *there is no rhyme for silver.* Atheneum, 1967. (E)

———— . "Markings: The Question," in *Finding a Poem.* Atheneum, 1970. (U)

Prelutsky, Jack. "A Dromedary Standing Still," in *Toucans Two and Other Poems.* Macmillan, 1970. (U)

Smith, Jay. "The Toaster," in *Laughing Time.* Atlantic, Little, Brown, 1955. (E-I)

Starbird, Kaye. "The Sleet Storm," in *A Snail's a Failure Socially.* Lippincott, 1966. (I)

Wylie, Elinor. "Velvet Shoes," in *Collected Poems.* Knopf, 1921, 1932. (I-U)

---

[1] "The Secret Sits" from *The Poetry of Robert Frost,* ed. Edward Connery Lathem (Holt, 1969).

[2] From Duncan Emrich, coll., *The Nonsense Book of Riddles, Rhymes, Tongue Twisters, Puzzles and Jokes from American Folklore* (Four Winds Press, 1970), p. 18. The answer is "a glove."

drinks the wind
and feeds
on sweat of the leaves.

Is little chinks
of mosaic floating
a scatter
of colored beads

Alighting pokes
with her new black wire
the saffron yokes

On silent hinges
openfolds her wings
applauding hands
Weaned

from coddling white
to lakedeep air
to blue and green

Is queen[1]

By Morning

Some for everyone
  plenty
  and more coming

Fresh   dainty   airily arriving
  everywhere at once
Transparent at first
  each faint slice
  slow   soundlessly tumbling

  then quickly thickly a gracious fleece
  will spread like youth   like wheat
  over the city

Each building will be   a hill
  all sharps made round

  dark worn noisy narrows made still
  wide   flat   clean   spaces

Streets will be   fields
  cars be   fumbling sheep
A deep bright harvest will be seeded
  in a night

By morning we'll be   children
  feeding on manna

  a new loaf on every doorsill[1]

---

[1]Both poems are from May Swenson, *Poems to Solve* (Scribner's, 1969).

Riddles in verse are scattered at crucial points throughout folk literature. These can be collected as introductions to their stories and used to stimulate children to compose stories that hinge on riddles. Note, for example, the riddle dialogue between the wicked queen and her mirror in "Snow White," the riddle at the center of the plot of "Rumpelstiltskin," and even the riddle of the Sphinx—the most famous riddle in all literature. In the fifth chapter of *The Hobbit* there are nine riddles, the first eight in verse and the final one the central question—"What have I got in my pocket?"—for the whole long narrative that follows:

> Voiceless it cries,
> Wingless flutters,
> Toothless bites,
> Mouthless mutters.[1]

The special appeal of a riddle, poetic or otherwise, is that it requires an immediate problem-solving response. Try removing the title of a poem so that children will use the lines of the poem as data for guessing the riddle. A simple example follows:

> His nose is short and scrubby;
>   His ears hang rather low;
> And he always brings the stick back,
>   No matter how far you throw.[2]

Some poems can be treated as riddles if you reveal one line at a time, permitting children to conjecture the answer based on the information given by the accumulation of lines. Try it with Elizabeth Madox Roberts's intriguing poem which begins like this:

"A little light is going by."

(What could it be? A bicycle with a light on it, an airplane, a man with a flashlight, the small pencil-size kind?)

"Is going up to see the sky."

(Now, what could it be? Which of the guesses based on the first line are supported by the information of the second line?)

"A little light with wings."

(A small airplane, a firefly, an elf?)

Eventually, the full text is presented, and by this time children have given so much attention to each line that the poem is practically memorized.

---

[1]J. R. R. Tolkien, *The Hobbit* (Houghton Mifflin, 1937, 1938), p. 86. (Wind.)
[2]Marchette Chute, "My Dog."

Firefly
A little light is going by,
Is going up to see the sky,
A little light with wings.

I never could have thought of it,
To have a little bug all lit
And made to go on wings.[1]

The following poem is more complicated. We presented each line on a separate strip of tagboard and asked children to assemble the lines into some logical
pattern. They scrutinized the lines for sound features, tried several readings to
determine whether a sequence of simple-to-complex lines or internal rhyme
lines at the end of stanzas or lines arranged to some sort of logic in meaning
(ground to sky, head to legs) worked best. It was an effortless sort of lesson
because the major attention was directed toward the riddle aspect of the poem.
Guesses included crane, heron, scarecrow, giraffe, windmill, and corn.

Stilted creatures,
Features fashioned as a joke,
Boned and buckled,
Finger painted.

They stand in the field
On long-pronged legs
As if thrust there.
They airily feed,
Slightly swaying,
Like hammer-headed flowers.

Bizarre they are,
Built silent and high,
Ornaments against the sky.
Ears like leaves
To hear the silken
Brushing of the clouds.[2]

You can use the riddle idea to bring out many facets of poetry. A study of
the difficulties people encounter in reading poetry disclosed that the prose
meaning, the literal meaning, of a poem is often missed.[3] Some people are
apparently so conditioned to "hear the pretty words" that they ignore the
contextual meaning. Your simplest poem-as-a-riddle activities can direct and
motivate attention to the literal meaning. But the activity in its more com-

---

[1]From Elizabeth Madox Roberts, *Under the Tree.* (Viking, 1922).
[2]Sy Kahn, "Giraffes," *Triptich* (Raymond College Press, 1964). Reprinted in *Reflections on a Gift of
Watermelon Pickle,* p. 31.
[3]See I. A. Richards, *Practical Criticism* (Routledge & Kegan Paul, 1929).

plicated stages can also help children search for the meaning behind imagery and metaphor.

Poems and Cloze Procedure

Cloze procedure, used primarily in measuring readability and in certain types of reading instruction involving context clue use, can be effective in teaching children about poetic diction. Poets, like all writers, are intent upon choosing the "right" word—the word that expresses thought most accurately, with metaphoric overtones. In cloze procedure crucial words are omitted; using the surrounding context, the reader attempts to supply the missing words. For example, study the following poem—"Late October" by Elizabeth Coatsworth[1]—and decide what words have been omitted.

> The cows are dressed in (1) _____,
> And the wild geese (2) _____ by
> Fleeing the cold; not so
> The (3) _____ butterfly
> Which o'er the dying grass
> And leaves and (4) _____ ferns,
> In (5) _____ delight
> (6) _____ and (7) _____.

Each blank presents its own challenge. In deciding how to fill it, you are placed in the role of the poet, attempting to communicate directly but uniquely. How,

booklist

Collections of Traditional Riddle Poems

Wood, Ray, comp. *The American Mother Goose.* Lippincott, 1939, 1940.

Withers, Carl, comp. *A Rocket in My Pocket.* Henry Holt, 1948. See this compiler's collection of freshly discovered oral tradition riddle rhymes.

Burroughs, Margaret Taylor, comp. *Did You Feed My Cow?* Follett, 1956, 1969. These verses collected from Chicago's South Side cover a wide range, from the bouncing ball rhymes and riddles of Middle English to black spirituals.

Opie, Iona and Peter, coll. *The Oxford Nursery Rhyme Book.* Oxford, 1955. A "happy heritage of oral tradition"—over 800 rhymes and ditties, including riddles.

---

[1]From Elizabeth Coatsworth, *The Sparrow Bush* (Norton, 1966), p. 57.

in the first blank, can you devise a unique but accurate way of "dressing" those cows? You can name a color—white, brown, even red—but that is hardly original; it hardly paints a poet's gleaming new picture to justify an eye-catching first line. A glance at the rhyme pattern in the second stanza discourages the use of a word that rhymes with *so.* You want somehow to connote the autumn season. What will you choose?

The second blank presents a different challenge. The geese can *fly* by, thus giving an internal rhyme to the line, or you might select *glide* which provides alliteration (*geese* and *glide*) as well as assonance (the two long *i* sounds in *glide* and *by*). (Actually, here, the poet has used *go,* which seems somehow an easy choice and has caused some children to express preference for their own choices!)

And so it goes. How do you describe that butterfly—uniquely but accurately? (One child suggested *foolish,* and gave good reasons.) How do you etch those ferns upon the memory with an adjective suitable for the fourth blank? The final blank, for the reader concerned with rhyme scheme, may be easy; but note that the meter (feet made up of an unaccented syllable followed by an accented syllable) is broken by the author's choice of *dances* for the sixth blank. When you present that word, ask why the poet has chosen to alter her meter.

When you and your co-poets have tested various blank-fillers, look at the poet's own choices. (See page 340.) You'll find that interest is high as you and the children attempt to justify those choices, or your own. In other words, you have become actively involved in the diction problems faced by poets.

Here's another brain-teaser, cloze-procedure poem. If you omit the title, it becomes a riddle as well:

booklist

Modern Collections of Riddle Poems

Stephenson, Marjorie, comp. *Fives, Sixes and Sevens.* Frederick Warne, 1968. Simple examples, some to be used with the preschool child.

de Regniers, Beatrice Schenk. *It Does Not Say Meow.* Illus. Paul Galdone. Seabury, 1972. (E) Even simpler than the Stephenson collection. These poems were composed by an individual poet. The answers are in picture form, appearing on the overleaf after each riddle.

Swenson, May. *Poems to Solve* and *More Poems to Solve.* Scribner's, 1969, 1971. Intriguing riddle poems for older children.

Catch and shake the (1) _____ garden hose.
Scramble on (2) _____ paws and flee
The hiss of tensing nozzle nose,
Or stalk that (3) _____ bee.

The back yard world is vast as park
With (4) _____ grass and stun
Of sudden sprinkler squalls that arc
Rainbows to the (5) _____ sun.[1]

The various clues—paws, something that shakes a garden hose, something that finds the back yard "vast as park"—contribute to a context that not only gives the title but also the point of view from which the missing words can be derived. But beware of the fifth blank—it's the crucial, surprise word on which the poem turns. When you discover it, try reading the poem so that all its force is directed at that word. (Many poems lend themselves to a unified reading in this way: you can find their center of meaning in a crucial word or phrase and read toward it.) Now check below to see how the poet filled those blanks.

Late October
The cows are dressed in suede,/And the wild geese go by/Fleeing the cold; not so/The tender butterfly/Which o'er the dying grass/And leaves and broken ferns,/In frivolous delight/Dances and turns.

Puppy
Catch and shake the cobra garden hose./Scramble on panicky paws and flee/The hiss of tensing nozzle nose,/Or stalk that snobbish bee./The back yard world is vast as park/With belly-tickle grass and stun/Of sudden sprinkler squalls that arc/Rainbows to the yap yap sun.

Parents and teachers have used cloze procedure for many generations whether or not they knew the term. It is a simple and effective manner of teaching rhyme: "Jack and Jill/Went up the_____." As we have shown, it can also be used for other components of diction—above all, it can help children place themselves in the role of the poet to discover the balance of unique sound and meaning that forms the heart of poetry.

teaching ideas

1. Select poems that lend themselves well to the poem-as-a-riddle device and to cloze procedure. Try your selections and the appropriate techniques with children. Urge hypothesis-making; ask children to justify their choices. Don't

[1]Robert L. Tyler, "Puppy," *The Deposition of Don Quixote and Other Poems* (Golden Quill Press, 1964). Reprinted in *Reflections on a Gift of Watermelon Pickle*, p. 86.

emphasize selecting the "right" answer, but accept and encourage well-defended choices.

2. Use cloze procedure in reverse to help children memorize poetry. Beginning with a complete poem, practice reading it together through choral verse. (See chapter 10 for help on this technique.) Then cover or erase crucial words, a few at a time scattered throughout the poem, so that they can be supplied through memory. Eventually, you can eradicate all but the *functors,* the minimum meaning-bearing but syntactically crucial words that bind the poem together. (See sample below.) You'll be surprised at the rapidity with which children's memories respond to this treatment. Try the first stanza of Arthur Guiterman's "Habits of the Hippopotamus," as an example:

> The hippopotamus is strong
> And huge of head and broad of bustle;
> The limbs on which he rolls along
> Are big with hippopotomuscle.[1]

After a few readings, with cumulative deletions, the following frame will suffice to stimulate the memory for the entire stanza:

> The _____ is _____
> And _____ of _____ and _____ of _____;
> The _____ on which he _____ _____
> Are _____ with _____.

Questions to Ask About a Poem

Discussing a poem with children can be a risky venture. Your intention and theirs may be strictly honorable: you want to clarify the poem and deepen their response to it through the discussion. But discussion often wanders and becomes boring, lapsing into abstract language that has little connection with a child's real world of response—and, perhaps worst of all, it sometimes builds a repertoire of stock answers ("I like the poem because it makes me feel happy") that have little to do with anything but winning approval.

Discussion shouldn't be too general—poems, and discussions about them, are built on specifics. Nor should it be too "picky." Too much emphasis on questions such as "What does this line say to you?" or "Exactly what does this word mean?" eludes the unity of a poem, which is its main reason for being.

Perhaps the most famous study of responses to poetry, I. A. Richards's *Practical Criticism,* disclosed the long-term results of misguided discussion. As mentioned earlier, Richards found that students were often unable to grasp even the literal meaning of poems. They were misled by irrelevancies. They produced stock

---

[1]From Arthur Guiterman, *Gaily the Troubadour* (Dutton, 1936). Reprinted in May Hill Arbuthnot, ed., *Time for Poetry* (Scott, Foresman, 1959).

responses drawn from random discussions and based on previously held convictions. These and other difficulties led Richards to suggest four "kinds of meaning" to be sought through discussion and other activities:

(1) The *sense* of a poem, its literal meaning;
(2) The *feeling* of the author relevant to his topic and theme;
(3) The *tone*—in this case, the poet's attitude toward his reader;
(4) The *intent*—the poet's purpose in creating his work.[1]

Richards's suggestions may help guide discussion, but you can't utilize them with children at this level of abstraction. You can't begin a discussion of poetry with children by saying, "What is the *sense* of this poem? What is the *feeling* of the poet?" If you do, you're likely to elicit more stock, abstract response.

What, then, can you do in discussion? What questions for discussion may help gain entrance to a poem? Perhaps more precisely, how can you examine the ideas Richards considers important and still retain the freshness and specificity of the work under discussion?

Let's begin the exploration by examining suggested questions from other sources. Robert Hillyer poses three critical questions to be asked about a poem:

(1) What is the author's intention?
(2) Has he succeeded in it?
(3) Was the intention worthwhile in the first place?[2]

Again, these seem a bit abstract if you are working with children. Note, too, that they do not include Richards's first item: getting the sense of the poem. You can, however, bring focus to the first two questions by point-of-view technique: simply ask children to respond by taking the first-person role of the poet. Discussing the first poem in this chapter ("No," page 308), say, "You are the poet: why did you write this poem?" Subsequent discussion asks the author to justify her or his choices in statement, word, and rhyme. Evaluation of the poem—Hillyer's third question—should wait till much data have appeared.

Three very lively and basic questions to apply to many poems are provided by Laurence Perrine in his fascinating exploration of poetry, *Sound and Sense:*

(1) Who is the speaker and what is the occasion?
(2) What is the central purpose of the poem?
(3) By what means is that purpose achieved?[3]

You may need to rephrase the questions so that they're understandable for your children, but try them out.

---

[1]Richards's findings and suggestions are summarized in Frederick B. Davis, "Psychometric Research on Comprehension in Reading," *Reading Research Quarterly* 7 (Summer 1972): 636–38.
[2]Robert Hillyer, *In Pursuit of Poetry* (McGraw-Hill, 1960), p. 13.
[3]Laurence Perrine, *Sound and Sense: An Introduction to Poetry,* 2nd. ed. (Harcourt, Brace & World, 1963), pp. 21–24.

Strawberries
Ripe, ripe Strawberries!
Who'll buy Strawberries?
Buy my Strawberries red and sweet
Then your child can have a treat,
And I'll trudge home and rest my Feet,
And cry no more in the dusty Street,
Ripe, ripe Strawberries!
Who'll buy Strawberries?[1]

Who is speaking—who is the "actor" in the poem? What is he or she trying to do? Why is there a poem about this? Why isn't it just a plain statement: someone is trying to sell strawberries? What does the poem do that a plain statement could not do?

We're attempting here to apply Perrine's basic questions to a specific poem. They permit room for conjecture and encourage divergent responses. They may also inspire point-of-view response, role-playing, and dramatization—techniques that readily suit many poems for children.

Our own recommended question sequence for use with many selections, derived from Perrine and others, is a little simpler. We've experimented with it at many ranges and levels—all the way from *Drummer Hoff* with kindergarten children to Milne's "The King's Breakfast" with nine-year-olds to the rather horrifying "Flight of the Roller-Coaster" by Raymond Souster[2] in middle school. Basically, we ask:

(1) *Who is the speaker (or who is the actor) in the poem?* Sometimes it's a good idea to note that the speaker isn't necessarily the poet himself, that the poet, in other words, can assume the point of view of someone else—an important realization in reading many poems.

(2) *What is the situation?* Some poems require discussion of the context in which they occur. You might ask what happened before, after, and during the amazing roller-coaster ride in "Flight of the Roller-Coaster."

(3) *Why is this a poem?* This question explores the aspects of the poem that make it a poem: its meter, its imagery, its sounds of language. In "Flight of the Roller-Coaster" you may note the grouping of lines, the length of lines like the swoop of the roller-coaster itself, the repeated sounds, the "cucumber-cool" and "movieland magic carpet" imagery.

Flight of the Roller Coaster
Once more around should do it, the man confided. . .

And sure enough, when the roller-coaster reached the peak

---

[1] See Eleanor Farjeon, *Poems for Children* (17), p. 14.
[2] From Mary Alice Downie and Barbara Robertson, comp. *The Wind Has Wings: Poems from Canada*, illus. Elizabeth Cleaver (Walck, 1968), pp. 12–13.

Of the giant curve above me—screech of its wheels
Almost drowned by the shriller cries of the riders—

Instead of the dip and plunge with its landslide of screams
It rose in the air like a movieland magic carpet, some wonderful bird,

And without fuss or fanfare swooped slowly across the amusement park,
Over Spook's Castle, ice-cream booths, shooting-gallery; and losing no height

Made the last yards above the beach, where the cucumber-cool
Brakeman in the last seat saluted
A lady about to change from her bathing-suit.

Then, as many witnesses duly reported, headed leisurely over the water,
Disappearing mysteriously all too soon behind a low-lying flight of clouds.

Try the questions on "No," the Dorothy Aldis poem found earlier in this chapter. Who are the actors? There's a boy: how old is he and how does he look? Who is the other actor? What is the situation? Read the poem aloud to show that the boy is obstinate and unreasonable; then read it to show sympathy for him. What is the reason for his rebellion? Why is he refusing? What is he refusing to do? (To go to bed? to hang up his clothes? to practice his piano lessons?) Is this the way he usually acts? Or is it the final straw, following a long period of acquiescence? Why is this a poem? Read the poem again to bring out the terse rhymes and the metrical pattern.

Note that you need to amplify each question, to pin it down to specifics unique to each poem. The questions suggested in this section are intended as guides to areas of questioning to be applied to particular poems.

Responding to Poetry through the Arts

In Chapter 10 we've included a section on choral reading. Not all poetry, of course, is suited to this technique. But, as one technique among others, it encourages discussion and shared valuing of a poem's sound and meaning.

Choral reading may also help highlight similarities in the interpretation of poems that may at first seem unrelated. Advanced choral speakers may enjoy and benefit from the paired examples of traditional and new poems presented in *Grandfather Rock* (18) collected by David Morse. For instance, Paul Kantner's rock lyric "We Can Be Together" can be matched in mood to Walt Whitman's "Song of Myself" (pp. 104–106 in that collection). Whether or not the group with whom you work is ready for these selections, you may wish to borrow the idea of paired poems—"How are these poems alike?" and "How are they different?"—as an impetus to choral speaking for interpretive effect.

THE LOOK OF POETRY. The way a poem sits on the page is one aspect of the why-is-this-a-poem question. It may also be used as a springboard to visual response to poetry.

Poets follow traditions of typography and placement to highlight unities within a poem: the poetic lines and stanzas, meter, and rhyme. Their arrangement may be unusual, as in A. A. Milne's highly rhythmical verses such as "The King's Breakfast" and "Hoppity."[1] E. E. Cummings goes even further, scattering lines to fit the mood, running words together, and varying spaces between words. (P. 346)

A poem's shape may literally fit its subject, as in the "Long Tale" of Lewis Carroll's Mouse in the third chapter of *Alice's Adventures in Wonderland.* (P. 347.) Or the poem may be entirely without words, depending on visual effect alone, as in "Night Song of the Fish." (P. 348.) Try the poem-as-a-riddle activity and interpretation questions on that one. Or the selection may attempt through its appearance to present the actor's visual style, as in "The Computer's First Christmas Card." (P. 349.) Try using the latter to suggest the creation of poems from various unusual points of view—an alarm clock's announcement, a windshield wiper's ditty, a mosquito or a firefly's evening out.

These examples illustrate a form called "concrete poetry," described rather enigmatically as "an ideogram . . . in which the sign and the thing signified are equatable."[2] But you don't have to define it if you simply show a few examples and invite children to try concrete poetry of their own. A recent collection by Eve Merriam called *Out Loud* (19) contains concrete poems, two of which appear in this chapter.

Concrete poetry can direct attention to visual arrangement as a device in interpreting any poem and can arouse interest in visual, nonverbal response to poetry.

POETRY AND MOVEMENT.   An up-tight generation fears spontaneous dance movements to the accompaniment of music or a poem, but you don't have to be part of an up-tight generation! Laura E. Richards's "The Baby Goes to Boston" (P. 350) at first may sound like rather syrupy nonsense, but if you move to its rhythm after a few readings, it begins to gather the force of a real locomotive. Movement and choral speaking may be combined to make a highly rhythmic poem a stimulating experience.

With younger children, you can get a good start with poetry-and-movement activity by using selections from *Children's Games in Street and Playground* (20). Many of these selections are in the form of games: acting games, chasing and pretending games, seeking games. For example:

> Mardy, mardy mustard,
> You can't eat custard;
> Hee, hee, hee,
> You can't catch me.

---

[1] A. A. Milne, *When We Were Very Young* (Dutton, 1924), pp. 57, 63.
[2] Eugene Wildman, ed., *The Chicago Review: Anthology of Concretism* (Swallow Press, 1967), p. 155.

IN JUST-

in Just-
spring   when the world is mud-
luscious the little
lame balloonman

whistles   far   and wee

and eddieandbill come
running from marbles and
piracies and it's
spring

when the world is puddle-wonderful

the queer
old balloonman whistles
far   and   wee
and bettyandisbel come dancing

from hop-scotch and jump-rope and

it's
spring
and
*   the*

*   goat-footed*

balloonMan   whistles
far
and
wee

E. E. Cummings

"Fury said to
a mouse, That
he met
in the
house,
'Let us
both go
to law:
I will
prosecute
you.—
Come, I'll
take no
denial;
We must
have a
trial:
For
really
this
morning
I've
nothing
to do.'
Said the
mouse to
the cur,
'Such a
trial,
dear sir,
With no
jury or
judge,
would be
wasting
our breath.'
'I'll be
judge,
I'll be
jury,'
Said
cunning
old Fury;
'I'll try
the whole
cause,
and
condemn
you
to
death.' ''

"The Long Tale" from the Heritage Club edition of *Alice's Adventures in Wonderland,* copyright 1941 by The Heritage Press, Avon, Connecticut; © renewed 1969.

From *CHRISTIAN MORGENSTERN'S GALGENLIEDER (Gallows Songs)*, translated by Max Knight. Originally published by the University of California Press; reprinted by permission of the Regents of the University of California.

You may aid freedom of movement by activities such as those in *Basic Rhythms* by Dorothy S. Ainsworth and Ruth Evans and *Movement and Drama in the Primary Schools* by Betty Lowndes.[1] The latter's sequence begins with "body awareness," then progresses to body activity, relationship of self to space and other people, and awareness of quality of movement. Such a sequence may lead to movement akin to modern dance, fully suited to serious poems and poems whose rhythm is varied to high lyric intent. But such sophistication will develop slowly, over a period of time devoted to more rhythmically predictable poetry. You might begin with the clear pantomime indicated in "House Moving" (p. 352) or the carefully described easy movement of "Run a Little" (p. 351).

---

[1]Dorothy S. Ainsworth and Ruth Evans, *Basic Rhythms* (Chartwell House, 1955), chapters 7 and 8; Betty Lowndes, *Movement and Drama in the Primary School* (B. T. Batsford, 1970). (Publisher's address is 4 Fitzharding St., London W1.)

THE COMPUTER'S FIRST CHRISTMAS CARD

jollymerry
hollyberry
jollyberry
merryholly
happyjolly
jollyjelly
jellybelly
bellymerry
hollyheppy
jollyMolly
marryJerry
merryHarry
hoppyBarry
heppyJarry
boppyheppy
berryjorry
jorryjolly
moppyjelly
Mollymerry
Jerryjolly
bellyboppy
jorryhoppy
hollymoppy
Barrymerry
Jarryhappy
happyboppy
boppyjolly
jollymerry
merrymerry
merrymerry
merryChris
ammerryasa
Chrismerry
aSMERRYCHR
YSANTHEMUM

EDWIN MORGAN

THE BABY GOES TO BOSTON

What does the train say?
  Jiggle joggle, jiggle joggle!
What does the train say?
  Jiggle joggle jee!
Will the little baby go
Riding with the locomo?
Loky moky poky stoky
Smoky choky chee!

Ting! ting! the bells ring,
  Jiggle joggle, jiggle joggle!
Ting! ting! the bells ring,
  Jiggle joggle jee!
Ring for joy because we go
Riding with the locomo,
Loky moky poky stoky
  Smoky choky chee!

Look! how the trees run,
  Jiggle joggle, jiggle joggle!
Each chasing t' other one,
  Jiggle joggle jee!
Are they running for to go
Riding with the locomo?
Loky moky poky stoky
Smoky choky chee!

Over the hills now,
  Jiggle joggle, jiggle joggle!
Down through the vale below,
  Jiggle joggle jee!
All the cows and horses run,
Crying, "Won't you take us on,
Loky moky poky stoky
  Smoky choky chee?"

So, so the miles go,
  Jiggle joggle, jiggle joggle!
Now it's fast and now it's slow,
  Jiggle joggle jee!
When we're at our journey's end,
Say good-by to snorting friend,
Loky moky poky stoky
  Smoky choky chee!

From *Tirra Lirra: Rhymes Old and New* by Laura E. Richards, originally published in 1902 by Dana Estes and Company; 1955 edition available from Little, Brown & Company.

RUN A LITTLE

Run a little this way,
    Run a little that!
Fine new feathers
    For a fine new hat.
A fine new hat
    For a lady fair—
Run around and turn about
    And jump in the air.

Run a little this way,
    Run a little that!
White silk ribbon
    For a black silk cat.
A black silk cat
    For the Lord Mayor's wife—
Run around and turn about
    And fly for your life!

James Reeves

From THE BLACKBIRD IN THE LILAC, published by E. P. Dutton. Used by permission of the author.

As you consider the suggestions presented in this chapter, remember that no activity fits all poems or all groups of children. Try them out, suiting the activities to the poems you select, and discard those that don't work for you.

CHAPTER REFERENCES

1. Belloc, Hillaire. *The Bad Child's Book of Beasts.* Knopf, 1965.
2. _____. *Cautionary Tales.* Knopf, 1931, 1941.
3. Roberts, Bertha E., and Beckman, Aneta T., comps. *Children's Voices.* Silver Burdett, 1939.
4. Jordan, June, and Bush, Terri, colls. *The Voice of the Children.* Holt, 1970.
5. Baron, Virginia Olsen, comp. *Here I Am!* Dutton, 1969.
6. Larrick, Nancy. *I Heard a Scream in the Street: Poetry by Young People in the City.* Dell, 1970.
7. Margolis, Richard J. *Only the Moon and Me.* Lippincott, 1969.
8. Giovanni, Nikki. *Spin a Soft Black Song: Poems for Children.* Hill and Wang, 1971.
9. Dunning, Stephen, Lueders, Edward, and Smith, Hugh, eds. *Reflections on a Gift of Watermelon Pickle and Other Modern Verse.* Scott, Foresman, 1966.

HOUSE MOVING

Look! A house is being moved!
    Hoist!
    Jack!
    Line!
    Truck!

    Shout!
    Yell!
    Stop!
    Stuck!

    Cable!
    Kick!
    Jerk!
    Bump!

    Lift!
    Slide!
    Crash!
    Dump!
This crew could learn simplicity from turtles.

Patricia Hubbell

10. Johnson, Edna, Sickels, Evelyn R., Sayers, Frances Clarke, eds. *Anthology of Children's Literature,* 4th ed. Houghton Mifflin, 1970.
11. Cole, William, ed. *Story Poems New and Old.* World, 1957.
12. MacLeish, Archibald. *Poetry and Experience.* Houghton Mifflin, 1961.
13. Benet, Rosemary and Stephen Vincent. *A Book of Americans.* Farrar and Rinehart, 1933.
14. Updike, John. *A Child's Calendar.* Knopf, 1965.
15. Potter, Charles F., ed. *Tongue Tanglers.* World, 1962.
16. Rasmussen, Knud, coll. and tr. *Beyond the High Hills: A Book of Eskimo Poems.* World, 1961.
17. Farjeon, Eleanor. *Poems for Children.* Lippincott, 1951.
18. Morse, David, coll. *Grandfather Rock: The New Poetry and the Old.* Delacorte, 1972.
19. Merriam, Eve, coll. *Out Loud.* Atheneum, 1973.
20. Opie, Iona and Peter. *Children's Games in Street and Playground.* Oxford, 1969.

BIBLIOGRAPHY

Carlson, Ruth Kearney. "The Creative Thrust of Poetry Writing." *Elementary English,* 49 December 1972, pp. 1177–86. All sorts of poetry forms to challenge prospective child poets.

Chisholm, Margaret. "Mother Goose—Elucidated." *Elementary English,* 49 December 1972, pp. 1141–44. Intriguing data about the historical political meanings behind well-known Mother Goose rhymes.

Hopkins, Lee Bennett. "Negro Poets: Through the Music of Their Words." *Elementary English,* 45 February 1968, pp. 206–8. Sketches and examples of black poets Paul Laurence Dunbar, Langston Hughes, and Gwendolyn Brooks.

Manzo, Anthony V., and Martin, Deanna Coleman. "Writing Communal Poetry." *Journal of Reading,* 17 May 1974, pp. 638–43. Description of a group writing process, in this case involving inner-city high school students.

Martin, Bill, Jr. "Helping Children Claim Language through Literature." *Elementary English,* 45 May 1968, pp. 583–91. The author, a well-known speaker, tells how poetry inspires language discovery.

Moore, Rosanna. "Poetry and Painting." *School Arts,* 70 January 1971, pp. 16–17. Lovely examples of the blending of visual arts with well-known poems. Examples are derived from the work of a high school class but ideas could apply to any level.

Nathan, Norman, and Berger, Allen. "The Building Blocks of Poetry." *English Journal,* 60 January 1971, pp. 42–46. Sophisticated use of cloze technique in teaching poetry.

Novak, Barbara. "Milne's Poems: Form and Content." *Elementary English,* 36 October 1957, pp. 355–61. Analysis of the enjoyment to be found in Milne's poetry.

Shapiro, Phyllis P. "The Language of Poetry." *Elementary School Journal,* 70 December 1969, pp. 130–34. A perceptive analysis of aesthetic experience through poetry, with references ranging from Arbuthnot to John Dewey.

Shay, D'Arcy C. "Creativity in the Classroom—Haiku." *Elementary English,* 48 December 1971, p. 1000. Description of haiku form and samples of fifth-graders' haiku.

Thompson, Phyllis. "How to Handle Children's Choices in Poetry Without Manhandling Them." *Elementary English,* 48 November 1971, pp. 849–55. Good taste, not children's preferences, is the criterion of this writer.

8 chapter

Nonfiction in the Curriculum

Until recently, nonfiction in children's literature has been neglected. Literature connotes artistry. The assembling of information into a nonfiction work doesn't at first appear to require artistic effort. But it does—or can. Nonfiction challenges the writer to go beyond the mere assembling of facts and create an artistic work. The product of such artistry may be as literary as any fiction.

The term itself hints of neglect, implying a negation of fiction. Other terms seem equally unsatisfactory. The term *informational materials* implies that fiction does not contain information or that nonfiction lacks dimensions beyond the factual. *Exposition* in its traditional sense excludes narrative; yet nonfiction can and does embody narration at times.

We are left with the not-quite-satisfactory term *nonfiction* and a growing sense of the importance of this literary type. Fortunately, children and publishers are not put off by the difficulty. Nonfiction is a major part of many a child's reading diet. Publishers' lists over the past few years contain as many nonfiction as fiction titles. Some of these are indeed attempts at artistry with a clear aim at lasting value: a biography intended to be authoritative for years to come, a celebration and explanation of some aspect of nature to enable future readers to appreciate and understand their world. Others explore a topic in less permanent detail, subject to change as time adds or alters information. Permanent or temporary, such works are worthy contributions to literature and require careful evaluation and selection.

Some of the elements that make up fiction can also be applied to a discussion of nonfiction. Some nonfiction, for example, contains characters. A biography may be examined for its characterization in a literary sense as well as its accuracy. But character is not an element in many books explaining a scientific process or depicting recent archaeological finds. In fact, the imposition of fictional characters may detract from, rather than contribute to, the effect. Setting and plot may likewise be distractions if they aren't integral to the work.

Theme in a nonfiction work remains a significant element in the sense that an author's attitude toward the subject is an important part of the communication. The theme-statement or theme-question that underlies the work reveals the author's reason for writing about the topic. In good nonfiction it is the keystone around which the information is assembled. But theme in nonfiction doesn't have the color and quality of theme in fiction. Fictional themes arise from the author's imagination; characters and events evolve to demonstrate the theme. In nonfiction, where information is only partially controlled by the author, the theme must be controlled by strict adherence to what is known. The artistry of free-ranging imagination is replaced by a different kind of artistry: that of communicating knowledge derived from observation and research.

Style is just as important in nonfiction as in fiction. An authority may write about a topic with a fine command of information and a worthy attitude or theme, but he or she must also have a command of language. The language must illuminate but not intrude. If you examine several nonfiction works about a common topic, you are likely to find that style is ultimately a major criterion for selection.

Reading nonfiction demands a wide range of abilities and knowledge. This is even more important when evaluating nonfiction. Like the author, the reader or reviewer must possess knowledge of the topic as well as the ability to appreciate literary quality. In a distinguished analysis of nonfiction, Margery Fisher has pointed out that many reviewers lack the necessary range.[1] They hold high standards of accuracy but fail to consider whether a work communicates an attitude or theme. They neglect other criteria: the appropriateness of tone, organization, diction, and style. These elements are as important in nonfiction as they are in any form of literature.

To help us examine nonfiction according to these criteria, we have drawn upon the knowledge of some authorities in various fields. In addition, we've confined our discussion to three major areas of the curriculum. Our aim in this chapter is not to cover the whole range of nonfiction but to present examples to help you devise criteria for examining it. By organizing our examples around these subject areas—science and mathematics, social science, and the arts— we've attempted also to show you the importance of nonfiction in developing children's independent learning. At times we have even illustrated the tie between nonfiction and other literary types to demonstrate their complementary nature. Our hope is that the criteria, together with the sample titles, will enable you to pursue the reading and presentation of nonfiction successfully.

CHILDREN'S BOOKS IN SCIENCE AND MATHEMATICS

By John P. Smith
University of Washington

New content, new formats for presenting content, new activities that emphasize concrete experience—these are some of the "news" in science and mathematics

---

[1] Margery Fisher, *Matters of Fact: Aspects of Non-Fiction for Children* (Brockhampton Press, 1972), pp. 9–17.

education. An effort to combine the knowledge of scientists and mathematicians with the know-how of educators has resulted in new curricula that present knowledge in the form of inquiry. Children are led to discover and interpret. They're led to extrapolate their experience into models, actual or theoretical, to represent the relationships among things and ideas.

All of this has changed the roles of teachers, textbooks, and nontext materials. A problem-solving approach, an impetus to inquiry, is called for. As with many other curricular innovations, the change is slow to come and imperfect. There's room now as always for books that tell as well as ask. A search of children's books reveals a wide variety of approaches at work. You can make your selection on the basis of topic, difficulty, treatment, and your own philosophy.

Selection Criteria

Because of continuing changes in science and mathematics education, you'll need to consider whether materials are compatible with content and mode of presentation in the curriculum you plan to follow. For example, inquiry is the key-note of Isaac Asimov's *The Noble Gases* (1). Throughout this book Asimov asks the reader the same questions that scientists asked themselves as they pursued their investigations. The book therefore uses an inquiry mode in keeping with the philosophy of many new curricula.

A fine biography, *In the Steps of the Great American Herpetologist Karl Patterson Schmidt* (2) by A. Gilbert Wright, ends with a twenty-page handbook to guide the reader who wants to follow Schmidt's path (and the paths of assorted frogs, toads, turtles, salamanders, and snakes). The inquiry mode is thus served in biography.

How to Make Your Science Project Scientific (3) by Thomas Moorman is a no-non-sense invitation to utilize scientific methodology in collecting data—to be able to report methods as well as results. Such a presentation goes a good deal further than the look-how-the-egg-goes-into-the-bottle treatment.

Mathematics books, too, are often written in a spirit of inquiry. The Exploring Mathematics series published by Doubleday invites the reader to experiment by posing questions along the way. Each book explores a single concept: for instance, *Symmetry* (4) by Arthur G. Razzell and K. G. O. Watts.

There are modes other than inquiry too. A useful criterion in selection is whether the mode suits the topic. The range is great, and the number of books on most topics is large. We must explore them fully to make good selections. Consider first the books themselves and then their appropriateness for various purposes.

THE BOOKS THEMSELVES. Look for currency and accuracy of content. The publication date is of some help in determining currency. *A Book of Moon Rockets for You* (5) by Franklyn Branley, is recent enough to include information about lunar probes and early, manned moon-landings, and even lists lunar expeditions up through 1969. This topic might well lead you to look further for even more up-to-date information.

Shrubs grow beneath the understory. They are bushy plants that have many woody stems. In some kinds of forests, especially dense evergreen forests, there may be so little light that no shrubs can grow. In more open forests, shrubs may be so abundant that they are hard to walk through.

Plants called herbs grow at your feet. Herbs are green plants with soft stems. Most forest wildflowers are herbs. The herb layer also includes other low-growing plants, including mosses, ferns, and mushrooms.

Underfoot is the forest floor. In most forests it is carpeted with fallen leaves. The forest floor is a sort of wastebasket for all the layers of plants above. Each year in eastern North America, about ten million leaves fall onto an acre of forest floor.

DECIDUOUS FOREST—
EASTERN NORTH AMERICA

Reprinted with permission of Macmillan Publishing Co., Inc. from INTO THE WOODS by Laurence Pringle. Copyright ©1973 by Laurence Pringle.

Since few of us can be experts in all curricular fields, it's important to know where to turn to find reliable reviews of nonfiction books. On page 358 we've listed some sources of expert reviews of science and mathematics books (these are in addition to sources cited in chapter 1). In addition, you'll probably find authorities in your community who will be glad to answer your questions and help you evaluate potential choices.

Examine illustrations carefully. Some authors and editors plan the graphics to be integral to the text. Others may simply add graphics to brighten format, giving little thought to the deeper contribution these can make. Diagrams and photos may clarify and amplify a text. Laurence Pringle in *Into the Woods: Exploring the Forest Ecosystem* (6) places black-and-white photographs directly beside the explanations of the concepts and processes illustrated. Well-placed diagrams at two points in the book are used to augment complex descriptions. The graphs and charts in *Physical Fitness through Sports and Nutrition* (7) by Walter H. Gregg are more than explanatory; they invite the reader's involvement. The picture glossary that presents concepts in *Doctors and Nurses: What Do They Do?* (8) by Carla Greene is most helpful, as are the charts that accompany discussion in *Book of Venus for You* (9) by Franklyn Branley. The combination of graphics and text in David Macaulay's books, including his scientific exploration of ancient city planning in *City: A Story of Roman Planning and Construction* (10) may well inspire graphics designers for years to come.

Imaginative drawings and humanizing illustrations in which details are accurate though presented fancifully are surely welcome in many informational books. As Margery Fisher has pointed out in *Matters of Fact,*[1] fancy may indeed enhance fact, rather than denigrate it. Tabot the Automated Truck Driver adds a touch of fanciful speculation to *Computers: Tools for Today* (11) by Claude J. De

booklist

Sources for Reviews of Science and Mathematics Books

Appraisal—Children's Science Books, published three times each year by Children's Science Book Review Committee, Harvard Graduate School of Education and New England Round Table of Children's Librarians, Cambridge, Massachusetts. Ratings and reviews are provided by librarians and by scientists, parallel reviews for each book.

The Arithmetic Teacher, published by the National Council of Teachers of Mathematics, eight issues each year. See "New Books for Pupils" column.

Mathematics Teacher, published by the National Council of Teachers of Mathematics, eight issues each year. See "New Publications" column, books designated as "Supplementary."

Science Books: A Quarterly Review. American Association for the Advancement of Science, edited by Kathryn Wolff, Washington, D.C. Reviews are listed according to science subject; includes recommended titles.

---

[1]Margery Fisher, *Matters of Fact* (American edition, Crowell, 1972), pp. 106–107.

Rossi without distorting the factual information. The flow chart on "How to Go to the Junior Prom"[1] in *Computers! From Sand Table to Electronic Brain* (12) by Alan Vorwald and Frank Clark is an engaging project in the midst of what might otherwise be a dreary discussion.

Not everyone who writes nonfiction in science and mathematics is a specialist in those fields. The authors may be expert craftsmen, skilled in meeting the child audience. If so, you should inquire as you read whether they have done their homework! Weyman Jones, best known as a fiction writer, turned to nonfiction in *Computer: The Mind Stretcher* (13) and gave the topic an immediacy that other such works lack. "The computer is a machine that is changing you," he remarks at one point,[2] bringing the topic home to the reader. The book's information is accurate as well as interesting.

On the other hand, books written by specialists need to be examined for their appeal to children. An author such as Isaac Asimov can be both specialist and writer for children. His *Realm of Numbers* (14) is just one example of this prolific author's ability to make information appealing.

THE BOOKS AND THEIR READERS. Consider the match between readers' abilities and readability of the books. (See chapter 3.) While it's desirable for a nonfiction book to extend children's vocabularies, the new words should be made comprehensible. Most of the vocabulary should be at the appropriate reading level. Vocabulary in science and mathematics books is highly specific, highly denotative. Words such as *heat, pressure, number,* and *time* may seem common enough in everyday parlance; children may have little trouble decoding them. But their precise use in specialized material may still cause difficulty.

Does the book suit the child's interests? Listen to freely expressed interests and probe for other interests. Remember, the child may have several purposes for his reading. Recreational reading calls for a book with a lighter approach than that of a technical book for a more serious student.

Sometimes the format of a book and its content seem to be at odds when you're trying to estimate difficulty. Large print and clear pictures don't always indicate a simple text. *Born in a Barn: Farm Animals and Their Young* (15) by Elizabeth and Klaus Gemming contains fascinating information, including a chart summarizing essential data for comparing animals. The book looks simple, with large photos and typography. But the text is difficult, probably requiring oral reading by an adult. The brevity and large type in Ronald Syme's *Amerigo Vespucci: Scientist and Sailor* (16), and in Syme's other biographies, don't really simplify the rich and amazingly complex sentences. Similarly, mathematics books, especially those associated with the "new math," often couch difficult terminology in a format that appears disarmingly simple. The only sure guide to difficulty is to have children try to read the book.

---

[1] pp. 96–97.
[2] p. 18.

Types of Nonfiction Books in Science and Mathematics.   Children's books in these fields may include those giving straight factual information, those containing problems to be solved, books describing laboratory experiments, books attempting a Socratic problem-solving method, and biographies that give insight into science and mathematics processes and discoveries.

The need for factual material to be accurate and appealing to children has already been discussed, as has the need for seeking competent reviews. Sometimes you'll be aided by carefully compiled lists of materials. For example, eighty-one useful books are cited and discussed in "Children's Literature: An Aid in Mathematics Instruction" by Lucille B. Strain.[1] Brief but specific recommendations of *High Interest—Low Vocabulary Science Books* are available in pamphlet form, compiled by Margaret E. Gott and James R. Wailes.[2]

Here are some questions to ask about science and mathematics books containing problems to be solved:

(1) Does the book contain accurate directions enabling children to proceed with the problems without having to obtain help from adults?

(2) If children follow the directions, will the results be of real value in expanding their knowledge of the topic? (Some highly elaborate experiments lead to trivial results.)

(3) Does the procedure described in the book have an underlying inquiry base so that thinking skills as well as knowledge are affected?

(4) Does the book contain follow-up treatments of the problems? Children need to be able to relate their investigation to the narrative or to previous experiences.

The experiments in *What Happens If. . . ?* (17) by Rose Wyler are accompanied by pictures showing what does happen, eliminating the child's chance to discover. Furthermore, the book fails to encourage the experimenter to hypothesize about causes of the results. *Chemistry Experiments for Children* (18) by Virginia Mullin lacks information needed to complete the processes.

Fortunately, there are many books that do fulfill the above criteria. A few of them are listed below:

Musselman, Virginia. *Learning about Nature through Indoor Gardening.* Stackpole, 1972. (E)

Adler, Irving. *Magic House of Numbers.* Illus. Ruth Adler. Day, 1958. (I)

Meyer, Jerome S. and Hanlon, Stuart. *Fun with the New Math.* Hawthorn, 1965. (I-U)

Kadesch, Robert R. *Math Menagerie.* Harper, 1970. (I-U)

Cobb, Vicki. *Science Experiments You Can Eat.* Lippincott, 1972. (I-U)

[1]From *The Arithmetic Teacher* 16 (October, 1969): 451–55.
[2]Available from the Bureau of Educational Research, School of Education, University of Colorado, Boulder 80302.

Others are included in subsequent discussion.

A word of caution: examine the safety of the activities described in such books. Matches, acids, strong bases, and flammable materials are hazardous and must always be used with competent adult supervision.

And finally, don't assume that children will learn more from an experiment than is possible in terms of the operations actually performed. A simple activity of rock identification must be contained within the larger context of the study of rock types and how they are formed if children are to understand the nature of rocks and their origins. Children may learn the names of certain common rocks, but that doesn't mean that they know anything else about those rocks. (Note, for example, how Seymour Simon's *The Rock-Hound's Book* (19) builds on the foundation of knowledge provided through rock collecting.)

Socratic methodology requires on-the-spot reactions to a child's questions and responses, a probing strategy to elicit exploration and use of logic. That's a tall order for books, as compared with face-to-face sessions. Programmed texts that provide branching may attempt Socratic teaching, but this format is not widely used in children's books. The less structured approach of the expository writer can, however, pose questions, attempt to anticipate readers' reactions, and then lead them to examine each of several plausible solutions. Such an approach requires a sensitivity to readers that can seldom be maintained consistently. Perhaps, in the end, it must be admitted that Socrates can't be packaged, programmed, or put between the covers of a book.

Still, an awareness of Socratic methodology often inspires writers to a closer link with readers. Asimov, as previously mentioned, accomplishes his purpose with a closeness to the reader that invites questioning and conjecturing. In the midst of a lively discussion in *One, Two, Three and Many: A First Look at Numbers* (20) by Solveig Paulson Russell there's the challenge of devising a new number system based on *googolplex,* an imaginative touch that stimulates readers' inquiry. After a rather slow opening, *A New Mathematics Reader* (21) by Evelyn Sharp becomes lively and exciting during the presentation of probability, challenging the reader to question and explore this "science of leaping in the dark."

Biography can reflect Socratic methodology by showing how a scientist questioned and probed step by step, in order to arrive at an important discovery. The early chapters of *Robert Goddard: Father of the Space Age* (22) by Charles Spain Verral engage the reader in Goddard's early attempt to float an aluminum balloon filled with helium. The book also explores some of the reasoning that accompanied his attempts to build a rocket. *Robert H. Goddard* (23) by Milton Lomask carries the experiments further, still with emphasis on Goddard's attempts to reason through the problems blocking the success of his invention. In both books the moment of insight—when Goddard envisioned his rocket while perched in a cherry tree—is shown to be the inspiration for his dauntless pursuit of invention through reasoning.

Similarly, *Charles Babbage: Father of the Computer* (24) by Ian Halacy describes a similar process of discovery. This account also reveals that brilliance may be accompanied by a crochety, troublesome personality. The anecdotal portrayal of *Black Pioneers of Science and Invention* (25) by Louis Haber highlights the investigative process, often set against a social background of prejudice to be overcome. Here, too, the reader can recapitulate the scientists' inquiry processes. *Lise Meitner: Atomic Pioneer* (26) by Deborah Crawford, is a unique biography of a woman who accomplished her work with good cheer despite the double-edged prejudice of the men who thought women couldn't be scientists and the Nazis who persecuted her. *Margaret Sanger: Pioneer of Birth Control* (27) by Lawrence Lader and Milton Meltzer also describes a scientist's struggles on two fronts: the effort to pierce the frontiers of knowledge and the effort to alter public opinion.

Faced with the difficulties of simplification, authors aren't consistently successful in writing process-oriented biographies for younger readers. While some of the World Explorer series published by Garrard do portray real people struggling to solve real problems, most seem content with an after-the-fact recitation of accomplishments. *Fridtjof Nansen* (28) by Erick Berry tells the story of the Norwegian explorer's treks across Greenland and his attempts to find the North Pole. But the inquiry process that distinguished him as an oceanographer, and later as a statesman who won the Nobel Peace Prize, is not presented. Susan Heimann's *Christopher Columbus* (29) stresses Columbus's navigational skills, a useful scientific emphasis somewhat marred by a summary-type description of how Columbus used his knowledge in the midst of danger. Many process-type biographies can be read to children who aren't yet able to read them. The warm, personal account of *The Boy Who Sailed around the World Alone* (30) by Robin Lee Graham with Derek L. T. Gill, with its maps, actual pages of Robin's diary and logbook, and on-the-spot color photos of this appealing young man and his accumulation of fellow-traveling kittens, is the sort of reading that can be shared by almost everyone.

For upper ages and adulthood the array of biographical, process nonfiction dealing with the sciences is rapidly expanding. James D. Watson's *The Double Helix* (31) is considered one of the best examples: a no-holds-barred chronicle of the lives of people involved in discovering the DNA heredity molecule structure. George Gamow's unique *Biography of Physics* (32) is both biography and history, tracing the lives of those who contributed most to this field, seen against the social backgrounds that influenced them. Other composite biographies, often with a process approach, include *The Universe of Galileo and Newton* (33) by William Bixby and *The Telescope Makers: From Galileo to the Space Age* (34) by Barbara Land.

Now that we've examined some of the criteria for selecting science and mathematics books for use in and outside the curriculum, let's turn to a few more examples of works that appear to fit these criteria.

Science Books

The Let's Read and Find Out Science series published by Crowell presents various topics for younger readers with clear, appealing illustrations integrated

Illustration of a banana tree by artist Alan E. Cober. Copyright ©1969 by Alan E. Cober. Reprinted from Your Friend, the Tree by Florence M. White, illustrated by Alan E. Cober, by permission of Alfred A. Knopf, Inc.

into the text. *Weight and Weightlessness* (35) by Franklyn Branley graphically portrays weightlessness as having nothing to do with distance from the earth but rather with whether or not rocket power is being used in connection with

Illustration of a fruit fly from THE GOLDEN BOOK OF BIOLOGY by Gerald Ames and Rose Wyler, illustrated by Charles Harper. ©1967, 1961 by Western Publishing Company, Inc. Reprinted by permission of the publisher.

experiences of the astronauts. In *Hot As an Ice Cube* (36) by Philip Balestrino, a part of the kinetic-molecular theory is explained as the distinction between heat and temperature. Another book in this series, *At Last to the Ocean: The Story of the Endless Cycle of Water* (37) by Joel Rothman, explains the hydrologic cycle via photos with a minimum of text. These are not easy subjects, but young readers will find them intriguing and clearly presented.

What Did the Dinosaurs Eat? (38) by Wilda Ross poses an intriguing question for dinosaur lovers. That many of those gigantic ancient animals were plant eaters comes as a surprise to many children. This book capitalizes on this surprise and interest and provides a history of the plant kingdom during the Mesosozic Era.

Simple projects that require no equipment can be carried out as a result of working with the book by Seymour Simon, *Let's Try It Out . . . Hot and Cold* (39). This is but one of the wide selection of experiment books for younger readers.

Factual books for middle readers sometimes focus on the functioning of the human body. *The Human Body: The Skeleton* (40) by Kathleen Elgin discusses the usefulness of the entire skeletal structure, a topic of general interest likely to ensnare the reader even though its presentation seems limited to facts rather than inquiry. *Your Brain and How It Works* (41) by Herbert Zim gives insight into

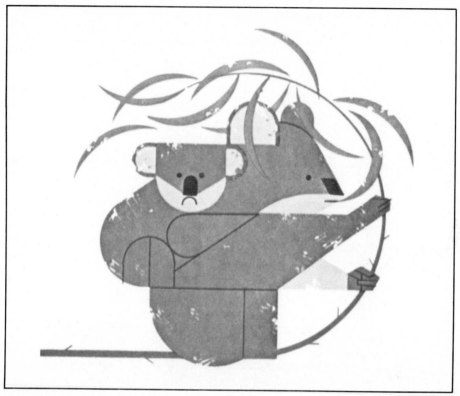

A mother koala bear and her baby. Illustration from THE ANIMAL KINGDOM by George S. Fichter, illustrated by Charles Harper. ©1968 by Western Publishing Company, Inc. Reprinted by permission of the publisher.

the formation of the brain, its growth structure, and the concept of mind. (Note, too, other science books by this able writer.)

Space Age Spinoffs: Space Program Benefits for All (42) by C. B. Colby brings awareness of products and devices used in everyday life that came about as a result of the space program, including shock-absorbing and fire-fighting equipment.

Science Experiments You Can Eat (43) by Vicki Cobb and *Grocery Store Botany* (44) by Joan Elma Rahn are inquiry-oriented, naturally motivating books that lead to gastronomical satisfaction.

Although the publication date is not current, *Bionics* (45) by Vincent Marteka is still distinguished for its clear definition and description of experiments in the bionics field. Several interesting examples of the results of bionic research are included: for instance, the study of the frog's eye developed into an electronic eye model for target systems, and research on dolphins resulted in a method of reducing the drag of a ship moving through water.

How Animals Learn (46) by Russell Freedman and James Morriss includes the landmark experiments of Pavlov, Konrad Lorenz, the monkey studies of Har-

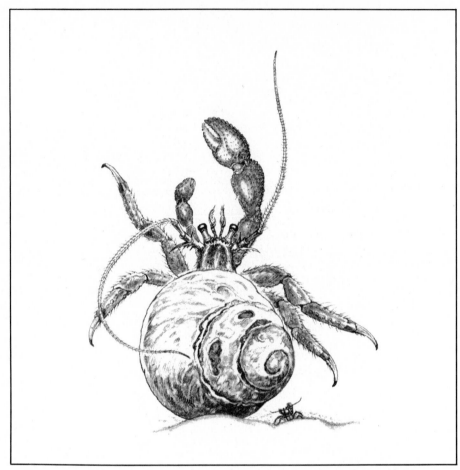

PAGOO **is the life story of a** ***pagurus,*** **or Hermit Crab.** Copyright ©1957 by Holling Clancy Holling. Reprinted by permission of the publisher, Houghton Mifflin Company.

low, and others. Sample experiments to be conducted with pets to test their problem-solving ability are also included, the most intriguing of which is "How to teach an earthworm to move over the correct course in a maze." A companion volume by the same authors, *Animal Instincts* (47), has a similar format and spirit of inquiry.

Snakes: The Facts and the Folklore (48) by Hilda Simon is an excellently illustrated, well-organized and highly informative book about venomous and non-venomous snakes. *Pieces of Another World: The Story of Moon Rocks* (49) by Franklyn Branley tells how rocks from the moon were gathered and describes techniques used for analysis, the results of analysis, and the questions raised by the discovery pertinent to theories of the moon's origin and history.

Illustration of mother prairie dog and her young. From THE ANIMAL KINGDOM by George S. Fichter, illustrated by Charles Harper. ©1968 by Western Publishing Company, Inc. Reprinted by permission of the publisher.

This is but a sampling of topics and selections offered to nonfiction readers in the field of science. With a bit of motivation (a selection read aloud, an initiating film), children can experience a variety of books based on related topics, permitting useful comparisons. For instance, a group of children with a wide range of reading abilities can examine and share their findings from books about whales, including *The Mother Whale* (50) by Edith Thacher Hurd, *The Whale Hunters* (51) by Joseph Phelan, *Little Calf* (52) by Victor B. Scheffer, and a related topic concerning archaeological discoveries about the Makah Indians of the Northwest, *Hunters of the Whale* (53) by Ruth Kirk with Richard D. Daugherty.

special activities

1. Examine and evaluate series books dealing with science. Use criteria discussed in the preceding section, as well as your own criteria. A good example is the Science I Can Read series published by Harper & Row, all aimed at the primary level. Titles in this series include the following:

   Shaw, E. *Alligator.* Illus. Frances Zweifel. Harper, 1972. (E)
   Myrick, Mildred. *Ants Are Fun.* Illus. Arnold Lobel. Harper, 1968. (E)
   Selsam, Millicent E. *Benny's Animals: How He Put Them in Order.* Illus. Arnold Lobel. Harper, 1966. (E)
   Selsam, Millicent E. *Greg's Microscope.* Illus. Arnold Lobel. Harper, 1973. (E)
   Shaw, Evelyn. *Octopus.* Illus. Ralph Carpentier. Harper, 1971. (E)
   Selsam, Millicent E. *When an Animal Grows.* Illus. John Kaufmann. Harper, 1966. (E)

   Many books in this series contain narratives or stories with factual material worked into the plot. How useful is this device? It is also used in the Beginner Book series published by Random House, which includes *Ann Can Fly* (54) and *The Whales Go By* (55) both by Fred Phleger. See also various titles in the Let's Read and Find Out series published by Crowell and the True Book series published by Grosset and Dunlap and Children's Press, all for early childhood. Compare your evaluations with those of other people.

2. Biographies for early childhood include the lives of scientists. Examine and evaluate several of these, applying previously discussed criteria. See, for example, *A Weed Is a Flower: The Life of George Washington Carver* (56) by Aliki and *The Heart Man: Dr. Daniel Hale Williams* (57) by Louise Meriwether. The latter will require reading aloud to young children. What concepts in these biographies will require expansion beyond that given in the text and illustrations? Discuss.

3. When you examine science books for young children, place yourself in the role of the child. Specific information presented with concrete detail is not so difficult as one might think. For instance, look at the details about the Ailanthus tree, the earthworm's activity, and the birds taking dust baths in Ruth Howell's *A Crack in the Pavement* (58). On the other hand, abstract vocabulary may be difficult, and at times it may mask rather simple concepts. In *A Walk in the Snow* (59) by Phyllis S. Busch, for instance, a discussion of snowflakes includes the statement: "A magnifier would make them appear larger." How useful, how understandable is such a statement? What criteria for evaluating concept load and vocabulary load can you devise?

4. Now use the criteria for evaluating an assortment of books for older children. There is a theme dealing with ecology in *Animal Invaders: The Story of Imported Wildlife* (60) by Alvin and Virginia Silverstein. How well is that theme illustrated through the chapter examples? The science of geochronology is his-

torically treated in *Clocks for the Ages: How Scientists Date the Past* (61) by Robert Silverberg. The presentation is not inquiry-oriented, but the factual information, including discoveries dealing with radioactivity and the hoax of the Piltdown Man, will arouse curiosity and broaden interest. Discuss the role of information-giving books, such as the following:

Simon, Hilda. *Dragonflies.* Viking, 1972. (I-U)

Hogner, Dorothy Childs. *Good Bugs and Bad Bugs in Your Garden: Backyard Ecology.* Illus. Grambs Miller. Crowell, 1974. (I)

Brown, Billye Walker, and Brown, Walter R. *Historical Catastrophes: Hurricanes and Tornadoes.* Addison-Wesley, 1972. (I-U)

Klopfer, Peter H. *On Behavior: Instinct Is a Cheshire Cat.* Illus. Martha Wittles. Lippincott, 1973. (I-U)

Spinar, Z. V. *Life Before Man.* Illus. Z. Burlan. American Heritage, 1972. (I-U)

Carlisle, Norman. *The New American Continent—Our Continental Shelf.* Lippincott, 1973. (U)

Berger, Melvin. *Oceanography Lab.* Day, 1973. (I-U)

Bova, Ben. *Starflight and Other Improbabilities.* Westminster, 1973. (I-U)

Laycock, George. *Wingspread: A World of Birds.* Four Winds, 1972. (I-U)

Headstrom, Richard. *Your Insect Pet.* McKay, 1973. (I-U)

Although inquiry is stressed in modern science curricula, the role of nonfiction books in stimulating discussion and providing a store of knowledge should not be overlooked. How might books such as these be used in an inquiry curriculum? How might you present them within an inquiry mode? How would you introduce them to expand interests as well as to meet expressed interests?

Mathematics Books

The format and complexity of mathematics series books aimed at younger readers vary greatly even within a series. Widely known are the Easy Book series published by Watts, the older True Book series published by Children's Press, and the Young Math books published by Crowell. Many of the Easy Book volumes are written by David C. Whitney, with various illustrators. Whitney involves the reader with questions and activities aimed at developing a concept; see, for example, *The Easy Book of Numbers and Numerals* (62). To some extent, the True Book series lacks appealing graphics, as in the bare silhouettes accompanying *The True Book of Numbers* (63) by Philip Carona, but the text is simple enough to be read by beginning readers. Young Math books explore more complex topics, using up-to-date, "new math" language and concepts, as in *Shadow Geometry* (64) by Daphne Harwood Trivett and *A Game of Functions* (65) by Robert Froman. Each book in these series can stimulate investigation, sharpen mathematics vocabulary by amplifying a single concept, and augment work done through texts and classroom activity. In fact, the vocabulary and concept load of many modern mathematics programs in early grades would seem to invite such supplementary reading and looking. In addition to the series, many single titles are available, including the clear, involving work of Irving and Ruth Adler—for example, *Numbers and Sets for the Very Young* (66).

The metric system has been the subject of a great number of books for intermediate and upper levels. Reviewers are of great help in making choices. *Meter Means Measure* (67) by S. Carl Hirsch is intended to persuade the reader that metric measure must be adopted universally, while in *Metric Measure* (68) Herbert S. Zim and James R. Skelly are content to present the history of metrics and a clear explanation of its use. For upper levels, two books give a full account of the manner in which the system will be used in the future: *The Metric System: Measures for All Mankind* (69) by Frank Ross, Jr. and *Metric Is Here!* (70) by William Moore.

Activities books in mathematics range from rather meaningless, catchy topics to real problems with pertinence to the development of thinking skills. To the layman, these are refreshing, since they are less encumbered with terminology associated with newer mathematics content; they seem better suited to inquiry. *Let's Play Math* (71) by Michael Holt and Zoltan Dienes exemplifies books written to be used by parents in playing math games with children of intermediate age levels. For children themselves, activities books include *Puzzles and Quizzles* (72) by Helen Jill Fletcher, *Math Menagerie* (73) by Robert R. Kadesch, and *A Miscellany of Puzzles* (74) by Stephen Barr—and there are many others. We'd especially recommend that you examine *Math Menagerie* for its great range of pertinent topics: optical transformers, a coded card deck, an investigation of Pascal's probability device, the binary system.

special activities

1. Compare children's book and textbook samples in mathematics. What different purposes are served by these two types?

2. Select a unit topic from a mathematics curriculum for any age level you wish. Using sources and reviews, devise a book list to use with this unit. Evaluate the books and share your findings with classmates or with teachers and parents—and with children.

CHILDREN'S BOOKS AND THE SOCIAL STUDIES CURRICULUM

by Mary Jett Simpson
University of Wisconsin–Milwaukee

Social studies curricula offer varied opportunities for using children's books to provide information and enjoyment, to inspire inquiry into values, and to promote problem solving. Here is a brief overview of some of the curricular changes in the social studies, followed by criteria for selecting children's books in this field and discussion of a few exemplary works.

Social Studies Curricula

Teaching materials in social studies vary greatly from area to area and school to school. You'll find classrooms in which a single traditional textbook is used and others in which a program such as MACOS[1] is used. This program includes student booklets, records, filmstrips, maps, posters, photomurals, games, cards, animals studies, observation projects, worksheets, journals, poems, songs, stories, and films—a veritable social science laboratory.

Curriculum content will vary even more than the materials themselves. Bruce Joyce has traced the evolution of the social studies curriculum from 1920 to the present, showing that the dominant pattern of expanding horizons (family, community, nation, world) has gradually been transformed into the broader problem-solving "study of man and his relationships with his social and physical environments."[2] The dimensions of the emerging social studies curriculum, according to Joyce, are intellectual, social, and personal. The intellectual emphasizes application of the tools of scholars, including analysis and problem-solving strategies. The purpose of the intellectual dimension is to assist children in using a solid knowledge-information base to identify and solve social problems. The social dimension emphasizes experiences that will help children operate effectively in society. The personal dimension includes activities to guide children in sorting out the confusion of the social world and finding meaning in their lives.

The array of disciplines, topics, and facets of exploration involved in the emerging curriculum is indeed wide. Disciplines involved include anthropology, sociology, history, political science, social psychology, economics, and geography. The social dimension includes concerns about racial attitudes, internationalism, interpersonal behavior and recognition of stereotypes, urban affairs, national heritage, and citizenship. The personal dimension is concerned with creativity, sensitivity, personality, mental health, and the development of open-mindedness.[3]

From this, it is apparent that the social studies constitute an amalgam. A variety of types of materials and a range in difficulty of materials must be sought to give a firm base for accomplishing the objectives of this field. In many cases, textbook materials provide insufficient coverage, and often these materials are too difficult for the average reader. Johnson and Vardian found, for instance, that over half the current social studies textbooks are one or more grade levels above that designated by the publishers.[4] This fact plus characteristics such as

---

[1]*Man: A Course of Study* (Curriculum Development Associates, 1970). Located in Washington, D.C.
[2]Bruce Joyce, *New Strategies for Social Education* (Science Research Associates, 1972), pp. 1–29.
[3]p. 26.
[4]Roger Johnson and Eileen B. Vardian, "Reading, Readability, and Social Studies," *Reading Teacher* 26 (February 1973): 483–88.

high fact load, difficult vocabulary, and abstract concepts indicate a need for other materials to supplement the texts. Here we'll cite a few suggestions, along with criteria for selection. Although our emphasis will be upon nonfiction, some fiction titles are included, for these, too, should be included in the study.[1]

Criteria for Selecting Children's Books in Social Studies

A well-written children's book may help increase a child's interest in the topic being studied. It may enlarge and deepen concepts, increasing understanding and acting as a catalyst for further exploration. Categories of useful books include information books, historical fiction, biography, autobiography, realistic fiction, folk tales, myths, and poetry.

The contribution of information books to a social studies program is obvious, but why include the other kinds mentioned above as potential resources? First, they reflect and illustrate samples of various cultures, and the values of peoples in each of the three dimensions suggested by Joyce. Second, many social studies concepts are not directly within children's past experience so teachers must work with children's books to build a vicarious experience base. Third, children's books can motivate a topic of study, drawing children irresistibly into enthusiastic pursuit of a topic.

The criteria discussed in conjunction with science and mathematics books in the preceding section are applicable here. In addition, consider the following:

- *Excellence in writing.* Search out books that capture reader interest and clearly communicate their contents.
- *Accuracy of information.* As with science materials, books pertaining to social studies must include facts without distorting events.
- *Levels of reading difficulty.* It's important to provide a range of difficulty in books selected and to aid children to select them according to difficulty.
- *Ease of locating information within a book.* Look for organizing features—headings, index, and style of presentation.

As you select books on a given topic, you'll need to consider other features. For example, look at books that present multi-ethnic groups. Is their treatment fair? Do they help to examine stereotypes without falling into stereotypical patterns themselves? David Gast has discussed some of the pitfalls of certain children's books dealing with minority ethnic groups, including the "noble savage" approach, the "queer customs" approach, and the "white man's burden" approach.[2] Such pitfalls are avoided when a book provides a balanced presentation, including positive aspects and problem areas in a way of life. For example, examine these balanced presentations:

---

[1]See "Notable Children's Trade Books in the Field of Social Studies" (no author cited), *Social Education* 37 (December 1973): 784–92.
[2]David Gast, "The Dawning of the Age of Aquarius for Multiethnic Children's Literature," *Elementary English* 47 (May 1970): 661–65.

Sidewalk Story (75) by Sharon Bell Mathis is a realistic fiction story of the ghetto, where one strong-willed child, Lilly Etta, uses friendship to subvert eviction of a neighbor.

Chicanos: The Story of Mexican Americans (76) by Patricia de Garza is a balanced, factual account of the history of Mexican Americans, their contributions to American culture, and their struggles for recognition.

American Indian Women (77) by Marion E. Gridley contains eighteen well-rounded, brief biographies of Indian women who excelled in various careers in history and modern life.

PROVIDING A BALANCE.   No single book or type of book can cover all facets of social studies. Your best strategy is to select an array of materials that complement each other, while insuring that most selections meet basic criteria such as those suggested above. A good selection often accomplishes more than mere coverage of its topic. The personal dimension is explored through human interaction in *Sidewalk Story,* involving a theme much broader than black Americans alone. The inspiring narratives of *American Indian Women,* depicting women seeking success in difficult circumstances, become an investigation of how people surmount obstacles universally. There is a universal balance to consider.

Now we'll illustrate the use of criteria in selecting children's books to achieve this kind of balance.

Mexican Americans: The Chicano Movement

In carefully guided reading and study, the strengths and weaknesses of materials about Mexican Americans and the Chicano movement can be turned into positive learning. But this kind of balanced analysis has to be kept in mind as the books are discussed.

For example, *Chicanos: Mexicans in the United States* (78) by Patricia Martin skirts some important issues and implies that the problems of migrant workers are virtually solved. If you contrast this book with others that include this topic, you'll have a basis for critical discussion and an impetus for further search. *Cesar Chavez* (79) by Ruth Franchere shows one man's efforts to improve the lot of migrant workers. Evelyn Lampman's fictional *Go Up the Road* (80) presents the topic from the point of view of a twelve-year-old Chicana heroine, while *Small Hands, Big Hands: Seven Profiles of Chicano Migrant Workers and Their Families* (81) by Sandra Weiner gives factual evidence through taped interview transcriptions and masterful photographs.

The emergence of Mexican-American culture patterns from their sources can be understood from a novel, *Crossroads for Chela* (82), by Dorothy Witton and an excellent autobiography, *Barrio Boy* (83), by Ernest Galarza. A recent biography, *Juarez, Man of Law* (84), by Newbery Medal winner Elizabeth Borton de Treviño, will add to the background. These are just a sampling of the excellent works available on this topic.

Black Americans

Nonfiction books can provide the knowledge to serve as a basis for decision making in the social and personal dimensions of the social studies. As contrasted with the more general treatment in textbooks, nonfiction books focus on a specific aspect of a topic. Consider American history and more specifically the Civil Rights movement—especially this plea from a nineteenth-century ex-slave:

> In all the books that you have studied you never have studied Negro history, have you? You studied about the Indian and white folks, but what did they tell you about the Negro? If you want Negro history, you will have to get it from somebody who wore the shoe, and by and by from one to the other, you will get a book.[1]

Tear Down the Walls! A History of the American Civil Rights Movement (85) by Dorothy Sterling is a dynamically written account of the movement's historical roots and major events prior to Martin Luther King's assassination. Julius Lester's *To Be a Slave* (86) contains specific oral testimony of slaves from the nineteenth century American Anti-Slavery Society, the Federal Writer's Workshop of the 1930s, and other sources. Here the social and personal dimensions of the social studies are served. But so is the intellectual dimension when children are asked to examine the data collection process in *To Be a Slave* and assess the accuracy of Lester's historical research in assembling the accounts under common headings. (See p. 375 for a list of other nonfiction books on this topic.)

The study of race relations also offers opportunity to explore personal emotions and values. Pertinent here are the various models for value clarification such as the Taba valuing model.[2] Taba's plan involves a series of questions for discussion. While these can be based on nonfiction books, they may also be directed at clarification through the use of fiction and poetry. For example, the level of "Exploring Feelings" begins with a literal re-statement of the information, followed by discussion of characters' feelings and readers' own conjectures about how *they* might have felt in the situation. Subsequently an "Analysis of Values" level is attempted, with questions aimed at discovering why people acted as they did and how their actions reveal differing value systems. The question sequence prescribed by Taba is intended to help the readers clarify their own value systems and, ultimately, to aid in the development of wholesome values, more clearly and rationally evolved. Note that informational accounts have their counterparts in fiction. For instance, Lorenz Graham's trilogy—*South Town* (87), *North Town* (88), and *Whose Town* (89)—depicts a family's early suffering, their move to a "promised land," and the eruptions of the 1960s.

---

[1]Quoted in Julius Lester, *To Be a Slave* (Dial, 1968), Frontispiece.
[2]See James A. Banks with Ambrose A. Clegg, Jr., *Teaching Strategies for the Social Studies: Inquiry, Valuing and Decision-Making* (Addison-Wesley, 1973), chapter 12, pp. 445–77.

Native Americans

Nonfiction history and historical fiction can often be successfully combined, as we mentioned in chapter 6. In fact, historical fiction may often be the best choice to initiate a topic of study. Scott O'Dell's *Sing Down the Moon* (90) tells, through fictitious characters, of the impact of the Navajo march three hundred miles to incarceration at Ft. Sumner, New Mexico. Its theme, the consequence of an act of oppression, is more vividly borne out than would be possible in nonfiction.

booklist

Nonfiction Books about Black Americans

Harnan, Terry. *African Rhythm—American Dance: A Biography of Katherine Dunham.* Illus. with photos. Knopf, 1974. (I-U) Biography of the great dancer; describes her research into authentic African and Haitian dance.

Jackson, Florence. *The Black Man in America, 1861–1877* and *The Black Man in America, 1877–1905.* Watts, 1972, 1973. (I-U) Two good basic books. Readers will be particularly interested in the nontraditional presentation of Lincoln's role in history portrayed here.

Feelings, Tom. *Black Pilgrimage.* Lothrop, Lee, 1972. (E-I) Autobiographical sketch of the artist's development and "black consciousness."

Jordan, June. *Dry Victories.* Holt, 1972. (I-U) The unusual format of this book is a dialog between two black teenagers, with focus on the Reconstruction and Civil Rights eras.

Banks, James A. *March toward Freedom: A History of Black Americans.* Fearon, 1970. (I-U) Resource book for students of black history.

Hamilton, Virginia. *Paul Robeson: The Life and Times of a Free Black Man.* Illus. with photos. Harper, 1974. (U) A biography that includes the subject's achievements as athlete and entertainer, as well as the political turmoil in the 1950s.

Halliburton, Warren. *The Picture Life of Jesse Jackson.* Watts, 1972. (E) The photographs give much support to this biography, which traces Jackson's early encounters with prejudice to his work as a peaceful resister to prejudice.

Mann, Peggy. *Ralph Bunche: UN Peacekeeper.* Coward, 1974. (I-U) Good biography of a great international peace leader.

Hirsch, Carl. *The Riddle of Racism.* Viking, 1972. (U) Historical and modern information on the problems of race relations and the concept of race.

Kaufman, Michael. *Rooftops and Alleys: Adventures with a City Kid.* Photos by Lee Romero. Knopf, 1973. (I) Semi-documentary adventures of a super street kid.

McGovern, Ann. *Runaway Slave, the Story of Harriet Tubman.* School Book Service, 1965. (E-I) Biography of Harriet Tubman—how she led hundreds of slaves to freedom through the Underground Railroad.

An intermediate-level biography of a famous Native American and great ballet dancer, Maria Tallchief. From MARIA TALLCHIEF by Tobi Tobias, illustrated by Michael Hampshire. Copyright © 1970 by Tobi Tobias; illustrations copyright ©1970 by Michael Hampshire; with permission of Thomas Y. Crowell Co., Inc., publisher.

It focuses on the personal dimension. One way to examine this focus is to relate specific events to feelings: the hunt, accompanied by feelings of boldness and confidence; the Spaniard attack by anger; the incarceration and deprivation of food by defeat and shame; the escape by hope and renewed self-respect. Such a comparison can be graphically portrayed on a time line as you read the book with children.

In similar manner, other fiction can be introduced. For example, *Ride the Crooked Wind* (91) by Dale Fife tells of a twelve-year-old Paiute reared by his grandmother to respect the "old ways" as part of ideal life. When the grandmother becomes ill, the boy must go to boarding school, where he faces the inevitable conflict of value systems. *High Elk's Treasure* (92) by Virginia Driving Hawk Sneve describes a youth's reservation life and an important historical discovery. Sneve's *Jimmy Yellow Hawk* (93) won first prize in the category of Indian stories written by an Indian in the 1971 Council on Interracial Books for Children

booklist

Nonfiction Books about Native Americans

Hoyt, Olga. *American Indians Today.* Abelard-Schuman, 1973. (U) Excellent reference for use in discerning the problems of many tribes in the United States today.

Baker, Betty. *The Big Push.* Coward, 1973. (E-I) True incident in Hopi Indian history, when children were forced to go to school and experienced severe conflict between two cultures.

Baldwin, Gordon. *How the Indians Really Lived.* Putnam, 1967. (I-U) Information about major Indian tribes in nine large areas.

Hofsinde, Robert (Gray Wolf). *Indian Music Makers.* Morrow, 1967. (I) A wealth of information on the role of music under topics such as games, crafts, beadwork, and horses.

Marriott, Alice. *Indians on Horseback,* rev. ed. Illus. Margaret Lefranc. Crowell, 1968. (I) Plains Indians and the development of their culture from the sixteenth century to mid-nineteenth century.

Carlson, Sherrill. *The Northwest Coast Indians ABC Book.* Photos Charles K. Peck. State Street Press, Pullman Washington, 1972. (E) A lovely book showing the Northwest Indians today with the influence of their historical culture.

Lampman, Evelyn. *Once upon the Little Big Horn.* Illus. John Gretzer. Crowell, 1971. (I) Battle of the Little Big Horn told first from one point of view, then the other.

Tamerin, Alfred A. *We Have Not Vanished: Eastern Indians of the United States.* Follett, 1974. (I) Documentary study, historical and modern.

Brown, Dee. *Wounded Knee: An Indian History of the American West.* Adapted by Amy Ehrlich. Holt, 1974. (U) Simplified version of *Bury My Heart at Wounded Knee.*

Kirk, Ruth. *David, Young Chief of the Quileutes.* Harcourt, 1967. (E) Through this biography of David Hudson (Hoheeshata), readers can view the customs of the Quileutes, a Northwest tribe, and the life of a Native American in contemporary settings of the wider culture.

contest. The strength of these books is that they break the stereotypical "tepees and feathers" image and at the same time provide a pleasurable story with believable characters.

Poetry can also provide a fine entry to a study of Native Americans. There is a growing collection of Indian poetry, including Hettie Jones's *The Trees Stand Shining* (94), Terry Allen's collection, *The Whispering Wind* (95), and *Songs of the Chippewa* (96) edited by John Bierhorst. You will find, side by side, poems of protest and poems celebrating life with a deep reverence for nature.

Nonfiction books—histories and biographies included—are more readily available than they were a few years ago. These are a remarkable addition to children's books and their effect may be as important as any other in refocusing American values. We have listed a few such works on p. 377.

Native American history and biography form the subjects of many volumes to be found among the entire lists of three distinguished series: the Challenger Books for intermediate and upper levels, published by Random House, the Crowell Biographies for Children Just Beginning to Read, and the Firebird Library, paperbacks for the intermediate and upper levels, published by Scholastic.

Women's Roles and the Feminist Movement

As you read of women's struggle to define their roles along humanistic lines and to have these roles accepted by the total society, you may gain the impression that this concern is a new one. History shows otherwise. A long tradition of women who struggled for equality is disclosed through biographies of the past as well as the present. The women in American history whose biographies are briefly told in Johanna Johnston's *Women Themselves* (97) sought recognition in many fields. They were aware of the ruling society's attempts to subordinate them and they set out valiantly to overcome prejudice. Many—from Anne Hutchinson to Phillis Wheatley to Nellie Bly to Carrie Chapman Catt—succeeded in furthering the cause of women's rights. Full-length biographies, such as Ellen Wilson's *American Painter in Paris: A Life of Mary Cassatt* (98), reveal that women in the past, as today, recognized their problems as akin to those of unaccepted minorities.

Today the role perceptions of women as homemakers, child caretakers, teachers, nurses, and secretaries is expanding to include women as participants in all careers. The options for participation in all phases of life are viewed by society in a new light. The struggle for equality has its bitter moments, but at least it does seem that society is seeking to correct its weaknesses, to act upon its stated tenets of equality.

Not long ago, books for children, particularly textbooks, were predominantly male-oriented. The argument ran that one must appeal to male interests: "Please the boys and the girls will go along with it." Various studies of children's books

Emma Willard, seated at center of table, leads her students from the Troy Female Seminary through an eight-day public examination. Reprinted by permission of Dodd, Mead & Company, Inc. from *WOMEN THEMSELVES* by Johanna Johnston, illustrated by Deanne Hollinger. Copyright ©1973 by Johanna Johnston.

of the recent past attest to such discrimination.[1] As many have pointed out, literary works contained a majority of male characters in central roles. They cast female characters in subordinate, passive roles. They often included as "typical" disparaging comments about females: "I'm just a girl, but I can climb a tree almost as well as a boy can." Recognized now is the fact that such values are unfair to women and, in addition, are not conducive to the full development of males.

So, belatedly, the total view of women's roles as they might be and should be is permeating children's books. We find, first, an outpouring of books directed at equalizing and re-defining women's roles. Just as important, though more difficult to assess at the moment of change, books on nearly all topics begin to reflect a broadened, deepened sense of womanhood.

We've attempted throughout our book discussions to present some of the works that portray women in central active roles in fiction. You might briefly review these—works such as those by Carole Bolton, Sylvia Louise Engdahl, Jean Craighead George, and others. In addition to biographies cited above, look for recent composites such as *An Album of Women in American History* (99) by Claire and Leonard Ingraham, *Women of the West* (100) by Dorothy Levenson, and *Young and Female* (101) edited by Pat Ross. The latter is especially noteworthy, containing accounts taken directly from autobiographies of eight modern women (Shirley MacLaine, Althea Gibson, Margaret Bourke-White, and others) at times when a conflict with traditionally assigned roles was displayed. Biographies of volume length include excellent, non-sexist material; see, for example, *Marian Anderson* (102) by Tobi Tobias, *Felisa Rincon De Gautier: The Mayor of San Juan* (103) by Ruth Gauber, *Martha Berry* (104) by Mary Kay Phelan, and *Israel's Golda Meir: Pioneer to Prime Minister* (105) by Iris Noble.

Factual accounts of women's career opportunities today are an important facet of the social studies. An excellent collection of first-hand statements of women in such occupations as physician, oceanographer, carpenter, and bank vice-president is *Saturday's Child: 36 Women Talk about Their Jobs* (106) compiled by Suzanne Seed. The "What Can I Be?" series includes *What Can She Be? An Architect* (107) by Gloria and Esther Goldreich and others. Norma Klein's *Girls Can Be Anything* (108) opens the possibility of varied careers, this time for the reading enlightenment of children of early years. In addition, see appropriate topics in *Subject Guide to Children's Books,* including "Women as Physicians," "Women in Aeronautics," "Women as Scientists," and "Women in Politics."

Free But Not Equal: How Women Won the Right to Vote (109) by Bill Severn is one of several histories of the women's suffrage movement,[2] a topic that is also

---

[1]See, for example, Betty Levy and Judith Stacey, "Sexism in the Elementary School: A Backward and Forward Look," *Phi Delta Kappan* 55 (October 1973): 105–9+. This article summarizes other studies of stereotyping in textbooks. See also "A Feminist Look at Children's Books" by Feminists on Children's Literature, *School Library Journal* 17 (January 1971): 19-24.

[2]See also Elaine Landau, *Woman, Woman!: Feminism in America* (Julian Messner, 1974). This upper level book reviews the achievements of women in America, including advancements in employment, sex roles, health care, and education.

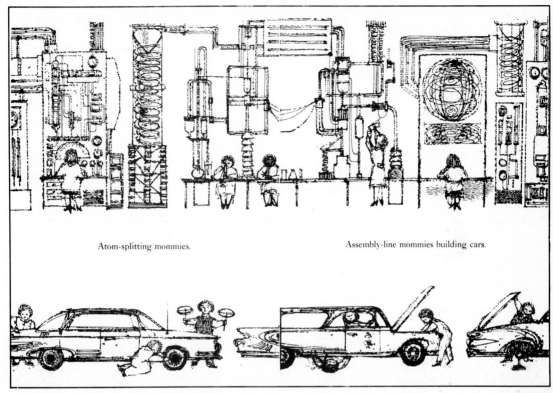

Atom-splitting mommies.

Assembly-line mommies building cars.

From MOMMIES AT WORK by Eve Merriam, illustrated by Beni Montresor. Copyright ©1961 by Eve Merriam and Beni Montresor. Reprinted by permission of Alfred A. Knopf, Inc.

receiving increasing coverage in fiction. *Girls Are Girls and Boys Are Boys So What's the Difference?* (110) by Sol Gordon is a candid look at the myths of sexism. Janet Harris's *Single Standard* (111) and Lucy Komisar's *New Feminism* (112) are confrontations with the issue, while *Girls Are Equal Too: The Women's Movement for Teenagers* (113) by Dale Carlson puts the conflict in stronger language, asserting that "a woman can be a woman without being treated like a slave, an inferior, a possession, or a child."[1] Such a statement should also alert protectors of children's rights.

Ecology

Consciousness of people's impact on the environment has at last become an important topic of study and of action. There's a great range in the materials about ecology. Bill Peet's *The Wump World* (114) is a blatant "hard sell" fiction book in which fanciful creatures must figure out what to do when they're invaded by polluters. Didactic though it is, the book can be easily dramatized

---

[1]p. 112.

—one class used it effectively for a puppet play—and can have impact when you want a source for motivating interest in the subject. Similarly, *Who Cares? I Do* (115) by Munro Leaf and *Dinosaurs and All That Rubbish* (116) by Michael Foreman are calls to action—sometimes useful motivators to a deeper study of ecological problems.

It's heartening to find that ecology-minded authors and illustrators haven't neglected early childhood as an audience for their works. Of many fine examples, several are especially noteworthy. For instance, Virginia Lee Burton's semi-fanciful *The Little House* (117) remains an effective, honest study of the effects of environmental change. *Ladybug, Ladybug, Fly Away Home* (118) by Judy Hawes is aglow with appreciation for small living things in the world, an appreciation that underlies ecological consciousness. *All upon a Stone* (119) by Jean Craighead George is a fictional account in narrative form of a mole cricket, but it provides relevant information to the budding ecologist. Harris Stone's *The Last Free Bird* (120) is perhaps too severe in its projection of the effects of man's domination. Isaac Asimov's *ABC's of Ecology* (121) is a book-length glossary, an excellent base for deepening study.

The field of ecology is an instance of merging curricula: science and social studies must be combined to study it realistically. There is, for example, a scientific emphasis in some ecology-oriented materials about biological life: *Life in a Bucket of Soil* (122) by Richard Rhine, *Good Bugs and Bad Bugs in Your Garden: Backyard Ecology* (123) by Dorothy Childs Hogner, *Animal Territories* (124) by Daniel Cohen, and *Animal Invaders: The Story of Imported Wildlife* by Alvin and Virginia Silverstein. But these are also sources of data to use in problem-confrontation in social studies. Scientific knowledge is the foundation but not the major theme of non-propagandist, objective books that explore the social dimensions of ecological problems. *Who Will Drown the Sound?* (125) by C. M. Hutchins and *Pollution: The Noise We Hear* (126) by C. Jones are important for presenting an often neglected part of the topic, each with an emphasis on the social and personal dimensions. *The Shrinking Outdoors* (127) by Gary Jennings compares today's environment with that of earlier times and makes its point: that immediate concern and action are necessary if we are to save the natural world. The implicit theme of *Wild Green Things in the City: A Book of Weeds* (128) by Anne Dowden and *City Lots: Living Things in Vacant Spots* (129) by Phyllis Busch is that a society facing increasing urbanization must also face new problems in conserving nature.

Not all of these books, nor the many others on ecology, meet the criteria for high quality literature. Since widespread recognition of ecological problems is comparatively new, there are, inevitably, books that create an awareness but fail to provide a sound knowledge base. But if you search, you can find well-informed, balanced, well-written presentations.

Our emphasis in this brief review of books pertinent to the social studies has been on issues—of minorities' rights, of the need to re-define women's roles, and of the issue of correcting the balance in our environment. Issues are only a part of the full scope of the social studies. Included also are understandings of interpersonal relations, the recognition and appreciation of the broad cultural heritage, the concepts of law and total patterns of living together to attain maximum potential. These are the themes in a wide variety of nonfiction. If freely available, children's books can promote independent learning in the social studies.

special activities

1. Select one ethnic group not discussed in this section. Using sources described in chapter 1, list titles in nonfiction, fiction, and poetry that pertain to the topic. Share your list. Discuss availability of titles. Which ethnic groups are in need of additional materials in children's literature? Study recent reviews to determine whether these needs are being fulfilled.

2. Plan a sequence of reading and related activities for exploring a topic in the social studies. The topic may be historical, modern informative, or related to a cause. Which type of book will you present first, in order to motivate? What activities will you use along with it? What type of book, what specific titles, would be suitable for helping define the issue and for bringing to bear information about the topic?

3. Two types of questions or activities are especially pertinent to nonfiction in the social studies. The first can be called "translation"—the conversion of information into another form. The information from a portion of a nonfiction book might be converted into a collage, a chart, a simple outline, a dramatization, a demonstration of a process, a dance, a mobile, a mural, or any number of other products. The problem is to match a translation activity with information in such a manner as to bring new understanding coupled with creativity. List titles and portions of selected works and, beside them, note translation activities that might aid in enlivening the information contained in them. The second type of question is "synthesis"—in this case, the production of a problem-solving work that takes into account the information as well as the cause-effect process involved. For example, what ideas for solving a noise-pollution problem can you and your children originate as a result of reading about the problem? Again, the problem-solving ideas should be expressed in some appropriate manner: a letter to authorities, a puppet play to inform others, a story or poem written for a specific audience. Devise a synthesis activity to go with a nonfiction book you've selected for use in the social studies. Discuss the values of translation and synthesis items in eliciting response to books such as those discussed in this section.

4. In addition to published reviews, authorities in various areas of the social studies are needed to help select good materials. List authorities who might help you in selecting books for your social studies curriculum.

5. Compare a textbook treatment and a children's book treatment of a topic in the social studies. How, for instance, do the two categories of books present problems of immigrants in modern America? How do they portray the shifting life styles of people who move from rural areas to the city? How do they examine career choices open to young people? Choose a specific topic or theme; tell how you might use textbooks and children's books to complement each other.

CHILDREN'S BOOKS AND THE ARTS

A mockingbird perches on the topmost twig of the tallest tree in the neighborhood and begins just after midnight to sing an incredible song, pausing at the double-bars to fly straight up ten feet and back again to his perch, continuing his aria until well after summer dawn, then flying away as the cars begin to roll along the streets.

Why is he doing that? What is his effect on other birds or on himself or on the people who live below? Can you compare him to the teenage rock group that practices publicly long into the night, or to a perfect human voice that suddenly brings a hush to the filled concert hall? Who's to decide?

Science will tell you about the sound and the practical reasons why the sound is made. Social science will tell you whether the mockingbird has an effect upon the social group who hears him, if there is social significance in this effect. But the song as a song—its process and product as an artistic expression—is a matter for the arts. The arts may reject it as a happy accident of noise lacking skill or self-awareness or perceive it as a creation of beauty. The point is that this concern with "the aim of beauty or aesthetic pleasure"[1] lies in the domain of the arts.

Broadly speaking, the arts are regarded as components of the humanities, as distinguished from the physical and social sciences. The importance of this segment of knowledge was noted in the 1964 federal Report of the Commission on the Humanities, as is apparent in the following excerpt:

> The humanities are the study of that which is most human. Throughout man's conscious past they have played an essential role in forming, preserving, and transforming the social, moral, and aesthetic values of every man in every age. . . . The humanities may be regarded as a body of knowledge and insight, as modes of expression, as a program for education, as an underlying attitude toward life. The body of knowledge is usually taken to include the study of history, literature, the arts, religion, and philosophy. The fine and the performing arts are modes of expressing thoughts and feelings visually, verbally, and aurally. . . . The attitude toward life centers on concern for the human individual: for his emotional development, for his moral, religious, and aesthetic ideas, and for his goals—including in particular his growth as a rational being and a responsible member of his community.[2]

---

[1]Thomas Munro, *The Arts and Their Interrelations* (Case Western Reserve Univ., 1949, 1967), p. 59.
[2]Report of the Commission on the Humanities, cited in Sheila Schwartz, sel., *Teaching the Humanities* (Macmillan, 1970), p. 1; the entire report appears as Appendix A, pp. 395–404.

The humanities, then, include more than the arts, although definitions vary. (Francis Bacon in 1623 limited the humanities to music, painting, and other "arts of the eye and ear.") But the broad aim of the humanities, as "the study of that which is most human," epitomizes the intent of the arts. This intent lies at the heart of our discussion here even though we'll limit our discourse to children's books relating to *visual art* and *music*.

Now go back to the mockingbird. If his song is a work of art aiming at beauty and aesthetic pleasure, it can be felt and thought about in these ways:

* as a *process,*
* as a *product,* and
* as a focus of *response.*

All three ways of examining and appreciating visual art and music are present in children's books about the arts. It's important to note that these books include nearly all types of literature. Artistic process, product, and response are included in fiction and nonfiction (including biography), as well as poetry.

For example, Don Freeman's *Norman the Doorman* (130) is a fanciful picture-book bulging with information about the process of creating modern art, the products of art displayed in a large museum, and the response of art judges and critics. When the museum guard captures the mouse-hero Norman, he exclaims: "Say, are you the rascal who's been taking my mousetraps every day and using them for artistic purposes?"[1] Here is a parody of some people's attitude toward objects of art as contrasted to objects of practical utility. The same author-artist's "Magic Flute" parody in *Pet of the Met* (131) is equally delightful and insightful.

In E. L. Konigsburg's comic Newbery Medal book, *From the Mixed-Up Files of Mrs. Basil E. Frankweiler* (132), two runaway children hide out in the Metropolitan Museum of Art, responding somewhat haphazardly to its contents and becoming involved in research to discover whether an "Angel" statuette really is the work of Michelangelo Buonarroti.

Certainly fiction can be misleading when describing artistic process, product, and response. It can deal with art in a superficial manner, a teasing reminder that the escapist misconceives art as a flash of inspiration unaccompanied by skill and hard work. For example, the three heroines in Noel Streatfeild's *Ballet Shoes* (133) dance and act their way to stardom with quite unbelievable lack of effort. In *Pennington's Last Term* (134) the obstinate hero performs Mendelssohn brilliantly at the piano, but most of his waking hours seem to be spent in school brawls and adventuring about in boats. The simple matter of honesty, when arts are presented in fiction as well as in factual accounts, ought to be examined with care.

Biographies of artists, composers, and musicians can be helpful in understanding and appreciating art. They can present the authentic setting in which artistic process has occurred. Under some circumstances, they can give insight

[1]p. 52.

into the process of artists as they develop their works as well as into the responses to their works. Perhaps most important for the child reader, they can present artists as real acting and reacting individuals not separated from the rest of humanity. These and other characteristics of good artist biographies are illustrated by Margery Fisher in her chapter on Johann Sebastian Bach in *Matters of Fact.*[1]

But there are pitfalls in biography as well as in other literature about the arts. The creative process is an inner process, not necessarily replete with drama that can be honestly communicated through words about the work or about the artist. All visual art and much musical art are nonverbal; so sometimes questions are raised about the appropriateness of verbal literature for examining these arts. When biography and expository literature attempt to explain artistic process or product, some accompanying experience may need to be provided. Books about the dance present photographs and drawings showing dance creations. A few books about music are accompanied by recordings: for example, a 45 rpm record is included with *Musical Instruments of Africa, A Little Schubert,* and *American Indians Sing.*[2] It's well to remember that books about nonverbal art aren't an end in themselves. Direct experience with visual art and music ought to accompany reading about artistic experience.

Let's now take a closer look at a sampling of books about visual art and music. There are many examples from which to choose, as you will see when you consult the sources listed in chapter 1. We'll present only a few, with emphasis on the need for artistic integrity, for aiding rather than confining children's understanding and appreciation, and for arousing interest.

Books about Visual Art

You don't have to be a snob to observe that the arts do not enjoy the highest priority in our culture. Perhaps the art appreciation curriculum in the past did little to help. Some children today may be growing up without any help whatsoever in appreciating or understanding visual art. Fortunately, an increasing amount of assistance is being provided through children's books written by skillful, devoted author-artists.

Books on visual arts encourage concentration: taking time and investing attention in order to *see.* Authors of books about art can act as guides. Questions and comments may direct attention.

But the response of a visually literate person requires more than concentration. John Hospers in "Meaning in Painting" presents a contrast between painting as illustration and the *essence* of a painting: its existence as a thing in itself, its composition, its form. Although Hospers doesn't believe the two aspects can

---

[1]Margery Fisher, *Matters of Fact,* pp. 312–37.
[2]Betty Warner Dietz and Michael Babatunde Olatunji, *Musical Instruments of Africa,* illus. Richard M. Powers (Day, 1965) (I); M. B. Goffstein, *A Little Schubert,* recording by Peter Schaaf (Harper, 1972) (E); Charles Hofmann, *American Indians Sing,* illus. Nicholas Amorosi (Day, 1967).

or should be separated, he notes that the long-term goal of education in the art of painting should be to deepen appreciation of its essence. The form of a painting brings viewers nearer to the artist's primary process and intention, ultimately yielding a more fulfilling response.[1]

Artists themselves hope that viewers will see beyond surface illustration. For instance, Hospers cites the example of James MacNeill Whistler who changed the title of his famed *Portrait of His Mother* to *Arrangement in Grey and Black* to direct viewers' attention away from the illustrational aspect of his painting to its composition, its essence, and its form.

You may argue that sophisticated response to the form of art requires long training and experience. Yet the young child, inexperienced and unsophisticated, will discern and enjoy the form of Karel Appel's painting, *Cry for Freedom,* more readily than the adult who reads the caption and then spends his time wondering why one arm in the painting is pink and the other is yellow. Marc Chagall's headless woman and floating violin players interest but do not surprise most children, who are quite content to accept these "unrealities" within the framework of the composition.

Should you then relax and rely on untutored, child-like visions? The answer is no. Children's responses to art aren't likely to be fully mature responses, even though they are spontaneous and real. This is where children's books come in: they should aid growth and maturity without dampening spontaneity or unnecessarily raising cultural barriers to the way children see.

Not all books on art for children provide this kind of aid. We need to set some literary standards for children's books about the visual arts—in addition to the usual standards for layout, color reproduction, and general tone of the writing.

First, commentary in a book about art ought to include a concern for the essence of the art—for its form, its composition. The commentary shouldn't give the impression that an art work's total intent is representational.

Second, commentary about the form of a work should not be difficult and abstract. It is true that we don't have a ready language for examining form. You'll have to look carefully to discover how a book about art handles this delicate matter.

Third, the book shouldn't over-emphasize culturally conventional interpretations of the content of art. If that happens, children may decide that art awareness lies in conformity. Ideally perhaps, a book about art interpretation ought to give a number of interpretations, then invite the readers to formulate their own. (You might show children that interpretations differ. We found, for example, that one book reproduced Darrel Austin's tiger in *The Gathering Storm* with the comment that this showed the little animal's innocence and peace, while another book presented the same painting with the comment that the terror of the approaching storm is revealed in the tiger's eyes.)

---

[1]John Hospers, "Meaning in Painting," *Aesthetics and the Arts,* ed. Lee A. Jacobus (McGraw-Hill, 1968), pp. 216–31.

PICTURE BOOKS AND VISUAL ART.   In chapter 4 we suggested some ways to help children appreciate picture books. These are often the best entry to appreciation for the visual arts. The best picture books combine illustrational and compositional appeal.

Good Books for Children, edited by Mary K. Eakin, and its successor *The Best in Children's Books,* edited by Zena Sutherland,[1] index a considerable number of picture books under "Art—Study and Teaching" with annotations relevant to their use for this purpose. Brian Wildsmith, Leo Lionni, Celestino Piatti, Maurice Sendak, Blair Lent, Marcia Brown, and many others deserve such study. Recent wordless books, their sole effect dependent on pictures, invite intensive visual art examination. Ezra Jack Keat's *Psst! Doggie* (135) and his *Skates!* (136) are excellent for seeing how an artist portrays motion in subject as well as composition. David McPhail's *Oh, No, Go (A Play)* (137) is a remarkable wordless book. Here the compositional aspect of the drawing overshadows the illustrative aspect so that it becomes believable that a passenger balloon is transformed into a theater and that the theater, in turn, becomes a flooding river.

The compositional aspect is most readily apparent in various "gimmick" picture books where holes, cut-outs, and inserts emphasize the artist's intent. Such devices are often discredited by critics, but Peter Newell's *The Hole Book* (138) has a long history of popularity. A hole through every page is meant to represent results of a gunshot. Eric Carle's *The Very Hungry Caterpillar* (139) and *The Secret Birthday Message* (140) use cut-outs to provide tactile and visual novelty. Bruno Munari's *The Circus in the Mist* (141) begins and ends with translucent pages as we go through the mist, while inner pages are appropriately printed on heavy colored paper like circus posters.

If you wish to intensify your own study of picture books for their contribution to visual art, there are a number of sources to help you. *Illustrators of Children's Books,* a series compiled by Lee Kingman, Joanna Foster, and Ruth Giles Lontoft[2] presents biographical information and thoughtful articles by illustrators themselves. For instance, Marcia Brown's "One Wonders" takes a critical look at recent picture book developments, while the same volume includes technical material on color separation and the working relationship between illustrators and editors in the picture book field.[3] Special issues of the magazine *Graphis* (written in English, German, and French) survey picture book innovations on the international level.[4]

EXPOSITORY BOOKS ABOUT VISUAL ART.   Art survey books differ widely in selection of examples, in quality of reproduction and layout, and in type and quality of

---

[1]Mary K. Eakin, ed., *Good Books for Children,* 3rd ed. (Univ. of Chicago, 1966); Zena Sutherland, ed., *The Best in Children's Books* (Univ. of Chicago, 1973).
[2]Horn Book, various dates.
[3]*Illustrators of Children's Books: 1957–1966* (Horn Book, 1968), pp. 3–28.
[4]Information about *Graphis* can be obtained by writing Walter Herdeg, The Graphis Press, 45 Nuschelerstrasse, 8001 Zurich, Switzerland.

commentary. Marion Downer's books in this field are readily available in many libraries, and their titles reveal a variety of topics: *The Story of Design, Discovering Design, Long Ago in Florence,* and *Children in the World's Art* (142). Pictures are reproduced in black and white. Commentary is in large, uncrowded print and is generally confined to historical detail and the *what* of the picture's representation rather than the *how* of its composition.

Pictures to Live With (143), compiled and edited by Bryan Holmes, is notable for its excellent selection and grouping—a difficult project, since this brief book attempts to sweep across all the world's art, from primitive cave paintings to modern surrealism. Arrangement by topics that will hold a child's interest is a great help: Cowboys, Animals, Athletes, Machines, The Weird and the Wonderful. There's little here to guide the eye for composition, but this is an exciting volume nonetheless.

A pair of art survey books with a very personal "you are here at our side" style is *Shapes and Stories—A Book about Pictures* (144) by Geoffrey and Jane Grigson and *Shapes and People: A Book about Pictures* (145) by Geoffrey Grigson. These books contain blessedly little abstract, over-general commentary. Sometimes the remarks are surprisingly appropriate and original: "noiseless light" refers to Rousseau's *The Jungle*—and, as you look at the painting, the phrase suddenly makes sense. The latter volume begins with the reader himself as the art work: "Think about heads and faces, have a long look at your head, face forward, in a looking-glass."[1] A few pages later we're marveling at the full-page color *Self-Portrait* of Leonardo da Vinci. This pair of books diminishes distance between the reader and the artist.

There is wisdom and a balance between illustrational components and compositional components in *The Many Ways of Seeing* (146), the remarkable collection by Janet Gaylord Moore. This is a book to be owned and referred to often. "Whether we are aware of it or not, our ways of seeing are affected by artists whose names or work we may never have known," begins the second chapter.[2] Ensuing examples range from the "austere and spare language" of the paintings of Mondrian to Renoir to Japanese art and its influence on van Gogh. There is discussion of elements in a painting—line, form, and color—and the author provides helpful ideas for making a visit to an art museum worthwhile. No pretense suggests that words alone can convey a complete feeling for art; instead, we are told at the end that" . . . a day may come when you will feel that you can apprehend the meaning of a work of art directly without the intervention of words, when you can put down the books and respond directly to the visual images before you."[3]

Even wider in coverage, though with a somewhat narrower scope in commentary, are *The Pantheon Story of Art for Young People* (147) by Adriane Ruskin and *Looking at Art* (148) by Alice Elizabeth Chase. The latter compares the different

---

[1]p. 8
[2]p. 16
[3]p. 120.

perspectives of paintings and photographs to reveal the artist's attempt to achieve certain psychological effects. This discussion usefully foreshadows the author's subsequent presentation of works by modern impressionists, cubists, and surrealists.

An interesting experiment is Cornelia Spencer's attempt to examine the interrelationship among the arts in *How Art and Music Speak to Us* (149). The two forms sometimes appear side by side in this book but do not really seem related; yet there are striking comparisons, as when a Martha Graham dance photo stands in juxtaposition to an ancient Egyptian mural of dancing figures.

Series books that survey visual art are plentiful. The best-known series of this type is probably that of Shirley Glubok—more than twenty-five volumes including the following:

The Art of Ancient Greece. Atheneum, 1963. (E-I)
The Art of the North American Indian. Harper, 1964. (I-U)
The Art of Africa. Harper, 1965. (E-I)
The Art of Japan. Macmillan, 1970. (I-U)
The Art of the Spanish in the United States and Puerto Rico. Macmillan, 1972. (I-U)
The Art of China. Macmillan, 1973. (I-U)

Despite the variety of publishers, each book in the series is similar to the others in layout and style. There is somewhat limited use of color but the commentary is clear in its reference to the pictures at hand. Early volumes, though simpler in style, lack illuminating comment on either an illustrative or compositional level. The words *wonderful, graceful, perfect,* and *magnificent* all appear on the first page of the description of Greek art—these are pleasant but empty. Later, however, this author rises to her task: she seeks out the universal and the unique in the contributions of each culture.

Others include the Art for Children series published by Doubleday (including, for example, *Pablo Picasso* (150) by Ernest Raboff), the Art Tells a Story series by Carella Alden, published by Parents' Magazine Press, and various authors' contributions to the Made In . . . series published by Knopf (for example, *Made in India* (151) by Cornelia Spencer).

Sculpture as a visual art form appears rather infrequently in art survey books. The Glubok volumes are rare exceptions. Note the placement, shape, and coloring of sculpture photographs in this series. The effect is as close to three-dimension as a photograph can attain.

But sculpture is meant to be examined from many angles. It is meant to be touched, just as the dance is meant to be seen in motion and not pinned to the page. Byrd Baylor's *When Clay Sings* (152) concentrates on shards of clay pottery of the Southwest and, within this small realm, develops through repetition a feeling for objects that is missing in book presentations of more complex sculptured subjects. A wild and colorful idea is *Ephemeral Folk Figures: Scarecrows, Harvest Figures, and Snowmen* (153) by Avon Neal, with photographs by Ann Parker. This "people's art" book will entertain any child and stimulate ideas for using the found object in extemporaneous sculpture.

The brief, photo-filled books of Shay Rieger deserve special mention because they engage the reader in the sculpting process. They invite him to give it a try, carefully avoiding the encouragement of imitation. *Gargoyles, Monsters and Other Beasts* (154) with a tempting "Crawlers and Creepers" section is a good one to begin with. Others include *The Stone Menagerie* (155) and *Animals in Clay* (156). To these you can add Bruno Munari's *From Afar It Is an Island* (157) with its ideas for drawing and painting on stones and for making stone sculpture.

The topic of architecture as a visual art deserves more space than we can afford to give it. Look for children who have a special interest in this field. Treat them to *Modern Art in America* (158) by Robert Myron and Abner Sundell even if it's necessary to read this rather difficult book to them. Architecture is the book's focus and other art forms are related to it. The book is up-to-date and observant. For example, the WPA art projects of the Depression years are called "a unique and important chapter in the history of American art,"[1] and the final chapter goes through the "cool sixties" and the antics of Andy Warhol. As a contrast, see Helen and Richard Leacroft's *The Buildings of Ancient Man* (159).

You'll make your own discoveries in children's books about architecture—a topic that holds fascination for certain children. We'll mention two we consider classic. *Shakespeare's Theater* (160) by C. Walter Hodges re-creates in simple language and clear watercolors The Globe Theater as it was in exciting Elizabethan days: "a little thatched building which disappeared long ago will always be one of the unforgettable places in the history of the human imagination." This book shows why.

Cathedral: The Story of its Construction (161) by David Macaulay is one of those rare children's books, like *The Wind in the Willows,* in which the author's enthusiasm amounts to an obsession and his skill is up to the task of communicating that obsession. Finely detailed pen sketches tell you how to build a Gothic cathedral—an eighty-six-year job. Certainly as you read and view the book, you'll begin to view cathedrals in a new light. Here's an example of this American author's controlled and detailed, but energetic style:

> Each stone was marked three times, once to show the future location in the cathedral, once to show which quarry it came from—so that the quarry man would be paid for every stone he extracted—and once to show which stone cutter had actually cut the stone, so that he would be paid as well.[2]

BOOKS THAT EMPHASIZE VISUAL ART PROCESS.   Elements of the art process are dealt with simply and attractively in a number of books for children. *Going for a Walk with a Line* (162) by Douglas and Elizabeth MacAgy relates line perspective to fine painting. Form, texture, and color are presented in a clear manner in *The Seeing Eye* (163) by Victor B. Scheffer, while media used in picture-making are examined for their unique properties in Helen Borten's *A Picture Has a Special Look*

---

[1] p. 122.
[2] p. 102. (p. 17 in American edition.) Original edition, published by Oxford Press in England, was awarded the Kate Greenaway Medal in 1965.

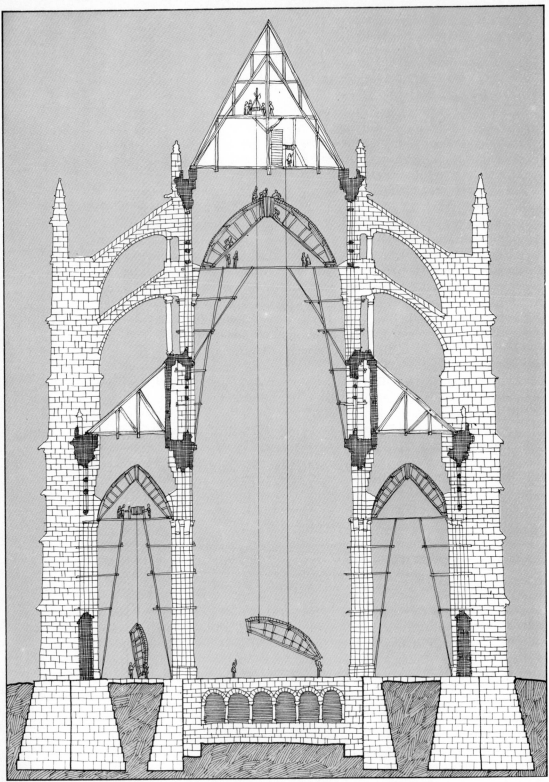

From CATHEDRAL: THE STORY OF ITS CONSTRUCTION by David Macaulay. Copyright ©1973 by David Macaulay. Reprinted by permission of the publisher Houghton Mifflin Company.

(164) and *Do You See What I See?* (165). An unusual book with page cut-outs to give "visual metaphors" is composed of photographs: Tina Hoban's *Look Again!* (166).

How-to-do-it books move a step further in exploring the art process. In our opinion, they're best when they describe a process explicitly but stop short of dictating subject and actual composition. One book we examined included patterns for carving and another included patterns for puppets. There can be little transfer in understanding the art process from that sort of imitation. Even Ed Emberley's charming *Drawing Book of Animals* (167) seems more set on imitation than invention.

Look for books that present genuinely new ideas dealing with process, or those that leave room for creativity along with a set process. In *Op-Tricks: Creating Kinetic Art* (168) a pencil, ruler, and compass are used to create designs pleasing or surprising to the eye, later to be elaborated with ink markers and other media, finally to be expanded into three-dimensional figures made from plastic, cork, and other available materials. The effect sought is an optical illusion of motion.

Collage-making as a process requiring minimal equipment, yet permitting experimentation, is well presented in books for children. "Collage may be the single most important thing to happen in art in our time," state Corrine and Robert Borja in *Making Collages* (169). Their examples and suggestions show the versatility of this form and its appropriateness to modern life. David Rosenfeld's photographs in *Collage* (170) by Mickey Klar Marks and Edith Alberts add variety of subjects. Best of all is *Collage and Construction* (171) by Harvey Weiss, one of the books in this author's Beginning Artists series. The style is pleasant but business-like, the definitions are clear but simple, and Weiss tells children that the most important ingredient is imagination—a theme that he is able to sustain throughout the book.

You won't have to look far to find other how-to books about almost any visual art process under the sun. These are good sellers, and each year brings lively additions. Hawthorn publishes annual crafts ideas from *Pack-o-Fun* magazine (for example, *Make It from Odds and Ends* (172) by Edna and John Clapper). Even the art of shadowgraphy has a book: *The Art of Hand Shadows* (173) by Albert Almoznino. A wider, steadier look at the processes of drawing and painting is presented in John Hawkinson's *Paint a Rainbow* (174) and in the Creative Play Series headed by Ernst Rottger and others (published by Van Nostrand). The Beginning Artist's Library series presents technical matters very clearly, as in *How to Make Your Own Movies* (175) by Harvey Weiss. Good writers familiar with an art process know better than to over-simplify for children: they write clearly, explain further with close-up photos and diagrams, and treat the reader as a fellow artist, as Yvonne Andersen does in *Make Your Own Animated Movies* (176).

Books about Music

What can you learn about music from a book? You can find out about the *process* of composition and performance. Musical elements such as pitch, duration, intensity, and tone color can be studied through literature, contributing to knowledge about musical *product*. Some helpful information can also be obtained in regard to ways of *responding* to music. Basically, this is another instance of a verbal medium commenting on a nonverbal medium. The strengths and limitations must be recognized: words may clarify but they can't substitute for the musical experience itself.

Behind every literary work about music there must be a philosophy of what music is. The best works include a sense of aesthetic distance, which might be translated as respect for an individual's ability to interpret music in his unique way. They don't presume to dictate the image or mood requisite for understanding music. They may suggest, they may provide helpful information—but that's the limit.

An aesthetic philosophy of music further warns that the majority of compositions and their performance are not intended to be onomatopoetic; that is, they aren't intended to be imitations of natural sounds. So-called "program" music, it's true, may consciously set out to imitate running water or galloping horses or gunshots or sparkling flowers—images a child may be urged to associate with the composition. But it's a mistake to imply that all music is of this type. A book about music or a music education sequence shouldn't emphasize image association.

Likewise, the theory that music is a "language of feeling" to be taught primarily as a means to arouse emotion is questioned by such philosophers as Susanne Langer. *"Sheer self-expression requires no artistic form,"* she remarks.[1] A composer, a performer, and a listener must objectify feelings. The ultimate response to music, says Langer, is "not emotional response, but *insight.*"[2]

Books can clarify such philosophy, making it their theme, opening up avenues for active participation and active listening. Other criteria will emerge as we cite examples, beginning with books that deal with stories in musical settings (a species, one might say, of program-type music), proceeding to items discussing specific musical topics such as rhythms, jazz, and instruments, and ending with survey-type books that attempt to synthesize the entire world of music.

STORIES IN MUSIC.   To take a story identified with music and to translate the story into picture book form can be an exciting, legitimate venture. The simplest way is to do this with a song, usually one that is likely to be familiar to children. The idea is especially pleasing to the pre-reading child, who discovers that he can "read" the book from memory. The quality of the work depends, of course, on the selection and upon the integrity of the artist's contribution, as well as his skill and invention.

Robert Quackenbush has wisely selected songs whose spirit suits his lively

---

[1]Susanne K. Langer, "On Significance in Music," in *Aesthetics and the Arts,* ed. Lee A. Jacobus (McGraw-Hill, 1968) p. 191.
[2]p. 196.

but unvarying style: *Old MacDonald Had a Farm* (177), *Go Tell Aunt Rhody* (178), and *She'll Be Comin' 'Round the Mountain* (179). The latter is really a double story in the Quackenbush version—a Wild West account to be read by a narrator, while a chorus echoes the verses of the folk song. In this book the "she" of the title is Little Annie O'Grady. Annie captures train robbers with her lasso and saves her hero, Handsome Larry Lackawanna.

These single-song picture books are just a step away from song collections. Social studies teachers attempting to broaden their units to include the arts should be aware that such collections are readily available in many libraries. *Songs of the Dream People* (180), edited and illustrated by James Houston, contains the lyrics for Indian and Eskimo chants, and musical settings for these may be adapted from *Songs and Stories of the North American Indians* (181). Music and bilingual lyrics are included in *Children's Songs from Japan* (182) by Florence White and Kazuo Akiyama, Anne Rockwell's *El Toro Pinto and Other Songs in Spanish* (183), and others. Frequently the illustrations in such books are distinguished: for instance, the full-color decorations by Maurice Sendak in *Lullabies and Night Songs* (184).

Opera as a wedding of visual art with music isn't readily available to most children, so it's rather surprising to find that picture books and collections of opera stories appear frequently among children's books. The purpose may be to acquaint children with opera narrative so that they'll be ready to see a performance or perhaps simply to present the stories, which are enjoyable in themselves. At any rate, *The Story of Aida* (185), retold by Florence Stevenson with illustrations galore by Leonard Everett Fisher, is a dramatic rendition of Verdi, filled with treason, victory in battle, love, and entombment alive. (There are other versions, including *Aida* (186) illustrated by Halmut Luckmann, but they are less attractive.) Mozart's *The Magic Flute* is present in a number of editions. The story's elements are certainly childlike, though the plot is very confusing. Stephen Spender's retelling isn't very clear, but Beni Montresor's paintings, based on his New York City Opera sets, are sufficient reason for celebration in *The Magic Flute* (187). *The Magic Flute* (188) adapted and illustrated by John Updike and Warren Chappel more appropriately treats the narrative as a book in itself rather than a commentary on the opera. The clearest presentation of all is *The Magic Flute* (189) illustrated by Riera Rojas, one of Watts's Curtain Raiser series, providing major melodies with English lyrics. (To accompany any of these versions, try *The Magic Flute: Mozart's Opera and How It Was Written* (190) by Eric Crozier, illustrated by Erica Macfadyen. It consists of fifty-six pages of fictitious letters by Mozart explaining his work. This is one volume in Walck's Young Reader's Guides to Music series.)

The four-opera cycle *The Ring,* based on Germanic folklore, contains heroic adventure with great appeal. Children who might rebel at a full rendition of Richard Wagner's music will appreciate the Siegfried portion of the story as adapted and illustrated by John Updike and Warren Chappell in *The Ring* (191), though the illustrations themselves are little better than those in a comic book.

The Ring and the Fire (192), by Clyde Robert Bulla, with woodcuts by Clare and John Ross, is something else again—a dramatic telling, meant to be read aloud, with equal strength in the visual presentation. This book is dedicated to Lauritz Melchoir, a great operatic Siegfried.

Clyde Robert Bulla has also produced three long collections of opera plots: *Stories of Favorite Operas* (193), *More Stories from Favorite Operas* (194), and *Stories of Gilbert and Sullivan Operas* (195). Each selection is done in good story form, with lively conversation. The Gilbert and Sullivan volume contains sixty-one pages of lyrics, but none of the books contain music from the operas. In these—as in all presentations of opera stories—you really ought to provide a sampling of an opera performance available on fine recordings; you'll find, as we have, that children are very receptive to an aria once they know what the singing is about.[1]

A most distinguished modern composer of opera is Gian Carlo Menotti, whose *Amahl and the Night Visitors,* a classic Christmas work, is adapted into book form (196) very beautifully by Frances Frost (who preserves the dialogue of the opera) and illustrated by Roger Duvoisin. Menotti's *Help, Help, the Globolinks!* tells how music defeated the UFOs who invaded the town of Thistle Glen. Menotti described it as "an opera for children and those who like children," and it's adapted in a fine, funny book (197) by Leigh Dean, illustrated by Milton Glaser.

Classical ballet offers several well-known stories that are widely performed. *Coppelia* with its doll motif delights children and is well served in *Coppelia—the Girl with Enamel Eyes* (198) adapted and illustrated by Warren Chappell with excerpts from Leo Delibes's music and in *Coppelia* (199) adapted by E. T. A. Hoffman, illustrated by Malada Mikulova (one of Watts's Curtain-Raiser series). A most distinguished rendition of a ballet story is *Giselle, or the Wilis* (200) adapted from Gautier by ballerina Violette Verdy of the New York City Ballet and hauntingly illustrated by Marcia Brown. Warren Chappell's treatment of Tchaikowsky's *The Nutcracker* (201) includes themes from the musical score and ought to be accompanied by a good recording. Walck's Young Reader's Guides to Music series includes editions of *The Nutcracker, Swan Lake, Sleeping Beauty,* and *The Firebird;* the first three of these are also included in *The Russian Ballet and Three of Its Masterpieces* (202) by Dorothy and Joseph Samachson. *Tales from the Ballet* (203) adapted by Louis Untermeyer, with rather stiff but colorful illustrations by A. and M. Provenson, is one of the few editions to include modern ballet stories: *Fancy Free, Billy the Kid,* and *Rodeo.*

You'll find many fiction books with a ballet motif. Of those we've read, Jean Ure's *Ballet Dance for Two* (204) is most enjoyable. This is a tasteful story dealing with the relationship between a British girl and a thirteen-year-old Belgian boy, both aspiring to be ballet dancers. Love of dance, not eagerness for fame, is the motivation here. It's gratifying to find a book that includes acceptance of males

---

[1]See also David Ewen, *Opera: Its Story Told Through the Lives and Works of Its Foremost Composers* (Watts, 1972). (U)

Art work from THE DANCERS, copyright ©1972; art by Anne Rockwell. Used by permission of Parents' Magazine Press.

in ballet. *The Dancers* (205) by Walter Dean Myers, pleasantly illustrated by Anne Rockwell, also includes male interest in ballet: a Harlem child named Michael befriends a ballerina named Yvonne.[1]

BOOKS DEALING WITH SPECIFIC MUSICAL TOPICS.   If you know children who have special interests in certain instruments, certain types of music, or certain musical careers, help them use sources such as those cited in chapter 1 to discover whether their reading can add information on the topic. You'll probably find something, but all in all, we're forced to admit that much of the material is disappointing. This is particularly true, we think, in regard to current topics.

---

[1] A very useful article and bibliography on ballet and modern dance in children's books is Amy Kellman, "Wallflowers and Winners," *School Library Journal* (October 1973): 88–93.

For instance, *How to Form a Rock Group* (206) by Leslie Lieber ought to be a winner, but its theme seems to be how much money you can make if your rock group is lucky. *The Rock Revolution* (207) by Arnold Shaw is much better, but reading it today, you become aware of a difficulty in books about the current musical scene: they're often destined to become quickly out of date. *Golden Guitars, the Story of Country Music* (208) by Irwin Stambler and Grelun Landon keeps historical perspective in its theme and is therefore less dated. But many current musical topics are probably better dealt with in periodicals rather than books.

Recently books have been published that examine musical instruments—their construction, their contribution to musical performance, technique, and leading artists. *The Violin Book* (209) by Melvin Berger does all these things and even includes related experiences with sound, using home-made devices. *The Violin* (210) by Bill Ballantine covers somewhat the same material a shade more technically and includes a longer list of recommended violin recordings. The latter, by the way, is a Keynote Book, a series that includes Ballantine's *The Piano* (211) and *The Flute* (212).

Musical instruments of various cultures are also represented in recent books. The aforementioned *Musical Instruments of Africa* enthusiastically describes traditional African instruments and then reveals some modern variations: "Rattles are made from the caps of Coca-Cola bottles. Gasoline cans are fashioned into drums. The metal stays of discarded umbrellas are made into tongues for thumb pianos. Enterprising Africans continue to make musical instruments of anything and everything."[1] One chapter in this book gives explicit directions for using the most available instrument of all: the body as a percussion instrument. To some extent, *The Music of Africa* (213) by Fred Warren with Lee Warren develops the theme of music in African ritual.

Although not new, the First Book series explores some current interests in a clear, engaging manner. *The First Book of Rhythms* (214) and *The First Book of Jazz* (215), both by poet Langston Hughes, relate music to visual art and, for that matter, to life itself. These are models of fine writing about the arts. Like the others in the series, *The First Book of Bells* (216) is succinct and yet comprehensive.

special activities

Here are two suggestions for further exploration of special topics in music and other art fields:

1. *The Bulletin of the Center for Children's Books,* published at The University of Chicago, consists of reviews of new books in the entire children's book field. Examine recent issues to see what is recent and recommended relevant to

---

[1] p. 100.

special interests. What topics are fairly well covered? Which ones need more material written about them?

2. Because the field of contemporary music is innovative and constantly chang-
    ing in its emphasis, written material about its progress is often confined to
    periodicals, sometimes limited to material with adult readability and com-
    plexity. Here is an area in which you may try rewriting such material for
    children. To do so, read more than one source on a topic. Then, keeping your
    child audience firmly in mind, write a feature to be read by children. Simplify
    structure, use diagrams and definitions and any other techniques to promote
    clarity. Try your material on children, and get their reactions. It's a good idea
    to duplicate such material and file it for future use. The revised form may
    not result in great literature, but it can meet a need that is otherwise unful-
    filled.

SURVEY OF MUSIC BOOKS.   Some survey books choose one facet of music and
attempt to explore it as completely as possible. Walter Terry does this in just
sixty-four pages in *Ballet: A Pictorial History* (217)—and he does it well. He catches
the ballet spirit through history of the topic and through well-selected photographs from famous performances. This is no hack writer at work but a *Saturday
Review* dance editor whose life is devoted to his subject.

Likewise, *Through an Opera Glass* (218), written by Englishwoman Irene Gass
and American Herbert Weinstock, captures—perhaps more than any other book
of this type—the spirit of its subject. The personalities of these authors are felt
strongly throughout their book, as if they stood beside the reader and pointed
out their special enthusiasms and judgments. They're particularly keen on early
opera history, beginning with the first opera, *Euridice,* in 1600. They clearly enjoy
the surprise that accompanied John Gay's *The Beggar's Opera* in 1728, and they
almost relish Verdi's struggles with the censors. Their book is dated—how could
they have known that Bellini and Donizetti would suddenly assume importance
in the decade after this book was written?—and they firmly turn away from
moderns such as Menotti and Samuel Barber. But those matters aren't important
in a book such as this. By writing in a human, subjective style they tell the reader
that theirs is a book of opinion as well as fact. This informality is welcome and
too often missing in nonfiction books.

For the child who is already intent upon music *The Meaning of Music: The Young
Listener's Guide* (219) by Jean Seligmann and Juliet Danziger and *The Sounds of Time:
Western Man and His Music* (220) by Nancy Wise Hess and Stephanie Grauman
Wolf are highly informative, dealing as they do with musical performance and
product. Both are loosely organized around music history, confined to Western
cultures only. Would children sit down and read either of these books from
cover to cover? Perhaps. We shouldn't underestimate children's wonderful capacity for curiosity. But the personal touch is missing in these volumes—a more
serious shortcoming than their rather unattractive art format. A shorter book—

The Wonderful World of Music (221) by Benjamin Britten and Imogene Holst—is less comprehensive, though it doesn't shirk detail on the topics it chooses to present. Here music of the East and West are skillfully contrasted. Colorful illustrations and a lengthy, lively glossary help communicate a caring for music.

None of the books we've mentioned really digs into the process and product of musical composition. Words and illustrations can only go so far, and these books use the medium to examine music from the outside—how music is composed, how it is performed, by whom and with what type of instrument. It's much more difficult to go beyond that—to analyze, for example, the way a symphony is put together and how this process can achieve an aesthetic effect. Those television concerts combined with lectures by Leonard Bernstein demonstrated that depth in music appreciation for adults and children can be achieved.

booklist

Books about Art and Music Education

Field, Dick. *Change in Art Education.* Routledge and Kegan Paul, 1970. A British view of art education as it might be, with its roots in Herbert Read's *Education through Art* (Faber and Faber, 1943), arguing that art is a clue to a "total means of education." The apparent stifling of artistic development at the age of adolescence is of particular concern.

Jefferson, Blanche. *Teaching Art to Children: Content and Viewpoint,* 3rd ed. Allyn and Bacon, 1969. Chapter 2 ("Values of Art Education") and chapter 12 ("Response to Art") are pertinent. The major theme is that children who engage in the art process are best enabled to see art as an aesthetic experience.

Trogler, George E. *Beginning Experiences in Architecture: A Guide for the Elementary School Teacher.* Photographs by Marjorie Pickens. Van Nostrand, 1972. The concept of architecture as a shaper of human activity is presented in a group of activities accessible to any child, with guidance. A short book—a good how-to-do-it guide.

Leonhard, Charles and House, Robert W. *Foundations and Principles of Music Education.* McGraw-Hill, 1959, 1972. Part 2, "Foundations of Music Education," builds a philosophy of music education that encompasses both the absolute and referential components of the art, a difficult but useful discussion.

Smith, Robert B. *Music in the Child's Education.* Ronald, 1970. Good lists for listening are included throughout. Chapters 6 and 7 are useful guides for listening activities involving excellent selections for early, middle, and upper childhood.

The Greater Cleveland Humanities-for-All Program. Educational Research Council of Greater Cleveland, 1967. Includes multi-volume curriculum guides for arts and literature through many media. You can obtain information about it by writing to the Council at the Rockefeller Building, Cleveland, Ohio 44113.

The Infinite Variety of Music (222) by Bernstein presents some of his scripts in book form—a book rather difficult for most children, but one you will find useful in conjunction with live or recorded performance.

The Arts and the Curriculum

The arts are neglected in many school curricula. Attempts to include them, to give them scope and sequence in the curriculum, often place them in the context of humanities. In doing so, they emphasize social and personal values and cultural complexity rather than aesthetic benefit for its own sake. Perhaps this is as it should be, but there is the danger that such curricula continue to view art from the outside. "How does this painting make you feel?" and "Does this musical composition remind you of a crisp autumn morning?" are crutches to artistic experience, not real openings to artistic insight. It will take concerted effort between artists and educators to make a curriculum of the arts effective.

In the meantime, you can merge the experience of visual art and music performance with the enlightenment provided by discussions about these topics. Clues to making your arts program effective can be gained from good books about art and music education. We have listed a few examples on p. 400.

special activities

1. Suppose that social conditioning and stereotyping, coupled with lack of information, have caused a child to dislike a topic. What if the topic might in the long run benefit the child—or if it's an important part of the curriculum? Select one or more of the following topics to show how you'd attempt to increase interest through using nonfiction:

opera	Asian dance motifs	Aztec culture
ballet	ancient architecture	metric system
jazz	study of another country	plane geometry

   (a) What books and other materials would you use?
   (b) What motivation/preparation would you provide?
   (c) What experiences, based on these materials, would you attempt to generate?
   (d) What outcomes would you aim for in terms of cognitive, affective, and psycho-motor learning?

2. Terms used in discussing children's literature sometimes neglect nonfiction. If you wish to open the full range of choices to a child selecting a book, what can you say instead of: "What type of stories do you enjoy?" or "If you want to know more about that topic, you might look for more stories about it."

Lepanto, October 7, 1571; Christians vs. Turks.
456 vessels engaged. 60,000 rowers.
Twilight of galley warfare.

3. It takes up to a year for a book to be published once the author has prepared the manuscript. What limits does this place upon the content of nonfiction children's books? What topics of interest to children are probably better treated in nonbook media? Which items in the selected bibliography for this chapter are of special interest to the person seeking information on a current topic?

4. In this chapter we have focused our attention on only three major areas of study in considering the use of nonfiction children's books in the classroom. The following is a list of titles compiled by a teacher, Dana Harmon, who read reviews and perused catalogs of recent nonfiction in order to gather a beginning supplementary list of nonfiction titles covering a wide range of topics. Following his example, what titles can you add for the topics covered in this list? What topics not listed might be of interest to children? See how many books you can add to this list for use with your children.

Carrick, Carol. *Beach Bird*. Dial, 1973. (E)
Lawrence, Jacob. *Harriet and the Promised Land*. Windmill, 1968. (E)
Kaufmann, John. *Bats in the Dark*. Crowell, 1972.
Langstaff, Nancy and John. *Jim along Josie: A Collection of Folk Songs and Singing Games for Young Children*. Harcourt, 1970.
Lobel, Arnold. *On the Day Peter Stuyvesant Sailed into Town*. Harper, 1971. (E)
Rinkoff, Barbara. *Guess What Grasses Do*. Lothrop, Lee, 1972. (E)
Tresselt, Alvin. *The Dead Tree*. Parents, 1972. (E)
Atwood, Ann. *Haiku: The Mood of the Earth*. Scribner's, 1971. (I)
Baylor, Byrd. *Before You Came This Way*. Dutton, 1969. (I)
Fisher, Aileen. *Jeanne D'Arc*. Crowell, 1970. (I)
Gruenberg, Sidonie. *The Wonderful Story of How You Were Born*. Doubleday, 1970. (I)
Rahn, Joan. *How Plants Travel*. Atheneum, 1973. (I)
Wahl, Jan. *The Norman Rockwell Storybook*. Simon & Schuster, 1969. (I)
Coolidge, Olivia. *Tales of the Crusades*. Houghton, Mifflin, 1970. (U)
Crawford, Deborah. *Four Women in a Violent Time*. Crown, 1970. (U)
Goldston, Robert. *The American Nightmare: Senator Joseph R. McCarthy and the Politics of Hate*. Bobbs-Merrill, 1973. (U)
Greenfield, Howard. *The Impressionist Revolution*. Doubleday, 1972. (U)
Karen, Ruth. *Song of the Quail: The Wondrous World of the Maya*. Four Winds, 1972. (U)
McHargue, Georgess. *Facts, Frauds and Phantasms: A Survey of the Spiritualist Movement*. Doubleday, 1972. (U)
Simon, Hilda. *Milkweed Butterflies: Monarchs, Models, and Mimics*. Vanguard, 1969. (U)
Suskind, Richard. *The Sword of the Prophet: The Story of the Moslem Empire*. Grosset, 1972. (U)

THE ROLE OF CHILDREN'S BOOKS IN THE CURRICULUM

As demonstrated through these three fields of study—science and mathematics, social studies, and the arts—books can broaden and deepen children's learning experiences. Although the textbook remains the principal medium for instruction in the elementary school—legitimately so—it does have limitations. As we have emphasized, children's books can extend and complement textbooks.

The primary objective of the whole elementary school curriculum is to help children become independent learners: to gain a sense of responsibility for determining why something should be learned, what the substance of the desired learning is, and how to go about learning it. Ready access to children's books will help develop that kind of independence. Children's books are available in a wide array and can make independent learning feasible and attractive.

In helping children become independent learners, the key condition is ready access. Every elementary school should have a well-stocked library and a well-trained children's librarian. That goal is far from being attained, but those of us who work with children should lobby long and loud to see that it receives the priority it deserves. Meanwhile, you can at least see to it that your classroom is brimming with children's books. The supply should change as the current studies change, providing constant opportunities to complement in children's books the topics being studied. At the same time, there should be a generous supply of books that have little or nothing to do with what is being studied, tempting children to pursue knowledge that is not specifically taught. And, of course, children should be encouraged to share their own books or those borrowed from libraries.

An additional incentive to stimulate children's reading is the model offered by someone they admire and respect. Bring your own reading to class and try to schedule an individual reading time during the day. When the children read, you read. Talk about your reading. When appropriate, read aloud from a book you're currently reading. Let children see the genuine pleasure you get from books. You might also encourage parents, grandparents, or other members of the family or community to come to class and talk about the books they read. Other models could include older children, possibly a well-read student leader or athlete from the high school. Anybody who will exemplify the genuine satisfaction to be gained from reading will help establish for children the role books can play in their lives.

CHAPTER REFERENCES

1. Asimov, Isaac. *The Noble Gases.* Basic Books, 1966. (U)
2. Wright, A. Gilbert. *In the Steps of the Great American Herpetologist Karl Patterson Schmidt.* Illus. Matthew Kalmenoff. Lippincott, 1967. (I)
3. Moorman, Thomas. *How to Make Your Science Project Scientific.* Atheneum, 1974. (I)
4. Razzell, Arthur G., and Watts, K. G. O. *Symmetry.* Illus. Ellen Raskin. Doubleday, 1964, 1968. (I)
5. Branley, Franklyn. *A Book of Moon Rockets for You.* Illus. Leonard Kessler. Crowell, 1970. (E)
6. Pringle, Laurence. *Into the Woods: Exploring the Forest Ecosystem.* Macmillan, 1973. (I)
7. Gregg, Walter H. *Physical Fitness through Sports and Nutrition.* Scribner's, 1974. (U)
8. Green, Carla. *Doctors and Nurses: What Do They Do?* Illus. Leonard Kessler. Harper, 1963. (E)

9. Branley, Franklyn. *Book of Venus for You.* Crowell, 1969. (E-I)
10. Macaulay, David. *City: A Story of Roman Planning and Construction.* Houghton, 1974. (All ages)
11. DeRossi, Claude J. *Computers: Tools for Today.* Children's Press, 1972. (U)
12. Vorwald, Alan, and Clark, Frank. *Computers! From Sand Table to Electronic Brain.* Whittlesay, 1961, 1964. (I-U)
13. Jones, Weyman. *Computer: The Mind Stretcher.* Dial, 1969. (I-U)
14. Asimov, Isaac. *Realm of Numbers.* Houghton Mifflin, 1959. (U)
15. Gemming, Elizabeth and Klaus. *Born in a Barn: Farm Animals and Their Young.* Coward, 1974. (E-I)
16. Syme, Ronald. *Amerigo Vespucci: Scientist and Sailor.* Illus. William Stobbs. Morrow, 1969. (I-U)
17. Wyler, Rose. *What Happens If. . . . ?* Illus. Daniel Nevins. Walker, 1974. (E)
18. Mullin, Virginia. *Chemistry Experiments for Children.* Dover, 1968. (I)
19. Simon, Seymour. *The Rock-Hound's Book.* Viking, 1973. (I)
20. Russell, Solveig Paulson. *One, Two, Three, and Many: A First Look at Numbers.* Walck, 1970. (E-I)
21. Sharp, Evelyn. *A New Mathematics Reader.* Dutton, 1967. (I-U)
22. Verral, Charles Spain. *Robert Goddard: Father of the Space Age.* Illus. Paul Frame. Prentice-Hall, 1964. (E)
23. Lomask, Milton. *Robert H. Goddard.* Illus. Al Fiorentino. Garrard, 1972. (E-I)
24. Halacy, Daniel. *Charles Babbage: Father of the Computer.* Crowell-Collier, 1969. (I-U)
25. Haber, Louis. *Black Pioneers of Science and Invention.* Harcourt, 1970. (I-U)
26. Crawford, Deborah. *Lise Meitner: Atomic Pioneer.* Crown, 1969. (U)
27. Lader, Lawrence, and Meltzer, Milton. *Margaret Sanger: Pioneer of Birth Control.* Crowell, 1969. (I-U)
28. Berry, Erick. *Fridtjof Nansen.* Illus. William Hutchinson. Garrard, 1969. (E-I)
29. Heimann, Susan. *Christopher Columbus.* Watts, 1973. (E-I)
30. Graham, Robin Lee, with Gill, Derek L. T. *The Boy Who Sailed Around the World Alone.* Golden, 1973. (All ages)
31. Watson, James D. *The Double Helix.* Atheneum, 1968. (U)
32. Gamow, George. *Biography of Physics.* Harper, 1961. (U)
33. Bixby, William. *The Universe of Galileo and Newton.* American Heritage, 1964. (U)
34. Land, Barbara. *The Telescope Makers: From Galileo to the Space Age.* Crowell, 1968. (U)
35. Branley, Franklyn. *Weight and Weightlessness.* Illus. Graham Booth. Crowell, 1972. (E)
36. Balestrino, Philip. *Hot as an Ice Cube.* Illus. Tomie de Paolo. Crowell, 1971. (E)
37. Rothman, Joel. *At Last to the Ocean: The Story of the Endless Cycle of Water.* Photos Bruce Roberts. Crowell, 1971. (E)
38. Ross, Wilda. *What Did the Dinosaurs Eat?* Coward, 1972. (E)
39. Simon, Seymour. *Let's Try It Out . . . Hot and Cold.* McGraw-Hill, 1972. (E)
40. Elgin, Kathleen. *The Human Body: The Skeleton.* Watts, 1971. (I)
41. Zim, Herbert. *Your Brain and How It Works.* Morrow, 1972. (I)
42. Colby, C. B. *Space Age Spinoffs: Space Program Benefits for All.* Coward-McCann, 1972. (I)
43. Cobb, Vicki. *Science Experiments You Can Eat.* Lippincott, 1972. (I)
44. Rahn, Joan Elma. *Grocery Store Botany.* Atheneum, 1974. (I)
45. Marteka, Vincent. *Bionics.* Lippincott, 1964. (U)
46. Freedman, Russell, and Morriss, James. *How Animals Learn.* Holiday, 1969. (U)
47. _____. *Animal Instincts.* Holiday, 1970. (U)
48. Simon, Hilda. *Snakes: The Facts and the Folklore.* Viking, 1973. (U)
49. Branley, Franklyn. *Pieces of Another World: The Story of Moon Rocks.* Crowell, 1972. (U)
50. Hurd, Edith Thacher. *The Mother Whale.* Illus. Clement Hurd. Little, Brown, 1973. (E)

51. Phelan, Joseph. *The Whale Hunters.* Time, Inc., 1969. (U)
52. Scheffer, Victor B. *Little Calf.* Illus. Leonard Everett Fisher. Scribner's, 1970. (I)
53. Kirk, Ruth, with Daugherty, Richard D. *Hunters of the Whale.* Morrow, 1974. (I-U)
54. Phleger, Fred. *Ann Can Fly.* Illus. Robert Lopshire. Random, 1959. (E)
55. _____. *The Whales Go By.* Illus. Paul Galdone. Random, 1959. (E)
56. Aliki. *A Weed Is a Flower: The Life of George Washington Carver.* Prentice-Hall, 1965. (E)
57. Meriwether, Louise. *The Heart Man: Dr. Daniel Hale Williams.* Illus. Floyd Dowell. Prentice-Hall, 1972. (E)
58. Howell, Ruth. *A Crack in the Pavement.* Photos by Arline Strong. Atheneum, 1970. (E)
59. Busch, Phyllis S. *A Walk in the Snow.* Photos by Mary M. Thacher. Lippincott, 1971. (E)
60. Silverstein, Alvin and Virginia. *Animals Invaders: The Story of Imported Wildlife.* Atheneum, 1974. (I-U)
61. Silverberg, Robert. *Clocks for the Ages: How Scientists Date the Past.* Macmillan, 1971. (I-U)
62. Whitney, David C. *The Easy Book of Numbers and Numerals.* Illus. Anne Marie Jauss. Watts, 1973. (E)
63. Carona, Philip. *The True Book of Numbers.* Illus. Mary Gehr. Children's Press, 1964. (E)
64. Trivett, Daphne Harwood. *Shadow Geometry.* Illus. Henry Roth. Crowell, 1974. (E)
65. Froman, Robert. *A Game of Functions.* Illus. Enrico Arno. Crowell, 1974. (E)
66. Adler, Irving and Ruth. *Numbers and Sets for the Very Young.* Illus. Peggy Adler. Day, 1969. (E)
67. Hirsch, S. Carl. *Meter Means Measure.* Viking, 1973. (I)
68. Zim, Herbert S. and Skelly, James R. *Metric Measure.* Illus. Timothy Evans. Morrow, 1974. (I)
69. Ross, Frank, Jr. *The Metric System: Measures for All Mankind.* Illus. Robert Galster. Phillips, 1974. (U)
70. Moore, William. *Metric Is Here!* Putnam, 1974. (U)
71. Holt, Michael, and Dienes, Zoltan. *Let's Play Math.* Walker, 1973.
72. Fletcher, Helen Jill. *Puzzles and Quizzes.* Illus. Quentin Blake. Abelard-Schuman, 1971. (E)
73. Kadesch, Robert R. *Math Menagerie.* Harper, 1970. (I-U)
74. Barr, Stephen. *A Miscellany of Puzzles.* Crowell, 1965. (I-U)
75. Mathis, Sharon Bell. *Sidewalk Story.* Viking, 1971. (I)
76. de Garza, Patricia. *Chicanos: The Story of Mexican Americans.* Messner, 1973. (I-U)
77. Gridley, Marion E. *American Indian Women.* Hawthorn, 1974. (E-I)
78. Martin, Patricia. *Chicanos: Mexicans in the United States.* Parents' Magazine, 1971. (E-I)
79. Franchere, Ruth. *Cesar Chavez.* Crowell, 1970. (E)
80. Lampman, Evelyn Sibley. *Go Up the Road.* Atheneum, 1972. (I)
81. Weiner, Sandra. *Small Hands, Big Hands: Seven Profiles of Chicano Migrant Workers and Their Families.* Pantheon, 1970. (All ages)
82. Witton, Dorothy. *Crossroads for Chela.* Washington Square, 1969. (U)
83. Galarza, Ernest. *Barrio Boy.* Univ. Notre Dame, 1971. (I-U)
84. de Trevino, Elizabeth Borton. *Juarez, Man of Law.* Farrar, Straus, 1974. (I-U)
85. Sterling, Dorothy. *Tear Down the Walls! A History of the American Civil Rights Movement.* Doubleday, 1968. (I-U)
86. Lester, Julius. *To Be a Slave.* Dial, 1968. (I-U)
87. Graham, Lorenz. *South Town.* Follett, 1958. (I-U)
88. _____. *North Town.* Crowell, 1965. (I-U)
89. _____. *Whose Town.* Crowell, 1969. (I-U)
90. O'Dell, Scott. *Sing Down the Moon.* Houghton, Mifflin, 1970. (I-U)
91. Fife, Dale. *Ride the Crooked Wind.* Coward, 1973. (I)
92. Sheve, Virginia Driving Hawk. *High Elk's Treasure.* Holiday, 1972. (I)

93. _____. *Jimmy Yellow Hawk.* Holiday, 1972. (I)
94. Jones, Hettie. *The Trees Stand Shining.* Dial, 1971. (All ages)
95. Allen, Terry, coll. *The Whispering Wind.* Doubleday, 1972. (All ages)
96. Bierhorst, John, ed. *Songs of the Chippewa.* Illus. Joe Servello. Farrar, Straus, 1974. (All ages)
97. Johnston, Johanna. *Women Themselves.* Illus. Deanne Hollinger. Dodd, Mead, 1973. (I)
98. Wilson, Ellen. *American Painter in Paris: A Life of Mary Cassatt.* Farrar, Straus, 1971. (I-U)
99. Ingraham, Claire and Leonard. *An Album of Women in American History.* Watts, 1972. (I-U)
100. Levenson, Dorothy. *Women of the West.* Watts, 1973. (I-U)
101. Ross, Pat, ed. *Young and Female.* Random, 1972. (I-U)
102. Tobias, Tobi. *Marian Anderson.* Crowell, 1972. (I)
103. Gauber, Ruth. *Felisa Rincon De Gautier: The Mayor of San Juan.* Crowell, 1972. (I)
104. Phelan, Mary Kay. *Martha Berry.* Crowell, 1972. (E-I)
105. Noble, Iris. *Israel's Golda Meir: Pioneer to Prime Minister.* Messner, 1972. (I)
106. Seed, Suzanne, comp. *Saturday's Child: 36 Women Talk about Their Jobs.* J. Philip O'Hara, 1973. (I-U)
107. Goldreich, Gloria and Esther. *What Can She Be? An Architect.* Photos by Robert Ipcar. Lothrop, 1974. (E)
108. Klein, Norma. *Girls Can Be Anything.* Dutton, 1973. (E)
109. Severn, Bill. *Free But Not Equal: How Women Won the Right to Vote.* Messner, 1967. (U)
110. Gordon, Sol. *Girls Are Girls and Boys Are Boys, So What's the Difference?* Illus. Frank Smith. Day, 1974. (E)
111. Harris, Janet. *Single Standard.* McGraw-Hill, 1971. (U)
112. Komisar, Lucy. *New Feminism.* Watts, 1971. (U)
113. Carlson, Dale. *Girls Are Equal, Too: The Women's Movement for Teenagers.* Atheneum, 1973. (I-U)
114. Peet, Bill. *The Wump World.* Houghton, Mifflin, 1970. (E)
115. Leaf, Munro. *Who Cares? I Do.* Lippincott, 1971. (E)
116. Foreman, Michael. *Dinosaurs and All That Rubbish.* Crowell, 1973. (E)
117. Burton, Virginia Lee. *The Little House.* Houghton, Mifflin, 1942. (E)
118. Hawes, Judy. *Ladybug, Ladybug, Fly Away Home.* Crowell, 1967. (E)
119. George, Jean Craighead. *All upon a Stone.* Illus. Don Bolognese. Crowell, 1971. (E)
120. Stone, Harris. *The Last Free Bird.* Illus. Sheila Heins. Prentice-Hall, 1967. (E)
121. Asimov, Isaac. *ABC's of Ecology.* Walker, 1972. (E-I)
122. Rhine, Richard. *Life in a Bucket of Soil.* Illus. Elsie Wrigley. Lothrop, 1972. (I)
123. Hogner, Dorothy Childs. *Good Bugs and Bad Bugs in Your Garden: Backyard Ecology.* Illus. Grambs Miller. Crowell, 1974. (I)
124. Cohen, Daniel. *Animal Territories.* Illus. John Hamberger. Hastings, 1974. (I-U)
125. Hutchins, C. M. *Who Will Drown the Sound?* Coward, 1972. (E-I)
126. Jones, C. *Pollution: The Noise We Hear.* Lerner, 1972. (I-U)
127. Jennings, Gary. *The Shrinking Outdoors.* Lippincott, 1972. (I-U)
128. Dowden, Anne. *Wild Green Things in the City: A Book of Weeds.* Crowell, 1972. (U)
129. Busch, Phyllis. *City Lots: Living Things in Vacant Spots.* Photos by Arline Strong. World, 1970. (E-I)
130. Freeman, Don. *Norman the Doorman.* Viking, 1959. (E)
131. Freeman, Don and Lydia. *Pet of the Met.* Viking, 1953. (E)
132. Konigsburg, E. L. *From the Mixed-Up Files of Mrs. Basil E. Frankweiler.* Atheneum, 1967. (I)
133. Streatfeild, Noel. *Ballet Shoes.* Random House, 1937. (I-U)
134. Peyton, K. M. *Pennington's Last Term.* Crowell, 1971. (U)
135. Keats, Ezra Jack. *Psst! Doggie.* Watts, 1973. (E)
136. _____. *Skates!* Watts, 1973. (E)

137. McPhail, David. *Oh, No, Go (A Play).* Little, Brown, 1973. (E-I)
138. Newell, Peter. *The Hole Book.* Harper, 1908. (E-I)
139. Carle, Eric. *The Very Hungry Caterpillar.* World, 1970. (E-I)
140. _____. *The Secret Birthday Message.* World, 1972. (E-I)
141. Munari, Bruno. *The Circus in the Mist.* World, 1968. (E-I)
142. Downer, Marion. *The Story of Design, Discovering Design, Long Ago in Florence,* and *Children in the World's Art.* Lothrop, Lee, 1963, 1947, 1968, 1970. (I-U)
143. Holmes, Bryan, comp. and ed. *Pictures to Live with.* Viking, 1959. (I-U)
144. Grigson, Geoffrey and Jane. *Shapes and Stories—A Book about Pictures.* Vanguard, 1964. (I-U)
145. Grigson, Geoffrey. *Shapes and People: A Book about Pictures.* Vanguard, 1969. (I-U)
146. Moore, Janet Gaylord. *The Many Ways of Seeing.* World, 1968. (I-U)
147. Ruskin, Adriane. *The Pantheon Story of Art.* Pantheon, 1964. (U)
148. Chase, Alice Elizabeth. *Looking at Art.* Crowell, 1966. (U)
149. Spencer, Cornelia. *How Art and Music Speak to Us.* Day, 1963. (I)
150. Raboff, Ernest. *Pablo Picasso.* Doubleday, 1969. (E-I)
151. Spencer, Cornelia. *Made in India.* Knopf, 1946. (I)
152. Baylor, Byrd. *When Clay Sings.* Scribner's, 1972. (E-I)
153. Neal, Avon. *Ephemeral Folk Figures: Scarecrows, Harvest Figures, and Snowmen.* Photos by Ann Parker. Clarkson N. Potter, 1969. (All ages)
154. Rieger, Shay. *Gargoyles, Monsters and Other Beasts.* Lothrop. 1972. (E)
155. _____. *The Stone Menagerie.* Scribner's, 1970. (E-I)
156. _____. *Animals in Clay.* Scribner's, 1971. (E-I)
157. Munari, Bruno. *From Afar It Is an Island.* World, 1971. (E-I)
158. Myron, Robert, and Sundell, Abner. *Modern Art in America.* Crowell-Collier, 1971. (I-U)
159. Leacroft, Helen and Richard. *The Buildings of Ancient Man.* Addison-Wesley, 1973. (I)
160. Hodges, C. Walter. *Shakespeare's Theater.* Coward, 1964. (I-U)
161. Macaulay, David. *Cathedral: The Story of Its Construction.* Houghton, Mifflin, 1973.
162. MacAgy, Douglas and Elizabeth. *Going for a Walk with a Line.* Doubleday, 1959. (E)
163. Sheffer, Victor B. *The Seeing Eye.* Scribner's, 1971. (E)
164. Borten, Helen. *A Picture Has a Special Look.* Abelard-Schuman, 1961. (E)
165. _____. *Do You See What I See?* Abelard-Schuman, 1959. (E)
166. Hoban, Tina. *Look Again!* Macmillan, 1971. (All ages)
167. Emberley, Ed. *Drawing Book of Animals.* Little, Brown, 1970. (E)
168. Marks, Mickey Klar, and Alberts, Edith. *Op-Tricks: Creating Kinetic Art.* Illus. David Rosenfeld. Lippincott, 1972. (All ages)
169. Borja, Corrine and Robert. *Making Collages.* Whitman, 1972. (I-U)
170. Marks, Mickey Klar, and Alberts, Edith. *Collage.* Photos by David Rosenfeld. Dial, 1968. (E-I)
171. Weiss, Harvey. *Collage and Construction.* Young Scott, 1970. (All ages)
172. Clapper, Edna and John. *Make It from Odds and Ends.* Hawthorn, 1973. (I-U)
173. Almoznino, Albert. *The Art of Hand Shadows.* Stravon, 1971. (All ages)
174. Hawkinson, John. *Paint a Rainbow.* Whitman, 1970. (E)
175. Weiss, Harvey. *How to Make Your Own Movies.* Addison-Wesley, 1973. (I-U)
176. Andersen, Yvonne. *Make Your Own Animated Movies.* Little, Brown, 1970. (I-U)
177. Quackenbush, Robert. *Old MacDonald Had a Farm.* Lippincott, 1972. (E)
178. _____. *Go Tell Aunt Rhody.* Lippincott, 1973. (E)
179. _____. *She'll Be Comin' 'Round the Mountain.* Lippincott, 1973. (E)
180. Houston, James, ed. and illus. *Songs of the Dream People.* Atheneum, 1972. (All ages)
181. Glass, Paul, ed. *Songs and Stories of the North American Indians.* Illus. H. B. Vestal. Grosset and Dunlap, 1968.

182. White, Florence, and Akiyama, Kazuo. *Children's Songs from Japan.* Edward B. Marks, 1960. (E-I)
183. Rockwell, Anne. *El Toro Pinto and Other Songs in Spanish.* Macmillan, 1971. (All ages)
184. Wilder, Alex. *Lullabies and Night Songs.* Illus. Maurice Sendak. Harper, 1965. (All ages)
185. Stevenson, Florence. *The Story of Aida.* Illus. Leonard Everett Fisher. Putnam's, 1965. (E)
186. *Aida.* Illus. Halmut Luckmann. Watts, 1970.
187. Spender, Stephen. *The Magic Flute.* Illus. Beni Montresor. Putnam's, 1966. (I)
188. Updike, John, and Chappel, Warren, adapt. and illus. *The Magic Flute.* Knopf, 1962. (E-I)
189. *The Magic Flute.* Illus. Riera Rojas. Watts, 1970. (I-U)
190. Crozier, Eric. *The Magic Flute: Mozart's Opera and How It Was Written.* Illus. Erica Macfadyen. Walck, 1965.
191. Updike, John, and Chappell, Warren, adapt. and illus. *The Ring.* Knopf, 1964. (I)
192. Bulla, Clyde Robert. *The Ring and the Fire.* Illus. Clare and John Ross. Crowell, 1962. (I-U)
193. _____, coll. *Stories of Favorite Operas.* Illus. Robert Galster. Crowell, 1959. (I-U)
194. _____, coll. *More Stories from Favorite Operas.* Illus. Joseph Low. Crowell, 1965. (I-U)
195. _____, coll. *Stories from Gilbert and Sullivan Operas.* Illus. McCrea. Crowell, 1968. (I-U)
196. Frost, Frances, adapt. *Amahl and the Night Visitors.* Illus. Roger Duvoisin. McGraw-Hill, 1952. (I-U)
197. Dean, Leigh. *Help, Help, the Globolinks!* Illus. Milton Glaser. McGraw-Hill, 1970. (All ages)
198. Chappell, Warren, adapt. and illus. *Coppelia—the Girl with Enamel Eyes.* Knopf, 1965. (I)
199. Hoffman, E. T. A., adapt. *Coppelia.* Illus. Malada Mikulors. Watts, 1971. (I-U)
200. Verdy, Violette, adapt. *Gisell, or the Wilis.* Illus. Marcia Brown. McGraw-Hill, 1970. (I)
201. Chappell, Warren, adapt. *The Nutcracker.* Knopf, 1958. (I)
202. Samachson, Dorothy and Joseph. *The Russian Ballet and Three of Its Masterpieces.* Lothrop, Lee, 1971. (U)
203. Untermeyer, Louis, adapt. *Tales from the Ballet.* Illus. Alice and Martin Provensen. Golden Press, 1968. (I)
204. Ure, Jean. *Ballet Dance for Two.* Watts, 1960. (I-U)
205. Myers, Walter Dean. *The Dancers.* Illus. Anne Rockwell. Parents' Magazine Press, 1972. (E)
206. Lieber, Leslie. *How to Form a Rock Group.* Grosset and Dunlap, 1968. (U)
207. Shaw, Arnold. *The Rock Revolution.* Crowell-Collier, 1969. (U)
208. Stambler, Irwin, and Landon, Grelun. *Golden Guitars, the Story of Country Music.* Four Winds, 1971. (I-U)
209. Berger, Melvin. *The Violin Book.* Lothrop, 1972. (I-U)
210. Ballantine, Bill. *The Violin.* Watts, 1971. (U)
211. _____. *The Piano.* Watts, 1971.
212. _____. *The Flute.* Watts, 1971.
213. Warren, Fred, with Warren, Lee. *The Music of Africa.* Illus. Penelope Naylor. Prentice-Hall, 1970. (I-U)
214. Hughes, Langston. *The First Book of Rhythms.* Watts, 1954. (E)
215. _____. *The First Book of Jazz.* Watts, 1955. (E)
216. Fletcher, Helen Jill. *The First Book of Bells.* Illus. Marjorie Auerbach. Watts, 1959.
217. Terry, Walter. *Ballet: A Pictorial History.* Van Nostrand, 1970. (I-U)
218. Gass, Irene, and Weinstock, Herbert. *Through an Opera Glass.* Abelard-Schuman, 1958. (I-U)

219. Seligmann, Jean, and Danziger, Juliet. *The Meaning of Music: The Young Listener's Guide.* Illus. Donald Leake. World, 1966. (I-U)
220. Hess, Nancy Wise, and Wolf, Stephanie Grauman. *The Sounds of Time: Western Man and His Music.* Lippincott, 1969. (U)
221. Britten, Benjamin, and Holst, Imogene. *The Wonderful World of Music.* Illus. Ceri Richards. Doubleday, 1958, 1968. (I-U)
222. Bernstein, Leonard. *The Infinite Variety of Music.* Simon and Schuster, 1966. (I-U)

BIBLIOGRAPHY

There is a shortage of perceptive commentary about nonfiction for children. The best reference is Margery Fisher's *Matters of Fact,* containing criteria derived from intensive examination of various books, good and bad examples, on selected topics. Dewey W. Chambers, *Children's Literature in the Curriculum* (Rand McNally, 1971) discusses the role of trade books in curricular areas including reading, social studies, science, and the arts.

Brown, Ralph Adams, and Brown, Marian R. "Biography and the Development of Values." *Social Education,* 36 January 1972, pp. 43–48. Ideas for using biographies to clarify the goals of upper age children; has sample bibliography.

Chambers, Dewey W., and O'Brien, Margaret H. "Exploring the Golden State through Children's Literature." *Elementary English,* 46 May 1969, pp. 590–95+. Lists trade books for topics, both fiction and nonfiction, with carefully stated basic concepts for each book category.

Consuela, Sister Mary. "Latin America: Materials for the Knowledge Gap." *Social Education,* 34 October 1970, pp. 673–81. Shows how to collect and arrange books and other materials to form the basis for a teaching unit.

Dieterich, Daniel J. "World Literature for World Understanding." *Elementary English,* 50 March 1973, pp. 479–86. A report on available literature resources for promoting international good will.

Endres, Raymond J. "The Humanities, the Social Studies, and the Process of Valuing." *Social Education,* 34 May 1970, pp. 544–48+. Quotations from Sandburg, Frost, and Farjeon are brought to bear on valuing in the social studies.

Feldman, Martin. "Art: A Social Study." *The Social Studies,* 49 December 1968, pp. 325–28. Suggests a marriage of social studies and the arts, with implications for choosing literature materials.

Gray, Charles E. "Value Inquiry and the Social Studies." *Education,* 93 November/December 1972, pp. 130–37. An extensive taxonomy of questions to be used in analyzing, comparing, and valuing cultures.

Gross, Franklin, and Rago, Francis. "Teaching about Energy." *Scholastic Teacher,* 40 April/May 1974, pp. 37–39. How to set up a mini-course on a current topic, using multi-media resources.

Mathews, Judy. "Magazines and Newspapers for Children." *Childhood Education,* 50 April/May 1974, pp. 349–59. Lists a hundred periodicals covering diverse interests from forestry, cars, and cats to skin diving, travel, and zoos. Gives addresses and prices.

Monjo, F. N. "Monjo's Manifest Destiny." *School Library Journal,* 99 May 15, 1974, pp. 1454–55. A noted historical writer states his objections to the censorship moves of some representatives of some ethnic groups.

Scott, Dorothea. "Chinese Stories: A Plea for Authenticity." *School Library Journal,* 99 April 15, 1974, pp. 21–25. Some surprising evaluations of the authenticity of books about China. This article should send you on a search for nonfiction about China.

Van Orden, Phyllis. "Humanities: Resources for Teaching." *School Libraries,* 21 Winter 1972, pp. 33–39. Lists visual arts resources in various media to accompany literature.

part **III**

Exploring Literature

9 chapter

Guiding the Literary Experience

Literary experience is personal and individual. No two people have exactly the same response to a book they read, a poem or story they hear, a television program, or a movie. "Reading, however one wishes to define it, is not an act that can be performed in a group," writes Miriam Wilt. "Reading is communication between an author and an individual."[1]

Still, there is a community of response. Otherwise, there would never be the sort of agreement that makes a book well-loved or well-hated. Children as well as adults seem to seek this commonality. They talk over their reactions to last night's TV special or to this week's bestselling book. This raises an important question for those who work with children and literature. How much should you do to promote and guide literary experience? If you become "pushy" in this area, will you be intruding on the personal and individual nature of literary experience? If you do nothing (except perhaps leave a lot of books lying about), will literary experience just happen?

We've already suggested in chapter 3 that you should help a child survey options and select from them according to his needs and abilities. Was that going too far?

Obviously, we don't think so. There's no such thing in a literate culture as an uninfluenced child! The media bombard us all—*see* this, *hear* this, *read* this, *do* this, and even *think* this. If children withdraw (or attempt to) from these sources of influence, they are faced with a random harvest of materials—such an array that they can't hope to make an informed choice. Some influence is needed, and in most cases, it will be welcomed—but it must be fair, wise, and enthusiastic.

In this chapter we've made a list of some of the things you can do to guide children's reading. Our suggestions don't form a complete theory and practical

---

[1]Miriam E. Wilt, "Grouping for Reading or for Reading Instruction," *Educational Leadership* 24 (February 1967): 445.

guide to literary experience for everyone. No one has accomplished that yet: neither the "self-selection" proponents who write books and articles about not doing anything for fear of interfering with the literary experience, nor the "fail-safe" proponents who define objectives for intended literary response and then design packets of lessons that "guarantee" those objectives will be met.

Basic to a positive literary experience is the selection of a good and appropriate work. Selection depends on how the options are introduced. We'll give examples of ways of making choices, generally based on books, but with some application to other media. Next, we'll suggest ways for stimulating literal responses. Then we'll turn to what we call *intensive* work with literary experience: a presentation of a tentative sequence of questions and activities that may be used as launching vehicles. Finally, we'll see how these procedures can be used to stimulate other literary experiences.

SELECTING GOOD AND APPROPRIATE LITERATURE

A *good* work and an *appropriate* work may not be the same. In some stages, both terms are relative to the needs and wishes of the child. This doesn't mean, however, that no other criteria are needed. When you select a work for intensive use in developing literary experience, the criteria become even more important.

What Is Good Literature?

Selection can begin at the gut level, for only in rare instances can you succeed with a book that neither you nor the children like. Beyond this, criteria such as the following are needed (most of which are recapitulated from previous chapters):

THEME. Is it important? Is the author asking a significant question? Is he attempting to persuade? Is he "celebrating"—lighting fires of idyllic enthusiasm? Does he balance sanctuary and encounter to entice listeners or readers? Is what he says honest and important?

CHARACTER. Do the characters invite projection or identification? Later, can you expect children to infer details and generalizations about the characters? If these factors seem weak, is there still something about the characterizations to make the work worth presenting despite its difficulty? Or, lacking characters, does the work (a poem, an informational account) still offer something of exceptional worth?

SETTING. Does the work give a sense of place, increasing sensitivity to place or introducing new places? Is there psychological as well as physical reality to the setting?

PLOT.   If the work presents a narrative, does its action make the reader want to turn the page to discover what happens next? Does the plot illuminate theme and character? Does it increase predictive power?

STRUCTURE.   This literary term is defined by Brooks and Warren as the "ordering of the larger elements such as statements, episodes, scenes, and details of action."[1] A natural structure is chronological order from a central character's point of view. Yet, for capturing interest or psychological effect, authors sometimes juxtapose episodes or change points of view. Does the ordering of events sustain interest and provide clarity?

STYLE.   The choice of words and ordering of language (style in written literature) are a kind of litmus test of an author's involvement in his work. Is he so involved in his material that the language, its sounds and its connotations, echo and augment what he's attempting to say? Children are sometimes shocked to learn that an author has worked for several days on a page that can be read in two minutes, or that, once an author "knows" his story, he works for months to get it right on paper. When selecting books with children, sample the style.

It's useful to develop a few relevant, short lessons in examining style. For example, take two or three passages from a favorite book—one the children have read. Look at these passages from a you-are-the-author frame of reference. Each child, representing the author, can be asked to justify and explain his choice of words. This can be done with several different authors, and a contrast can be made. For example, using the above procedure we contrasted Sid Fleischman's *By the Great Horn Spoon* (1) and Walt Morey's *Canyon Winter* (2). Some aspects of style quickly appeared: one example is filled with direct conversation, while the other is not. But other appropriate stylistic devices are not so easily seen until the contrast is examined: Fleischman's sentences and phrases are more staccato, to coincide with comic action, while Morey uses more even sentences and, as one child put it, "words you don't notice."

The style of a book is changed when it is transferred to another medium, such as film. Perhaps it's appropriate to ask children to compare a film's style with a book's style when the occasion arises. To film *Charlotte's Web,* or *From the Mixed-up Files of Mrs. Basil E. Frankweiler,* or *Pippi Longstocking,* or any other well-known book selection, the film maker must reconceptualize the story and translate it into a visual style. Some readers are disappointed if the film style doesn't coincide exactly with the written style, but such an achievement is impossible. Instead, ask children: how is film style different from book style? What are some of the things that make a film good? How did the film maker change the style when he changed the emphasis from words to pictures? (This is better than stating preferences, since either medium can produce a good literary work.)

---

[1] Cleanth Brooks, Jr., and Robert Penn Warren, *Understanding Fiction* (Crofts, 1943), p. 605.

FORMAT.   The visual arrangement and texture of a book are definitely important. Although many readers are unaware of the painstaking work that goes into selection of type, picture placement, and design, publishers know that these factors affect a book's popularity. The appearance and feel of a prospective selection may well determine whether it invites involvement.

To demonstrate the criteria we have discussed, we'll use a detailed example. "Mitzi Sneezes" is the second of three stories in *Tell Me a Mitzi* (3) by Lore Segal, illustrated by Harriet Pincus. A brief introduction to each story tells the reader that the child Martha requests a story. What does this introduction do for the story's *setting* and *structure?*

Observe the story's *format.* As reproduced here, it is altered somewhat from the book itself, but observe the arrangement of type and placement of illustrations. Are they suitable for conveying this story?

How about the *plot* and its structure? Once the story begins, it is told sequentially. It's not just a string of unrelated incidents. There's an accumulation of parallel incidents, a problem with a build-up, and a solution. Will this plot hold attention? Does it draw the reader onward to find out what happens next?

Which *characters* do you remember after you've finished the story? Is Mitzi's mother the fussy type? Are the children spoiled? Is the father too demanding, or just funny? Are these flat characters? Are they merely types without individuality, such as those in a folk tale? If not, do the characters invite specific projection and identification? Why would they or wouldn't they appeal to children?

Is there a theme? An epidemic of colds hits a family. Is that the theme? Things happen in patterns, and each variation in the pattern is more emphatic than the preceding. Is that the theme? In this story is the theme an implied question, an emphatic statement, or an idyllic statement?

A summary of any story is almost certain to divest it of its *style:* "A whole family got sick and the grandmother came and took care of them, and then she got sick too." That's the story? What has the author's style done for it? What are the components of her style?

Now compare your observations about the above criteria with those of others. Compare these judgments with the observations of children. Tastes do vary. We're trying to base taste on solid criteria that remove judgment from mere whim. We want to help children use such criteria and find that their judgment is growinig—and, further, that they're discovering more in a story such as "Mitzi Sneezes" than they did previously.

For older children (middle years) you might try applying the criteria to a straightforward book—something children recommend from their own reading, such as a story by Beverly Cleary or Walt Morey. Later, suggest a risk-taking book and see what it does to (or with) these criteria: try, for example, E. L. Konigsburg's *A Proud Taste for Scarlet and Miniver* (4) or Madeleine L'Engle's *A Wind in the Door* (5).

MITZI SNEEZES

"Tell me a Mitzi," said Martha.

"Later I will," said her mother. "Now I've got a headache."

In a little while Martha asked her mother, "Mommy, now is it later?"

"No," said her mother. "It's still now."

In a little while Martha asked her mother if she had a headache.

"No," said her mother, "Why?"

"Tell me a Mitzi," said Martha.

Once upon a time (*said her mother*) there was a Mitzi and she had a mother.

One morning Mitzi sneezed and her mother said, "Mitzi! You've got a terrible cold." She took Mitzi's temperature and put her to bed and gave her two baby aspirins and Mitzi said, "Tell me a story."

"Later I will," said her mother. "Now I've got to see what's the matter with Jacob."

Jacob was sitting on the floor, crying, and his mother picked him up and said, "You feel hot, Jacob."

She took his temperature and put him to bed and gave him a baby aspirin. Then she went out into the kitchen and brought Mitzi some orange juice in a glass and a bottle of orange juice for Jacob.

Mitzi said, "Now tell us a story."

Her mother said, "I've got to get you some lunch."

Mitzi's mother went into the kitchen and made
a bowl of soup for Mitzi and one for Jacob and when
she brought them in, Mitzi said, "While we're having
our lunch, tell us a story."

"I will," said her mother. "Only I've got to go and
see who's at the door."

Mitzi's mother went to the door and it was Mitzi's
father. "I've got a terrible cold," he said.

"I've got a cold, too," said Mitzi's mother.

"I said it first," said Mitzi's father.

"I've got it worst," said Mitzi's mother.

"Where's the thermometer?" asked Mitzi's father. He took his temperature and said, "I'm going to bed. Get me the aspirin, please."

Mitzi's mother got Mitzi's father the aspirin and brought him a glass of orange juice and some for Mitzi and some in a bottle for Jacob. Mitzi's father said he was hungry, so her mother went into the kitchen and made him a bowl of soup and then she gave Mitzi and Jacob some more baby aspirin and Mitzi said, "You said you would tell us a story!"

But Mitzi's mother said, "I'm going to bed."

Jacob and Mitzi and their father sat up in their beds and said, "You can't."

"It's not your turn to be sick," said Mitzi's father.

"Who would take our temperature?" said Mitzi.

"And give us aspirin?" said Jacob.

"And get us orange juice?" said Mitzi's father.

"And make us soup?" said Jacob.

"And tell us stories?" said Mitzi.

"I've got to go and see who's at the door," said her mother.

Mitzi's mother went to open the door and it was Mitzi's grandma.

She looked at Mitzi's mother and said, "You've got a terrible cold. Where's the thermometer?" Grandma took Mitzi's mother's temperature and put her to bed and gave her some aspirin.

Then Grandma went into the kitchen and brought everybody some more orange juice. For a snack she made them cinnamon toast, and noodle soup for supper, and she took their temperatures and gave them their aspirins and told them stories and the next day they were all better.

Only Grandma sneezed. They took her temperature and put her to bed. Mitzi's mother got the aspirin and brought her a bowl of nice hot soup and Mitzi's

father made his special cinnamon toast and Jacob
took in the orange juice without spilling it and
Mitzi told her a story she made up all by herself.

Mitzi's grandma said it was the best cold she
ever had.

special activities

1. No pat formula works when selecting a good book. One librarian, however, reports satisfactory results from having pupils assign "grades" to factors related to book selection and justifying the grades, for example:

Plot—A	Characterization—F	Satisfying Conclusion—A
Conversation—D	Action—A	Fidelity to Real Life—F
Setting—C		

   "There's a Hardy Boys book for you," concludes the librarian, Rowan Bryant.[1]

   Such grading might help initially in book selection. After grading a book, compare your conclusions with those of another reader. To test the system further, ask children to use the system on the same book or on some familiar selection. The grading can become a kind of book review to help other readers make appropriate selections.

   Are there dangers in this system of grading? If discussion and debate arise from them, is the resulting conversation a better developer of taste than other types of evaluation, such as random comments? Discuss.

2. Some very good books fall short in one way or another. Howard Pease's *Long Wharf* (6) seems to have an undistinguished style. The conversation and action are reported without the salty vernacular one might hope for in a mid-nineteenth-century San Francisco setting. So far as the style is concerned, the story might just as well have occured in any frontier setting. But we use this book nearly every year with a new group of fifth or sixth-graders. Why? Because the plot presents ingenious solutions to serious problems encountered by Danny, the hero. Danny's growing independence is convincing and admirable. Intermediate-grade students identify with him. One former pupil recently told us that when his own father died, he was comforted by reading about Danny's sorrow and recovery after the supposed loss of his father. What similar books do you know that lack something but compensate for the lack? How could you use them in working with children?

What Is an Appropriate Literary Work?

The information about finding a suitable match between children and literature (chapter 3) is one guide to appropriate selection. This should be combined with quality of literature to complete the task.

Interests and developmental levels sometimes limit selection, at least initially. *The Wind in the Willows* (7) lacks instant appeal for some listeners because of the complexity of its plot, setting, and style. Several Newbery Medal and Honor

---

[1] Rowan Bryant, "About Book Reports," *Elementary English* 48 (February 1971): 221–23.

books also present too great a challenge for some children to read independently, although these young readers may respond favorably when they are given some help and encouragement. *Secret of the Andes* (8) by Ann Nolan Clark, Virginia Sorenson's *Miracles on Maple Hill* (9), *I, Juan de Pareja* (10) by Elizabeth Borten de Treviño and *The Tombs of Atuan* (11) by Ursula K. Le Guin are all good selections, but they may have to wait until intensive work with literature builds requisite readiness.

Suppose a selection fares badly on literary criteria but is thought by children (and perhaps by adults) to be utterly appropriate. The book cited in the grade card example might fit that description. Some critics would quickly place Roald Dahl's *Charlie and the Chocolate Factory* (12) in this category. Run-of-the-mill series books have so often been faulted for lack of literary quality that they threaten to make people condemn all series; yet many series books are best sellers, their young readers insisting that they're completely appropriate!

Many times an appropriate book is chosen over one with high literary quality. If a child seeks above all else a story with a fast-moving plot or books that seem to reflect a distorted sense of values, you can—within our suggested framework —help him examine these works. You can choose books of high quality for intensive examination, hoping that your teaching will influence the child's later independent selections. This, we believe, is the best resolution.

A taste for high literary quality—for selecting good works—is desirable if the great benefits literature offers are to be reaped. But taste must be developed through freedom. Many an adult or child, after enjoying a fine literary experience, will sometimes turn happily to purely escapist, low-quality materials. You should accept this occasional preference as long as it's only a part of the child's extensive reading program. A work that seems appropriate, whatever its quality, can often generate enthusiasm and meet a need. Make sure you leave the options open and continue to work for understanding of literary criteria. Realistically accept the reader for where he is at the moment, then direct him toward alternatives and increasingly rewarding options.

INTRODUCING AN OPTION OR A SELECTION

Many good literary works fail to gain an audience because they seldom get an honest introduction. A book doesn't speak for itself. Motion pictures do clamor for attention, but their advertising slogans are all too often indiscriminate: the film with no quality at all may be proclaimed as "this year's greatest achievement!" Book jackets with glowing promises often broadcast the same kind of exaggeration. The man who returned the book to its publisher with a note, "The man that writ the cover should have writ the book," obviously wanted a more valid preview of its contents.

Children must be taught how to introduce themselves to literature, not to depend on a title, a cover, a first paragraph or an ad. They need to learn how to use a good book list, a card catalog, and some of the sources mentioned in chapter 1, in addition to recommendations from friends. Children should be taught to skim and scan, to preview and reflect, before making a final choice from among the options.

There's an entirely understandable tendency to judge a book by its opening pages. Many good writers know this and use it: they start with a cliff-hanger. Other writers can't begin their books honestly without taking time to build information that lacks initial clout. If you think their books are worth presenting, then you'll need to give them the aid of a proper introduction. A look at the following examples may prove helpful.

Sylvester and the Magic Pebble (13) by William Steig doesn't launch the reader into the plot on the first page, but the cartoon-style picture of a happy donkey family (father reading the paper, mother sweeping, Sylvester sorting his pebble collection) will interest most individuals. By the sixth page Sylvester is in enough trouble to prevent readers or listeners from turning away. Perhaps no introduction beyond a brief discussion of the first picture will be necessary.

Brinton Turkle's *The Fiddler of High Lonesome* (14) begins as follows:

> Yonder mountain is called High Lonesome. Nowadays nobody lives up there—nobody but the critters. Not the big critters, just the little bitty ones like squirrels and rabbits and maybe a skunk or two. There's a old cabin without a roof on it and a dry well—all that's left of the last folks that lived up there. Name of Fogle.

Interest may be aroused by reading this opening. What happened to the Fogles? How about the language—"critters," "*a* old cabin?" Some listeners will know that this beginning presents a flashback and has a mountaineer sytle. But they are unlikely to perceive the force of the story—its tragic theme and characters. The beginning may, in fact, misinform—may lead the reader to believe that he's embarking on a Little Abner sort of comedy. Your introduction might then be used to highlight the book's real components. For example:

Show the book's format: muted blue, uncrowded pictures and text that certainly don't indicate a comic tale. Preview the central character, Lysander Bochamp, by examining his picture in the early pages of the book. In reading the book aloud, give the opening paragraphs the serious tone needed to foreshadow the mood of what is to happen.

An object or an activity can introduce a book. Doris Gates's *Blue Willow* (15) ought to be introduced with a Blue Willow plate. Ezra Jack Keats's collages for *The Snowy Day* (16), for example, invite visual feasting. Children are more likely to enjoy the feast if the book has been introduced by sharing the experience of making a collage. One group of seven-year-olds photographed their own collage pictures to discover how texture and color are reproduced, and then turned to the Keats books to see how a fellow artist fared.

The introduction to some books should clarify setting. For instance, the "Map of the Run—as Described by Cinnabar" might be put on a large chart for viewing before you start reading *Cinnabar, The One O'Clock Fox* (17) by Marguerite

six. For you and I can split the back and breast; and that is all there is."

Now everyone gathered about the table, letting their eyes wander over the bowls of beetles and crickets and sauces and seasonings. But mostly they fixed upon the bright red mounds

From *CINNABAR, the One O'Clock Fox* by Marguerite Henry, illustrated by Wesley Dennis. Copyright 1956 by Rand McNally & Company.

Henry. The book's antic adventures (which include spirited talking animals and a cameo appearance by George Washington) get a good warm-up from an introduction that includes the hunting song (on page 51 of the book). The travel structure of Elizabeth Janet Gray's *Adam of the Road* (18) also requires a map. One is included in the flyleaf of the original edition. Share it prior to and during the reading. Use landscapes of thirteenth-century English countryside to help children visualize this setting in which a boy minstrel searches for his father.

Many stories of other lands require an introduction to setting, both in time and place. If possible, use nonfiction source books, maps, and objects to introduce *Earthfasts* (19) by William Mayne, *Black Jack* (20) by Leon Garfield, and Howard Pyle's classic tale of knighthood, *Men of Iron* (21). If settings are used effectively, such books bring history to the imagination as nothing else can.

Some good books have characters who need an introduction. Karana, the lone girl on the Island of San Nicholas in Scott O'Dell's *Island of the Blue Dolphins* (22), tells her own story in laconic, plain speech. Her dignity and bravery may be pointed out when the book is introduced. By all means include, as part of the introduction, a reading of the Author's Note printed at the end of the book. The strange mixture of prehistoric and modern qualities in Harry Behn's characters in *The Faraway Lurs* (23) needs introductory discussion. Sometimes, too, preparation is needed just to keep characters straight. For modern readers the opening of *Half Magic* (24) by Edward Eager is rather slow and confusing in its introduction to the characters. (Sometimes listing the characters and their ages is a great help.) The hilarious payoff (by chapter 2) is worth the effort of a slow start.

A theme is an outcome, not an introduction. But there are times when children need to know something of the issues at stake. Do not introduce a good book, however, by delivering a sermon. Marguerite de Angeli's *Bright April* (25), though now somewhat dated, remains a good early effort at presenting a racial issue. The confrontation that underlines the theme, however, doesn't occur until the final tenth of the book. It might be advisable to begin by relating the oncoming issue to similar issues in familiar books or current events.

When theme hangs on an allusion, children should be made aware of the allusion. *The Strange Story of the Frog Who Became a Prince* (26) by Elinor Lander Horwitz is best enjoyed if the reader knows the folk tale "The Frog Prince." You might tell the folk tale as an introduction to this book, or even tell related tales to show variations on the idea: for example, "The Fairy Frog" in *Black Fairy Tales* (27) by Terry Berger and "The Frog Princess" in *One Hundred Favorite Folktales* (28) collected by Stith Thompson. Similarly, Mary Stolz's satire, *Belling the Tiger* (29) is funnier if the listener is freshly familiar with the "belling the cat" fable.

Some literary works need to be introduced with a brief mention of the literary type to which they belong. The lively science fantasy works of Eleanor Cameron begin as realistically as the stories of *Henry Huggins* and *Ramona the Pest* by Beverly Cleary (see chapter 5). To know at the outset that these stories will change from realism to fantasy will not spoil the suspense but rather will prepare the reader for what he may expect.

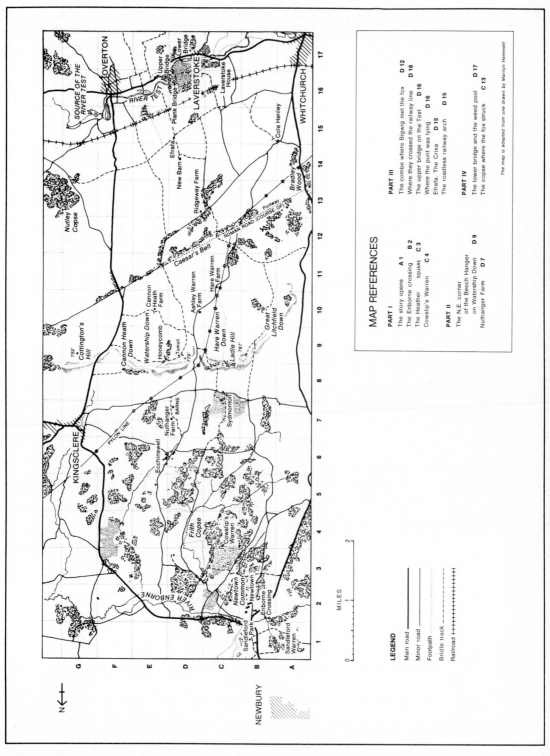

Displaying a good map of the setting is an effective way to heighten interest in the story being read. Reprinted with permission of Macmillan Publishing Co., Inc. and Rex Collings Ltd. from WATERSHIP DOWN by Richard Adams. Copyright ©1972 by Rex Collings, Ltd.

You should ask yourself: Does this selection require an introduction to insure that children will become involved in the literary experience? If so, what are the important components of the selection that need highlighting or explaining? If an introduction is in order, it should be direct and brief.

special activities

1. Many years ago the great storyteller Marie Shedlock explained with an example how *not* to introduce a literary work. After you've read her report, explain why this introduction failed:

> "Yesterday, children, as I came out of my yard, what do you think I saw?"
> The elaborately concealed surprise in store was so obvious that Marantha rose to the occasion and suggested, "an el-phunt."
> "Why, No. Why should I see an elephant in my yard? It was not *nearly* so big as that—it was a little thing."
> "A fish," ventured Eddy Brown, whose eye fell upon the aquarium in the corner. The ranconteuse smiled patiently.
> "Now, how could a fish, a live fish, get into my front yard?"
> "A dead fish," says Eddy.
> He had never been known to relinquish voluntarily an idea.
> "No; it was a little kitten," says the story-teller decidedly. "A little white kitten. She was standing right near a big puddle of water. Now, what else do you think I saw?"
> "Another kitten," suggests Marantha, conservatively.
> "No; it was a big Newfoundland dog. He saw the little kitten near the water. Now, cats don't like water, do they? What do they like?"
> "Mice," said Joseph Zukoffsky abruptly.
> "Well, yes, they do; but there were no mice in my yard. I'm sure you know what I mean. If they don't like *water, what* do they like?"
> "Milk," cried Sarah Fuller confidently.
> "They like a dry place," said Mrs. R. B. Smith. "Now, what do you suppose the dog did?"
> It may be that successive failures had disheartened the listeners. It may be that the very range of choice presented to them and the dog alike dazzled their imagination. At all events, they made no answer.
> "Nobody knows what the dog did?" repeated the story-teller encouragingly. "What would you do if you saw a little kitten like that?"
> And Phillip remarked gloomily:
> "I'd pull its tail."
> "And what do the rest of you think? I hope you are not as cruel as that little boy."
> A jealous desire to share Philip's success prompted the quick response:
> "I'd pull it too."[1]

2. Write the title of a book:
   a. that will probably need no introduction.

---

[1] Marie L. Shedlock, *The Art of the Storyteller*, 3rd ed. (Dover, 1915, 1936, 1951), pp. 11–12.

b. whose plot structure will require an introduction.

c. whose place-setting will require introduction.

d. whose central character will require introduction.

e. with an issue or confrontation that will require introduction in order to clarify.

Explain how you'd begin a literature lesson to present each book on your list.

3. Consider the latest Newbery or Caldecott Medal Book. Will either of them require an introduction? If so, when, and what kind? How might the introductions contribute to the popularity of these books?

4. Design a lesson to acquaint children with options for reading so they can then make selections from these options. What sources will you make available to them? What directions can you give to help them?

SHARING GOOD NEWS: THE LITERAL LEVEL

Whether or not a literary selection rates high on literary criteria, it may capture a child's interest so that he wishes to share it. He may gain great satisfaction from telling what happens in a plot through dramatizing an incident or drawing a picture of an event. This recapitulation is a literal level of response. The basic intent is simply to reproduce some part of the content of a selection.

The literal level, it is true, adds little to the message. Its motive is to "spread the good news," to involve the reader or listener only as an intermediary, not as a fellow creator. It has little to do with interpreting the literature through drawing upon one's own experience or synthesizing components. It is also true that this level is overworked and overused: Frank Guszak's research showed that 70 percent of teachers' questions in reading class were aimed at this level.[1] Considering the higher levels of response that we'll illustrate later, this proportion is obviously too large.

Literal level questions, when used alone, do not do justice to literary response, but they're a welcome beginning. It is safe and often pleasant—pleasant to respondents if not to their audience. Variety, however, can make it satisfying to the audience as well.

Literal Level Activites

At the early childhood level (and sometimes later) children may need the experience of repeating a story in their own words but using, where they wish, portions of the original. Their memories are likely to be excellent: a story or poem that commands their attention may be recalled flawlessly. You probably

---

[1]Frank J. Guszak, "Teacher Questioning and Reading," *The Reading Teacher* 21 (December 1967): 227–234.

know children who can repeat *The Three Bears* (a good illustrated version (30) was done by Paul Galdone), *Rosie's Walk* (31), "A Visit from St. Nicholas," or any number of other stories with considerable zest and satisfaction. Two excellent collections of warmup activities are *With a Deep Sea Smile* and *Juba This and Juba That*, both selected by Virginia A. Tashjian.[1]

What is gained from such recitals? They promote initial enthusiasm for literature and may lead to higher interests. They provide early experience with "book language," which, unlike the language of conversation, is sustained monolog or dialog, often with more complex word other and sentence expansion. They offer experience with the patterns of literary form and the ordering of incidents and details to form a unity.

The satisfaction of communicating a story or poem to an audience unfamiliar with its content can be fostered at any point in childhood. At a prereading level, children can be encouraged to rehearse and then tell a wordless book, such as Fernando Krahn's *How Santa Claus Had a Long and Difficult Journey Delivering His Presents* (32) or any of the wordless picture books by John S. Goodall.[2] Later, children may tell stories from a folk tale collection or review the content of a nonfiction selection. In a sense, this is supplementing literal recall with contributions of their own: their own language and perhaps their own elaboration. There is some creation as well in the audience awareness factor: the teller learns to fashion his telling to appeal to his audience.

To these activities you can help children add dramatic activity, which encourages elaboration and interaction. An impromptu dramatization of a simple folk tale helps in visualizing the setting, the sequence of actions and certain features of character (such as innocence, shrewdness, or stupidity). Thus the literal level response begins to grow beyond itself into inference and interpretation. Literal-based dramatic activity can and should be continued into later years, when selections are more complex. In the Winnetka schools, for example, a group of sixth-graders substituted for the traditional book report their dramatization of a crucial incident in a Nancy Drew story. Later they used their experience with the dramatic mode to share favorite myths from several cultures. (For more specific information about relating creative dramatics to literary response, see chapter 10).

From the above examples, it should be obvious that activities that satisfy the literal level of response can quickly develop into more creative avenues leading to higher levels. We'll examine this development more closely later in this chapter.

Literal Level Questions

Sometimes literal level questions are needed for a basic understanding of a selection and as a base for higher-level questions and activities. These are

---

[1] *With a Deep Sea Smile: Story Hour Stretches for Large or Small Groups,* illus. Rosemary Wells (Little, Brown, 1974); *Juba This and Juba That,* illus. Victoria de Larrea (Little, Brown, 1969).
[2] For example, *The Adventures of Paddy Pork* (Harcourt, 1968) or *Shrewbettina's Birthday* (Harcourt, 1970).

memory items, eliciting recall, recognition, and relationships. The following categories, illustrated with sample items based on "Mitzi Sneezes," may be helpful for use with children.

1. *Recalling events and their sequence.* Who had a cold first? What was done about it? Who had a cold next? What was done about it? Who was next . . .? (Or: turn the question into a recall activity: "Tell what happened in each of these pictures.")

2. *Recognizing relationships among events.* Each person in the story went somewhere and each person wanted something. Did they go to town, to the kitchen, to bed? Who wanted a story—Jacob, Mitzi, Mother, Father, Grandma? (Or: Tell all the troubles Mother had in the story.")

3. *Noting important details of setting or character.* Look at the pictures: what did the children in the house have to play with? What in the pictures shows that the family members helped each other? (Or: Draw from memory the things in the house that helped the family get over their colds. Act out one part of the story that shows they tried to help each other get over their colds.)

4. *Recalling examples of style.* Who is telling the story? How does she begin it? When in the story are we told exactly what people said? (Or: Find the places in the story where people talked to each other. Read or tell just what they said.)

Such items are on a data-retrieval level, although the respondent must sort the data and organize them in order to give an acceptable answer. Usually, recall and recognition information (whether based on story, poem, or nonfiction) should be used subsequently to interpret and evaluate the work beyond the literal level. Frank Smith's definition of reading as "the reduction of uncertainty"[1] highlights the need for understanding beyond the "givens" in a story of exposition. The same definition can also be applied to literary experience derived from listening and viewing.

From experience we have developed some simple guidelines for literal-level items:

• Try to avoid the *trivial* and *obvious.* Triviality in literary discussion can get to be a habit and pattern—for example, "Mitzi feels bad in the story, doesn't she? Why is she feeling so bad? Don't we feel terrible when we have a bad cold? . . ." There's no thinking going on here, just passive agreement. If recall or recognition of important information requires a long succession of questions and activities, the selection may be unsuitable for the group. The sequence of events in some dreary stories is difficult to recall because the events don't matter. Children will probably welcome a different story.

• Strive to elicit recall that is pertinent to discussion and activity for higher levels of understanding and response. For example, "Find the places in the story

---

[1]Frank Smith, *Understanding Reading* (Holt, Rinehart and Winston, 1971), p. 12.

where people talked to each other" would be pertinent for a later examination of a family's interrelationships.

- Watch your language. Avoid using overly pedantic phrases. "Tell what happens in 'Mitzi Sneezes'" will get a response, but "Summarize the sequence of events in 'Mitzi Sneezes'" won't.

special activities

1. Literal-level questions are often considered "right answer" questions: their answers are supposed to be recalled or recognized in the text of the story. But you should be prepared to consider answers that diverge from the ones you've chosen. Asked to recall a happening from "Mitzi Sneezes," a child might say that in the story people had their temperatures taken with a thermometer. Even though this doesn't fit into your list of the sequence of important events, you ought to be prepared to work with the answer as given. Reexamine the question examples given above. Which questions might elicit good, original answers that are unexpected? Choose a question and show that it could have two or more acceptable answers.

2. As you continue through this sequence, give yourself practice in using the ideas presented. Select a book or story and determine three or four main purposes for giving extensive attention to your selection. Jot these down. Then do sample literal-level activities and questions that work toward those purposes. Make them flexible enough to permit unexpected answers and to allow for adding and changing purposes as your actual lesson progresses.

INTENSIVE WORK WITH LITERATURE

The literary types presented in chapter 2 all contain some examples of excellent stories and nonfiction that may not immediately appeal to children. The folklore of unfamiliar cultures will sometimes fit into this category, as will some of the fanciful stories of Hans Christian Andersen, Walter de la Mare, and L. M. Boston. Some of the finest Newbery and Caldecott books, some worthwhile books dealing with social and psychological issues, and some biographies and other nonfiction present an initial challenge that many deserving readers can't accept without help. In such cases, an introduction to these works and a provision for literal-level sharing may be all that is needed. Or it may quickly become clear that a selection fails intrinsically to meet the requisite match and ought to be discarded, postponed, or left for a different audience.

But often a difficult or strange literary selection holds the potential for intense literary experience if it can capture children's attention and fire their imagination. What is more, such a selection can light the way to others of its type. Julius Lester's *Black Folktales* (33) lay undisturbed on the library table for a year before a lively teacher picked it up and read "Jack and the Devil's Daughter" to a group of sixth-graders just before Halloween. Before long, these children, inspired by Julius Lester's bright modern style, were searching out other folk tales and translating the stories into their own vernacular to tell to the class. Other teachers have reported similar experiences. A brief but intensive study of a Lloyd Alexander book, for example, triggered immediate and sustained interest in the entire Prydain series.

If you want to see how a bit of intensive literary experience affects a primary-level group, design a few lessons to help children look at pictures. Try, "You are the artist; tell us how you made your pictures; tell why you chose to make a picture of this part of your story." Block out part of a picture, asking children to tell what the masked portion should contain. Try having the children take the same positions as characters in a crucial picture and then ask them to go on with the action in pantomime or spontaneous dramatization. Contrast and compare picture books. Then watch the results. You should find that children will spend more time on a particular picture book, studying its illustrations more closely and entering into its contents with greater enthusiasm.

Research on children's responses to literature shows that they can be complex and deeply rewarding. A summary of this research points out some of the important factors in response:

> During the past fifty years, researchers have slowly dissected the complex phenomenon which is response to literature. They have shown that it contains cognitive aspects related to the ability to read and the possession of certain kinds of information as well as to the logical processes of thinking and of decoding complex messages. They have found that it consists of certain abilities to perceive sensuous aspects of language, particularly its sound and its image-making aspects, and that these abilities are only partially related to the cognitive ones. They have found that it consists of certain judgmental acts, which are based primarily upon liking or pleasure that the individual derives from the experience. They have found that a great deal of the 'interference' or the difference between responses can be accounted for by the experiential, psychological, and conceptual baggage that the reader already has before picking up the book or scanning the poem. It is what the reader brings to the text as much as the text itself that determines the nature of the response. The model of literary response is quite different from an oversimple view of the communication model of *sender/message/ receiver.* The reader takes as active a role in determining the message as does the sender.[1]

Cognition is drawing upon information, using one's logic, appreciating language or style, making informed judgments: the "capacity for and habit of making use of all that one knows or can find out in interpreting or construing

---

[1] Alan C. Purves and Richard Beach, *Literature and the Reader: Research in Response to Literature, Reading Interests, and the Teaching of Literature,* Final Report to the National Endowment for the Humanities, Project Number 1169-0-129 (National Council of Teachers of English, 1972), p. 177.

The Master Cat

THERE WAS A MILLER
who left no more estate to the three sons he had than his mill,
his donkey and his cat. The division was soon made. Neither
scrivener nor attorney was sent for; they would soon have
eaten up all the poor patrimony. The eldest had the mill, the
second the donkey, and the youngest nothing but the cat. The
poor young fellow was quite comfortless at having so poor a
lot.

'My brothers,' said he, 'may get their living handsomely
enough by joining their stocks together. But for my part, when
I have eaten my cat, and made me a muff of his skin, I must
die of hunger.'

The cat, who heard all this, said to him with a grave and
serious air, 'Do not thus afflict yourself, my good master. You
need only give me a bag, and have a pair of boots made for
me that I may scamper through the brambles. You shall see
you have not so bad a portion with me as you imagine.'

The cat's master had often seen him play a great many cunning tricks to catch rats and mice; he used to hide himself in
the meal, and make as if he were dead; so he did not altogether
despair. When the cat had what he asked for, he booted him-

154

Illustration by Gustave Doré, 1892.

self very gallantly, and putting his bag about his neck, he held
the strings of it in his two forepaws and went into a warren
where was a great abundance of rabbits. He put bran and let-
tuce into his bag and, stretching out at length as if dead, he
waited for some young rabbits, not yet acquainted with the
deceits of the world, to come and rummage for what he had
put into his bag.

Scarce had he lain down but he had what he wanted: a rash
and foolish young rabbit jumped into his bag. Monsieur Puss,
immediately drawing close the strings, killed him without pity.
Proud of his prey, he went with it to the palace, and asked to
speak with his majesty. He was shown into the king's apartment and, making a low reverence, said to him:

'I have brought you, sir, a rabbit from the warren, which
my noble lord, the Master of Carabas'—for that was the title
Puss was pleased to give his master—'has commanded me to
present to Your Majesty from him.'

'Tell your master,' said the king, 'that I thank him, and that
he gives me a great deal of pleasure.'

Another time the cat hid himself among some standing corn,
holding his bag open. When a brace of partridges ran into it,
he drew the strings and so caught them both. He made a present of these to the king as he had the rabbit. The king, in like
manner, received the partridges with great pleasure, and or-
dered some money to be given to him.

The cat continued thus for two or three months to carry to
his majesty, from time to time, game of his master's taking.
One day in particular, when he knew for certain that the king
was to take the air along the riverside with his daughter, the
most beautiful princess in the world, he said to his master:

'If you will follow my advice your fortune is made. You

have nothing to do but wash yourself in the river, where I shall show you, and leave the rest to me.'

The Marquis of Carabas did what the cat advised him to do, without knowing why or wherefore. While he was washing, the king passed by, and the cat began to cry out:

'Help! Help! My Lord Marquis of Carabas is going to be drowned.'

At this the king put his head out of the coach window, and finding it was the cat who had so often brought him such good game, he commanded his guards to run immediately to the assistance of his lordship the Marquis of Carabas. While they were drawing him out of the river, the cat came up to the coach and told the king that, while his master was washing, there came by some rogues, who went off with his clothes, though he had cried out, 'Thieves! Thieves!' several times, as loud as he could.

This cunning cat had hidden them under a great stone. The king immediately commanded the officers of his wardrobe to run and fetch one of his best suits for the Marquis of Carabas.

The fine clothes set off his good mien, for he was well made and very handsome in his person. The king's daughter took a secret inclination to him, and the Marquis of Carabas had no sooner cast two or three respectful and tender glances upon her than she fell in love with him to distraction. The king would needs have him come into the coach and take the air with them. The cat, quite overjoyed to see his project begin to succeed, marched on before, and meeting with some countrymen, who were mowing a meadow, he said to them:

'Good people, you who are mowing, if you do not tell the king that the meadow you mow belongs to my Lord Marquis of Carabas, you shall be chopped as small as herbs for the pot.'

The king did not fail to ask the mowers to whom the meadow belonged.

'To my Lord Marquis of Carabas,' they answered altogether, for the cat's threat had made them terribly afraid.

'You see, sir,' said the marquis, 'this is a meadow which never fails to yield a plentiful harvest every year.'

The Master Cat, who still went on before, met with some reapers, and said to them, 'Good people, you who are reaping, if you do not tell the king that all this corn belongs to the Marquis of Carabas you shall be chopped as small as herbs for the pot.'

The king, who passed by a moment after, wished to know to whom all that corn belonged.

'To my Lord Marquis of Carabas,' replied the reapers, and the king was very well pleased with it, as well as with the marquis, whom he congratulated thereupon. The Master Cat, who went always before, said the same words to all he met, and the king was astonished at the vast estates of the Marquis of Carabas.

Monsieur Puss came at last to a stately castle, the master of which was an ogre, the richest ever known. All the lands which the king had then gone over belonged to this ogre. The cat, who had taken care to inform himself who this ogre was and what he could do, asked to speak with him, saying he could not pass so near his castle without paying his respects to him.

The ogre received him as civilly as an ogre could and made him sit down.

'I have been assured,' said the cat, 'that you have the gift of being able to change yourself into any sort of creature. You can, for example, transform yourself into a lion or elephant and the like.'

'That is true,' answered the ogre briskly, 'and to convince you, you shall see me now become a lion.'

Puss was so badly terrified at the sight of a lion so near him that he immediately got into the rain gutter, not without abundance of trouble and danger, because of his boots. They were of no use walking upon the tiles. A little while after, when Puss saw that the ogre had resumed his natural form, he came down and owned he had been very much frightened.

'I have been moreover informed,' said the cat, 'but I know not how to believe it, that you have also the power to take on the shape of the smallest animal; for example, to change yourself into a rat or a mouse; but I must own to you I take this to be impossible.'

'Impossible!' cried the ogre. 'You shall see that presently.'

At the same time he changed himself into a mouse and began to run about the floor. Puss no sooner perceived this than he fell upon him and ate him up.

Meanwhile the king, who saw, as he passed, this fine castle of the ogre's, had a mind to go into it. Puss, who heard the noise of his majesty's coach running over the drawbridge, ran out, and said to the king:

'Your Majesty is welcome to this castle of my Lord Marquis of Carabas.'

'What, my Lord Marquis!' cried the king. 'And does this castle also belong to you? There can be nothing finer than this court and all the stately buildings which surround it. Let us go in, if you please.'

The marquis gave his hand to the princess and followed the king, who went first. They passed into a spacious hall, where they found a magnificent collation, which the ogre had prepared for his friends, who were that very day to visit him, but dared not enter, knowing the king was there. His majesty was charmed with the good qualities of the Lord Marquis of Carabas, as was his daughter, and seeing the vast estate he possessed, said to him:

'It will be owing to yourself only, my Lord Marquis, if you are not my son-in-law.'

The marquis, making several low bows, accepted the honor which his majesty conferred upon him, and forthwith, that very same day, married the princess.

Puss became a great lord, and never ran after mice any more.

[Charles Perrault.]

the meaning of the ideas read."[1] These are high skills in the literary experience. They aren't discovered effortlessly by all capable readers, but there is growing evidence that they can be taught. Intensive work with a few selections can help develop them. The following ideas for above-literal questions and activities are intended to give suggestions pertinent to this sphere of literary experience. Select a few from them and try them out, using a suitable story.

Inference and Extrapolation Questions and Activities

Like all other arts, literature derives its power from its ability to suggest. It triggers the imagination, which draws upon past experience. No story gives all the details of its setting; some must be provided from the reader's or listener's past experiences. No story tells all about the characters; again it is necessary to read into the characters, to draw upon personal experience, sharing the act of creating with the author. Plots suggest crucial actions, but the reader must harness his or her imagination to the task of filling in the actions, determining their importance in the total structure of the story. Similarly, the reader infers a theme from a total work. (Often when readers are told the theme or lesson of a story, they feel cheated, and rightly so: they weren't allowed to use their powers of inference to discover a theme connected to their own experience.)

Inference takes place within the structure of the literary work. To go beyond the structure requires extrapolation. Both of these interpretation techniques are based on literary components. Applied to stories, they are based on setting, character, plot, and theme. Both should be relevant to literary purposes.

To illustrate the progression from literal to inference and extrapolation items, consider Andrew Lang's version of the Charles Perrault story best known as "Puss in Boots."[2] You may want to examine *Puss in Boots* (34), freely translated and cleverly illustrated by Marcia Brown, or *Puss in Boots* (35) told by Hans Fischer, adapted from Charles Perrault, and humorously illustrated with charcoal sketches by Fischer.

Read the story and then work along with us as we identify, somewhat randomly, two purposes that will serve as a guide as we work intensively with the story. Then, to provide a base, we'll give sample literal-level items, and demonstrate inference extrapolation ideas. These, remember, are examples. You are encouraged to create your own.

LITERARY PURPOSES FOR "PUSS IN BOOTS":

1. To observe the central character's ingenuity;
2. To recognize that the story's elements of fantasy are presented consistently.

---

[1] William S. Gray and Bernice Rogers, *Maturity in Reading: Its Nature and Appraisal* (University of Chicago Press, 1956). Chapter 3 is reprinted in Sam Sebesta and Carl Wallen, eds, *The First R* (Science Research Associates, 1972), pp. 14–23.

[2] The version reprinted here, titled "The Master Cat," first appeared in 1889 in *The Blue Fairy Book*. A modern edition of this version is "Puss in Boots," in Andrew Lang's *The Blue Fairy Book*, illus. Grace Dalles Clarke (Random House, 1959), pp. 15–21.

The terminology *behavioral objective* or *performance objectives* (or whatever the current parlance) would no doubt be different from the language we use here.[1] For example, the first purpose might read, "Asked to list examples of Puss's ingenuity, the child responds with at least six such examples, inferring the reasons for Puss's action." We think this is sterile and arbitrary language. It would not, however, alter the substance of our statements or our efforts.

Literal-level Items for "Puss in Boots"

1. What did Puss want Carabas to give him? What did Puss do with the sack? To whom did he give the rabbits? (Recalling events and their sequence.)
2. Puss seemed to want to help his master. List the things he did to help. (Recalling relationships among events).
3. Which characters could do something unusual—something you wouln't expect to happen in real life? Which characters did something that was clever? (Noting important details)
4. Puss often talks and acts like a person. What does the author tell us during the story to remind us that he is a cat? (Recalling examples of style)

Now, look back at the purposes. Have these been applied in the literal items? What should be added?

Inferring Puss's Ingenuity

1. Puss must have done some planning. When did he start? Where's the first clue that tells you he might be planning to please the king? What were his reasons for tricking the king and the ogre? Who benefited from his trickery? Who did not benefit? Is this the way Puss planned it? Could his plans have gone wrong? What might have happened? Was he an honest cat? To whom was he dishonest?
2. Who made mistakes in the story? Did Puss know that they would make mistakes?

Inferring Consistency among the Elements of Fantasy

1. Is this a story of magic? Who, if anyone, has magic? Why doesn't Puss just call on his fairy godmother to help him? How is the story different from those in which wishes are granted by magic?
2. How early in the story do you know that Puss won't find some magic way to solve his problems?
3. An unusual thing in the story is that a cat can talk. What other unusual things occur? One person in the story can change his shape. Can the other characters do that? What would happen if they could? Who in the story has no unusual abilities? What would happen if these other characters had unusual abilities? How would the story be different?

---

[1] See Robert Zoellner, "Behavioral Objectives for English," *College English* 33 (January 1972): 418–32.

EXTRAPOLATING

1. Let's go on with the story. What might happen in the kingdom to cause Carabas to need the help of Puss, who is now a "great lord"? Make up a new adventure for Puss in Boots. (Or act it out.)
2. Did the king ever discover that he had been tricked? What did he do?
3. Tell the story of the other two brothers. What happened to them? Does the story give you any clues to help in answering this question?
4. Explain how the ogre got his power to change into a lion or a mouse.
5. Were there any other unusual animals in the kingdom? If so, tell about one. Which of them would fit best into another story about Puss in Boots and the rest of the kingdom? Why?

Remember, extrapolation items go beyond the story. They require creative responses by the reader based on the tone and literary components within the story. You may ask, "What in the story led you to think that?"

You must be selective with your questions, of course. You don't want to make a career of any story. Watch carefully to see what the traffic will bear.

special activities

1. Add a literary purpose (to those already given) for "Puss in Boots" and construct literal questions or activities to develop that purpose. Then develop inference and extrapolation items to develop it further.

2. Go back to "Mitzi Sneezes" and design an inference item and an extrapolation item to be used with that story.

3. If possible, test your questions and activities. Can a child respond to them? If so, are the responses pertinent? Do they derive from the story and retain the story's tone? If not, why not? Is the language of your items concrete enough so that a child can understand them? Higher level questions aren't necessarily difficult in themselves, but you must guard against difficulty arising from language that is too abstract or a tendency to question in a stilted, forbidding manner. Learn, also, to wait for a response; don't rush on from item to item for fear that no one will respond.

We noted earlier the Guszak study showing that teachers use above-literal level questions infrequently. Other studies reinforce this conclusion. Why aren't more inference and extrapolation items included in intensive work with literature? Why should they be? What is their use? And how are you to evaluate their results? Consider these matters as you go on. We'll return to them at the end of this section.

POINT-OF-VIEW TECHNIQUE, BRAINSTORMING, AND ROLE-PLAYING

These techniques can be used to enliven and sustain inference and extrapolation based on a story. The point-of-view technique (sometimes referred to as taking a character's *stance*)[1] requires a response to be stated in first-person from the point of view of a story character. Brainstorming, which can be used in any open-question situation, simply clears the air for fluent response. Role-playing is a dramatization technique focusing on a specific problem derived from the story in an attempt to clarify the problem and to try out and evaluate solutions. We'll now illustrate each of these techniques, still basing the illustrations on "Puss in Boots."

Point-of-View Items for "Puss in Boots"

You can prepare your students for point-of-view technique by saying, "When I snap my fingers, you must magically *become* the character whose name I say first. Tell (or act) your answer as you would if you were that character."

1. You *be* Puss. Now, Puss, tell what you were trying to do. Who was it you wanted to help? How did you figure out your scheme? Didn't you trick the king? Why did you do it? Was that an honest thing to do? How did you know about the ogre's magic ability? Didn't you have any magic yourself?
2. Puss, after this story ended, did you ever help Carabas again? What did you do this time? Tell us about it.
3. You *be* the king. King, what do you think of Puss today? Was it smart of him to trick you? Was it honest? Have you been tricked before—are you the sort of person who gets tricked often? Weren't you suspicious when a talking cat wearing boots came into your palace?

Note that some of these are "yes-no" items. You can, of course, encourage a child to continue his response. You'll find that this is no great problem: most children step effortlessly into a role once they understand the basic point-of-view requirement: that the item is to be answered in the first person. The self-consciousness and struggle for language that often accompany less direct inference and extrapolation questions tend to disappear when point-of-view technique is used.[2]

special activities

1. Restate two questions (any level) from the "Puss in Boots" examples in the preceding section, applying the point-of-view technique.

---

[1] See John S. Simmons, "The 'Stance' Approach in Responding to Literature," *Journal of Reading* (October 1968): 13–17.
[2] Sam Leaton Sebesta, "The Neglected Art: Thought Questions," *Elementary English* (December 1967): 888–95.

2. Restate two or more of your questions for "Mitzi Sneezes" using this technique.
3. Select a book or story to work with independently during this sequence and make up point-of-view questions for it.
4. Note that sometimes the character for point-of-view can be a minor one or even one not mentioned in the story but somehow inferred to be in it. For instance, let the family doctor tell about Mitzi's family, recapitulating the incidents of the story and adding to them. Can you create a character who might throw light on characters' motives and reactions? Who might it be?

Brainstorming

Point-of-view technique usually works best if it requires instant response. Otherwise, it loses spontaneity. A useful technique for encouraging instant fluency is brainstorming. Its "rules" were set forth by the originator of the term, Alex Osborn.[1] Here are some of his suggestions:

1. Encourage children to express any idea that comes immediately to mind.
2. Don't criticize or place a value judgment on any other person's expressed idea.
3. As the response develops, seek to combine, adapt, and expand several of the ideas that have been presented. (You might encourage several children to take the point of view of Puss and then combine and develop their ideas.)

As you can see, brainstorming has but one aim: *fluency*. If such fluency promotes unconsidered, slipshod thinking, you can go back later and help the children reconsider their responses. In fact, brainstorming does include eventual review, evaluation, and further development of fluently produced ideas derived from an earlier stage of the discussion. For instance:

You might ask an extrapolation question on "The Three Bears," with each child *being* Goldilocks—"Goldilocks, what did you do after you ran away from the Bears' house?" Try to get answers as quickly as possible. Let some respondents develop their ideas or those of others; also encourage new ideas. (Sometimes, just to warm up a group and underline the fluency idea, show them that you're keeping tally of the number of responses and put a plus-sign over each response that represents a new idea). When fluency has been achieved, you suggest combination and development—such as, "We've had several ideas that might be put together to show more about what Goldilocks did. Goldilocks, tell us more about your story." Then keep track of how many combinations and elaborations are used. This needn't be accurate, but it should be done by the group during evaluation of the brainstorming session. It simply calls attention to the manner in which fluently produced ideas are refined and more fully elaborated at a later stage.

To re-examine the production, you can shift the point-of-view and begin

---

[1]Alex F. Osborn, *Applied Imagination*, rev. ed. (Scribner's, 1957), pp. 84, 244–45.

again: "Now, Mrs. Bear, is that what really happened? What do you know about what Goldilocks did after she ran away?"

Out of our experience we offer two suggestions:

1. The flat characters of folk literature present a challenge in point-of-view and brainstorming techniques. On the one hand, they seem to encourage response, since too little is given about them. Almost anything goes. But on the other hand, response can get out of hand. You'll discover respondents (children or adults) who force a folk tale character into a modern setting or into a comic role when that isn't his tone at all in the story. At first, you might accept this. After all, it does promote fluency and familiarity with the techniques. Once this has been done, if you shift the example to a story with greater depth of character, you"ll be likely to get more satisfying, productive results.

2. If you are working in a classroom, use these techniques instead of, or as a preface to, individual creative writing or drawing assignments. At each grade level—first through sixth—we have used these techniques successfully to the extent that children can work independently in small groups to construct point-of-view items of their own and explore them through brainstorming. It takes careful guidance at first, but interest is usually sufficient to develop it from there.

Role-playing

Sometimes inference and extrapolation items explored through point-of-view technique and brainstorming converge to reveal a central problem within a story or one suggested by the story. It may be an indicator of the story's theme. As such, it's worth more intensive exploration than the levels and techniques discussed thus far can provide. What's next?

The next step should be neither an adult sermon nor an attempt to get a child to state an abstract moral (though some children, to please an adult, become proficient at this). You must not let an abstract thematic statement kill a story's spirit. (We did this a few times, but stopped the day a child mumbled, "Here comes the commercial.")

Still, you don't want to drop the matter when it's at a high point of interest. The moral level—the level at which a character must choose between doing what's right and doing what works—is of concern to all of us. (See Kohlberg's discussion in chapter 3.)

Suppose your discussion has intensified around these questions: "Puss, did you help Carabas the next time he was in trouble? . . . Carabas, we hear you have a helpful cat; now that you are king, can you call on him for help?" Brainstorming has followed, until there are several idea combinations and an implicit debate. Here are some responses from Puss:

I always help Carabas. He's good but he isn't smart. He didn't eat me, so I've always been grateful. And I'm smart.

He's king so now all he has to do is call his soldiers and he has a couple of bombers and nobody else has got any. So who needs me? I'm starting up a magic act. I learned it from an ogre I met one time. I stole his book.

I got married and then I went and lived with one of Carabas's brothers. I like him better anyway. I just did that other stuff for kicks.

Carabas is all right and I help him when I get the chance, but he laughs at me when I walk in these boots and I can't get them off.

Here are responses from Carabas:

Actually, Puss never was a very good helper. He lied a lot and later I had to pay the ogre's wife a million dollars to keep her from suing me.

Puss would help if I needed him. But now I settle things myself. I had a big battle a week ago and I won it. I used the ogre's sword and turned the other army into mice.

Puss is the best man in my kingdom, even if he is a cat. He makes all the laws.

You have to be careful of a friend who plays tricks on people.

At this point—where point-of-view technique results in focus on an implied theme—the interpretation session can be shifted to the more focused process called *role-playing*. Role-playing steps are designated and described by Fannie R. Shaftel and George Shaftel in *Role-Playing for Social Values: Decision-Making in the Social Studies.*[1] Here they are applied to literary experience:

PROBLEM DEFINITION.   In this first step, the role-playing leader draws from the point-of-view discussion a thematic problem and sets it before the group. In this case, the value of a friend who tricks opponents is being debated. The problem might be stated in this way: "Let's find out if Puss really was a good friend to Carabas both in the story and afterwards. Were his actions wise? Can he be counted on to be helpful?"

DELINEATION OF ALTERNATIVES.   Before the actual role-playing session can begin, negative and positive ideas for solving the problem need to be put forth. This calls for focused brainstorming. You might guide this step by saying, "Go back to the start of the story. We've just found out that Puss is able to talk. He knows that Carabas is sad. Let's have a discussion between Puss and Carabas. You don't have to follow the plot of the story this time. Let's see if there are other ways the story might have developed."

---

[1](Prentice-Hall, 1967), pp. 183–88.

EXPLORING ALTERNATIVES.   To consider the alternatives, assign roles: one child plays Puss, one plays Carabas. Set the stage. Decide where the characters are. Briefly discuss how the scene might begin. For instance, Carabas might begin by asking Puss what they can do about his problem: what is he to do when his possession is a cat? The actors make up the dialogue and action as they go along, illustrating one of the alternatives. Repeat the process, with other enactments, using other actors to play the characters. Explore several alternatives.

First Enactment

PUSS: I'd like to help you, but I'm just a cat. You could hire me out to catch mice in the mill.
CARABAS: I don't think that would bring in much money.
PUSS: Well, a talking cat is something to own. I could be on television.
(*Observers objected that television doesn't fit the setting of the story.*)

Second Enactment

CARABAS: I'm going to be king. It won't be easy, but you can help me.
PUSS: How? If you don't get me any nice clothes, I won't do you any good. You'll be sorry you ever got me.
CARABAS: Okay, but you've got to promise to do what I say. I want you to trick everybody so they think I'm the most important person in the kingdom, next to the king.

Having inferred alternatives within the story, try refocusing the problem to role-playing outside the story, hence to an extrapolated situation: "A moment ago we brainstormed to decide whether Puss was a good friend after the story ended. Now there's new trouble. A whole kingdom of ogres seems headed for Carabas's land. Use what you know of Puss's actions within the story to decide what he'll do now." Again, roles are assigned and the stage set.

First Enactment

PUSS: I'll trick every ogre into changing into a mouse again.
CARABAS: I don't think that will work the second time. They've probably heard about you. Thanks for trying, though.
PUSS: Maybe the ogres will win.
CARABAS: If they do, will you go over to their side?
PUSS: No, I'll always be your friend.

Second Enactment

CARABAS: I don't know what to do. I guess I could raise some money and try to pay them.

Puss: Okay. I'll sell my boots and give you the money.

Carabas: That won't be enough. You'll have to go to my brothers and have them sell the mill and the donkey. Bring the money here.

Puss: All right. Maybe I'll think of something along the way.

Carabas: I think you brought this all on. Your tricks made the ogres mad at us.

Puss: I just did what would help you, and I got something to boot.

Evaluating Alternatives in Light of the Problem.   Return to the problem or problems as stated: "In the first situation, which enactments showed that Puss was a good friend? When did you doubt that he was a good friend? Was there anything in your role-playing that showed Puss had not acted wisely? What do you think now: was Puss wise?"

The evaluative discussion should help children reflect on the story's theme: whether Puss's actions were wise ones. The discussion is facilitated by the enactments based on inference and extrapolation.

Decision-Making and Generalizing.   The decision here, within the context of the story, is whether Puss is a good friend and whether he has acted wisely. It's unlikely that role-playing will yield a "yes-no" decision; the purpose is rather to clarify the issue and to invite reflection on it. Beyond this, there is a broader theme: whether real friendship includes or justifies trickery. You need not belabor a moral (or depart too far from the story's portrayal of ingenious action) to arrive, through discussion, at some generalization about the appropriate actions of friendship. You might ask, "What has our role-playing shown us about friendship in this story?" But in our view you shouldn't go further than that. Your role as leader consists of helping define a problem, setting a specific role-playing situation, guiding the evaluative discussion, and opening the way to generalization.

We used "Puss in Boots" as an example partly because it's a playful story, well removed from modern realism. It doesn't tempt you to seek out a lesson and drive it home. We recommend that your early role-playing situations be of this type. Later, you and your children may examine more pertinent issues through role-playing. Remember, though, that an issue involves various points of view and a number of reasonable alternatives. Role-playing should be used as an aid to reasoning, not to propagandizing.

teaching ideas

In keeping with their themes, most stories offer opportunities for role-playing. Here are a few that we've used with apparent success in the early stages of role-playing sessions:

EARLY CHILDHOOD

1. Hoban, Russell. *A Bargain for Frances.* Illus. Lillian Hoban. Harper & Row, 1970. Stop at the foot of page 39. At this point Frances, having discovered that Thelma tricked her out of a tea set, is planning to do something about it. "What is Frances going to do? What should she do?" Elicit comments and discuss; then assign parts, try out the alternatives, and evaluate.

2. Bertol, Roland. *Charles Drew.* Illus. Jo Polseno. Crowell, 1970. One place to stop this biography for role-playing is at the end of page 31, where the U.S. Army's white doctors are attacking Dr. Drew for refusing to separate blood plasma by race. Select a Dr. Drew, a group of antagonistic doctors (as shown in the illustration on that page), and perhaps a sympathetic doctor. Then proceed with role-playing before going on with the narrative.

3. Beim, Lorraine and Jerrold. *Two Is a Team.* Illus. Ernest Cricklow. Harcourt, 1945. Stop where the two boys have created mayhem on their scooter ride: a lady has dropped her shopping bag, a little girl's doll has been injured, and a man's dog has escaped. Start with the confrontation between the boys and these three angry people. Role-play the situation before proceeding with the story.

INTERMEDIATE CHILDHOOD:

4. Babbit, Natalie. *Knee-Knock Rise.* Farrar, Straus & Giroux, 1970. "You are Egan and have learned what the much feared Megrimum really is. Will you tell Ada and the others?" Role-play alternatives from which Egan can choose. Let the role-playing session continue until the consequences are clear.

5. MacGregor, Ellen. *Miss Pickerell Goes to the Arctic.* Illus. Paul Galdone. Whittlesey House, 1954. Stop at the end of chapter 14, where Miss Pickerell is afloat alone on an iceberg. Set the scene and let the role-playing determine what Miss Pickerell might do.

6. Cleary, Beverly. *Ramona the Pest.* Illus. Louis Darling. Morrow, 1968. Stop in the midst of chapter 7 (page 164) where Miss Binny, the kindergarten teacher, says: "You will have to go home and stay there until you can make up your mind not to pull Susan's curls. . . . I'm sorry, Ramona, but we cannot have a hair puller in our kindergarten." What does Ramona do? With whom does she interact? What is the outcome? Play several versions, then discuss.

LATER CHILDHOOD:

7. Meigs, Cornelia. *Jane Addams: Pioneer for Social Justice.* Little, Brown, 1970. You might try a hypothetical talk show between Jane Addams and Ralph Nader, their major question being "What are this nation's most pressing problems?" Chapter 15 provides a chance for an interesting confrontation between Jane Addams and the visitors who are demanding to see the "Devil Baby" at Hull House—a challenge to the protagonist. Try playing this scene.

special activities

1. Select one of the works cited above. Briefly state the following: a literary purpose for using the work, literal-level questions and activities as a base for examining the purpose, inference and extrapolation items for directing attention to the purpose or for other purposes that may emerge in the discussion, and point-of-view evolving into role-playing situations that may develop out of the preceding discussion. If possible, try out your plan with a group of children or adults.

2. The procedures discussed here are somewhat sequential, as has already been noted. Sometimes they are lively preliminaries to full-scale creative dramatics sessions. After you study creative dramatics in chapter 10, consider whether our work with "Puss in Boots" might lead to creative dramatics. Would your plan for your own selection build to a creative dramatics session? What would you need to consider before proceeding?

Activities That Relate Self to Story

The various literary types differ in their distance from everyday experiences. The folk tale and the modern fanciful story may at first seem distant in their content (and sometimes in their themes) from readers' lives. The modern realistic story may, on the other hand, appear to be quite close. The procedures for intensive work with literature heretofore described are all likely to bring a story within the range of known experience, making the literary experience itself a personal one. "Change the names and the story is about you" then becomes a meaningful statement.

Don't ask relating-self-to-story questions too early or the response will be superficial. First, explore the story using some or all of the techniques that have been discussed. Don't make your items too general, or they'll fail to challenge the respondent to find a real parallel. "Have you had a good friend who helped you?" is too general to relate one's life to "Puss in Boots."

Of course you can't ask who has met a talking cat, but that isn't the point of "Puss in Boots" anyway. Try, instead, something similar to these examples:

> You've just done something that caused your friend to say, 'You are a real Puss in Boots.' What did he mean? What have you done? Now, can you tell about a time when you really did solve a problem as if you were a Puss in Boots? Tell about it. Explain how you were like Puss. Did you act wisely?

> Tell about a time when you needed a Puss in Boots to help you. Would the situation have turned out well? Is there another character in another story who might have been more helpful? Why or why not?

Try to get specific real-life incidents that parallel thematic movements in the story. Take time to observe the parallels.

As we've said, this becomes easier as you move toward more realistic stories. Try constructing a relating-self-to-story item to use with "Mitzi Sneezes." Use this technique with your own selection. If practical, exchange your items with someone, and test your responses through mutual criticism.

SEQUENCE FOR FACILITATING LITERARY EXPERIENCE

We've described a sequence for facilitating literary experience based on intensive work with a good selection. The sequence begins with an understanding at the literal level: ability to recall or recognize pertinent information contained in a selection. It then moves to the use of inference and extrapolation questions and activities, point-of-view technique using brainstorming, and sometimes evolving into role-playing, and items aimed at relating the selection directly to one's own experience. Three questions need to be answered about using this sequence.

- *Does the sequence apply to stories only, or might it be used with other literary types?* The procedure as we've described and illustrated it applies to narrative—to stories and other literary types when they describe events, for example, biography, historical accounts, poetry that tells a story. The focus of your questions and activities must highlight the major qualities of each type. For instance, biography is likely to bring emphasis on point-of-view and on role-playing. Because it attempts to be factual, it may not work so well with extrapolation. Role-playing has been especially effective in exploring historical and current social and psychological issues, as the Shaftels' book shows. Ideas for intensive work with poetry and nonfiction forms are presented in chapters 7 and 8, respectively.

- *Does the sequence cover factors known to exist in literary response research?* Only partially. Look at the summary of research quoted from Purves and Beach (p. 433). The cognitive factor and the interpretive factor are the major components explored in our sequence. Attention to language and style have not been dealt with extensively here but have been considered in the discussion of literary types, and elsewhere. Certainly a work such as Walter de la Mare's *The Three Royal Monkeys* (see chapter 4) invites intensive involvement with the author's language and style; many other works are equally rewarding in this area.

  Judging the value of a work leads back to consideration of literary criteria. Informed judgment should, we believe, come after other intensive exploration. To begin a discussion with "Did you like the story?" will invite superficial judgment and may close avenues for further exploration.

- *How can results be measured?* Perhaps the measurement question is at the root of the trouble. Teachers and others working with literature often over-emphasize literal-level questions because they yield right or wrong answers that can be measured quickly. Interpretation items do not. Current concern over accountability seems to encourage right answer measures.

But some general ways of measuring interpretation are feasible. (1) You can measure *fluency* and *productivity*. Give a point, if you choose, for every reasonable response to an open interpretation item. (2) You can judge *quality* of responses: devise a point system to differentiate between the stock response and the response that demonstrates greater creativity. Included in this differentiation might be evidence of "change of set": that is, a response qualitatively different from other responses, yet within the context or tone of the work, should receive higher evaluation. (3) Although subjective, the quality of enthusiasm ought to be included in your evaluation of the results of your intensive sessions with literature. How enthusiastically do children pursue the study? Is there evidence that the sessions increase children's literary pursuits? Experimentation will yield more objective ways of judging enthusiasm: measured increase in amount of

booklist

Aids for Evaluating Literary Experience

"A Look at Literature." National Council of Teachers of English. Educational Testing Service, 1968. An NCTE Cooperative Test of Critical Reading and Appreciation, available from Educational Testing Service, Box 999, Princeton, New Jersey 08540. There are two forms of the test, making it possible to study changes in response and appreciation over a period of time. Geared for intermediate-age children, it attempts to measure (1) perception of literary qualities and devices, (2) comprehension of meaning (literal and interpretive), (3) extension and application of meaning.

Cooper, Charles R. *Measuring Growth in Appreciation of Literature.* Where Do We Go? Series. International Reading Association, 1972. (Address of I.R.A. is 800 Barksdale Rd., Newark, Delaware 19711.) A critical survey of measures used over the years to determine quality of literary experience. Cooper's substantiated opinion is that measurement has been slow and misguided in most cases, but he gives constructive suggestions for improving the situation.

Purves, Alan C. and Rippere, Victoria. *Elements of Writing about a Literary Work: A Study of Response to Literature.* Research Report Series, No. 9. National Council of Teachers of English, 1968. (Address is 1111 Kenyon Road, Urbana, Illinois 61901.) Booklet includes a categorization of types of response with descriptions of the categories to help in devising a response checklist.

Cooper, Charles R., and Purves, Alan C. *Responding: Ginn Interrelated Sequence in Literature: A Guide to Evaluation.* Ginn, 1973. A pamphlet describing measures of literary response at the secondary-school level.

reading, measured increase in comments about selections read, measured increase in the variety and types (and even the quality) of literature independently selected.

special activities

1. Select a literary type from those discussed in chapter 2. How might the sequence described in this chapter be modified to bring out response to that type? Which strong unique qualities of that literary type ought to be highlighted as you devise purposes for your work and activities to apply to those purposes? If possible, select one literary example from the type and use it to illustrate your modified sequence.

2. Go back to the sequence as we've described it and show how style might be included in your questions and activities. This will require use of a specific story, such as the one you used as you studied this section.

3. Devise a checklist or quantitative instrument for evaluating the role-playing responses given for "Puss in Boots." What can you add to our comments on evaluation as given here?

INTENSIVE AND EXTENSIVE LITERARY EXPERIENCE

Not all literary selections should be handled in the way we've just described. The sequence is meant to facilitate an experience that can be transferred to other situations. A child's *extensive* reading should be affected through what you've done in an intensive literature lesson.

Relating One Story to Another: Basic Plots

Much has been written about the commonalities of all literature, even to the claim that all plots are basically derived from one central plot. That is probably an over-statement, but it does point up the possibility that a child's understanding of one selection may enable him to understand others.

Northrop Frye, in *Anatomy of Criticism,* notes in early theories about plot that many plots are about a hero's quest for something valuable: a return to a Golden Age or efforts to bring a Golden Age into reality. Certainly that idea does operate in many traditional stories as well as many modern ones. Then Frye states an even more abstract central theme and plot: "This story of the loss and regaining of identity is, I think, the framework of all literature." Lest we jump to the conclusion that the common plot rules out variation in literature, Frye observes:

"I'm not saying that there's nothing new in literature: I'm saying that everything is new, and yet recognizably the same kind of thing as the old, just as a new baby is a genuinely new individual. . . ."[1]

Less abstractly, some critics have attempted to designate *basic plots:* those used over and over again with considerable variation in characters, settings, and even themes. For instance, there is the basic plot identifiable as a *travel* story. A character goes away from home and meets an adventure (a monster to be overcome, a quest to be fulfilled, a person to be rescued, a character deficiency to be corrected). He undergoes the experience: he either overcomes the difficulty or it overcomes him. You'll have no difficulty citing examples, from the *Odyssey* to "The Gingerbread Man" to Ursula K. Le Guin's *The Farthest Shore* (36) and Lloyd Alexander's *The Cat Who Wished to Be a Man* (37). Perhaps you'll spot the travel-story element in "Puss in Boots."

Another basic plot is the *contrast* story. Two or more characters have opposing points of view, or come from contrasting settings, or meet contrasting adventures or experience the same adventure in contrasting ways. They may confront each other; the plot results from their conflict and sometimes its resolution. Folk literature abounds in such confrontations. The country mouse meets the city mouse or Cinderella encounters the wicked new inhabitants of the house. One modern author says that in his books all conversation scenes are confrontations, with two or more characters presenting opposing beliefs.

There is also the *episodic* story. Incident after incident reveals the adventures of central characters, sometimes with a recurrent problem. Many series books present parallel episodes—the Nancy Drew books, the Hardy Boys books, the Oz books, and others.

Another common plot is the *pourquoi* or *origin* story. The plot gives an explanation of some observed phenomenon. The classic myths, as well as some modern ones, are of this type.

Do these basic plots really describe the breadth of literature? As in the case of the travel story, they aren't limited by age boundaries. They are combined and intertwined in the plot structure of many stories. *The Wind in the Willows,* for instance, presents Toad's travels and Mole's long adventure into the unknown world. Hence it is a travel plot. But there is contrast, too: the refined aristocratic Badger against the devil-may-care Toad; the naïve Mole against the worldly Rat. Then, too, the story is episodic; each chapter consists of a central incident sometimes unrelated to the others. And there are mythical elements: the origin of dawn and a visit to the origins of nature herself.

Such combinations reveal commonalities in most fiction. But there are limits. To distill stories into one central plot or combination of basic plots ignores uniqueness—the "everything is new" that Northrop Frye mentions. Attempts to sum up a story by listing its basic plots result in over-generalization. *The*

---

[1]Northrop Frye, *Anatomy of Criticism* (Princeton University Press, 1957), p. 55.

Odyssey is not *The Wind in the Willows* even if there are similarities in basic plot. Finding similarities from one plot to another clarifies form and does show unity in literature. It may help in the development of what is called "form consciousness." But the flavor of a work—its tone, its unique way of handling plot and other components—is not revealed by a basic plot study.

Recurrent story parts, smaller than whole plots, are exhaustively tallied and compared in the six-volume *Motif-Index of Folk-Literature* by Stith Thompson.[1] Major motif topics in this index include: Creation, Fanciful Animals, Tabu, Magic, Ideas about the Dead, Marvels, Dreadful Beings, "Tests," Wisdom, Cleverness, Foolishness, and a miscellany of categories such as reversals of fortune, bargains and promises, gifts, social systems, rewards and punishments, captives and fugitives, cruelty, and numerous others. You may find this index helpful when you search for comparable stories from the folklore of many cultures. (It would be helpful, by the way, if someone would compose a motif list based on modern children's literature.)

One basic plot, a number of basic plots, a long list of recurrent motifs—being aware of these factors increases our awareness of the commonalities that run through all literature. But don't begin with them, as if they were lists for children to consume and apply. Instead, ask children questions such as, "How is this story similar to other stories?" Later you may want to ask, "How is the plot similar to the plot of another story?" Still later, specifically: "We've talked about trickery in 'Puss in Boots'; in which other story do you find trickery as a main part of the plot?"

Eventually, you and your children might devise your own list of familiar plot elements—basic plots or motifs—derived from your literature sessions. This is an inductive way of examining commonalities, and it will be far more applicable to extensive literary experience than a deductive use of someone else's plot lists.

Now you may ask, why? What's the good of discerning basic plots, the recurrent underlying structure that exists in the literary field? Here are three reasons:

1. Discernment of basic plots increases a reader's sense of expectation and his ability to hypothesize about a story's components. A story is a shared experience, a transaction between a creator and recipient. When children read or hear a story, they need to "cast ahead"—to anticipate what is to come, and then to check the accuracy of their predictions. Perhaps this facet of literary experience—more than any other—accounts for interest and elicits continued reading and listening. Some knowledge of plot structures will promote expectation and hypothesis-making.

2. Discernment of basic plots or motifs directs a child's thinking toward the totality of a work. Other components, their details and the style of their

---

[1]Stith Thompson, *Motif-Index of Folk-Literature,* rev. ed. (Indiana University Press, 1958).

presentation, are then viewed in better perspective, their relationship to the whole made clearer. James R. Squire refers to this aspect of literary experience as *form consciousness*. His comments here applied to the writer of literature could, if slightly reworded, apply just as aptly to the reader:

> The good writer worries about organization, about form, about having no clearcut purpose in his writing, about not being specific and to the point; whereas the poor writer worries about none of these things. . . . In the good writer, then, concern for content is paralleled by an equal concern for form. . . .[1]

3. Such discernment helps a reader to feel more comfortable with many literary types. A child whose experience is confined to one type of story, or who seeks one type whenever he has a choice, is helped to see a wider range of choices through understanding the commonalities among all types.

special activities

1. In our discussion above we listed examples of a few basic plots. Most often, these plot patterns are derived from and applied to folklore. Do they also apply to modern stories? Our examples seem to suggest they do. But try them out for yourself—look for these basic plots in Caldecott and Newbery books or even in television narratives or movies.

2. In chapter 3 we suggested that children's interests aren't always described by a topic. Excitement about a "girl-tames-horse" story may not indicate a child's interest in horses but rather a broader, plot-based interest, that of achieving some control over a known environment. How might an understanding of basic plots—by you and by children—result in a better match between children and their literature? Discuss.

Our major theme in this chapter is this: we'd like you to try to facilitate intensive literary experience by using a limited number of good selections so that the result may be a deeper and broader literary experience for each child. The main source of examples has been narrative as it is presented in books. But there is no reason whatever that literary experience as we've discussed it cannot be derived from stories presented through other media. The important thing is the overall literary experience that is derived from a work. Ultimately, you may find that your work with intensive literary experience, using one good selection and teaching it well, has a far wider, deeper result than you've ever dreamed.

---

[1]James R. Squire, "New Direction in Language Learning, *Elementary English* (October 1962): 535–44.

CHAPTER REFERENCES

1. Fleischman, Sid. *By the Great Horn Spoon.* Little, Brown, 1963. (I)
2. Morey, Walt. *Canyon Winter.* Dutton, 1972. (I–U)
3. Segal, Lore. *Tell Me a Mitzi.* Illus. Harriet Pincus. Farrar, Straus & Giroux, 1971.
4. Konigsburg, E. L. *A Proud Taste for Scarlet and Miniver.* Atheneum, 1973. (I–U)
5. L'Engle, Madeleine. *A Wind in the Door.* Farrar, Straus & Giroux, 1973. (I–U)
6. Pease, Howard. *Long Wharf.* Dodd, Mead, 1939. (I–U)
7. Grahame, Kenneth. *The Wind in the Willows.* Scribner's, 1960. (I–U)
8. Clark, Ann Nolan. *Secret of the Andes.* Viking, 1952. (I)
9. Sorenson, Virginia. *Miracles of Maple Hill.* Harcourt, 1956. (I)
10. de Treviño, Elizabeth Borten. *I, Juan de Pareja.* Farrar, Straus & Giroux, 1965. (U)
11. LeGuin, Ursula K. *The Tombs of Atuan.* Atheneum, 1971. (U)
12. Dahl, Roald. *Charlie and the Chocolate Factory.* Knopf, 1964.
13. Steig, William. *Sylvester and the Magic Pebble.* Windmill Books/Simon and Schuster, 1969. (E)
14. Turkle, Brinton. *The Fiddler of High Lonesome.* Viking, 1968. (I)
15. Gates, Doris. *Blue Willow.* Viking, 1940. (I)
16. Keats, Ezra Jack. *The Snowy Day.* Viking, 1963. (E)
17. Henry, Marguerite. *Cinnabar, The One O'Clock Fox.* Rand McNally, 1956.
18. Gray, Elizabeth Janet. *Adam of the Road.* Viking, 1942. (I)
19. Mayne, William. *Earthfasts.* Dutton, 1966. (U)
20. Garfield, Leon. *Black Jack.* Pantheon, 1968. (U)
21. Pyle, Howard. *Men of Iron.* Harper, 1891. (U)
22. O'Dell, Scott. *Island of the Blue Dolphins.* Houghton Mifflin, 1960. (I–U)
23. Behn, Harry. *The Faraway Lurs.* World, 1963. (U)
24. Eager, Edward. *Half Magic.* Harcourt, 1954. (I)
25. de Angeli, Marguerite. *Bright April.* Doubleday, 1946. (E–I)
26. Horwitz, Elinor Lander. *The Strange Story of the Frog Who Became a Prince.* Illus. John Heinly. Delacorte, 1971. (E)
27. Berger, Terry. *Black Fairy Tales.* Atheneum, 1969. (E–I)
28. Stith Thompson, coll. *One Hundred Favorite Folktales.* Indiana Univ. Press, 1968. (I)
29. Stolz, Mary. *Belling the Tiger.* Harper, 1961. (U)
30. *The Three Bears.* Illus. Paul Galdone. Seabury, 1972.
31. Hutchins, Pat. *Rosie's Walk.* Macmillan, 1968.
32. Krahn, Fernando. *How Santa Claus Had a Long and Difficult Journey Delivering His Presents.* Delacorte, 1970.
33. Lester, Julius. *Black Folktales.* Illus. Tom Feelings. Baron, 1969. (I)
34. *Puss in Boots.* Illus. Marcia Brown. Scribner's, 1952.
35. Fischer, Hans, adapted from Charles Perrault. *Puss in Boots.* Illus. Hans Fischer. Harcourt, n.d.
36. LeGuin, Ursula K. *The Farthest Shore.* Atheneum, 1972. (U)
37. Alexander, Lloyd. *The Cat Who Wished to Be a Man.* Dutton, 1973. (I)

BIBLIOGRAPHY

Aborne, Carlene. "The Newberys: Getting Them Read (It Isn't Easy)." *Library Journal,* 99 April 15, 1974, pp. 1195–97. The author describes multi-media approaches to gain reactions to Newbery Award books.

Artley, A. Sterl. "Reading Instruction and Cognitive Development." *Elementary School Journal,* 72 January 1972, pp. 203–11. Questioning techniques for teaching children to think and to apply the products of thought.

Bernat, Edwinna. "We Drew a Movie." *Grade Teacher,* 86 February 1969. pp. 110–13. Simple description of film activity for application to literary experience.

Champagne, David W., and Hines, John F. "Role Play Simulation Activities as a Teaching Strategy: Suggestions for New Uses." *Educational Technology,* 11 August 1971, pp. 58–60. A broad range of role-playing activities for use in content areas.

Cianciolo, Patricia. "The Role of Children's Books in the Open School." *Elementary English,* 50 March 1973, pp. 409–16. The personalized open school concept affords strong support for literature; this article illustrates the idea with good titles and discussion.

Crystal, Josie. "Role-Playing in a Troubled Class." *Elementary School Journal,* 69 January 1969, pp. 169–79. How one teacher used role-playing despite doubts and mistakes; good background material for use of role-playing in conjunction with literature.

Dillner, Martha H. "Affective Objectives in Reading." *Journal of Reading,* 17 May 1974, pp. 626–31. With *Huckleberry Finn* as the example, the author suggests objectives for "receiving," "responding," "valuing," and "evaluating."

Fennimore, Flora. "Creative Ways to Extend Children's Literature." *Elementary English,* 48 April 1971, pp. 209–14. Helpful discussion of the creativity factors inherent in various activities: fluency, flexibility, adaptiveness.

Giovanini, Gail M. "Children's Literature and More." *Elementary English,* 49 November 1972, pp. 981–85. A series of learning experiences to explain and illustrate characterization in the story, "The Emperor and the Kite."

Goldberg, Edward D. and Ann T. "Teaching Problem-Solving Skills." *Instructor,* 81 November 1971, pp. 88–89. Techniques used to teach problem-solving skills, with application to children's literature selections.

Greer, Margaret. "Affective Growth through Reading." *Reading Teacher,* 25 January 1972, pp. 336–41. Activities to enhance emotional response to literature.

Hall, Maryanne. "Literature Experiences Provided by Cooperating Teachers." *Reading Teacher,* 24 February 1971, pp. 425–31+. Research report whose findings suggest that many student teachers receive little help in presenting or obtaining literature in their classrooms.

Hoskin, Barbara, and Swick, Kevin. "Questioning and Learning." *Clearing House,* 47 May 1973, pp. 567–68. Reviews research on the importance of teacher questioning techniques as a learning tool.

John, Martha Tyler. "Role Play into Thinking." *Instructor,* 83 March 1974, p. 56. Uses role-playing to accent particular kinds of thought processes.

Kaltsounis, Theodore. "Teach with Questions." *Instructor,* 82 May 1973, pp. 43–45. Based on social studies teaching about cities, incorporating various materials. The author illustrates use of different types of questions and strategies.

Ladas, H., and Osti, L. "Asking Questions: A Strategy for Teachers." *High School Journal,* 56 January 1973, pp. 174–89. Questioning strategies applied to many fields, with implications for teaching literature.

Odell, Lee. "Teaching Reading: An Alternative Approach—Use of Role-Playing and Value Judgment." *English Journal,* 62 March 1973, pp. 454–58+. Relates incidents of "decentering," or role-playing, in which students become more competent at understanding other people's perspective, going beyond the present moment to examine and clarify their own values.

Rogers, Virginia M. "Modifying Questioning Strategies of Teachers." *Journal of Teacher Education,* 25 Spring 1972, pp. 58–62. Reviews research to serve as a basis for developing games to improve classroom questioning techniques.

Sanders, Norris M. "Second Look at Classroom Questions." *High School Journal,* 55 March 1972, pp. 265–77. Questioning techniques as a means of improving curriculum, with implications for teaching literature.

Sullivan, Joanna. "Literating Children to Creative Reading." *Reading Teacher,* 25 April 1972, pp. 639–42. Sample questions to illustrate methods for encouraging divergent thinking (fantasy, invention, sensory awareness, and speculation).

Swynehardt, Mary and Hatlestad, Carolyn. "Extending Children's Appreciation of Book Illustration through Creative Activity." *Elementary English,* 49 February 1972, pp. 235–39. Specific methods and books appropriate mainly at primary level.

Ter Louw, Adrian L. "Look Beyond the Picture." *Instructional Materials,* 1 March 1956, pp. 44–46. Helpful ideas to aid presentation of picture books through questioning.

Wright, Lin. "Creative Dramatics and the Development of Role-Taking in the Elementary Classroom." *Elementary English,* 51 January 1974, pp. 89–93+. Values and procedures based on role-playing to broaden cultural understanding.

Zahorik, John A. "Questioning in the Classroom." *Education,* 91 April 1971, pp. 358–63. Suggests that children themselves should be the questioners; the adult should serve as responder and facilitator of children's inquiry.

Creative Techniques for Exploring Literature

We have proposed a general teaching sequence for increasing children's enjoyment of literature: you select and introduce literature to stimulate children to respond and relate to it. As we've said, this teaching sequence need not be followed every time a child reads a book, but there is a place for it with selected books to help increase the pleasure children gain from the literary experience. The object always is to stimulate further independent reading in which children may realize for themselves the joys of reading which effective teaching have opened to them.

In teaching literature, certain avenues to enjoyment are particularly useful. We think the following are among the most important:

> Reading aloud
> Storytelling
> Creative Dramatics
> Puppetry
> Choral Verse

Each technique provides a somewhat different access to literature. Reading aloud brings to life and voice the exact words of the author. When the reading is skilled, it seems almost as if the author were telling the story in person. In storytelling the teller is actually the author, because a good storyteller takes a story and makes it his own. Although he usually did not originate the narrative, he chooses how he begins the story, leads to the climax, and ends the tale. The characters speak as he wishes; the setting is of his devising.

In both reading aloud and storytelling, the encounter between sender and receiver is a very personal, one-to-one relationship. The reader or teller speaks directly to each person in the listening circle. Together, the sender and receiver make new artistry: literature comes alive through a unique bond wrought when the two join the story for a few magic moments.

Creative drama, on the other hand, is a group encounter. The group plays out a story or a poem without using a script. Children become the characters and create the drama. No one knows exactly what the other may say—except that it must be true to the spirit of the story as they all heard it or read it. Literature gains reality and impact which ordinary discussion simply cannot achieve. Creative drama permits children to explore freely the potentialities of intonation, sound, and rhythm in literature. They can extend their life space through the infinite variety of roles which literature provides. They can sense more deeply the power of literature to stir, to calm, to anger, to mollify. They will be stimulated by the unpredictable dialogue to try to find their own language suited to the context of the drama being created that very moment. They will, in short, find a new perspective on literature.

Puppetry can be used in creative drama as well as in playing out written scripts. In either case, it adds another dimension to the interpretation of literature. It offers a freer realm to the actors. The puppet and the simple stage provide a shield between their own vulnerable selves and the audience. If the puppet fluffs a line or forgets some necessary stage business, it is not quite so personal an error. Nor need the actors themselves move about in full view of the audience. Children who feel self-conscious or awkward need not parade themselves before others. Puppetry can also free children in a larger-than-life sense—puppets can be super-women, super-men, and super-children. They can move mountains, fly through the air, and perform all sorts of powerful magic. Children can become fireflies or elephants in a much more facile transformation than their own bodies would ever permit. They can try out ways of behaving—speaking, singing, dancing—which most of them would otherwise hesitate to try before a group. Puppetry offers a wide range of opportunities that can involve children more deeply in literature.

Choral verse similarly makes immediate the power of literature to mold ideas and feelings. Uncomplicated choral verse can make the sounds of poetry more real to the ear. John Ciardi puts it this way:

> For years I have read poetry as a sensual act, sounding each cadence in my head and often saying the lines aloud. Good poetry . . . carries with it a notation as detailed and specific as that of music. . . . Like music, poetry gives signals to indicate its own tempo, emphasis, pauses, stresses, modes and moods; like music, it must be taken as indicated. To speed up either one (music or poetry) simply for the sake of speed would be disaster. The best conductor is not the man who gets the orchestra through a score in the shortest elapsed time. . . . The best conductor is the one who leads the orchestra through the score in the most sensitive way.[1]

Now let us look at each of these creative activities in greater detail. Keep in mind that these techniques should be employed as part of a teaching sequence, not as ends in themselves. Your aim should be to help children become more

---

[1]From *Saturday Review* (November 15, 1969): 14.

aware of the joys of literature. If you are wise and economical in your guidance, children will learn to select books, introduce themselves to books, respond to books, and relate books to their own lives with increasing satisfaction.

READING ALOUD

Of the many techniques for presenting literature, the ability to read aloud is basic. Let's assume that you've introduced your selection. The literary experience is getting underway. On this particular occasion, you're reading aloud. Now it's appropriate to ask a personal question: *how well do you read?*

Most teachers, librarians, parents, aunts, and uncles would like to think that they're effective oral readers. After all, most of us at one time or another have really moved a listener. When was that? Think back to an example in your own life. Wasn't it a time when your mind seemed wonderfully clear, your selection seemed really "right," and your audience (whether it consisted of one or a multitude) magically seemed to be tuned in? When and how did it all happen, and can you make it happen again and again?

It's unlikely that you can afford the time to "make it happen again" by rehearsing every oral reading as if it were to be a stage performance. Even if you did, the result might well be a self-conscious disaster. But you do want to avoid a flat reading that will break the invisible thread leading from reader to listener. You're seeking a way to read that will make your audience realize that you, the reader, are undergoing the literary experience, too. All the technical guidelines about voice quality, diction, pauses, and rate are meant to facilitate this effect. Here is how a great novelist, Ivy Compton-Burnett, discusses good oral reading through a conversation between a wealthy dowager named Miranda and a prospective companion:

> "Have you a good voice for reading aloud?" said Miranda. . . .
> "It would hardly be different from my ordinary voice."
> "Would you read as if you had written the books yourself, and felt self-conscious about them?"
> "No, I should only try to interpret them."
> "You cannot just read simply and clearly what is before your eyes?" said Miranda, giving a sigh.
> "Yes, if that is what you want."
> "Well, it naturally is. Why should I wish for your implied opinion? I could ask for it."
> "Well, I would remember that."
> "And you would not sit as if you had a host of thoughts seething within you?"
> "It is not likely I should have a host of them."
> "Or as if your mind were a blank?"
> "I would try to strike the mean."[1]

---

[1] Ivy Compton-Burnett, *Mother and Son* (Victor Gollancz, Ltd., 1967).

The music was furnished mostly by the Musical Soup Eaters. They marched
with big bowls of soup in front of them and big spoons for eating the soup.
They whistled and chuzzled and snozzled the soup, and the noise they made

Illustration ©1967 by Harriet Pincus. Reproduced from her illustrated volume of THE WEDDING PROCESSION OF THE RAG
DOLL AND THE BROOM HANDLE AND WHO WAS IN IT by Carl Sandburg; by permission of Harcourt Brace Jovanovich, Inc.

Apropos to oral reading, there are three important areas of concern that the
applicant in that passage had better attend to if she is to succeed at her job, and
that will help you succeed at yours. First, you must cultivate the elusive quality
of *concentration*. Whatever the distractions—milk money to be collected, the child
who has decided on a thorough desk cleaning for the moment's business, the
fleeting thoughts about what you should wear to dinner—you have to place
them aside during your oral reading. It's not easy, especially since some of us
were trained to read aloud from the basal reader automatically when called
upon. Figure out how to cut down on distraction. You may need to assert a
"rule"—pleasantly but firmly—that all desks be cleared during the presentation
of literature. You may need to make a conscious effort to attend to bothersome
details before you start reading. You may need to plan to do your oral reading

could be heard far up at the head of the procession where the Spoon Lickers were marching. So they dipped their soup and looked around and dipped their soup again.

and William Collins Sons, Ltd. (See p. 466 for discussion of how to prepare for reading it aloud.)

in a certain part of the room, in a certain chair, even at a certain time. (There are effective oral readers who sit on the floor with the children or on a child's desk.) Perhaps the best single suggestion for cutting down distraction and being able to concentrate on the task is to have your listeners near you. Body closeness and direct eye contact aid concentration.

Second, if you are going to "strike the mean," you need *prior information* about where the book is going. To discover the theme, the plot, the characters, and the setting at the same time your listeners discover them isn't dependable. It doesn't permit the planning you will need to do to enrich the experience. Your oral reading is likely to find a balance between conscious interpretation and the sense of discovery if you have read over the book prior to reading it aloud. Depth will come as you re-experience it during the reading. The fresh discoveries will be accompanied by a sense of security, of knowing the quality of the literature you are offering.

Look at some examples. If you don't know that Thelma in *A Bargain for Frances* (1) is a schemer (and not a totally honest one at that), you'll fail to give her those qualities in the conversation that begins on page 10. A fine contrast between naïve Frances and scheming Thelma won't emerge in your reading until it's too late. Your audience will be amused, but the tension of empathy will be missed. Heaven help the reader who picks up Carl Sandburg's wild book, *The Wedding Procession of the Rag Doll and the Broom Handle and Who Was in It* (2), and tries to read it aloud before a group without prior knowledge of its substance. You have to know that the entire plot is taken care of in the title, that the Sandburg humor lies in the way you chew, shriek, grunt, and mumble the description of that curious procession. Try it. *Portrait of Ivan* (3) by Paula Fox is just what the title says it is and nothing more. Most reviewers seemed to be looking for heavy drama. Instead, the book presents Ivan's portrait, a memorable face that is softened and changed by the portrait painter. From the third line onward, you must in your oral reading make that painter what he is—the book's single source of warmth, even its sanity. The first speaker in Rosemary Harris's *The Moon in the Cloud* (4), a Carnegie Medal winner, is God Himself, and the Great Flood is just around the bend. You have to know this—and about the book's comic tone—if your oral reading is to get off to a good start.

Third, as an oral reader imparting a literary experience to an audience, you should be concerned with some techniques, though they shouldn't become the main focus. Useful techniques include attention to vocal quality (planning how and where to alter your pitch and loudness to highlight meaning), variation in rate (planning where to slow down for emphasis and where to glide along quickly to give the feeling of action), and, most difficult for most readers, the use of pauses. A pause puts emphasis on what is to follow, and sometimes an extra long pause permits your listeners some happy anticipation of what is about to happen. A pause can develop into a brief conversation with your listeners. For example, before you turn the page to reveal the audience of Tizuvthee in Ellen Raskin's surprise climax to *The World's Greatest Freak Show* (5), stop and ask who the audience will be. (See illustration on pp. 468–69.)

Such techniques require prior reading and sometimes concentrated practice —and even a simple marking system. Hanley and Thurman, in writing about vocal techniques for interpretive reading, suggest such marking.[1] A short line drawn in pencil at the beginning of a sentence or paragraph indicates rapid rate, while a longer line marks a slower rate. Small drawn squares and rectangles amid or above key words or phrases can indicate brief or longer pauses. Such aids, derived from careful reading of the material, may help recapture your interpretation when you read aloud to the group.

---

[1] Theodore D. Hanley and Wayne L. Thurman, *Developing Vocal Skills,* 2nd ed. (Holt, 1970).

These suggestions for facilitating literary experience through oral reading focus on meaning. They're aimed at helping you communicate the reasons you chose the book in the first place and went to the trouble of introducing it.

Many adults who work with children are surprised to discover that their audiences are uncritical, accepting, appreciative, and ready to respond. The most skilled actor on tape is no match for the live, known teacher (or librarian or parent) who reads aloud to the child, especially for him. Cultivate your own oral reading skill, for it, more than any other factor, is basic to the personalized, independent transaction involved in the literature you are imparting.

The best proof that you've been effective in reading aloud will be the increasing desire children have to read aloud themselves. Encourage that desire. This kind of oral reading will, of course, differ from the diagnostic reading that is characteristic of basic reading instruction, in which the emphasis is on checking accuracy in literal word identification and literal comprehension of sentences. In this case, concentrate on the children's ability to communicate impact beyond literal meaning: their enjoyment of language, their pleasure in passages which evoke emotion, and their joy in the sensitivity of a writer to the textures of experience.

To achieve this kind of literary communication, children who read aloud must have adequate time to prepare. They need help in choosing stories or poems that are within their abilities. They must have practice, guided by the same principles and techniques that you use. During this practice, they need someone to work with them. You may not always have that time, but judicious pairing with classmates having good oral reading ability will sometimes help. Arrangements can sometimes be made to release older children in the school to assist younger children. Parents and other volunteers, especially retired people with strong interests in children, can often assist. Tape recording of practice reading is, of course, another valuable means for helping children realize how they sound to others.

Passing around the opportunity to read aloud poses some problems. One child reader shouldn't immediately follow another. If you schedule more than one reader on a given day, plan a generous amount of time between them. In the primary years, the opportunity to read aloud should be family-like in quality, reducing the physical distance between reader and audience. Shy and self-conscious children especially will profit from the privilege of sitting rather than standing. You may sit side-by-side with the reader and the listeners, all offering clear, visible support to the reader. As children mature in their effectiveness, these kinds of support become less necessary. But with all children your whole demeanor should project warm, friendly reception. An effective way to diminish a child's chance to succeed as a reader is to let your mind wander as soon as the child opens his mouth.

Sharing of readers among the classes is obviously desirable. For example, older children may prepare readings for the kindergarten and primary children. These early opportunities need careful supervision. The first readings should be to

The audience of Tizuvthee in *The World's Greatest Freak Show.* **Prepare your listeners for this surprise.** See discussion on p. 466. Copyright ©1971 by Ellen Raskin. From THE WORLD'S GREATEST FREAK SHOW. Used by permission of Atheneum Publishers.

groups of two or three people. Gradually the size of the group can be increased. The rewards, of course, are twofold: the younger children furnish a powerful incentive to an older child to read well while the older child personifies to the younger ones the joys of reading.

special activities

1. "Inviting Jason," the story reprinted in chapter 1, is well suited for reading aloud. Practice reading it aloud, following the suggestions you have just read:

(a) *Concentration.* You need to cut down all distractions in your own and the children's minds. What can you do to bring concentration to a maximum?

(b) *Information.* You don't want your reading to sound "canned," but instead, you want children to feel as if you are discovering the elements of the story at the same moment they are. At the same time, you do want to prepare for the real feelings of ten-year-old Stanley in inviting Jason. How can you keep this balance?

(c) *Techniques.* Consider how the techniques of tone, pitch, loudness, rate, and pauses can make your reading aloud more effective. In deciding tone, for example, remember that although this story contains some humor, it is basically a serious story. Moreover, it is told in first person by a ten-year-old. How will you develop an appropriate tone for Stanley? In considering pitch, look for key words or phrases to be emphasized; for example, where might Stanley raise or lower his pitch? Loudness can be used to underscore certain words and to indicate emotion. A sudden shift in volume may indicate envy, excitement, or irritation—all emotions displayed by Stanley in this story. Rate, another important technique, might be increased during the first bit of dialog between Stanley and his mother. At what other points can you speed up or slow down your rate to help interpret the meaning? Where can you use pauses to heighten your audience's anticipation? (Consider, for example, what effect you might achieve by pausing after Stanley tells his mother that Jason has dyslexia.)

2. Read "Inviting Jason" to a small group of children or record your reading on tape (or do both). Follow the teaching sequence suggested in chapter 9:
   (a) *Selecting.* At the end of chapter 1 you were encouraged to think of purposes for sharing the story with children. Review your thoughts. What might be the purposes of the author in writing the story? Your purposes in reading it aloud to children? The purposes of the children in listening to it?
   (b) *Introducing.* Review the discussion in chapter 9 about introducing a story. How much introduction will you use in view of the purposes you thought of in the item above? How will you introduce this story?
   (c) *Responding.* In talking with children about this story—whether or not you actually read it to them—what kinds of literal-level questions might you use? What kinds of inferential questions could you discuss? If you are able to read the story to children, briefly critique your discussion of it.
   (d) *Relating.* In relating this literary experience to others, what kinds of connections can you make? If you do read the story to children, summarize the bridges that you built to other literature or other experiences.

STORYTELLING

Storytelling has survived the Gutenberg galaxy; it will survive the electronic age; and it will survive accountability. Scheherezade, remember, was held accountable for telling a rouser every night for 1001 nights, under penalty of losing her head. Scheherezade did just fine, as did Odysseus who was, perhaps, a wilier storyteller than hero, though this trait did not detract from his magnetism.

There is evidence from McLuhan and others that society is heading toward a broader concept of comprehension—not just reading comprehension but that involved in visual literacy and in oral expression. If this is the case, the art of storytelling will gain in reputation. Even in the midst of electronic wonders, storytelling is still one of the best ways of comprehending literature.

Storytelling and Acting

Storytelling is often contrasted with acting in the theater. The contrast may be superficial, arising from the comparison of good storytelling with bad acting. A good actor has to be three persons. First, he has learned to be the author of the play. He knows the structure and how the plot will turn out. He knows the theme or themes, and how each scene fits into the whole. He recapitulates the author's process.

Second, the actor has learned to be a character in the play. He acts out the character, or more accurately, interprets the character. The difference is like the difference between a newsphoto and an Andrew Wyeth painting. The actor must interpret how the character fits into the whole pattern.

Third, the actor must learn to be part of the audience and watch the play unfold. In this function he does not know or unduly anticipate what will happen until it happens. He makes guesses and responds to false leads on the basis of what has gone before, not on what is yet unknown.

Structuring the Story

Like the actor, the storyteller recapitulates the creative process of the author. As author, he knows how the story is going to turn out. He senses its structure, including elements such as theme, character, plot, and setting. Moreover, he is capable of living through the story again and again, as authors live their stories when they create them and as actors live through plays when they play them. Like the author, the storyteller must sense how and to what degree each segment fits into the whole pattern.

The storyteller is all the characters in the story, yet he is really none of them. His role-playing is less direct, though by this indirection he aims for an effect similar to that of the actor. Like the actor, he entices his audience to catch the image of characters going about the business of living within the cause-and-effect of narrative. He, too, interprets characters.

The storyteller is also the audience. The best storytellers have a grace and manner that says, "I know what you think will happen. I know your opinion of this and that character. I know the image in your mind. You want to know if you're right? Well, we'll just have to wait and see, won't we?"

This is the manner that persuaded Alice of *Through the Looking Glass* (6) to believe six impossible things before breakfast. It invites camaraderie. Not all actors can manage it—those who try and fail are called *hams*. There are, unfortunately, ham storytellers, too, who are spawned when audience-pleasing takes precedence over carrying out the author's intent and concentrating on character. Mark Twain describes the ham problem best in comparing the teller of a *humorous* story to the teller of a *comic* story:

The humorous story is told gravely; the teller does his best to conceal the fact that he even dimly suspects that there is anything funny about it; but the teller of the comic story tells you before hand that it is one of the funniest things he has ever heard, then tells it with eager delight, and is the first person to laugh when he gets through. And sometimes, if he has had good success, he is so glad and happy that he will repeat the "nub" of it and glance around from face to face, collecting applause, and then repeat it again. It is a pathetic thing to see.[1]

Twain concluded that witnessing such a performance "makes one want to renounce joking and lead a better life."

The Broadway production, *Story Theatre,* exemplifies the close relationship between actor and storyteller. The actors in this show effortlessly step out of character to tell the story, then just as effortlessly pick up the character again to dramatize. It can be done. The intents of the two arts are very similar. The techniques of the storyteller and the actor, however, differ somewhat.

Technique of Storytelling

One technical suggestion for storytelling is "Don't memorize." This is a recent ruling. Storytellers in ancient times memorized, as do some today. Greek schoolboys learned the *Odyssey.* Too many people were forced to memorize the wrong way and got sick of it. But often when a story is worked on so that you recapitulate the author's process, the story begins to stick in the memory like a song. If memorized effortlessly in this way, the story is aided rather than blocked in the telling, as happens with favorite stories. The rule might be changed to say, "Don't memorize—if it hurts."

Another bit of technical advice might be phrased this way: "Don't use props and don't wave your arms about." Yet a prop can help. A leaf can make a forest. One authentic ax or ax model can bring focus on the blurred panorama of Ithaca. A prop can begin a story—"thereupon hangs a tale"—and it can supplant some tiresome description, but don't drag in a prop inappropriately or use too many of them.

Arm waving, head wagging, and jumping up and down are certainly distractions to be avoided. But some storytellers are lifeless because all the action has been trained out of them. It seems somehow uninteresting to sit primly with one's hands carefully in place when one is conjuring a jolly tailor sewing up the sky with a hundred miles of thread to make the rain stop. It would be easy if we were all Ruth Sawyers or Gudrun Thorne-Thomsens or May Arbuthnots or Bill Martins—able to convey almost unbearable immediacy with voice alone.

Marie Shedlock says that Anglo-Saxons move in solid blocks, that is, are gross in gestures.[2] They cannot "gesture" getting on a horse without lifting a leg over their heads and clutching at something. But many people of other cultures are

---

[1] From "How to Tell a Story," in *Writings of Mark Twain,* vol. 22 (Underwood edition, American Publishing, 1901).
[2] Marie L. Shedlock, *The Art of the Story-Teller* (Appleton, 1915, Dover, 1952).

artists of the gesture. An almost imperceptible movement of the head can say in Greece, "It is sunny and pleasant today. I am going to drink two glasses of retsina and enjoy the view. I hope you are enjoying it, too."

Shedlock says that we should learn sparing use, not non-use, of gesture. This is important advice. If you are not Greek, you might begin grossly. Practice with big gestures that fit the story and then gradually make them more subtle.

Of all techniques for aiding this art, vocal technique is the most important. Two suggestions regarding vocal technique have proved useful: the use of *crescendo* and the use of the *pause*. Both can be planned ahead of time, even marked on the printed story or outline, and then practiced.

Crescendo is sometimes defined as "getting louder," but perhaps it is better described as "starting softer." There is a difference. If you start a story low-pitched and softly, you have some dynamics in reserve. If you must begin fortissimo in order to capture attention, find a place early in the story to retreat. Incidentally, this technique is known to good actors as well. You may have an actor who seems excellent the first ten minutes but eventually you realize that there is no heightening of dramatic tension to come. In all art, much depends upon aroused expectations—that which is to come, rather than that which now exists.

Pause is also a means of arousing expectation. Mark Twain in "How to Tell a Story" considers it indispensable. So do others. The pause lets listeners wonder and hope, giving them a chance to be surprised.

A description of storytelling in Russia over the centuries says simply that "The telling of a tale is primarily an art, a special skill, accessible to the artists of the poetic word, to persons who are especially gifted for this kind of work."[1] Those gifted ones among Russian storytellers took their work seriously. They were in demand. The mills and marketplaces hired them to draw customers. These artists were not concerned about repeating a story. In fact, some had only two or three stories in their entire repertoire, but they were effective ones. These storytellers knew how to use gesture, pause, and voice effectively. In 1649 they were adjudged so effective that a royal rescript to governors commanded severe penalties for storytelling. As reported by Sokolov, the edict read in part:

> Many men senselessly believe in dreams, in encounters, and in the evil eye, and in the calling of birds, and they propound riddles and tell tales of things unheard-of, and by idle talk and merry-making, in blasphemy they destroy their souls with such benighted deeds. For all this the most serene Tsar commands the governors to impose the severest penalties.[2]

Few of us can pose so great a threat today. Those who can have learned to beguile with words just as a ballet dancer has learned to beguile with movement.

---

[1] Y. M. Sokolov, *Russian Folklore,* tr. Catherine Ruth Smith (Macmillan, 1950), p. 404.
[2] pp. 381–82.

The storyteller shortens the distance between words and feelings, between a word and its referent. Ultimately, this art eludes technique.

If it is really such an elusive art, should a teacher or librarian or parent attempt it? Shouldn't you rely on recordings or locate the town storyteller? Those might be good things to do, but they are not substitutes. Children respond best to a voice they know, to a voice performing for them "at a given time in a given place."[1] If our voices bring only half the magic, children will supply the other half.

Shedlock suggests that you learn seven stories a year—just seven—and see how over the years these become a fine repertoire. Mae Benne at the University of Washington makes another useful suggestion: Have each teacher in a school learn to tell *one* story and at an appointed hour each week have them rotate to tell their stories to different classes. The class is maintained, and the offering is vastly multiplied. This is a good way to get started.

Should children tell stories? There can be no doubt that they do—personal experiences, movies and television shows, and more. It may be surprising to learn that at the turn of the century there arose a whole movement to encourage children to repeat a story after it was told by the teacher. Various claims were made for this practice: that it contributed to good speech and good listening, that it increased knowledge of literature, and the like.

Nowadays there is less enthusiasm about such close modeling, although you shouldn't be surprised to learn that children go home and repeat a story at the dinner table. In 1913, McManus said:

> Storytelling is superior to the written story chiefly because the man who writes is not in touch with the audience. The storyteller talks to you and has to make a story from beginning to end, and every sentence has to be a part of the story, because he is within range of a brickbat—and subject to the recall at any minute.[2]

Children respond well to practice and guidance in storytelling. With a little thought and manipulation of words, you should have no difficulty in providing accountability in this matter. Make sure to provide access to good stories to tell.[3]

If one child tells a story to an entire class, practice is limited and attention is sometimes strained. It is better to divide the class into groups of three or four and have storytellers all around the room and in the corridor. (Incidentally, encouragement to tell stories in childhood will most certainly pay off in adult-hood.)

Storytelling is tough fibered. Stories hold the reins of continuity and the consciousness of all cultures. Stories live on, even when history is forgotten. There can be no doubt that storytelling is strong enough to survive history itself.

---

[1]Dewey W. Chambers, "Storytelling: The Neglected Art," *Elementary English* 43 (November 1966): 715–19+.

[2]William Byron Forbush, *Storytelling in the Home* (American Institute of Child Life, 1913) p. 190.

[3]*Elementary English* is a useful source. See, for example, Gwendella Thornley, "Storytelling is Fairy Gold," *Elementary English* 45 (January 1968): 67–79+.

special activities

1. You can see that the art of storytelling is close to the art of reading aloud, whether you memorize a tale or create your own narrative. Storytelling, like reading aloud, demands concentration, information about the story, and the effective use of techniques such as tone, pitch, loudness, rate, and pauses.

    Choose a story you'd like to tell—perhaps a favorite folk tale. (See the discussion of folk tales in chapter 4 for ideas.) Try telling the story your own way. Tell it aloud, even if your practice audience is imaginary. You can't gauge the effects of beginnings and endings, dialog, or a turn of a phrase without giving voice to the language. Experiment with the techniques you used in reading aloud.

2. Now you're ready to tell the tale to children. If that's not feasible, tell it to a compassionate tape recorder. Place the story within a teaching sequence, as you did with the oral reading earlier. Allow yourself the risk and the pleasure of the unexpected—don't rehearse so much that you never have to search for a word. Risk waiting for creative additions to the story as you tell it. When you have told your story, briefly evaluate its effectiveness.

Listening to Literature

In listening to stories, whether read aloud or told, the visualizing skills are uniquely illuminating. Listening helps children to "see between the lines." Certainly listeners must first understand what is directly stated and recognize the organizing structure of the story. But to enjoy the full power of literature, children as listeners must go beyond the writing structure to the imagery behind it, extending their imaginative response beyond *what* happened to visualize *how* it happened, *where* it happened, and, most importantly, to *whom* it happened. In this kind of visualizing, they must be helped to react to what is only suggested and encouraged to lend their own creative additions to whatever is directly stated.

For example, in reacting to plot, children must go beyond simply naming the events. They must be helped to lend their own imaginations to visualizing the action. Suppose, for instance, you are reading Kipling's story of the renegade elephant Moti Guj. As a regular ritual Deesa and Moti Guj go to the river for a bath. Your listeners can be encouraged to visualize:

> *how* Deesa gave Moti Guj the bath: earnestly, gaily, silently, singingly?
> *how* they left the river: the author reports they left with a song. What kind of song? How rendered?

Similarly, in reacting to setting, the children when listening should be helped to cut the bonds of the classroom and to involve their imaginations in the realm of the story. For example, each child listening to *Treasure Island* (7) ought to be encouraged to tell the images *he* sees. Remember Stevenson's suggestions of sight and sound surrounding the Little Green Dell where Long John Silver murders the honest seaman?

> Stevenson mentions the *sight:* of the bulrushes, the wild ducks, the live oaks, the steaming marsh, the sun beating down, the flowering plants, the sword grass, the ledges of rocks, the snakes. Just how does each sight appear in the individual's mind as he reads?
> And the *sounds:* Stevenson mentions the boom of distant sea surges, the quack and screaming of the ducks, the whirr and rustle of the redescending birds. Just how are these sounds heard in the individual's imagination?

Stevenson might have employed smells, tastes, and textures to lend dimension to the setting. How could these sensory accesses have lent a sense of setting?

Finally, and most importantly, children ought to be helped to visualize the characters of fiction. Remember the clues to character projection:

> How does he look?
> How does he speak?
> How does he act?
> How does he think and feel?
> How does he appear to others?
> How do others speak to him and about him?
> How do others act toward him?
> How do others think and feel about him?

Suppose the character is Tom Sawyer in the episode in which he and Huck and Joe pretend to be pirates and run away to an island in the river and are mourned as drowned. Your task is to help the children to respond to Tom's speech and action. How do the following clues help to visualize Tom?

> His lively imagination as revealed by the pirate's names which he furnishes.
> His qualities of leadership as he commands the raft on the journey to the island.
> His sensitivity to the sound, touch, color, shape, and texture of the surroundings on the island.

Another part of your task is to help the children use the reactions of others to Tom:

> The talk of the boys and girls back home when Tom is believed drowned.
> Becky Thatcher wishes she had kept a brass door knob which Tom had given her.
> A boy takes pride in the beating he once received from Tom.

Much of the emphasis in literary listening should be devoted to these visualizing skills, especially as they relate to setting and character. At the same time, of course, don't neglect poetry. This kind of visualizing is even more important in listening to poetry than it is in responding to prose fiction:

Single out the image-making words.

Talk over the effectiveness of the figures of speech.

Underline with your voice the sounding and rhythm-making qualities of the verse.

Discuss the over-all effect or mood of the piece.

In all cases, whether story or verse, try to get individual responses. Try to establish securely that no two listeners need see, hear, feel, taste, smell or touch the images in the same way. So long as the children do not gravely distort the spirit of the writer, they are in fact doing what every writer wishes—lending their own unique responses to give to "airy nothing a local habitation and a name."

CREATIVE DRAMATICS[1]

by Burdette S. Fitzgerald

Creative dramatics is the theatre of the child, because it is a dramatic art form that allows the participants freedom of mind and movement. They are not restricted by the written drama, with the playwright's conception of dialogue, characterization, and action. Given a stimulus, such as a story, the children in a group act it out, using their own interpretation, words, and actions. It is their creative activity—their drama. Since they are not producing a play for an audience, they are not concerned with the techniques or disciplines of the adult stage. Their actions occur from a natural impulsive feeling; their stage is wherever they may be at the *moment*. It is this "moment," when thoughts are created and exchanged, when the emotions and inner feelings of people are sincerely felt, that is the child's drama. A group of twelve-year-olds, who had progressed to being allowed on the stage, and had learned terms and techniques for producing a play, were one day told the story of Ivan in "The Deserted Mine." As they developed the escape from the caved-in mine, they became so absorbed in the treacherous flight to safety that they forgot the stage completely and used the entire auditorium floor for the dark narrow passages of the tunnel. Adult standards were cast aside; they did not have to stay behind the proscenium arch, for there was no audience to inhibit or restrict their movements. This is the child's creative drama.

The role of the adult in creative dramatics is that of a leader who gives the proper stimulation for creative thinking. This process of the mind develops the ideas for active self-expression by the players. The leader prepares the mind or sets the mood, presents material for thinking, gives the opportunity

---

[1]Reprinted from Burdette S. Fitzgerald, *World Tales for Creative Dramatics and Storytelling* (Prentice-Hall, 1962), pp. 1–14.

for complete freedom of response, and guides intellectual appraisal. The purpose is to excite the mental and emotional state that manifests itself in bodily feelings and actions. Drama which presents the various and complex reactions of life readily offers an art form that challenges the mind. The leader who uses it wisely will achieve for the child and himself a feeling of self-confidence that comes only from the creative inner self.

The height and depth of this dramatic experience for the child depends first upon the leader's ability to establish the proper atmosphere and material for stimulation of the imagination. It is the imaginative mind that produces the various art forms. This is especially true of the drama, which is concerned with the portrayal of the feelings and actions of others. To stimulate the imagination, so that it will become active and creative, is the initial goal of the leader. Just as the teacher of the adult uses emotional and sensory devices, pantomimes and improvisations to train the mind and body, the leader of children also uses motivations to stir the mind and body of the child. Some of these motivating methods are dramatic play, imaginative situations and objects, and pantomimes.

Motivations

Dramatic play is used primarily with the younger child, as it is a group activity based upon familiar experience that allows the child to just "be" in a situation, doing whatever he wants. A visit to the beach or going on a picnic are popular situations. The preparation for playing is simple. Certain plans are made, such as the location of the beach, or what they are taking on the picnic. As they play, they are recalling the memory of a past experience, using their imaginations to relive and extend those feelings and actions. A beginning class of six-year-olds took a walk around the room one day on the way to the planned picnic at the beach, and stopped to look at an imaginary tree. There were many faces looking up, but very little comment. On the way home from the beach, after they had dug in the sand, hunted shells, swam, ate their lunch, and listened to a story, the room became full of trees, flowers, cats, dogs, squirrels, and even a snake. The creative mood had been established.

As the child learns first through his five senses—hearing, seeing, smelling, tasting, and touching—it is natural that these abilities be used for beginning motivations. As he looks at the sky, the child might be asked what he sees, and if he can imagine anything else that might be there. A smell from the kitchen might be . . . The chocolate drink which was going to be so good is . . . A sound in the night storm is. . . . The sound of music suggests . . . Not only does the child tell what his mind has created by the imagery of words, but he shows as well. Tommy's mind began to work one day as he sat looking skeptically at the rest of the class, which was having a good time feeling the gooey, sticky substance they imagined was on their hands. They

were saying it was gum, tar, and honey, when he suddenly smiled and presented us with the best taffy pull ever beheld. When I commented upon the
candy, he put his hands behind his back and said, "It's not here, it's home."
The imaginative moment of creative freedom was gone, but became much
easier to arouse the next time. Motivational material based on the reaction
of the senses is unlimited for the creative leader.

Imaginative situations or objects allow a wide range for development of the
creative mind. A trip in a glass ball to the bottom of the ocean presents many
ideas of sight and sound that may be formed into a story. Magic shoes may
travel around the world in a few minutes, or they may go home with the child,
as was once requested by a little girl. The telescope may see the faraway palace
of the North Wind or the nest of the bird in the near-by tree. The floor of
the room may become a lake, the desert sands, or a mountain top. Chairs can
suddenly become the homes for sleeping elves, who will be awakened by the
tap of their king's stick. There is a happy excitement about the imaginative
land created by the child. The leader supplies the point of departure for the
journey, going along only to encourage and stimulate further expansion.

The use of pantomime (action or gestures without words as a means of
expression) generally enters into these creative situations, since it is largely
by *doing* that the young child first expresses himself. The skilled leader, therefore, uses the art of bodily action as another form of motivation. An example
is the act of eating something, which is a favorite with children. An imaginary
tray holding things to eat may be passed around. Each child takes whatever
he wants and holds it in his hands until all have been served. One by one
they eat what they have taken, and the rest of the class tries to guess what
it is. The one who guesses correctly gets the next turn. This becomes a game,
which is what the pantomime should be in the first attempts. Other activities
include showing what you like to do in the summer time; selecting a toy;
finding an object you are looking for in the room; and any sports activity.
After beginning experiences of this kind, the leader may introduce the next
step in pantomimic action: feeling. The action should show how a person feels
while he is doing it; the game of eating could be extended to find out if the
person likes or dislikes what he eats. This opens up a variety of participation
activities to stimulate the emotional state of mind and the physical response.
If the movement is not accurate in detail, it is of no concern in this motivational period. The art of pantomime comes at a later stage in the child's
progress. The purpose here is the stimulation of the imagination.

The selection of the motivation to be used will depend upon the age level
of the group, the purpose or objective of the leader's planned session, or the
story that is to be told. Whether the method used is dramatic play, sensory
concepts, imaginary situations, pantomimic action, or other devices from the
resources of the leader, such as music and rhythms, the result should be that
the mind of the child is prepared for more extensive creativity.

The Story

When the imagination has been set to work, the happy recreation atmosphere established, it is time for the story, which may be either read or told. The tale will be enhanced by telling rather than reading; the responsive faces of the children will show this to be the preferred method.

Selection of the tale should be based primarily on finding something in the story of vital interest to the teller, as well as to the children. It is assumed that the leader of a children's class in creative dramatics will be aware of the interests, ages, and comprehensive abilities of the children concerned. To be able to see clearly the word pictures, to feel the intensity of the emotions of the people in the story, and to recreate them, requires an inner will that responds with understanding and a genuine liking for the story. It is the power of the spoken word that touches the feelings of children. A powerless teller will never reach the soul of the child. When the story is told with the self-possession that uses the imagination in recreating a work of art, there is beauty in the creative force . . . and there is response in the faces of the listeners. Whether it be fact or fantasy, the leader must enjoy the story in order to tell it with this result.

After selecting a story that will appeal, it should be carefully read for words that are unfamiliar, for secondary characters and sub-plots that may slow up the main action of the story, and for long passages of description. These should be eliminated, as the straight line of action is important in telling a story. It is the action that produces suspense, which is the keynote of listening to a story or play.

In preparing the story, it is helpful to memorize the structure of sequences of action. The entire story should not be memorized word for word because if the mind refuses to remember, the story-teller is lost. The story must be so much a part of the teller that it flows like conversation. The chronological order of events in the story, and also the first and last sentences, should be memorized. This gives the teller a base around which he can weave the mental pictures through the imagery of the words. These should be selected carefully, since children like sensory impressions, color words, and the repetition of words. Each word is important in this art; there must be an economy which eliminates such unnecessary terms as ah, uh, so, and well-a. When dialogue is used, it should be placed in the present tense, which makes it more dramatic. If the words of the author are of a specific style, as many of them as possible should be mastered. The story should be practiced out loud; the sound of the voice is quite different from the quiet thought of mind.

When telling the story, a circle or semi-circle of children is the best physical arrangement, since eye contact is essential. It is easier to make each child feel the story is directed at him if he is at eye level. The approach must be enthusiastic and positive, with a quiet persuasiveness that lets the children know the story is for them. The voice quality should be pleasing, gestures used only when related to the story, and interpretation heightened by use of the dramatic techniques of the pause, variety of vocal pitch, and varying rates of speed.

Children do not need to have the story explained. The principal purpose of literature is to touch the feelings of the child, and to let him see the ideals, struggles, and values of life. Stories of literary quality will have this effect. Many of the folk tales emphasize the moral; the fable bases its form upon it. It is in acting out the story that the values of life will be emphasized through the dynamics of the living play.

The Playing of the Story

The leader guides the children in planning the part of the story to be acted by asking leading questions based upon the following: 1) the main points in the scene; 2) the setting; 3) the people in the scene; 4) general ideas for dialogue; 5) the necessary properties. After these have been discussed, with the leader clarifying and summarizing the ideas in order to give the players security of feeling, the parts are chosen. The leader must have an organized plan for selecting the children who are going to play, as every child must be given an opportunity. One simple method is to begin at one end of the semi-circle or row, allowing each child to choose the part he wants to play. The next time, the leader starts wherever he left off.

After the playing, evaluation or positive critical thinking about what has just happened takes place. This is the time for appreciation of what they have watched or done, and the time for suggestions for improvement. The scene is repeated again with different children playing the parts. It may be repeated a number of times; the leader extends the abilities of the children in dramatic art as the need and opportunities arise.

Dramatic Knowledge

As the children progress in confident freedom of expression, the leader guides them into using their abilities on a wider scope. Expansion and deepening of capabilities is part of the learning process in creative dramatics. It is accomplished, as in the stimulation of the imagination, through motivational devices, experiences which will make them more aware of other creative possibilities. These are not to be confused with acting techniques such as "sharing a scene" or "dressing the stage," which are theatrical disciplines for staging a play. Just as the adult actor in his training grows in bodily control, sensitivity to the feeling from within, and the mastery of the interpretive word, so the child learns more accurate movement, a greater power to express his feelings and the thoughts of others, and a more fluent speech skill.

The leader who is perceptive and accurately responsive to the children will know when to apply these experiences. The philosophy of children's librarians, "The right book for the right child at the right time," may well be used here. The creative spirit may be deadened if they are not applied at the right time. The leader must pick the moment when the children present a suggestion, question, or answer which opens the way for further exploration of the idea. As the impetus has come from them, there is no thought of inadequacy, disapproval, or unwanted direction which can close the creative mind. Generally, opportunities will arise during the evaluation period, when the children are discussing what they have just watched or played. In this atmosphere of talking over what can be done to improve the scene, the leader suggests things that will aid in understanding the situation. It is the right time for the intellectual appraisal.

Movement

The movements of children are delightful to watch; they are uninhibited and swing with abandon. In beginning work in creative drama, children tend to move together, to imitate, to crowd together in a small area. This is particularly true of the younger children. A favorite place to play is under the table. Such stories as "The Cat and the Mice" lend their settings to such a situation, but the need for movement around the room by the mice in this story makes it an excellent one for widening the concept of use of space. "How can the mice file past the cat if the table is used for the home?" is a leading question for the discussion. Exercises, such as movement to music, the large physical actions of horses, airplanes, kangaroos, and birds are some of the ways awareness of space and freedom of movement may be realized.

Although bodily action is easier for the young child than the spoken word, accuracy is still lacking. As the child progresses in his ability to act out a part, he needs to grow in this ability. The mother in "Salting the Puddin'" must make the puddin' and place it in a believable manner. The actions must be detailed and correct for the rest of the plot. This fact, discovered by the children themselves, opens up the field of pantomime. If pantomimic exercises have been used earlier, they may be used again with the emphasis placed upon clarity and exactness of movement. There is a need to know immediately and convincingly what the person in the play is doing. Incidents from the story may be concentrated upon until the actions of everyone can be believed. The dishing up of the puddin' must be accurate, and the first bite must be real in order to give reason for the reaction of feeling that follows. A story such as "Juan Goes to Heaven" presents the problem of opening the gates of Heaven, which gives an opportunity for the study of opening and closing doors in pantomime. Practice in detail of body movement is essential for dramatic growth.

Characterization

Development of the understanding of characterization may be encouraged through the asking of leading questions as to how the person feels, looks, talks, walks, and the reasons for his behaviour. After the discussion, a group activity should be presented, such as everyone sitting in his throne as the mighty King Kunz in "The Story of Kunz and His Shepherd," or dancing as the cats in "Another Haunted Mill," or as the body of armed men moving toward the Castle of Dunbar in the story, "Black Agnace of Dunbar." Following the group activity, there can be individual attempts at characterization, provided the leader knows that the children are ready for single flight. In order to deepen the intensity of feeling in the character of a little girl who was glued magically to her chair, a group of seven-year-olds was allowed to show individually what each one would do. All of the group of twenty struggled violently to get off the chair, many crying for their mothers. Three of them went beyond this initial step. The first asked for a pair of scissors to cut her dress and so get off. The second picked up the chair, went to an imaginary telephone, and phoned the magician; the third screamed, "Help! Help! Get me off this bloomin' thing!"

Absorption in the belief of the character is the drama of the child. Sincerity of feeling that can be sustained is the important part of characterization. This will not happen in the beginning, since children are easily distracted by the unusual, the funny, or the actions of others. As the child learns that each mood must not be broken as long as he is playing, his powers of concentration increase. One afternoon a group of sixth graders was playing out a story about a king. The boy who was the page held an imaginary tray in his two hands. The door of the room opened and a boy (not in the play) walked up to him and gave him a note. Instead of being distracted, he kept it in his hand and carried the tray across the room to the king. After bowing himself out of the room, he opened the note. This shows understanding of the feelings of others, and the ability to forget oneself in the pleasure of being someone else.

Short improvised scenes based upon the emotions or feelings of people may be used to train the will to respond when the imagination calls on it. Group situations, such as being cold, hot, thirsty, lonely, frightened, or happy, may be the mood around which a scene is played. Older groups like to develop their own plot line, after being given just the feeling. As characterization depends upon the inner-self and sensitivity to the understanding of a person's driving force, the development of this dramatic awareness will require a long period of time. The leader's encouragement is especially essential in intensifying this ability.

Dialogue

The child's capabilities in the art of dialogue run all the way from very little (in the very young) to too much dialogue in the advanced. The problems of encouraging the child to think and respond to the situation by speaking is difficult until he has become completely free. The child who can react as did the little girl of six who was playing the mother in the story of "The Three

Bears" has learned this significant part of life. The bears had returned to find their porridge eaten and their chairs sat in. When the little bear cried, "Someone's broken my chair," the Mother said immediately, "Papa bear, you better fix that right away!"

It is only by first giving the child situations of group activity with a minimum of dialogue that the foundation for later creative powers in the spoken word will be created. Short exercises in situations that are familiar to them, such as an argument as to whose doll or train it is or buying an ice cream or a pair of shoes from the store, will aid in this development. A story such as "Ashiepattle and the Troll" is excellent material, not only strong in actions but so emotionally strong that the dialogue is easily remembered. To encourage original dialogue the leader may ask in the evaluation period if there was anything else the troll or the lads could have said. This is the help the child needs for growth in verbal expression.

The other aspect of dialogue is the period when everyone wants to talk at the same time, or the conversation stretched out merely for the sake of talking. These situations are readily apparent to the children in creative dramatics, and correction of the faults comes from them. The leader has only to ask what the trouble was. Situations can be given to illustrate the point: three friends are talking about a fourth, who suddenly appears; a family is taking an automobile ride; three friends are having lunch in a restaurant. The rest of the class listens for polite conversation and equality of the scene.

Another aspect of dialogue is quality of thought. This must be in keeping with the characterization. If silliness, unrelated or improbable ideas creep in, the leader must guide the group to a discussion of what is silly in contrast to humor, and the difference between the realistic and the unrealistic. In playing "Juan Goes to Heaven" (nineteenth century), one of the girls said she was Marilyn Monroe. The reply from a boy was, "That's silly! She's not dead yet!" The development of this quality is not difficult because children are sincere. They need the quick observance of the leader to encourage freedom of speech, knowledge of when to speak, and growth in the quality of the created dialogue.

Dramatic Awareness

An awareness of the total effect of the scene played becomes apparent to the group as learning progresses. They are stimulated by the well-done achievement or are impulsively honest when it is not a good one. A cooperative consciousness is felt, and they are ready for an understanding of what is drama. This may be accomplished by discussions, or by performing a scene showing the conflict necessary in a dramatic play. Two members of the class may be asked to approach each other from opposite sides of the room. They pass by without speaking. Is this drama? No, nothing happened. The next time they approach each other, they bump shoulders and go on their way.

Is this drama? No, not enough happened. The next time they approach, they bump shoulders and react, their reactions involving spoken dialogue. Is this drama? Yes, because there was physical conflict which caused an emotional reaction. If their reactions caused the group to laugh, they had created a comic scene. If their reactions were so strong that one of them was hurt with the emotional response caused by pain, they had created a serious drama. Improvised scenes in groups of two or three will give practice in the understanding that drama depends upon the emotional and physical struggles of life. Suggestions for scenes should be based on subject matter within the comprehension of the group. Typical children's situations would include washing the dishes, flying a kite, playing ball, hiking, fishing, riding in an automobile, and going to the movies. The problem for the improvisation is to develop some action that will make the scene dramatic. Time is allowed for planning what is going to happen. After each group has participated, the action is evaluated in terms of plot structure. Did it have a good beginning, middle, and end? Was there suspense, and was it believable? A dramatic awareness has now been learned.

Developing the Story into the Play

If it is necessary to present a story for an audience, as it is in certain situations, the creative dramatics approach is far more rewarding to the child than use of a written play. The introduction of the audience transposes the purpose from that of art for the child to art for the spectators. Such a transposition makes it necessary to observe the techniques required for staging a play, and may restrict naturalness of spirit. This is the reason it is better not to use the written script, as the memorization of words is a skill in itself. It becomes more important than interpretation of words and development of character. This danger may also occur in playing a story that has an unfamiliar name or song that cannot be left out of the plot. In the Mexican story of "The Hunchback," the song "Lunes, y martes y miércoles—tres" (Monday and Tuesday and Wednesday—three), is the keynote in the conflict. The words need to be chanted over and over in the planning period so that the attempt to remember will not stultify the children's joy in playing. In the created play the naturalness of speech will remain, as it has become spontaneous. Although this is not a problem, the performance for an audience requires observance of all other stage disciplines which are comparable in every aspect to the adult theatre. The play is still the child's creation, but no longer just his.

The problems of developing the story into a stage play lie in the concern of dramatic action, change of scenes, time lapses, and keeping the story told by what the actors are saying and doing. This means there may have to be additional action for dramatic suspense, elimination of unnecessary incidents and characters, combining scenes or telescoping them into one incident, and maintaining time and space unity. . . .

The leader approaches the development of the story into play form for an audience . . . [using] question and answer discussion. The group plans together, with the leader summarizing its ideas. If there has been a true learning experience of the dramatic art, they will have no difficulty in putting the story into play form. When this has been accomplished, the first scene is discussed, following the steps of the planning period. The scene is played and evaluated over and over again until the group is satisfied with the incidents, dialogue, and characterizations. When the entire play is ready and the cast has been chosen, the leader becomes the director. This is the point when the play no longer belongs entirely to the child. It is now ready for the refinements necessary in a production for an audience. These must be done by someone who can look at the whole play objectively, with the eyes of the audience. This is the director, who focuses his attention upon the stage techniques, demanding that the actors utilize the skills of the theatre.

These skills are the details of any production which the director and the actors must plan and execute for clarity of the play and intensification of the emotions involved. Stage business, which is the visual activity of the actor other than movement, cannot just happen. Its purpose is to contribute action that will give emphasis or aid in telling the story. This demands that the stage business must be definite, motivated, varied, unified, accurately timed, and visibly clear. Creativity lies in the imagination and taste of the business selected by the director and the actors. Other skills, such as opening and closing doors, kneeling, gesturing, sitting and rising, falling, crying, and laughing require specific techniques. An audience not only expects pleasing and exciting stage pictures that have meaning, but also that the play be audible. This calls for the skills of speech and voice projection.

Although these are skills and not a creative process, they fit naturally into creative dramatics because they are needed to transmit the creation to an audience. They are not an end in themselves, but will have been assimilated into the genuine expression of each individual and of the group as a whole. This acquiring of knowledge aids in the creative imagination; it is the refining and verifying of the act. Creative play again proves its value as it gives the opportunity for extension and expansion of the learning possibilities of this dramatic art. Although the play is for an audience, the main purpose of creative dramatics should not be lost. It is an art that concerns itself with what is happening to the child while he is experiencing the art. . . .

special activities

1. On page 172 of chapter 4, there are brief directions for a story theater experience and on pages 446–51 of chapter 9, you'll find a brief description of role-playing. How do these two techniques differ from creative dramatics? How might you use one to augment the other? Suppose, for example, that

you were creating an activity to bring dramatic experience to a simple folk tale. For the purpose of discussion, select a folk tale you'd use and discuss which techniques you'd use and why.

2. Tone is important in creative dramatics presentations. The tone of the activity ought to match the tone of the work dramatized. What, for instance, is the tone you'd attempt to sustain if you were presenting "Inviting Jason"? If you were to portray all or part of "Puss in Boots"? One might argue that, above all else, creative dramatics provides the opportunity to study the tone of a work. How might such learning be useful in developing literary taste and appreciation?

3. Most people tend to think first of folk literature when relating creative dramatics to literature. What other literary types might you use? What realistic fiction would be suitable for creative dramatization? What criteria are important in selecting a narrative for creative dramatics presentation? Can nonfiction ever be used in such a performance? Discuss.

4. If you are unfamiliar with this technique, a good way to begin creative dramatics is with yourself. Together with a few classmates, other teachers, or a room full of other interested adults, try a brief creative dramatics session, using the ideas in the previous section. Afterwards, discuss your feelings openly. This will help you approach the technique with children.

5. Choose a selection for creative dramatization with children. Discuss the rationale for selecting the work. Summarize the main elements, such as plot, character, setting, tone, theme. Tell how you plan to begin the activity after you read or tell the selection. Speculate ahead of time on what problems you may encounter. What will you do to overcome problems such as those connected with dialog, movement, dramatic awareness, failure to recapture the work's tone? Now, having made your plans, carry out the session and evaluate it.

A CREATIVE APPROACH TO PUPPETRY AND LITERATURE

by Hans J. Schmidt[1]

Place a puppet on the hand of a child, and things begin to happen. He or she will wriggle the puppet and speak for it or to it, assuming a voice or accent other than their normal one. These spontaneous reactions springing from the dynamics of puppetry can be used creatively to motivate children to read, discuss, enact, create, and enjoy literature. We want now to look into the nature of puppets and puppetry as an art form in order to achieve these goals.

---

[1]Hans J. Schmidt, a well-known professional puppeteer from Chicago, has performed and conducted puppetry workshops for many years throughout the Chicago area as well as in many other parts of the country.

The Puppet as an Actor

A puppet is a figure of a person, animal, superhuman being, or object, made of any kind of material, and so constructed that it appears to have a life of its own when manipulated. It is not a thing merely to be made. The primary purpose of a puppet is to be an actor.

Some of the ways of making a puppet are quite simple. They are fun to do, using familiar materials available in art rooms—paper, paste, scissors, cloth, or whatever. Many are suitable for the young child—stick puppets, puppets from found objects, paper and bag puppets.

But puppetry is more than gimmickry, more than bits and patches and paste and sticks. Puppetry is an expanding art form, a sculptural art and a performing art—a medium that explores the potential of the human hand and arm in interpreting literature and an aid in the appreciation of language. Does this sound like an impossible kind of a marriage? Not if you consider a puppet from the beginning of its construction as a character representing one existing in literature, endowed with whatever nature its literary creator has given it. Since the puppet is an instrument to express a character from literature, and since you are going to substitute the puppet for the live body of an actor in a dramatic performance, each puppet must be expressive in form and action.

A puppet should be able to do more than point, bow, nod his head (both "yes" and "no"), jump, pop up and down, in and out. He should be able to depict inquisitiveness, shyness, anger, fear, surprise, happiness, pleasure, love, hate, timidity and a host of other moods and emotions. He should be able to indicate his reactions to heat, cold, wind, water, and the feel of the ground he is walking on.

The Hand Puppet

Out of the many many ways to make a puppet, one kind of puppet is especially useful and attractive to children. That is the hand puppet, also called the glove or fist puppet. Fortunately, this kind of puppet is among the easiest to make. It is also adaptable to wide differences in manual skills, both in its making and performing.

A simple bit of human behavior translated into puppet action will illustrate the advantages of fist puppets. When you say, "There it is!", you may accompany the words with a pointing gesture that involves the arm, hand, and an extended finger. The puppeteer translates this arm-hand-finger movement to the movement of a single finger, since that finger is the "arm" and "hand" of the puppet. Similarly, when you say, "Hello" or "How do you do?", you may do one of several things, (1) extend a hand in greeting, (2) nod the head, or (3) bow slightly. A puppeteer translates these movements to (1) extending a finger as the "arm" of the puppet, (2) crooking the forefinger on which the puppet's head rests, or (3) tilting the wrist as the waist of the puppet. These are controlled gestures, adding emphasis to the spoken word. How the gestures are manipulated can indicate a state of mind, an emotion, a reaction to another character's speech.

Manipulating a puppet in this way immediately gets you away from aimless hand wriggling to controlled movements motivated by and accompanying speech. The puppeteer suits the action to the word in order to be a better actor. There is a large gamut of movements by which a puppet becomes more expressive and life-like. Finding these movements increases the fun of puppetry, and in the finding there may be the beginnings of an awareness of the richness of language, of experimentation with words and combinations of words out of which literature is built. There can be a search for words and phrases that lend themselves to manipulative reinforcement. Indeed, this becomes a circular phenomenon, with words leading to manipulation and the need to manipulate leading to words.

This power of fist puppetry to motivate the creative process is what you will want to develop and promote. Through puppets, the scale of the human and animal-sized world is brought down to the size of the fist. It becomes, literally, within a child's grasp. It is his size. Gestures are reduced to a flick of the finger. A small cardboard box becomes a huge crate superhumanly handled by a puppet. He can uproot and drag a tree. He can fling stars into the heavens, dig into the earth, swim the oceans, transcend time and space. Nevertheless, in doing these things, because the child wears the puppet as he would a glove, he is the one who gives it life. The "acting" of the puppet is really that of its manipulator. It is an extension of himself. Real life is inextricably mixed with fancy to the enrichment of both.

Attributes of a Good Hand Puppet

The puppet should fit the hand of the manipulator so that he feels secure enough to manipulate. Conversely, it should not constrict any finger or hand movements he may want to make. The head should fit snugly on the forefinger as far as the large knuckle. The arms of the puppet are the thumb and middle finger. (Many younger children will feel more comfortable inserting the index finger for head, thumb for one arm, and the remaining three fingers for the other arms.) Fingers not used as neck and arms are curled up inside the puppet (see illustration on p. 491.)

The puppet's costume should drape loosely over the hand and entire forearm. Commercially made puppets, and alas, many puppets illustrated in "how-to" books, have such short costumes that they barely cover half the arm, spoiling the illusion upon which the puppet depends. Costumes should not be so elaborate as to inhibit movement. If you try to make them look too realistic, such as using shirt and trousers, the puppet will look misshapen because of the shape of the hand. Try it! Clench your hand, open up the three fingers used for manipulation. Where is the puppet's shoulder line? One arm is much lower than the other, and as a result, the puppet lists to one side. So the best costume is a loosely draped one that camouflages the puppet's lack of figure and hides the human arm and hand. Collars, capes, a few buttons, tie, scarf, and brooch all make very acceptable costume accessories. Simplicity and suggestion are the motifs for puppet costuming.

Second, the size of the puppet head is of key importance. Too large a puppet head is difficult for children to manipulate and is too out of proportion with the small arms made by the child's fingers. The best head size is about three inches in diameter.

The materials used to make the head should not be too heavy. A heavy puppet is tiring and not conducive to manipulation, and it is apt to sink lower and lower during a scene. Lightness in weight, however, does not mean a flimsily made figure. On the contrary, a puppet should be durably constructed (but not brittle) so that it won't inhibit freedom of action. There are rehearsals, accidents of dropping and bumping, storage, and the rigors of performance to consider.

Lastly, the more the physical appearance of the puppet can be identified with the character it portrays, the better. Just looking at the puppet should cause the viewer to identify and respond to its character. This is of importance not only to the viewer but to the manipulator. It is easier to play at being grumpy, for example, if the puppet looks grumpy. The appearance of the puppet is also an aid to vocal expression. Because it looks a certain way, it seems natural to talk the way the puppet looks.

The most successful puppets have some of the characteristics of caricatures or of masks. Features can be distorted or out of proportion, colors can be used to portray emotional mood, shapes and lines can be arranged to indicate expressions. What is it that makes a face show anger, joy, jealousy, craftiness, innocence, fate, greed? The making of a puppet can be used to make children aware of the variety of faces and expressions of the people around them, or those they see in pictures and cartoons, or even in their own faces in the mirror. This is part of that whole universe that is brought down to their size through puppetry.

The kind of puppet we have been talking about should not be too difficult to construct. Moreover, construction techniques and material used should be within children's capabilities. If the techniques and materials used can be the same for younger children as for older ones, all the better. Children's puppetry can then keep pace with their literature. It does them little good to be constantly learning a little about a lot of ways of making puppets. Smatterings of puppet knowledge will not give them better instruments of expression. Very simple puppets will do for "The Three Bears," but it takes puppets of a higher order to do "Rumpelstiltskin," if you want to do more than just the bare bones of the story.

The criteria to follow in making a puppet can be summarized easily. It should (1) fit the hand of its manipulator, (2) be proportioned to his hand, (3) be light in weight, (4) be durable, (5) express character in its appearance, and (6) be

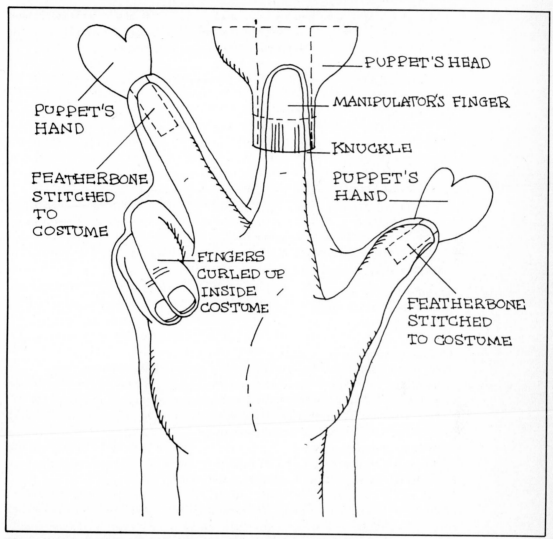

PUPPET'S HAND

PUPPET'S HEAD

MANIPULATOR'S FINGER

KNUCKLE

PUPPET'S HAND

FEATHERBONE STITCHED TO COSTUME

FINGERS CURLED UP INSIDE COSTUME

FEATHERBONE STITCHED TO COSTUME

The puppeteer's hand fits inside the puppet costume as shown above.

relatively easy to construct. The ultimate goal is to insure that the puppet can become an effective actor.

special activities

1. You might begin with a puppet who serves merely as a singer or storyteller. What materials can you use to make a puppet that fulfills the criteria above

to use for leading action songs, such as those in Tom Glazer's lively bright-red collection, *Eye Winker, Tom Tinker, Chin Chopper; Fifty Musical Fingerplays* (8)? Use your puppet to teach these songs.

2. Before you go on, consider occasions for using puppets to enhance experience with various types of literature. List some works that might be introduced by a puppet skit, even though the plots themselves may not lend themselves to total puppet presentation. E. L. Konigsburg's *(George)* (9) has a title character who never appears in the story; he lives inside Howard Carr and speaks through Howard's lips. Try the puppet medium for bringing (George) into the open, letting him tell about the situation. The inanimate central characters in *Paddle-to-the-Sea* (10) by Holling C. Holling and *Hitty: Her First Hundred Years* (11) by Rachel Field are instant invitations for puppetry. Their puppet selves can tell a bit about their adventures to introduce the books. Ankhsenamon, the title character in Lucile Morrison's *The Lost Queen of Egypt* (12), may speak across the centuries in puppet form. List other works to be introduced or played by puppets to enhance literary tone.

Making the Hand Puppet

THE BASIC FORM.   A papier-mâché puppet made on an armature fits the requirements discussed above admirably. An armature is a simple form on which an artist molds a three-dimensional figure. Of all the kinds of materials that may be used for this armature (clay, wire, inflated balloon, wood, light bulb, crushed newspapers), a 3-inch styrofoam ball, such as those used for Christmas decorations, is the best. The important thing is for the face to remind you of a being or creature, and the ball is a good simple form to begin with.

To begin the puppet, make a hole to accommodate the index finger up to the large knuckle by inserting a stick or stout pencil into the center of the ball. Make this hole in stages, testing its diameter and depth.

ADDING FACIAL FEATURES.   Make the nose first. But what kind of nose? What shape? Long? Pointy? Stubby? Upturned? Broad? Narrow? How large or small? These questions bring you into direct contact with the physical attributes of the character each puppet will portray. To whom does the nose belong: person, animal, superhuman, witch, giant, ogre, space creature? That takes you into the story, for you will want to know what kind of character the puppet is going to be in terms of its role in the story. Lead this discussion carefully, for too much of it can inhibit the creativity that makes children's art so fascinating.

To fashion the nose, use styrofoam that is available commercially in various shapes.[1] One of the best shapes is called a "pigeon egg." Apply white glue to the place on the armature where the nose is to go. It will usually be positioned

---

[1] Look for it in art and craft supply stores, large variety stores and school supply firms.

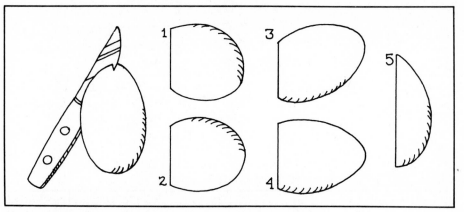

Some possible nose shapes from a styrofoam "pigeon egg."

on the line in the center of the ball. Push the nose firmly on to the ball so it makes a good glue joint. Insert a toothpick or two to hold it firmly.

The pigeon egg can be applied with the rounded end out, or the rounded end glued to the ball. Note that you already have two different shaped noses. The pigeon egg can be squeezed slightly on one or two sides or gently upwards. It can be cut lengthwise and glued down on its flat length. A little experimentation, which should be encouraged, can result in all sorts of noses. (See illustration.)

For beginners and young children, this is all that needs to be done to model a head. The rest of the features can be painted on. It is often best to start puppetry with this simple head, for every feature that is added to the armature requires more skill when giving the puppet its skin of papier-mâché (directions on page 494). Older children can model eye sockets and mouth. Eye sockets can be made simply by pressing into the head with the thumbs or a tool, such as the handle of a paring knife. To construct the mouth, insert a popsicle stick in the appropriate place, and rock it sideways. Move the stick up and down to open the mouth, starting at the center line and diminishing the opening towards the two ends. The mouth helps depict character—a straight line (anger, severity), upturned at the ends (smiley, happy), or downturned (grim, mean, unhappy). (Remember that two layers of papier-mâché are going to be worked onto both the upper and lower lips. Leave enough space for the thicknesses of paper.)

It is seldom necessary to construct human ears, but they are important for animal heads. A human type head is easily converted into an animal one by the addition of ears that stick up like that of a cat, fox, bear, pig or rabbit. Round ears are made by two slices of cane styrofoam or cut from a half-inch styrofoam sheet and compressed. Two slits on the top or side of the ball armature accommodate the ears, fastened with glue. Long ears for a rabbit or donkey are made by slicing a 3-inch length of round styrofoam lengthwise, then tapering each half and hollowing out the flat center. These are inserted into matching holes, glued, and covered with paper (see illustrations on p. 494.)

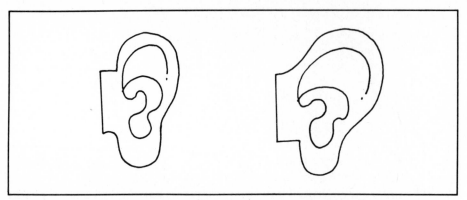

Puppets' ears should have tabs as illustrated above to fit into slits on the head.

Leather and felt can also be used for making ears. Cut out the desired shape, make a slit in the armature, insert, and glue. When painted, these ears will be stiff. Dangling ears should be left unpainted. To make an animal head, it may sometimes be necessary to depart a bit from the roundness of the ball. Jaws can be formed out of styrofoam, glued on, and covered with paper.

THE PAPIER-MÂCHÉ SKIN.   Take a piece of wrapping paper or light weight bagging paper about the size of a piece of construction paper. Soak it in water for a minute, then crush it thoroughly into as small a wad as possible, getting rid of the excess water. Lay the paper out flat in front of you on several layers of newspaper. Smooth out the damp paper and tear off a small piece about one-inch square. Larger pieces of paper will wrinkle when applied to the armature; smaller pieces actually save time and make a better finish. The paper should be torn, not cut, because the tearing makes feathered edges that not only adhere better, but eliminate a bandaged look on the finished product.

Apply wall paper paste with a finger tip to one side of the paper. The paste should be applied liberally enough to be seen on the surface of the paper. Paste the paper down on the back section of the head, rubbing it down with a finger tip and a very little paste. You should not be able to see paste on the outside surface. Do not pat the paper or it may lift off. After rubbing the piece down thoroughly so it adheres well, especially at the edges, repeat the process with other pieces of paper, overlapping the edges. If the pieces do not adhere readily to the armature, check the amount of paste on the pasted side—you may not be using enough, or, you may be using too much on the exposed side.

When you get to the nose or other protruding features, use a narrow strip of paper. Apply paste as before. Now place the strip so half of it lies loosely on the armature, the other half on the nose. Work the paper down on the armature as far as the nose, usng a fingernail or a popsicle stick to get firm adhesion at the point where the nose meets the ball. Then paste the paper down on the nose. It is important to have a continuous strip of paper running from the ball onto the nose in order to give the nose strength. You may have to use smaller pieces of paper in order to cover the nose without undue wrinkling.

Similarly, when you reach the neck hole or other depressions in the armature, lay the paper strip half on the ball, half over the hole. Work the paper down onto the ball first, then into the hole, using your little finger. For shallow depressions use a popsicle stick.

When the armature is completely covered, no white styrofoam should be seen peeking out between the paper pieces. The armature should appear to be one piece of paper, with no loose edges, lumps, or wrinkles. You should be able to feel the hard surface of the styrofoam under the paper. It should not be soft or mushy. The paper should adhere especially closely at the juncture of the head and protrusions. Give the entire head a good rubdown. Then paste contrasting colored pieces of paper to cover the first layer. Lay the head aside to dry.

special activities

1. Help children study illustrations to obtain ideas for puppet making. Encourage them to depart from exact reproduction of illustrations and instead to create their own interpretations. The wonderful compositions of a master illustrator, John Bauer, reproduced in *Great Swedish Fairy Tales* (13) show a great imagination at work. Without direct copying, see how these illustrations inspire puppetry—to produce, for instance, Lady Skinflint (p. 35), the ugly troll people (p. 66), and the witch of Hulta Wood pursued by the phantoms (p. 180). The simple but amazing characters in each of the folk tales of the Antilles in *Greedy Mariani* (14) are drawn by Trina Schart Hyman in such a way as to inspire the creative puppeteer.

2. Which Caldecott Medal books and Caldecott Honor books contain characters suitable for puppetry? Choose one, and suggest procedure.

PAINTING.   When the head is dry, it's ready for painting. Mix tempera color with white liquid latex paint (the kind of water-based paint you use on interior walls). The latex paint will waterproof the tempera and the painting will be almost as effective and easy as the use of acrylic colors, and far cheaper.

Water color brushes, the kind usually used in schools, will handle this tempera mixture. Use a #6 brush or larger, and paint the entire head a coat of white. To hold the head while painting, make a tight roll of 8-inch-wide newspaper and insert it into the neckhole.

While the white layer is drying, lay the head aside and mix the colors to suit the character you are making. Painting can be very straightforward and simple. A single hue is used for the skin, a contrasting color for the lips (usually red), a third color for the eyes (blue, green, black, or brown), and another hue for eyelashes and eyebrows (usually black or deep brown). Exact reproduction, however, is not necessary and should be discouraged. Young children will like to decorate their faces, making the nose a different color just because it sticks out, or freckling it with green dots or the like. Apply the paint sparingly so it can dry quickly. (A word of caution: discourage dipping brushes directly into the supply can of paint—it takes only a brush or two that have not been properly washed out to contaminate the white paint. Take a little paint and put it into a 3-ounce paper cup, bottle or jar lids, or the like. You only need a tablespoon or so.

Painting in eyes and lips presents the greatest problem to puppet makers. Eyes in particular are crucial in giving the puppet expression and seeming life. Avoid eyes that are made by a dot of color placed in the center of a white shape (see illustration). This kind of eye stares forward like a zombie. It is expressionless,

and yet that is the way most children will paint eyes. Ask the class to look at each other's eyes. Do you see the whole roundness of the eye? Where is it placed in relation to the white of the eye? What covers the eyeball so it can't be seen as completely round? Move the eyes left, right, up, down. What happens to the expression on the face? From this demonstration it can be seen that the eyeball is almost never seen in its full roundness. A good rule to follow is that the eyeball must touch the skin on one or two sides. Before painting the eye, discuss what kind of eyes the literary character might have. (See examples below for some ideas to start with.) Practice some eyes on a flat piece of paper before attempting to paint the ones on the puppet. To actually paint the eyes, use a finer brush, and handle it as you would a pencil. Be careful not to overload the brush with paint. And if a mistake is made, overpaint it, allow it to dry, and try again.

Use a finer brush to paint in lips, eyebrows, eyelashes. A good way to explain how to paint lips is to tell the children to think of it as putting on lipstick. Encourage children to paint these features with sharp outlines. This will help increase the expressiveness of the face.

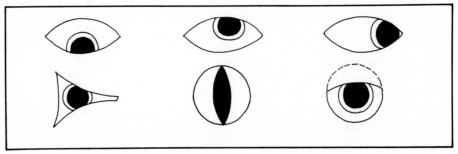

Some possible eye shapes to add expression to puppets' faces.

HAIR. When the paint is dry, it is ready for a wig. Rug yarn of 25% cotton, 75% synthetic fiber is a good material for wigs. Discuss what kind of hair suits the character being portrayed. One girl who made a puppet of a modern mother in fiction completed the wig with hanks of yellow yarn to represent blond hair, and then took a black felt pencil and marked in the black hair roots. Look around the room and at book illustrations to see how hair can be arranged. A faint pencil line can be drawn on the puppet head to indicate the limits of hair growth. To apply the yarn hair, use a bit of glue applied with a toothpick to the hairline, beginning at the middle of the forehead. Glue only an inch or so at a time. The yarns are then glued one at a time, patted down, and the next piece glued down right next to the first one, crowding it a bit.

To show parted hair, glue on one side of the part first, then the other. When the yarns are glued and dried, arrange them in sequence, and put a line of glue parallel to the hairline and about one inch away, and pat the wig down. This will allow the hair to follow the curve of the head and to be shaped around the scalp. When all is glued down, the ends should fall in a bob; trim these with scissors. Beards and moustaches are made in similar fashion. A small piece of yarn can be glued above the eye for a three-dimensional eyebrow, and around the whites for eyelashes. Stubble or short-cropped; hair is glued on by covering the scalp or face area with glue applied with a brush, and short snips of yarn applied in pinches of 4 or 5 pieces.

COSTUMING. The size of the costume is determined by the size of the hand and forearm. Of great importance is the length of the costume—from fingertip to the crook of the elbow so that the entire forearm is covered. The forefinger of the three-fingered costume should fit the finger snugly, because that is the finger that fits into the hole in the puppet's head. The ends of the other two fingers (the "arms" of the puppet) should fit fairly snugly. A few buttons, lace, or other trim can be added to the costume to enhance it.

The sewing of costumes presents a problem to young children. Parents, older relatives, or other helpers may make the costumes. If so, furnish a pattern cut out of newspaper (see illustration on p. 498). Turn out a batch of these by measuring the dimensions of the pattern on the fold of several thicknesses of paper. Cut out on the line, holding the paper firmly so the sheets do not slip, and you have your patterns.

When children are able to run a sewing machine, a master pattern can be cut out of tagboard. Outline the costume on a double thickness of the cloth. Instead of cutting out the costume and then sewing it, reverse the process and sew along the line first, much as a carpenter cuts along a line, and then cut out the costume. This may drive a seamstress out of her mind, but it works.

When the costume is done, turn it right side out and paint the ends of the "arms" with the same color used on the head. These become the puppet's hands. Place the puppet head on the forefinger. Line the hole with a little felt if it is too big.

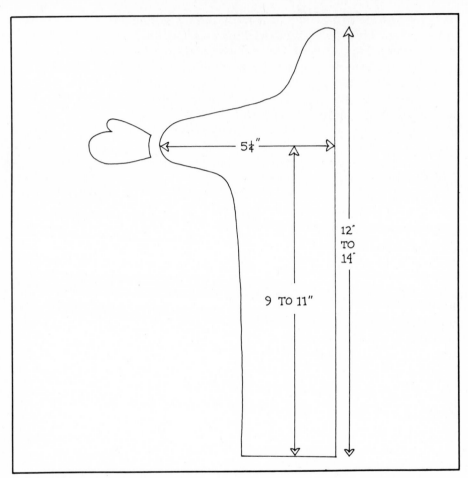

5¼"

12″
TO
14″

9 TO 11"

Basic pattern for puppet costumes.

Preparing for the Performance

Now plunge into the dramatization of your story. Doing a few simple exercises first, however, will give the puppeteer some working knowledge of how a puppet can "come alive."[1] Place a puppet on a child's hand and instantly the puppet will begin to nod, wriggle, bow and, most surprising, strike other puppets aggressively. All this haphazard kinetic energy needs to be harnessed and controlled, a value in itself. If manipulation is the secret of making a puppet expressive, control is the key to manipulative success.

So begin by doing the obvious things the children are already doing, only now do them with conscious direction. Start by suggesting simple movements as follows:

---

[1]See Larry Engler and Carol Fijan, *Making Puppets Come Alive* (Taplinger, 1974).

Action	*How done*
Nod the head "yes"	Crook the forefinger.
Shake the head "no"	Move the forefinger sideways, or rotate wrist to and fro.
Bow	Keeping the hand straight, bend the wrist forward.
Look around	Combination of rotating wrist and bending forefinger so head inclines up or down. Each movement should be clear and sharp with a little pause in between.
Enter and exit	Pop up or down, keeping the puppet vertical.
Walking	With either a slight twisting of the wrist, slight bobbing up and down, or simply gliding the puppet smoothly.

In all these movements, especially in the walking movement, the puppet is held vertically as though a stick were tied up and down the length of the forearm, hand, and forefinger. As the puppet walks, swing out the upper arm from the body, and swing the torso when necessary. There is a vast difference in keeping the puppet vertical at all times by putting your body into the action, or in standing stock still so that the puppet leans over, for then its head is where you want it to be, but its "feet" are still near where it began its walk.

A great deal of fun and creativity goes into discovering the full range of puppet movement. Try these—running, jumping, leaping, sidling, slumping, crawling. Try clapping hands; scratching nose, ear, scalp; fixing up hair; applying lipstick or wiping mouth; patting and scratching stomach; doubling up in pain; hiding eyes; indicating large size, small size, and lengths of time. Experiment; try to do the impossible. What you can't do in close imitation, you might be able to suggest.

teaching ideas

1. Ask the children to make their puppets jump for joy, jump over something, creep fearfully or furtively, scratch head thoughtfully, scratch in response to an itch, enter uncertainly, look around perplexedly. It may help the child to say suitable phrases to himself, such as (matching the actions described above), "Oh, I'm so glad I could burst!", "Got to keep my feet out of this puddle," "This place gives me the creeps," "Now let me think, where could I have lost that money," "Ouch! That darn dog has given me its fleas!", "I'm not sure I'm in the right place," "Should I go this way, or that way?" These pantomimes may be invented by each child, performed before the class who may try to guess the puppeteer's intent. Discussion can follow as to why it was or wasn't successful, and improvements tried out. Discuss, too, how these pantomimes fit into a story.

2. Play "Simon Says" with the puppets. The leader's puppet is Simon, who tells the children to follow his actions only when he says "Simon says." Play this as you play the well-known game, accompanying "Simon says hands up" with the puppet gesture: when you say "Simon says hands down," the puppet puts his hands down, and so on until you say "hands up" or "hands down" to catch the unwary who move without the command of "Simon says." Then vary this with other gestures, such as "Simon says point left . . . point right, bow down . . . stand up, head down . . . head up," and so on.

3. Now use the puppet more creatively. Try this jingle:

Words	*Action*
When Suzy is sleepy	Rubs her eyes.
Her head begins to droop,	Bow the head down in slow degrees.
And if she isn't careful	Continue bowing lower.
She'll drop it in the soup.	Hold cupped hand near waist of the puppet and pop her head in it on the word *soup.*

4. Ask children to write four-line jingles for puppet actions. Verbal and nonverbal language are intertwined in puppetry. The words open up a world of imagination; the self-same words can also tell the puppeteer what to do to enliven the manipulation of the puppet. Look for adjectives, adverbs and verbs that can be depicted by puppet action. Children literally start talking with their fingers. There is no need for the puppet to stand stock still or to wriggle meaninglessly as it performs.

THE STAGE.   The simplest type of puppet stage is the table top theater, for it uses a table as its chief component. A cloth is thrown over the table to hide the puppeteer's legs. (Puppeteers can work standing or seated.) The table holds puppets and props. When the show is over, the theater is folded up and stored like an ironing board (see illustration on next page).

Whatever kind of stage you use, it must have a *playboard,* also referred to as a *wristboard.* This is a ledge in front of the acting space on which the puppeteer's arm can rest lightly. It is also the shelf on which props and furniture can be placed. It must be sturdy.

SELECTING THE STORY.   In a dramatization, children are primarily interested in "what happens next?" They may accept the happenings uncritically unless the matter is brought up at story's end. To some, however, the story is over. "So what" may be the attitude. "I've been entertained; let's get on with another story." This attitude may result because the discussion is abstract. Children frequently are asked to talk about a character that exists on the printed page. It is at this point that the puppet becomes a great aid. When children are asked to talk about the *puppet* character as opposed to an imaginary concept of the character, the abstract becomes tangible and real. The puppet is a handle, so to

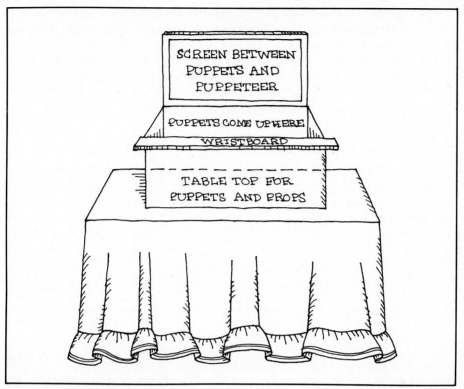

The table top puppet theater.

speak, to the concepts being discussed. It gives the discussion an immediate purpose because something definite is going to come out of it. The "what does he look like" question is now supplanted by "What does he do and why does he do it?" This process goes on whether you make up your own story, select one to fit the puppets at hand, or work on a pre-selected story for which specific puppets have been made.

Science fiction, especially that for younger children, is often suited for puppetry. So are the action-filled picture books of Robert Kraus (with various illustrators), Leo Lionni, Peggy Parish's *Amelia Bedelia* (15), and the "Curious George" books (16) by H. A. Rey. Even the antics of *Runaway Ralph* (17) or of *Homer Price* (18) are good puppet material, as are some modern fanciful stories with unusual, not-quite-human characters, such as *The Borrowers* (19) by Mary Norton and *The Return of the Twelves* (20) by Pauline Clarke. The encounter between Asa and Rambo and the friendly tiger in Mary Stolz's *Belling the Tiger* (21) presents some problems for portraying farcical action, but these can be solved with amusing results. The "monsters" in Peter Dickinson's *Emma Tupper's Diary* (22) in an underwater setting and a cave will challenge puppeteers and may add imaginative substance to this portion of the story.

Folk tales are excellent vehicles for dramatization for the reasons stated in chapter 3. Virginia Haviland's collections, for example, make a good starting point for selecting exciting puppetry fare with wide ethnic variety. Folk tales do not indulge in the inner subtleties of a character; instead, a good rendering of a folk tale may crystallize selected facets of a character in a short phrase. Here are some phrases taken at random from *Grimm's Fairy Tales,* based on the translation of Margaret Hunt, revised by James Stern (23):

> There were once upon a time two brothers, one rich and the other poor. The rich one was a goldsmith and evil-hearted. The poor one supported himself by making brooms, and was good and honorable. ("The Two Brothers," p. 290)

> A certain father had two sons, the elder of whom was smart and sensible, and could do everything, but the younger was stupid and could neither learn nor understand anything, and when people saw him they said, "There's a fellow who will give his father some trouble!" ("The Story of the Youth Who Went Forth to Learn What Fear Was," p. 29)

> A farmer once had a faithful dog called Sultan, who had grown old, and lost all his teeth, so that he could no longer hold on to anything. ("Old Sultan," p. 230)

> A King had a daughter who was beautiful beyond all measure, but so proud and haughty withal that no suitor was good enough for her. She sent them away one after the other, and ridiculed them as well. ("King Thrushbeard," p. 244)

The very flatness of these descriptions is an asset, for the flat characters can be rounded out in the process of dramatization. You can take a sparsely described character and supply him with appearance, motives, feelings, and behavior. Look deeply and closely at the story in order to remain as true to the intent and tone as possible. In turn, the child brings to his discussion of character his

booklist

Stories Suitable for Puppet Dramatization

Woods, Betty. *A Wall Around My Yard.* Reilly and Lee, 1965.
Steig, William. *Roland, the Minstrel Pig.* Windmill Books, 1968. (Distributed by Harper)
Titus, Eve. *Anatole.* Whittesley House, McGraw-Hill, 1956.
Steig, William. *Sylvester and the Magic Pebble.* Windmill Books, Simon and Schuster, 1969.
Flack, Marjorie. *Ask Mr. Bear.* Macmillan, 1932, Collier, 1971.
Elkin, Benjamin. *The Loudest Noise in the World.* Viking, 1955, 1964.
Elkin, Benjamin. *Gillespie and the Guards.* Viking, 1956, 1965.
Schlein, Miriam. *The Big Cheese.* Wm. R. Scott, (1958).

own observations of human behavior, of people he knows, has read about, seen on TV or in the movies, and most importantly, about himself.

We shall use the story of "Rumplestiltskin" to illustrate the process of choosing and dramatizing literature. (Unless noted, we will use the version in the Hunt-Stern collection already referred to.) "Rumplestiltskin" is suitable for puppets for several reasons: (1) the plot is not involved. "What happens next" carries the action along without subplots, long descriptive passages, or sedentary action. In other words, the story moves. (2) Characters are clear-cut and suitable for puppets. There are few of them so that neither the stage nor backstage areas are cluttered. Also, only a few puppets appear on the stage at any one time. (3) Scenery, furniture, and props are interesting and manageable without too much reliance on gimmicks. (4) There are few changes of locale where the action takes place. (5) Though the characters are flat, they can have motivations ascribed to them that come from the kind of questions listed in chapter 9. (6) An added bonus is the existence of a character who is superhuman and can do a superhuman thing, a real advantage, as we shall see, when the straw is spun into gold. (7) The story offers an opportunity for jingles, songs or music.

In staging this story, first make a list of characters and make a preliminary decision as to whether they are essential for the telling of the story.

Characters in story.	Must have?	Other characters that could be added.
King	Yes	Councilor, servant
Miller	Yes	Farmer with grain, Crony
Daughter	Yes	Lady in waiting when Queen, Nurse for her Baby
Rumplestiltskin	Yes	None; he lives alone.
Servant	Yes	Other servants.

No character in the story can be eliminated, as they all play a part in it. Nor can they be combined. On the other hand, if needed, there are other characters that could be added to help tell the story, to supply atmosphere, or provide comedy.

If you must present the story with just a few puppeteers, several characters can be played by one child. Analyze the story to see which characters do not appear at the same time. Rumplestiltskin never appears with the Miller, King, or Servant. The King never appears with the Servant or Rumplestiltskin. The Daughter appears with each of them. Therefore, one puppeteer could play Rumplestiltskin and the Miller; another could play the King and the Servant. The play can be performed by three puppeteers.

The better the children know the story, the more fruitful will be their discussion of character. In the discussion, it is a good idea to brainstorm characteristics and make a chart on the blackboard. Out of this quick analysis of the characters, you might get something like this:

Miller
Was poor.
Wants to impress King: because he is afraid of him;

> can't help it, he boasts;
> covers up his feelings of being
> in the lower class

Tells gold story because he has no dowry for his daughter.
Is a braggart.

King
  Greedy
  Cruel (would kill girl if she fails to spin gold)
  Getting more just feeds his greediness.
  Does not want to marry a poor girl.
  Is stupid—falls for the Miller's straw-into-gold story.

Daughter
  Beautiful
  Very obedient
  Too obedient—Couldn't deny her father because it would get him in trouble.
  Shows how women were dominated by men.
  Very dumb to agree to giving away her child so quickly.
  Pretty smart to make the bargain because she might not have a child.
  Showed intelligence by sending out for names.

Rumplestiltskin
  Was very lonely living in forest alone.
  Wanted a baby to raise.
  Had it in for the King.
  Went around tricking people.
  Had soft spot in his heart because he did give Queen a chance to guess his name and so keep baby.
  Was just toying with the Queen about his name—he knew he had her over a barrel.
  A show-off.
  Took it out on humans because he was small and grotesque.

Servant
  Faithful.
  Character doesn't make any difference—all he does is bring in the correct name.
  Could be comic, nervous, pompous.

The children should be encouraged to support their ideas with passages from the story, their knowledge of the times, or how it would add to the enjoyment of the play. Quick forays can be made into the realm of real life by asking: "Why do people boast?" "Have you ever boasted?" "Why?" "What was the result?" "Are there people like Rumplestiltskin who take advantage of a situation by driving a hard bargain?" "Are there lonely people who would take a baby?"

"What would you do if you were faced with making the kind of bargain the Queen made with Rumplestiltskin?" "Is it always easy to know what will happen when you are faced with a problem?"

Of all the characters in the story, perhaps Rumplestiltskin is the most fascinating. He should be considered as human when his motivations are discussed.

This process is not all of one piece, for conclusions are only tentative. They will be tested against the dramatizations. So don't overdo the questioning. Let the dynamics of puppetry take over.

When dramatizing folk tales, an opportunity arises that does not exist in other types of literature. You can compare the *same story* in several versions. Here children have an opportunity to see how slight differences in words or phrases can change the character involved and even alter the action. For example, compare the Hunt-Stern version of "Rumplestiltskin" with the one from *Favorite Stories Old and New* (24) selected by Sidonie Matsner Gruenberg. In the Hunt-Stern version, the story begins: "Once there was a Miller who was poor, but who had a beautiful daughter." The Gruenberg version begins: "There once was a Miller who was always boasting." Nothing is said about his being poor. The emphasis is on his boasting, because he boasts to his friends about his daughter's supposed skill in spinning. The story spreads about the country and reaches the ears of the King. The King then sends for the Miller. In the Hunt-Stern version, the Miller "had to go and speak to the King, and in order to make himself appear important, he said to him, 'I have a daughter who can spin straw into gold.' "

The motivations for the Miller's story are not alike. Depending upon which version is used, the Miller will be a different kind of person. These variations allow for a choice or a combination of characteristics, for the Miller could be poor, boastful, or both or he might be boastful only on this occasion and sorry for it later.

The tentative conclusions reached by the children in the brainstorming session should be tried out with simple improvisations. Children put their puppets on and begin to talk for them, not necessarily in a stage. Let's follow the two versions to show what could happen.

First Version.   The King is on his throne. It is the day that he listens to his subjects' problems, grants boons, decides controversies. He opens the scene by asking who else there is for him to see. A councilor, invented for this pupose, replies, "The Miller." Now we have to invent a reason for his appearance before the King. To pay his taxes? Did he short-weight someone? Is his milling below standard? Is he to get a reward for excellent work? Whatever the reason, it should lead naturally to his straw-into-gold boast. The Miller appears, his reason for coming disposed of, and the boast made. A great stir fills the throne room! The councilor and King confer, ask questions, the Miller may embroider his story, or may now try to get out of it. Too late! The King orders him to produce the daughter. As the Miller goes, the scene closes with the King gloating over the event and ordering that straw be brought in preparation for the spinning. There are many ways of embellishing the story. Much depends upon how many children want to be involved with their puppets in the story, but no matter how many extras are invented, they must help to move the story along, and not clutter up the stage in big crowds.

SECOND VERSION.   The story may open in the mill, or in a tavern. The Miller, in talking with a farmer who has brought grain to be ground, makes his boast. Or he may be talking with a crony or two as he drinks in the tavern. He boasts; the others ridicule him, but he continues with his story. He may boast that this way his daughter will have a fine dowry. His friends may point out that the story is getting about the country and the King might hear of it. What is the Miller's reaction—pleasure or fear? Later, the King himself may arrive to investigate the story and may end up ordering the Daughter to come to the palace to spin. Or a courier may come to order the Miller to appear before the King.

There are countless variations open to you. The children can weigh them, play with them, and then adopt a course of action. After going through the story using simple improvisations, scenes can be added, amplified or deleted. The play need not ever be written down, but can be kept on the improvisational level. There is a value to this, for it keeps the children's focus on the puppets instead of on a written script. If the play is written, it *must* be memorized. If puppeteers are reading a script behind the scenes, the rendition of the play will sound stilted and flat. Moreover, with their eyes on the script, the puppeteers will pay scant attention to the puppet, and manipulation will be forgotten. A written *scenario,* or outline of the action, will, however, help keep the play moving smoothly.

Younger children will get on with the story more directly than suggested here. You work at whatever level the children can handle. Their simple dramatizations can be effective when told without benefit of scenery. Often, one side of the stage is one locale, the other side another. The audience will assume this convention of collapsing time and space.

Puppets can do one thing that is often denied to live actors: they can establish direct contact with the audience. Puppets do not need the "theatrical distance" that sets off live actors from the audience. They can look directly at an audience and even speak directly to them. This can be done effectively when the character is "thinking out loud." A puppet character facing a choice can say to his audience, "What would you do if you were standing up here?" Be prepared, of course, for an unexpected reply, especially from young audiences. But oftentimes the storyline will cause some vocal member of the audience to make an appropriate reply. In that case, a genuine rapport has been created that makes the presentation immediate and spontaneous. Few other dramatic forms can do this.

If you are using the thrust type puppet stage, where scenery and furniture changes are performed in view of the audience, use a neutral colored background. Begin with a throne for the throne room. Remove the throne, bring up a heap of straw and a spinning wheel, and you are in the spinning room. Try to concentrate as much action as possible into a few locales. In the scene where the servant discovers Rumplestiltskin's name, use a set piece showing a pot over a fire, and put a huge tree trunk to one side behind which the servant can peek.

The existence of interesting and manageable props and furniture invests a story with puppet possibilities. Some of these are obvious. The King should have a throne. There must be a spinning wheel, straw, and gold in some form. The presence of a baby indicates a cradle. The names read off by the Queen can be on scrolls. Look over the story carefully to see where props can fit in. It helps to give the puppets something to do and adds to the charm of the performance. Props often suggest things for puppets to do or say. For example, when the Queen is naming names, a long length of adding machine tape can be unrolled so it hangs down over the edge of the playboard. Additional scrolls can be brought in just as Rumplestiltskin thinks she has come to the end. The scene can end with paper all over the place, thus adding comedy and making what could be a dreary recitation of names more lively. (Note that the story as written does away with the name business with three names each time; the rest of the names are merely described.)

Often a story will present technical problems, such as working a spinning wheel and transforming straw into gold. A spinning wheel that actually runs can be constructed, either in the round or flat. Making such a prop appeals to the mechanically minded child, and this could be his or her particular contribution to the play. The straw could be real hay or straw bound up at one end so it is easy to handle. Shredded cellophane similar to Easter basket grass, straw glued to a cardboard background to look like a straw heap, or even a drawn representation of straw are suitable substitutes. As the spinning goes on, the straw is slowly lowered below the playboard, while the gold comes up. The action is partially hidden by the wheel or by Rumplestiltskin himself. With practice, this transformation can appear quite realistic. The gold can be decorative tinsel, gold ribbon, or cord. One version of the story says it was wound on reels. These can be built and wound up by the Queen, or the gold can be just heaped up, and left to hang partially over the edge of the playboard.

All furniture and props that are placed on the playboard should have little handles fixed to them so they can be placed, held if necessary, and removed without showing a puppeteer's hand.

If you are going to use a story whose characters are rounded, use the same process. There may be fewer choices about what a character is like, since the author may have provided more details. Dig into the story to get the facts; brainstorm, list, and put the clues together. There can be little doubt that seeing the characters on the stage will enliven what children read.

Perhaps an anecdote will serve as an example:

There is a famous puppet show called *Punch and Judy*. Punch is a monstrous creature who disguises his lack of morals behind a grinning, swaggering, funny facade. He manages, with complete aplomb, to do away with his baby, his wife, his dog, the policeman, and the hangman, until the Devil comes to take him away to meet his just desserts—he ends up in Hell.

One day this show was performed in a church hall. The children cheered the villain in bloodthirsty fashion. But when the Devil came and carried Punch away on a pitchfork, the room became very quiet. The puppeteer raised a replica of a huge flame in the place where Punch had last been seen. The Devil ended the show by indicating the flame and saying, "This is the end of Mr. Punch."

As the puppeteer was striking his stage, a woman approached him, her voice seething in indignation, and said, "How dare you bring this kind of show into the church!" It turned out that she objected to the presence of the Devil. But the puppeteer, accustomed to making quick recoveries, said, "Madam, does your church teach the existence of the Devil?"

"Yes, we do," she answered.

"And do you teach that those who do wicked things will end up in Hell?"

"We certainly do!" she said with great conviction.

"And you teach this in Sunday school?"

"We do."

"Then," suggested the puppeteer, "your children have *read* about being punished for wickedness, they have *seen* pictures in the Sunday school manuals, and have *heard* sermons on the subject. But today, they actually *saw it happen.* Which of these means do you think has left them with the greatest impression?"

She looked at the puppeteer shrewdly and relaxed. "I hadn't thought of it in that way," she said, and walked away.

Do think of puppets in that way. From nonsense stories to works of great morality and everything that lies in between, the puppet can leave a lasting impression upon those who use it and see it.

CHORAL VERSE

Choral verse derives originally from ancient Greek drama where the chorus, speaking sentences in unison and sometimes in parts, commented on the play. More recently verse choirs were revived in England at the suggestion of poet John Masefield. Perhaps the one person who took his suggestion most earnestly was Marjorie Gullan.[1] First in Scotland and later in England she directed choruses with great success and trained teachers to carry on her work in their classes. Later she came to America, where she generated more enthusiasm. Today, in some sections of the country, regular concerts are given by school groups.

---

[1]See Marjorie Gullan, *The Speech Choir* (Harper, 1937).

Choral Verse at the Primary Level

Choral work with poetry can be started in the early grades by reading verse that has a refrain. Read the main substance and have the children come in on the refrain, as in the following example:

> A farmer went trotting upon his grey mare,
>   Bumpety, bumpety, bump!
> With his daughter behind him so rosy and fair,
>   Lumpety, lumpety, lump!
>
> A raven cried, Croak! and they all tumbled down,
>   Bumpety, bumpety, bump!
> The mare broke her knees and the farmer his crown,
>   Lumpety, lumpety, lump!
>
> The mischievous raven flew laughing away,
>   Bumpety, bumpety, bump!
> And vowed he would serve them the same the next day,
>   Lumpety, lumpety, lump!

Later the teacher may try simple division into parts with perhaps half the class doing a first stanza and the other half the next, alternating stanzas until the whole poem has been recited. Edward Lear's "The Owl and the Pussy-Cat" lends itself to this approach:

> The Owl and the Pussy-Cat went to sea
>   In a beautiful pea-green boat:
> They took some honey, and plenty of money
>   Wrapped up in a five-pound note.
> The Owl looked up to the stars above,
>   And sang to a small guitar,
> "O lovely Pussy, O Pussy, my love,
> What a beautiful Pussy you are,
>   You are,
>   You are!
> What a beautiful Pussy you are!"
>
> Pussy said to the Owl, "You elegant fowl,
>   How charmingly sweet you sing!
> Oh! let us be married; too long we have tarried:
>   But what shall we do for a ring?"
> They sailed away, for a year and a day,
>   To the land where the bong-tree grows;
> And there in the wood a Piggy-wig stood,
> With a ring at the end of his nose,
>   His nose,
>   His nose,
> With a ring at the end of his nose.
>
> "Dear Pig, are you willing to sell for one shilling
> Your ring?" Said the Piggy, "I will."
> So they took it away, and were married next day

By the Turkey who lives on the hill.
They dined on mince and slices of quince,
    Which they ate with a runcible spoon;
And hand in hand, on the edge of the sand,
    They danced by the light of the moon,
        The moon,
        The moon,
    They danced by the light of the moon.

Still later some solo voices may be introduced, as in the following example:

The Mouse, The Frog, and The Little Red Hen

All: Once a Mouse, a Frog, and a Little Red Hen
Together kept a house.
The Frog was the laziest of frogs,
And lazier still was the Mouse.

The work all fell on the Little Red Hen,
Who had to get the wood,
And build the fires, and scrub, and cook,
And sometimes hunt the food.

One day, as she went scratching round,
She found a bag of rye.
Solo 1: Said she, "Now who will make some bread?"
Solo 2: Said the lazy Mouse, "Not I."

Solo 3: "Nor I," croaked the Frog, as he drowsed in the shade.
Red Hen made no reply,
But flew around with bowl and spoon
And mixed and stirred the rye.

Solo 1: "Who'll make the fire to bake the bread?"
Solo 2: Said the Mouse again, "Not I."
And, scarcely op'ning his sleepy eyes,
Frog made the same reply.

The Little Red Hen said never a word,
But a roaring fire she made.
And while the bread was baking brown,
Solo 1: "Who'll set the table?" she said.

Solo 3: "Not I," said the sleepy Frog with a yawn.
Solo 2: "Not I," said the Mouse again.
So the table she set and the bread put on.
Solo 1: "Who'll eat the bread?" said the Hen.

Solo 3
  &
Solo 2: "I will!" cried the Frog. "And I!" squeaked the Mouse.
As they near the table drew.
Solo 1: "Oh no, you won't!" said the Little Red Hen.
And away with the loaf she flew.

Action accompaniments to the chorus are also very satisfying: soft clapping of hands to the beat of the verse, bodily movements, galloping, marching. "The Grand Old Duke of York" is especially suited to this activity:

> The grand Old Duke of York
> He had ten thousand men,
> He marched them up a very high hill
> And he marched them down again.
> And when he was up he was up
> And when he was down he was down
> And when he was only halfway up
> He was neither up nor down.

Choral Verse at the Intermediate Level

In the intermediate grades, narrative poetry introduces the possibility of dialog either by solo voice or by separate chorus. "Godfrey Gordon Gustavus Gore" by William Brightly Rands works well in this way:

> Godfrey Gordon Gustavus Gore—
> No doubt you have heard the name before—
> Was a boy who never would shut a door!
>
> The wind might whistle, the wind might roar,
> And teeth be aching and throats be sore,
> But still he never would shut the door.
>
> His father would beg, his mother implore,
> Solo 1 (boy   "Godfrey Gordon Gustavus Gore,
> and girl):   We really *do* wish you would shut the door!"
>
> Their hands they wrung, their hair they tore;
> But Godfrey Gordon Gustavus Gore
> Was deaf as the buoy out at the Nore.
>
> When he walked forth the folks would roar,
> Solo 2 (several   "Godfrey Gordon Gustavus Gore,
> boys and girls):   Why don't you think to shut the door?"
>
> They rigged out a Shutter with sail and oar,
> And threatened to pack off Gustavus Gore
> On a voyage of penance to Singapore.
>
> Solo 3:   But he begged for mercy, and said, "No more!"
> Pray do not send me to Singapore
> On a shutter, and then I will shut the door!"
>
> Solo 1:   "You will?" said his parents; "then keep on shore!
> But mind you do! For the plague is sore
> Of a fellow that never will shut the door,
> Godfrey Gordon Gustavus Gore!"

By this time, more sophisticated effects are possible—loudness and softness, building toward a crescendo, slowing and hastening rhythm, exaggerating consonant qualities, such as sibilance, liquids, gutterals, emphasizing the tonal values in vowels.

In general, however, your interest as a teacher in securing more sophisticated effects should be tempered by a sensitivity to long-term results in children's affection for poetry. For example, children who would rebel at solo recitation in front of the class may be lured into speaking poetry aloud protected by the anonymity of a group. Gradually within the group they may learn to hear their own voices lent to rhythm and sound and imagery. But this slow-budding affection could easily be killed by the perfectionist who presses too grimly toward performance results. The principal goal for the children is not performance for others but satisfaction for themselves.

A sense of easy informality, touched now and then with humor, should be carefully preserved. At the same time no burlesquing of serious poetry need be tolerated.

Probably the best insurance that this attitude will be furthered resides in your own reading or reciting aloud. If you read or recite with ease and naturalness—without excessive formality or effusiveness—then probably your efforts in directing choral verse will be accepted as normal and natural and satisfying.

In beginning to train your class, read the verse aloud several times in the manner you wish to be emulated. Talk about the poem a little, mentioning its rhythm or its sound or its imagery. Then have the children open their books. Read it aloud with them. That may be as far as you go in a single session with young children—with older children, you may begin the division into parts or begin to practice certain effects.

What kinds of poems will you choose? Poems with pronounced rhythm, sound, imagery; poems with contrasts in mood and idea; poems that lend themselves to the use of different voices, choirs, and characters; poems of a somewhat public nature rather than private communications; poems of a virile quality rather than those of a delicate nature.

Be careful not to overdo choral verse. It is not the only avenue to poetry appreciation. Avoid excessive emphasis on rhythm or sound or imagery. Don't let yourself become too performance-minded. Most of your work should be a part of regular classroom instruction.

THE ROLE OF CREATIVE TECHNIQUES IN TEACHING LITERATURE

In all these creative techniques place your greatest faith in what children do for themselves: reading aloud, telling stories, dramatizing, choral speaking. Place in an ancillary role—important but not enjoying first priority—those activities where the initiative, the shaping, and in fact most of the doing is by others. No one denies, for example, the power of the media in our time: television, motion picture, other projected material, radio, recording. But try to remember that the power is best employed if it is a stimulant and not simply a tranquilizer. Instead, seek always to use the medium primarily as an incentive. Let the children assume the initiative, the shaping, the doing.

Especially if a particular medium is used to project literature, don't choose material that is so explicit that each child does not see in the imagination—hear, taste, touch, or other sensory appeal—in a way that is uniquely his own. The prime invitation of literature is to add creatively out of children's own imaginations to that which is only suggested. No literature should be presented through any medium so comprehensively that children cannot add individual, imaginative extensions. There is never only one correct response in literature. It is absolutely essential for each child to know he can and should respond with his own image, each image different yet true to the spirit of the writing. If children feel they must yield to responses completely supplied by the medium—with every child's response completely paralleling that of his classmates—then attraction to individual reading in literature is reduced, not enhanced. Children must feel the privilege and proprietary interest in giving their own responses out of the invitations they sense in literature.

Whatever you do to engage children in literature, remember that the key word is "perspective." Whatever else you do, help children know where the lasting power of literature is and try to avoid anything that subverts the private discoveries each child can make.

CHAPTER REFERENCES

1. Hoban, Russell. *A Bargain for Frances.* Harper, 1970.
2. Sandburg, Carl. *The Wedding Procession of the Rag Doll and the Broom Handle and Who Was in It.* Illus. Harriet Pincus. Harcourt, 1967.
3. Fox, Paula. *Portrait of Ivan.* Bradbury, 1969.
4. Harris, Rosemary. *The Moon in the Cloud.* Faber and Faber, 1968.
5. Raskin, Ellen. *The World's Greatest Freak Show.* Atheneum, 1971.
6. Carroll, Lewis. *Through the Looking Glass and What Alice Found There.* St. Martin's, 1927.
7. Stevenson, Robert Louis. *Treasure Island.* Dodd, Mead, 1972.
8. Glazer, Tom. *Eye Winker, Tom Tinker, Chin Chopper: Fifty Musical Fingerplays.* Doubleday, 1973. (All ages)
9. Konigsburg, E. L. *(George).* Atheneum, 1970. (I)
10. Holling, Holling C. *Paddle-to-the-Sea.* Houghton, Mifflin, 1941. (I)
11. Field, Rachel. *Hitty, Her First Hundred Years.* Illus. Dorothy Lathrop. Macmillan, 1929. (I)
12. Morrison, Lucile. *The Lost Queen of Egypt.* Stokes, 1937. (U)
13. Olenius, Elsa, sel. *Great Swedish Fairy Tales.* Illus. John Bauer. Delacorte, 1973. (I-U)
14. Carter, Dorothy Sharp, sel. and adapt. *Greedy Mariani.* Illus. Trina Schart Hyman. Atheneum, 1974. (I)
15. Parish, Peggy. *Amelia Bedelia.* Harper, 1963. (E)
16. Rey, H. A. *Curious George.* Houghton, Mifflin, 1941. (E)
17. Cleary, Beverly. *Runaway Ralph.* Illus. Louis Darling. Morrow, 1970. (I)
18. McCloskey, Robert. *Homer Price.* Viking, 1943. (I)

19. Norton, Mary. *The Borrowers.* Harcourt, 1952.
20. Clarke, Pauline. *The Return of the Twelves.* Coward, 1963. (U)
21. Stolz, Mary. *Belling the Tiger.* Illus. Beni Montresor. Harper, 1961. (I)
22. Dickinson, Peter. *Emma Tupper's Diary.* Little, Brown, 1971. (U)
23. Hunt, Margaret, tr. *Grimm's Fairy Tales.* Rev. James Stern. Random.
24. Gruenberg, Sidonie Matsner, sel. *Favorite Stories Old and New.* Doubleday, 1955.

BIBLIOGRAPHY

Allison, Eileen. "Growth with Puppets." *Instructor,* 81 November 1971, p. 36. How to construct shadow puppets; bibliography of stories and records that may provide script material for puppet plays.

Brown, Jennifer. "Reading Aloud." *Elementary English,* 50 April 1973, pp. 635–36. Techniques for selection and oral reading, with annotated bibliography of suitable items.

Burch, Robert. "Why Read Aloud to Children Today." Instructor, 82 November 1972, pp. 121–22. Guidelines for reading aloud; suggestions for appropriate situations; significance of storytelling.

Confino, R. J. "Puppetry as an Educative Media." *Elementary English,* 49 March 1972, pp. 450–56. Theory of puppetry as applied to literary selections.

Dovey, Irma. "Puppets Are Simple." *Elementary English,* 51 January 1974, pp. 52–54. Personal experiences in creating puppets to develop oral reading skills.

Filstrup, Janie. "Children + Picture Books = Story Making and Telling." *Top of the News,* 29 November 1972, pp. 1–6. Good how-to-do-it article that could be used with many picture books.

Garthwaite, Marion. "Stories to Shorten the Road." *Elementary English,* 49 April 1972, pp. 600–3. Criteria for selecting stories for storytelling.

Hansen, Harlan and Ruth. "Let's Read to Children." *Instructor,* 82 April 1973, pp. 69–70+. Storytelling and reading aloud to children fulfill three purposes: introducing literature, imparting information, and developing language-related skills (memory, sequence, and analysis).

Heins, Ethel L. "Literature Bedeviled: A Searching Look at Filmstrips." *Horn Book,* 50 June 1974, pp. 306–13. Author weighs the use of filmstrips based on books, with specific examples of good ones and bad ones.

Hinds, Nadine. "Puppet Power." *Arts and Activities,* 74 January 1974, p. 36. Good guide to construction of puppets to be used with stories.

Niedermeyer, Fred C., and Oliver, Linda. "The Development of Young Children's Dramatic and Public Speaking Skills." *Elementary School Journal,* 73 November 1972, pp. 95–100. Behavioral research that gives convincing evidence that pantomime and dramatization experience contributes to a child's development.

Ottley, Reginald. "On Storytelling." *Elementary English,* 49 February 1972, pp. 279–80. Essay regarding value of storytelling as a means of communication.

Paston, Herbert S. "Puppets are Personalities." *School Arts,* 70 November 1970, pp. 28–29. Help in avoiding stereotypes in puppets used to portray stories.

Price, Ed. "Filmmaking in the Classroom." *Teacher,* 91 May/June 1974, pp. 28–31. Clear directions for simple filmmaking activities. These can be applied to literary favorites.

Reed, Linda. "Creative Drama in the Language Arts Program, or 'Catch the Crab Before He Finds a Hole!' " *Elementary English,* 51 January 1974, pp. 103–10. Annotated bibliography of recent references for using drama in language arts curricula.

Stewig, John W. "Pictures: Impetus to Dramatize." *Elementary English,* 50 March 1973, pp. 393–96+. Discusses kinds of pictures most likely to capture children's interest and elicit dramatic response.

Volc, Judy, and Stuart, Allaire. "Storytelling in the Language Arts Program." *Elementary English,* 45 November 1968, pp. 958–65. Extensive discussion of the art of storytelling, its values, ideas for procedure, sample references suitable for storytelling.

Weiger, Myra. "Puppetry." *Elementary English,* 51 January 1974, pp. 55–65. Diagrammed instructions for making puppets, discussion of methods for presenting puppetry.

Yawkey, Thomas D., and Aronin, Eugene L. "Creative Dramatics for Teaching Career Concepts to the Young Child." *Elementary English,* 51 January 1974, pp. 38–40. Useful extension of creative dramatics into career-planning; might be integrated with books about careers.

II chapter

Literature and the Creative Process

There is a quality in children's literature that overshadows all the others and goes a long way toward explaining the creative process: that quality is generosity.

Writers and artists must be generous in exploring and expanding their original inspirations, fashioning them into creations quickened with a vitality all their own. Readers and listeners must be generous in giving them audience in order to travel in wider realms.

The job of sharing literature with children is basically one of revealing the fruits of generosity, and our inquiry in the preceding chapters has really been directed toward this purpose. Now we are suggesting that you go one step further: to examine the creative process through which such generosity is transmitted.

This step must not be perceived as an attempt to coax children to be kind to dull books by telling them all about when authors lived, how hard they worked, and how fine their intentions were. Knowledge of the rigors of production must not be expected by itself to arouse enthusiasm in reception. To know, for example, that Ruth Sawyer was an "indefatigable worker" in writing *Roller Skates* (1) is of no use to readers unless it increases their own generosity and releases their own creative energy.[1]

But somewhere along the way toward experiencing the beauty attained in literature, you need to consider how that beauty was achieved. The enjoyment of literature is enhanced by becoming sensitive to the process of creation. A brief glance at Gerald McDermott's *Anansi the Spider* (2) shows a brief folk tale with what might appear at first to be garish illustrations; but inquiry into the author/ artist's creative process reveals the integrity of the designs with which he transmitted this solid and enduring Ashanti tale. As you read about a spider whose

---

[1]Bertha Mahoney Miller and Elinor Whitney Field, eds., *Newbery Medal Books: 1922–1955* (Horn Book, 1955), pp. 147–560.

six children saved him from the belly of a fish, you see how the colors and even the stylized animals and plants are derived from a rich culture. You realize, in the end, that this brief bright book can tell more about that culture than a mound of anthropologist's notes. Just as wondrous is McDermott's intricate design and storytelling in *Arrow to the Sun* (3). This Pueblo myth is illustrated in shades of yellow, orange, and brown.

Likewise, Roger Duvoisin's amusing drawings of animals—for instance, the full-page backside of a hippopotamus in *Veronica* (4)—take a new perspective when you learn that one of this artist's central purposes in creation is "counterbalancing the too great love that children have for mechanical things in opposition to things of nature."[1]

The inquiry into the tantalizing mysteries of genius may increase the generosity of the reader's response. When you read Beatrix Potter's *The Tale of Tom Kitten* (5), you come upon a line which is particularly apt. Tom and his sisters, sent to bed because they've been naughty when guests are about to arrive, make a shambles of the bedroom. Potter depicts the situation in this half-sentence: "very extraordinary noises over-head, which disturbed the dignity and repose of the tea party." Why does such language live? It lives for a four-year-old who doesn't understand it, later to be resurrected to life again as he gathers referents for the words, even later to be chuckled over by him as an adult who sees a milieu of drawing-room manners in the phrases. But why? We aren't likely to find out exactly why. Even the experts on creativity have only some hypotheses about the why. Yet you can gain some insight into the process and, concomitantly, into your own process of enjoyment. Beatrix Potter, for example, made quite clear her serious purpose and effort in writing:

> I think I write carefully because I enjoy my writing, and enjoy taking pains over it. I have always disliked writing to order: I write to please myself. . . . My usual way of writing is to scribble, and cut out, and write it again and again. The shorter and plainer the better. And read the Bible (unrevised version and Old Testament) if I feel my style wants chastening.[2]

Let's look for a few moments at how authors and artists go about their work, obtain their insights, and join in the creative process that produces literary works.

AUTHORS AT WORK

It has been said that deep within everyone is the inspiration and material for a good book. The successful children's author, however, has somehow recog-

---

[1] Roger Duvoisin, "Acceptance Paper: Outwitting the Comics," in *Caldecott Medal Books: 1938–1957,* ed. Bertha Mahoney Miller and Elinor Whitney Field (Horn Book, 1957), p. 173.
[2] Quoted in Margaret Lane, *The Tale of Beatrix Potter* (Warne, 1946, 1968), p. 135.

nized that inspiration and its appropriateness and has found the craft for evolving the inspiration into an artistic product. The process by which this is done varies a good deal from author to author, so much so that many books that attempt to tell how to write for children are rudimentary at best and at worst downright misleading. They often attempt to make rules where rule-breaking is the only recourse. Yet a pattern in the creative process, however vague, does begin to emerge as you listen to authors comment about themselves.

The Inspiration

Most authors acknowledge a beginning to their work that defies close analysis. They didn't sit down with an empty mind and ask, "Now what shall I write about?" Some components in their experience kept reappearing and growing, offering themselves as central ideas—for a setting, an episode, or a theme.

Jean Craighead George, arriving in Barron, Alaska, to write about wolves for *Reader's Digest,* happened to see "a small fur-clad child who was walking into the wilderness over which we had just flown" and to hear her son's remark, "She's awfully little to be going that way alone."[1] It was this vision and not the magazine assignment that drew the author to her work and resulted in *Julie of the Wolves* (6).

Evaline Ness dug out a half-forgotten drawing of a "shabby misplaced child," combined it with a newspaper article about a baby kangaroo, and then added her memories of her childhood self as "a liar and a profitable one," and the eventual result of this synthesized inspiration was *Sam, Bangs & Moonshine* (7).[2]

Lloyd Alexander found his inspiration for the famous five-volume Prydain series while working on a smaller, less significant book, *Time Cat* (8).[3] But he is quick to acknowledge that inspiration is never derived from just one source: "Everything," he remarks of authors, "is grist for their mill."[4]

Many authors go back to memories of childhood for their initial spark, although editors and critics warn that it is freshness of vision and not just nostalgia which transforms memory into a new creation. Many writers acknowledge the life-long inspiration of early literary experience. Sometimes the connection between such experience and the author's published work is difficult to discern. For instance, Maurice Sendak cites Dickens as one of his sources of inspiration. He also credits the influence of George Macdonald (an early writer of fantasy), the film classic *King Kong,* and the early animations of Walt Disney.[5]

Similarly, William Steig tells of his indebtedness to such seemingly diverse

[1]Jean Craighead George, "Newbery Award Acceptance," *Horn Book* 49 (August 1973): 338.
[2]Evaline Ness, "Caldecott Acceptance Speech," *Horn Book* 43 (August 1967): 434–38.
[3]Lloyd Alexander, "Newbery Award Acceptance," *Horn Book* 45 (August 1969): 379.
[4]Lloyd Alexander, "No Laughter in Heaven," *Horn Book* 46 (February 1970): 12.
[5]Maurice Sendak, "Questions to an Artist Who Is Also an Author," *The Quarterly Journal* (October 1971): 263–280. Reprinted and expanded in Miriam Hoffman and Eva Samuels, eds., *Authors and Illustrators of Children's Books* (Bowker, 1972).

childhood heroes as Charlie Chaplin, the Brothers Grimm, and the comic strip Katzenjammer Kids—and especially to his childhood reading of *Pinocchio*. In commenting on his writing of *Sylvester and the Magic Pebble* (9), Steig remarked: "And it is very likely that Sylvester became a rock and then again a live donkey because I had once been so deeply impressed with Pinocchio's longing to have his spirit encased in flesh instead of in wood."[1]

Certainly, early memories are for some authors so vivid that they amount to almost an obsession. Mary Norton, whose Borrowers series gives thousands of readers the delight of her shortsightedness, explains: "I think the first idea—or first feeling—of the Borrowers came through my being shortsighted: when others saw the far hills, the distant woods, the soaring pheasant, I, as a child, would turn sideways to the close bank, the tree roots and the gangled grasses."[2]

Elizabeth Enright, author of *Thimble Summer* (10) and *Gone-away Lake* (11), illustrates the concepts of observation, experience, wish, and memory that she believes lie at the heart of inspiration:

> When I was a child I was once severely reprimanded by one of my teachers before the whole class. As I listened, humiliated, my eye was fastened to a triangular jet button on her dress. It rocked on her indignant bosom like a hard little boat. What caused the scolding I have long since managed to forget, but that button is buttoned to my memory forever.[3]

The constant present—not a surprise occurrence or a distant persistent memory—is the basis of inspiration for some. Lucy Boston's Green Knowe books were begun when the author was sixty years old, and they might not have been written at all without the inspiration of Mrs. Boston's house: "I am obsessed by my house. . . . It is in the highest degree a thing to be loved." And she adds, "I believe that one place closely explored will yield more than continents passed through."[4]

And yet—to place all these alleged sources of inspiration aside for a moment —one can't help wondering if they are merely the shadows projected by the creative process. The images of the dream recalled by the dreamer are said to be only the symbols of the emotions and cognitions that lie behind them. Similarly, the real inspiration at the heart of a literary work may be in the context behind the image identified by the writer.

Scott O'Dell, discussing the origins of his Newbery Award book, *Island of the Blue Dolphins* (12), reports that the book "began in anger, anger at the hunters who invade the mountains where I live and who slaughter everything that creeps or walks or flies."[5] The book isn't about those hunters, and its focus

---

[1] William Steig, "Caldecott Award Acceptance," *Horn Book* 46 (August 1970): 359.
[2] Cited in *Chosen for Children: Carnegie Medal Award Books, 1936–1965* (The Library Association, 1967), 68. (Address of publisher is Ridgemont St., London, W.C.1.
[3] Elizabeth Enright, "Realism in Children's Literature," *Horn Book* 43 (April 1967): 165.
[4] Quoted in John Rowe Townsend, *A Sense of Story* (Longman, 1971), p. 36.
[5] Quoted in *A Sense of Story,* p. 160.

isn't really the anger; but the strongly felt emotion and the image behind the emotion may indeed be the source of the inspiration.

And Philippa Pearce, author of *Tom's Midnight Garden* (13), which one critic has called the single masterpiece in children's literature of the past twenty-five years, describes the heart of the thematic inspiration of her work: "One of the things most difficult to believe . . . is the change that Time makes in people. . . . I tried to explore and resolve this non-understanding."[1]

Inspiration derives from a symbol: a memory from childhood, a strong emotion, a chance incident, a present circumstance, an urgently felt theme. Perhaps the best that can be said is that authors or artists, unlike others, have been "gifted" or skilled to the point of concentration where inspiration can be recognized and nurtured. Or, possessing strong impetus to create but lacking a clearly defined inspiration, they may simply produce in order to discover something which satisfies that drive. Virginia Hamilton, author of *The House of Dies Drear* (14) and *The Planet of Junior Brown* (15), describes this kind of search: "You might well ask, what is it I'm getting at. Not actually knowing, I sense that finding out is the reason I persist."[2]

The Craft

The comments of many authors emphasize that the process of evolving inspiration into a transactable work is difficult. Few speak of it so lightly as does Eleanor Estes: "My kind of writing is for me the easy kind and does not involve pilgrimages of any sort except into the mind, my own and the minds of others."[3] Most encounter the difficulty with a certain fondness, however, and agree with at least the first half of Maurice Sendak's pronouncement, "I love my work very much, it means everything to me."[4]

Craft doesn't consist of setting down precisely what inspiration dictates. In fact, a recurrent comment of authors is that objectivity must be attained in treating the inspiration, a constant attempt to view the on-going work from the standpoint of the reader. Betsy Byars, author of *The Summer of the Swans* (16), describes four stages in her craft. She begins by staring at her thumbnail, reflecting upon the inspiration. Then, "gripped with enthusiasm," she writes eagerly and swiftly. At the third stage, she finds herself slowing down, forcing the words until they come to a stop. Then she comes to grips with the task, "reading what I've written and trying to make something of it." On this final level she comments: "I have never read a manuscript in this stage without becoming aware again of the enormity of the gap which exists between the brain and a sheet of paper."[5]

---

[1]Quoted in *Chosen for Children: Carnegie Medal Award Books, 1936–1965,* p 96.
[2]Virginia Hamilton, "Portrait of the Author as a Working Writer," *Elementary English* 48 (April 1971): 302.
[3]Eleanor Estes, "My Teacher's Blue Crayon," *Chicago Tribune Books Today* (May 7, 1967): 4A.
[4]"Questions To an Artist Who Is Also an Author," reprinted in *Authors and Illustrators of Children's Books,* p. 377.
[5]Betsy Byars, "Newbery Award Acceptance," *Horn Book* 47 (August 1971): 355–57.

IV

By Daylight

THE next morning, when Tom woke, he could not think why he felt so happy, until he remembered the garden. The appearances in the hall seemed less likely than ever; but the impression on his mind of what he had seen through the garden door remained unchanged. Yet now he began to think that visiting the garden would be less easy than he had reckoned last night. His aunt and uncle would certainly do all they could to stop him; they did not want him to use the garden, else why had they kept him in the dark about its very existence?

That made Tom remember his anger against them, and he determined to shame them. He would have to play a very careful game: by innocent-seeming references he

25

Authors are, above all, self-critical at the craft level. Nearly all, like Beatrix Potter, assume the burden of writing a projected work many times, trying many different ways. "I sometimes think that some of the people who assure me that their verses come to them without any trouble would be astonished if they saw the sheets and sheets of paper that I use in writing one short poem," wrote Rose Fyleman some years ago,[1] and most modern authors would concur.

Even Eleanor Estes, who remarked that her work is the "easy kind," has stated elsewhere that "It is only after the fourth revision that I feel I know my book."[2] Apparently, ease doesn't rule out rewriting and revising. And even Dr. Seuss, the ebullient Theodor Seuss Geisel of apparently effortless drawing and tireless rhyme, reveals, "The 'creative process' consists for me of two things—time and sweat."[3]

The seeming paradox behind craft is that, however burdensome, it is attended with joy. Not all authors will call it that, and some will use words that are quite the opposite; but eventually you will discover from their conversation and performance that their craft brings them joy, that the generosity of time and spirit which must go into their work is somehow intrinsically rewarding to them.

They are, whether they recognize it or not, close kin to the game-player, who brings all his energy to bear upon the process of the game even when the outcome is perceived as negligible or when extrinsic reward is unlikely. Or to the ballet dancer who practices many hours each day just for the joy of dancing. Or, for that matter, to any other artist striving to create.

Most are aware that the process grows no easier with practice. Rosemary Sutcliff, in fact, notes that "with each book one becomes more and more a perfectionist" so that each of her great historical tales presents a new, more difficult problem.[4] And Madeleine L'Engle, author of *A Wrinkle in Time* (17) and *The Arm of the Starfish* (18), observes, "The hardest part of writing a book is making yourself sit down at the typewriter and bat out a first page, any kind of first page, knowing that it will be changed over and over again before the book is done."[5] This comment comes from an author who has practiced the rigor over and over again.

How They Learned.   Experts in the field of creativity attempt to pinpoint steps in problem identification and solution operating in the creative process. They have documented the artist's process of working with a total structure rather than with a narrowly conceived sequence of unrelated detail. But the inner creative process is still somewhat mysterious and likely to remain so, since it appears to be unique with individuals. Our few comments are intended to give

---

[1] Rose Fyleman, "Writing Verse for Children," *Horn Book* 13 (May 1937): 145.
[2] Quoted in *A Sense of Story*, p. 87.
[3] Quoted in Donald Freeman, "Who Thunk You Up, Dr. Seuss?" *San Jose Mercury News* (June 15, 1967): 12–13.
[4] Quoted in *A Sense of Story*, p. 200.
[5] p. 127.

you some clues as to the task faced by authors. Should you wish to pursue the matter further, you might read books discussing the writer's craft in the juvenile field, such as those listed below. These books are concerned with the patterns of authorship that sell, however, and tacitly assume that the art, the inner creative process itself, must come from the writer's own experience and practice.

It is fortunate that some excellent authors and artists sometimes do write about their own creative process. Wanda Gág's diary, *Growing Pains,* is the most delightful of all authors' accounts, filled with the joy of creation in the midst of orphanhood and poverty.[1] Elizabeth Yates, whose *Amos Fortune, Free Man* (19) won a Newbery Medal in 1951, has written a charming and helpful account of the creative process in a book addressed to her daughter, *Someday You'll Write.*[2]

Authors who have succeeded are often as puzzled as anyone about how they learned their craft. Some seem to have succeeded almost at once and almost by accident; but most point to a long struggle in which seemingly endless practice paid off. Some got practical experience through steady jobs that required writing, as Joan Aiken, author of *The Wolves of Willoughby Chase* (20), did in her six years of practical writing for *Argosy* magazine. Some point to the influence of teachers: Andre Norton, author of *Breed to Come* (21), mentions an inspiring teacher in a high school creative writing class. The prolific picture-book writer Margaret Wise Brown was taught by Lucy Sprague Mitchell at Bank Street School, where classes of aspiring writers constantly tried their efforts on groups of children. Others appear to have been less fortunate. Meindert de Jong, author of *The House of Sixty Fathers* (22), and *Journey from Peppermint Street* (23), was employed

booklist

Books about the Writer's Craft

Hinds, Marjorie M. *How to Write for the Juvenile Market.* Frederick Fell, 1966. A valuable section of this book contains a completed story with the author's annotations tracing the process of the writing.

Wilson, Barbara Ker. *Writing for Children.* Watts, 1960. This author gives sound advice, after warning would-be writers that the profession is "a solitary pursuit" and that you "cannot go fishing for a story with tackle and bait." Elsewhere emphasis is placed on the author's development through reading and through "unconscious imitation."

Whitney, Phyllis A. *Writing Juvenile Fiction.* The Writer, Inc., 1947, 1960. Contains a case study showing how this author produced a published story.

---

[1] Wanda Gág, *Growing Pains* (Coward McCann, 1940).
[2] Elizabeth Yates, *Someday You'll Write* (Dutton, 1962).

at "tinning and grave digging," and tried teaching (which he didn't like) and farming. Paula Fox once had a job punctuating Italian madrigals of the fifteenth century.

A trait of many authors is to accept with humor the random experiences and pitfalls that apparently led them to their level of skill, to smile at the vagaries of their lives and their art. Writes Lloyd Alexander: "With a strong distaste for hard work, but without any particularly useful skills, it was only natural for me to become a writer. Melancholy, sour-tempered, and gloomy, it was only natural for me to become a humorist."[1]

AND WHY THEY WRITE.   Some children's authors, it is true, write for money and fame. But children's literature presently has, fortunately or unfortunately, a built-in safety factor against the too-greedy, too-commercial entrepreneur. Publications for children simply don't pay that well. Movie rights and television rights that help line the pockets of writers for adults are far less common in the juvenile field. The aspiring author who wants to create a *Charlotte's Web* to get rich doesn't really share the central motive that lies within most children's authors.

Fame is another matter, but here the fame that brings light to the eyes of children's writers comes not primarily from the wide public or even from the critics but from the children themselves. Most writers speak sincerely of children's enthusiasm for their books as their greatest reward. Many accept quite happily the invitation to talk with groups of children, even when they refuse to encounter groups of adults in an audience situation.

Beyond this, writers for children write for the same reasons that all artists create. Many state that they write not for children, or only incidentally for children, but for themselves. What is probably nearer the truth is that author/ artists in the children's literature field create their works with two aims: they create for an audience (in this case, children), and they create for the clarification and unity that the process brings within themselves. There is no reason that the two aims should not be compatible. Language is, after all, not only an instrument for communication with others but a vehicle for one's own inner thought.

Basic to the author's reasons for writing, in fact, is her or his obsession with the reality of words. It's a difficult matter to explain, though one senses it when authors try to explain themselves. It's as if the author's world cannot be adjusted until he can form it into negotiable language—language that establishes the relationship among events and their significance, language that makes this reality clear to others and to the author himself. Such is Madeleine L'Engle's summation of the matter as she discusses the words that are her trade:

> It is with these slippery, changing creatures, then, that we must try to reach each
> other, here, now, in this age that has been labeled the 'age of anxiety' and the 'aspirin

---

[1]Lloyd Alexander, "No Laughter in Heaven," p. 11.

age,' in which we live in a 'lonely crowd,' in which we flee from the pain of imagination and truth by setting our sights on a new television set or a second car (or is it a third car?) or an electric wastebasket. As the electric wastebaskets chew papers we do not want anyone to see, our conversations with each other chew up the things we do not want to reveal. In confronting each other we slide cosily around the periphery and talk about things being 'meaningful' and 'relevant' in order to escape meaning and relevance, but when we are alone again, we are anxious, we are lonely.

She concludes with the hope that, in her work as an author, she along with others has "helped to tear down a little of the wall that we have built to shield us from the brilliant power of approaching words as they were meant to be approached, of using language that helps our imagination grow so that our knowledge can expand into wisdom, and from wisdom to the truth that will make us free."[1]

CHILDREN AND AWARENESS OF THE CREATIVE PROCESS

Perhaps you will decide that the foregoing information is interesting and that it is handy information for getting to know authors or even for selecting their work. But still, you may wonder just what place it has in the work you do with children. We'll suggest some possibilities.

Knowing How Things Are Done

Just as children learn how governments operate or how the weather works, they have a need to know how their literature is composed—or, for that matter, how a painter goes about his work or a musician learns to perform. It is simply a matter of becoming aware of the world, specifically in this case of how a profession accomplishes its purpose. In most fields, this is information that just serves the general education of children.

In art, however, the understanding of its creation goes a step further in that knowledge of the process becomes knowledge to aid children in their reception of the work.

Reception: a Creative Process

Many critics and philosophers believe that the first and foremost way of understanding art is not to ask "What does it mean?" but "How was it made?" This is a recapitulation of the idea at the end of chapter 2 that understanding a work's form and structure helps one understand the synthesis of parts that comprise the work.

When you examine a work's components with emphasis on how the author assembled them, and the emerging theme that might have guided the author

---

[1]Madeleine L'Engle, "Before Babel," *Horn Book* 42 (December 1966): 670.

in selecting and presenting those components, you are examining his creative process. It is as if you are given a way to see the work from the author's point of view, sensing to the fullest the author's intent.

This is perhaps the only way that so-called "literary analysis" can be profitable. It is not the same as assigning a reader to analyze plot, character presentation, and the like. Instead, he looks at the components from the standpoint of their creation by learning something about the author or by bringing to bear his knowledge of how authors go about their work. It is parallel to a situation in which an individual develops understanding and appreciation of music by learning a bit of the process of making music himself, through playing the piano, through dancing, or even by composing some tunes for himself.

What is more, there seems to be some transfer from learning to enjoy one art form through its creative process to learning to enjoy another art form. The structure and creation of a painting, a concerto, or a folk tale are different in the tools used and the craft involved; yet there are similarities in their effects and in the manner in which the receiver must "live through" the creative process in order to get at the heart of the work. As Susanne Langer observes, "Expressiveness, in one definite and appropriate sense, is the same in all art works of any kind. What is created is not the same in any two distinct arts—that is, in fact, what makes them distinct—but the principle of creation is the same."[1]

This interrelationship among the arts presents an interesting opportunity for those who work with children in the arts. Perhaps it suggests an alliance among the humanities—not treating them as separate subjects of music, art, and literature—and a need for new strategies to help children understand them through learning about the creative process. Still, you don't have to redesign the whole curriculum to begin to do this. Like so many facets of education, it isn't a matter of either/or.

teaching ideas

Here are some suggestions for ways to present the creative process in conjunction with your literature or humanities program. They don't need to displace other activities we've suggested, but they may be used to augment what you do.

1. Present some material about the author as you present his or her work. Use some of the sources mentioned in chapter 1 as well as the annual Newbery and Caldecott Award acceptance speeches that appear in *Horn Book,* usually in the August edition. Sometimes you and your children may arrange a visit to or from an author. The Children's Book Council has on occasion supplied lists of local authors for communities in various parts of the country.

---

[1]Susanne Langer, *Problems of Art* (Scribner's, 1957), p. 14.

2. When a work has been particularly well received, when its possibilities for role-playing or other interpretive work have been partially explored, stop and ask, "How did the author do this book? What might he have seen or heard that got him started? What might he have been like as a child to lead him to produce this book? Which parts might have given him the greatest 'kick' in writing? Where do you think he got an especially exciting idea? Where in the finished product do you think he might have changed his mind from what he first wrote?" To make the discussion more intense, use the point-of-view technique, asking children to pose as the author to answer such questions. (If nothing else, such discussion may dispel the notion that authors simply sit down and dash off a book as you'd dash off a letter. As one pair of writers puts it, "A rather common belief of college students as well as youngsters seems to be that children's books are written overnight."[1])

3. Compare or contrast familiar works of approximately the same type: folk tales, fantasies, humorous realistic fiction, biographies. Ask children, "If you were writing 'guidelines' for an author about to write a book of this type, what would your advice be about how to begin the book; about how to end it; which episodes to select; what type of reader to write for?" You can ask, too, how and where an author may have obtained the information needed to write the book. One of the best adolescent novels about ancient Greece, *The Spartan* (24) by Caroline Dale Snedeker, was written before the writer had ever left the United States. How did she collect the information? How do you get that specific about the Greek topography, the dress and customs, even the phase of the moon, without going there?

4. A difficult task, but an enlightening one: find a painting, a book, a photograph, and a selection of music that have a commonality of theme or even of form. For example, Kate Seredy's *The Good Master* (25) is episodic, each chapter playing a little melody of its own (sometimes a folk melody and sometimes one based on current incident, always filled with action). There's a recurrent, rising theme of the city girl Kate learning to direct her tremendous energy to rural peaceful living. It's a Mozart spirit musically, and perhaps a creation that Paul Klee or Miro reflects in painting. Talk about the interrelationships among the art forms.

5. Provide an opportunity for mixing art forms. We did this with "Gilgamesh," the ancient Sumerian epic, whose various children's editions make it especially useful for the purpose.[2] Children were divided into groups and told to transmit the story nonverbally, communicating it across the ages and across languages, so that its meaning would come through. One group sketched the story on a long roll of shelf paper, using arrows to show its

---

[1]Miriam Hoffman and Eva Samuels, *Authors and Illustrators of Children's Books*, Preface, pp. ix.–x.
[2]See Bernarda Bryson, *Gilgamesh* (Holt, 1967) and Jennifer Westwood, *Gilgamesh and Other Babylonian Tales* (Bodley Head, 1968).

sequence and brightening climactic scenes with felt-pen color. One group pantomimed, using quickly devised visual signs to indicate characters. One group transformed the story into a highly stylized dance that derived in part from the authentic drawings in both editions. Ensuing discussion was based not only on the question, "Did the story come across?" but on the more important item, "Did this version keep the feeling and the theme of the story?" (One group observed that their comic book version was a cop-out!) A particularly fine source for activity of this type, especially suited for younger children, is any work by Wanda Gág, beginning with *Millions of Cats* (26). In addition, James A. Smith has provided a list of children's poems with appropriate "other form" activities.[1]

6. Pause occasionally in the midst of a good book which your group is reading and ask, "If you were the author, what would you put next in your book? How would you build suspense? How would you create a new episode?" Obviously you won't want to interrupt the flow of the book too often. But once in a while this kind of speculation is very revealing to the children.

PROMOTING RECEPTION THROUGH PRODUCTION

The theme of this chapter is the link between the production of literature and its reception through the creative process. By viewing a work from the standpoint of the creator, children bring their own creative power to it. This is not the mode of a "passive culture," where viewers or readers are conditioned to sit back and expect the art form to overwhelm them without effort on their own; but, instead, it treats the literary experience as an active process.

As we've discussed, one way to promote the creative response is to focus attention on how a work was created as well as what it represents. Another way is to encourage children to engage in the creative act itself. Creative writing and speaking activities may play a part in literary understanding and appreciation.

There are two rather opposite theories concerning the processes and products of children's creation. The first holds that children should be given complete freedom in creative writing and speaking and that all production is to be enthusiastically received. Hughes Mearns in *Creative Power: The Education of Youth in the Creative Arts* defines this strategy. As you read his description, however, you realize that a fair amount of guidance is provided in the form of recognizing and pointing out original and effective work, ignoring products that are imitative or less successful. As Mearns puts it, you must be able to point to successful accomplishment and say, "This is the real thing!"[2]

---

[1] See his *Creative Teaching of Reading and Literature in the Elementary School* (Allyn and Bacon, 1967), pp. 249–52.

[2] Hughes Mearns, *Creative Power: The Education of Youth in the Creative Arts* (Dover, 1958), p. 39. This theory is expanded and documented in other works such as Alvina Treut Burrows, Doris C. Jackson, and Dorothy O. Saunders, *They All Want to Write*, 3rd ed. (Holt, 1964) and A. B. Clegg, ed., *The Excitement of Writing* (Chatto and Windus, 1964).

The expressed view of Mearns and other such writers is that children learn to enjoy writing and speaking from having such freedom. The transfer to enjoyment of literature is not so well defined. On the other hand, the *Curriculum for English,* a series of grade level units devised by The Nebraska Curriculum Development Center[1], specifies emulative speaking and writing activities based directly on examples drawn from children's literature. This exemplifies the opposite theory: that the creative process promotes literary understanding when it is tied to the literature itself.

For example, the *Curriculum for English* unit for first grade based on *Millions of Cats* suggests that children expand the story to describe one of the cats, supplying adjectives and descriptive phrases. They're asked to devise a new ending for the story, to think up new wording to imitate unusual sentence patterns in the story, such as "Walking along the road, the old man saw a pond." At the third grade level, the unit based on *Mr. Popper's Penguins* (27) urges that children experiment with difficult vocabulary found in the story *(heathen, prostrate, irritable).* The major goal in composition recommended through this program seems to be that through good examples children learn the attributes of various literary forms and then create their own works using such forms. Research on the *Curriculum for English* has shown that the program does indeed lead to somewhat greater language sophistication, and perhaps to somewhat greater ability to emulate accepted forms of literature, than seems to result from a free-wheeling creative program.

There is also some evidence, however, that imitation need not be so heavily encouraged; that children nurtured by good literary models do show the effects of language and form stimulation in their creative processes and that, in turn, children who create "literature" of their own become more avid and productive readers and listeners.

Whichever point of view you prefer, we'd encourage you to stimulate children's creative processes, seizing opportunities to relate what they create to literature. One way to make this relationship explicit is to examine the way in which authors have produced their literature, as we did earlier in this chapter.

We suggest three stages of guidance to aid children's creative activity. While most of our suggestions are based on writing examples, you might consider their application to other arts, including painting or drawing, the dance, and production of music.

First Stage: Feeling Free to Begin

"I'd write something if I could just get started!" is the complaint of many would-be writers, whether children or adults. You need to realize first of all that this difficulty is real. Writing is the culminating art in language, coming out of experience shaped through listening, speaking, and reading.

Listening, for example, is a pre-condition to writing. The effects of hearing

---

[1]Univ. of Nebraska Press, Lincoln, Nebraska.

language well spoken and well read are pervasive. Listening helps a child to know how the words ought to go. Similarly, speaking has a lasting influence on writing. Children who master—even modestly—the art of telling a story know better how to say what they want to say, especially if they have taken their budding art to a new clientele. They may be third graders who tell their tales to the first grade or second graders who read aloud to the kindergarten. These speaking experiences will clearly ease their way into writing.

And, as we have stressed, a store of remembered reading helps guide the pen. Good readers of literature conduct a dialog with the writer as they read. Reading is no passive process. Affirming, qualifying, identifying, rejecting, supporting, denying as they go, readers are at the same time shaping their own tools for writing.

But while wide, general experience in listening, speaking, and reading is basic to writing, some specific aids may be helpful. Many teachers pool their lists of brief, stimulating ideas for getting the process on its way. Helen Danforth's six fine ideas have served well in workshops for children and adults. In at least one instance a Danforth "stimulator" led to the writing of a published story.

FIRST AID IN CHILDREN'S WRITING[1]

by Helen Danforth

Never in the history of the world has it been more essential that people think straight and deep, and express their thoughts convincingly. A strong language arts program is the prime need in all education today, since acquiring and sharing knowledge are almost wholly dependent on the spoken and written word.

Writing skills will be embellished by spelling insight and practice, assistance in producing rapid, legible, and lovely handwriting, and attention to the conventions of word usage, capitalization, and punctuation. But these are tools, not substance.

Real writing will be done for many purposes, all of which can be classified as either communicative or personal expression, with the boundary between the two not rigidly fixed.

Communicative writing clearly includes reports, letters, newspaper and magazine features, and certain stories and poems. Personal writing includes other stories and poems, diaries, introspective essays, dreams, reminiscences, and various art forms with which the writer experiments for his own satisfaction, much as a composer, painter, or photographer attempts many works which will never be shared with the public.

With pre-adolescents the teacher's aim, transcending all lesser considerations, is to keep each child writing. One hopes, of course, that most children's written expression will well up from within, based on experience, awareness,

---

[1]From *Elementary English* 37 (April 1960): 246–47.

and the undeniable urge to create. Every teacher knows, however, that there are times when a child's own resources fail, and he needs befriending so that the flow of creativity may reestablish itself in its own good time.

A teacher properly has at her disposal first aid equipment to help the child when he is disabled. I like to think of the equipment as splints, crutches, and antibiotics. I never use them on well children (and they do not want them), and the treatment is reduced and withdrawn as healthy expression begins to flow.

Here is the current inventory of my growing collection:

1. Picture file.   I am collecting "pictures with a story in them" which a child may leaf through until he feels a stirring of ideas. Strangely, the ideas are, as often as not, unrelated to any picture, but the child has been spared the panicky blocking of waiting helplessly for thoughts to come.

2. Phrase file.   On small oak tag cards I have nearly a hundred phrases. A child may select one, two, or three (face up), or draw three unknowns and weave them into a story plot. Typical examples: a bag of popcorn, a magic potion, a winged creature, noise in the night, an unexpected visitor.

3. Opening sentence file.   These are culled regularly from successful compositions of previous years, plus any I am able to concoct or steal. The ones below are all from pupils:

> "Once there was a little boy who loved snow, until one day."
> "Mr. Jones had a car, and what a car it was!"
> "Even the other ghosts were frightened!"
> "The Smiths are a most unusual family."
> "Willie the whale was just an ordinary whale, except that
> he wore a top hat and drove a taxicab."

4. Title file.   Some of the phrase cards make good titles, and in addition former pupils have given me the following:

> The Runaway
> The Little People
> What I See from My Front Door
> Enchanted Haircut
> The Trouble with Grownups

5. Stock stimuli.   All of the following, properly presented, have helped individuals and groups to more varied, more penetrating observation and writing:

> the feel of autumn
> what it means to be trustworthy
> memories of another grade
> rain in November
> "I used to think . . ."

6. Other devices are rather too mechanical, but have served a purpose when widely spaced and used with appropriate caution:
   (a) Home work assignment. Retell to your family the anecdote about Miss Danforth's father and the rattlesnake. Ask them to tell you some of *your* family's stories. In class, write a good story you heard.
   (b) The following is put on the board: "A little boy/girl stood in the doorway of the kindergarten. She/he held her/his hands behind her/his back. The teacher came forward, smiling. 'What do you have?' she said." Through the group discussion we develop that the kindergartner and the teacher may be made vivid and interesting, and that a fine climax is possible when the hidden object is divulged. Then the children write.
   (c) Pretend you are an animal or another person and describe yourself. Perhaps you could tell one of your adventures.
   (d) The situation is this. A space ship has circled our playground and come in for a landing. A hatch opens, and something or someone emerges. How do you feel and what do you do?

More and better items for the infirmary are always welcome. However, like the public health nurse, I count those seasons most successful when the splints, crutches, and antibiotics are hardly ever used!

A very useful booklet of similar ideas is Ruth Kearney Carlson's *Writing Aids Through the Grades*.[1] The fourth chapter presents a variety of Oriental verse forms, including tanka, cinquain, lanterne, and haiku. The fifth chapter is alive with challenging and unusual poetry forms—"pop art" poems, sound poetry, and "poems with a visual analogy." Along with this, you might use "Excerpts from 'Write Me Another Verse' " by David McCord, who defines unusual verse forms by explaining them in the context of the verse itself. Take, for example, his "Clerihew," "Cinquain," and "Haiku":

The Clerihew
The clerihew
Is a tricky form for you.
The first two lines state a fact;
The second two, how you react.

Cinquain
This is
The form of the
Cinquain. The five lines have
2, 4, 6, 8, 2 syllables
As here.

---

[1] Ruth Kearney Carlson, *Writing Aids through the Grades* (Teachers College Press, 1970).

Haiku
Count the syllables!
Five each in lines one and three,
Seven in line two.[1]

For suggestions for extending technique—for developing the beginning of craft—follow ideas to help children begin writing in *Slithery Snakes and Other Aids to Children's Writing* by Walter T. Petty and Mary E. Bowen.[2]

These sources are more than simply random collections. Most of them include examples drawn from children's writing. Most make it quite clear that the aids are just that—stimulators designed to release the writers to begin their flow of thoughts, to focus ideas through form, even to dart out on their own as soon as inspiration and craft can begin to take over.

For the child who seems unable to get started, even with an aid such as those suggested, word games may be a good beginning. *Word Play* by Joseph T. Shipley is a book of riddles, puns, anagrams, and other word games, written especially for children.[3]

The primary goal of this first stage is getting started, producing something, that will strike the creator as unique and worthwhile. This is not a time for heavy pressure, either through imposition of unmanageable form or through criticism. Fluency and pride in having accomplished something are sought.

Can this stage relate to the creative process of accomplished authors to enhance literary experience? Surely it can. The writer who has struggled, however briefly, with a haiku form will have a better appreciation of Elizabeth Coatsworth's cow dressed in suede and all the cleverness of Harry Behn's *Cricket Songs.*

Second Stage: Developing Craft and Learning to Evaluate

In very early writing, when children are working in a group, creating what is sometimes called an "experience chart" or story, it gives them a better start if the activity is immediately preceded by the telling of a story, the reading of a poem, or the playing of an episode of creative drama. Children should then have time to plan and talk before beginning. This will help the group develop a proprietary interest in recasting and revising until all are satisfied with the finished product.

When children begin to write independently, they need increasing support to sustain them while their craft slowly develops. Personal conferences are usually more helpful than written commentary, enabling a sensitive teacher to tell at once how much suggestion would be liberating and how much would be constricting.

---

[1]David McCord, "Excerpts from 'Write Me Anoter Verse'," *Horn Book* 46 (August, 1970): 367, 368, 369.
[2]Walter T. Petty and Mary E. Bowen, *Slithery Snakes and Other Aids to Children's Writing* (Appleton-Century-Crofts, 1967).
[3]Joseph T. Shipley, *Word Play* (Hawthorn, 1972).

Hughes Mearns believes children's creations should be evaluated only through praising what is good in them. To say, "This is good," and then to ask, "How could you make it better?" are probably the major ways to improve a work. These questions soon become a part of the child's self-evaluation.

Even so supportive a question may be threatening at the beginning. Only after the process has begun and fluency has begun to develop is evaluation more likely to help. But evaluation must begin, for creation is difficult, and would-be artists who believe that each act is finished and perfect will sooner or later learn that they're short-circuiting their own abilities.

After some fluency has begun to develop, the relationship between production and reception can be profitably sought. If you have attempted to define a landscape in writing or speech, or describe the way someone searches for a lost wallet, or find an image to reveal utter but seemingly unexplainable happiness, your awareness of the need for craft has been sharpened. Your eagerness to see just how an author has achieved a successful product can help you look more keenly at his creative process.

In the early stage of creativity, fluency is a major goal, but after a time it must be subjected to judgment. The ability to tell a straight narrational tale skillfully requires selection and pace. The child who has attempted such a feat will turn to Margery Clark's *The Poppy Seed Cakes* (28) and to Lloyd Alexander's *The Marvelous Misadventures of Sebastian* (29) with increased wonder at how both authors achieved such a quick, convincing flow of narrative. His perception of the craft of writing will have been sharpened.

Craft is only partially a matter of imitation. The skillful author must take risks as well. He must often surprise the knowledgeable reader by breaking rules to achieve certain effects. The child who has attempted to discern the "rules" by matching his talents to those of other writers will discover that the uniqueness of a work derives in part from the surprises that result from the risk taking. This factor is apparent in the Alexander book noted above. At the conclusion of a wild and humorous narrative, the author injects a note of the supernatural and slows his story a bit to suggest that there has been a serious theme all along. Sebastian's marvelous violin, which has brought him joy and escape throughout his misadventures, endangers his sanity. It's a risk to introduce such a theme in the story, and the author's craft in succeeding with that risk is worth notice. The child who understands the risk-taking will appreciate it all the more.

All of this suggests that evaluation and the introduction of craft into the creative process can't be handled by any simple formula. The usual book about how to write may go too far in assuming that there are unbreakable rules. The teacher or other adult working with children must be far more sensitive to the possibilities for altering the rules, for encouraging the creation of a unique work.

Third Stage: Looking at Process and Product

It seems a shame to suggest that children as artists aren't often destined to achieve a finished, first-rate work. But for purposes we're suggesting here, such an achievement really isn't necessary. To enhance children's receptive process for good books doesn't require that they produce a good book, but only that they have attempted the creative process with sufficient intensity to increase their sensitivity to the process of the author at work.

As they develop their craft, children should have the right to throw away some of their works. The waste baskets of professional writers bulge with discarded writing. Children should not be forced to polish their failures. True, we must help some children recognize small successes, but some throwing away can stimulate true creativity, for the discards force writers to begin anew.

That willingness to risk the ego again is crucial to writing. Otherwise long before the high school years, children learn to play it safe. They may not commit many offenses against accepted images, and spelling may be almost perfect. But they say nothing.

We realize that if writing is to be viewed publicly—placed on the bulletin board or sent home to the family—the mechanics must be in order. But that consideration should intervene much later, not in the act of creating.

Writing should be a personal act of creative human interchange. Children's writing can and should become as personal as their speaking. Indeed writing should be a child's other voice. As Robert Frost once said:

> A dramatic necessity goes deep into the nature of the sentence. Sentences are not different enough to hold the attention unless they are dramatic. No ingenuity of varying structure will do. All that can save them is the speaking tone of voice somehow entangled in the words and fastened to the page for the ear of the imagination. That is all that can save poetry from sing-song, all that can save prose from itself.[1]

As children write, they should be encouraged to entangle themselves in the words they use, to discover that writing can be as personal as speaking. They must feel free to invest themselves when they write, becoming involved in the all-important process of self-discovery. Their products may not be great, but the accumulating sense of personal resource will serve them well all their lives.

The emphasis, then, is on the process and not the product. Somewhere along the line, children can discard the aids of the first stage and overcome some of the basic difficulties inherent in craft. They can begin to seize on a real inspiration, something that is of value and urgency in their lives that can be expressed in some conceptual form, an image grasped in words or in painting or in dance. And they can become preoccupied by the problems of craft needed to manifest that conception. Some children can even find interest in revising and altering— the scribbling between the lines, the cutting and pasting, the admission of defeat and trying again—that recapitulate the process well known to the authors of the books they read.

At such time, a guiding adult may help by being an audience and assisting in publication, helping with the details of manuscript and duplicating. Many schools now make it possible for a child to bind his work into a booklet and

---

[1] Robert Frost, *A Way Out* (Harbor Press, 1929).

place it in the library so that others can check it out and read it. In one Spokane school a wise teacher, Jean Anderson, has helped high school students to write and bind their stories for younger children and to visit elementary schools to present these books to a suitable audience.

The goal in encouraging and guiding children's writing is to develop a creative process that is on-going, that doesn't stop with the completion of a grade or the completion of a brief work, but that continues to thrive and grow for the sake of its doing—and, beyond this, for the enlightenment it provides in experiencing the work of other artists.[1]

The creative process must continue to survive and to be valued in all the arts, whatever their medium. The sensitivity and sensibility derived from the creative process—the awakening of joy in a shared generosity released through the process—these are the goals we seek in emphasizing this process. The enjoyment of art—whatever its medium—releases the spirit from some of its confines. That is why any inquiry into literature has to encompass the creative process.

CHAPTER REFERENCES

1. Sawyer, Ruth. *Roller Skates.* Viking, 1936. (I)
2. McDermott, Gerald. *Anansi, the Spider.* Holt, 1972. (E)
3. _____. *Arrow to the Sun.* Viking, 1974. (All ages)
4. Duvoisin, Roger. *Veronica.* Knopf, 1961. (E)
5. Potter, Beatrix. *The Tale of Tom Kitten.* Warne, 1907.
6. George, Jean Craighead. *Julie of the Wolves.* Harper, 1972. (I-U)
7. Ness, Evaline. *Sam, Bangs and Moonshine.* Holt, 1966. (E)
8. Alexander, Lloyd. *Time Cat.* Holt, 1963. (I)
9. Steig, William. *Sylvester and the Magic Pebble.* Simon and Schuster, 1969. (E-I)
10. Enright, Elizabeth. *Thimble Summer.* Farrar & Rinehart, 1938.
11. _____. *Gone-Away Lake.* Harcourt, 1957.
12. O'Dell, Scott. *Island of the Blue Dolphins.* Houghton, Mifflin, 1960.
13. Pearce, Philippa. *Tom's Midnight Garden.* Lippincott, 1959. (U)
14. Hamilton, Virginia. *The House of Dies Drear.* Macmillan, 1968.
15. _____. *The Planet of Junior Brown.* Macmillan, 1971.
16. Byars, Betsy. *The Summer of the Swans.* Viking, 1970.
17. L'Engle, Madeleine. *A Wrinkle in Time.* Farrar, Straus, 1962.
18. _____. *The Arm of the Starfish.* Farrar, Straus, 1965.
19. Yates, Elizabeth. *Amos Fortune, Free Man.* Dutton, 1950.
20. Aiken Joan. *The Wolves of Willoughby Chase.* Doubleday, 1963.
21. Norton, Andre. *Breed to Come.* Viking, 1972.
22. de Jong, Meindert. *The House of Sixty Fathers.* Harper, 1956.
23. _____. *Journey from Peppermint Street.* Harper, 1968.
24. Snedeker, Caroline Dale. *The Spartan.* Doubleday, 1912. (I-U)
25. Seredy, Kate. *The Good Master.* Viking, 1935. (I)
26. Gág, Wanda. *Millions of Cats.* Coward, 1928.
27. Atwater, Richard and Florence. *Mr. Popper's Penguins.* Little, Brown, 1938. (E-I)
28. Clark, Margery. *The Poppy Seed Cakes.* Doubleday, 1924. (E-I)
29. Alexander, Lloyd. *The Marvelous Misadventures of Sebastian.* Dutton, 1970. (I-U)

---

[1]For a useful sequence of activities leading to this stage, see James Moffett, *A Student-Centered Language Arts Curriculum, Grades K-13: A Handbook for Teachers* (Houghton Mifflin, 1968).

BIBLIOGRAPHY

Aiken, Joan. "How to Keep the Reader on the Edge of the Chair." *The Writer,* 86 March 1973, pp. 9–13. Citing instances of suspense techniques used by Coleridge, James, and Stevenson, this excellent writer gives insight into how she creates suspense in her books for children and adults.

Arbuthnot, May Hill. "Puss, the Perraults and a Lost Manuscript." *Elementary English,* 46 October 1969, pp. 715–21. A manuscript printed in 1697 and lost until 1953 reveals amazing sketches of a popular story.

"Augusta Baker." *School Library Journal,* 99 March 15, 1974, pp. 75–77. Illustrations portray the life of a great storyteller and librarian, with evidence that librarians are a part of the creative process.

Bradbury, Ray. "How to be Madder than Captain Ahab." *The Writer,* 87 February 1974, pp. 21–22. How his childhood reading influenced one of the best living science fiction writers.

Brown, Marcia. "My Goals as an Illustrator." *Horn Book,* 43 June 1967, pp. 305–16. A famed artist tells what it takes to produce distinguished work in the picture book field.

Burch, Robert, and Duff, Annis. "Editors and Children's Book Writers: Two Sketches." *Horn Book,* 50 June 1974, August 1974, pp. 249–55. Funny dialog in role-playing situation between a fictitious editor who wants to "try for a bigger market" and a "not too bright" author.

Chambers, Adrian. "Reviewers' Railments: A Game for Children's Game People." *Horn Book,* 48 April 1972, pp. 129–33. Playful but lethal, this article points out what's wrong with the way people review books for children.

"Charlotte Zolotow." *Publishers Weekly,* 205 June 10, 1974, pp. 8–9. How an editor-author combines her two roles, with a few remarks about censorship.

Deksnis, Almo. "Beatrix Potter." *Elementary English,* 35 November 1958, pp. 431–40. A very intimate portrait of Beatrix Potter, her life and work.

Freedman, Florence B. "Ezra Jack Keats: Author and Illustrator." *Elementary English,* 46 January 1969, pp. 55–59. The writer draws upon her long acquaintance with Keats, describing his methods and work.

Hamilton, Virginia. "Literature, Creativity and Imagination." *Childhood Education,* 49 March 1973, pp. 307–10. The author discusses her craft, especially as it was used in writing *The Planet of Junior Brown.*

Lindgren, Astrid. "A Short Talk with a Prospective Children's Writer." *Horn Book,* 49 June 1973, pp. 248–52. The author of *Pippi Longstocking* tells you gently, as if over a cup of coffee, how *not* to try writing for children.

Norton, Eloise. "An 'Exposition' to Christopher Robin's Home." *Top of the News,* 29 January 1973, pp. 146–50. Over seven million copies of the Christopher Robin books have been sold, but the real house and farm where Milne's son grew up are neglected.

"Profile of an Author Harve Zemach and an Illustrator Margot Zemach." *Top of the News,* 27 April 1971, pp. 248–55. This is one of the frequent "profiles" of authors and artists presented in this publication. The Zemachs, who later won a Caldecott Medal, discuss their style of collaboration.

Sayers, Frances Clarke, and Horovitz, Carolyn. "Remembrance and Re-creation: Some Talk about the Writing of a Biography." *Horn Book,* 28 October 1972, pp. 444–51. A dialogue about Anne Carroll Moore, who changed the tone and recognized purpose of children's libraries; some perceptive comments about the task of writing a biography.

Southall, Ivan. "Real Adventure Belongs to Us." *Top of the News,* 30 June 1974, pp. 373–93. Australian author Southall delivered the May Hill Arbuthnot Honor Lecture in Seattle in 1974. This article is a transcript of what he said: as he describes his way of working, perceptive readers will discover the sources of each of his books as he tells incidents from his life.

A appendix

Publishers' Addresses[1]

Abelard-Schuman, Ltd., 257 Park Ave. S., New York, NY 10010
Abingdon Pr., 201 Eighth Ave. S., Nashville, TN 37202
Harry N. Abrams, Inc., Pubs., 110 E. 59 St., New York, NY 10022
Addison-Wesley Pub. Co., Inc., Reading, MA 01867
Allyn and Bacon, Inc., 470 Atlantic Ave., Boston, MA 02210
Appleton-Century-Crofts, 440 Park Ave. S., New York, NY 10016
Atheneum Pubs., 122 E. 42nd St., New York, NY 10017
Ballantine Books, Inc., 201 E. 50 St., New York, NY 10022
Bantam Books, Inc., 666 Fifth Ave., New York, NY 10019
Beacon Pr., 25 Beacon St., Boston, MA 02108
The Bobbs-Merrill Co., Inc., 4300 W. 62 St., Indianapolis, IN 46206
R. R. Bowker and Co., 1180 Ave. of the Americas, New York, NY 10036
Bradbury Pr., Inc., 2 Overhill Rd., Scarsdale, NY 10583
Bro-Dart Foundation, New Brunswick, NJ 08901
William C. Brown & Co., Pubs., 2460 Kerper Blvd., Dubuque, IA 52001
Coward, McCann & Geoghegan Inc., 200 Madison Ave., New York, NY 10016
Criterion Books, Inc., 257 Park Ave. S., New York, NY 10010
Crowell Collier and Macmillan, Inc., 866 Third Ave., New York, NY 10022
Thomas Y. Crowell Co., 666 Fifth Ave., New York, NY 10019
The John Day Co., Inc., 257 Park Ave. S., New York, NY 10010
Delacorte Pr. *See Dell*
Dell Pub. Co., 1 Dag Hammarsjold Plaza, New York, NY 10017
The Dial Pr., Inc. *See Dell*
Dodd, Mead & Co., 79 Madison Ave., New York, NY 10016
Doubleday & Co., Inc., 277 Park Ave., New York, NY 10017
Dover Pubns., Inc., 180 Varick St., New York, NY 10014
E. P. Dutton & Co., Inc., 201 Park Ave. S., New York, NY 10003
Farrar, Straus & Giroux, Inc., 19 Union Sq. W., New York, NY 10003
Follett Pub. Co., 1010 W. Washington Blvd., Chicago, IL 60606
Four Winds Pr. *See Scholastic*
Golden Pr., Inc. *See Western*
Grosset & Dunlap, Inc., 51 Madison Ave., New York, NY 10010
Harcourt Brace Jovanovich, Inc., 757 Third Ave., New York, NY 10017
Harper & Row, Pubs., 10 E. 53 St., New York, NY 10022
Hastings House Pubs., 10 E. 40 St., New York, NY 10016
Hawthorn Books, Inc., 260 Madison Ave., New York, NY 10016
Hill & Wang, Inc., 72 Fifth Ave., New York, NY 10011
Holt, Rinehart & Winston, Inc., 383 Madison Ave., New York, NY 10017
Horn Book, Inc., 585 Boylston St., Boston, MA 02116
Houghton Mifflin Co., 2 Park St., Boston, MA 02107
Alfred A. Knopf, Inc., 201 E. 50 St., New York, NY 10022

[1] For addresses of publishers not listed here consult the latest *Books in Print* or *Literary Marketplace*.

J. B. Lippincott Co., E. Washington Sq., Philadelphia, PA 19105
Little, Brown & Co., 34 Beacon St., Boston, MA 02106
Longman Canada Limited, 55 Barber Greene Rd., Don Mills, Ont.
Lothrop, Lee & Shepard Co., Inc., 105 Madison Ave., New York, NY 10016
McGraw-Hill Book Co., 1221 Ave. of the Americas, New York, NY 10020
David McKay Co., Inc., 750 Third Ave., New York, NY 10017
Macmillan Co., 866 Third Ave., New York, NY 10022
Charles E. Merrill Pub. Co., 1300 Alum Creek Dr., Columbus, OH 43216
Julian Messner, Inc. *See Simon & Schuster*
Methuen Pubns., 2330 Midland Ave., Agincourt, Ont.
William Morrow & Co., Inc., 105 Madison Ave., New York, NY 10016
National Council of Teachers of English, 1111 Kenyon Rd., Urbana, IL 61820
New American Library, 1301 Ave. of the Americas, New York, NY 10019
W. W. Norton & Co., Inc., 500 Fifth Ave., New York, NY 10036
Odyssey Pr. *See Bobbs-Merrill*
Oxford Univ. Pr., 200 Madison Ave., New York, NY 10016
Pantheon Books, 201 E. 50 St., New York, NY 10022
Parents' Magazine Pr., 52 Vanderbilt Ave., New York, NY 10017
Parnassus Pr., 2721 Parker St., Berkeley, CA 94704
Pergamon Pr., Inc., Maxwell House, Fairview Park, Elmsford, NY 10523
Pitman Pub. Corp., 6 E. 43 St., New York, NY 10017
Platt & Munk, Inc., 1055 Bronx River Ave., Bronx, NY 10472
Praeger Pubs., Inc., 111 Fourth Ave., New York, NY 10003
Prentice-Hall, Inc., Englewood Cliffs, NJ 07632
Press of Case Western Reserve University, Quail Bldg., Cleveland, OH 44106
G. P. Putnam's Sons, 200 Madison Ave., New York, NY 10016
Rand McNally & Co., P.O. Box 7600, Chicago, IL 60680
Random House, Inc., 201 E. 50 St., New York, NY 10022
Reilly & Lee Books, 114 W. Illinois St., Chicago, IL 60610
The Ronald Press Co., 79 Madison Ave., New York, NY 10016
Roy Pubs. Inc., 30 E. 74 St., New York, NY 10021
St. Martin's Pr., Inc., 175 Fifth Ave., New York, NY 10010
Scholastic Book Services, 50 W. 44 St., New York, NY 10036
Scott, Foresman and Co., 1900 E. Lake Ave., Glenview, IL 60025
Charles Scribner's Sons, 597 Fifth Ave., New York, NY 10017
Simon & Schuster, Inc., 630 Fifth Ave., New York, NY 10020
Univ. of Calif. Pr., 2223 Fulton St., Berkeley, CA 94720
Vanguard Pr., Inc., 424 Madison Ave., New York, NY 10017
Van Nostrand Reinhold Co., 450 W. 33 St., New York, NY 10001
The Viking Pr., Inc., 625 Madison Ave., New York, NY 10022
Henry Z. Walck, Inc. *See McKay*
Frederick Warne & Co., Inc., 101 Fifth Ave., New York, NY 10003
Franklin Watts, Inc., 730 Fifth Ave., New York, NY 10019
Western Pub. Co., Inc., 1220 Mound Ave., Racine, WI 53404
H. W. Wilson Co., 950 University Ave., Bronx, NY 10452
Windmill Books, 201 Park Ave. S., New York, NY 10010
World Pub. Co. *See Harry N. Abrams*
Young Scott Books. *See Addison-Wesley*

B appendix

Children's Book Awards

HANS CHRISTIAN ANDERSEN AWARD

Given biennially since 1956 by the International Board on Books for Young People to one author and one illustrator (since 1966) in recognition of his or her entire body of work.

1974 Author: Maria Gripe (Sweden); Illustrator: Farshid Nesghali (Iran)
1972 Author: Scott O'Dell (U.S.A.); Illustrator: Ib Spang Olsen (Denmark)
1970 Author: Gianni Rodari (Italy); Illustrator: Maurice Sendak (U.S.A.)
1968 Authors: James Krüss (Germany), José Maria Sanchez-Silva (Spain); Illustrator: Jiri Trnka (Czechoslovakia)
1966 Author: Tove Jansson (Finland); Illustrator: Alois Carigiet (Switzerland)
1964 René Guillot (France)
1962 Meindert DeJong (U.S.A.)
1960 Erich Kästner (Germany)
1958 Astrid Lindgren (Sweden)
1956 Eleanor Farjeon (Great Britain)

LAURA INGALLS WILDER AWARD

First awarded in 1954, this medal is now given every five years (since 1960) in recognition of an author or illustrator whose books, published in the U.S., have over a period of years made a substantial and lasting contribution to literature for children. Administered by American Library Association, Children's Services Division.

1975 Beverly Cleary
1970 E. B. White
1965 Ruth Sawyer
1960 Clara Ingram Judson
1954 Laura Ingalls Wilder

JOHN NEWBERY MEDAL

Donated by the Frederic G. Melcher family, the Newbery Medal has been awarded annually since 1922 under the supervision of the American Library Association, Children's Services Division, to the author of the most distinguished contribution to literature for children published in the U.S. during the preceding year. Announced in January, the award is limited to residents or citizens of the U.S.

1975 *The Grey King* by Susan Cooper (Atheneum). *Honor Books: The Hundred Penny Box* by Sharon Bell Mathis (Viking); *Dragonwings* by Lawrence Yep (Harper)
1974 *The Slave Dancer* by Paula Fox (Bradbury) **Honor Book:** *The Dark Is Rising* by Susan Cooper (Atheneum)

1973 *Julie of the Wolves* by Jean Craighead George (Harper)   **Honor Books:** *Frog and Toad Together* by Arnold Lobel (Harper); *The Upstairs Room* by Johanna Reiss (Crowell); *The Witches of Worm* by Zilpha Keatley Snyder (Atheneum)

1972 *Mrs. Frisby and the Rats of NIMH* by Robert C. O'Brien (Atheneum)   **Honor Books:** *Annie and the Old One* by Miska Miles (Atlantic-Little); *The Headless Cupid* by Zilpha Keatley Snyder (Atheneum); *Incident at Hawk's Hill* by Allan W. Eckert (Little); *The Planet of Junior Brown* by Virginia Hamilton (Macmillan); *The Tombs of Atuan* by Ursula K. LeGuin (Atheneum)

1971 *Summer of the Swans* by Betsy Byars (Viking)   **Honor Books:** *Knee-Knock Rise* by Natalie Babbitt (Farrar); *Enchantress from the Stars* by Sylvia Louise Engdahl (Atheneum); *Sing Down the Moon* by Scott O'Dell (Houghton)

1970 *Sounder* by William H. Armstrong (Harper)   **Honor Books:** *Our Eddie* by Sulamith Ish-Kishor (Pantheon); *The Many Ways of Seeing: An Introduction to the Pleasures of Art* by Janet Gaylord Moore (World); *Journey Outside* by Mary Q. Steele (Viking)

1969 *The High King* by Lloyd Alexander (Holt)   **Honor Books:** *To Be a Slave* by Julius Lester (Dial); *When Shlemiel Went to Warsaw & Other Stories* by Isaac Bashevis Singer (Farrar)

1968 *From the Mixed-Up Files of Mrs. Basil E. Frankweiler* by E. L. Konigsburg (Atheneum)   **Honor Books:** *Jennifer, Hecate, Macbeth, William McKinley, and Me, Elizabeth* by E. L. Konigsburg (Atheneum); *The Black Pearl* by Scott O'Dell (Houghton); *The Fearsome Inn* by Isaac Bashevis Singer (Scribner's); *The Egypt Game* by Zilpha Keatley Snyder (Atheneum)

1967 *Up a Road Slowly* by Irene Hunt (Follett)   **Honor Books:** *The King's Fifth* by Scott O'Dell (Houghton); *Zlateh the Goat and Other Stories* by Isaac Bashevis Singer (Harper); *The Jazz Man* by Mary H. Weik (Atheneum)

1966 *I, Juan de Pareja* by Elizabeth Borten de Treviño (Farrar)   **Honor Books:** *The Black Cauldron* by Lloyd Alexander (Holt); *The Animal Family* by Randall Jarrell (Pantheon); *The Noonday Friends* by Mary Stolz (Harper)

1965 *Shadow of a Bull* by Maia Wojciechowska (Atheneum)   **Honor Book:** *Across Five Aprils* by Irene Hunt (Follett)

1964 *It's Like This, Cat* by Emily Cheney Neville (Harper)   **Honor Books:** *Rascal* by Sterling North (Dutton); *The Loner* by Ester Wier (McKay)

1963 *A Wrinkle in Time* by Madeleine L'Engle (Farrar)   **Honor Books:** *Thistle and Thyme* by Sorche Nic Leodhas (Holt); *Men of Athens* by Olivia Coolidge (Houghton)

1962 *The Bronze Bow* by Elizabeth George Speare (Houghton)   **Honor Books:** *Frontier Living* by Edwin Tunis (World); *The Golden Goblet* by Eloise McGraw (Coward); *Belling the Tiger* by Mary Stolz (Harper)

1961 *Island of the Blue Dolphins* by Scott O'Dell (Houghton)   **Honor Books:** *America Moves Forward* by Gerald W. Johnson (Morrow); *Old Ramon* by Jack Schaefer (Houghton); *The Cricket in Times Square* by George Seldon (Farrar)

1960 *Onion John* by Joseph Krumgold (Crowell)   **Honor Books:** *My Side of the Mountain* by Jean George (Dutton); *America Is Born* by Gerald W. Johnson (Morrow); *The Gammage Cup* by Carol Kendall (Harcourt)

1959 *The Witch of Blackbird Pond* by Elizabeth George Speare (Houghton)   **Honor Books:** *The Family under the Bridge* by Natalie S. Carlson (Harper); *Along Came a Dog* by Meindert DeJong (Harper); *Chucaro: Wild Pony of the Pampa* by Francis Kalnay (Harcourt); *The Perilous Road* by William O. Steele (Harcourt)

1958 *Rifles for Watie* by Harold Keith (Crowell)   **Honor Books:** *The Horsecatcher* by Mari Sandoz (Westminster); *Gone-Away Lake* by Elizabeth Enright (Harcourt); *The Great Wheel* by Robert Lawson (Viking); *Tom Paine, Freedom's Apostle* by Leo Gurko (Crowell)

1957 *Miracles on Maple Hill* by Virginia Sorensen (Harcourt)   **Honor Books:** *Old Yeller* by Fred Gipson (Harper); *The House of Sixty Fathers* by Meindert DeJong (Harper); *Mr. Justice Holmes* by Clara Ingram Judson (Follett); *The Corn Grows Ripe* by Dorothy Rhoads (Viking); *Black Fox of Lorne* by Marguerite de Angeli (Doubleday)

1956 *Carry on, Mr. Bowditch* by Jean Lee Latham (Houghton)   **Honor Books:** *The Secret River* by Marjorie Kinnan Rawlings (Scribner's); *The Golden Name Day* by Jennie Lindquist (Harper); *Men, Microscopes, and Living Things* by Katherine Shippen (Viking)

1955 *The Wheel on the School* by Meindert DeJong (Harper)   **Honor Books:** *Courage of Sarah Noble* by Alice Dalgliesh (Scribner's); *Banner in the Sky* by James Ullman (Lippincott)

1954 *. . . and now Miguel* by Joseph Krumgold (Crowell)   **Honor Books:** *All Alone* by Claire Huchet Bishop (Viking); *Shadrach* by Meindert DeJong (Harper); *Hurry Home Candy* by Meindert DeJong (Harper)

1953 *Secret of the Andes* by Ann Nolan Clark (Viking)   **Honor Books:** *Charlotte's Web* by E. B. White (Harper); *Moccasin Trail* by Eloise McGraw (Coward); *Red Sails to Capri* by Ann Weil (Viking); *The Bears on Hemlock Mountain* by Alice Dalgliesh (Scribner's); *Birthdays of Freedom, Vol. 1* by Genevieve Foster (Scribner's)

1952 *Ginger Pye* by Eleanor Estes (Harcourt)   **Honor Books:** *Americans before Columbus* by Elizabeth Baity

(Viking); *Minn of the Mississippi* by Holling C. Holling (Houghton); *The Defender* by Nicholas Kalashnikoff (Scribner's); *The Light at Tern Rocks* by Julia Sauer (Viking); *The Apple and the Arrow* by Mary and Conrad Buff (Houghton)

1951 *Amos Fortune, Free Man* by Elizabeth Yates (Aladdin)   **Honor Books:** *Better Known as Johnny Appleseed* by Mabel Leigh Hunt (Lippincott); *Gandhi, Fighter without a Sword* by Jeanette Eaton (Morrow); *Abraham Lincoln, Friend of the People* by Clara Ingram Judson (Follett); *The Story of Appleby Capple* by Anne Parrish (Harper)

1950 *The Door in the Wall* by Marguerite de Angeli (Doubleday)   **Honor Books:** *Tree of Freedom* by Rebecca Caudill (Viking); *The Blue Cat of Castle Town* by Catherine Coblentz (Longmans); *Kildee House* by Rutherford Montgomery (Doubleday); *George Washington* by Genevieve Foster (Scribner's); *Song of the Pines* by Walter and Marion Havighurst (Winston)

1949 *King of the Wind* by Marguerite Henry (Rand)   **Honor Books:** *Seabird* by Holling C. Holling (Houghton); *Daughter of the Mountains* by Louise Rankin (Viking); *My Father's Dragon* by Ruth S. Gannett (Random); *Story of the Negro* by Arna Bontemps (Knopf)

1948 *The Twenty-One Balloons* by William Pène du Bois (Viking)   **Honor Books:** *Pancakes—Paris* by Claire Huchet Bishop (Viking); *Li Lun, Lad of Courage* by Carolyn Treffinger (Abingdon); *The Quaint and Curious Quest of Johnny Longfoot* by Catherine Besterman (Bobbs); *The Cow-Tail Switch, and Other West African Stories* by Harold Courlander (Holt); *Misty of Chincoteague* by Marguerite Henry (Rand)

1947 *Miss Hickory* by Carolyn Sherwin Bailey (Viking)   **Honor Books:** *Wonderful Year* by Nancy Barnes (Messner); *Big Tree* by Mary and Conrad Buff (Viking); *The Heavenly Tenants* by William Maxwell (Harper); *The Avion My Uncle Flew* by Cyrus Fisher (Appleton); *The Hidden Treasure of Glaston* by Eleanore Jewett (Viking)

1946 *Strawberry Girl* by Lois Lenski (Lippincott)   **Honor Books:** *Justin Morgan Had a Horse* by Marguerite Henry (Rand); *The Moved-Outers* by Florence Crannell Means (Houghton); *Bhimsa, the Dancing Bear* by Christine Weston (Scribner's); *New Found World* by Katherine Shippen (Viking)

1945 *Rabbit Hill* by Robert Lawson (Viking)   **Honor Books:** *The Hundred Dresses* by Eleanor Estes (Harcourt); *The Silver Pencil* by Alice Dalgliesh (Scribner's); *Abraham Lincoln's World* by Genevieve Foster (Scribner's); *Lone Journey: The Life of Roger Williams* by Jeanette Eaton (Harcourt)

1944 *Johnny Tremain* by Esther Forbes (Houghton)   **Honor Books:** *These Happy Golden Years* by Laura Ingalls Wilder (Harper); *Fog Magic* by Julia Sauer (Viking); *Rufus M.* by Eleanor Estes (Harcourt); *Mountain Born* by Elizabeth Yates (Coward)

1943 *Adam of the Road* by Elizabeth Janet Gray (Viking)   **Honor Books:** *The Middle Moffat* by Eleanor Estes (Harcourt); *Have You Seen Tom Thumb?* by Mabel Leigh Hunt (Lippincott)

1942 *The Matchlock Gun* by Walter D. Edmonds (Dodd)   **Honor Books:** *Little Town on the Prairie* by Laura Ingalls Wilder (Harper); *George Washington's World* by Genevieve Foster (Scribner's); *Indian Captive: The Story of Mary Jemison* by Lois Lenski (Lippincott); *Down Ryton Water* by Eva Roe Gaggin (Viking)

1941 *Call It Courage* by Armstrong Sperry (Macmillan)   **Honor Books:** *Blue Willow* by Doris Gates (Viking); *Young Mac of Fort Vancouver* by Mary Jane Carr (Crowell); *The Long Winter* by Laura Ingalls Wilder (Harper); *Nansen* by Anna Gertrude Hall (Viking)

1940 *Daniel Boone* by James Daugherty (Viking)   **Honor Books:** *The Singing Tree* by Kate Seredy (Viking); *Runner of the Mountain Tops* by Mabel Robinson (Random); *By the Shores of Silver Lake* by Laura Ingalls Wilder (Harper); *Boy with a Pack* by Stephen W. Meader (Harcourt)

1939 *Thimble Summer* by Elizabeth Enright (Rinehart)   **Honor Books:** *Nino* by Valenti Angelo (Viking); *Mr. Popper's Penguins* by Richard and Florence Atwater (Little); *Hello the Boat!* by Phyllis Crawford (Holt); *Leader by Destiny: George Washington, Man and Patriot* by Jeanette Eaton (Harcourt); *Penn* by Elizabeth Janet Gray (Viking)

1938 *The White Stag* by Kate Seredy (Viking)   **Honor Books:** *Pecos Bill* by James Cloyd Bowman (Little); *Bright Island* by Mabel Robinson (Random); *On the Banks of Plum Creek* by Laura Ingalls Wilder (Harper)

1937 *Roller Skates* by Ruth Sawyer (Viking)   **Honor Books:** *Phebe Fairchild: Her Book* by Lois Lenski (Stokes); *Whistler's Van* by Idwal Jones (Viking); *Golden Basket* by Ludwig Bemelmans (Viking); *Winterbound* by Margery Bianco (Viking); *Audubon* by Constance Rourke (Harcourt); *The Codfish Musket* by Agnes Hewes (Doubleday)

1936 *Caddie Woodlawn* by Carol Brink (Macmillan)   **Honor Books:** *Honk, the Moose* by Phil Stong (Dodd); *The Good Master* by Kate Seredy (Viking); *Young Walter Scott* by Elizabeth Janet Gray (Viking); *All Sail Set* by Armstrong Sperry (Winston)

1935 *Dobry* by Monica Shannon (Viking)   **Honor Books:** *Pageant of Chinese History* by Elizabeth Seeger (Longmans); *Davy Crockett* by Constance Rourke (Harcourt); *Day on Skates* by Hilda Van Stockum (Harper)

1934 *Invincible Louisa* by Cornelia Meigs (Little)   **Honor Books:** *The Forgotten Daughter* by Caroline Snedeker (Doubleday); *Swords of Steel* by Elsie Singmaster (Houghton); *ABC Bunny* by Wanda Gág (Coward); *Winged Girl of Knossos* by Erik Berry (Appleton); *New Land* by Sarah Schmidt (McBride); *Big Tree of Bunlahy* by Padraic Colum (Macmillan); *Glory of the Seas* by Agnes Hewes (Knopf); *Apprentice of Florence* by Anne Kyle (Houghton)

1933 *Young Fu of the Upper Yangtze* by Elizabeth Foreman Lewis (Winston) **Honor Books:** *Swift Rivers* by Cornelia Meigs (Little); *The Railroad to Freedom* by Hildegarde Swift (Harcourt); *Children of the Soil* by Nora Burglon (Doubleday)

1932 *Waterless Mountain* by Laura Adams Armer (Longmans) **Honor Books:** *The Fairy Circus* by Dorothy P. Lathrop (Macmillan); *Calico Bush* by Rachel Field (Macmillan); *Boy of the South Seas* by Eunice Tietjens (Coward); *Out of the Flame* by Eloise Lownsbery (Longmans); *Jane's Island* by Marjorie Allee (Houghton); *Truce of the Wolf and Other Tales of Old Italy* by Mary Gould Davis (Harcourt)

1931 *The Cat Who Went to Heaven* by Elizabeth Coatsworth (Macmillan) **Honor Books:** *Floating Island* by Anne Parrish (Harper); *The Dark Star of Itza* by Alida Malkus (Harcourt); *Queer Person* by Ralph Hubbard (Doubleday); *Mountains Are Free* by Julia Davis Adams (Dutton); *Spice and the Devil's Cave* by Agnes Hewes (Knopf); *Meggy Macintosh* by Elizabeth Janet Gray (Doubleday); *Garram the Hunter* by Herbert Best (Doubleday); *Ood-Le-Uk the Wanderer* by Alice Lide and Margaret Johansen (Little)

1930 *Hitty, Her First Hundred Years* by Rachel Field (Macmillan) **Honor Books:** *Daughter of the Seine* by Jeanette Eaton (Harper); *Pran of Albania* by Elizabeth Miller (Doubleday); *Jumping-Off Place* by Marian Hurd McNeely (Longmans); *Tangle-Coated Horse and Other Tales* by Ella Young (Longmans); *Vaino* by Julia Davis Adams (Dutton); *Little Blacknose* by Hildegarde Swift (Harcourt)

1929 *The Trumpeter of Krakow* by Eric P. Kelly (Macmillan) **Honor Books:** *Pigtail of Ah Lee Ben Loo* by John Bennett (Longmans); *Millions of Cats* by Wanda Gág (Coward); *The Boy Who Was* by Grace Hallock (Dutton); *Clearing Weather* by Cornelia Meigs (Little); *Runaway Papoose* by Grace Moon (Doubleday); *Tod of the Fens* by Elinor Whitney (Macmillan)

1928 *Gayneck, the Story of a Pigeon* by Dhan Gopal Mukerji (Dutton) **Honor Books:** *The Wonder Smith and His Son* by Ella Young (Longmans); *Downright Dencey* by Caroline Snedeker (Doubleday)

1927 *Smoky, the Cowhorse* by Will James (Scribner's) **Honor Books:** No Record

1926 *Shen of the Sea* by Arthur Bowie Chrisman (Dutton) **Honor Book:** *Voyagers* by Padraic Colum (Macmillan)

1925 *Tales from Silver Lands* by Charles Finger (Doubleday) **Honor Books:** *Nicholas* by Anne Carroll Moore (Putnam's); *Dream Coach* by Anne Parrish (Macmillan)

1924 *The Dark Frigate* by Charles Hawes (Atlantic-Little) **Honor Book:** No Record

1923 *The Voyages of Doctor Dolittle* by Hugh Lofting (Lippincott) **Honor Book:** No Record

1922 *The Story of Mankind* by Hendrik Willem van Loon (Liveright) **Honor Books:** *The Great Quest* by Charles Hawes (Little); *Cedric the Forester* by Bernard Marshall (Appleton); *The Old Tobacco Shop* by William Bowen (Macmillan); *The Golden Fleece and the Heroes Who Lived before Achilles* by Padraic Colum (Macmillan); *Windy Hill* by Cornelia Meigs (Macmillan)

RANDOLPH J. CALDECOTT MEDAL

Donated by the Frederic G. Melcher family, the Caldecott Medal has been awarded annually since 1938, under the supervision of the American Library Association, Children's Services Division, to the illustrator of the most distinguished picture book for children published in the U.S. during the preceding year. Announced in January, the award is limited to residents or citizens of the U.S.

1975 *Why Mosquitoes Buzz in People's Ears: A West African Tale* by Leo and Diane Dillon (Dial) Honor Books: *Strega Nona* by Tomie de Paola (Prentice-Hall); *The Desert is Theirs* by Byrd Baylor (Scribners)

1974 *Duffy and the Devil* by Margot Zemach (Farrar) **Honor Books:** *Three Jovial Huntsmen* adapted and ill. by Susan Jeffers (Bradbury); *Cathedral: The Story of Its Construction* by David Macaulay (Houghton)

1973 *The Funny Little Woman* retold by Arlene Mosel, ill. by Blair Lent (Dutton) **Honor Books:** *Anansi the Spider* adapted and ill. by Gerald McDermott (Holt); *Hosie's Alphabet* by Hosea, Tobias and Lisa Baskin, ill. by Leonard Baskin (Viking); *Snow White and the Seven Dwarfs* translated by Randall Jarrell, ill. by Nancy Ekholm Burkert (Farrar); *When Clay Sings* by Byrd Baylor, ill. by Tom Bahti (Scribner's)

1972 *One Fine Day* by Nonny Hogrogian (Macmillan) **Honor Books:** *Hildilid's Night* by Cheli Durán Ryan, ill. by Arnold Lobel (Macmillan); *If All the Seas Were One Sea* by Janina Domanska (Macmillan); *Moja Means One* by Muriel Feelings, ill. by Tom Feelings (Dial)

1971 *A Story, a Story* by Gail E. Haley (Atheneum) **Honor Books:** *The Angry Moon* by William Sleator, ill. by Blair Lent (Atlantic-Little); *Frog and Toad Are Friends* by Arnold Lobel (Harper); *In the Night Kitchen* by Maurice Sendak (Harper)

1970 *Sylvester and the Magic Pebble* by William Steig (Windmill/Simon & Schuster) **Honor Books:** *Goggles* by

Ezra Jack Keats (Macmillan); *Alexander and the Wind-Up Mouse* by Leo Lionni (Pantheon); *Pop Corn & Ma Goodness* by Edna Mitchell Preston, ill. by Robert Andrew Parker (Viking); *Thy Friend, Obadiah* by Brinton Turkle (Viking); *The Judge* by Harve Zemach, ill. by Margot Zemach (Farrar)

1969   *The Fool of the World and the Flying Ship* by Arthur Ransome, ill. by Uri Shulevitz   **Honor Book:**   *Why the Sun and the Moon Live in the Sky* by Elphinstone Dayrell, ill. by Blair Lent (Houghton)

1968   *Drummer Hoff* by Barbara Emberley, ill. by Ed Emberley (Prentice)   **Honor Books:**   *Frederick* by Leo Lionni (Pantheon); *Seashore Story* by Taro Yashima (Viking); *The Emperor and the Kite* by Jane Yolen, ill. by Ed Young (World)

1967   *Sam, Bangs and Moonshine* by Evaline Ness (Holt)   **Honor Book:**   *One Wide River to Cross* by Barbara Emberley, ill. by Ed Emberley (Prentice)

1966   *Always Room for One More* by Sorche Nic Leodhas, ill. by Nonny Hogrogian (Holt)   **Honor Books:** *Hide and Seek Fog* by Alvin Tresselt, ill. by Roger Duvoisin (Lothrop); *Just Me* by Marie Hall Ets (Viking); *Tom Tit Tot* by Evaline Ness (Scribner's)

1965   *May I Bring a Friend?* by Beatrice Schenk de Regniers, ill. by Beni Montresor (Atheneum)   **Honor Books:** *Rain Makes Applesauce* by Julian Scheer, ill. by Marvin Bileck (Holiday); *The Wave* by Margaret Hodges, ill. by Blair Lent (Houghton); *A Pocketful of Cricket* by Rebecca Caudill, ill. by Evaline Ness (Holt)

1964   *Where the Wild Things Are* by Maurice Sendak (Harper)   **Honor Books:**   *Swimmy* by Leo Lionni (Pantheon); *All in the Morning Early* by Sorche Nic Leodhas, ill. by Evaline Ness (Holt); *Mother Goose and Nursery Rhymes* ill. by Philip Reed (Atheneum)

1963   *The Snowy Day* by Ezra Jack Keats (Viking)   **Honor Books:**   *The Sun Is a Golden Earring* by Natalia M. Belting, ill. by Bernarda Bryson (Holt); *Mr. Rabbit and the Lovely Present* by Charlotte Zolotow, ill. by Maurice Sendak (Harper)

1962   *Once a Mouse . . .* by Marcia Brown (Scribner's)   **Honor Books:**   *The Fox Went Out on a Chilly Night* ill. by Peter Spier (Doubleday); *Little Bear's Visit* by Else Holmelund Minarik, ill. by Maurice Sendak (Harper); *The Day We Saw the Sun Come Up* by Alice E. Goudey, ill. by Adrienne Adams (Scribner's)

1961   *Baboushka and the Three Kings* by Ruth Robbins, ill. by Nicholas Sidjakov (Parnassus)   **Honor Book:** *Inch by Inch* by Leo Lionni (Astor-Honor)

1960   *Nine Days to Christmas* by Marie Hall Ets and Aurora Labastida, ill. by Marie Hall Ets (Viking)   **Honor Books:**   *Houses from the Sea* by Alice E. Goudey, ill. by Adrienne Adams (Scribner's); *The Moon Jumpers* by Janice May Udry, ill. by Maurice Sendak (Harper)

1959   *Chanticleer and the Fox* adapted from Chaucer and ill. by Barbara Cooney (Crowell)   **Honor Books:** *The House That Jack Built* by Antonio Frasconi (Harcourt); *What Do You Say, Dear?* by Sesyle Joslin, ill. by Maurice Sendak (Scott); *Umbrella* by Taro Yashima (Viking)

1958   *Time of Wonder* by Robert McCloskey (Viking)   **Honor Books:**   *Fly High, Fly Low* by Don Freeman (Viking); *Anatole and the Cat* by Eve Titus, ill. by Paul Galdone (McGraw)

1957   *A Tree Is Nice* by Janice May Udry, ill. by Marc Simont (Harper)   **Honor Books:**   *Mr. Penny's Race Horse* by Marie Hall Ets (Viking); *1 Is One* by Tasha Tudor (Walck); *Anatole* by Eve Titus, ill. by Paul Galdone (McGraw); *Gillespie and the Guards* by Benjamin Elkin, ill. by James Daugherty (Viking); *Lion* by William Pène du Bois (Viking)

1956   *Frog Went A-Courtin'* ed. by John Langstaff, ill. by Feodor Rojankovsky (Harcourt)   **Honor Books:** *Play with Me* by Marie Hall Ets (Viking); *Crow Boy* by Taro Yashima (Viking)

1955   *Cinderella, or the Little Glass Slipper* by Charles Perrault, trans. and ill. by Marcia Brown (Scribner's) **Honor Books:**   *Book of Nursery and Mother Goose Rhymes* ill. by Marguerite de Angeli (Doubleday); *Wheel on the Chimney* by Margaret Wise Brown, ill. by Tibor Gergely (Lippincott); *The Thanksgiving Story* by Alice Dalgliesh, ill. by Helen Sewell (Scribner's)

1954   *Madeline's Rescue* by Ludwig Bemelmans (Viking)   **Honor Books:**   *Journey Cake, Ho!* by Ruth Sawyer, ill. by Robert McCloskey (Viking); *When Will the World Be Mine?* by Miriam Schlein, ill. by Jean Charlot (Scott); *The Steadfast Tin Soldier* by Hans Christian Andersen, ill. by Marcia Brown (Scribner's); *A Very Special House* by Ruth Krauss, ill. by Maurice Sendak (Harper); *Green Eyes* by A. Birnbaum (Capitol)

1953   *The Biggest Bear* by Lynd Ward (Houghton)   **Honor Books:**   *Puss in Boots* by Charles Perrault, ill. and trans. by Marcia Brown (Scribner's); *One Morning in Maine* by Robert McCloskey (Viking); *Ape in a Cape* by Fritz Eichenberg (Harcourt); *The Storm Book* by Charlotte Zolotow, ill. by Margaret Bloy Graham (Harper); *Five Little Monkeys* by Juliet Kepes (Houghton)

1952   *Finders Keepers* by Will, ill. by Nicolas (Harcourt)   **Honor Books:**   *Mr. T. W. Anthony Woo* by Marie Hall Ets (Viking); *Skipper John's Cook* by Marcia Brown (Scribner's); *All Falling Down* by Gene Zion, ill. by Margaret Bloy Graham (Harper); *Bear Party* by William Pène du Bois (Viking); *Feather Mountain* by Elizabeth Olds (Houghton)

1951   *The Egg Tree* by Katherine Milhous (Scribner's)   **Honor Books:**   *Dick Whittington and His Cat* by Marcia Brown (Scribner's); *The Two Reds* by Will, ill. by Nicolas (Harcourt); *If I Ran the Zoo* by Dr. Seuss (Random); *The*

Most Wonderful Doll in the World by Phyllis McGinley, ill. by Helen Stone (Lippincott); *T-Bone, the Baby Sitter* by Clare Newberry (Harper)

1950 *Song of the Swallows* by Leo Politi (Scribner's)   **Honor Books:** *America's Ethan Allen* by Stewart Holbrook, ill. by Lynd Ward (Houghton); *The Wild Birthday Cake* by Lavinia Davis, ill. by Hildegard Woodward (Doubleday); *The Happy Day* by Ruth Krauss, ill. by Marc Simont (Harper); *Bartholomew and the Oobleck* by Dr. Seuss (Random); *Henry Fisherman* by Marcia Brown (Scribner's)

1949 *The Big Snow* by Berta and Elmer Hader (Macmillan)   **Honor Books:** *Blueberries for Sal* by Robert McCloskey (Viking); *All Around the Town* by Phyllis McGinley, ill. by Helen Stone (Lippincott); *Juanita* by Leo Politi (Scribner's); *Fish in the Air* by Kurt Wiese (Viking)

1948 *White Snow, Bright Snow* by Alvin Tresselt, ill. by Roger Duvoisin (Lothrop)   **Honor Books:** *Stone Soup* by Marcia Brown (Scribner's); *McElligot's Pool* by Dr. Seuss (Random); *Bambino the Clown* by George Schreiber (Viking); *Roger and the Fox* by Lavinia Davis, ill. by Hildegard Woodward (Doubleday); *Song of Robin Hood* ed. by Anne Malcolmson, ill. by Virginia Lee Burton (Houghton)

1947 *The Little Island* by Golden MacDonald, ill. by Leonard Weisgard (Doubleday)   **Honor Books:** *Rain Drop Splash* by Alvin Tresselt, ill. by Leonard Weisgard (Lothrop); *Boats on the River* by Marjorie Flack, ill. by Jay Hyde Barnum (Viking); *Timothy Turtle* by Al Graham, ill. by Tony Palazzo (Welch); *Pedro, the Angel of Olvera Street* by Leo Politi (Scribner's); *Sing in Praise: A Collection of the Best Loved Hymns* by Opal Wheeler, ill. by Marjorie Torrey (Dutton)

1946 *The Rooster Crows* (traditional Mother Goose) ill. by Maud and Miska Petersham (Macmillan)   **Honor Books:** *Little Lost Lamb* by Golden MacDonald, ill. by Leonard Weisgard (Doubleday); *Sing Mother Goose* by Opal Wheeler, ill. by Marjorie Torrey (Dutton); *My Mother Is the Most Beautiful Woman in the World* by Becky Reyher, ill. by Ruth Gannett (Lothrop); *You Can Write Chinese* by Kurt Wiese (Viking)

1945 *Prayer for a Child* by Rachel Field, ill. by Elizabeth Orton Jones (Macmillan)   **Honor Books:** *Mother Goose* ill. by Tasha Tudor (Walck); *In the Forest* by Marie Hall Ets (Viking) *Yonie Wondernose* by Marguerite de Angeli (Doubleday); *The Christmas Anna Angel* by Ruth Sawyer, ill. by Kate Seredy (Viking)

1944 *Many Moons* by James Thurber, ill. by Louis Slobodkin (Harcourt)   **Honor Books:** *Small Rain: Verses from the Bible* selected by Jessie Orton Jones, ill. by Elizabeth Orton Jones (Viking); *Pierre Pigeon* by Lee Kingman, ill. by Arnold E. Bare (Houghton); *The Mighty Hunter* by Berta and Elmer Hader (Macmillan); *A Child's Good Night Book* by Margaret Wise Brown, ill. by Jean Charlot (Scott); *Good Luck Horse* by Chin-Yi Chan, ill. by Plao Chan (Whittlesey)

1943 *The Little House* by Virginia Lee Burton (Houghton)   **Honor Books:** *Dash and Dart* by Mary and Conrad Buff (Viking); *Marshmallow* by Clare Newberry (Harper)

1942 *Make Way for Ducklings* by Robert McCloskey (Viking)   **Honor Books:** *An American ABC* by Maud and Miska Petersham (Macmillan); *In My Mother's House* by Ann Nolan Clark, ill. by Velino Herrera (Viking); *Paddle-to-the-Sea* by Holling C. Holling (Houghton); *Nothing at All* by Wanda Gág (Coward)

1941 *They Were Strong and Good* by Robert Lawson (Viking)   **Honor Book:** *April's Kittens* by Clare Newberry (Harper)

1940 *Abraham Lincoln* by Ingri and Edgar d'Aulaire (Doubleday)   **Honor Books:** *Cock-a-Doodle Doo* by Berta and Elmer Hader (Macmillan); *Madeline* by Ludwig Bemelmans (Viking); *The Ageless Story* ill. by Lauren Ford (Dodd)

1939 *Mei Li* by Thomas Handforth (Doubleday)   **Honor Books:** *The Forest Pool* by Laura Adams Armer (Longmans); *Wee Gillis* by Munro Leaf, ill. by Robert Lawson (Viking); *Snow White and the Seven Dwarfs* by Wanda Gág (Coward); *Barkis* by Clare Newberry (Harper); *Andy and the Lion* by James Daugherty (Viking)

1938 *Animals of the Bible* by Helen Dean Fish, ill. by Dorothy P. Lathrop (Lippincott)   **Honor Books:** *Seven Simeons* by Boris Artzybasheff (Viking); *Four and Twenty Blackbirds* by Helen Dean Fish, ill. by Robert Lawson (Stokes)

NATIONAL BOOK AWARD CHILDREN'S BOOK CATEGORY

In March 1969 the National Book Awards included for the first time a prize in the category of children's books. The award, contributed by the Children's Book Council and administered by the National Book Committee, is presented annually to a juvenile title that a panel of judges considers the most distinguished by an American citizen published in the U.S. in the preceding year.

1975 *M. C. Higgins, the Great* by Virginia Hamilton (Macmillan)

1974 *Court of the Stone Children* by Eleanor Cameron (Dutton)

1973 *The Farthest Shore* by Ursula K. LeGuin (Atheneum)   **Other Finalists:** *Children of Vietnam* by Betty Jean Lifton and Thomas C. Fox (Atheneum); *Dominic* by William Steig (Farrar); *The House of Wings* by Betsy Byars (Viking); *The Impossible People* by Georgess McHargue (Holt); *Julie of the Wolves* by Jean Craighead George (Harper);

Long Journey Home by Julius Lester (Dial); *Trolls* by Ingri and Edgar Parin d'Aulaire (Doubleday); *The Witches of Worm* by Zilpha Keatley Snyder (Atheneum)

1972   *The Slightly Irregular Fire Engine* by Donald Barthelme (Farrar)   **Other Finalists:**   *Amos & Boris* by William Steig (Farrar); *The Art and Industry of Sandcastles* by Jan Adkins (Walker); *The Bears' House* by Marilyn Sachs (Double-day); *Father Fox's Pennyrhymes* by Clyde Watson, ill. by Wendy Watson (Crowell); *Hildilid's Night* by Cheli Durán Ryan, ill. by Arnold Lobel (Macmillan); *His Own Where* by June Jordan (Crowell); *Mrs. Frisby and the Rats of NIMH* by Robert C. O'Brien (Atheneum); *The Planet of Junior Brown* by Virginia Hamilton (Macmillan); *The Tombs of Atuan* by Ursula K. LeGuin (Atheneum); *Wild in the World* by John Donovan (Harper)

1971   *The Marvelous Misadventures of Sebastian* by Lloyd Alexander (Dutton)   **Other Finalists:**   *Blowfish Live in the Sea* by Paula Fox (Bradbury); *Frog and Toad Are Friends* by Arnold Lobel (Harper); *Grover* by Vera and Bill Cleaver (Lippincott); *Trumpet of the Swan* by E. B. White (Harper)

1970   *A Day of Pleasure: Stories of a Boy Growing Up in Warsaw* by Isaac Bashevis Singer (Farrar)   **Other Finalists:**   *Pop Corn & Ma Goodness* by Edna Mitchell Preston (Viking); *Sylvester and the Magic Pebble* by William Steig (Windmill/Simon & Schuster); *Where the Lilies Bloom* by Vera and Bill Cleaver (Lippincott); *The Young United States* by Edwin Tunis (World)

1969   *Journey from Peppermint Street* by Meindert DeJong (Harper)   **Other Finalists:**   *Constance* by Patricia Clapp (Lothrop); *The Endless Steppe* by Esther Hautzig (Crowell); *The High King* by Lloyd Alexander (Holt); *Langston Hughes* by Milton Meltzer (Crowell)

COUNCIL ON INTERRACIAL BOOKS FOR CHILDREN AWARD

Established in 1968, the award is made annually to encourage the publication of children's books by minority writers. Since its inception, the number of categories for the award has been expanded. As of 1973 the Council on Interracial Books for Children offers five awards for unpublished manuscripts by writers who are Black, Chicano, American Indian, Puerto Rican, and Asian American, and who have not yet published a book for children. In some cases, the manuscripts selected for awards have subsequently been published; where publication has occurred or will soon take place, the publisher is named in the annotation.

1971–1972   Asian-American: *Morning Song* by Minfong Ho; Black: *The Rock Cried Out* by Florenz Webbe Maxwell; Puerto Rican: *The Unusual Puerto Rican* by Theodore Laquer-Franceschi

1970   American Indian: *Jimmy Yellow Hawk* by Virginia Driving Hawk Sneve (Holiday); Black: *Sneakers* (orig. title *Warball*) by Ray Anthony Shepard (Dutton); Chicano: *I Am Magic* by Juan Valenzuela (Indian Historian Press)

1969   Ages 3–6: *ABC: The Story of the Alphabet* by Virginia Cox (Wayne State U.); Ages 7–11: *Sidewalk Story* by Sharon Bell Mathis (Viking); Ages 12–16: *Letters from Uncle David: Underground Hero* by Margot S. Webb

1968   Ages 3–6: *Where Does the Day Go?* by Walter N. Myers (Parents'); Ages 7–11: No Award; Ages 12–16: *The Soul Brothers and Sister Lou* by Kristin Hunter (Scribner's)

CARNEGIE MEDAL

Given annually in May since 1937 by the British Library Association for a children's book of outstanding merit written by a British subject and published in the United Kingdom during the preceding year. The year cited in the listing that follows is the year in which a book was published, not the year in which the honor was bestowed.

1974   *The Stronghold* by Mollie Hunter (Harper)
1973   *The Ghost of Thomas Kempe* by Penelope Lively (Dutton)
1972   *Watership Down* by Richard Adams (Rex Collings)
1971   *Josh* by Ivan Southall (Angus & Robertson)
1970   *The God Beneath the Sea* by Leon Garfield & Edward Blishen (Longmans)
1969   *The Edge of the Cloud* by Kathleen Peyton (Oxford)
1968   *The Moon in the Cloud* by Rosemary Harris (Faber)
1967   *The Owl Service* by Alan Garner (Collins)
1966   No Award
1965   *The Grange at High Force* by Philip Turner (Oxford)
1964   *Nordy Bank* by Sheena Porter (Oxford)
1963   *Time of Trial* by Hester Burton (Oxford)
1962   *The Twelve and the Genii* by Pauline Clarke (Faber)
1961   *A Stranger at Green Knowe* by Lucy Boston (Faber)

1960 *The Making of Man* by I. W. Cornwall (Phoenix House)
1959 *The Lantern Bearers* by Rosemary Sutcliff (Oxford)
1958 *Tom's Midnight Garden* by Philippa Pearce (Oxford)
1957 *A Grass Rope* by William Mayne (Oxford)
1956 *The Last Battle* by C. S. Lewis (Bodley Head)
1955 *The Little Bookroom* by Eleanor Farjeon (Oxford)
1954 *Knight Crusader* by Ronald Welch (Oxford)
1953 *A Valley Grows Up* by Edward Osmond (Oxford)
1952 *The Borrowers* by Mary Norton (Dent)
1951 *The Wool-Pack* by Cynthia Harnett (Methuen)
1950 *The Lark on the Wing* by Elfrida Vipont Foulds (Oxford)
1949 *The Story of Your Home* by Agnes Allen (Transatlantic)
1948 *Sea Change* by Richard Armstrong (Dent)
1947 *Collected Stories for Children* by Walter de la Mare (Faber)
1946 *The Little White Horse* by Elizabeth Goudge (Brockhampton Press)
1945 No Award
1944 *The Wind on the Moon* by Eric Linklater (Macmillan)
1943 No Award
1942 *The Little Grey Men* by B. B. (Eyre & Spottiswoode)
1941 *We Couldn't Leave Dinah* by Mary Treadgold (Penguin)
1940 *Visitors from London* by Kitty Barne (Dent)
1939 *Radium Woman* by Eleanor Doorly (Heinemann)
1938 *The Circus Is Coming* by Noel Streatfeild (Dent)
1937 *The Family from One End Street* by Eve Garnett (Muller)
1936 *Pigeon Post* by Arthur Ransome (Cape)

KATE GREENAWAY MEDAL

Given annually in May by the British Library Association to the most distinguished work in the illustration of children's books first published in the United Kingdom during the preceding year. The year cited in the listing that follows is the year in which a book was published, not the year in which the honor was bestowed.

1975 *The Wind Blew* by Pat Hutchins (Macmillan)
1973 *Father Christmas* by Raymond Briggs (Coward)
1972 *The Woodcutter's Duck* by Krystyna Turska (Hamilton)
1971 *The Kingdom under the Sea* by Jan Pienkowski (Cape)
1970 *Mr. Gumpy's Outing* by John Burningham (Cape)
1969 *The Quangle-Wangle's Hat* by Edward Lear, ill. by Helen Oxenbury (Heinemann); *Dragon of an Ordinary Family* by Margaret Mahy, ill. by Helen Oxenbury (Heinemann)
1968 *Dictionary of Chivalry* by Grant Uden, ill. by Pauline Baynes (Longmans)
1967 *Charlie, Charlotte & the Golden Canary* by Charles Keeping (Oxford)
1966 *Mother Goose Treasury* by Raymond Briggs (Hamilton)
1965 *Three Poor Tailors* by Victor Ambrus (Hamilton)
1964 *Shakespeare's Theatre* by C. W. Hodges (Oxford)
1963 *Borka* by John Burningham (Cape)
1962 *Brian Wildsmith's ABC* by Brian Wildsmith (Oxford)
1961 *Mrs. Cockle's Cat* by Philippa Pearce, ill. by Antony Maitland (Longmans)
1960 *Old Winkle and the Seagulls* by Elizabeth Rose, ill. by Gerald Rose (Faber)
1959 *Kashtanka and a Bundle of Ballads* by William Stobbs (Oxford)
1958 No Award
1957 *Mrs. Easter and the Storks* by V. H. Drummond (Faber)
1956 *Tim All Alone* by Edward Ardizzone (Oxford)
1955 No Award

Acknowledgments

The authors and publisher gratefully acknowledge permission to reprint the following material:

From *When We Were Very Young* by A. A. Milne. Illustrated by Ernest H. Shepard. Copyright, 1924 by E. P. Dutton & Co. Renewal copyright, 1952 by A. A. Milne. Reprinted by permission of the publisher, E. P. Dutton & Co., Inc.

From *THE WIND IN THE WILLOWS* by Kenneth Grahame. Copyright 1933, 1953 Charles Scribner's Sons; renewal copyright © 1961 Ernest H. Shepard. Used by permission of Charles Scribner's Sons, Methuen & Co. Ltd., and the Bodleian Library Oxford.

From "How Is Your Folklore Quotient?" by Sister Margaret Mary Nugent, from the May 1968 *ELEMENTARY ENGLISH*. Copyright © 1968 by the National Council of Teachers of English. Reprinted by permission of the publisher.

Art work from *A Story, A Story* by Gail E. Haley. Copyright © 1970 by Gail E. Haley. Used by permission of the author and Atheneum Publishers.

Art work from *May I Bring a Friend?* by Beatrice Schenk de Regniers. Pictures copyright © 1964 by Beni Montresor. Used by permission of Atheneum Publishers and William Collins Sons & Co., Ltd.

Art work from the book *DRUMMER HOFF* by Barbara and Ed Emberley. © 1967 by Edward R. Emberley and Barbara Emberley. Published by Prentice-Hall, Inc., Englewood Cliffs, New Jersey.

Art work from *The Funny Little Woman* by Arlene Mosel, illustrated by Blair Lent. Text © 1972 by Arlene Mosel. Illustrations © 1972 by Blair Lent. Reproduced by permission of the publishers, E. P. Dutton & Co., Inc.

Art work from *SAM, BANGS & MOONSHINE* written and illustrated by Evaline Ness. Copyright © 1966 by Evaline Ness. Reproduced by permission of Holt, Rinehart & Winston, Inc.

Art work from *THE STORY OF BABAR*, by Jean de Brunhoff. Copyright 1933 and renewed 1961 by Random House, Inc. Reprinted by permission of Random House, Inc. and Methuen & Co. Ltd.

Art work from *HOMER PRICE* by Robert McCloskey. Copyright 1943, Copyright © renewed 1971 by Robert McCloskey. Reprinted by permission of The Viking Press, Inc.

Louis Darling illustration reproduced by permission of William Morrow & Co., Inc. from *RIBSY*. Copyright © 1964 by Beverly Cleary.

Art work from *RAGGEDY ANN STORIES* by Johnny Gruelle, copyright 1918 by P. F. Volland Company, 1946 by Myrtle Gruelle, 1947 by the Johnny Gruelle Company; used by permission of the publisher, The Bobbs-Merrill Company, Inc.

Reprinted by permission of G. P. Putnam's Sons and Jonathan Cape Ltd. from *MISTRESS MASHAM'S REPOSE* by T. H. White. Copyright 1946 by T. H. White.

From *WILLIAM'S DOLL* by Charlotte Zolotow. Text copyright © 1972 by Charlotte Zolotow. Reprinted by permission of Harper & Row, Publishers, Inc.

From *CHARLOTTE'S WEB* by E. B. White. Copyright, 1952 by E. B. White. By permission of Harper & Row, Publishers, Inc. and Hamish Hamilton, Ltd.

From "McLuhan, Youth, and Literature: Part II" by Eleanor Cameron in the December 1972 *Horn Book*. By permission of the author and publisher.

548

From *The Here and Now Story Book* by Lucy Sprague Mitchell. Copyright 1921 by E. P. Dutton & Co. Copyright renewed, 1952, by Lucy Sprague Mitchell. Reprinted by permission of the publishers, E. P. Dutton & Co., Inc.

Reprinted with the permission of Farrar, Straus & Giroux, Inc. and the Ann Elmo Agency, Inc. from *A WRINKLE IN TIME* by Madeleine L'Engle; copyright © 1962 by Madeleine L'Engle Franklin.

From "A Thinking Improvement Program through Literature" by Sara W. Lundsteen in the April 1972 *Elementary English.* Copyright © 1972 by Sara W. Lundsteen. Reprinted by permission of the author.

From "The Cloze Readability Procedure" by John R. Bormuth, from *Readability in 1968,* A Research Bulletin Prepared by a Committee of the NCRE. Published for the NCRE by the National Council of Teachers of English. Reprinted by permission.

"Wordless Book Bibliography" by William A. Brochtrup. Reprinted by permission of the author.

From *RAIN MAKES APPLESAUCE* by Julian Scheer and Marvin Bileck. By permission of the publisher, Holiday House, Inc.

From *THE FOLKTALE* by Stith Thompson, published by Holt, Rinehart and Winston, Inc., 1946.

Reprinted by permission of Lothrop, Lee & Shepard Co., Inc. and the author from *PROVERBS OF MANY NATIONS* by Emery Kelen. Copyright © 1966 by Emery Kelen.

From "The Wild Swans" by Hans Christian Anderson in *IT'S PERFECTLY TRUE AND OTHER STORIES* translated by Paul Leyssac. By permission of the publisher, Harcourt Brace Jovanovich, Inc., and Alfred J. Bedard.

From "The Three Royal Monkeys" by Walter de la Mare, by permission of The Literary Trustees of Walter de la Mare, and The Society of Authors as their representatives.

From the book *LITTLE FUR FAMILY* by Margaret Wise Brown. Text copyright © 1946 Margaret Wise Brown. By permission of Harper & Row, Publishers, Inc.

From *THE SAILOR DOG* by Margaret Wise Brown, copyright 1953 by Western Publishing Company, Inc. Reprinted by permission of the publisher.

From *MADELINE* by Ludwig Bemelmans. Copyright 1939 by Ludwig Bemelmans, Copyright © renewed 1967 by Mrs. Madeleine Bemelmans and Mrs. Barbara Bemelmans Marcian. Reprinted by permission of The Viking Press, Inc.

From "Worlds as They Should Be: Middle-earth, Narnia and Prydain" by Mary Lou Colbath from the December 1971 *Elementary English.* Copyright © 1971 by the National Council of Teachers of English. Reprinted by permission of the publisher and the author.

Extracted from "Silver" and "A Child's Day" by Walter de la Mare by permission of The Literary Trustees of Walter de la Mare, and The Society of Authors as their representative.

Excerpted from "Waiting," "Near and Far," and "Hallowe'en" from *THE LITTLE HILL,* copyright 1949, by Harry Behn. Reprinted by permission of Harcourt Brace Jovanovich, Inc.

"No" and "Bad" by Dorothy Aldis. Reprinted by permission of G. P. Putnam's Sons from *ALL TOGETHER* by Dorothy Aldis. Copyright © 1952 by Dorothy Aldis.

"The Pickety Fence" from *EVERY TIME I CLIMB A TREE* by David McCord, by permission of Little, Brown and Co. Copyright 1952 by David McCord.

From "The world was meant to be peaceful" in *HERE I AM.* Reprinted by permission of Julian Bach Literary Agency, Inc. Copyright © 1969 Voice of the Children, Inc.

From *ONLY THE MOON AND ME* by Richard J. Margolis. Copyright © 1969 by Richard J. Margolis. Reprinted by permission of J. B. Lippincott Company.

"Mommies Do" reprinted with the permission of Farrar, Straus & Giroux, Inc. from *SPIN A SOFT BLACK SONG* by Nikki Giovanni, illustrated by Charles Bible; text copyright © 1971 by Nikki Giovanni, illustrations © 1971 by Charles Bible.

From "How to Eat a Poem" by Eve Merriam. Copyright © 1964 by Eve Merriam. From *IT DOESN'T ALWAYS HAVE TO RHYME.* Used by permission of Atheneum Publishers.

"Incident" from *ON THESE I STAND* by Countee Cullen. Copyright 1925 by Harper & Row, Publishers, Inc.; renewed 1953 by Ida M. Cullen. Reprinted by permission of Harper & Row, Publishers, Inc.

"Elfin Berries" reprinted with permission of Macmillan Publishing Co., Inc. from *POEMS* by Rachel Field. Copyright 1926 by Macmillan Publishing Co., Inc.

"Lone Dog" from *SONGS TO SAVE A SOUL* by Irene Rutherford McLeod. Reprinted by permission of the Author's Literary Estate and Chatto & Windus, publishers.

"My Dog" from the book *Around and About* by Marchette Chute. Copyright © 1957 by E. P. Dutton & Co. Reprinted by permission of the publisher, E. P. Dutton & Co., Inc.

Excerpted from "The Lost Cat" from *THE FLATTERED FLYING FISH & OTHER POEMS* by E. V. Rieu. Used by permission of Penelope Rieu.

"The Night Will Never Stay" and "Strawberries" from POEMS FOR CHILDREN by Eleanor Farjeon. Reprinted by permission of J. B. Lippincott Company and Harold Ober Associates Incorporated. Copyright 1920 by E. P. Dutton. Renewed by Eleanor Farjeon 1948 and 1951.

"A Tree Toad" by Charles Potter from *TONGUE TANGLERS*, edited by Charles Potter. Used by permission of William Collins + World Publishing Co., Inc.

Reprinted by permission of William Collins + World Publishing Company from *BEYOND THE HIGH HILLS, A BOOK OF ESKIMO POEMS* by Knud Rasmussen. Copyright © 1961 by The World Publishing Company.

"Parting Gift" Copyright 1923 by Alfred A. Knopf, Inc. Reprinted from *COLLECTED POEMS OF ELINOR WYLIE*, by permission of the publisher.

"Elegy for Jog" from *AS IF* by John Ciardi, published by Lothrop, Lee & Shepard. Used by permission of the author.

"The Secret Sits" from *THE POETRY OF ROBERT FROST*, edited by Edward Connery Lathem. Copyright 1942 by Robert Frost. Copyright © 1969 by Holt, Rinehart and Winston, Inc. Copyright © 1970 by Lesley Frost Ballantine. Reprinted by permission of Holt, Rinehart and Winston, Inc. and Jonathan Cape Ltd.

"Was Worm" and "By Morning" (Copyright © 1969 by May Swenson) are reprinted by permission of the author and Charles Scribner's Sons from *POEMS TO SOLVE* by May Swenson.

From *THE HOBBIT* by J. R. R. Tolkien. Used by permission of Houghton Mifflin Company and George Allen & Unwin Ltd.

"Firefly" from *UNDER THE TREE* by Elizabeth Madox Roberts. Copyright 1922 by B. W. Huebsch, Inc.; Copyright renewed 1950 by Ivor S. Roberts. Reprinted by permission of The Viking Press, Inc.

"Giraffes" from *TRIPTICH* by Sy Kahn, published by Raymond College Press. Used by permission of the author.

"Late October" reprinted from *THE SPARROW BUSH* by Elizabeth Coatsworth. Copyright © 1966 by Grosset and Dunlap, Inc. Published by Grosset and Dunlap, Inc., New York. Reprinted by permission of the publisher.

"Puppy" by Robert L. Tyler from *THE DEPOSITION OF DON QUIXOTE & OTHER POEMS.* Used by permission of Golden Quill Press.

"Habits of the Hippopotamus" by Arthur Guiterman. Copyright E. P. Dutton in *Gaily the Troubadour* 1936; © renewed by Vida Lindo Guiterman.

"The Flight of the Roller Coaster" from THE COLOUR OF THE TIMES/TEN ELEPHANTS ON YONGE STREET by Raymond Souster. Reprinted by permission of McGraw-Hill Ryerson Limited.

Marie L. Shedlock: *The Art of the Story-Teller.* Copyright 1915, 1951. By permission of Dover Publications, Inc., New York.

Reprinted from *Saturday Review,* November 15, 1969 by permission of the author, John Ciardi.

From *MOTHER AND SON* by Ivy Compton-Burnett. By permission of Curtis Brown Ltd. London on behalf of the Estate of Ivy Compton-Burnett.

Burdette S. Fitzgerald, *WORLD TALES FOR CREATIVE DRAMATICS AND STORYTELLING,* © 1962. Reprinted by permission of Prentice-Hall, Inc., Englewood Cliffs, New Jersey.

Excerpts from *GRIMM'S FAIRY TALES*, translated by Margaret Hunt and James Stern. Copyright © 1972. By permission of Pantheon Books, a Division of Random House, Inc.

"First Aid in Children's Writing" by Helen Danforth from the April 1960 *Elementary English.* Copyright © 1960 by the National Council of Teachers of English. Reprinted by permission of the publisher and the author.

From *Pen, Paper and Poem* by David McCord. Copyright © 1973 by Holt, Rinehart and Winston, Inc. Used by permission of the publisher.

"Before Babel" reprinted with the permission of Farrar, Straus & Giroux, Inc. and Garnstone Press Ltd., London, from *A CIRCLE OF QUIET* by Madeleine L'Engle. Copyright © 1972 by Madeleine L'Engle Franklin.

Index

AUTHORS AND ILLUSTRATORS OF CHILDREN'S BOOKS

TITLES

SUBJECTS[1]

---

[1]Critics and other authorities who write about children's books are included in this listing.

Literature for Thursday's Child was set in 10 point Compano, a version of Palatino, on the RCA Videocomp (CRT) and then printed and bound, all by Kingsport Press of Kingsport, Tennessee. Display type is Delphin, a typositor face. The book and cover were designed by Judith Olson with special cover art by Ralph Mapson. Sponsoring editor was Karl J. Schmidt and project editor was Barbara L. Carpenter.